Conversational Statistics for Business and Economics

Second Edition

L. Van Jones, Ph.D.
Texas Christian University

Kendall Hunt
publishing company

Works Cited:
Over the years, I have used several other author's works to prepare some materials in my course, this textbook and the companion workbook. My thanks go to the following who have helped develop even my understanding of the field of statistics.

L. Van Jones, Ph. D.

David R. Anderson, Dennis J. Sweeney, Thomas A. Williams. *Statistics for Business and Economics.*

Wayne W. Daniel and James C. Terrell. *Business Statistics for Management and Economics.*

David M. Levine, Mark L. Berenson and David Stephan. *Statistics for Managers.*

Douglas A. Lind, Robert D. Mason, William G. Marchal. *Basic Statistics for Business and Economics.*

Patrick W. Shannon, David F. Groebner, Phillip C. Fry, Kent D. Smith. *A Course in Business Statistics.*

Andrew F. Siegel. *Practical Business Statistics.*

Allen L. Webster. *Applied Statistics for Business and Economics.*

Interior design images:
Text image © 2010 JupiterImages Corporation.
Judge image © Junial Enterprises, 2010. Used under license from Shutterstock, Inc.

Kendall Hunt
p u b l i s h i n g   c o m p a n y

www.kendallhunt.com
Send all inquiries to:
4050 Westmark Drive
Dubuque, IA 52004-1840

Copyright © 2007, 2009 by Loyde Van Jones

ISBN: 978-0-7575-7758-1

Printed in the United States of America
10 9 8 7 6 5 4 3

Contents

Preface

Twenty Years' Experience

I don't know about you, but for over 20 years I have read and looked at hundreds of statistics textbooks. Some are better than others, but there seems to be one common denominator. They all look pretty much the same.

Many students complain, among other things, about the pace of a statistics class. They tell me it is too rapid for them. While they are taking notes from one part of the board, I have moved to another part of the board with new information. About three years ago, I wrote a series of notes for my classes at TCU. I began passing them out to the students before my lectures. After the first semester, many students complimented me (even after grades were in) about how helpful the notes were. I continued to pass out the notes from semester to semester as a student aid. The notes tend to slow down the pace of the class, since the notes often reflect what I am writing on the board. I probably win the award for most notes in any class in any school in any country but can't empirically demonstrate that to be true (just a gut feeling).

One semester about a year ago, I began thinking. Maybe, just maybe, my notes could be converted to a textbook I could publish and actually make a buck or two. About six months ago, Kendall/Hunt showed up in my office soliciting me to write, of all things, a statistics textbook. I thought about it for a few days, reviewed their contract, and came to the conclusion "this could work." So I began converting my notes to a textbook, a task that was more formidable than I had envisioned. The result of the conversion is what you are holding in your hand right now—my textbook.

Clever Marketing

On the cover you will notice some clever marketing phrases. One of them claims this textbook is *"like no other."* That is really a true statement. I have written the textbook as if I were speaking with my classes at TCU. The book has a logical flow to it and is in a conversational tone. I often use contractions because I speak in contractions as do many of us. Using those gave the editor fits, but I finally reminded her that the book was "conversational." She would edit them out, and I would put them back. I finally won the argument or she just gave up.

Why This Book?

You might ask, *"Why should I choose this textbook over another, especially since I already have one that works pretty well?"* Good question, I respond. Apart from the fact that I need the royalties to retire to the Bahamas, I think there are better reasons. This textbook has a logical and continuous flow of material written in language which allows the student to follow a clear, concise explanation of basic concepts and processes. Most textbooks are written in a staccato style where the thought process is interrupted by a multitude of examples. I call that clutter. For me, it is sometimes hard to follow the logical flow, even if it is well written. I use examples but tend to keep them constant throughout the entire chapter.

Over the past 20 years of teaching, I think I have heard all of the questions a student can possibly ask, so I have inserted the most often-repeated questions at appropriate times to keep the thought process flowing logically and consistently.

My wife suggests to me one of the shortfalls of the textbook is that I tend to insert my dry sense of humor. While some of these insertions are rarely spoken aloud in a class, I certainly think them from time to time. Some of you may actually grow to like my sense of humor.

Miracles for the Professor?

My approach can work miracles for the professor because it relieves the professor from repeating explanations on basic material. I think the consistent and logical flow of my explanations will lead to more students understanding the basic material with less help from the professor. Don't get me wrong, the professor will not be worked out of a job with my textbook; however, oftentimes the professor is kept from moving beyond the basics into other important areas because of the ubiquitous doctrine of repetition. There is a saying I have heard repeated from my youth. Only by iteration and reiteration can an alien concept be imparted to a reluctant mind. I have no clue who said this originally, but think it is most apropos for many statistics students.

By using my textbook, students will achieve a level of basic understanding (if they read it). This leaves room for professors to supplement the basic material with other material they believe is important. This will, in turn, provide an opportunity for the professor to challenge the student with other aspects of statistical knowledge. My intent is to cover the basics yet leave room for expansion. Think about it for a moment. If the professor had the basic material covered in an understandable and logical format, then there would be freedom to raise the bar, add additional material, or emphasize the material the professor deems to be the most relevant. By raising the bar, the course takes on new meaning and value to the student and the university as the student matures into a valued member of the business community. There is ample room for professors to expand the course and make it their own.

Are All Subjects Covered?

This leads to the question, *"Do you cover all subjects?"* Simply said, nope, but I do cover the basics in great detail and touch on many subjects in lesser detail. Many statistics textbooks move from formula to answer without intervening steps. This can be very frustrating for most students. Often the biggest challenge for the student is to remember the order of operation. To solve this issue, I work all example problems on a step-by-step approach. I also dwell on interpretation. I often tell my students that the numbers are really meaningless unless you know what to do with them (read "interpret them"). Interpretation should include a detailed decision. It is not enough to say you reject the null hypothesis unless you can tell someone in manufacturing or marketing or management what this means to them directly.

Material Covered

To let you know what I cover, I have included a table of material covered. I have listed it chapter by chapter.

Chapters	Material Covered

□ **Chapter 1**

Introduction to Definitions, Concepts, and Graphics

- ◆ Why Study Statistics? Application Examples
- ◆ Sampling Error and Bias
- ◆ Population and Sample
- ◆ Parameter and Statistic
- ◆ Introduction to Descriptive Statistics
  - *Central Tendency*
  - *Dispersion*
  - *Raw Data Sets*
  - *Grouped Data Sets*
- ◆ Conversion from Raw to Grouped Data Sets
- ◆ Introduction to Inferential Statistics
- ◆ Random Sampling
- ◆ Charts Using Excel Chart Wizard

□ **Chapter 2**

Descriptive Statistics Raw Data

- ◆ Calculations of Central Tendency
  - *Mean*
  - *Median*
  - *Mode*
  - *Weighted Mean*
  - *Geometric Mean*
- ◆ Calculations of Dispersion
  - *Range*
  - *Average Deviation*
  - *Variance*
  - *Standard Deviation*
  - *Percentiles*
  - *Quartiles*
  - *Deciles*
- ◆ Contrast of Calculations for Populations and Samples
- ◆ IQR and Outliers
- ◆ Excel Calculation of Descriptive Statistics
- ◆ Explanation of Excel Output
- ◆ Skewness
- ◆ Kurtosis

Chapter 11

Forecasting Simple and Multiple Regression

- ◆ Linear and Non-Linear Regression
- ◆ Concentration on Simple Linear Regression
- ◆ Cause and Effect Examples
- ◆ Contrasting Simple Linear and Multiple Linear Regression
- ◆ Deterministic Model
- ◆ Stochastic or Random Model
- ◆ Problem Example of Stochastic Model
- ◆ Regression Using Excel
- ◆ Excel Output with Detailed Explanations of Values
- ◆ Goodness of Fit
  - • *Coefficient of Determination*
  - • *Standard Error of Regression*
- ◆ Strength: Coefficient of Correlation
- ◆ Manual Calculations of Stochastic Model Using Ordinary Least Squares Method
- ◆ Beta and Rho Testing as Applied to Stochastic Example Problem
- ◆ Confidence Intervals and Predicting Intervals with Calculation Examples
- ◆ Multiple Linear Regression
- ◆ Example of Multiple Regression for Four Independent Variables Using Excel
- ◆ Excel Output and Interpretation of Values
- ◆ Parsimonious Model Working with the Four Independent Variable Example Eliminating Independent Variables and Measuring the Impact.
- ◆ Beta Testing for Multiple Regression
- ◆ Additional Concepts
- ◆ Multi-co-linearity
- ◆ Dummy Variables
- ◆ Curvilinear Relationships
- ◆ Model Misspecification
- ◆ Heteroscedasticity
- ◆ Autocorrelated Errors
- ◆ Tear-Out In-Class Problem Sheets

Chapter 12

Smoothing Techniques and Time Series Qualitative and Quantitative Methods of Forecasting

- ◆ Business Forecasting and Planning
- ◆ Qualitative Approaches
  - • *Delphi Approach*
  - • *Scenario Writing*
  - • *Brainstorming*
- ◆ Quantitative Approaches
- ◆ Time Series: Multiplicative Model

My Dry and Warped Sense of Humor

I am a Texan by natural birth, so you will also find my sense of humor poking fun at my fellow Texans and me. Each chapter ends with a Jeff Foxworthy approach "you know you are a Texan if." My source for that material was the Internet. In your search engine, type in the phrase "you know you are a Texan if" and you will be surprised at how many sites appear. I was surprised. Multiple sites contain similar quotations so to identify the originating source is quite impossible. Fellow Texans, please do not take offense at my stereotyping Texans. In reality, you can regionally stereotype most Americans in some fashion. As a native Texan, I am poking fun in this insanely politically correct world where you have to be careful not to offend anyone at the expense of forgetting to laugh at ourselves. Have fun, laugh, and take it the way I intend it.

At the beginning of each chapter, I have inserted some actual courtroom humor. I figure if you begin a chapter with humor and end the chapter with humor, perhaps you won't be totally grossed out by the stuff in between. This material comes from a book written by Charles M. Sevilla entitled "Disorder in the American Courts." Numerous attorneys contributed to his book, so attorneys are poking fun at themselves. Some of the stuff is really funny and at the same time a bit scary, since most of our politicians are lawyers. Wow.

Lab Assignments

Included at the end of each chapter (except Chapter 1) are tear-out sheets which may be used in a lab setting. These problems reinforce the chapter material just read. The student should remove the sheet from the book, work the problems and turn them in to the professor. I have included a typical schedule I use in my classes. This schedule provides for lab time in class when these tear-out sheets can be most effectively used. I will provide the answers to these problems for the professor for reproduction or as an aid in working the problems. I simply reproduce the answers and hand them out to the students.

Typical 15-Week Lecture and Lab Schedule

Listed below is my typical schedule for a 15-week course (16 including spring/fall break). Notice I give five examinations plus the final. For me, this breaks the material into enough subsets so I can cover more material. It is very difficult to properly test a student in 1 hour and 20 minutes, when you only give a mid-term and a final. Since I have up to four sections, I use scantrons for grading. I also give pop quizzes from time to time. The pop quizzes are meant to encourage attendance since they cannot be made up. You take them or get a zero. Before each examination, I like to set aside time which I refer to as lab time. During this time, I can get up close and personal with many of the students. This schedule shows how I am able to cover the material included in this textbook. It might provide a useful guide for any professor and, then again, it may not. I am certain there are other excellent ways in which this material may be covered just as effectively.

Schedule of Classes ** Tuesday/Thursday ** 1 hour 20 minute All Day Classes

Week	Class #	Day & Date	Chapter	Material	Test Wt.
Week 1	1	Tu Jan 17	1 & 2	Introduction	
	2	Th Jan 19	3	Ungrouped Data	
Week 2	3	Tu Jan 24	3	Grouped Data	
	4	Th Jan 26	4	Probabilities	
Week 3	**5**	**Tu Jan 31**	**Lab**	**Lab**	
	6	*Th Feb 2*	*Test*	*Test #1*	10%
Week 4	7	Tu Feb 7	5	**Return Graded Test #1** Probability Distributions	
	8	Th Feb 9	6	Sampling Distribution of Sample Means	
Week 5	9	Tu Feb 14	7	Confidence Intervals	
	10	**Th Feb 16**	**Lab**	**Lab**	
Week 6	*11*	*Tu Feb 21*	*Test*	*Test #2*	10%
	12	Th Feb 23	8	Hypothesis Testing—1 Pop.	
Week 7	13	Tu Feb 28	8	**Return Graded Test #2** Hypothesis Testing—1 & 2 Pop	
	14	Th Mar 2	9	Hypothesis Testing—2 Pop	
Week 8	**15**	**Tu Mar 7**	**9**	**Lab**	
	16	*Th Mar 9*	*Test*	*Test #3*	25%
Week 9	*No*	*Tu Mar 14*	*Spring*	*Spring Break—No Class*	
	Class	*Th Mar 16*	*Break*	*Spring Break—No Class*	
Week 10	17	Tu Mar 21	9.9 & Notes	**Return Graded Test #3** *F* and Chi-Square as a Parametric Test	
	18	Th Mar 23	10	ANOVA	
Week 11	19	Tu Mar 28	11	Simple Regression	
	20	Th Mar 30	12 & Notes	Multiple Regression Chi-Square (nonparametric)	
Week 12	**21**	**Tu Apr 4**	**Lab**	**Lab**	
	22	*Th Apr 6*	*Test*	*Test #4*	15%

Week	Class #	Day & Date	Chapter	Material	Test Wt.
Week 13	23	Tu Apr 11	13	**Return Graded Test #4** Index Numbers	
	24	Th Apr 13	13	Time Series & Smoothing	
Week 14	25	Tu Apr 18	15	Quality Control	
	26	**Th Apr 20**	**Lab**	**Lab**	
Week 15	*27*	*Tu Apr 25*	*Test*	*Test #5*	10%
	28	Th Apr 27	Review	**Return Graded Test #5** Review for Final	
Week 16	29	Tu May 2	Review	Review for Final – Last Class Day	
Final		**Per Below**	**Final**	**Date & Time Per TCU Schedule**	**25%**
Five Examinations from the Solutions Manual—Cumulative Percentage					5%
				Total Test Weights	100%

Supplemental Homework Book

One of the problems most professors have is how to handle homework. Working homework in class takes away from lecture time. If you are like me, there is never enough time in class to lecture and do homework problems on the board. This means the student must come to your office one at a time (usually) and tell you the sad story as to why they can't work some (or any) of the homework problems. The solution has been to prepare a very detailed homework assignment book. Most statistics textbooks will provide the answer to the odd or even problems in the back of the book, but it is just that—a one-line answer. There is no attempt to show the detailed step-by-step solutions (order of operation). There is absolutely no attempt to interpret the results. Most students have difficulty with the order of operation and really need a step-by-step solution. The homework solutions manual provides just that. For each problem in the book, there is a detailed solution on a step-by-step basis. And, more importantly, there is an "interpretation" of the results. Both my textbook and the homework book will really give any professor a head start handling the routine and repetitive process of teaching statistics. Both will be provided as a package or sold separately.

Tables

In the back of the textbook are eight tables. I find one of the most interesting challenges is to explain to a student how to properly read a table. I write some great explanations. This instruction alone is worth the price of the textbook—well, maybe not that much, but it will provide reference material that just might keep students from asking the same question over and over again. Isn't it strange how, as the professor, you answer a question only to have a second student ask the same question again within a span of 30 seconds? I think one of Murphy's Law has been uncovered. I just need a name for it.

That's about all I can think of right now for a preface. Oh, I guess I should thank everyone without whose help this book would not be possible, but in reality that is me, so I think thanking myself is really irrelevant, don't you? I could thank my publisher, my wife, my daughters, my cat and dog, and my proofreader (to whom you can attribute any errors not caught, since professors never make errors, right?).

However, this does bring up a question about who I am

I will start with a picture.

© Matthew Mendelsohn/CORBIS

Okay, okay!!! So the picture may not really look like me. Okay, I guess I better tell you something about myself. This stuff you can believe, well . . . mostly!

Work Experience

I have worked for large to medium sized corporations in various financial capacities including financial analyst, controller, and vice president of development. I have successfully worked for myself for the past 25+ years in various capacities which include general contracting, land development, restaurant owner, and as an insurance agency owner. My wife, brother-in-law and I, about a year ago, opened up a securities uniform and embroidery business which is still struggling at this writing. We do expect it to do okay since we think the growth industry of the next five years or so is security (since 9/11). I have a very strong entrepreneurial background but have also worked for multi-million dollar corporations. I prefer the entrepreneurial side of the equation.

Teaching Experience and Publications

I currently teach four sections of statistics for TCU each semester. I have been with them for at least seven years. I have taught for the University of Dallas for over 20 years such courses as statistics, marketing management, financial accounting, and risk management. I have taught quantitative analysis and statistics for Dallas Baptist University and managerial accounting and accounting for Texas Women's University (TWU). I have taught in both live classroom and asynchronous online settings. I have written two online courses and two books and a couple of articles.

Education

I have an undergraduate degree in business from TCU as well as a Masters Degree from TCU. I have two earned Doctorates. One is from Louisiana Baptist Theological University. Both advanced degrees are in Eschatology (look it up, if you want to know).

Personal

I have two daughters and four grandchildren—two boys and two girls. One daughter owns her own business and one is a stay-at-home mom. I live in Southlake, Texas, and have two animals—one cat and one dog, who do not get along but tolerate each other. The dog thinks it is playtime with the cat. The cat views it differently, as a life and death match. Luckily for the dog, the cat has no front claws.

I lost my wife to pancreatic cancer in 2009 and really miss her. From the time she was diagnosed to her death was a very short 4-and-a-half months. I was lucky to be married to her. She was active in the Miss Texas Scholarship Pageant having been a former Miss Texas herself. She was third runner up to Miss America. Currently I am still active in the Miss Texas system and am on the board of directors of the Miss Southlake Scholarship Organization. We provide scholarship monies for young ladies to help pay for their college.

Well, I guess that about does it for me. For copies of my full story forward your check to me for $5.00 and I will expand the story to a couple of more pages of boring and dull reading. I am not serious about the $5.00 since $1.00 will get you the same expanded write-up.

L. Van Jones, Ph.D.

Words of Wisdom for Men to Help Them Understand What Women are Really Saying. (Women should not read this section)

I am obviously older than most who will read this book as students, but the other day something came across the Internet I thought was pretty descriptive of how to listen, really listen to women, especially that special one in your life. There are nine words/phrases that a man must put into his vocabulary. In fact you will do well to write these on an index card, keep them with you, and refer to them often.

Fine:	This is the word women use to end an argument when they are right and you need to stop talking.
Five Minutes:	If she is getting dressed, five minutes means a half an hour. Five minutes is only five minutes if you have just been given five more minutes to watch the game before helping around the house.
Nothing:	This is the calm before the storm. This means something and you should be on your toes. Arguments that begin with "Nothing" usually end in "Fine."
Go Ahead:	This is a dare, not permission. Don't do it.
Loud Sigh:	This is not actually a word, but is a non-verbal statement often misunderstood by men. A loud sign means she thinks you are an idiot and wonders why she is wasting her time standing here and arguing with you about "Nothing." (See above for the meaning of "Nothing.")
That's Okay:	This is one of the most dangerous statements a woman can make to a man. "That's Okay" means she wants to think long and hard before deciding how and when you will pay for your mistake.
Thanks:	A woman is thanking you, do not question or faint. Just say "You're welcome."
Whatever:	This is ultimate disgust. You are in deep trouble. Even flowers or candy won't help.
Don't Worry About It, I Got It:	This is another dangerous statement, meaning there is something that a woman has told a man to do several times, but she is now doing it herself. This will later result in a man asking "What's wrong?" For the woman's response see the word "Nothing."

Men, this is a battle you cannot win, so best be armed with these critical words so you can at least know when to retreat. ☺

Introduction to Definitions, Concepts and Graphics

1

Attorney:	This myasthenia gravis, does it affect your memory at all?
Witness:	Yes.
Attorney:	And in what ways does it affect your memory?
Witness:	I forget.
Attorney:	You forget? Can you give us an example of something you forgot?

Introduction

If you are the normal student, you are probably approaching the study of statistics with much fear and trembling. Maybe you have postponed the course; then postponed it a second time, only to find you are finally being forced to take statistics now. You may be a freshman or a sophomore who is being dragged kicking and screaming into the course because you want to be admitted to the school of business. No matter what your status, the time is here and the time is now.

Actually, statistics should be one of the first courses you take. Statistics ties to many other courses such as Marketing Research, Financial Accounting, Financial Management, Forecasting, and many others. Most of you who fear the course do so because you have heard a horror story of someone who knew someone who took the course and found it to be cruel and unusual punishment ranking with the death penalty.

Truth be known, many times this is the case, but usually that is because the statistics course is taught by a statistician who expects you to have completed integral and differential calculus as a minimum requirement. Even though you may have taken these courses, they rarely form the basis for making daily business decisions. Don't get me wrong, there are many fine and talented statisticians teaching this course, but sometimes it seems as though they try to mystify it and only allow you to "see through a glass darkly."

What you will experience in this textbook is an emphasis on applying statistics to daily business decisions. You will also understand some of the concepts behind statistical procedures. This textbook is not written to emphasize mathematical solutions and proofs. Instead, you are expected to gain a working knowledge of the *language of statistics* and enough familiarity to understand the most basic solutions to real life business challenges.

Suddenly, my finely tuned "mind reading" talent awakens. I sense you are forming a question as you silently lament: Okay, I have read the first couple of paragraphs but am still wondering what I can really learn from a statistics course that will be helpful to me in real life?

While I do not want to get too far ahead of myself, let's take a minute or two and look at just how you might really use the information learned in a statistics course. (You are somewhat amazed that I seem to have read your mind, but say nothing at this point.)

Uses of Statistical Techniques

Some of the techniques and concepts you will be introduced to include the following: regression, ANOVA, averages (mean, median, mode), variability (variance, standard deviation, percentiles), two-population comparison (mean product life), normal distribution, and chi-square as a nonparametric test, among other techniques. I know you have no clue what any of these are at this point, although you might have studied regression before and you probably understand averages.

Let's see how some of these can be used.

Finance

You have no interest in simply blindly investing your money, so you may want to calculate the average return on investment over a period of time to determine which option is the best investment. Under these circumstances, the geometric mean, not the arithmetic mean, enables you to determine the correct return. The geometric mean is appropriately used when looking at percentage returns.

You may want to find a safe investment for one of your clients. This may be done through the use of the normal distribution and standard deviation to measure the risky nature of an investment. If you are investing money for a client and the client is risk averse, you would want to make sure you choose the safest investment (least risky). The investment with the smallest variability (standard deviation) around the mean would be the least risky.

Let's say you have $100,000 to invest for your client. You decide that you want to invest in mutual funds, but since there are hundreds, you wonder who manages their fund the best. You might wonder if there is a relationship between the performance of the fund and the manager's education and experience. Here you might be able to use probability or ANOVA to aide you in evaluating the question.

Human Resources

As a manager, you know employee turn-over is a problem that needs to be addressed, since high turn-over can lead to higher training expenses. The human resource manager may be able to use regression analysis to predict turn-over. Regression may also be able to predict employee absence by day of the week or to predict worker's compensation claims. You may be able to better budget worker's compensation insurance payments, especially if your company has chosen to retain part of the risk.

Marketing

One of the most important decisions in marketing is how to effectively spend your advertising dollar. No budget bucket is bottomless, so you may want to allocate your advertising budget among alternative sources. Of course you would want to select the type of media that yields the best exposure to your target market. This can be done by using an average exposure calculation.

You may want to introduce a new product to the marketplace. You identify your target market, but you know it can be expensive to rush to the market without proper planning. You may want to carefully design a focus group study from a group of potential customers whose demographics represent the target market. From this focus group you might extrapolate the results and imply the results of the focus group will be the same as those of the entire target market. This is known as inferential statistics and if the sample is properly designed reduces the probability of making bad decisions.

Properly pricing your product is an important function of any marketing operation. You may find a statistical technique known as ANOVA to be quite helpful as you make the decision on how to properly price your product. For example, you may manufacture a cell phone. The cell phone may have the possibility of several feature choices. It may have a camera, calculator, text messaging center, Internet access, and other features. By using a focus group, you may find that your customers will pay for certain features but will not pay for others. By using ANOVA, you can help isolate those features which lead to the proper price.

This same technique can be used in determining marketing strategy where a marketing manager wants to know if changes in the marketing mix (design of the product, design of the package, different advertising strategies) will lead to differences in how the consumer will react to your product. When you think about strategy and have competitors in the marketplace, you have to give the customer a reason to change to your product. That reason may be something as simple and effective as a redesign of the product or a repackaging of the product. Cheese Whiz remarketed their product in 4-ounce microwaveable containers years ago and found that their sales rose dramatically right after the repackaging.

Operations Management

In a manufacturing situation, you may be faced with measuring the average completion time of assembly process A versus the average completion time of assembly process B to determine which process yields the best results. The mean completion time may be useful in making this evaluation.

As the general manager of several plants, you might be faced with determining if Plant *A* produces more product than Plant *B*. Here average production output will form the starting point in your analysis. Assuming the two plants have very similar processes, you may want to know if the difference in the process of Plant *A* produces more (or less) product than Plant *B*. This might lead you to better production design and ultimately lead to a competitive advantage.

Projects must be completed on time and within budget. To aid you in managing the project, you might use techniques such as PERT/CPM which are beyond the scope of this course; however, they lend themselves to use of the normal distribution to make sure the project is completed on time and within budget (expected value).

Quality is extremely important as you offer your product or service to your customers. Quality is determined by how variable your service or product is to a standard. There is one hotel which has the slogan "Simply the Best." This slogan challenges the employees and management to seek the highest level of service, but at the same time it raises customer expectations. If your quality of service is inconsistent, you will have complaints, so you strive to reduce the variability of that service from a given standard. The standard may be a mean value or it may be set at a much higher threshold. The more tightly your employees and managers adhere to the standard, the higher the propensity of your customers will be to return to purchase your product or to seek your services.

Your customers will come to your place of business for service. Let's assume you own a trucking company and want to know how many employees to hire to unload the trucks as they arrive at your loading dock. How many do you hire? If the trucks arrive too quickly, you might not have enough personnel on the docks to unload. If you hire too many and the trucks arrive slowly, the employees may be standing around waiting. This is a waiting line or queue problem. The same issues exist for restaurants or telephone companies or customer service operations. What you want to know is the probability of a customer arriving and the time lapse between the arrival of the first customer and the second. Two important probability distributions are helpful: the Poisson and the exponential distributions. Properly using these distributions will enable you to predict the probability of the truck's arrival time and the lapse time between the arrival time of other trucks. This in turn aids you as the manager in making proper staffing decisions.

Accounting

You are employed by a CPA firm and your first job is to help conduct an audit of a manufacturing firm. The firm has a number of receivables and payables. Normally you would send out confirmation letters to those who owe money to verify the amount shown on the balance sheet. The same would be true about the accounts payable. From your initial examination, you determine there are over 5,000 customers involved. By using a properly designed sampling technique, you can limit your inquiries to a sample rather than processing 5,000 letters. Proper design hinges on random selection.

Managerial accounting is a branch of accounting where decisions are made using the numbers generated by the financial accountant. Fixed, variable, and mixed costs are important in any operation. The managerial accountant may make use of regression analysis to forecast each of these costs. Regression can also be applied to forecast sales or expenses, so the manager can better budget future years.

Wow, you say, I had no idea that statistical techniques were so useful in making business decisions.

I have shown you only a few uses. There are more, but sharing with you ad infinitum would be rather boring and unproductive. What I have shared should give you a flavor of the relevance of statistics. A statistics course is not meant to destroy the meaning of life for you; in fact, if you apply yourself, you will find some very helpful techniques which are useful in making better business decisions.

More General Ideas and a Couple of Specific Thoughts

As you read through this section, take special note of the definitions but less attention to the details of the calculations. The techniques will be repeated in Chapter 2.

Statistics surround us every day. Can you name some that come to mind?

How about:

Inflation Rate	Business Cycle
Government Debt	Budgets
Gallup Polls	Batting Averages
Unemployment Rate	Crime Rate
Interest Rate	U.S. Census Bureau

The major problem with statistics is not mathematical, because nothing more than basic algebra will be required. Taking the square root of a number and solving an algebraic equation with one unknown is probably the toughest math you will face in this textbook. You will be required to do a lot of adding, subtracting, squaring, dividing, and looking up values in a table. The mathematics is straightforward, but learning statistics is really the study of a new language. Statistics is a foreign language. You are going to have to learn it.

A major goal of this textbook will be to make you "statistically literate." You should be able to communicate with and better understand statisticians or those who routinely apply statistical techniques. By reading this textbook and taking a statistics course, you will not be a statistician. In most cases, you will find that you know formulas intuitively before you actually see them written in statistical language and symbols.

For example, if I ask you how to calculate the **arithmetic mean** of a data set, you would probably tell me you would add up all the numbers in the data set and then divide that sum by the number of observations in the data set.

You would be correct. That formula, however, is written as follows:

$$Mean = \frac{\Sigma X}{n}$$

where X is any data set value and n is the number of observations in that data set. Σ is the capital Greek letter sigma. When you see it you would say to yourself "the sum of a column headed ..." In this instance, the column is headed "X". The column heading could be X or Y or XY or X^2 or almost anything. The point is that it simply means to add up a column of numbers.

For example, assume that the following data set consists of the examination grades for the semester of a student in economics.

Let X represent the examination grades. After arranging them in a column, we have the following data set.

Table 1.1 A Semester of Examination Grades for a Student in Economics.

X
85
90
87
83
92
Total 437

The 437 would be the sum of a column headed X, which is ΣX. Each test score would be called $X_1 = 85$, $X_2 = 90$, $X_3 = 87$, etc.

If you were asked to calculate an arithmetic mean, you would intuitively know to simply sum the numbers (437), and then divide the sum by the number of grades (5). This would yield an average of 87.4 (437 divided by 5).

You have done exactly what the formula written above required you to do. The column would be headed X. The sum of a column headed X is the numerator of the equation, which in this case is 437. The number of observations is 5 (the value n), which in this case is the denominator of the equation.

By the way, I have used the term data set often. What is a **data set?** It is simply a *set of data*. There is nothing foreign or foreboding associated with the term data set. A data set is a set of data. In my example above, the data set is the five grades for the student. Data sets can be small or rather large (thousands of data points).

Bias

In statistics there is something called **bias**—the tendency to favor the selection of certain sample elements or events over other sample elements or other events.

Bias could be *unintentional or intentional.* An example of **unintentional bias** might occur during an interview. Assume that the interviewer is white and the person being interviewed is African American. Let's further assume that a white athlete has been accused of raping a woman. Let us assume that the question is "Do you think this white athlete is guilty or innocent?" Would you get a biased answer? Maybe or maybe not, but the potential is in place to receive a slanted, and thus biased, answer to the question.

What if the reporter is African American and the person being interviewed is white. What if the white respondent is asked the question "Do you favor or do you not favor African American reporters?" Remember, the question is being asked of a white respondent by an African American reporter. Would there be the potential for bias with the white respondent saying what he or she thinks the African American reporter wants to hear? Maybe or maybe not, but again the potential is there to receive a slanted, and thus biased, answer to the question.

What if the same two questions were asked by a white reporter and the respondent was also white? Would the results be the same in both instances? A questionnaire must be designed with the idea of guarding against bias regardless of the source.

An example of **intentional bias** might exist if the question is slanted toward a particular answer. For example, in a recent Democratic National Committee questionnaire, one question was "Are you in favor of the rich receiving a tax cut to the exclusion of the working man?" What do you think the answer to that question will be?

Another example of intentional bias would be if the interviewer selects all males and excludes females. Either way the results of the survey might be slanted in one direction or the other, thus biasing the results.

There is also unintentional bias that may occur. As an example, assume you are the marketer for a new magazine, which is targeting the more affluent market. You select North Dallas and identify the zip codes of the more affluent homes in the area. You then begin a marketing survey of those people in that area to determine if they would be interested in your new magazine. You take the telephone book and select at random the names of people in the particular area of interest. Have you biased your survey?

The answer is yes, but it is unintentional. Since your source document is the telephone directory, you have not included those with unlisted telephone numbers or with no telephone.

You might rightly ask the question, so what? I have been able to select a large sample from the designated population, so why would my survey sample be considered invalid?

Good question, I respond.

For a sample, any sample, to be statistically accurate it must conform to a very important rule of randomness.

Random Sample

Each and every element (purchaser of magazines) in the population (North Dallas) must have an equal and independent chance of selection (included in the sample).

In my example of the magazine survey, does each and every member of the population have an equal and independent chance of selection?

Hint: The answer is no.

Those without telephones or with unlisted telephone numbers could not be included; therefore, the results of the sample were biased. This is the very thing that happened during the 1948 Truman-Dewey presidential election. The interviewers selected their survey from a group of people who had a very large proportion of registered Republican voters. This led to the published headline in the *Chicago Tribune* the morning after the vote stating "Dewey Defeats Truman." The vote count, however, revealed Truman was the winner. A picture of Truman holding the "Dewey Defeats Truman" newspaper captured the attention of newspaper readers all across America, much to the embarrassment of the *Chicago Tribune.*

The whole purpose of developing a statistically accurate, random sample is to apply other statistical techniques to the research and imply something about the population from the sample.

Of course, there are samples which are not statistical samples. For example, some sampling procedures use mall intercept interviews which usually involve the selection of the first candidate who meets certain criteria. The interviewer may select a person who looks like they would talk to the interviewer about your questionnaire. When working with data from mall intercept samples, the use of statistical inference would not be proper and must be avoided. Other techniques will be examined in later chapters which would be helpful in these circumstances.

My desire as the researcher is to develop a sample that is drawn from a population where the sample accurately represents that population. This allows me to apply the statistical inference procedures, which are essential in making informed and accurate business decisions.

Let's move on with some definitions and other important distinctions.

Population versus Sample

One of the most important concepts in the field of statistics is the difference between a **population** and a **sample.**

Population

The entire collection of all observations of interest to the researcher.

One of the first questions you might ask is who is the researcher? The researcher is the one conducting the research. (Duh). This means the researcher could easily be anyone including me or you. It logically follows that the one doing the research has absolute control over *the definition of the population.*

For example, I could be conducting a survey to determine the average age of those enrolled in a class. My population is, therefore, defined by me as those who have enrolled, paid their fees, and attended the first class. If there were 20 students enrolled in the class who met the above criteria, the 20 students would comprise the population. This becomes a data set or a set of data of 20 students, which is defined as the population by me, the researcher. I, in turn, will conduct the study.

Sample

A sample is a representative portion of the population selected for study.

Logically I can conclude that, from this definition, a sample represents the population. I can further conclude that the sample is a portion of the population and not all of it. The sample data set will then be different and apart from the population data set. The sample data set is a *sub-set of the population* data set and is, therefore, less than the population data set. The sample is represented by small "*n*" while the population is represented by capital "*N*". Remember this distinction for future reference.

There is something else very critical about a sample. For a moment, let's assume I have two populations. I will label one Population *A* and the other Population *B* (Isn't that clever?). Population *A* is composed of the students in my class. Population *B* is composed of the students who are enrolled in a graduate level financial management class. I want to determine the average age of the students in my class (Population *A*). Is it okay for me to take a sample of the students in Financial Management (Population *B*) and imply that the average age of the students in Population *A* (my class) is the same as the average age of the students in Population *B* (Financial Management)?

The answer is no. It is not okay for me to take the sample from *B* and imply something about *A*. Clearly the sample must come from the population of interest (*A* in this instance) to imply anything about that population. Said another way, you cannot take a sample from Population *B* and imply anything about Population *A* or from Population *A* and imply anything about Population *B*.

For further clarification, the sample is a smaller part which comes from the population. For example, I have a list of 20 students (population) and I selected the *first three* students from the list of 20 students and determined their average age. The three students would be a sample from the defined population of 20 students. The average age of the sample of the three should be representative of the average age of the entire population of 20.

You might ask, why would I want to take a sample since the population is so small?

You are correct, the data set of 20 students is quite small, so I could very easily gather the information on the age of each student, total them and determine an average age for all 20 students. However, most population data sets far exceed 20. Many populations might have a data set of hundreds or thousands. When this occurs, the population data set may be too large for me to do a 100% survey. It may either take too long or cost too much or be so geographically spread out that I cannot reach them within a reasonable cost. I then opt for a *random sample of the population data set*. Less time and money is then invested in achieving my desired result of determining the average age of the students in the population.

I need to ask you a question. By selecting the *first three* on the list from the population of 20 students, have I violated any rule that I have given you to this point?

Go back and look at the way I selected a sample (random selection).

The answer is yes. I have violated the rule of randomness. Remember, I told you that *each and every element in the population must have an equal and independent chance of being selected*? Did the fourth or the twentieth student on the list have the same chance of selection as did the first three? The answer is no. By simply selecting the first three listed, I have excluded students 4 through 20.

To be completely random, each of the 20 students must have *an equal and independent chance of being selected in the sample.*

Ignoring your dumbfounded expression I ask, how do you think I might accomplish randomness?

There are several ways. I could assign a unique number to each student, place that number in a hat, stir the numbers up and draw three out, or I could use a random number generator or random table to accomplish the same thing (more about this process in a later chapter).

Concept of Inferential Statistics

There are two branches of statistics—descriptive and inferential. With **descriptive statistics,** you will use various techniques to describe the data sets. With **inferential statistics,** you will infer something about the population from a properly designed sample. In the next chapter I will cover descriptive statistics, but for now I want to give you a glimpse of the concept of inferential statistics.

A population is defined by the researcher. Because of time or budgetary constraints, a sample may be selected from the population. The purpose of the sample is to use less time and less money yet come up with the same results as if you did a 100% survey. In doing this I am making the claim that the sample is representative of the population. If the sample is representative of the population, then I must conclude that the difference in the sample mean and the population mean is insignificant and due to something called "sampling error." I will make a bold, yet accurate statement. I do not know the true population mean, and I never will know the true population mean.

Okay, I notice that dumbfounded expression again. I continue:

I am claiming that the sample value is the same as the population value. If I knew the population value, I would have no need for a sample at all. When I use the phrase "is the same as" I am referring to the statistical value of the sample, not necessarily the mathematical value of the sample. If the average age of the population is 20 and the sample average age is 19.5, no one is saying $20 = 19.5$.

I am trying to achieve statistical accuracy and not necessarily mathematical accuracy. I know you probably are lost at this point, but I promise to cover this in more detail a bit later in the textbook. In essence, I will never know the true population mean.

Remember one key fact: For a sample to be statistically valid, it must be *selected randomly* from the population it purports to represent, thus *each and every element in the population must have an equal and independent chance of being selected.* (I have said this before, so you might consider this an important issue.)

Let me illustrate what I mean. Assume I have calculated the average age of the sample to be 19.6 years of age. The arithmetic mean of the sample is designated $\overline{X}$ called *X*-bar.

$$\overline{X} = \text{arithmetic mean of the sample.}$$

Assume that the mean of the population, which is unknown, is designated the Greek letter, μ, mu.

μ = arithmetic mean of the population.

By taking a properly designed random sample, I am inferring that $\overline{X}$ represents μ. What do I mean by inferring? By definition, a sample is a representative portion of the population. By taking a correctly designed random sample, I can infer something about the population from the sample. What I infer is that the sample mean and the population mean are statistically equal. This is called inferential statistics. I do not know the population mean, so my sample represents or infers that the two values are equal.

I have said a couple of times that I do not know the population mean and so far you haven't really challenged me. Why not, I ask?

Okay, you say, consider yourself challenged. What do you mean you do not know the true population mean?

This is best illustrated by an example. Let's suppose you have purchased a soft drink in a can that has a label net weight of 12 ounces. My question to you: How do you know there are 12 ounces in the can? You don't, I respond to myself.

As a matter of fact, I doubt you even think about it when you purchase most any product with a net weight label on the package. In fact, you can never know the true mean weight of the contents of the soft drink can. To know the true, population weight of the liquid in the soft drink can, you would have to measure the liquid in 100% of the production. To do that you might have to destroy the entire production, which is something the marketing department might not think a good plan.

There are times, however, when you must use destructive sampling. Suppose you purchase mortar shells for the army. To test them you would have to fire several. You could not fire them all or you would have no product left.

Sampling Error

Just above I used an example about average age. I determined that the average age of the students included in the sample is 19.6 years of age. Assume for a minute that I *do know* the population mean. Assume it is 20.1 years of age. From my explanation above, the sample mean of 19.6 represents (statistically, that is) the population mean of 20.1. As I have already indicated, any mathematical student would quickly point out that 19.6 does not equal 20.1. However, from a statistical inference viewpoint, I am claiming that the two equal each other statistically.

All of you have heard about surveys. Some more recent ones claim that a political candidate for office has 42% of the vote $\pm$ 3 percentage points. This is called margin of error and allows the researcher to make the claim that the mean of the sample is statistically equal to the mean of the population within the stated margin of error.

Sampling error by definition is the difference between the sample mean and the population mean. Here the sampling error would be 0.5 years of age (20.1 less 19.6 = 0.5 years of age). In later chapters I will show you how to evaluate this difference, since I have suggested that you really do not know the population mean. Once again, if I knew the population mean (average age), there would be no need for a sample, would there? There are two possible ways of having sampling error.

1. **Luck of the Draw** This will be addressed later when I discuss sampling distributions of sample means (which means nothing to you at this point, so don't even try to remember it now).

2. **Bias** I have told you that drawing a sample may be intentionally or unintentionally biased.

The accuracy of the estimate of the population from a sample depends on two things.

1. The manner in which the sample is taken, i.e., is it randomly selected where each and every element in the population has an equal and independent chance of selection or is it not randomly drawn?

2. How careful one is to ensure that the sample provides a reliable image of the population. This will be discussed more at length in a later chapter.

Keep in mind that no matter how careful you may be in randomly selecting elements from the population or in designing the sample, there is always a chance for sampling error. Sampling error exists if the unknown population parameter does not equal the sample statistic used to estimate the parameter.

Whoops, two more new terms—parameter and statistic. I guess I had better define them. See what I mean, this course is a language course, a fact about which you will be painfully aware.

Parameter and Statistic

Parameter: Any *descriptive* measure of the entire population.

Statistic: Any *descriptive* measure of the sample.

The parameter is associated with the population and the statistic is associated with the sample. Population begins with the letter "P" as does parameter. Statistic begins with the letter "S" as does sample. This letter association should help you keep the two better organized in your mind. Notice that both are descriptive measures.

Keep these two ideas in mind and I will re-introduce them to you shortly.

There are two more very important concepts which apply to our data set. One is called measures of **central tendency** and the other is called measures of **dispersion** or variability.

Oh, no, more language definitions, you complain. I am just getting into the idea of population and sample and now you want to overload my brain. Oh, well, press on. I can hardly wait.

Do I detect some sarcasm? And I am not through the first chapter yet!

Central Tendency

Any distribution can have a measure of central tendency. What I mean by central tendency is the tendency of the distribution to fall close to a central point or middle point. The middle point or central point is useful in describing the data set. There are several measures of central tendency which describe the data set. These measures apply both to a population or a sample. The three measures of central tendency are the arithmetic mean, the median, and the mode.

Mean: the arithmetic value of any data set. This is the most commonly used and most easily understood value. This is simply the arithmetic average.

Median: the value in the middle with 50% above the value and 50% below the value. This value provides a good estimate of central tendency if the data set contains extreme values (high or low).

Mode: the value that occurs most often.

Dispersion

Any distribution that has a central tendency will have measures of dispersion. Some distributions will be more widely dispersed from the central point than other distributions.

Range: the difference between the high and low values.

Average deviation: this is the difference between the mean and each of the individual values in the data set. This value is always zero. It is the first step in determining the variance.

Variance: the mean of the squared deviations around the mean. (And I know you have no clue what this is, but trust me, you will understand it shortly.) However, one problem exists with the variance. The units are in terms of *units squared* (remember this). Do you know what grades squared or dollars squared or people squared is? Neither do I. This value is calculated only to allow me to determine the standard deviation, which is the value most useful to me as I make statistical inferences.

Standard deviation: the square root of the variance is the standard deviation. This term is one of the most important values and will be used often in the balance of this textbook and any statistics course. The units of measure are not in units squared like the variance but are in terms of units—grades, dollars or people.

Percentiles: any data set may be subdivided into subsets. Percentiles divide the data set of interest into 100 equal pieces. Each piece is equal to 1% of the total data set.

Quartiles: just as any data set may be divided into percentiles, any data set may also be divided into quarters. There are four quarters known as quartiles. Each represents 25% of the distribution. A value known as the **inter-quartile range (IQR)** is the mid-fifty percent of the data set. The IQR is the difference between the 25th and the 75th percentile value.

The IQR is a valuable calculation. If you multiply the IQR times 1.5 (a fixed value), you will generate a number which is useful in identifying outliers. An outlier is a value in a data set that is an aberration or deviant value. The presence of outliers might signal that the data set needs adjusting, since the presence of an outlier will distort the result of any forecasting you do.

For example, let's assume your data set has a value of 40 for the 25th percentile and 60 for the 75th percentile. The difference ($60 - 40 = 20$) is the IQR. Next multiply the IQR times 1.5. This gives you $1.5 \times 20 = 30$. Next subtract the 30 from the 40 (25th percentile) to get 10 and then add the 30 to the 60 (75th percentile) to get 90. Now any value in the data set that falls below 10 or above 90 is considered to be an outlier or aberrant data point. You would then want to adjust it by seeing if you have made a data entry error. If the entry is an aberrant one, you might want to eliminate it from your data set. This concept is important as you "clean" your data.

Deciles: the division of any data set into ten equal increments is known as a decile. There are ten deciles in a data set. Each decile represents 10% of the total distribution.

The measures of dispersion are available to tell you, the researcher, just how much the data set distribution varies or disperses around or from the center point usually measured by the arithmetic mean.

All data sets will have a measure of central tendency and a measure of dispersion.

Data sets also have something called variables.

Oh, my gosh, more definitions, you lament.

Yep, I smile sadistically, more definitions. Need I repeat that this is a language class and not so much a math class?

Variables

Variable: This is any *characteristic* of the population or sample that is being examined in the statistical study.

Variables may be expressed in two ways:

1. **Quantitatively,** which are expressed numerically.

   Examples: weights, heights, number of cars sold, number of defects. (All are characteristics of interest).

   Quantitative variables can be further expressed two ways.

   Continuous data sets: A continuous data set is one where the values can take on a whole range of values. Think of these as having decimal points after or with the whole number.

   Examples: Height, weight, age, money (characteristics of interest).

   Discrete data sets: Generally expressed in whole numbers. Think of these as being measured in whole numbers without decimal points.

   Examples: Number of students, number of cars sold, number of children at school, number of defects in a unit (characteristics of interest).

One Interesting Distinction

Even though a discrete data set is measured in whole numbers, this does not mean a discrete data set cannot have decimals. Let's take an example. Let us say that the Federal Reserve will raise or lower interest rates only 25 basis points at a time. Even though the interest rates are not truly whole numbers, they act as whole numbers because they move in fixed increments of one-quarter of a point. The rates of 6.25, 6.50, and 6.75 are not whole numbers, yet they are treated as discrete data points because they cannot take on a "range of values." The values are limited to a movement of one-quarter point at a time.

You must have a clear understanding of the two types of quantitative data sets—discrete and continuous. This distinction is vitally important in learning how to apply various statistical techniques.

2. **Qualitative,** which are expressed non-numerically. This is the second major type of variable.

Examples: Marital status, hair color, religious preference, gender.

Question to You: In my example of determining the average age (mean age) of the student members of this class, remember I determined the sample average was 19.6 years of age. In this example, which one is the statistic and which one is the variable?

Think about it before reading on.

Average and Age are the two items of interest. Average is the arithmetic average, thus it is the measure of central tendency. A measurement of central tendency is a descriptive measure. A descriptive measure may be a statistic (sample value) or a parameter (population value). In this case, average is the statistic.

Knowing this certainly narrows your choice to make a correct identification of the variable, right? The characteristic (variable) of interest is age. Age is a continuous variable. Age can take on a range of values.

This leads us to a generalization which is true. You can apply the term parameter or statistic to a measure of central tendency or a measure of dispersion.

Raw (Ungrouped) and Grouped (Frequency Distribution) Data Sets

For any data set, I can calculate measures of central tendency and measures of dispersion. These measures are descriptive. They describe data sets. When I say these measures describe data sets, I still must do calculations, but the result is a description of the data set. Describing a data set does not solely imply you are describing it with words alone. The data set can be described as the arithmetic mean or the standard deviation or as a percentile or as the range. In broad categories these calculations are measures of central tendency and measures of dispersion.

As you will later learn, the two most important measures are the arithmetic mean and the standard deviation. This will become more evident as the text material unfolds.

There are two branches of statistics—descriptive and inferential—as you have already been told. When you calculate a measure of central tendency or a measure of dispersion, you are calculating a value that *describes the data set* (set of data). When you calculate a measure of central tendency for a population, it is referred to as parameter. When you calculate a measure of dispersion for a sample, it is referred to as a statistic.

To further complicate things, I now want to introduce you to the concepts of **raw (ungrouped) data sets** and **grouped (frequency distribution) data sets**.

Enough, you say, I am still having trouble staying mentally organized as it is.

Chill, I say. In a hundred years neither one of us will remember this stuff anyway. So let's give it a try.

Raw, ungrouped data is just that. It is raw and unorganized. For example, if you wanted to determine the average age of a group of 100 students, the raw data set would consist of a listing of the 100 ages in no particular order. Grouped data, however, is a data set that has been organized into some useable form. For example, you might want to classify the students' ages into categories of 15 to 18, 19 to 21, 22 to 25, etc. This would require that you take the raw data and rearrange it into organized categories. The rearranged data is often referred to as a frequency distribution. The idea of frequency distributions is an important one.

Raw data or grouped data can be either a population or a sample. Knowing if a data set is a population or a sample is important, because some of the calculations are different for a sample than they are for a population. Variance is one in which the value will actually change. For a sample, the denominator is $n - 1$. For a population the denominator contains N. You must identify if your data set is a population or a sample. Ask the question: Is this data set a population or a sample? I will cover this information more shortly.

Let's look at examples of both a raw data set and a grouped data set.

Raw (Ungrouped) Data Set

Let's assume the following data set for the number of passengers who took a Southwest Airlines flight from Dallas Love Field to Austin at 7:00 AM each day for 50 consecutive days. The first question you should ask yourself is "Is this a population or a sample?" Since this is not a representative portion but a total listing of 50 consecutive days, you should identify this as a population data set.

What are some observations you can easily make about this data set?

Table 1.2 Number of passengers on a Southwest Airlines flight, recorded over 50 days.

69	70	78	83	79
73	73	57	67	69
51	60	70	67	76
70	84	82	75	93
64	72	84	79	71
83	85	59	75	95
78	73	79	93	94
77	81	78	90	83
81	83	91	101	86
92	94	103	80	68

The data set is listed in an unorganized fashion. There are five columns and ten rows making a total of fifty observations, which equals the number of flights at 7:00 AM for 50 consecutive days. I can calculate an arithmetic mean by simply adding up all the numbers and dividing the sum of those numbers (3,918) by the number of observations (50). (3,918 / 50 = 78.36) I can now interpret the arithmetic mean I just calculated. There are, on average, 78.36 passengers per day on the Southwest Airlines flight from Dallas to Austin at 7:00 AM.

Without making any changes to the data set, can I tell anything more about the data set?

Yes, I can determine the range—the highest number is 103 and the lowest is 51; therefore the range is 52. If this data set included 5,000 observations, would the range be as easily determined?

Perhaps, but so much data would leave room for observation error. A solution would be to arrange the data set in ascending or descending order. This would place the highest value at one end and the lowest value at the other end.

Another question of interest to you is: Am I dealing with a discrete or continuous data set? Remember, continuous data can take on a range of values while discrete data is measured in whole numbers.

Hint: The answer is a discrete data set (number of passengers is a whole number). Do you agree?

Since the data set is not in an ordered array, determining the median, a quartile, decile, or percentile would be impossible. It is difficult to determine the mode from this un-arranged data set but not impossible. It would be difficult, but not impossible to determine the standard deviation of this data set.

However, if I place the data set in ordered array (arrangement), there are a couple of other observations that I can make. I can now calculate the median, percentiles, quartiles, and deciles and more easily determine the mode. But remember I have placed the data set in ordered array first (lowest to the highest is the most usual arrangement).

You can't really tell much more about the data distribution, but if the raw data were grouped into classes, could I then gain more information that would be helpful in making decisions about the number of passengers flying on the 7:00 AM flight?

The answer is, yes, but more on that shortly.

The bottom line is that without re-arrangement of the raw (unorganized) data set, I can't tell very much about the raw data set. The data set does not yield sufficient information to aid management in making service decisions such as food, beverages, flight attendants, estimated turn-around time, etc.

Best Rule When Analyzing Raw Data

For any raw data set (population or sample), the first thing you should do is to arrange the raw data set in an ordered array. *Always* (strong word) arrange the data set into an ordered array before attempting to make any descriptive calculations about the data set.

As a reminder, you now have two important questions to ask about any data set. First, is the data set a population or sample and second, is the data set discrete or continuous? Ask these each time.

So do I have other options as I analyze the data set? Yep. For one, I can organize the data set into something referred to as a frequency distribution, which is also referred to as a grouped data set. The data will be divided into classes and from the raw data you will record the number of observations in each class. The data will be presented in a more organized fashion, which in turn will be more usable. Let's take a look at converting the raw data in Table 1.2 into a grouped data presentation.

Grouped (Frequency Distribution) Data Sets

Assume the following classes have been developed from the raw data set above. I will show you how to develop the classes a bit later. Remember the low was 51 and the high was 103.

50 to 59

60 to 69

70 to 79

80 to 89

90 to 99

100 to 109

Notice there is no overlap in classes. That is important. If they overlapped like 50 to 60 and 60 to 70, what would you do with a value of 60?

I am waiting. This is not a rhetorical question.

The answer is that you would not know where to place 60—in the first category or the second.

Remember these are discrete data, since the units of measure are people (whole numbers).

If this were miles flown, what kind of data would I be analyzing?

I am waiting. This, too, is not a rhetorical question.

That's right, continuous. Continuous data can take on a range of values.

Okay, let's go back to the original question. How do I convert the raw data set in the Table 1.2 into a frequency distribution?

Easy, there is nothing too complicated here. Just look at each of the raw data values and record a "chicken scratch mark" in that class each time the number falls within those boundaries. For example, reading down the first column of Table 1.2, the first value is 69, so I simply record a "chicken scratch" next to the 60 to 69 class. The next value is 73, so I record a "chicken scratch" next to the 70 to 79 class. The next value is 51, so I record a "chicken scratch" next to the 50 to 59 class. I continue this process until all of the 50 observations have been organized into the grouped data set. I have recorded those values below. Go through Table 1.2 and count the number of values that occur in the 50 through 59 class. You will find there are three (51, 57, and 59), which is reflected in Table 1.3 below.

The final result is as follows, where "f" is the number of passengers in each of the following classes. Here "f" represents the frequency distribution of the raw data set in the table below.

Notice that the first class begins close to the lowest value in the raw data set (Table 1.2). The lowest value is 51, but I begin the class with 50. There is some latitude in where to start the classes, but generally try to begin as close to the lowest value as possible. Also observe that the frequency distribution is in an ordered array from 50 to 109. Notice that the total frequency of

Table 1.3   The Southwest Airlines passengers data set grouped into classes.

Classes	Frequency (f)
50 through 59	3
60 through 69	7
70 through 79	18
80 through 89	12
90 through 99	8
100 through 109	2
Total	50

50 is the same as the total number of raw data observations. If it does not total 50, then I need to review my tabulations since I have made a mistake somewhere.

One disadvantage of a frequency distribution is that once it is completed, I will lose the original values. For example, the first class is from 50 through 59. As I have already said, there are three values in that class. From the frequency distribution I cannot tell what they are, but from the raw data set I can determine that the three values are 51, 57, and 59. However, from the frequency distribution I cannot see those three numbers. I know only that there are three numbers somewhere in the class of 50 through 59.

This leads me to have to make some assumptions about the distribution of the value in each class. *It is assumed that the values in the class are equally distributed within that class and that the midpoint of the class is a good representation of the average value in each class.* For example, there are eight values in the 90 through 99 class. For purposes of later calculations, I will assume those eight numbers are equally spread in the class 90 through 99.

Can I observe additional things about my frequency distribution that I cannot observe from my raw data set?

Yes, I can add several other columns. I can show a cumulative frequency distribution (cf) and a relative frequency distribution (rf) and a cumulative relative frequency distribution (crf). Let's expand the table to include those calculations.

Table 1.4   Distribution of Southwest Airlines passenger data.

Grouped Data Set Classes	Frequency Distribution (f)	Cumulative Frequency Distribution (cf)	Relative Frequency Distribution (rf)	Cumulative Relative Frequency Distribution (crf)
50 through 59	3	3	6%	6%
60 through 69	7	10	14%	20%
70 through 79	18	28	36%	56%
80 through 89	12	40	24%	80%
90 through 99	8	48	16%	96%
100 through 109	2	50	4%	100%
Total	50	N/A	100%	N/A

Observations and Conclusions from the Table

1. 36% of the flights have between 70 and 79 passengers.
2. 60% of the flights have between 70 and 89 passengers. (36% + 24%)
3. 76% of the flights have between 70 and 99 passengers. (36% + 24% + 16%)
4. 90% of the flights have between 60 and 99 passengers. (14% + 36% + 24% + 16%)
5. 80% of the flights have between 50 and 89 passengers. (6% + 14% + 36% + 24%)

From the grouped data set (frequency distribution) I can gain more insight into the data set. From a managerial point of view, this allows me to better plan staffing and meals. You can observe more about a grouped data set (frequency distribution) than you can about raw data. Consider grouping your raw data into frequency distributions whenever possible.

Determining the Number of Classes and Class Interval

Even though you are struggling, you manage to frame a question. You ask, was the determination of the number of classes or the interval within each class arbitrary?

The answer is no, but a very good question.

But in my highly trained mind (and warped sense of humor), I sense you want more of an answer than just "No."

I begin my explanation. Determining the classes and the **interval** (the distance from the lowest value in the class to the highest value in the class) is a two-step process.

From your raw data set, the *first step* is to determine the number of classes by the following method.

$$2^C \geq N$$

where "c" is the desired number of classes and "N" is the number of population observations. This would be "n" for a sample data set.

For the example problem this would be as follows:

$$2^C \geq 50$$

Usually the easiest way to determine the power of 2 is to use trial and error.

What, you wonder, trial and error? I thought this was a sophisticated statistics course?

I ignore you for the time being and move on with my explanation. In this example, I would multiply the following:

$$\underline{\mathbf{2}} \times \underline{\mathbf{2}} = 4 \times \underline{\mathbf{2}} = 8 \times \underline{\mathbf{2}} = 16 \times \underline{\mathbf{2}} = 32 \times \underline{\mathbf{2}} = 64.$$

That is as far as I need to go. The value 64 meets your criterion, which was that 2^C must equal or exceed 50. I need go only as far as the first number that meets my criterion.

This first number was 64. $64 \geq 50$.

What I do next is count the number of twos I have in the multiplication string.

I have **bolded the twos** and underlined them for ease of counting. Notice there are six which means I have six classes (C).

The second step is to determine the **interval width.** What do I mean by interval width? The class interval is the spread (distance) between the lower and the upper number of any class. The interval width should be consistent for all classes. There are six classes and the frequency distribution reflects six classes, but I need to determine the interval within those classes.

I will let "CI" stand for the class interval.

CI = (Largest Value − Smallest Value) ÷ Number of Desired Classes From the raw data, I previously determined that the smallest value was 51 and the largest was 103.

CI = $(103 - 51) \div 6 = 8.66$ which I can round to 9.

The class interval should be nine.

However, being an astute student, you challenge my conclusion. Professor, this is discrete data so don't I have to count the 50 and the 59? If I do count them both (inclusive) the interval is ten, not nine as the calculation indicates. (50, 51, 51, 53, 54, 55, 56, 57, 58, and 59)

I am impressed, I admit. My explanation is simple, however. I do have some latitude in adjusting the interval width. I rounded the interval to ten simply because the person or group to whom I may present my findings will not "think" in terms of an interval of 8.66 or even nine. As the researcher, you have some latitude in setting the interval width at a reasonable value.

So what does this mean? Do I have an insurmountable problem?

The answer is no, but if rounded too high, there could be some data calculation issues.

In this instance, classes established with an interval of nine would have yielded the following.

50 − 58   59 − 67   68 − 76   77 − 85   86 − 94   95 − 103

Would this affect our calculations?

Yes, it would.

Are the effects significant?

In this case, the results are not affected materially. Repeated: Most supervisors and managers would rather think in terms of an interval of ten than an interval of nine.

Compare the two classes: 50 through 59 versus 50 through 58.

Which makes more sense as you present the data to upper management? The answer to that question will dictate the adjustment you make to the class interval. Adjusting by this small amount does not create a material difference in the descriptive measure calculations.

Other Terms and Calculations

Midpoint: For purposes you will understand in the next chapter, the class midpoint must be calculated in order to determine a center point within each class. The calculation is as follows:

Class Midpoint (M) = the lowest value of the class + highest value of the class divided by 2. (Lowest + Highest) ÷ 2

Midpoints for this distribution

$(50 + 59) \div 2 = 54.5$
$(60 + 69) \div 2 = 64.5$
etc.

Once you have made descriptive calculations, you might want to present the data set pictorially. Here Excel is the software of choice. In Excel there is an icon named "Chart Wizard" in the upper toolbar. I need you to find a computer that has Excel on it.

I will wait.

Oh, I see you are back. Let's take a quick look at some presentations.

Pictorial Displays

Important displays include histograms, line charts, bar charts, pie charts, side by side bar charts, Pareto charts, stacked bar charts, and many other pictorial displays. These displays will help communicate key points to management in a graphic manner. Often a picture is really worth a thousand words. You might want to spend some time reviewing the various displays. The Chart Wizard allows you to graphically present your data in dozens of formats.

Under Tools > Data Analysis you can also find the all-important histogram. If Data Analysis does not appear, you need to click on Tools > Add > then check the two VBA boxes. Now go back to Tools > Data Analysis (it should now be available).

Using the data set on the airline flight, I can present the following graphical displays (Figures 1.1 through 1.5).

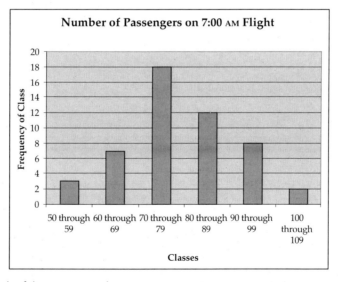

Figure 1.1   A bar graph of the passenger data.

Using Excel, this took me about two to three minutes to develop. All I did was to open my Excel software. I then typed in the data from Table 1.3—the classes with their corresponding frequencies. I next highlighted all the columns and rows I just entered into the Excel spreadsheet. I next opened the Chart Wizard (on your tool bar). I then selected a bar chart (there were five from which I could choose). I selected the first bar chart. I clicked next until I was able to name the table, the x-axis and the y-axis. I decided to save it in the worksheet into which I entered the Table 1.3 data. I then copied it and went to this textbook and pasted it into this area. You see the result. After being copied, you can paste it in a report or presentation.

I could have chosen a line chart and the result would be as follows:

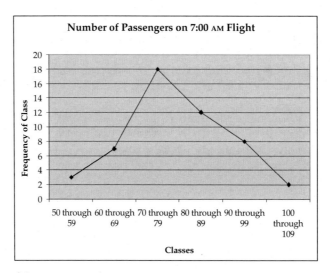

Figure 1.2   A line chart of the passenger data.

I could have created a pie chart as follows:

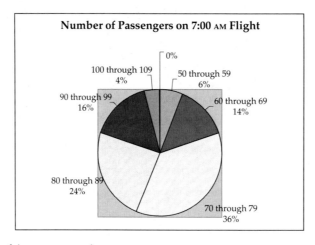

Figure 1.3   A pie chart of the passenger data.

I could have created an area chart.

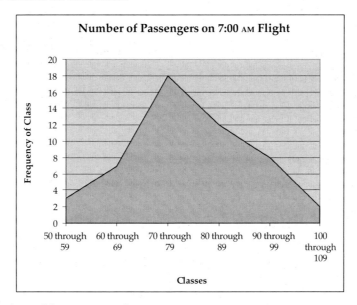

Figure 1.4   An area chart of the passenger data.

The area chart is a most interesting chart and provides me with a graphic presentation of the area under the curve. The area under any curve equals 100% of the observations of the data set. This is an important idea.

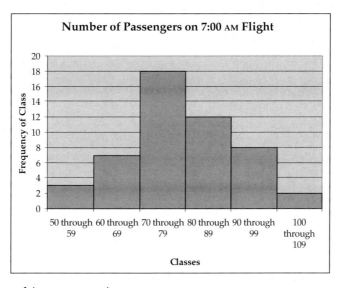

Figure 1.5   A histogram of the passenger data.

Let's say I want to create a histogram (bars will be touching). You can do this by using the Chart Wizard *if you already have the frequency distribution*. If you are working with the *raw data*, you cannot use the Chart Wizard to create a histogram, but must use Tools > Data Analysis > Histogram. In my example, I already have the frequency distribution so I will show you how to create the histogram from the Chart Wizard.

First create a bar chart like that shown in Figure 1.1 above. Next, right click on the bars until a small diamond shows on each bar. Then right click on one of the diamonds and select Format Data Series. Six tabs will appear. Select the "Options" tab. Next change the "Gap Width" to zero. The result is a histogram as shown in Figure 1.5.

Pie Charts in General

I differ with most textbook authors when it comes to creating pie charts. When working with pie charts apart from a frequency distribution, they should start at noon and move in a clockwise manner with the largest category of data shown as the first "slice" of the pie. Next following would be the next largest category proceeding in a similar order down to the smallest category.

Side by side pie charts would create an exception. Once you have determined that the largest category for Pie Chart 1 is category *A*, you need to keep *A* as the first category in Pie Chart 2, even if category *B* has become larger in the second pie chart. This will enable you to glance at the pie chart and visually determine a relative size from year 1 to year 2. Below is an example of 2003 compared to 2004 in the production of various crops (Figures 1.6 and 1.7).

Notice that at a glance you can determine that cotton production dropped from 2003 to 2004, while wheat production increased when comparing 2003 to 2004. By having a common starting point (noon) and following certain rules, the meaning of the pie chart can be more easily interpreted.

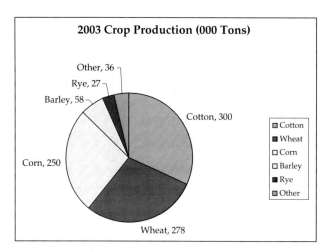

Figure 1.6   Pie chart of 2003 crop production.

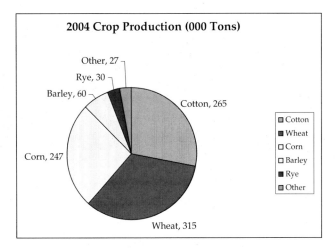

Figure 1.7   Pie chart of 2004 crop production.

Stem and Leaf Display

The stem and leaf display will present the values of the original data set. When I go to a frequency distribution from raw data, I lose the original values. The stem and leaf display is one way to present the data in a format that still holds the original values. You will find the stem and leaf graphic in the Chart Wizard of Excel.

Tick and Tab Display

The tick and tab display is primarily used in financial markets to reflect the high-low-close values for such things as the money market, interest rates, stock prices, etc. It is a graph showing time on the horizontal axis (x) and the value or percentage on the vertical axis (y). For each unit of time, say daily, the high point of a stock is plotted as well as the low point of the stock. Also included is the closing point of the stock.

Caveat (Keep in Mind for Chapter 3)

As already pointed out, one of the things that happens to you when you start developing frequency distributions is you lose track of the original data values. For example, let's take the frequency distribution in the 50 through 59 class for the airline passenger data problem. There are three values in that class, but I do not know what they are. I must make some assumptions about how to calculate their value. The midpoint of the class, which is 54.5, might best represent the average values in that class.

Since I do lose the original values, I must use the midpoint as an estimate of the values in each particular class. In this instance, there are three frequencies. My representation of the values works this way. $3 \times 54.5 = 163.5$. The raw data had three values that would have naturally fallen into the 50 through 59 class. I happen to know what they are, but if you convert from raw data sets to grouped data sets you will not. In this instance they are 51, 57, and 59. By adding these three numbers you have a sum of 167.0. Obviously 163.5 does not equal 167.0.

The plusses and minuses associated with each class as represented by the midpoint will tend to neutralize each other, thus leaving you with totals that are reasonably close to the original (raw data) values. Even though this presents a minor problem, the error is not usually significant and tends to balance out throughout the entire distribution.

Next in our quest is to actually learn how to make the calculations for all of the descriptive measures (central tendency and dispersion) for ungrouped (raw data sets) and grouped data sets (frequency distributions), populations, and samples. What you find in most instances is that the only thing that changes in most calculations is the symbols and not the value of the calculation. An exception exists—the variance of the sample and the variance of the population will differ in value.

You know You are a Texan If:

- You use "fixin to" in daily conversation.

- You know the value of a parking space is not determined by distance to the door but by the availability of shade.

Descriptive Statistics—Raw Data

2

| Attorney: | Now Doctor, isn't it true that when a person dies in his sleep, he doesn't know about it untill the next morning? |
| Witness: | Did you actually pass the bar exam? |

My next step in this marathon is to take you through calculations for raw data sets. Remember, raw data sets are unorganized. I will show you how to make calculations for the mean, median, and mode as measures of central tendency and show you how to make calculations for the range, average deviation, variance, standard deviation, percentiles, quartiles, and deciles as measures of dispersion.

Central tendency and dispersion are useful in describing data sets. I want to know how much the data set tends to focus about a center point (usually the mean) and just how far it is dispersed from that center point (usually the standard deviation).

In this chapter I will deal exclusively with raw data sets. In the next chapter, I will deal exclusively with grouped data sets.

Measures of Central Tendency for Raw (Ungrouped) Data Sets

Let's assume that Bill Smith earned the following grades in a full semester of statistics.

Let "X" represent the variable, grades.

Table 2.1   Bill Smith's grades in statistics class.

Test	Grade (X)
#1	63
#2	59
#3	71
#4	41
#5	32
Total	266

The first question you should ask yourself is "Is this a population or a sample?" To be a sample these must be a representative portion of the population. Since these are all of the grades for Bill Smith for the entire semester, this is a population of Bill's grades. This distinction will be important when I calculate the variance.

Arithmetic Mean

In order to calculate the arithmetic mean, you would simply add up the numbers, which total 266, and then divide 266 by the number of observations (N), which is 5 in this case.

$$266 \div 5 = 53.2 \text{ average grade}$$

Can you write a formula for this calculation?

The column is headed "X" and you totaled the "X" column, so this would be the sum of a column headed "X". If I let μ (Greek letter mu) represent the arithmetic mean of the population, the formula is as follows:

$$\mu = \frac{\Sigma X}{N} \text{ population mean}$$

If this were a sample rather than a population would the formula change?

The answer is yes, but the changes would be only notational. The μ would become $\overline{X}$ and the capital N would become small n. The calculation methods would not change—just the symbol notations.

$$\overline{X} = \frac{\Sigma X}{n} \text{ sample mean}$$

Special Note

As you will see later, this is true about almost all of the calculations for the population or the sample. The exception to the rule is the variance and, subsequently, the standard deviation.

Median

Let's now tackle the second value in central tendencies, which is the median. The median is the one in the middle—50% above and 50% below.

The formula for the *position of the median* is as follows:

$$\text{Median} = (N + 1) \div 2$$

What is the median in this example?

$$\text{Remember } N = 5$$

So $(5 + 1) = 6$ and $6 \div 2 = 3$ which I am identifying as the median position.

My next step is to count down three positions in the data set and determine the value of the median. In this case that value is 71, but is this correct?

Think about it.

The answer is no, the median is not 71. Remember, I told you earlier that any time you have a data set that is ungrouped, the first thing you must do is to arrange the data set in some logical sequence from ascending order to descending order or vice versa. The position is determined *only after you place the data set in an ordered array*. The reordered data set is as follows.

Table 2.2 Bill Smith's grades in ascending order.

Test	Grade (X)
#1	32
#2	41
#3	59
#4	63
#5	71
Total	266

So now if I count down three positions, I find the number 59. Fifty-nine is the median value. Don't get the position (3) and the value (59) mixed up. The first is a position and the second is a value. It should be rather clear that three is not a value since three does not appear in the data set at all. Three (3) is not the median value.

Would the same approach work if I had an even numbered data set? In Table 2.3, notice that I have added another 63 to the original data set. This is an arbitrary addition to illustrate a couple of points.

Table 2.3 The data set with 63 added.

Test	Grade (X)
#1	32
#2	41
#3	59
#4	63
#5	63
#6	71
Total	**329**

The answer is "yes", although you have probably forgotten the question by now.

The position of the median would be determined the same way.

$$\text{Median} = (N + 1) \div 2$$

$N = 6$ So $6 + 1 = 7 \div 2 = 3.5$ (which is the position not the value).

The value of the median would fall between 59 and 63 (after you count down). This tells us that the median is between the third and fourth position. You simply average the two values: $(59 + 63) = 122 \div 2 = 61$. So even though the value of 61 does not appear in the distribution, the value in the middle of the distribution is 61. The median is the one in the middle with 50% above and 50% below.

Mode

Using the data in Table 2.3, what is the mode? By definition, the mode is the value that occurs most often, so the mode would be the value 63 using the data from Table 2.3. Sixty-three is the only value that repeats itself and must be the mode value. What if I had a third distribution and it looked like the following?

$$32, 41, 41, 59, 63, 63, 71$$

Now what is the value of the mode?

There are two modes. One is 41 and the other is 63, so this distribution is **bi-modal.** In the very first distribution (Table 2.1), when $N = 5$, there was no mode. So for ungrouped data sets there can be no mode, one mode, or two modes or more, depending on the observations made from the data set.

Weighted Mean

How would you go about calculating a mean if I told you that the tests are arranged in sequence and that the first test is to be weighted (valued) as if it were equal to one test, the second with the weight of one, the third with the weight of two, the fourth with the weight of two, and the last test with the weight of three? In other words, the tests are progressively more important. The distribution is as follows:

Table 2.4 Distribution of test grades and their weights.

Test	Grade (X)	Weight (W)
First	32	1
Second	41	1
Third	59	2
Fourth	63	2
Fifth	71	3
Total	**266**	**9**

The first thing you would do is multiply the test score times the weight to get a weighted value for each test. By doing this you are considering each test's relative importance in the course. What you get is as follows.

Table 2.5 The weighted score for each test grade.

Test	Grade (X)	Weight (W)	Weighted Score (XW)
First	32	1	32
Second	41	1	41
Third	59	2	118
Fourth	63	2	126
Fifth	71	3	213
Total	**266**	**9**	**530**

Now the next step is to divide 530 by 5 to get a value of 106.

Wait a minute, you astutely observe. How can the value jump so drastically from 53.2 to 106? That does not make too much sense to me.

You have made an excellent observation. Congratulations. In reality, no matter how you weight the grades, you could never get a grade that exceeded 71, so I must have made an error somewhere. Care to guess what it was?

Okay, you say, why didn't you divide by the weight rather than the number of grades?

That is exactly what I should have done. The sum of the column headed "W" is nine. The approach I should have used was to divide 530 by 9, which equals 58.8.

This is called a **weighted mean.** I could have a weighted mean for a sample or for a population. Here the data set is a population, so can you write a formula for the weighted mean of a population?

Think about it and try it before glancing at the answer below.

$$\mu_w = \frac{\Sigma XW}{\Sigma W}$$

This is the sum of a column headed XW divided by the sum of a column headed W. If this were a sample the only change would be to replace μ_w with $\overline{X}_w$.

Geometric Mean

There may be times when you may want to determine the average change for percentages. When this occasion arises, the arithmetic mean does not yield the most accurate result.

For example, assume the growth rate of an investment has yielded rates of return for the past four years of 1.21%, 1.12%, 0.90%, and 1.25%. You could calculate the arithmetic average, which would be 4.48 ÷ 4 = 1.1200%. However, this would overstate the return since your calculations are in percentages. The correct calculation would be the **geometric mean,** which would be determined as follows.

$$\text{Geometric Mean} \;=\; \sqrt[4]{(1.21)(1.12)(0.90)(1.25)} = 1.1112\%.$$

The geometric mean is always less than the arithmetic mean unless the percentage change is equal each time period.

I have shown you how to calculate the mean, median, mode, weighted average, and geometric mean for raw data sets. Remember, these are measures of central tendency and all describe the data set of interest.

Calculations for Measures of Dispersion for Raw (Ungrouped) Data Sets

Dispersion is associated with the variability of the data set from its center point (usually the mean). The calculations are designed to tell us to what degree the individual observations disperse or spread from or about the mean. Let's examine the measures of dispersion one at a time.

Range

The range is the difference between the high and the low values in the data set. In the grade distribution given above in Table 2.2, the high value is 71 and the low value is 32. The difference between these two is the range.

$$71 - 32 = 39 \text{ (which is the range)}.$$

The range is a rather quick calculation, but has minor use. Later I will use the range more extensively when I show you quality control techniques.

New Data Set Example

The following grades were the grades for *the first test for all eight students in a statistics class.*

Table 2.6   Test grades earned by the students in a statistics course.

X
73
82
64
61
63
68
52
73

What is the first thing I told you to do to any ungrouped data set?

That's right! Put the raw data set into an ordered array. I hope you remembered.

The revised data set looks like the following table.

Table 2.7   Statistics students' test grades, in ascending order.

Student	X
1	52
2	61
3	63
4	64
5	68
6	73
7	73
8	82
Total	536

Calculate the mean, median, and the mode for this ungrouped data set.

Check Answers: mean = 67; median = 66; mode = 73. Take a few minutes and make sure you can get these answers.

Average Deviation

Let's say that I want to calculate the average deviation for the new data set. How do I accomplish that? First, I need to ask myself if the data set is a population or sample.

It is a population, because it consists of all the test scores for all the students for the first test.

The formula is as follows. Let AD = average deviation.

$$AD = \frac{\Sigma(X - \mu)}{N}$$

This would be the average deviation for the population data set. If the data set was a sample, the symbols would change but not the actual calculation.

I need to calculate the sum of a column headed "$X - \mu$". To do this, I need to add two columns to my Table 2.7 data set.

Table 2.8   Data set showing the mean and average distribution.

Student	X	Mean (μ)	X − μ
1	52	67	−15
2	61	67	−6
3	63	67	−4
4	64	67	−3
5	68	67	+1
6	73	67	+6
7	73	67	+6
8	82	67	+15
Total	536	N/A	Zero

The average deviation is a key concept. The value of the average deviation is zero. Think about it. It makes logical sense. If the mean is the balancing point, then the deviations around the mean *must equal zero*. Of course, if you had a continuous number for the mean (33.33333), you would never have an average deviation that would exactly equal zero, but if you carry the mean to enough decimal points (usually four) you would be very close.

The last column in Table 2.8 shows the deviations around the mean. Remember this. I will tell you why shortly.

Variance and Standard Deviation

The most important measure of the dispersion (or variability) of a data set is the standard deviation. You need to know what it is. If I assume the mean of any distribution is zero, I can then measure variability around the mean in a standard unit of measure, which is called the standard deviation. This idea will become more meaningful as you continue reading. In order to calculate the standard deviation, I must first calculate the variance. The standard deviation is simply the square root of the variance.

The variance is defined as *the mean of the squared deviations around the mean*. Not one of you has a clue what I am talking about, I am sure. It sounds like a lot of statistical double-talk. To calculate the variance I will do the following:

1. I must find the amount by which the observations deviated around or away from the mean. Wait a minute, that sounds like the average deviation, doesn't it? (Of course, most of you have forgotten what the average deviation is by this point in your reading.)

2. I must then square those deviations. No sweat, I can do that. Since I am going to use a tabular approach, I will simply create another column headed $(X - \mu)^2$. This new column will be the deviations around the mean which are squared.

3. Then, using the total in the column calculated in step 2, I must find the average or the mean of the squared deviations.

I am not naïve enough to believe you understand what you just read. Well, most of you did not.

Let's take another approach to it.

To better understand, let's take a look at the formula for variance.

$$\sigma^2 = \frac{\Sigma(X - \mu)^2}{N}$$

This is the population variance. The symbol σ is the Greek symbol lowercase sigma. The summation sign (Σ) is also a Greek symbol called sigma, but it is capital sigma. Do not be confused because you have two symbols referred to as sigma—one is lowercase and the other is its capital counterpart (like A and a).

If this were a sample the formula would look like the following:

$$S^2 = \frac{\Sigma(X - \overline{X})^2}{n - 1}$$

This is the sample variance. Here I let S^2 be the symbol of the sample variance.

Notice here the denominators of the population formula and the sample formula. Assuming I am working with the same data set, I will actually have a different value for the sample variance and population variance. Let's take an example of a data set in which I will make the calculation as if it was a population, and then I will make the calculation as if it was a sample. The purpose is to illustrate the difference in values.

I will use the data from Table 2.8. Let's first calculate the population variance. Repeating the formula, I have the following:

$$\sigma^2 = \frac{\Sigma(X - \mu)^2}{N}$$

I need a column headed $(X - \mu)^2$. To get that I will square the values in the column headed $(X - \mu)$. For example $-15^2 = 225$, which is the first value in the last column. When completed, I will sum the column I just calculated.

Table 2.9   The population variance for the data in Table 2.8.

Student	X	Mean (μ)	$X - \mu$	$(X - \mu)^2$
1	52	67	−15	225
2	61	67	−6	36
3	63	67	−4	16
4	64	67	−3	9
5	68	67	+1	1
6	73	67	+6	36
7	73	67	+6	36
8	82	67	+15	225
Total	536	N/A	Zero	584

Next I substitute the value (584) from the last column in Table 2.9 into the formula.

$$\sigma^2 = \frac{584}{8} = 73 \text{ grades squared.}$$

One problem I have with the variance is that the units of measurement are squared. Here the variance is 73 grades squared. I personally have great difficulty understanding grades squared, so that is why *I never use the variance to calculate anything.* I always use the standard deviation. The standard deviation is the square root of the variance. To get the standard deviation I take the square root of 73. This value is 8.54 grades $= \sigma$, which is the square root of the variance.

Let's assume for a minute that the data set I am using is a sample rather than a population.

What would change?

First the formula would change. Let's compare them.

$$\text{sample: } S^2 = \frac{\Sigma (X - \overline{X})^2}{n - 1} \qquad \text{population: } \sigma^2 = \frac{\Sigma (X - \mu)^2}{N}$$

Wait a minute, you say, they look much the same.

Right on—but notice that the denominator includes $n - 1$ for the sample rather than N as shown in the population. The numerator is still the sum of a column headed either $(X - \overline{X})^2$ or $(X - \mu)^2$. The numerator would be the same either way, but the symbols would be different. $\overline{X}$ changes place with μ.

The population variance would be:

$$\sigma^2 = \frac{\Sigma (X - \mu)^2}{N} = \frac{584}{8} = 73 \text{ grades squares}$$

The standard deviation would be the square root of the variance and would be:

$$\sigma = \sqrt{73} = 8.54 \text{ grades}$$

The difference lies in the denominator. If I were to calculate the variance as a sample, I would have 584 (same numerator) divided by 7 (which is $n - 1$) = 83.4 grades squared. The standard deviation of the sample would then be the square root of 83.4 grades squared, which is 9.13 grades.

The denominator for a sample is $n - 1$, which is referred to as degrees of freedom. Because you are working with a sample, you would lose one degree of freedom (free choice) in any sequence of numbers. A couple of paragraphs below I discuss more fully the idea of degrees of freedom.

Notice that the sample standard deviation is larger than the population standard deviation. (9.13 versus 8.54) This will always be the case.

Why, you wonder silently?

Being clairvoyant, I continue my explanation. When I take a sample, I am prone to make an error, wouldn't you agree?

The answer is yes, in case that stumps you a bit. I compensate for this error with a larger sample standard deviation. If this were a population value, there would be no error so I do not need to make the same compensation. Using degrees of freedom for the denominator for sample calculations provides a useful adjustment.

Summary Chart for the Symbols I Am Using

Table 2.10   Symbols for some measures of populations and samples.

	Mean	Variance	Standard Deviation	Size of the ...
Population	μ	σ^2	σ	N
Sample	$\overline{X}$	S^2	S	n

Degrees of Freedom Is $n - 1$

What do I mean by **degrees of freedom?** Let's assume that you have four numbers that add to 100. Once you have selected three of the four numbers, the fourth number is automatically selected for you. My freedom in selecting the fourth number is not available.

For example, let's say that I designated those four numbers by A, B, C, and D.

$$A + B + C + D = 100.$$

I have complete freedom in selecting three of the numbers. They could be 25, 30, and 10. The sum of these four numbers is 65. The fourth number must therefore be 35. No other choice is possible. That is why I can say that my degrees of freedom is $n - 1$, which is $4 - 1$ or 3 in this example. I have three free choices but do not have free choice for the fourth number. The fourth number is predetermined.

Percentiles, Quartiles, and Deciles

The only remaining measure of dispersion I need to show you is how to calculate the values for percentiles, quartiles, and deciles. Once you understand percentiles, understanding quartiles and deciles will be a snap.

Percentiles divide the data set into equal increments of 1%. Quartiles divide the distribution into four equal increments of 25% each, and deciles divide the distribution into ten equal increments of 10% each. The first quartile is the 25th percentile, the first decile is the 10th percentile, and the third quartile is the 75th percentile.

Example

Let's assume I have determined the number of shares of stock that traded on the New York Stock Exchange (NYSE) for the past 50 days for a particular stock. (Shares are in thousands.)

The resulting data set is listed in an ordered array with five days listed (going down) in the first column and five in the second column and so forth. The total observations would be 50 ($N = 50$). Table 2.11 shows the raw data source for the shares sold during that 50-day period.

Table 2.11   Raw data for shares sold on the NYSE over the past 50 days.

2	12	18	28	34	38	47	57	66	74
5	12	20	29	35	39	48	58	67	75
8	14	21	31	35	42	51	62	70	76
8	15	26	32	36	44	52	63	72	78
11	16	28	34	37	46	55	65	73	81

Suppose that I wanted to calculate the 25th percentile for the distribution of stock sales listed above.

The formula is as follows

$$L_P = (n + 1)[P \div 100]$$

where

L_P is the *location* in the ordered array of the desired percentile.
n is the number of observations.
P is the desired percentile.

The calculations look like this:

$$L_{25} = (50 + 1)[25 \div 100] = 51 \times 0.25 = 12.75.$$

Does this mean that 12.75 is the value of the 25th percentile?

No, it does not. L_p is the location of the desired percentile by definition, not the value. What I need to do is count down from the first position in the distribution, which starts with the number 2, to the twelfth number in the distribution, which is the value 20. I am not finished yet, however, because I am not looking for the twelfth position, which is the value 20. I am looking for a value between the twelfth and the thirteenth positions. The value I need will be between 20 and 21.

How far between, you ask?

To answer that question, I must return to the positional calculation of 12.75. I will count down 12 full positions and then go 75% (0.75) of the way into the next position. Remember, the data set is assumed to be divided into 100 equal pieces that are each equal 1%.

The calculations are as follows

$$20 + (0.75)(21 - 20) = 20 + (0.75)(1) = 20 + 0.75 = 20.75$$

20.75 is the VALUE of the 25th percentile, while 12.75 is the POSITION of the 25th percentile.

I have shown you a very important distinction—the difference between position (location) and value. Keep that distinction in mind.

What would the value be if the thirteenth number in the data set was changed from 21 to 24?

This is not a rhetorical question, so calculate it. You should be doing this math in your head.

The answer is 23.0.

The position remained the same at 12.75, but the value changed to 23 from 20.75 because of the gap between the twelfth and thirteenth positions.

$$20 + (0.75)(24 - 20) = 20 + (0.75)(4) = 20 + 3.0 = 23.0$$

Let's try a quartile. I can use the same formula shown above for quartiles and deciles.

Try to calculate the first quartile using the original data set (Use 21 and not 24 as the thirteenth value).

Scratching your head about this one? Think about it.

You have already done that calculation. The answer is 20.75. The first quartile is the same as the 25th percentile.

The same is true with regard to the first decile. The first decile is the tenth percentile. The second decile would be the 20th percentile and so on.

If you understand percentiles you will easily understand quartiles and deciles. You use the percentile calculation for determining quartiles or deciles.

What do you suppose the 25th percentile (first quartile) means?

It simply means that 75% of the observations in the data set fall above the value of 20.75 (in the first example). It also means that 25% of the observations in the data set lie below that value. This will become more important as you look at the concept of the inter-quartile range (IQR).

Inter-quartile Range

The inter-quartile range is the *difference between the first and third quartile.* To determine the IQR you would calculate the first quartile value (25th percentile) and the third quartile value (75th percentile) and then subtract the *values* to get the inter-quartile range.

Fifty percent (50%) of the observations in the data set are found between the two values (first quartile and third quartile). Knowing the first and third quartile values provides a basis for determining if outliers are in the data set. Outliers are deviant data points which fall outside the normal pattern of the other data points. If outliers do exist, they should be examined, adjusted if an error exists or eliminated if truly aberrant.

I have already calculated the first quartile and found the value is 20.75 (using Table 2.11 with 21 as the thirteenth listed value). The third quartile is determined as follows.

$$L_{75} = (50 + 1)\,(0.75) = 38.25 \text{ position.}$$

Counting down the data set, I find the third quartile falls between 62 and 63 (38th and 39th positions respectively).

Calculating the value I find the following:

$$62 + (0.25)\,(63 - 62) = 62.25 \text{ value of the third quartile.}$$

The IQR itself is 62.25 minus 20.75, which is 41.50. This value is a range which is referred to as the inter-quartile range.

The interpretation is that fifty percent (50%) of the observations fall between the two values of 20.75 and 62.25, but the IQR itself is 41.50. The value of the IQR helps us determine aberrant data points called outliers. I mentioned this briefly in Chapter 1.

The process of identifying the outliers is as follows.

Outliers would be determined by multiplying the IQR times 1.5 (fixed value) to get a number which will be used to add and subtract from the first and third quartile value.

Wow, that's confusing, I say. I think I confused myself.

What I am trying to say is best illustrated by the following. The IQR just calculated of 41.5 is multiplied by 1.5 = 62.25 (a coincidence that it equals the third quartile value also).

Next, subtract that 62.25 from 20.75 and you will get a negative number (which you can call zero). Adding the 62.25 just calculated to the 62.25 (previously calculated) for the value of the third quartile, I have 124.5 as an upper value. I next look at my data set. I see that no value in Table 2.11 falls below zero, so there are no outliers on the lower end of the distribution. I check to see if any of the data set values are above 124.5. If they do, I identify those as outliers (aberrations or deviant data points). By inspecting my data set in Table 2.11, I find no points are above 124.5, thus concluding my data set has no outliers or aberrant data points.

If you found outliers, you would have to examine the aberrant data points. You might find you made a recording error (data should have four weeks but only has three weeks). If you can, adjust the data set. If there is no error to be found, you might want to eliminate the aberrant data point from consideration. Take it out of your data set and use only those which tend to conform to a pattern. In short, you need to examine the data set and adjust the aberrant point for errors or eliminate it from your calculations. Leaving them in the data set will cause the data set to be distorted and the result obtained to be less reliable. All data sets need to be cleaned.

Outliers may exist for data sets that are or are not normally distributed. If normally distributed, logically there should be fewer outliers. For non-normally distributed data sets, however, there may be more outliers since the data is skewed. The number of outliers will depend on the severity of the skewness. A highly skewed data set will often contain more than one that approaches a normal distribution.

Excel Calculations

Let's stop for a minute and look at how to use the descriptive statistics calculator in Excel. Find a computer with Excel on it. I will use the data from Table 2.9 and show you the results of the Excel calculator.

You will enter the data (Table 2.9) into an Excel worksheet. It does not matter where you begin, but put the data in column format. Once the data set is entered, go to tools > data analysis > descriptive statistics. Under descriptive statistics, you will place your cursor in the input range box. Now, highlight the column of grades you entered (click one corner and drag

Table 2.12   Excel's summary statistics for the data in Table 2.9.

Grades	
Mean	67
Standard Error	3.229329873
Median	66
Mode	73
Standard Deviation	9.133924208
Sample Variance	83.42857143
Kurtosis	0.295618315
Skewness	0.031494813
Range	30
Minimum	52
Maximum	82
Sum	536
Count	8

through the data). Next, if you have named the column (I used grades), then check the box which says label in the first row. Check that your data is in columns. Select summary statistics. Select as the output new worksheet ply, which means you will create another tab in the current worksheet. Click okay and you have the following results.

If you have tried it, you will be amazed at how fast the calculation actually is. Everything in the output that was created you have been exposed to except standard error, kurtosis and skewness. I will tell you about standard error later.

Kurtosis is a measure of the degree of peakedness of a distribution. A positive value is more peaked than a negative number. A distribution that has a positive kurtosis is said to be leptokurtic (more peaked). A distribution that has a negative kurtosis is said to be platykurtic (flatter peaked). A distribution with a value of zero is a normal distribution and is referred to as mesokurtic.

The following formula can be used to calculate kurtosis:

Figure 2.1 Leptokurtic and platykurtic distributions.

$$Kurtosis = \frac{\Sigma \left(X - \mu \right)^4}{n\sigma^4} - 3$$

Skewness is the measure of the how much the distribution is pulled in one direction or the other. A distribution is skewed if one of its tails is longer than the other. The first distribution shown in Figure 2.2 (below) has a positive skew (skewed right). This means that it has a long

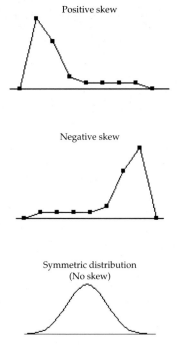

Figure 2.2 The skewness of some three typical distributions.

tail in the positive direction. The distribution below it has a negative skew since it has a long tail in the negative direction (skewed left). Finally, the third distribution is symmetric (normal distribution) and has no skew.

Pearsonian Coefficient of Skewness

The following formula is used to calculate the Pearsonian coefficient of skewness.

$$Skewness = \frac{3(mean - median)}{S}$$

If the coefficient of skewness is negative, the distribution is negatively skewed (pulled in the direction of the smaller values). If the coefficient of skewness is positive, the distribution is positively skewed (pulled in the direction of the larger values). If the coefficient of skewness is zero, the distribution is normal.

$P < 0$ negative skew (left)
$P > 0$ positive skew (right)
$P = 0$ normal distribution (mean and median are equal)

A normal distribution is a key concept in statistical circles. A normal distribution has several characteristics—bell shaped, symmetrical (50% to the right of the mean and 50% to the left of the mean), asymptotic (never touches the x-axis), associated with continuous data, the mean $=$ the median $=$ the mode, subject to the Empirical Rule for interpretation.

Let's look at a couple of examples of the Pearsonian skewness calculation.

The closer to 0, the less the distribution is skewed. The higher value of the coefficient (positive or negative), the more the distribution is skewed.

Example One

Given: $\overline{X} = 78.3, S = 10.8$, median $= 77.9$. What can you say about the skewness of this distribution?
The Pearsonian coefficient is $P = 3(78.3 - 77.9) \div 10.8 = 0.11$.
The distribution is skewed right, since the coefficient is positive ($+0.11$).
You may also say the distribution appears to be narrowly dispersed and tends toward a normal distribution (moves toward zero).
A normal distribution would have occurred if the Pearsonian coefficient equaled 0. If the Pearsonian coefficient is closer to 0, then the distribution tends toward normality. If the Pearsonian coefficient is greater or less than 0, then the distribution is more prone to dispersion.

Example Two

Given: $\overline{X} = 85.9, S = 10.8$, median $= 77.9$. What can we say about the skewness of this distribution?

The Pearsonian coefficient is $P = 3(85.9 - 77.9) \div 10.8 = 2.22$.

The distribution is still skewed right, since the coefficient is $+2.22$.

This distribution appears to be more broadly dispersed since the Pearsonian coefficient is much larger than the previous one ($+0.11$ versus $+2.22$). The second one does not tend toward a normal distribution.

Let's look at the three types of distributions again.

Types of Distributions

Distributions are not all normal distributions. Some will be pulled in one direction or the other. Distributions are skewed when they depart from the normal distribution. Generally all distributions follow the shape of one of three configurations. Figure 2.3 shows the three main types of distributions.

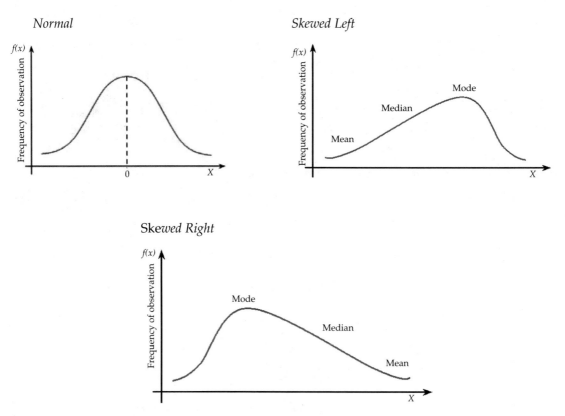

Figure 2.3 The three main types of frequency distributions.

From these distributions, you can get a good idea of the relative position of the mode, median, and mean in any skewed distribution. The mode will appear at the highest point (most often). The median will be found between the mean and the mode with the mean drawn in the direction of the skew (lower or higher values). As shown in Figure 2.3, the positions are exaggerated, since in practice they would cluster closer to the center of the distribution. Here, for emphasis, I am spreading them out.

In a normal distribution, the mean, median, and mode are all equal to each other. With those distributions skewed left or right, the mean is pulled in the direction of the skew. The mode will be the highest point and generally the median will fall between the mean and mode.

In the Pearsonian coefficient of skewness formula shown below, notice that if the mean is greater than the median, the distribution will be skewed right (positive coefficient of skewness). If the mean is less than the median, the distribution will be skewed left (negative coefficient of skewness).

$$Skewness = \frac{3(mean - median)}{S}$$

Both kurtosis and skewness are descriptive measures. They are useful in further describing the data set. As I have repeatedly said, the other descriptive measures are central tendency and dispersion.

Coefficient of Variation

A quick analysis of the relative value of two population or sample distributions can be accomplished by the calculation of a coefficient of variation for each distribution. The **coefficient of variation** is a relative (percentage) measure of dispersion. It assesses the degree of dispersion in two data sets by comparing the standard deviation divided by the mean for each data set.

One Warning: The standard deviation is one of the most important measurements in statistics. Some care is needed when comparing two or more distributions (populations or samples) if certain conditions exist. Under these conditions, be careful not to draw too many conclusions based on the relative size of the standard deviation as a percentage of the mean (coefficient of variation).

Those conditions include: If the means are significantly different or the units of measurement are in different units (apples to oranges or dollars to yen, etc.), the coefficient of variation does not work well. When either of these conditions exist, you will be better off not using the coefficient of variation.

The formula is a simple one:

$$CV = \frac{S}{\overline{X}} \text{ times 100, where } S \text{ is the sample standard deviation.}$$

This formula is the sample standard deviation divided by the sample mean with the resultant multiplied by 100. Let's look at an example.

Assume you have two sets of tires which are priced approximately the same. The manufacturer of Tire *A* claims a mean life of 40,000 miles with a standard deviation of 6,000 miles. The manufacturer of Tire *B* claims a mean life of 50,000 miles with a standard deviation of 9,000 miles. Which tire has the least relative variability as measured by the coefficient of variation?

You need to calculate two separate coefficients of variation (*CV*).

$$\text{Tire } A \ CV = (6{,}000 \div 40{,}000) \text{ times } 100 = 15\%$$

$$\text{Tire } B \ CV = (9{,}000 \div 50{,}000) \text{ times } 100 = 18\%$$

Assuming no other tests were appropriate and price is not a major consideration, you would select Tire *A* over Tire *B* since the relative variability is less for *A* than *B*.

**You know
You are
a Texan
If:**

- You have ever had to switch from "heat" to "a/c" in the same day.
- You think eveyone from North Dallas has an accent.
- You describe the first cool snap (below 70 degrees) as good chili weather.

Tear-Out Sheet Chapter 2

Student Name: _____

Day and Time of Class: _____

Please remove the sheets marked tear-out sheets from the book. Then work the problems in class, if the professor allows you lab time during class, or work them as homework.

Raw Data Set and Outlier Problems

1. You are advising your mother how she can invest her money in the safest way possible. The investment consultant has narrowed the decision to two investment funds, which have been in existence for five years. He gives you the following data on the return on investment (ROI) to help you in making the decision

Year	Fund A	Fund B
2004	12%	13%
2003	10%	12%
2002	13%	14%
2001	9%	10%
2000	11%	6%

   a. Is this a population or a sample?
   b. Which fund is the safest for your mother and why? There may be many different calculations, but the solution really boils down to variability. However, make all other calculations you think helpful. Do not use the Geometric mean since the variability will determine the safest investment. Use the percentages as whole numbers.

2. The *Los Angles Times* regularly reports the air quality index for various areas of southern California. A *sample* of the air quality index for Pomona provided the following data:

   28, 42, 58, 48, 45, 55, 60, 49, and 50

   a. Compute the mean.
   b. Compute the range.
   c. Compute the inter-quartile range.
   d. Explain the meaning of the inter-quartile range.
   e. Determine the upper and lower values for outliers and indicate if any of the points are outliers.
   f. Compute the variance.
   g. Compute the standard deviation.
   h. Compute the Pearsonian coefficient of skewness.

      i. Interpret the meaning of each of the calculations made above.

        Hypothetically, what would happen (change) if the data set in problem #2 was a population rather than a sample?

3. Given the following data set of the weights of 92 college students, determine if the data set contains any outliers (if yes, what are they) based on the IQR approach. Notice the data set has been put into an ordered array, which is the first step in working with any ungrouped or raw data set.

96	117	125	133	141	150	154	160	173	194
103	118	125	135	142	150	154	161	175	217
107	119	125	135	145	150	155	161	180	
108	121	125	136	145	150	155	162	180	
111	121	130	136	145	151	155	163	181	
111	122	131	137	145	151	155	164	184	
113	122	131	138	146	151	155	171	190	
114	122	132	139	147	152	155	171	190	
115	124	132	140	150	153	155	171	191	
116	125	133	140	150	154	157	171	192	

Descriptive Statistics— Statistics— Grouped Data

Attorney:	The youngest son, the twenty-year-old, how old is he?
Witness:	He's twenty, much like your IQ.

In Chapter 2, I showed you how to describe your raw data sets with the calculation of measures of central tendency and dispersion. In Chapter 3, I will show you how to calculate measures of central tendency and dispersion for grouped data sets. Raw data sets, as I pointed out, tend to give us less descriptive information than grouped data sets. Grouped data sets are also referred to as frequency distributions. A frequency is developed by counting the number of times something occurs in a particular category.

Remember, when you convert the raw data set to a group data set, you lose the original data. The grouped data set is referred to as a frequency distribution. I determine the number of classes by using the $2^c \geq n$ and, then, determine the class interval (*CI*) by using the range divided by the number of classes (*C*).

Measures of Central Tendency for Grouped Data Sets

Assume I have made a study of 50 customers and the average dollars they spent when shopping.

The data is shown in the following table.

Table 3.1   Fifty customers and the average dollars they spent.

Categories	Frequency (f)
$50 through $59	3
$60 through $69	7
$70 through $79	18
$80 through $89	12
$90 through $99	8
$100 through $109	2
Total	**50**

Table 3.1 is grouped data since there are categories. I should be able to calculate descriptive measures of central tendency and dispersion and I can.

Mean

The formula for a population of a grouped data set is as follows:

$$\mu = \frac{\Sigma fM}{N}$$

This is the mean of the population for a grouped data set. Here f = the frequency, M = the midpoint, and N = total number of observations.

The formula for the mean of a sample for grouped data sets is as follows:

$$\overline{X} = \frac{\Sigma fM}{n}$$

Here, f = the frequency, M = the midpoint, and n = total number of observations.

Okay, you say, they look the same.

Essentially they are, I reply. The only difference is in the symbols. An arithmetic average for either a population or sample is calculated the same way. The symbols will change depending on identity of the data set as a population or sample.

I must make one major assumption when making grouped data set calculations. For example, in the first category ($50 through $59), there are three customers but I have no clue how much each person spends. I only know there are three customers who spend between $50 and $59 dollars. *The assumption is that the midpoint of the class is equal to the average dollars spent in that class.* The midpoint of the class is a good approximation of the average for that class. The midpoint of the first class is determined by adding ($50 + $59) ÷ 2 = $54.5.

The midpoints are shown in the following table (cleverly labeled midpoint).

Table 3.2 Customer spending data.

Categories	Frequency (f)	Cumulative Frequency (cf)	Midpoint (M)	fM
$50 through $59	3	3	54.5	163.5
$60 through $69	7	10	64.5	451.5
$70 through $79	18	28	74.5	1,341.0
$80 through $89	12	40	84.5	1,014.0
$90 through $99	8	48	94.5	756.0
$100 through $109	2	50	104.5	209.0
Total	**50**			**3,935.0**

Also shown is the cumulative frequency. The cumulative frequency column is easily determined. You simply add the frequency in the 50 through 59 class (3) to the frequency in the 60 through 69 class (7), which yields the cumulative frequency of 10(3 + 7 = 10). This would be repeated by adding 18 to the previous cumulative frequency of 10 for a cumulative frequency of 28 and so forth. The last cumulative value must equal 50, since you started with 50 observations.

From the formula, I am interested in a column headed *fM*, which is shown as the last column. The last column is developed by multiplying the frequency (*f*) of the class (*not the cumulative frequency*) by the midpoint (*M*) of the class. This would be $f \times M = fM$. Once this column is totaled (last column on the right-hand side of Table 3.2), you can then determine the arithmetic mean.

Let's see how this works.

$$\mu = \frac{\Sigma fM}{N}$$ The numerator is the sum of a column headed "*fM*".

This happens to be a population, since it does not meet the criterion for a sample (representative portion), so the correct calculation would be as follows:

$$\mu = \frac{3,935}{50} = \$78.70$$

Were this a sample data set, the value would be the same at $78.70 but the symbols would be different.

Let's take a minute to review some of the important symbols (Table 3.3).

Table 3.3   Some important symbols for measures of populations and samples.

	Mean	**Variance**	**Standard Deviation**	**Size of the . . .**
Population	μ	σ^2	σ	N
Sample	$\overline{X}$	S^2	S	n

Median

The formula for the median probably scares some of you to death but it is not as difficult as it looks.

$$Median = L_{md} + \left[\frac{(n \div 2) - F}{f_{md}} \right] CI$$

Where:

L_{md} = Lower limit of the median class.

F = Cumulative frequency of the class preceding the median class.

f_{md} = Frequency of the median class.

CI = Class interval.

So where do I start, you ask?

Remember, one of the first things I told you to do is place your data set in an ordered array when determine the value of the median and the mode. Here I still abide by that rule. In Table 3.2, the data set categories are from $50 to $109, which is an ordered array.

By definition, the median is the one in the middle. I have 50 observations. If I multiply 50 times 0.50 (50%) or divide 50 by 2, I will find the middle *position* is 25. The median is in the 25th *position*. Observe this is the *position* and *not the value*.

Let's go back to Table 3.2. I want to find the 25th position. The best way to find that position (and the value) is to use the column headed cumulative frequency. Where is the median class? By observation, I determine the median class is the $70 through $79 class, which means the value will fall between $70 and $79.

I do not understand, you comment.

Okay, follow this closely, I reply. In the cumulative column in Table 3.2, the last value in the $60 through $69 class is the tenth cumulative item (position). The beginning of the next class ($70 through $79) is the 11th position. The end of the $70 through $79 class is the 28th position, so the median value (25th position) falls somewhere between the 11th and the 28th position.

What I have just determined is the class for the 25th position. However, what I want is the value of that 25th position.

Median Class = $70 through $79

Let's next apply the formula to determine the *value* of the median. Make sure you review the definitions of the elements in the formula carefully. I am showing you all of the numbers to make it easier for you to follow.

Follow the calculations by going back to look at the definitions of each of the terms in the formula.

$$Median = L_{md} + \left[\frac{(n \div 2) - F}{f_{md}} \right] CI$$

The lower limit of the median class is 70; n is equal to 50; f_{md} is equal to 18. F is the most difficult to see. F is the cumulative frequency of the class preceding the median class. Use the cumulative frequency in Table 3.2 and find the class preceding the median class. If the median class is $70 through $79, the class preceding that class is $60 through $69. The cumulative frequency of the class preceding the median class is 10. CI is the class interval. Counting $50 and $59 the interval is 10.

You now have all of the numbers, so substitute the values into the formula as follows:

$$Median = 70 + \left[\frac{(50 \div 2) - 10}{18} \right] 10$$

$$Median = 70 + \left[\frac{(25) - 10}{18} \right] 10$$

$$Median = 70 + \left[\frac{15}{18} \right] 10$$

$$Median = 70 + \left[\frac{150}{18} \right]$$

$$Median = 70 + 8.33$$

$$Median = \$78.33$$

You must understand the difference between *position* and *value*. The position is the 25th, but the value is $78.33. It would make no sense for me to identify 25 as the value because 25 is not within the range of my data set (low of 50 and high of 109). The 25 would fail a "smell test."

Mode

This one looks tough too, but it is not if you stay mentally organized. The formula is as follows:

$$Mode = L_{mo} + \left[\frac{(D_a)}{(D_a + D_b)} \right] CI$$

Where:

L_{mo} = Lower limit of the modal class.

D_a = Difference between the frequency of the modal class and the class *preceding* it.

D_b = Difference between the frequency of the modal class and the class *following* it.

CI = Class interval.

The mode is the value that occurs most often, so the modal class is the one with the highest frequency. In this case, it is also the $70 through $79 class.

Why is the modal class $70 through $79, you ask?

Because, I answer, the $70 through $79 class has a frequency of 18, which is the largest number in the frequency distribution for any one class. The median and the modal class will not always be the same, but in this instance they are.

Let's do the math. Refer back to the definitions of the terms in the formula.

$$Mode = 70 + \left[\frac{(18-7)}{(18-7)+(18-12)}\right]10$$

The rest is just math and order of operation. Do the work inside the brackets first, then multiply, then add. The result would be a mode of $76.47.

Advantages and Disadvantages

Mean

Advantages:

Most Commonly Known.

Most Easily Understood (widely used)

Easily Determined in Grouped or Ungrouped Data

Easily Managed Algebraically/(Add and Divide)

Easily Interpreted

Disadvantage:

Affected by the Extreme Values (pulled toward extreme values)

Median

If some of the values are extreme (very big or very small relative to the other values), the median represents the data set better than the mean.

Mode

The mode is least affected by the extremes but its use is confusing. For raw data sets some distributions have two or more modes and some distributions may have no mode at all. I determine the mode in raw data sets by observation. A mode is calculated for grouped data sets, so a mode will always exist for grouped data sets.

Let's look next at the variability of grouped data sets. I am not as interested in the range or the average deviation for grouped data sets but the variance and standard deviation are extremely important.

Variance and Standard Deviation for Grouped Data Sets

The variance and the standard deviation are calculated as follows. For these calculations it is important to know if this is a population or sample.

Why you may ask?

Let's look at the two formulas.

Population

$$\sigma^2 = \frac{\Sigma fm^2 - N\mu^2}{N}$$

Sample

$$S^2 = \frac{\Sigma fm^2 - n\overline{X}^2}{n - 1}$$

Do you notice the difference between the two formulas that will result in different answers? This is true for both raw and grouped data sets. The variance for a population is determined by using "N" while the variance of the sample uses "$n - 1$" (degrees of freedom) for the denominator. The variance for a sample will always, repeat, *always* be larger than the variance of the population. Mathematically no other conclusion is possible. This is due to the nature of sampling. Sampling has inherent error; so to compensate, I make the variance of the sample larger and thus the standard deviation (taking the square root of the variance) larger as well.

I am going to arbitrarily work this problem as both a sample and a population to show you the differences in values. This is actually a population since it is not a representative part of the population selected randomly. I will develop the entire table, then explain it. The table is as follows (Table 3.4):

Table 3.4 Customer spending data.

Categories (Column 1)	Frequency f (Column 2)	Midpoint M (Column 3)	Freq. Times Midpoint fM (Column 4)	Freq. Times Midpoint Squared fM² (Column 5)
$50 through $59	3	54.5	163.5	8,910.75
$60 through $69	7	64.5	451.5	29,121.75
$70 through $79	18	74.5	1341.0	99,904.50
$80 through $89	12	84.5	1014.0	85,683.00
$90 through $99	8	94.5	756.0	71,442.00
$100 through $109	2	104.5	209.0	21,840.50
Totals	50	N/A	3,935.0	316,902.50

You are given columns one and two. Column three is the midpoint, which is ($50 + $59) ÷ 2 = 54.5 and so forth for the other classes.

Column four is found by multiplying column two times column three. For example, 3 times 54.5 (for the first class) is 163.5. For the second class the value is 7 times 64.5 = 451.5 and so forth for the other classes.

Okay, some of you do not have your calculator in hand checking my numbers. My question is why not? You will not understand any of this stuff, if you don't try to follow the calculations.

Get your calculator. I will wait.

By now you should have your calculator in hand cross checking my numbers. Good!

The last column (fifth column) is found by multiplying the third column by the fourth column. For example, for the first class, 54.5 × 163.5 = 8,910.75. The second class is found by 64.5 × 451.5 = 29,121.75 and so forth for the other classes.

It is this fifth column that I really need to begin my calculation of the variance.

Before I make that calculation, I will need one more thing—the mean. If you go back to the mean section of this chapter you would find the mean is the total of the fourth column divided by the number of observations. Here it is: 3,935.0 ÷ 50 = 78.70.

Remember, this is really a population, but I am going to illustrate the difference between the final values of the variance for a population and a sample. Let's first work through the formula for a sample.

$$S^2 = \frac{\sum fm^2 - n\overline{X}^2}{n - 1}$$

The formula calls first for the sum of a column headed fM^2. Find that value in Table 3.4.

Okay, you say as you look back to Table 3.4.

Found it, you answer. It is 316,902.50.

Brilliant, I respond. Now let's put that number to work in the formula.

$$S^2 = \frac{316,902.50 - (50)(78.70)^2}{50 - 1}$$

Where

$n = 50$ (total number of observations or total frequency)

$\overline{X} = 78.70$, which was calculated earlier.

The only thing left is for me is to solve the formula. I will first square $\overline{X}$, which is $(78.70)^2 = 6,193.69$, then I will multiply this value by 50. 6,193.69 × 50 = 309,684.50.

Completing the entire solution, you will have the following.

$$S^2 = \frac{316,902.50 - (50)(6,193.69)}{50 - 1}$$

$$S^2 = \frac{316{,}902.50 - 309{,}684.50}{50 - 1}$$

$$S^2 = \frac{7{,}218}{49} = 147.31, \text{ which is the variance (dollars squared)}$$

The standard deviation is the square root of the variance.

$$S = \sqrt{147.31} = \$12.14 \text{ dollars.}$$

If solved as if the data set is a population, the only difference in the calculations for the variance and standard deviation for the population is the denominator. For a population, I use N rather than $n-1$ (sample). I will divide 7,218 (shown above) by 50 rather than 49. The resultant would be 144.36 dollars squared. The standard deviation is the square root of 144.36 = \$12.01 dollars.

Remember, the variance is in squared units. The standard deviation is in units. I use the standard deviation, not the variance coupled with the mean, in drawing additional conclusions about my data set. This allows me to work with units to units (the mean in units and the standard deviation in units). For example, the mean is \$78.70 dollars. I could not use \$147.31 dollars squared with it but I could use \$12.14 dollars, since the units would be equivalent. More on how I use this later.

Also notice that the population standard deviation is *always smaller* than the sample standard deviation. This will always be true.

One observation should be made at this point. In the formula for the sample variance above, the numerator consists of two terms. One is on the left and is 316,902.50 (which comes from Table 3.4). The other is on the right in the numerator and is the product of 50 times 78.7^2, which in this case is 309,684.50. *The second term on the right can never be greater than the first term on the left.* Were this condition to exist, the variance would be negative and a mathematical impossibility. If you end up with a negative variance, you have made an error somewhere, so check your math.

Setting Up Classes

One word about setting up classes needs to be mentioned. Whatever you do, do not have overlapping classes. The following would be unacceptable.

50 to 60 followed by

60 to 70

70 to 80 etc.

If 60 is in your data set, where would you place it—the first or the second class? With overlapping classes, you have no way of making an accurate determination.

Setting up classes can use different language such as:

50 but less than 60

60 but less than 70 etc.

Neither of these would present an opportunity to overlap if 60 were selected. It would fall in the second class. The same would be true for the following language.

50 up to but not including 60

60 up to but not including 70 etc.

Let's look at percentiles, quartiles, and deciles. When calculating percentiles, quartiles, and deciles for raw data sets, understanding percentiles was the key. The same logic applies when you work with grouped data sets.

Percentiles, Quartiles, and Deciles

Let's keep using the same data set from Table 3.4, but now I really need only two columns—the frequency and the cumulative frequency.

I have included as the third column the cumulative frequency. The cumulative frequency is determined by adding the frequencies (f) 3 + 7 = 10, then adding the next frequency 18 to the 10 = 28 and so forth. Follow how I did this in Table 3.5.

Let's say I am looking for the 70th percentile in the distribution.

So where do I start, you ask?

I need to first determine the *position* of the 70th percentile (not the *value*).

50 observations $\times$ 0.70 = 35th position.

Next I must determine into which class the 35th position falls.

The class is 80 to 89. The value will be between 80 and 89.

Okay, you question. How did you know that?

I make use of the cumulative frequency column. By going down that column I notice that the third category (class) ends with the 28th item (28th position).

Go to Table 3.5 and observe what I am telling you. I will wait.

Good, now you see it.

Logic tells me that if the third class ($70 through $79) ends with the 28th position then, by observation, the fourth class ($80 through $89) must end with the 40th item (position). Once again look at Table 3.5. I will wait.

Okay, is it soaking in? Good.

Table 3.5 The classes, frequency, and cumulative frequency from Table 3.4.

Categories	Frequency f	Cumulative Frequency F
$50 through $59	3	3
$60 through $69	7	10
$70 through $79	18	28
$80 through $89	12	40
$90 through $99	8	48
$100 through $109	2	50
Totals	50	N/A

If the third class ends with the 28th item and the fourth class ends with the 40th item, the 35th item must fall somewhere in the fourth class. I logically selected the $80 through $89 class.

Using logic, I will now make the calculation. I am looking for a value that falls in the fourth class. To make the calculation, *I must make an assumption that the frequencies of any class are equally spread though the class.* Said differently, there are 12 frequencies in the fourth class ($80 through $89). I will make the assumption that these 12 frequencies (numbers) are evenly spread through the class, which has an interval of 10 (inclusive of $80 and $89). Count them if you are confused: 80, 81, 82, 83, 84, 85, 86, 87, 88, 89.

Now for the application of logic: To end up somewhere in the class of $80 through $89, I must find a value equal to or higher than $80 but less than $90.

Okay, you say, so what now?

Let's begin with the lower limit of the class, which is 80.

$80 + (7 \div 12)(10) = 80 + 5.83 = 85.83$, which is the value of the 35th position.

That's cool, you say, I understand the $80 and I understand the 10, which is the class interval, but where did you get the 7/12 fraction?

Good question, I respond. Most students have difficulty with that fraction.

Using the cumulative frequency distribution, the reason for the 7/12 fraction is as follows:
The cumulative frequency of the class just preceding the $80 through $89 class is 28. Go look at Table 3.5. Since the $70 through $79 class ends in 28, I must go into the next class by seven items. This is simply a matter of counting or subtracting ($35 - 28 = 7$). I go from the 28th

position to the 35th position, which is where I will convert the position to value. I get the numerator 7 (35 − 28 = 7) from this logical process.

The denominator of 12 comes from the *frequency* in the 70th percentile class (35th position). Since the class has been identified at the $80 through $89 class, the frequency of that class is 12.

Since there are 12 frequencies in the $80 through $89 class, I must go 7/12 of the distance into the $80 through $89 class. This is 7/12 of 10 (class interval).

This might seem a bit confusing at first, but if you will take it a step at a time you will find it works. If you do not understand what I just did, then go back and walk through the explanation again.

Deciles and quartiles work the same way as percentiles. The second decile is the 20th percentile. The first quartile is the 25th percentile.

Okay, you say, so now we know how to make the calculation of the mean and standard deviation, so what?

I am glad you asked. First, let's look at two rules which are important *interpretative* rules. These rules will help you actually use some of this stuff (very secret statistical word—stuff).

Empirical Rule and Chebyshev's Theorem

Let's say I want to make use of the mean and standard deviation I have just calculated. As a reminder the mean is 78.70 and the sample standard deviation is 12.14 (population is 12.01). I will use the sample to illustrate the following point. The 78.70 is a point estimate, which simply means it is an estimate at a given point. It is what I might expect on average. A point estimate is, however, not likely to exactly occur. Since I know the chances of 78.70 exactly occurring, I wonder if I can set an expected range (interval)? Suppose I made a calculation of the mean plus and minus the standard deviation. I might want to move one or two or three standard deviations from the mean in both directions to see what sort of interval might result. The calculation might look like the following. The number two (2), in this calculation, was arbitrarily chosen to illustrate my point.

$$\overline{X} \pm (2)(12.14) = 78.70 \pm 24.28 = 54.42 \text{ to } 102.98 \text{ or } 54 \text{ to } 103 \text{ rounded}$$

Okay, now I have an interval estimate of spending between $54 and $103, but I still have a problem. How do I interpret the result - Empirical Rule or Chebyshev's Theorem?

The **empirical rule** and **Chebyshev's theorem** provide us with two distinct *methods of interpretation* for the one calculation. The standard deviation provides a standard measurement of the movement from or around the mean, which in a normal distribution is in the middle. For skewed distributions, this presents a different issue, but more on that shortly.

There is only one calculation for either interpretation rule. The one calculation is as follows:

$$\overline{X} \pm 1S \quad \text{Where 1, 2, and 3 are the number of standard deviations}$$

$$\overline{X} \pm 2S \quad \text{And S is the standard deviation}$$

$$\overline{X} \pm 3S$$

I begin the calculations with the mean, and then add and subtract an interval from the mean. The interval is composed of two parts: 1, 2, or 3 and S. S is the standard deviation. 1, 2, and 3 are the number of standard deviations (K).

Even though there is only one calculation, there can be two interpretations depending on the data set.

For example, if the data set is normal with continuous data (data that can take on a range of values), then I would use the empirical rule to interpret the result. Chebyshev's theorem, however, can be used to interpret any data set but it is particularly useful with skewed data sets or discrete data (whole numbers). The following table (Table 3.6) summarizes the use of the two rules of interpretation.

Table 3.6 Use of the empirical rule and Chebyshev's theorem.

Interpretation: Empirical Rule Applies to Normal Distributions and Continuous Data Sets.	Calculations: Calculations Are the Same for Either Approach.	Interpretation: Chebyshev's Theorem Applies to Any Data Set (Skewed or Normal; Continuous or Discrete). Best Use is for Discrete Data Sets.
68.3 %	$\overline{X} \pm 1(S)$	Calculation = Zero
95.5%	$\overline{X} \pm 2(S)$	At least 75%
99.7%	$\overline{X} \pm 3(S)$	At least 88.89% (round to 89%)
These exist by definition.	The 1, 2, and 3 are the number of standard deviations (K), while S is the standard deviation itself.	$1 - \left[\dfrac{1}{K^2}\right]$ where K is the *number* of standard deviations, *NOT* the standard deviation. K must be greater than 1. This is the calculation for the interpretation percentage shown above.

Listed below is a broader discussion of the two rules and when to use them. Both interpretation rules apply to population or sample, raw or grouped data sets.

Empirical Rule

One of the two most important rules in statistics is known as the empirical rule. The other is the central limit theorem (CLT). The CLT idea will come later, but for now I want you to understand the empirical rule. The empirical rule (ER) applies as follows:

1. ER applies to a normal distribution, which is bell shaped and symmetrical (50% to the left of the mean and 50% to the right of the mean).

2. ER applies to continuous data sets.

3. Any distribution will only encompass 100% of the observations in your data set. In other words, the area under the curve is equal to 100%.

4. The interval is composed of movement to the left of the mean and to the right of the mean. To the left is designated as a negative direction. To the right is designated as a positive direction. The signs, however, are directional indicators only. Negative means left and positive means right, nothing more.

5. The interpretation of the Empirical Rule provides that if you move from the mean ± 1S, you will encompass 68.3% of the area under the curve. If you move from the mean ± 2S, you will encompass 95.5% of the area under the curve. If you move from the mean ± 3S, you will encompass 99.7% of the area under the curve. These values are given, so for now accept them. Later I will show you their derivation.

6. A normal distribution is asymptotic, which means the curve will never touch the horizontal axis.

How far can I move away from the mean, you might ask?

Any distribution can equal only 100% of the observations (100% of the area under the curve).

By moving three standard deviations in either direction, I have identified 99.7% of the area under the curve. If I go four standard deviations on either side of the mean, I will be able to identify only a very small additional area. There is only 0.3% left (100.0% − 99.7% = 0.3%). Since the normal distribution is symmetrical, this means 0.15% in the left tail and 0.15% in the right tail.

Think about it, there is no practical reason for moving beyond ±3 standard deviations. There is no real value in identifying more of the area at this point. When I cover quality control, I will cover the idea of Six Sigma™ (which is ±6 standard deviations from the mean). Most business challenges are restricted to ±3 standard deviations, however.

Using the information in Table 3.6, I can draw a normal distribution and draw some conclusions about my data set using the two rules of interpretation.

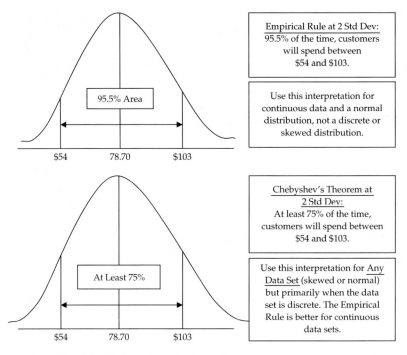

Figure 3.1   Comparison of Empirical Rule and Chebyshev's Theorem.

For discrete data sets, Chebyshev's theorem is a more practical interpretation.

Chebyshev's Theorem

The empirical rule does not work for all distributions, only normal distributions with continuous data sets. Chebyshev's theorem works for *any distribution*, but is more effectively used for discrete data sets or skewed distributions.

Continuous data sets can take on a range of values, such as height, weight, age, etc. Discrete data sets primarily involve whole numbers.

So what do I do when I have a discrete data set, you may ask?

The Russian mathematician, Pafnuty Chebyshev, discovered the following relationship in all data sets.

$$1 - \frac{1}{K^2}$$

Where:

K equals the number of standard deviations and not the standard deviation (S). K equals 1, 2, or 3 for now. K must also exceed one, since substituting one into the formula above will yield zero. Look at the formula and make that calculation.

S is the calculated standard deviation.

I will show you more on this shortly.

More Thoughts on the Interval Estimate

I calculated the mean as $78.70 for the shopping spending example presented in Table 3.2. Calculated as a sample, the standard deviation was 12.14. If you have forgotten how I got these numbers go back and look at the calculations. Both of these values, used together, tell management something about the data set. They are further descriptive measures of the data set. The average amount spent by these 50 customers was $78.70 with a standard deviation of $12.14.

The mean of $78.70 is a point estimate. I can, however, develop an interval estimate around the point estimate. This interval, when interpreted, will give me more insight into my data set.

The calculation of an interval is simple and straightforward.

$$\overline{X} \pm 2(S) \quad \text{(I arbitrarily chose } K = 2).$$

$$\$78.70 \pm (2)(12.14) = 54.42 \text{ and } 102.98.$$

Rounded: $54 to $103.

My dilemma is that I don't know if I should use the empirical rule or Chebyshev's theorem to interpret the results of the calculation.

I am working with dollars, so this is continuous data. From this fact alone, I would generally use the empirical rule to interpret my results, but I have another problem. The distribution is not a normal distribution, so the empirical rule interpretation will not work. However, Chebyshev's theorem interpretation Theorem works for any data set, so it is more appropriate.

Okay, you say, how do you know it is not a normal distribution?

Simple, I say. Go back to the frequencies as shown in Table 3.2. They are 3, 7, 18, 12, 8, and 2. For there to be a normal distribution, it should be symmetrical—the same on each side of a peak.

I chose the value of K to be two, since I am interested in the area two standard deviations from the mean. I could have chosen three, but not one. K must be greater than one. I must now use Chebyshev's formula to determine my percentages. The correct interpretation calculation is as follows.

$$1 - \frac{1}{K^2}$$

$$1 - \frac{1}{2^2}$$

$$1 - \frac{1}{4}$$

$$1 - 0.25 = 0.75$$

I can now assert that at least 75% of the time, the customers will spend between $54 and $103. Notice the words "at least." See the information in Table 3.6, but those two words are an important part of the interpretation.

First, $78.70 is a point estimate. Second, the rounded values $54 to $103 are an interval estimate.

Repeating, this is interpreted as follows. At least 75% of the time, the dollars spent shopping will be between $54 and $103. This information is quite helpful to management in planning inventory, ordering products, and staffing a retail outlet.

Here I chose two as K. I could have chosen three, which would have widened my interval. Remember, Chebyshev's theorem applies to any distribution, including a normal distribution, but K must be greater than one.

When you have a distribution that meets the criteria for a normal distribution (continuous data, symmetrical, etc.), use the empirical rule to interpret the interval, because it is more accurate. If a distribution is skewed to the left or to the right; or if the data set is discrete, use Chebyshev's theorem as the best interpretation.

See Table 3.6 above for a full summary of the uses. Remember there is only one calculation, but two possible interpretations.

You know You are a Texan If:

- You know all four seasons: almost summer, summer, still summer and Christmas.
- Someone you know has used a football schedule to plan their wedding.
- You have owned at least one belt buckle bigger than your fist.

Tear-Out Sheet Chapter 3

Student Name: _____

Day and Time of Class: _____

　　Let's take a brief time out and look at some examples for you to calculate the area under the curve using the normal distribution and continuous data and the empirical rule.

Examples of Calculations of Area Under the Curve for a Normal Distribution:

1. Given the following distribution:

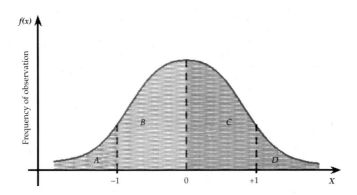

　　Using the Empirical Rule:

　a. Calculate the Area in *A* and *D*.

　b. Calculate the Area in *A* or *D*.

　c. Calculate the Area in *B* or *C*.

　d. Calculate the Area in *A*, *B*, and *C*.

　　Check Answers:

31.7 in *A* and *D*

15.85 for *A* or *D*

34.15 in *B* or *C*

84.15 in *A*, *B* and *C*

2. Let's expand problem #1 to all of the empirical rule possibilities. There are many ways to determine the areas you are being asked to determine. The solutions will use one method, but you may find other combinations more appropriate for your understanding.

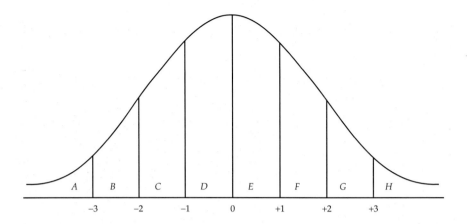

Determine the area under the normal curve in the following areas:
Note: Use the Empirical Rule Approach.

a. *A*

b. *B*

c. *C*

d. *D*

e. *D + E*

f. *D + F*

g. *H + A*

h. *F + G*

3. First: *Draw a normal curve* as a visual aid of what area under the curve you are seeking.
   Second: Assume the units of measurement are inches and the product is steel rebar.

   a. Assume $\overline{X}$ = 100 and S = 40. What is the area under the curve containing steel rebar between 60 inches and 140 inches? *Note:* This is determined by developing the area under the curve between those two points using the empirical rule. Remember S is the standard deviation.

   b. Assume $\overline{X}$ = 200 and S = 50. What is the area under the curve between 100 inches and 300 inches? (This is both sides of the curve so add the values).

   c. Using the data from "*b*," what is the area under the curve *less than* 100 inches? (This is the far left of the curve.)

   d. Using the data from "*b*," what is the area under the curve *greater than* 300 inches? (This is the far right of the curve.)

   e. Using the data from "*b*," what is the area between 200 inches and 300 inches?

4. Grouped Data Set Problems

   The following is a set of sample datum of the monthly starting salaries of recent finance graduates from TCU.

Starting Salaries	f	Cum F	M	fM	fM^2
1,400 < 1,500	2				
1,500 < 1,600	4				
1,600 < 1,700	3				
1,700 < 1,800	1				
1,800 < 1,900	1				
1,900 < 2,000	0				
2,000 < 2,100	1				
Total	12				

USE 100 FOR THE CLASS INTERVAL.

Complete the table and calculate the following:

    a. Compute the mean.
    b. Compute the median.
    c. Compute the mode.
    d. Compute the variance.
    e. Compute the standard deviation.
    f. Compute the 90th percentile.
    g. Using the frequencies listed above, draw a rough picture of the distribution of the data set. Show the relative positions of the mean, median and mode.
    h. Using the Pearsonian Coefficient of Skewness approach, determine which way the distribution is skewed. Does your calculation and drawing support each other?
    i. Are there any calculated values that will change if this were a population rather than a sample or are the only changes symbols? Why?

Learning to manipulate the empirical rule information is crucial to your understanding of the next few chapters and most of the concepts associated with inferential statistics.

Probability I
—The Basics

4

| Attorney: | Were you present when your picture was taken? |
| Witness: | Are you sh---ing me? |

Probability is a necessary evil if you are to understand some of the underlying principles associated with inferential statistics. I have introduced you to the ideas of describing data sets, or descriptive statistics. Inferential statistics, the second branch of statistics, infers something about a population data set from a sample data set. Two important applications are confidence intervals and hypothesis testing which will be covered in subsequent chapters, but first I need to introduce you to the basics of probability.

All inferential statistical testing is referred to as **parametric testing** (usually testing the *mean* or the *variance* of the population). Parametric testing is accomplished by using a statistic (sample mean or sample variance). This is necessary since you never really know the population values. You must use samples, correctly designed, to represent the population.

Three Important Theorems

There are three theorems that are very important. One of them is the *central limit theorem*, another is the *empirical rule*, while the third is *Chebyshev's theorem*. All of these are extremely important. In the last chapter I discussed at length the empirical rule and Chebyshev's theorem of interpretation. The central limit theorem (CLT) is probably the most important or the three as it relates to inferential statistics. I will discuss the CLT shortly.

Again, the empirical rule and Chebyshev's theorem are two rules for interpretation. The calculations begin with the mean and place around the mean an interval using the standard deviation.

Empirical Rule

The empirical rule is useful with a normal curve and continuous data sets. Beginning with the mean and moving ±1 standard deviation (S) from the mean in any normal distribution, you will include 68.3% of the observations in your data set; ±2 S = 95.5% of the area under the curve; ±3 S = 99.7% of the area under the curve (observations in your data set).

Chebyshev's Theorem

Chebyshev's theorem works for any data set, including normal distributions. However, it is best used for discrete data sets and skewed distributions (non-normal). When the criteria of a normal distribution and continuous data are present, the empirical rule best describes the data set. Chebyshev's theorem, on the other hand, makes use of the relationship $1 - 1/K^2$, where K is greater than one and is *the number of standard deviations*, not the standard deviation itself. Chebyshev's theorem asserts that movement ±2 standard deviations from the mean will encompass *at least* 75% of the observations in the data set.

Reconciling the interpretation using Chebyshev's theorem and the empirical rule is done by using the words "at least" with Chebyshev's interpretation. For example, with an interval of ±2 standard deviations from the mean, the empirical rule encompasses 95.5% of the area under the curve. Chebyshev's, on the other hand, finds 75% of the area. By using the words "at least" I can reconcile the difference between the two since 95.5% is *at least* 75%.

Please keep these things in mind. Let's now look at basic probability.

Why Do You Study Probability?

The theory behind **probability** provides a basis for evaluating the reliability of the conclusions reached and the inferences made about a data set. Remember I introduced you to the concepts of population and sample. I said I wanted to infer something about the population from the sample. I told you that I took a sample because it might be too time consuming or too costly to do a 100% survey of the population.

What Is Probability? Some General Definitions

An experiment is composed of events. All of the events are considered to be the sample space or the collective exhaustive events. Once you have conducted the experiment you will have an outcome or result.

At the base, it is simply the numerical likelihood of an occurrence of an uncertain event, which is measured between 0 and 1.

So a virtually certain event will carry a high probability such as $P = 1$.

A virtually impossible event will carry a low probability such as $P = 0$.

There are two rules of probability. First, *each event* is measured between zero and one and, second, the sum of the probabilities of all events in an experiment must total one.

Helpful Definitions or "Your New Foreign Language" Section

You will tend to learn these words as you are exposed to examples, but refer back to these definitions when you are stumped.

Table 4.1   Inferential statistics terms.

Random	Each and every item in the population (as defined by the researcher) has an equal and independent chance of selection.
Experiment	A well-defined action, which leads to a single, well-defined outcome or result or event. For example, flipping a two-sided, balanced coin is the experiment.
Event	Flipping the coin yields two events: heads or tails. Heads = an event; Tails = an event.
Outcome	The result of an experiment is an outcome or result. For example, if the outcome of flipping a coin (the experiment) is heads then heads is the result or outcome of the experiment. There are two events—heads and tails, but the result or outcome will not be determined until the experiment is conducted.
Data Set	Set of data.
Objects in a Set	Elements or members in a data set are known as objects in a set of data (data set). Each object would be an event, while the entire collection of objects would be the data set or sample space or collectively exhaustive events.
Sample Space**	The set of all possible outcomes (all events) for an experiment. Sample space is also referred to as collectively exhaustive events. Let's take the coin flip I discussed earlier. The sample space is shown as SS {H, T}. There are only two possible outcomes: heads or tails in any one flip (experiment). Each possible event (*H* or *T*) is part of the sample space. Once the experiment is conducted, the event is referred to as an outcome or a result.

**Sample space is one of the most important concepts for you to understand.

Let's Look at Some Examples

What is the probability (*P*) of getting a six in rolling a single, six-sided, fair die? How many sides does a single, six-sided die have?

Tough question, I know.

I think you can safely conclude that a single, six-sided die has six sides.

Ya' think?

I shake my head as I decide if I am going to throw some really tough stuff at you on an examination to get even. I choose not to respond—immediately, that is.

Table 4.2   Die-Rolling experiment example.

What is the sample space?	SS {1, 2, 3, 4, 5, 6}
What is the experiment?	Rolling a single, six-sided die.
What is the outcome?	Once the die is rolled, the outcome would be the result, which would be one of the six elements in the sample space. You would experience either a 1 or 2 or 3 or 4 or 5 or 6. The occurrence of any one of the sides is a random variable. Any one may occur with any roll.
What are the events?	An event would be 1, 2, 3, 4, 5, or 6. Each possible outcome is considered to be an event. Do not confuse event with experiment.

A Couple of Simple Examples

Recall, Rule 1: The probability of an event is measured between zero and one. Rule 2: The sum of the probabilities of the experiment must total one.

Tossing a Single, Six-Sided, Fair Die

There are six sides which could possibly turn up. The probability (*P*) of any one side = one-sixth (1/6th), as long as the die is fair and balanced. One of the rules of probability is met—the events must be measured between zero and one.

The sum of all of the probabilities of the sample space must equal one. In this experiment, the probabilities of the sample space would be written as follows:

$$\sum P \{1, 2, 3, 4, 5, 6\} = 1. \text{ (adding } 1/6 + 1/6, \text{ etc gives you } 6/6 = 1)$$

Both rules of probability are met in this experiment.

Defective Parts

There are only two possible outcomes: a defective part or a non-defective part. Let's call the outcome defective which is written D and the outcome non-defective which is written $\overline{D}$, (pronounced non-D). If the probability of $D = 0.10$, what is the probability of a non-defective part?

The answer is 0.90.

Why?

The rule is that the sum of the probabilities of the sample space must total one.

Since the sample space has only two possible outcomes, the sum of D and non-D must total 1.

The sample space would be SS $\{D, \overline{D}\}$ and the probabilities would be $(0.10 + 0.90 = 1.00)$.

Deck of Cards

A deck of cards has 52 cards. There are 4 suits with 13 cards each ranging from the ace through 10 and then jack, queen, and king. For purposes of this textbook the J, Q, and K are defined as face cards, which means there are 12 face cards in a 52-card deck.

SS = $\{A, 2, 3, 4, 5, 6, 7, 8, 9, 10, J, Q, K$ of hearts, then the same for clubs, diamonds, and spades$\}$ The total sample space includes all 52 cards.

The probability of drawing any one card from the deck of 52 cards is 1/52, so the rule is met that stipulates that the probability of each event in the sample space must be greater than zero but less than one.

The other rule specifies that the sum of the probabilities of each event in the sample space must total one. Since there are 52 cards and the probability of drawing any one card is 1/52, this rule is also met $(52/52 = 1)$.

Three Generally Accepted Approaches to Probability

Relative Frequency Approach

The **relative frequency approach** is an **historic** approach. This approach is one in which data are collected over a period of time. Let's assume I manufacture radios. During the past five years I have determined that 500 radios have been defective out of the 5,000 I have produced. The sample space is the 5,000 radios. Let's further assume I am interested in determining the probability of randomly selecting a defective part from my assembly line.

How would you write the relative frequency relationship?

$$P(E) = \frac{\text{Number of Times an event Occurred}}{\text{Total Number of Observations}}$$

The number of times an event occurred in this example is 500 defective parts.

The total number of times the event could occur (total number of observations) is 5,000 (the sample space).

So the probability of obtaining a defective part (*D*) is 500 ÷ 5,000 = 0.10.

Since there are only two possible outcomes, what is the probability of obtaining a non-defective part?

$$1 - 0.10 = 0.90.$$

When there are only two possible outcomes, the events are considered **complementary.** They are also **mutually exclusive.** (There will be more on these definitions shortly.)

Oh no, I just told you there would be more definitions. Sorry about that, I was just going to surprise you later.

Other examples of the relative frequency approach would be mortality tables or claims in the insurance industry, both used to set insurance rates.

One warning: Let's assume that I went to the Dallas-Fort Worth (DFW) Airport to pick up my cousin. The flight was 20 minutes late, so I make the claim that American Airlines is late 100% of the time. Unfortunately this claim in not valid, since I have too few observations to make this a valid claim. Historic means that I must have a history and it must be adequate for me to make certain judgments. Too few observations will not allow the historic method to work in an unbiased manner.

Subjective Approach

The **subjective approach** is just that—subjective. Past data are not available and the classical approach (just below) does not lend itself to use in most business settings. Here probability is determined based on personal beliefs or expertise which is bolstered by some facts that will influence the outcome. This approach is based on the best available evidence. It is often referred to as an educated guess approach or best guess approach. In the business community this is a very valid approach to making judgments about delivery dates to a customer or supplier performance or closing ratios for sales people as they make sales calls.

For example, if the Dallas Cowboys' star running back and star quarterback are hurt for a particular football game, the probability of winning would be less than if both were healthy and playing.

The results of this approach can be, and many times are, very biased. There are techniques that are useful for narrowing subjective probability to determine the accuracy of pure "gut" feeling probability. These approaches are, however, beyond the scope of this course.

The Classical Approach

The **classical approach** is an a priori approach, meaning the probabilities can be determined before the fact. In other words, the probability is determined before the experiment occurs. Contrast this approach to the relative frequency approach. One is historic and one is when the probabilities are determined before the event occurs.

The classical approach is most often associated with games of chance or gambling. The relationship is stated as follows.

$$P(E) = \frac{\text{Number of Ways the Event Can Occur}}{\text{Total Number of Possible Outcomes}}$$

The total number of possible outcomes is the sample space. This differs from the relative frequency approach in that the classical approach uses all possible outcomes where the relative frequency approach uses the total number of observations. The total number of observations may change from time to time, whereas the total possible outcomes in the classical approach do not change.

For Example

The probability of selecting a queen [$P(Q)$] from a deck of 52 cards on the *first draw* is 4/52. (4 Q and 52 cards)

$P(Q)$ from a deck of 52 cards on a *second draw*, if the first card drawn is not a queen and is not placed back into the deck, is 4/51 (without replacement).

OR

$P(Q)$ from a deck of 52 cards on a second draw, if the first card drawn is a queen and is not placed back into the deck, is 3/51 (without replacement).

The second draw is a dependent event if on the first draw the card drawn is not replaced.

The outcome depends on not replacing the card.

$P(H)$ on the flip of a two-sided coin $= 1/2$ (0.50).

$P(3)$ on the roll of a single, six-sided die $= 1/6$ (0.1667).

All of these probabilities can be determined before you actually have to draw the card, flip the coin, or roll the die. This is a priori probability, before the fact.

Table 4.3   The sample space for shooting craps.

		1	2	3	4	5	6
			1st Die Outcome				
1		2	3	4	5	6	7
2	2nd Die Outcome	3	4	5	6	7	8
3		4	5	6	7	8	9
4		5	6	7	8	9	10
5		6	7	8	9	10	11
6		7	8	9	10	11	12

Playing Craps

If you have ever been to a gambling center such as Las Vegas, Nevada, you have seen the dice table. Playing dice or shooting craps is when a person, called a roller, has two six-sided dice that are rolled simultaneously. Two faces are exposed when two dice are rolled simultaneously. The sum of the two dice turned up is equal to either a winning or losing roll.

Let's develop a table to represent all possible outcomes of rolling two dice at the same time. First of all, you are looking at the sample space for playing craps. There are 36 possible outcomes (6 times 6).

Let's assume you can win if on the first roll of the dice, you get a 7 or an 11. What is the probability of winning using the classical approach?

There are 6 − 7's and 2 − 11's so from the classical calculation the probabilities are 6/36 + 2/36 or 8/36 to win on the first roll. (Count them in the table.)

Let's simplify the game. Let's say that 7 and 11 are the winning numbers on the first roll of the two dice. Let's further say that I do not roll a 7 or 11 on the first roll, but instead roll a 6. On the second roll, 6 is my point, meaning I must make a 6 before I roll a 7 or an 11 on the second roll (my rules for illustration purposes). If I roll a 6 on the second roll, I win, but if I roll a 7 or 11 on the second roll, I lose.

Table 4.4   The sample space for shooting craps.

Sample Space Possible Outcomes Column 1	Probability of Any One Outcome Happening Column 2	Comments Column 3
2	1/36	Do you notice anything about the distribution?
3	2/36	
4	3/36	
5	4/36	
6	5/36	
7	6/36	You should see that it is a normal distribution.
8	5/36	
9	4/36	
10	3/36	
11	2/36	
12	1/36	
Total Sample Space	36/36 = 1	This is the sample space or collection of all events (collectively exhaustive events).

What is the probability of rolling a 6 on the second roll of the dice?

Count the 6's. There are five, so the classical approach tells me that the probability is 5 out of 36 to win on the second roll if my point is 6.

Which has the higher probability on the second roll—winning or losing?

Think about it.

The answer: There is a higher probability of losing on the second roll (8/36) versus winning on the second roll (5/36). There is a higher probability of getting a 7 or 11 on the second roll than getting a 6.

Let's now display the entire sample space for shooting craps in a different manner.

Remember there are two rules of probability. Each outcome in the sample space must be measured between zero and one. Is this rule met? Each of the probabilities in the center column is greater than zero and less than one.

The answer is yes. (See Column 2 in Table 4.4.)

The second is that the sum of all of the outcomes in the sample space must total 1.0. Is this rule met?

The answer is yes.

The total of the sample space is 36/36 which is 1.0.

Now that you have developed the sample space, I can ask you some *tougher questions.*

For example, what is the probability of *eight or less*? Using the center column in Table 4.4, I would add up the probabilities of 8 + 7 + 6 + 5 + 4 + 3 + 2 = 26/36.

If this question had been framed in the terms of *less than eight,* what would the answer be? (21/36).

What if I ask you the probability of more than eight? (10/36).

The point I am driving at is simply this. You can determine any probability by knowing the probability distribution, if you listen carefully to the question and then simply count the probability of success.

You comment, why does this seem so simple?

It is because you have captured the sample space. In general if you can identify the sample space, most probabilities will be very simply determined.

Let's take a short breather from probabilities, before continuing, and look at a fun idea.

Let's look at odds making, which may be helpful as you visit Lone Star Park (a thorough bred horse racing track in Texas) for you horse racing enthusiasts.

Odds Making—The Basics

If the odds that some event (E) will occur are estimated to be three to one, written 3:1, then the probability it will occur can be determined as follows:

$$P(E) = \frac{A}{A + B}$$

where the form is $A{:}B$ or A to B

Calculations of winning are: $3 \div (3 + 1) = 0.75$.

The odds of the event *occurring* are, therefore, set at 0.75 or 75%. Stated either way is correct. This is a complementary event; therefore the odds of the event *not occurring* are set at 0.25, since the probability of the entire sample space must equal 1.0.

Calculations of losing are: $1 \div (1 + 3) = 0.25$.

For example, in southern California, the odds that it will rain on any given day were given by a local radio station as 1 to 37. What is the probability it will rain today?

$P = 0.0263$ (Calculate it and see if you agree.)

Probability or Decision Tree

Another very useful way of looking at sample space uses a probability tree. I think the concept is best understood by looking at an example. Let's assume you are trying to decide to file a lawsuit or not to file a lawsuit—two choices: sue or not sue. You decide to use a probability tree to aid you in making the decision. There are many possibilities, such as you may sue and win. You may sue and lose. If you win, they could appeal. If you lose, you could appeal. How far you go depends on how much you want to spend on lawyers.

In developing your sample space, you want to determine what the probability is of you being successful. You must use subjective probability (best educated guess) to determine the germane probabilities. You can also estimate what you might gain if you are successful. You can also estimate what it might cost you if you are not successful. These values are referred to as payoffs. Payoffs are real numbers and are what you expect to happen for each leg of the decision tree. For example if you sue, win, and win the appeal you might expect to gain $100,000. If you sue, lose, and lose the appeal you might expect it to cost you $90,000. Both of these values are payoffs.

I will not walk through each and every step in the calculation, but will show you the results of two approaches. Since there are three possible initial outcomes—winning, losing, and the judge throwing the suit out, I need probabilities associated with those three outcomes. I want to show you two different probability trees and adjust the probabilities to show how the outcome changes based on sensivity to probabilities.

In the first tree (Figure 4.1) the probabilities for the three possibilities will be set at 25%, 70%, and 5% for winning, losing, and being thrown out. In the second tree (Figure 4.2) I will set the probabilities for the three possibilities at 70%, 25%. and 5% for winning, losing, and being thrown out. Essentially I am flip-flopping two probabilities and holding everything else constant.

Figure 4.1 is the probability tree (also known as the decision tree) using the subjective probability of initially winning of 25%. (Case 1).

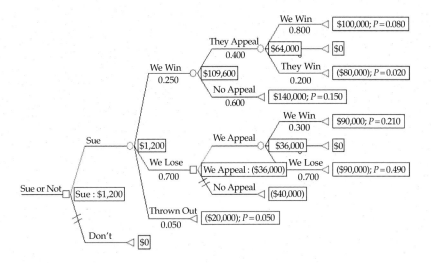

Figure 4.1 Probability tree for the 25% case for winning.

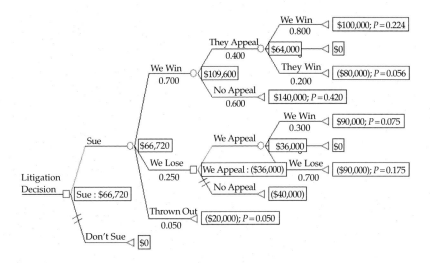

Figure 4.2 Probability tree for the 70% case for winning.

Figure 4.2 is the probability tree using the subjective probability of initially winning of 70%. (Case 2).

Notice that every time a probability is given for a leg of the tree, the total is equal to one and the individual parts are measured between zero and one.

I will not take you through all of the decision possibilities. You can list them. For example, looking at Figure 4.1, you could win, they could appeal, they could lose their appeal, and you would be rewarded by a payoff. The payoffs are estimates of the monetary value of each decision path. Notice some are positive values and some are negative values. This reflects the reality of winning—a positive outcome and thus a positive monetary value—or the reality of losing—a negative outcome and thus a negative monetary value (real cost). The two trees are shown in their entirety as follows. You would develop them leg by leg if you were creating them from the beginning.

Let's take a moment to analyze the results. Notice the values at the far right do not change in either approach. If you sue, win, they appeal, and you win, you stand to gain a real monetary value of $100,000. This is one of the legs of the decision tree. Assume attorney fees are properly added to or netted from the payoff values for the sake of simplifying the presentation.

The worst situation for you would be to sue, lose, you appeal, and you lose the appeal. This carries with it a real monetary loss of $90,000.

For both trees, the probabilities are identical except for the first leg. In Figure 4.1 (25% Case), the initial probabilities are set at 25% for winning, 70% for losing, and 5% for the case being thrown out. In Figure 4.2 (70% Case) the initial probabilities are set at 70% for winning, 25% for losing, and 5% for the case being thrown out. The remainder of the probabilities for each leg and decision remain the same.

I know this may be a bit confusing, but if you take the time to trace each leg you will notice what I am saying is correct. Also notice that the probabilities of each level (winning the appeal or losing the appeal) also are measured between zero and one with the sum total of that level equaling one. The two rules of probabilities remain the same. The probability of an event is measured between zero and one and the sum of the probabilities of the sample space equals one.

Without beating a dead horse, let's focus on the outcomes on the right and then look at the last value on the left. I will address those two values. One is a monetary value (real payoff) and the other is an expected monetary value (weighted expected outcome).

Have you wondered where the idea of beating a dead horse arose?

Not really, you think, but in hoping to impress the professor, you actually reply. Yes, professor, I was wondering about that phrase just the other day.

I look skeptically at you and go on with my wealth of knowledge.

Robert Hendrickson in the *Encyclopedia of Work and Phrase Origins* (Facts on File, New York, 1997) attributes the phrase to British politician and orator John Bright as he railed for the passage of the Reform Bill of 1867, which called for more democratic representation, claiming it would never be passed by Parliament. Trying to rouse Parliament from its apathy on the issue, he said in a speech, would be like trying to "flog a dead horse" to make it pull a load, which is often used as trying to revive interest in an apparently hopeless issue or forcing an issue that is already closed. A dead horse will not get up and pull a load regardless of how much or how often you beat it.

How interesting, you say with tongue in cheek. Umm, ever wondered where the expression tongue in cheek was first used? Oh well, that is another story and I won't digress further. (You cheer silently. Can that really be done—cheering silently?)

Let's go back to the decision trees. In Table 4.5 I will contrast the outcomes of the 25% case and the 70% case to show you how sensitive decisions are to probabilities. I am going to simply list the outcomes of each leg of the decision tree. MV stands for monetary value and is the payoff for each leg.

Notice that the payoffs or the monetary values do not change. The probability of the outcomes does, however, change. Under the Sue, Win, They Appeal, You Win the probabilities

Table 4.5 Outcomes of the 25% case versus the 70% case.

Each Possible Outcome Leg These are Decision Paths flowing from the left to the right.	Tree 1 or 2: 25% or 70% Case MV	Tree 1: 25% Case Probability	Tree 2: 70% Case Probability
Sue, Win, They Appeal, You Win	$100,000	0.080	0.224
Sue, Win, They Appeal, They Win	−$80,000	0.020	0.056
Sue, Win, No Appeal	$140,000	0.150	0.420
Sue, Lose, You Appeal, You Win	$90,000	0.210	0.075
Sue, Lose, You Appeal, You Lose	−$90,000	0.490	0.175
Sue, Judge Throws Out the Case	−$20,000	0.050	0.050
Summary of All Possible Legs	N/A	1.000	1.000
Expected Monetary Value	N/A	$1,200	$66,720
Probability: All Positive Outcomes	N/A	44%	71.9%
Probability: All Negative Outcomes	N/A	56%	28.1%

are more favorable for the 70% case than the 25% case. They move from 8% to 22.4%. Suing and winning with no appeal moves from a 15% chance of success to a 42% chance of success.

If you add the positive outcomes and the negative outcomes, you have an interesting picture. The probability of a positive outcome for the 25% case is only 44% while the probability of a positive outcome for the 70% case rises to 71.9%.

The shift is due to one, singular change in subjective probabilities at the initial stage of suing or not suing. The decision tree allows you to trace how sensitive your decision is to the probability of an event occurring.

Lastly, there is a value in the 25% case and a value in the 70% case in Table 4.5 called an expected monetary value (bolded). This value is a weighted average of the monetary values and the probabilities of each leg. The expected monetary value is not a real number (the monetary values are real), but the expected monetary value is a weighted average of all possible outcomes. See me if you want to know how to calculate it. *www.treeage.com* will allow you access to software that will calculate these values for you.

A higher expected monetary value is better than a lower expected monetary value. Expected monetary values are simply guides to how strong our decision is to sue or not. With an expected monetary value of $1,200 the case may be argued that the outcome is not strong enough to move forward with the suit (25% case). For the 70% case, the expected monetary value shifts to $66,720 which provides us with a stronger motive for suing.

As a matter of fact with an EMV of $66,720, I might find a person who would be willing to pay me $10,000 to assume my position in the law suit. I could take my $10,000 and take a nice vacation fo the Bahamas.

The decision tree is useful in making all sorts of business decisions. For example, let's assume you are considering an investment opportunity. You can invest $1,000 for a sure return of 5%, or $50. You can take the same $1,000 and invest it three other ways which are a bit more risky. One way yields a $500 return (large increase) with a probability of 30%. Another way yields a small increase of $100 with a probability of 40%. The third yields a large loss ($600) with a probability of 30%. (30% + 40% + 30% = 100%)

The investment decision tree is shown below. From the outcome you would find the best path to follow is to make the sure return of 5% since the expected monetary value is $50; whereas the expected monetary value of the risky investment is $10, based on the probabilities as given.

The $10 is a sum of the products of 0.30 × $500 + 0.40 × $100 − 0.30 × −600, which is $150 + $40 − $180 = +$10 (the expected monetary value of the risky decisions.

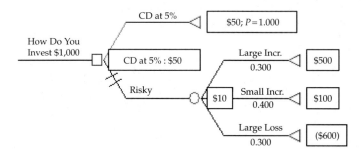

Figure 4.3 $1,000 investment decision tree.

However, shift the probabilities to 40% for the large increase, 50% for the small increase, and 10% for the large loss and you have quite a different result—an expected monetary value of $190 (compared to $10 for this path before). Here again you see how sensitive your decision is based on the subjective probabilities. In this instance, you would be influenced to make the risky investment bypassing the sure thing, the 5% return. Just for grins, you might try to figure out how I got the $190. Hint: It is a weighted average. Weigh each of the monetary values with the probability of outcome and then sum the results (yields an expected monetary value of $190). This is called rolling back the decision tree. (0.40 × $500 + 0.50 × $100 − 0.10 × −$600)

Let's spend a few minutes reading about the relationship between events in the sampling space (in an experiment).

Events, Unions, Intersections, Addition, and Subtraction Rules

Relationships Between Events

What you need now is more new language, so I have graciously inserted more definitions. These are important in understanding how to apply probabilities.

Mutually Exclusive

Events are said to be **mutually exclusive** if the occurrence of one event precludes (or shuts out or stops) the occurrence of another event. Remember events are part of the sample space. The entire sample space is composed of all of the events in an experiment.

Let's look at a couple of examples. Would the following be mutually exclusive events?

**Getting heads or tails on a single flip of a coin?

In the same experiment or the same flip, getting heads on a single flip of a coin precludes the occurrence of tails. If you get heads, you cannot get tails *on the same flip* of the coin. Yes, this is a mutually exclusive event.

**Rolling a 3 or a 5 on a single roll of a six-sided die?

In the same experiment or during the same roll, getting a 3 precludes getting a 5 *on the same roll* of a six-sided die. Yes, this is a mutually exclusive event.

**Queen or an ace from a deck of 52 cards?

In the same draw, getting a queen precludes getting an ace from a deck of 52 cards *on the same draw*. Yes, this is a mutually exclusive event.

**10 or a face card from a deck of 52 cards?

In the same draw, getting a 10 precludes getting a face card (J, Q, K) in a single draw from a deck of 52 cards. This too is a mutually exclusive event.

**Queen or a heart from a deck of 52 cards?

Whoops, this one is *not* mutually exclusive.
You ask, why not?
Because I could draw the queen of hearts from the deck, so the happening of the queen would not preclude the happening of a heart *during the same draw*.

**2 or an even number from a single, six-sided die.

This too is *not* a mutually exclusive event, because I could get a two and an even number *at the same time*.

Collectively Exhaustive Events

This concept is the same as sample space. To be **collectively exhaustive,** events must be all of the possible outcomes of an experiment. So this means that the sum of the probabilities of collectively exhaustive events will equal one, the same as the sample space.

Independent Events

Two events are **independent** *IF* the occurrence of one event has *NO* effect on the probability that the second event will occur.

For example, the outcomes of flipping a coin and rolling a single, six-sided die are independent from each other. Another would be the drawing of the queen of hearts and the probability of rain.

The probability of drawing a jack from a deck of cards is 4/52 on the first draw. On the second draw, the independence is determined by whether I replace the card or I do not replace the card drawn on the first attempt. If I replace the card, I return the deck to the original sample space of 52 cards. If I do not replace the card, then I change the sample space by reducing it to 51 cards. In the latter, a dependent event occurs and the sample space is modified. In the former, an independent event occurs on the second draw.

Rule: The data set must be finite (have predefined limits) and replacement must be done for events to be independent.

Dependent Events

If the occurrence of an event depends on the occurrence of another event then the events are considered dependent. The other event may be prior to, simultaneous with, or following the first event.

If you have a finite population without replacement, the event is said to be dependent. Dependency is conditional. It is conditioned on what happens to a prior, simultaneous, or following event.

Repeat: The occurrence of one event affects the occurrence of another event, *if you must consider the probability of the first event in determining the probability of the other event. The events have a relationship to each other when dependency exists.*

Complementary Events

If the failure of one event means the other must occur, the events are **complementary.** Complementary events exist when there are only two outcomes in the sample space.

$$P(A) + P(\overline{A}) = 1.$$

$\overline{A}$ is read A-bar which means any event other than A.

If there are only two events, the sum of the probability of the two events must equal one; therefore, the events are complementary.

For example, let's say I manufacture and assemble radios. Given the probability of a defective part of 0.10, what is the probability of a non-defective part?

Answer: 0.90.

These events are complementary. The same would be true for getting an odd or even in the roll of a single, six-sided die or the flipping of a coin.

Answer: 3/6 for odd and 3/6 for even.

Flipping a single coin: $1/2$ for heads and $1/2$ for tails.

All these examples are complementary events.

Complementary events are also mutually exclusive.

Unions and Intersections

I have a present for you: more foreign language definitions and a new concept.

Are you excited?

Okay, maybe excited is not the right description of your present emotion, but let's not go there. A **set** is any collection of objects. Sets may be related to each other. For example, let's define Set *A* as the students who are in statistics. Let's further define Set *B* as the students who are seniors. There would be a Set *C*, which would be all other students who are not seniors and not in statistics, but I have no interest in Set *C*. I will concentrate on Set *A* and Set *B*. Let's identify those students with the first initial of their last name, which in this case happens to be as follows.

Set A

A, B, C, D, E, F, G.

Defined as students who are taking statistics.

Set B

G, H, I, J, K.

Defined as those who are Seniors.

If I list the two sets in the following manner, you should notice something about the two sets that is interesting (at least to some of you).

Set *A* (Those in Statistics)

A

B

C

D

E

F

G   H   I   J   K   L   ← Set *B* (Those Who are Seniors)

Student *G* appears in Set *A* and Set *B*. This is called **intersecting probability**. It is also referred to as joint probability.

Intersection

By definition, **intersecting probability** *is the set of ALL of the elements that are in both Set A and in Set B.*

This is written as follows: $A \cap B$, which reads A *intersection B*.

The question would be: What element or elements in Set A and Set B meet or meets this criterion? The answer is student G. Student G appears in both A *and* B. Student G is in statistics (Set A) and is a senior (Set B).

Student G is said to be the intersection point of the two sets. Intersecting probability is often referred to as joint probability.

By definition, *joint probability is the probability of two events occurring simultaneously.* The **multiplication rule** is useful in finding joint probability. The connecting word *and* is the key. I will discuss this more shortly.

Union

By definition, **union** is the set of ALL elements that are in A *or* B.

This is written as follows: $A \cup B$, which reads A union B.

The question is: What elements or element in Set A and Set B meet or meets this criterion?

The answer is *all students* appear in either A or B, so Student A through Student L appear in A or B. The **addition rule** is helpful in determining union probability. The connecting word *or* is the key. I will discuss this shortly.

Okay, shortly is here. Notice the word "and" as it applies to intersection and the word "or" as it applies to union. The words "and & or" are important words when working with probabilities.

The questions would be phrased as follows. What is the probability of drawing an *ace **and** a king* in two successive draws from a deck of 52 cards? $8/52 \times 7/51 = 56/2{,}652$.

Why, you might ask?

First, there must be two draws and each must be successful. On the first draw the probability is 8 out of 52. You must draw either an ace or a king. Next you draw again. Now there is one less "target" card and one less card in the deck (assuming non-replacement) thus you have 7 out of 51 possible chances. These are independent events, so you would multiply the probabilities of independent events. Multiplied this would be $56/2{,}652$ chances of drawing an *ace **and** a king* on two successive draws from a deck of 52 cards Notice the connector word AND. Also notice that I multiplied the probabilities of two independent events (two independent outcomes).

The second question: What is the probability of drawing an *ace **or** a king* from a deck of cards? Here one draw will be done. There are four aces and four kings. Adding the two possibilities together you have eight possible "targets" out of 52 cards thus $8/52$ is the answer. Notice the connecting word OR and notice that I added the probabilities.

The connector words "and & or" are very important in knowing if you are going to multiply the probabilities or you are going to add the probabilities.

Another important method of working problems is to convert a frequency table to a probability table. This is probably the easiest method. Remember the craps table approach?

Once the sample space was identified, I could not come up with a question on probabilities you could not answer. The same is true for the probability table approach.

Frequency Table and Probability Table

A probability table flows from (comes from) a frequency table. To understand I have to throw some more definitions at you. Sorry about that. There are three types of probability present in any probability table.

Joint Probability

By definition **joint probability** is the probability that two events will occur simultaneously.

Marginal Probability

By definition **marginal probability** is the probability of a single event occurring.

Conditional Probability

By definition **conditional probability** is a ratio of joint probability divided by marginal probability.

Conditional probability is written as follows.

$P\langle A \mid B \rangle$, which reads from the right to the left (outside in). *Given B has occurred*, what is the probability of *A* occurring? Or if *B* has occurred, what is the probability of *A* occurring? *B* is a given occurrence. *B* is the condition that exists.

Summary of General Guidelines

Solutions to problems hinge on the following relationships.

$$A \cap B \quad \text{Intersection and Joint (And \& Multiplication)}$$

$$A \cup B \quad \text{Union and Marginal (Or \& Addition)}$$

Remember, I told you there are three generally accepted approaches to probability, which are the *relative frequency* approach, the *subjective* approach and the *classical* approach.

With the *relative frequency* approach you can use one of three methods to solve probability problems. Do not get the following three confused with the generally accepted approaches just because there are three of each one.

First, there is the use of a probability tree, also known as a decision tree. This is the most time consuming and difficult of the three approaches unless you use software like Treeage (*www.treeage.com*) or other similar software. In your Internet browser, you might type in decision tree and see what pops up. While the most difficult to set up, this approach yields excellent time-benefit results and it is highly recommended when you have a reasonably complex business decision to make. I showed you a decision tree approach on the sue or don't sue case as well as how to invest $1,000.

Second, there is the use of a probability table, which flows from a frequency table. This is a much simpler approach to probability calculations. The probability table captures all of the sample space. Once you have identified the sample space, it is relatively easy to determine any probability using joint, marginal, and conditional probabilities. I will show you an example of this approach shortly.

Third, there is the use of the rules of multiplication and addition. The summary chart below (Figure 4.4) summarizes how to make use of these rules. The chart hinges on use of the words "and" and "or."

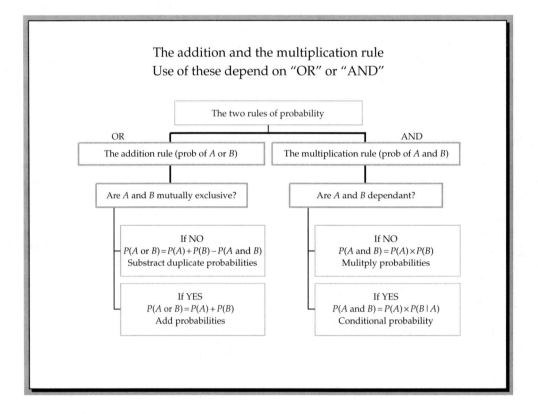

Figure 4.4 Chart summarizing the multiplication and addition rules in probability.

Remember These Definitions

Mutually exclusive means the happening of one event precludes the happening of another event.

Dependent event means that the probability of one event depends on the probability of another event, for example, if probability is measured without replacement. This can be conditional probability. The outcome of one depends on the outcome of another. Events are independent if the occurrence of one event has no effect on the probability that the second will occur.

Figure 4.4 looks great, you say, but how the heck do I use it?

Good question, I respond.

Let's look at a couple of examples. I know it is a stretch, but you will actually have to look at Figure 4.4 as I go through this explanation.

What is the probability of selecting an *A* (ace) or *H* (heart) from a deck of cards?

Notice the word "or." This takes you down the *left side* of Figure 4.4. You must now ask yourself "Are *A* and *B* mutually exclusive?" Look back at the definition of mutually exclusive a couple of pages back.

The answer is "no, they are not" since I can draw the ace of hearts. This means, according to the rules of addition, that I will add the probability of A to the probability of B and subtract the overlapping probability of *A* and *B*. The answer is 4/52 for aces +13/52 for hearts = 17/52. But I have counted the ace of hearts in both the aces and the hearts. This double counting must be eliminated so the final answer is $17/52 - 1/52 = 16/52$.

I have already shown you an example where the answer was "yes, the events are mutually exclusive." Do you remember what it was?

Remember the craps example? I asked the question what is the probability of a 7 or an 11 on a single roll of two die? Since obtaining a 7 precludes obtaining an 11 in the same roll, these are mutually exclusive events. This, according to the chart rules, tells me to add P(7) and P(11), which is $6/36 + 2/36 = 8/36$. This is exactly what I did.

These two examples are associated with the left side of Figure 4.4, but what about the right side of the chart? That side is utilized when you have the connecting word "and."

Some slot machines, like those used in gambling casinos, have three wheels that rotate. Let's assume they have 40 positions on each wheel. Let's further assume that there is one seven on each wheel. To win the maximum prize all three sevens must line up on the payline. What is the probability of a seven on the first wheel *and* a seven on the second wheel *and* a seven on the third wheel at the same time? (7 and 7 and 7).

The solution is driven by the word "and." Going down the right side of Figure 4.4, you must ask yourself if the events are dependent. The answer is they are not. The occurrence of the first seven has no impact on the occurrence of the second seven which in turn has no impact on the occurrence of the third seven. This means the events are independent of each other. (If you are confused, look at the definitions of independent and dependent again).

What is the probability of all three sevens lining up on the payline? Figure 4.4 tells you to multiply the probability of independent events. The probability of a seven appearing on the payline for each wheel is 1/40. The probability of three lining up would be $1/40 \times 1/40 \times 1/40 = 1/64,000$ (0.00002). Are the odds in your favor here? I think not. Independent events always multiply probabilities.

The other leg of the right side of the chart is conditional probability. This approach is a bit more mathematical. In the tear-out sheets, I will address this type of problem in detail, although I rather doubt most of you will ever try to work this sort of probability mathematically.

By tracing these solutions to problems using Figure 4.4, I believe you can see how to use the chart. Pay particular attention to the words "and" and "or". *P(A and B)* works differently than the *P(A or B)*. Knowing if the probabilities are driven by the word "and" or the word "or" and knowing the definition of mutually excluding and dependent, you can make the calculations using the rules for addition or multiplication.

Let's now take a look at what is probably the easiest method of solving probability problems.

Frequency Table and Probability Table

One of the easiest methods for determining probabilities is to convert your data to a frequency table and then to convert the frequencies to a probability table.

Shown below is the result of an optometrist who keeps records on the kind of glasses he sells. He has determined that glasses have sold in small, medium, and large sizes. He has also determined the manufacturing methods for the frames: plastic, wire, or composite materials. The frequency table is set up from his raw data tabulations. The values in *italics* are the frequency numbers while the values in **bold** are the probability table values.

As a continued reminder, probability is measured between zero and one and the sum of all probabilities of the sample space (all the events in an experiment) will equal one.

Table 4.6   *Frequency table* / **Probability table.**

	Column D Plastic		Column E Wire		Column F Composite		Totals	
	F	*P*	*F*	*P*	*F*	*P*	*F*	*P*
Row A Large	*24*	**0.12**	*16*	**0.08**	*10*	**0.05**	*50*	**0.25**
Row B Medium	*46*	**0.23**	*62*	**0.31**	*2*	**0.01**	*110*	**0.55**
Row C Small	*12*	**0.06**	*12*	**0.06**	*16*	**0.08**	*40*	**0.20**
Totals	*82*	**0.41**	*90*	**0.45**	*28*	**0.14**	*200*	**1.00**

Notice that I have labeled the rows (*A* through *C*) and the columns *D* through F. This will be useful in identifying positional locations. The frequencies are necessary so that I can determine the probabilities. The concept is one with which you should be familiar—relative frequency. The sum of the probabilities will equal one (see the last number in the far right of Table 4.6). The table contains the sample space, which is all the possible outcomes. The total in the far right is one (1.00) thus reflecting that I have identified and captured the sample space. With the sample space in front of me, I cannot create a problem I cannot answer.

To complete calculations for Table 4.6, I would place the frequencies over the total possible occurrences. For the cell identified as *AD*, the percentage or probability is 24/200 = 0.12. For the cell identified as *BF*, the percentage or probability is 2/200 = 0.01. For the cell identified as *CF*, the percentage or probability is 16/200 = 0.08. Notice all cell frequencies are placed over the common total of 200. This allows you to convert from frequency to probabilities.

Intersecting Probability

What if I wanted to determine *A* ∩ *D*? Remember, this is read *A* intersection *D*. Intersecting probability occurs when you identify all of the elements in both *A* and *B* (*A* and *D*, in this case). Strangely that sounds like joint probability, because joint probability occurs where two events occur simultaneously.

I can now apply these definitions to the frequency table/probability table. A is the sale of a large pair of glasses. D tells me the large glasses are made of plastic material. The two events are large and plastic. They occur simultaneously, thus the probability is *intersecting probability*, which is also called *joint probability*. If I wanted to determine the probability straight from Table 4.6, what would it be?

$$P(A \cap D).$$

Answer: $P(A \cap D) = 0.12$. (Read this directly from the Probability Table 4.6).

Marginal Probability

Let's ask a different question. What is the probability of the glasses sold being large? Here, I am concerned with one event—large glasses. This is the probability of a single event occurring. Large framed glasses include plastic, wire, and composite construction.

I am also asking about the marginal probability. Marginal probability is the probability of a single event occurring.

What is the single event?

Large glasses would be the single event. From Table 4.6, what is the probability of large glasses being sold? $P(L)$, which is Row A.

Answer: $P(L) = 0.25$ (Read directly from the Table 4.6).

Make a note about joint and marginal probabilities: Joint or intersecting probabilities are found in the body of the table. Marginal probabilities are found in the margin of the table. Joint is the occurrence of two events simultaneously and marginal is the occurrence of a single event. Go to the table and observe what I am saying here. There are several joint probabilities: large-plastic, large-wire, large-composite, and so forth.

The third major probability other than joint and marginal is conditional probability.

Conditional Probabilities

Remember, conditional probabilities, by definition, are a ratio of joint (intersecting) probabilities divided by marginal (union) probabilities. The relationship can be stated as follows:

$$CONDITIONAL = \frac{(JOINT)}{(MARGIN)}$$

Conditional probability begins with a "condition" or "given" or an "if" statement. In other words, something has occurred. Now you want to determine the probability that event A will happen, given that event B has occurred already.

For example, given that a large pair of glasses was sold, what is the probability they were made of plastic material? Reading this directly from Table 4.6, you would have the following solution.

Answer: $P\langle P \mid L \rangle = 24$ (joint)/50 (marginal) or using the percentages $0.12/0.25 = 0.48$. This is the intersection of Row A and Column D.

You may use either the frequencies or the probabilities and get the same correct answer.

In effect, the sale of large glasses has occurred or is a given. I can now *completely forget about the medium and small glasses.* They are no longer of interest to me. I must, therefore, reset the 1.00 (100%) to be equal to the large glasses and the large glasses alone. This means that I must recalculate the probabilities using only the large glasses numbers.

Here again I have captured my sample space in Table 4.6. By knowing the sample space, I cannot come up with a question you cannot answer.

Okay, enough seriousness.

Let's do some fun stuff.

Fun Applications

No testing on this material.

Texas Hold 'Em

Need I say more? Since you probably have not lived in a cave the last few years you probably have been exposed to this card game. There are hundreds of online links in which you can learn about playing. The key to looking at the percentage or probability of success is wrapped up in the number of *outs* you have when trying to draw a particular card. I pulled Table 4.7 from the following site: *http://www.texasholdem-poker.com/odds_chart.php*.

Table 4.7 Texas hold 'em poker odds.

Outs	On the Flop for the Turn	On the Turn for the River	On the Flop for the Turn and River combined
1 Out	2.13%	2.17%	4.26%
2 Outs	4.26%	4.35%	8.42%
3 Outs	6.38%	6.52%	12.49%
4 Outs	8.51%	8.70%	16.47%
5 Outs	10.64%	10.87%	20.35%
6 Outs	12.77%	13.04%	24.14%
7 Outs	14.89%	15.22%	27.84%
8 Outs	17.02%	17.39%	31.45%
9 Outs	19.15%	19.57%	34.97%
10 Outs	21.28%	21.74%	38.39%
11 Outs	23.40%	23.91%	41.72%
12 Outs	25.53%	26.09%	44.96%
13 Outs	27.66%	28.26%	48.10%

(continued)

Table 4.7 Texas hold 'em poker odds *(Continued)*

Outs	On the Flop for the Turn	On the Turn for the River	On the Flop for the Turn and River combined
14 Outs	29.79%	30.43%	51.16%
15 Outs	31.91%	32.61%	54.12%
16 Outs	34.04%	34.78%	56.98%
17 Outs	36.17%	36.96%	59.76%
18 Outs	38.30%	39.13%	62.44%
19 Outs	40.43%	41.30%	65.03%
20 Outs	42.55%	43.48%	67.53%
21 Outs	44.68%	45.65%	69.94%

Of course, you must be of legal age in Texas to do any gambling, so don't try it unless it and you are legal, but once you reach the legal age, these ideas may help.

One of the nice things about the site I listed above is that it has odds calculators, so you can determine the probabilities based on every possible combination of pre-flop, flop, turn, and river card. I am not going to define these terms so I am pre-supposing you have some working knowledge of the game. For example, if you are dealt a Q–3 suited, the probabilities are shown in Table 4.8 of obtaining help on the flop.

Table 4.8 The Probability of obtaining help on the flop in Texas hold 'em.

Chance of getting 4-of-a-kind on the flop:	0.01%
Chance of getting a full house on the flop:	0.09%
Chance of getting a flush on the flop:	0.84%
Chance of getting a straight on the flop:	Not Measurable
Chance of getting 3-of-a-kind on the flop:	1.57%
Chance of getting 2 pair on the flop:	4.04%
Chance of getting 1 pair on the flop:	26.94%
Chance of getting a four flush on the flop:	10.94%
Chance of NO overcards coming down on the flop:	58.57%
Chance of ONE overcard coming down on the flop:	35.14%
Chance of TWO overcards coming down on the flop:	6.00%
Chance of THREE overcards coming down on the flop:	0.29%
Chance of ANY overcards coming down on the flop:	41.43%

The odds calculator allows you to select the deal or have it randomized. Try it. It is fun. Of course, winning at Texas hold 'em depends on a lot of factors, but one is knowing when you have the percentages in your favor.

Horse Racing

Horse Racing in the Fort Worth/Dallas, Texas area is at Lone Star Park in Grand Prairie. Their link is *http://www.lonestarpark.com/.*

Here the odds are a bit more difficult to calculate but, needless to say, going with the odds will improve your chances of winning.

The approximate payoff for a $2 bet is displayed in the following Table taken directly from the Lone Star Park website. If the odds are 1 to 9, the payoff for a $2.00 bet is $2.20.

Horse racing is paramutual betting, which means that all monies are pooled, and some of the bettors pick a horse to win and the other bettors pick the horse to lose. The house (the race track) takes a portion of the pool before distributing the remainder to the winners. Usually the track will take from 18% to 25% of the pool, so if the pool is $10,000 for a race, the house takes up to $2,500, then the remainder is distributed. It is a bit more complicated, but this oversimplification will explain the basics.

To calculate the payoff as shown above with odds of 1 to 9, a horse is expected to win 9 times and lose 1 time out of 10 races, a real favorite, so the payoff is very small $0.20 on a $2.00 bet. In other words, one person is betting $9.00 for the horse to win and someone else is betting $1.00 for the horse to lose. This is an odds of $1/(1 + 9) = 1/10 = 10\% \times \$2.00 = \$0.20 + \$2.00$ (get back original bet) = a $2.20 payoff.

At the race track you will see several odds posted—the morning odds (subjective odds of the experts) and the pre-race odds (determined by the betting pool), with the payoff coming from the final betting pool (frozen at the time the starting gate opens). Don't let those confuse you. The winnings are paid from the final betting pool after the gate opens and may be slightly different than the pre-race odds simply because of last-second betting.

Odds of 20 to 1 convert to probability based on the formula given to you early in this chapter, which is $a/(a + b)$. Here the probability of the horse losing is $20/21 = 95.24\%$. This is considered to be a long shot, but the payoff will be exceptional, if you bet the horse to win and it wins. You are, however, playing against the odds.

Table 4.9 Payoff for a $2.00 horse racing bet.

Odds	Pays	Odds	Pays	Odds	Pays	Odds	Pays
1−9	$2.20	1−1	$4.00	2−1	$6.00	5−1	$12.00
1−5	$2.40	6−5	$4.40	5−2	$7.00	6−1	$14.00
2−5	$2.80	7−5	$4.80	3−1	$8.00	7−1	$16.00
1−2	$3.00	3−2	$5.00	7−2	$9.00	8−1	$18.00
3−5	$3.20	8−5	$5.20	4−1	$10.00	9−1	$20.00
4−5	$3.60	9−5	$5.60	9−2	$11.00	10−1	$22.00

If you know the probability is $\frac{1}{45}$ this becomes odds of 1 to 44 to win, a really long shot. This is based on the same formula shown just above. Odds are stated in terms of how many times you expect the horse to win and lose. For example, 20 to 1 means you expect the horse to win 1 time but lose 20 times (1 out of 21 of winning or 0.0476 probability or 4.76%). 2 to 1 means you expect the horse to win 1 time and lose 2 times (1 out of 3 or 0.3333 probability or 33.33%). The payoff on a $2.00 bet would be $\frac{1}{2}$ = 50% × $2.00 = $1.00 + $2.00 (original bet returned) = $3.00.

This is probably enough to pique your interest and just enough to confuse you. The point is that probability and odds are heavy hitters in horse racing. Here too you must understand the odds so you can determine the favorite. The long shots pay more, but while the winnings are less, the favorites pay more often.

You know You are a Texan if:

- You know that "y'all" is singular and "all y'all" is plural
- A Jaguar is not a status symbol. A Ford 350 4 × 4 is.
- Your place at the lake has wheels on it.

Tear-Out Sheet Chapter 4

Student Name: _____

Day and Time of Class: _____

Sample Problems to be Worked:

Probability is a concept that needs to be brought together, and I feel the best way is to work several problems associated with the concepts I have just shown you.

Remember there are three generally accepted methods of solving probability problems: relative frequency, subjective, and classical. Under the relative frequency approach there are three methods of problem solving. One is the probability tree, the second is the chart for addition and multiplication, and the third is the probability table.

Solve these problems. Make a note of the approach you use, i.e., relative frequency, subjective, or classical. Also make note if you are using conditional probability, joint probability, or marginal probability.

1. From a single draw from a deck of standard playing cards: P (Jack).
2. From Table 4.6 using the data from the optometrist problem, what is the probability of a large being sold given it is made of composite material? P (Large | Composite).
3. From the same optometrist table: P (Plastic | Large).
4. From the same optometrist table: P (Large or Small).
5. From the same optometrist table: P (Large or Plastic).
6. From the single draw of one card from a deck of standard playing *cards* and the roll of a six-sided, balanced/fair *die*: P (King and 5).
7. From one attempt from a standard deck of playing cards: P (Ace | Not a Face Card). This reads as follows: Given the card drawn is not a face card, what is the probability it will be an ace?
8. From a single draw from a standard deck of cards: P (Ace or Heart).
9. In a single draw from a standard deck of cards: P (Heart or Diamond).
10. The sales records of an automobile dealer in Dallas indicate the following weekly sales volume over the last 200 weeks.

Number of Cars Sold	Number of Weeks	
0	8	
1	14	
2	25	
3	60	

Number of Cars Sold	Number of Weeks	
4	50	
5	23	
6	12	
7	8	
Total	200	

   a. Develop the sample space for the probabilities associated with number of weeks in the study.
   b. Which of the three approaches would you use?
   c. What is the probability of selling exactly three cars any week you are open for business using this 200-week study?

11. During the last several years the Dow Jones Industrial Average closing prices have been converted to probabilities and are shown below.

Close	Probability
Higher	0.60
The Same	0.10
Lower	0.20

   a. Is this distribution the entire sample space?
   b. Are the probabilities developed correctly? Why or Why Not?

12. The results of a survey of 800 married couples and the number of children they had is tabulated below. This distribution is listed in probabilities.

Number of Children	Probability
0	0.050
1	0.125
2	0.600
3	0.150
4	0.050
5 or more	0.025
Total	1.000

   a. What is the probability that a couple will have fewer than four children?

   b. What is the probability a couple will have more than two children?

   c. What is the probability a couple will have either two or three children?

13. A Daytona Beach nightclub has the following frequency data on the age and marital status of 140 customers:

		Marital Status		
		Single	Married	Total
Age	Under 30	77	14	
Age	30 and Over	28	21	
	Total			

   a. Complete the frequency table.

   b. Convert the frequency table to a probability table.

   c. Use the marginal probabilities to comment on the *age of customers* attending the club.

$$P(<30)$$

$$P(30+)$$

   d. Use the marginal probabilities to comment on the *marital status of customers* attending the club.

$$P(M)$$

$$P(S)$$

   e. What is the probability of finding a customer who is single and under the age of 30? If you label the rows A and B and the columns C and D, you need to find $P(A \cap C)$.

   f. If a customer is under 30, what is the probability that he or she is single?

$$P(S | < 30)$$

14. Let us assume you have taken a survey that yields the following results—120 are men and 80 are women. Out of the 120 men, 40 own stock. Out of the 80 women, 20 own stock. Develop a frequency table and a probability table showing the entire sample space.

   a. Given a man is selected, what is the probability that he will be a stockholder?

$$P(SH | M)$$

   b. If a woman is selected, what is the probability that she will be a stockholder?

$$P(SH | W)$$

    c. What kind of approach is used in the calculations in *a* and *b* above?

    d. Find: P(Man and Stockholder)

    e. Find: P(Woman and Non-Stockholder)

15. Using the information from problem 14, answer the questions below using the multiplication and addition rules (Use Figure 4.4 as your guide). (Hint: The table is much simpler, but the calculation is more mathematical). Problems 14 and 15 are two different approaches to the same problem.

    a. P (Male and Stockholder)

    b. Given a man is selected, what is the probability that he will be a stockholder? (conditional)

    c. P (Woman and a Non-Stockholder)

    d. Given a woman is selected, what is the probability that she will be a non-stockholder?

Probabilities II —Probability Distributions

Court Room Humor – Actual Exchanges Based on a Book by Charles M. Sevilla

Attorney:	She had three children, right?
Witness:	Yes.
Attorney:	How many were boys?
Witness:	None.
Attorney:	Were there any girls?
Witness:	Your Honor, I think I need a different attorney. Can I get a new attorney?

Before I cover probability distributions, I want to look at one basic idea behind inferential statistics, which most believe is the most important branch of statistics. Remember the other branch is descriptive statistics.

Before I do probability distributions, I want to spend some time on the arrangement of the population data set into subsets. I want to know how many arrangements of my population I can develop in smaller groupings (subsets).

Sounds complicated doesn't it?

Let's say I am interested in determining the average age of those reading my textbook. I could work with the entire population (all of you) who are reading the textbook, but I could also work with a sample of the population. Recall, the population is all of the elements of interest to the researcher and a sample is a representative portion selected at random from the population of interest.

Let's assume the population is 150 students. I want to know the average age of the 150 students, but do not want to speak with all 150. I select at random 10 students to represent the entire population and determine the age of those students. I now assert that the average age of the 10 students (the sample) represents the average age of the entire population.

However, it is clear that out of 150 students I could have selected several sets of 10 students.

You agree; but you wonder how I can determine the possible number of arrangements.

Not to worry, I all-knowingly respond. I will show you how.

There are four generally accepted methods of determining arrangements of data sets. Mercifully, I will address only the two that have the most relevance at this point.

Permutations and Combinations

Both of these techniques are designed to determine how many *subsets* into which your population data set can divide. As I said, it sounds rather complicated. It really is not, however. All I am asking you to do is to arrange a population data set into subsets or pieces given certain arrangement criteria.

For example, let's say that your data set consists of the population of students who are taking a class. Let's say there are 12. What I want to know is if I take a sample of three students, how many possible subsets (arrangements) of the data set of 12 can I have? *The answer depends on the concept of order.* If the order makes a difference, I would expect one subset arrangement. If the order makes no difference, I would expect another subset arrangement.

So, you quite naturally ask, what do you mean by the statement "order makes a difference"?

Good question, I respond.

For example, if a different prize award is given to the first three people to cross the finish line in a race, then the order of finish makes a difference. You would most certainly want to finish the race first to obtain the best prize. However, if the prize is the same for the first three finishers, then the order would not make any difference. If you finish first you get the same prize as if you finish third.

In any arrangement, you should first ask the question "Is order important?"

If the answer is "yes," then you will have a data set that must be arranged by using a **permutation.**

If the answer is "no," then you will have a data set that must be arranged by using a **combination.**

The number of permutations (arrangements) of a data set of 12 (n) arranged 3 (r) at a time would be determined as follows: The general statement is arrangement of n elements arranged r at a time.

In a permutation, order is important. In the formula below, "!" is read "factorial". So "n!" is read "n factorial." **Factorial** by definition is the product of all positive integers from 1 to n, with "0!" being defined as equaling 1. Without this last definition of 0!, you would have a formula that yielded zero if n and r are equal. "n" is always the population size and the largest number. "r" is always the sample size and the smaller of the two numbers. The calculation for 12 elements arranged 3 at a time when order matters is as follows:

$$_nP_r = \frac{n!}{(n-r)!}$$

$$= \frac{12!}{(12-3)!} = \frac{12*11*10*9!}{9!} = 12*11*10 = 1,320$$

From this you can see there are 1,320 possible arrangements of your population data set of 12 elements arranged 3 at a time. Notice you can cancel the 9! in the denominator and the 9! in the numerator without having to go to the trouble of multiplying all the numbers to their final product. This saves time.

What this says is that, as long as *order of finish is important,* the maximum possible arrangements of the population data set of 12 elements 3 at a time into subsets is 1,320. That is a lot of arrangements (subsets).

But let's say the *order is not important,* what then?

A combination approach will be used.

For combinations, order is not important.

It makes no difference to me if there are two people ahead of me at the finish line as long as the prizes for all three places remain the same. Arranging the same 12 elements 3 at a time will yield the following result.

$$_nC_r = \frac{n!}{r!(n-r)!} = 220$$

Work out the answer. You can use the permutation calculations as your benchmark. The only difference is you have one more term in the denominator ($r!$). Here $r!$ is $3 \times 2 \times 1 = 6$, so dividing 1,320 by 6 you have 220, but make sure you get the same number. Make sure you understand the process since the idea is a very important idea for inferential statistics.

Combinations will *always be less* than the permutations.

Solving the same problem for combinations, the result, as we have demonstrated, will yield 220 combinations while it yielded 1,320 permutations.

To recap, the permutations *will always be greater* than the combinations. For permutations, the order of finish is important. In combinations, the order of finish is not important.

Duplication is not allowed in either approach.

Okay, so what, you say. How is this practical to the expensive education I am paying for at this university? (Actually, it is my parents who are paying, goes flashing through your mind).

In Texas, as in other places, there is a taxation system called the lottery. The Texas Lottery can be won by having 6 out of 54 numbers drawn randomly. You have probably seen the ping-pong ball approach. What are the chances of this occurring, you wonder.

First question: Is order important?

Answer: No. It makes no difference if you have a one or a six or a fifty-four selected first or sixth.

Is duplication allowed?

No, so this means I can use a combination solution where order makes no difference. Here $n = 54$ and $r = 6$. The question is: How many arrangements of my data set of 54 can be obtained 6 at a time? The calculation would be as follows.

$$_nC_r = \frac{n!}{r!(n-r)!} = \frac{54!}{6!(54-6)!} = \frac{54*53*52*51*50*49*48!}{(6*5*4*3*2*1)(48!)}$$

$$\frac{18,595,558,800}{720} = 25,827,165$$

The probability of winning the Lottery is 1 in 25,827,165.

Wow, but can I improve my chances by purchasing two tickets?

Think about it. Does just purchasing another ticket improve your odds on the first ticket?

The first ticket is independent from the second. The odds of winning are still 1 in 25,827,165 for each separate ticket purchased.

I can win something with just five numbers, can't I?

Yep! Try using the same formula to determine the chances of winning using 54 numbers 5 at a time.

Solution: 1 in 3,162,510. Better, but still not very good.

54 numbers 4 at a time = 1 in 316,251. Getting better, but the payoff drops considerably ($54 versus $22 million). I don't know about you but I would rather win $22 million. How about you????

Some typical payoffs (which I took from the *www.texaslottery.com*) are shown in Table 5.1 above. Typically if there is no winner of the jackpot, it "rolls over" until someone wins. The other winnings are paid.

Okay, enough of the fun stuff. Check that: all of this is fun, I say!

You think, "this professor is really sick," but out of courtesy you say nothing.

Thanks for not saying anything, I incoherently mumble as I press on.

Okay, so how does this stuff tie to inferential statistics, you ask?

Think about it. I draw a random sample from the population of interest. A sample is a representative portion of the population. The sample I select has a mean which is meant to

Table 5.1   Some typical Texas Lottery payoffs.

Date	# Correct	Prize Amounts	Winners
06/21/2006		6 − 8 − 9 − 31 − 32 − 52	
	6 of 6	$22 Million	Roll
	5 of 6	$2,224	22
	4 of 6	$54	1,337
	3 of 6	$3	29,809
06/17/2006		6 − 26 − 29 − 39 − 43 − 50	
	6 of 6	$20 Million	Roll
	5 of 6	$1,975	28
	4 of 6	$58	1,406
	3 of 6	$3	30,799
06/14/2006		14 − 20 − 21 − 31 − 33 − 38	
	6 of 6	$19 Million	Roll
	5 of 6	$1,734	27
	4 of 6	$50	1,376
	3 of 6	$3	27,809
06/10/2006		24 − 28 − 41 − 42 − 44 − 47	
	6 of 6	$17 Million	Roll
	5 of 6	$2,531	21
	4 of 6	$59	1,330
	3 of 6	$3	29,046

represent the population mean. Depending on the size of my population data set I can have many different samples all of which represent the population mean. Each of these arrangements or samples is a subset of the population. I can determine the number of those subsets or arrangements by using permutations or combinations. This will become a bit clearer as the textbook unfolds.

For now I want to return to the idea of special probability distributions.

Probability Distributions

There are many types of probability distributions which are important in working with business decisions. Business decisions are made under conditions of uncertainty. Uncertainty must be measured. Uncertainty must be reduced and must be turned into higher certainty.

Nothing is absolutely certain, but in business settings I can cut off the downside risk and move my decisions away from negative results, and I can improve the probability of better outcomes.

Let's suppose that you want to market your new computer service. You know that the acceptance of your new service can be excellent, good, or fair. You want to determine the probability of each outcome. If all three have an equal chance of occurring, then no choice you make will be any better than any other choice. If, however, the chances of success are higher for one outcome than the other, you need to determine which decision is best. You want to improve your chances at a successful outcome. Some business problems and opportunities can be addressed with special probability distributions. The most common distributions are as follows:

> Binomial Probability Distribution – Discrete Data Set
> Poisson Probability Distribution – Discrete Data Set
> Hypergeometric Probability Distribution – Discrete Data Set
> Exponential Probability Distribution – Continuous Data Set
> Uniform Probability Distribution – Continuous Data Set
> Normal Probability Distribution – Continuous Data Set
> Standard Normal Probability Distribution – Continuous Data Set

A **probability distribution** is simply a list of all possible outcomes of an experiment coupled with the probabilities associated with each outcome [usually denoted as function of x or probability of x, written $f(x)$ or $p(x)$].

This sounds like the concept of sample space, doesn't it? If so, then the sum of the probabilities of the entire distribution, like sample space, will total one and each of the probabilities of each event will be measured between zero and one. The two rules of probabilities apply here also.

I will examine all seven probability distributions and the conditions under which you should use them. The three which will be mostly emphasized are the binomial, the uniform, and the standard normal distributions.

There are three basic kinds of probability distributions: uniform, continuous, and discrete. You must know the difference between each of these so you will know when you should use each. In the **uniform distribution,** the probability of all outcomes is the same across the entire distribution. A **continuous distribution** is one in which a range of values can occur (a normal distribution). A **discrete distribution** (a binomial distribution) is one in which only whole numbers can occur (simplified definition for this textbook).

Whenever you have multiple outcome possibilities, any one of them might occur at any time. Rolling a single, balanced, six-sided die has six possible outcomes. On any one attempt you can have an outcome of 1, 2, 3, 4, 5, or 6. Each of these outcomes is a random variable. A probability distribution is no different. Any of the outcomes can occur at random at any time. Assume you make 15 sales calls. You can have anywhere from zero sales to 15 sales in 15 attempts. Any one of the outcomes (a sale) is a random occurrence. For a probability distribution this is also referred to as a random variable. This is the result of a random event.

I can determine an expected value of the random event, which is also referred to as a variable. In other words, I can calculate the expected value of the random variable. The **expected value of the random variable** is the weighted mean of all possible outcomes in which the weights are the respective probabilities of the outcomes.

Table 5.2 Outcomes of 100 sales calls.

Successful Sales Call	Probability of Sale
0	0.0001
1	0.0005
2	0.0008
3	0.0150
4	0.0400
5	0.0600
Etc through all of the values up to 100	Etc
98	0.0004
99	0.0002
100	0.0001
Total	**1.0000 (Sample Space)**

I think I can best show you from an example.

Assume that I have 100 sales calls to make. I will define a success as a sale.

How many outcomes can I have out of the 100 sales calls? There are 101 if you include 0 as a no sale.

I can list the 101 outcomes in the sales calls example in the following manner (arbitrary probabilities for illustration purposes only).

I will let the first column represent all of the possible outcomes and the second column represents the probabilities of any one of the events shown in column one.

If I know the probabilities of each of the events and I multiply the probability of occurrence times the expected outcome, I would get an average outcome that I can expect.

Let's reinforce this by looking at another example.

Let's assume that you own an automobile dealership. During the past 300 days you have determined the following sales pattern. Table 5.3 shows all columns for my analysis, but some will be used and explained later.

The formula for determining the *expected value of the random variable* follows:

$$E(X) = \sum [x f(x)] \text{ (which is shown in the last column of Table 5.3)}$$

The formula reads the sum of a column headed $x f(x)$. This is the expected value of the random variable. In this example, the value is 1.5 as shown in Table 5.3.

Table 5.3   Automobile sales pattern.

X Sales Volume Per Day	Number of Days	f(x) or p(x)	X f(x)
0	54	0.18	0
1	117	0.39	0.39
2	72	0.24	0.48
3	42	0.14	0.42
4	12	0.04	0.16
5	3	0.01	0.05
Totals	300	1.00	1.50

The 1.5 is simply the weighted average of how many cars you expect to sell each day you are open based on the 300-day study.

The X column (0 through 5) represents the variable that might occur. This simply means on any given day any value from 0 to 5 sales could occur. On any given day I could sell zero cars, one car, two cars, three cars, four cars, or five cars. *Each value from 0 to 5 is a random variable.* What I expect, on average, is to sell 1.5 cars per day. This, as I have said, is a weighted average. It is weighted by the probability of the outcome of the sale of cars.

Another very important relationship is that the expected value of the random variable [$E(x)$] is equal to mu, μ. This is an important concept. Think about it.

To summarize, I am converting frequency (number of days) to probability (function of x). I then multiply the probability times the expected outcome, which will then give me a weighted average. I expect to sell 1.5 cars per day on average, if I sell many times (many days). Most statisticians generally believe that if an experiment is conducted 1,000 times it will approximate the expected value of the random variable.

Let's take another example. What is the expected value of rolling a single, six-sided die?

Answer: It is 3.5. (Try to calculate this.)

Does this mean I will ever roll a 3.5?

No.

What it does mean is that if I conduct the experiment of rolling the 6-sided die 1,000 times, I can expect the average to be 3.5. This value is the **measure of the central tendency** or the expected value.

If any distribution can have a measure of central tendency, and it can, the distribution can also have a measure of dispersion or variability. The measure of the central tendency of a probability distribution is called the expected value of the random variable. *To repeat, the expected value of the random variable is a weighted mean of the probability distribution. You weigh each possible outcome by the probability of that outcome and sum the results.*

The measure of dispersion is the variance, which can then be converted to the standard deviation. Remember, any variance is in units squared and the standard deviation is in units. Units are understandable. Units squared are not. The variance is the mean of the squared deviations around the mean. All variances are calculated the same way but the calculation can be for different purposes: variance of a sample, variance of a population, variance of the expected value of the random variable, and later, the variance of the standard error. All are variances. All are the mean of the squared deviations around the mean.

The formula for the variance of the random variable $= \sigma^2 = \sum(x - \mu)^2 f(x)$.

To make this calculation, I must add columns to the automobile dealer example and re-write the results as Table 5.4.

If you go back to the formula, you find that the variance is equal to 1.25. The last column in Table 5.4 is the formula: $\sigma^2 = \sum(x - \mu)^2 f(x)$.

The standard deviation is the square root of the variance.

The standard deviation is $\sqrt{1.25} = 1.118$.

Since this is a discrete distribution, I could place an interval around the mean of 1.5 by using the mean $\pm 2\,(S)$.

$$1.5 \pm 2(1.118) = -0.7360 \text{ to } 3.7360.$$

Since the lower number is negative, this is a practical range of 0 to 3.7 cars per day.

I have no evidence the distribution is normal and the data set is discrete, so I must use Chebyshev's theorem to interpret the result. Chebyshev's theorem tells us that *at least 75%* of the time your business is open you should expect to sell from 0 to 3.7 cars per day.

The expected value is quite helpful in planning how many cars I can expect to sell per month. Assume I am open 20 days per month, then I expect to sell 30 cars per month (20 times 1.5). This allows me to plan on the size of lot required, floor planning dollars, and replacement cars I must purchase. I also know this could vary. It could be as many as 74 cars per month (3.7 times 20 days) and as few as zero cars. While this is a rather large interval (0 to 74), it still gives me some valuable planning information.

Table 5.4   Automobile sales.

X Sales Volume Per Day	Number of Days	f(x)	X f(x)	μ	$x - \mu$	$(x - \mu)^2$	$(x - \mu)^2$ f(x)
0	54	0.18	0	1.5	−1.5	2.25	0.4050
1	117	0.39	0.39	1.5	−0.5	0.25	0.0975
2	72	0.24	0.48	1.5	0.5	0.25	0.0600
3	42	0.14	0.42	1.5	1.5	2.25	0.3150
4	12	0.04	0.16	1.5	2.5	6.25	0.2500
5	3	0.01	0.05	1.5	3.5	12.25	0.1225
Totals	300	1.00	1.5	N/A	N/A	N/A	1.2500

Mathematical Expectations

One use of the expected value of the random variable is mathematical expectation. As an outgrowth of probabilities and games of chance, you can determine if it is wise to play a particular game or not. If any of you have been to Las Vegas, the gaming capital of the United States, you can better understand games of chance. The house (casino) sets the probability of all the games, so the house has a better chance of winning. Their view is one of the long run. The key to all games of change is just that—the long run. If you play a game long enough the outcomes can be mathematically predicted. In the simplest form, I will show you an example.

Game

Let's assume that you flip a coin three times in sequence. There are three coins, but four outcomes since you want a head to occur.

The game is as follows:

If you get 3 heads, you win $20.
If you get 2 heads, you win $10.
If you get 1 head, you lose $12.
If you get 0 heads, you lose $20.

Should you play the game?

Is this game, in the long run, a fair game? To answer this you use mathematical expectation.

Let's set this up in columns for ease of evaluation. (The probabilities are given for now.)

Table 5.5   Coin toss game.

# of Heads	Probability [P(x)]	Gain or Loss (X)	Payoff [E(x)]
0	1/8	−$20.00	−2.50
1	3/8	−$12.00	−4.50
2	3/8	⏐ $10.00	+3.75
3	1/8	+$20.00	+2.50
Total	1.00		Net = −0.75

Should you play the game?

The mathematical expectation is negative; therefore, you should expect to lose in the long run. Don't play any game with a negative mathematical expectation.

Are you wondering how I got the probabilities of getting heads or tails?

Probably not, but I am going to stubbornly show you anyway.

The tossings of the coin are independent occurrences; therefore, the probabilities would be multiplied.

I find there are three ways two heads can occur on three flips. I can get a head on the first toss. I can get a head on the second toss. I can get a head on the third toss. All three tosses are independent of each other.

All eight possible outcomes are shown in Table 5.6.

Notice that I can get two heads in three different ways (HHT, HTH, THH). Because those events are mutually exclusive, I can now add the probabilities of tossing two heads on three sequential flips of a coin. (1/8 + 1/8 + 1/8 = 3/8 for two heads). The same is true for one head. No heads is the fourth possible outcome. See Table 5.6 for that calculation of these probabilities.

If you are interested in other games of chance, you would use this same approach. If a game has a zero mathematical expectation, the game is balanced and fair. Playing a zero balanced game is one of choice. As long as you play the game many times (usually at least 1,000), you should break even.

If a game has a positive mathematical expectation, the game is tilted in your favor. If you play a game with a positive mathematical expectation many times, you should make money in the long run.

If you take this concept to Las Vegas and win a bunch of money, I do expect a share of the winnings. Right?

Let's now visit several of the more important distributions.

Table 5.6 Possible outcomes of the coin tossing game.

Outcomes	# of Heads in 3 Independent Flips		Probabilities		Results
Three Heads	H H H	=	.5 × .5 × .5	=	0.125 which is **1/8**
Two Heads	H H T	=	.5 × .5 × .5	=	0.125 which is 1/8*
	H T H	=	.5 × .5 × .5	=	0.125 which is 1/8*
	T H H	=	.5 × .5 × .5	=	0.125 which is 1/8*
					*Total for Two Heads **3/8**
One Head	H T T	=	.5 × .5 × .5	=	0.125 which is 1/8**
	T H T	=	.5 × .5 × .5	=	0.125 which is 1/8**
	T T H	=	.5 × .5 × .5	=	0.125 which is 1/8**
					Total for One Head **3/8
No Heads	T T T	=	.5 × .5 × .5	=	0.125 which is **1/8**

Uniform Probability Distribution (Continuous Data)

A uniform probability distribution is a unique, special distribution. The uniform probability distribution is associated with *continuous data*. One of the unique features is that the probability of any one outcome is the same across the entire distribution. Examples are the rolling of a single, six-sided die (1/6) or the selection of any number from a random number table (1/10). The distribution is useful in evaluating such things as the fill weights of a soft drink can or soup can or box of cereal.

For example, when you purchase a regular soft drink in a can, the label reads a net weight of 12 oz of liquid.

How do you know?

Maybe there are only 11.95 oz in the can, or maybe there are 12.055 oz in the can.

The distribution is also helpful when you are determining the useful life of an electronic part or chip, the flight time of an airplane from Dallas to New York or Dallas to any destination, or the estimated depth of drilling required in an offshore platform to reach oil.

A discrete probability distribution uses the concept of *an exact number* as in the automobile dealer example. I found that I expected to sell *exactly 1.5 cars on average* each day I am open.

However, for continuous data sets, a new approach is required. I must use area under the curve as an estimate of the probability of an event occurring, since *I cannot determine an exact probability*. I can, however, determine a probability for a range of data.

The uniform distribution can be graphically displayed as follows:

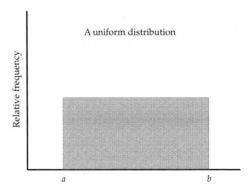

Figure 5.1   A uniform distribution.

As you look at the distribution, the left axis is the $f(x)$ or the $p(x)$, function of x or the probability of x. The high point is considered the height of the distribution. This point simply means that the probability is the same across the entire distribution. If this was rolling a single, six-sided die, the probability would be 1/6. This would also be referred to as the height of the distribution.

The total area under the curve (rectangle) is equal to $A = HW$, if you recall your basic geometry.

There is a maximum value, which is "b." There is a minimum value, which is "a."

Do you remember that any distribution has a measure of central tendency and a measure of dispersion, I rhetorically ask?

The same holds true for the uniform distribution. The mean is determined as follows.

$$\mu = \frac{a+b}{2}, \text{ where "}a\text{" is the minimum value and "}b\text{" is the maximum value}$$

From your basic mathematics courses, do you remember that the area of a rectangle is the height times the width? The relationship may be written as follows:

$$A = H \times W$$

I can re-write the relationship as follows (solving for H).

$$H = A \div W$$

Since the area under the curve is equal to 100%, I can next substitute the value 1 for the area. Since the W (width) is the maximum minus the minimum $(b - a)$, I can re-write the relationship again.

$$H = 1 \div (b - a)$$

The height of the distribution is the probability of $x[p(x)]$ or the function of $x[f(x)]$ and must be used in determining the probability of any outcome associated with the distribution.

Since I have said that each distribution can have a measure of central tendency, I can also determine the *standard deviation* of the uniform distribution, which is the measure of variability.

$$\sigma = \frac{b - a}{\sqrt{12}}$$

Let's look at a simple example.

Let's say that you manufacture cereal. You have a box of cereal labeled 32 oz.

You have determined the minimum is 28 oz and the maximum is 36 oz.

Using a simple random sample, you want to calculate the probability of obtaining a box of cereal weighing between 32 oz and 34 oz.

Where do you begin?

Let's start by determining the $p(x)$ or $f(x)$, which is the probability across the entire distribution. This also equals the height (H). In other words, the height is representative of the probability of occurrence throughout the entire distribution.

$$H = 1 \div (36 - 28), \text{ which is } 1/8.$$

So, the height is 1/8, or the probability across the entire distribution at any given point is equal to 1/8. This value is referred to as the $p(x)$ or the $f(x)$. It would be shown on a graph as follows:

Okay, now I have the height (H). I need to determine the area.

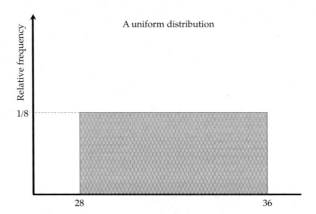

Figure 5.2   A uniform distribution showing the probability across the distribution.

The area of interest is from 32 to 34 ounces. These are my boundaries. These, in essence, are the new maximum and minimum values for the area of interest. You might want to refer to them as "a-prime" and "b-prime" to distinguish them from the original "a" and "b" values. See Figure 5.3 below.

If you draw a picture of the area of interest, it would look like this.

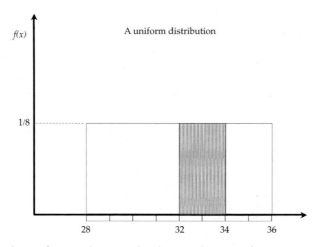

Figure 5.3   Uniform distribution for cereal net weight, showing the area of interest.

I can now calculate the area under the curve for the values of 32 and 34 oz.

$$A = H \times W$$
$$A = (1/8) \times (34 - 32)$$
$$A = (1/8)(2/1) = 2/8 = 0.25.$$

The probability of obtaining a box of cereal that weighs between 32 and 34 oz is 25% or 0.25.

This is the area under the curve. For a continuous distribution I cannot tell you the exact probability of a box of cereal weighing precisely 34 ounces. The best I can do is to determine the probability between two values. This is just the opposite of a discrete distribution, where I can give you the exact probability of an event occurring.

For an exercise, what is the probability of obtaining a box of cereal weighing between 28 and 30 oz? Try it before reading on.

I hope you came up with the same answer (0.25).

If the width is the same, then the probability is the same.

For any distribution, I can calculate a measure of central tendency, which in most cases is the mean (not the median or mode).

I can also calculate a measure of the variability or dispersion, which is best done with the standard deviation.

For this example, the calculation of the standard deviation of a uniform distribution is as follows.

$$\sigma = \frac{b - a}{\sqrt{12}}$$
$$\sigma = (36 - 28) \div 3.464 = 8 \div 3.464$$
$$\sigma = 2.309 \text{ oz.}$$

Since this is continuous data, the interpretation using the empirical rule applies. Using the mean $32 \pm (1)(2.309)$, I can place an interval around the expected value (32 ounces). Try this for an exercise.

The answer: 29.69 oz to 34.31 oz. From the empirical rule, 68.3% of the time a box of cereal will weight between these two values.

Other Probability Distributions

Three other probability distributions are of importance. At this point, I will mention them and give you examples of their use. Excel or other comparable software should be used to make probability calculations.

Before I cover those, I want to give you another new definition, as if you don't have enough already.

When there are two complementary events, one may be labeled success (π) and the other may be labeled failure ($1 - \pi$). These are complementary events. When one does not occur, the other must occur. This would exist in flipping a coin (heads or tails) or in the selection of a part from the assembly line (defective or non-defective) or in making a sale in a retail store (sale or no sale). *The definition of success does not always carry a positive outcome.* A sale is positive. A defective part is negative. Either may be defined as a success. The study you conduct will define the outcome. Success is neutral.

It should be noted that since the events are complementary, the sum of the probabilities of the two events equals one. The outcomes are also mutually exclusive (the occurrence of one precludes the occurrence of the other). If I know the probability of one event, I automatically know the probability of the other event.

Hypergeometric Distribution (Discrete Data)

The hypergeometric distribution is useful when the value of π (success) changes from one attempt to another attempt. This distribution is associated with discrete data sets.

For example, if a sample is taken *without replacement* from a small population, the probability of success will vary between attempts. Let's suppose I have a group of 30 people; 20 are men and 10 are women. I want to know the probability of selecting a female at random. On the first attempt, this probability will be 10 out of 30 or 0.3333. Since I do not replace the person selected, the probability of selecting a female on a second draw now becomes either 10 out of 29 or 9 out of 29 depending on if the person selected in the first attempt was a female or male. Since the probability of success does vary, the hypergeometric distribution is used. The **hypergeometric distribution** is a binomial distribution where the probability of success changes between attempts.

It is best to use an Excel function for calculating hypergeometric probabilities. In the example above, I would go into Excel and double click on $f(x)$ in the toolbar. I would then find the HYPGEOMDIST function. Opening it, I would then complete the four questions posed. Using the example from above, I would identify the Sample_s as 1; Number_sample = 1; Population_S = 10; Number_pop = 30. The result will be the 0.3333 as manually calculated above. You can expand the question to ask the probability that out of four attempts one will be female. The only change to the settings would be Number_sample = 4. The result is 0.4159. This can be interpreted as follows: The probability of exactly one female being selected from a population of 30 with a sub-stratum of 10 females given you draw four times = 0.4159. When you have the "function arguments" opened (the hypergeometric data entry window), you will see a "Help on This Function" link. Open it and it will walk you through what I have just told you.

Use Excel when confronted with the use of a hypergeometric probability distribution, where π changes between attempts.

Poisson Distribution (Discrete Data)

The **Poisson distribution** is a discrete data set and is useful in measuring the *relative frequency of some event over time and space.* In real English, this means that the Poisson distribution is useful when you want the probability of an exact number of customers arriving at your car wash within a time interval (each hour) or arriving at your retail store within a time interval (each minute). The Poisson distribution is useful when considering the number of repairs in 10 miles of highway, the number of leaks in a 100-mile-long pipeline, the number of telephone calls received in your retail business in one hour, the number of trucks arriving at your loading dock in one hour, or in considering to accept or reject a shipment of goods arriving at your loading dock (lot acceptance). The Poisson distribution is a discrete data set; thus it can estimate the probability of an *exact arrival time*. The Poisson distribution, however, does not tell you the lapse time between the arrival of each customer or truck for example. The Poisson distribution is most appropriate when a business is faced with a queuing business decision.

Like the hypergeometric distribution, you should use an Excel function in determining probabilities for the Poisson distribution. Open Excel. Double click on $f(x)$. Search for the function POISSON. Open it. You will have three inputs possible: X is the number of events; mean is the expected numeric value, a positive number; cumulative is the logical value—true for the cumulative probability and false for the probability mass function (exact probability). Here again use the "Help on This Function" link. Let us assume I want to know the probability of one defect in five miles of highway. The entries would be $X = 1$; Mean $= 5$; True or False depending on the format of your desired answer. Here true yields a probability of 0.0404, which is the probability of the random event being between zero and one defect in one mile of highway. False yields a probability of 0.0337, which is the probability of exactly one defect in five miles of highway.

The next distribution can be used in conjunction with the Poisson distribution to tell you the lapse time between those customers or trucks. It is the exponential distribution.

Exponential Distribution (Continuous Data)

While the Poisson distribution measures the arrival of trucks at your loading dock within an hour or the arrival of customers each minute during the lunch rush hour, the **exponential distribution** *measures the passage of time between the arrivals.* The exponential distribution is useful in queuing problems in business to aid you in determining how long a line you might expect at your business. This knowledge allows you to better staff to handle the crowds or trucks or telephone calls without the customer having to wait an excessive period of time.

As in the two previous distributions, use Excel in making the calculations for the exponential distribution. Open Excel. Double click on $f(x)$. Search for the function EXPONDIST. Open it. You will have three inputs: X = value of the function, a nonnegative number; Lambda = parametric value (a positive number); Cumulative—True for cumulative probability and False for the probability mass function. This function gives you the probability of obtaining a value less than or equal to X.

What is the probability that the next customer arrives within six minutes (0.1 hour) assuming a mean (λ) of 20? Answer the cumulative question as True. The answer is 0.8647. The probability of the next customer arriving in six minutes or less is 86.47%.

Here, as in the Poisson and exponential distributions, Excel proves to be the best approach to determining probabilities.

There are two other distributions which are quite useful and occur quite often in business decision making—the binomial distribution and the normal distribution (standard normal distribution).

Binomial Distribution (Discrete Data)

A special probability distribution that is very useful in working with discrete data sets is the **binomial distribution.** All binomial distributions exhibit four properties. They are:

- The probability of success is constant from one trial (attempt) to another.
- There are only two possible outcomes—success (π) and failure ($1 - \pi$).
- The trials (attempts) are independent of each other.
- The experiment can be repeated many times.

A binomial distribution is a mathematical model that is useful in business, in social and natural sciences, and in medical research. In working with a binomial distribution, you are able to develop an *exact number of successes in a given number of attempts*. Bankers may survey other bankers to determine if the interest rates will go up or down (two outcomes). Labor unions may survey workers to determine if they want a union to represent them or they do not want a union to represent them (two outcomes). A survey of potential customers wants to determine if a new product would be favorably or unfavorably received (two outcomes).

There is a rather complicated looking formula for determining probabilities via formula.

$$P(X) = \frac{n!}{x!(n-x)!} \cdot \pi^x (1 - \pi)^{n-x}$$

Looks tough, but fortunately someone up there loves you.

There are binomial tables which have been developed from this formula which allow you to look up most values rather than to manually calculate them. I will reproduce part of one here to use as an example, but suggest you go online to such sites as the following to find other binomial tables: *http://www.stat.sfu.ca/~cschwarz/Stat-301/Handouts/node120.html*

Presented here is a binomial table for $n = 5$ (Table 5.7). Across the top of this table is π. Down the left side is X. Listed are all possible outcomes from zero to five. The question might be as straightforward as "What is the probability of *exactly* two sales in five attempts given that the probability of success is 30% on any one attempt?"

Look at the table! What do you see under $\pi = 0.30$ and $X = 2$? Answer: 0.309.

Table 5.7   Probability table for sales calls.

X	Probability of Success (π)										
	0.05	0.10	0.20	0.30	0.40	0.50	0.60	0.70	0.80	0.90	0.95
0	0.774	0.590	0.328	0.168	0.078	0.031	0.010	0.002	0.000	0.000	0.000
1	0.204	0.328	0.410	0.360	0.259	0.156	0.077	0.028	0.006	0.000	0.000
2	0.021	0.073	0.205	**0.309**	0.346	0.312	0.230	0.132	0.051	0.008	0.001
3	0.001	0.008	0.051	0.132	0.230	0.312	0.346	0.309	0.205	0.073	0.021
4	0.000	0.000	0.006	0.028	0.077	0.156	0.259	0.360	0.410	0.328	0.204
5	0.000	0.000	0.000	0.002	0.010	0.031	0.078	0.168	0.328	0.590	0.774
Total	1.000	1.000	1.000	1.000	1.000	1.000	1.000	1.000	1.000	1.000	1.000

The probability of exactly two sales out of five sales calls, given the probability of success of 0.30 on any one sales call is 0.309 or 30.9%.

Also notice the total at the bottom of each column. What does it total?

That is not a rhetorical question. Answer: 1.000. When something adds to 1.00 and the events are measured between zero and one, what do you call it? That's right—sample space. This will also be true for any X-value. Here I am illustrating the binomial distribution using $X = 5$, but if you go to the website I referenced, you will find other X-values. There is also a more complete binomial table in the back of the textbook. In fact, you can have an infinite number of X-values. Most of the time, you can find a table from which you can determine probabilities. If your table does not contain all of the values of interest to you, you need to work with the formula or, better yet, Excel.

Go to trusty Excel and use the BINOMDIST function. Open Excel. Double click on $f(x)$. Find the BINOMDIST function. Open it and you will have four questions to answer:

> Number_S is the number of successes in trials;
> Trials are the number of independent trials;
> Probability_S is the probability of success on each trial (π);
> Cumulative can be answered True or False.
>> True returns the probability of at most a number of successes.
>> False returns the probability mass function or the probability of an *exact number* of successes in a given number of attempts. Most of the time, you will respond False.

What is the probability of exactly two sales out of five attempts given a probability of success of 0.30? From Excel the answer is 0.3087, which is the same answer I got from looking it up in Table 5.7 (0.309 rounded). Using a table is great; but if you do not have tables which have the correct numbers, you must resort to manual calculations using the formula or Excel. Excel is much easier.

If I ask you the question, "What is the probability of exactly five sales in 20 sales calls (attempts) given that the probability of success on any one sale call (attempt) is 0.10?" What is the answer from a table you pull up through an Internet site or the back of the textbook? I have copied one below for your use (Table 5.8); however, you should actually go to a website to make sure you can find this sort of table if you ever need it and do not have a textbook.

If the table for your desired "n" is not on an online site, you should use the Excel function to determine your probabilities.

The answer is 0.0319 or 3.19% chance of exactly five sales out of 20 sales calls given a probability of success of 0.10 on any one attempt.

If you are having difficulty with the answer, let's take a look at some hints. First, you are defining "n" as 20, the number of possible sales calls (attempts). Second, you are defining "x" as 5, an exact number of sales (successes). You are defining success as a sale. Third, in this instance, π is equal to 0.10, so you go to the binomial table and find the values under $n = 20$ under the heading of $\pi = 0.10$. Now trace that column to the intersection point of $X = 5$ under $n = 20$. You would find the value 0.0319 (3.19%), which would be the probability of exactly five sales in 20 sales calls given the historic (or subjective) probability of success of 0.10 on any one attempted sales call.

The interpretation is that there is *a 0.0319 (3.19%) chance of exactly five sales out of 20 attempts knowing the probability of a success (sale) equal to 0.10 on any one attempt.* Binomial distributions

Table 5.8   Binomial table for $n = 20$ and selected π values.

		Selected values of π						
n	X	**0.10**	0.20	0.30	0.40	0.50	0.60	0.70
20	0	0.1216	**0.0115**	0.0008	0.0000	0.0000	0.0000	0.0000
20	1	0.2702	**0.0576**	0.0068	0.0005	0.0000	0.0000	0.0000
20	2	0.2852	**0.1369**	0.0278	0.0031	0.0002	0.0000	0.0000
20	3	0.1901	0.2054	0.0716	0.0123	0.0011	0.0000	0.0000
20	4	0.0898	0.2182	0.1304	0.0350	0.0046	0.0003	0.0000
20	5	**0.0319**	0.1746	0.1789	0.0746	0.0148	0.0013	0.0000
20	6	0.0089	0.1091	0.1916	0.1244	0.0370	0.0049	0.0002
20	7	0.0020	0.0545	0.1643	0.1659	0.0739	0.0146	0.0010
20	8	0.0004	0.0222	0.1144	0.1797	0.1201	0.0355	0.0039
20	9	0.0001	0.0074	0.0654	0.1597	0.1602	0.0710	0.0120
20	10	0.0000	0.0020	0.0308	0.1171	0.1762	0.1171	0.0308
20	11	0.0000	0.0005	0.0120	0.0710	0.1602	0.1597	0.0654
20	12	0.0000	0.0001	0.0039	0.0355	0.1201	0.1797	0.1144
20	13	0.0000	0.0000	0.0010	0.0146	0.0739	0.1659	0.1643
20	14	0.0000	0.0000	0.0002	0.0049	0.0370	0.1244	0.1916
20	15	0.0000	0.0000	0.0000	0.0013	0.0148	0.0746	0.1789
20	16	0.0000	0.0000	0.0000	0.0003	0.0046	0.0350	0.1304
20	17	0.0000	0.0000	0.0000	0.0000	0.0011	0.0123	0.0716
20	18	0.0000	0.0000	0.0000	0.0000	0.0002	0.0031	0.0278
20	19	0.0000	0.0000	0.0000	0.0000	0.0000	0.0005	0.0068
20	20	0.0000	0.0000	0.0000	0.0000	0.0000	0.0000	0.0008
	Total	**1.0000**	**1.0000**	**1.0000**	**1.0000**	**1.0000**	**1.0000**	**1.0000**

yield an exact number of successes in a given number of attempts. This is not a range of success, but an exact number of successes.

Let's take a second example. I will again define a success as a sale. What is the probability of exactly two sales out of 15 sales calls (attempts) given the probability of success is 0.15 on any one attempt?

Answer from Excel: 0.2856 or 28.56%.

I hope you now see that the table approach is rather simple, as is using the BINOMINDIST function in Excel. Either way the answer is a 0.2856 or 28.56% chance of exactly two sales in

15 attempts given the probability of success of 0.15. Here is a quick look at the four questions you must answer using the BINOMINDIST in Excel. The questions: Number_s = successes in number of trials; Trials = number of independent trials; Probability_s = probability of success on each trial; Cumulative = True which returns the cumulative distribution function or False which returns the probability mass function (an exact probability). In the n = 2, X = 15, and π = 0.15 example from above, the values are inserted as follows.

Number_s = 2; Trials = 15; Probability_s = 0.15; False = 0.2856; True = 0.6042. False is an exact probability of two sales in 15 attempts, while True is the probability of 0, 1, or 2 sales in 15 attempts. Try it and see what you get.

Going back to the Table 5.8, notice that there is an X-value from 0 to 20 and an associated probability with each of those outcomes. This is the sample space and the total of the column will equal 1.000. Since I have captured the sample space, I can now ask you any question about probabilities and you can answer it. For example, what is the probability of two or fewer sales out of 20 sales calls given the probability of success is 0.20 on any one attempt?

Ouch, you say. That seems too complicated.

Not so, I say.

Since I am working with sample space, I will go to the column headed 0.20 for π and sum the values in that column for 0, 1, and 2 (two or fewer). (0.0115 + 0.0576 + 0.1369 = 0.2060) The probability of two or fewer successes (sales) is 20.60% or 0.2060 probability. If you can somehow capture the sample space, you can answer any question rather easily.

Mean of a Binomial Distribution

All random probability distributions have a mean. The binomial distribution is no exception. There is a mean or measure of central tendency for a binomial distribution. The mean is simply the following:

$$\mu = n\pi = (20)(0.20) = 4.00$$

Assume the following example, let n = 20 and x = 2 and π = 0.20. What is the mean of the distribution? Answer: 4.00. This is the expected value of the random variable of 20 sales calls given the probability of success of 0.20 on any one attempt. I expect, on average, to make 4.00 sales on 20 attempts (sales calls) with a probability of success of 0.20 on any one attempt.

There can also be a measure of dispersion for the binomial distribution. The variance and standard deviation are calculated as follows.

$$\sigma^2 = n\pi(1 - \pi)$$

Which in the last example would be 20(0.20) (0.8) = 3.20

$$\sigma = \sqrt{3.2} = 1.7889$$

What can I do with this?

The data set meets the criterion for a discrete binomial distribution. I can use Chebyshev's theorem to determine some level of confidence in my sales.

$$\mu \pm 2(\sigma) = \text{at least 75\% of the observations.}$$

In this instance, 4.0 ± 2 (1.7889) would give me an expected range for my sales. Mathematically it would be 0.4222 to 7.5778. I can expect that at least 75% of the time my sales successes will fall between 0.4222 and 7.5778, when I make 20 sales calls given the probability of success of 0.20 on any one attempt.

Forecasting Technique

The binomial process can be useful when making a forecast of the sales you expect. Let's assume you have a retail store in a shopping center. You place several big advertisements in the local newspaper. You are trying to conduct an annual sales event. You expect to draw 1,000 customers over the weekend. From your past experience, the probability of making a sale is 0.30.

How many sales would you expect? Since I have only two outcomes—sale or no sale—the binomial distribution will help me make a forecast. I can calculate the mean of the binomial distribution.

The mean would be:

$$\mu = n\pi = 1{,}000\,(0.30) = 300 \text{ sales out of 1,000 expected customers.}$$

The standard deviation would be $\sigma^2 = n\pi(1 - \pi) = 1{,}000(0.3)(0.7) = 210$, which would be a standard deviation of $\sigma = \sqrt{210} = 14.48$.

How do I use this?

$$\mu \pm 2(\sigma)$$

Begin with the mean of 300 (a point estimate) and add an interval.

$$300 \pm 2(14.48) = 271 \text{ to } 329 \text{ sales (an interval estimate).}$$

This is extremely helpful information for you to have as the owner of the store.

You can now forecast that your sales should be between 271 and 321 units 75% of the time given the probability of success in any one attempt of 0.30 and an expected crowd of 1,000 over the weekend. This information is helpful in staffing your store to maximize the best customer service and to stock for the expected sales.

Normal Distribution (Continuous Data)

I have often referred to the normal distribution. This distribution is one of the most important used by companies across America, no matter the type of business. The normal distribution consists of continuous data. This fact alone makes it impossible to determine the exact probability of an event occurring. In fact, the probability of a particular event is zero. This is directly opposite to the binomial distribution, where I can calculate the probability of exactly two successes out of 20 attempts given the probability of success on any one attempt.

How is the normal distribution useful to the business person, you ask?

I am glad you asked, I respond.

For example, suppose that a manufacturer of clothing wishes to determine how many of a particular men's blazer they wish to manufacture.

How do they start? They might start with a study of the sizes of men. When the study was completed, they would find that the sizes would approximate a normal distribution with a few small sizes and a few larger sizes and most of the sizes tending toward the middle of a distribution. The same is true for shoes, women's clothing, and many more articles or products.

The normal distribution is in fact a whole family of normal distributions with many different means and many different standard deviations. The shape of the normal distribution is determined by two parameters—the mean and the standard deviation. Some normal curves will be broader and some will be narrower. To determine the expected value of the random variable, I would find it necessary to make the calculations with integral calculus. I need a more civilized way to determine the probabilities. I have two approaches possible—tables from Internet or from an Excel function or the back of this textbook. I have calculated a normal table using the Excel function and am including it as Table 5.9 toward the end of this chapter. Tear it out of the textbook and use it, when possible.

If you use the Excel function NORMSDIST, open Excel, double click on $f(x)$ in the tool bar and find the NORMSDIST function. Open it. You will need a Z-value to determine probability. Let's assume you select a Z-value of 2.0 (more on the Z-value and how to calculate it shortly). The result would be a probability of 0.9772. This is the cumulative value from the far left of the curve to +2.0 standard deviations. The mean of a standard normal distribution is zero and the measures around the mean are in standard deviations measured as negative deviations to the left and positive deviations to the right. To determine the area to the right of the mean you would subtract 50% or 0.5000 from the 0.9772 = 0.4772. This is the same value you would get from looking up the value in Table 5.9 reproduced toward the end of this chapter.

For this function, you may enter negative numbers. For example, if I entered −2.0 rather than +2.0, I would get the value 0.0228 which is the cumulative value from the far left of the curve up to −2.0 standard deviations. Notice, if I add 0.9772 + 0.0228 = 1.0000 or if I add 0.0228 to 0.4772 = 50% or 0.5000, the Excel function returns a cumulative value and I must subtract or add to equal the Table 5.9 values reproduced below. Using the Excel function creates an extra step in the process that using Table 5.9 does not require. Either, however, is correct and will yield the same result.

Since I have a whole family of normal distributions, it would be best if I could come up with some method that allows me to use the normal distribution and quickly determine the probability of an event. More on this shortly, but first let's look at a normal distribution graphically.

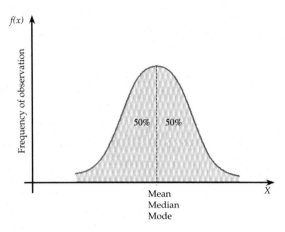

Figure 5.4 A normal distribution.

The characteristics of a normal distribution are as follows:

- It is bell shaped.
- It is symmetrical such that 50% is on the right of the mean and 50% is on the left of the mean.
- The measures of central tendency—the mean, median, and mode—equal each other.
- It represents continuous data, which tells us that the associated random variable has an infinite range.
- The empirical rule applies to a normal distribution. The empirical rule tells me than if I move ±1 standard deviation from the mean of any normal distribution, I will have an area that encompasses 68.3% of the observations in my distribution, ±2 standard deviations equals 95.5%, and ±3 standard deviations equals 99.7% of the observations.
- It is asymptotic with the curve never touching the X-axis.

I wonder what would happen if I converted from a value scale to something called a Z-scale (the empirical rule concept)? Perhaps I could develop a standard approach to my calculations, which would be based on standard deviations rather than value. As luck or good mathematics has it, there is a conversion formula which does just that. The normal distribution can be converted to a standard normal distribution.

Standard Normal Distribution

By applying a little logic, I can convert from a value scale where the values of the means and standard deviations are in unit values (pounds, dollars, weight, height) to a Z-scale where the mean is shown as 0 and the standard deviation is 1, meaning that the measurement around the mean is in terms of standard deviations. That sounds rather confusing, but this is how it works.

By using what is termed a **normal deviate formula,** I can arrive at a **standard normal distribution.** The conversion formula is shown below.

	Where Z is the normal deviate. The units of measurement are standard deviations.
$Z = \dfrac{X - \mu}{\sigma}$	X is some specified value along the curve.
	μ is the mean.
	σ is the standard deviation.

What this formula does is convert the mean of any values measured in units to zero and with the measurements around the mean in terms of standard deviations (measured by $\pm$ Z-units). Take a look at Figure 5.5 below.

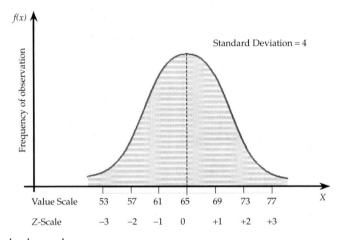

Figure 5.5   *Z-scale and value scale.*

What do I mean by a value scale and a Z-scale? Both scales are shown in Figure 5.5.

The units of the Z-scale and the Z-formula are in standard deviations. The $\pm$ is a directional indicator only. The minus will mean you are on the left of the mean and the plus will mean you are on the right of the mean.

Perhaps the best way to understand this concept is to look at a problem. Look at the formula for Z, just above. If X, the specified value, is greater than μ, then the value of Z is positive (to the right of the mean). If X, the specified value, is less than μ, then the value of Z is negative (to the left of the mean).

Let's assume that you are the owner and operator of a telephone answering service. During the past five years you have determined that the mean for each call is 150 seconds with a standard deviation of 15 seconds.

The question is this: "What is the probability that a phone call will last between 150 and 180 seconds?" I am interested in the area between 150 and 180 seconds. Since area under the curve is the same as probability, I can use the Z-formula to convert to a Z-value. From that I will use the normal table to convert to area under the curve (probability $=$ P).

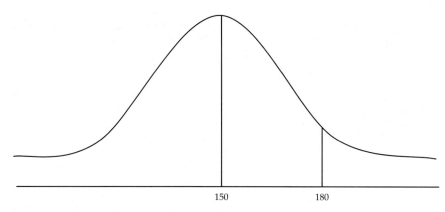

Figure 5.6   Normal distribution filled in with known values.

The solution is as follows.

$$Z = \frac{X - \mu}{\sigma} = \frac{180 - 150}{15} = 2.0 \text{ (these are plus standard deviations)}$$

This is 2.0 standard deviations from the mean. Logically 180 is greater than 150, so the value is positive (right of the mean).

> X is the specified value $= 180$.
> μ is the mean $= 150$.
> σ is the standard deviation $= 15$.

Okay, I have determined there are two standard deviations involved in something, but what is the something and what do I do next?

I now want to convert the Z-value, standard deviation, to a probability. This is nothing more than looking up the probability in a normal curve table. Don't make this a complex issue.

What do you need to know in order to use this table? Table 5.9 is shown toward the end of the chapter. Go to it now. I will wait.

Assuming you found the table let's walk through some important factors.

Look carefully.

The values along the left hand are called "Z" and the values at the top of the table are also "Z." By using this table I can now carry Z to two decimal places rather than be stuck with 1.0, 2.0, and 3.0 as in the empirical rule. I can determine a probability for values of 1.57 or 2.06 or 2.98. This increases my ability to be more accurate in my calculations of area under the curve (probability).

Also, notice that the value in the far right bottom of the table is 0.5000 (if your table goes to 3.99, Table 5.9 does). This means that Table 5.9 is one-half of the area under the normal curve.

If this is one-half of the area, how do I know when I am on the left of the mean or on the right of the mean?

I have previously answered that, but I will repeat the answer.

Notice the Z-formula.

$$Z = \frac{X - \mu}{\sigma}$$

If the specified value (X) is larger than (μ) the mean, the Z-value will be positive, which means I am to the right of the mean. If the specified value (X) is smaller than (μ) the mean, the Z-value will be negative, which means I am to the left of the mean.

Now back to the question. What is the probability that a phone call will last between 150 and 180 seconds?

I previously calculated Z to be 2.0. Using Table 5.9, I look up the corresponding area associated with the standard deviation of $Z = 2.00$.

What I find is the number 0.4772. (Make sure you find this number, since the majority of the course hinges on your ability to look up values like this in tables).

This is the probability. This means I have a 0.4772 chance (probability) of a phone call lasting between 150 and 180 seconds. This can also be stated as 47.72% chance. Decimals or percentages are the same thing.

One clarification is necessary at this point. You have previously used the empirical rule. Is there a relationship between the empirical rule and the standard normal table (Table 5.9)?

Let's take one example of the empirical rule. Let's say I am dealing with two standard deviations from the mean. From the empirical rule I know the area under the curve will be 95.5%.

Does this tie to the normal distribution in Table 5.9, you ask?

The answer is, yes it does.

From the normal Table 5.9 I see that two standard deviations equals 0.4772 (previously shown).

I know that the normal table is one-half of the area, so if I double the 0.4772 I get 0.9544, which is amazingly close to the 95.5% of the empirical rule.

What this means is the empirical rule comes from the normal distribution in Table 5.9.

Try one and three standard deviations and see what you get.

Isn't that interesting, you muse. How does this impact me, you ask?

This simply means that I will stop using the empirical rule (for now), since the normal table allows me to carry Z to two decimal points rather than just using $Z = 1, 2,$ or 3. As previously stated, I can now calculate the probabilities for 1.25, 2.37, 2.46, and others. The empirical rule limited me. The normal table allows me to carry the Z-value to two decimal points. This is a big help in fine-tuning the probabilities.

In the future, all of my calculations (until further notice) will make use of the Z-value with the probabilities coming from the normal distribution table and not the empirical rule.

You know You are a Texan If:

- You are not surprised to find movie rental, ammunition and bait all in the same store.

- You can properly pronounce the towns of Mexia and Mesquite.

Tear-Out Normal Distribution Table

$$0 \quad z$$

Normal Distribution Table
Area between 0 and Z

The following calculations may be made using the Excel formula NORMSDIST and subtracting 0.5000 from each result to get the area between 0 and Z, where Z is taken to within two decimal points. In Excel find the $f(x)$ area. Double click on that symbol and the functions will appear. From that you can select the proper function. The NORMSDIST function is a cumulative distribution with a mean of 0 and a standard deviation of 1. *There is another helpful Excel function: NORMDIST (X, Mean, Standard Deviation, Cumulative). This calculation is for a specific Z value, but is cumulative also.*

Table 5.9 Normal table.

Notice that Z is down the left side of the table, but Z is also across the top of the table. I can now carry Z to two decimal points. Reading the table below: if Z, for example, is 1.96, the corresponding area between 0 and Z is 0.4750.

Z	0.00	0.01	0.02	0.03	0.04	0.05	0.06	0.07	0.08	0.09
0.0	0.0000	0.0040	0.0080	0.0120	0.0160	0.0199	0.0239	0.0279	0.0319	0.0359
0.1	0.0398	0.0438	0.0478	0.0517	0.0557	0.0596	0.0636	0.0675	0.0714	0.0753
0.2	0.0793	0.0832	0.0871	0.0910	0.0948	0.0987	0.1026	0.1064	0.1103	0.1141
0.3	0.1179	0.1217	0.1255	0.1293	0.1331	0.1368	0.1406	0.1443	0.1480	0.1517
0.4	0.1554	0.1591	0.1628	0.1664	0.1700	0.1736	0.1772	0.1808	0.1844	0.1879
0.5	0.1915	0.1950	0.1985	0.2019	0.2054	0.2088	0.2123	0.2157	0.2190	0.2224
0.6	0.2257	0.2291	0.2324	0.2357	0.2389	0.2422	0.2454	0.2486	0.2517	0.2549
0.7	0.2580	0.2611	0.2642	0.2673	0.2704	0.2734	0.2764	0.2794	0.2823	0.2852
0.8	0.2881	0.2910	0.2939	0.2967	0.2995	0.3023	0.3051	0.3078	0.3106	0.3133
0.9	0.3159	0.3186	0.3212	0.3238	0.3264	0.3289	0.3315	0.3340	0.3365	0.3389
1.0	0.3413	0.3438	0.3461	0.3485	0.3508	0.3531	0.3554	0.3577	0.3599	0.3621
1.1	0.3643	0.3665	0.3686	0.3708	0.3729	0.3749	0.3770	0.3790	0.3810	0.3830

(continued)

Table 5.9   Normal Table (*Continued*).

1.2	0.3849	0.3869	0.3888	0.3907	0.3925	0.3944	0.3962	0.3980	0.3997	0.4015
1.3	0.4032	0.4049	0.4066	0.4082	0.4099	0.4115	0.4131	0.4147	0.4162	0.4177
1.4	0.4192	0.4207	0.4222	0.4236	0.4251	0.4265	0.4279	0.4292	0.4306	0.4319
1.5	0.4332	0.4345	0.4357	0.4370	0.4382	0.4394	0.4406	0.4418	0.4429	0.4441
1.6	0.4452	0.4463	0.4474	0.4484	0.4495	0.4505	0.4515	0.4525	0.4535	0.4545
1.7	0.4554	0.4564	0.4573	0.4582	0.4591	0.4599	0.4608	0.4616	0.4625	0.4633
1.8	0.4641	0.4649	0.4656	0.4664	0.4671	0.4678	0.4686	0.4693	0.4699	0.4706
1.9	0.4713	0.4719	0.4726	0.4732	0.4738	0.4744	**0.4750**	0.4756	0.4761	0.4767
2.0	0.4772	0.4778	0.4783	0.4788	0.4793	0.4798	0.4803	0.4808	0.4812	0.4817
2.1	0.4821	0.4826	0.4830	0.4834	0.4838	0.4842	0.4846	0.4850	0.4854	0.4857
2.2	0.4861	0.4864	0.4868	0.4871	0.4875	0.4878	0.4881	0.4884	0.4887	0.4890
2.3	0.4893	0.4896	0.4898	0.4901	0.4904	0.4906	0.4909	0.4911	0.4913	0.4916
2.4	0.4918	0.4920	0.4922	0.4925	0.4927	0.4929	0.4931	0.4932	0.4934	0.4936
2.5	0.4938	0.4940	0.4941	0.4943	0.4945	0.4946	0.4948	0.4949	0.4951	0.4952
2.6	0.4953	0.4955	0.4956	0.4957	0.4959	0.4960	0.4961	0.4962	0.4963	0.4964
2.7	0.4965	0.4966	0.4967	0.4968	0.4969	0.4970	0.4971	0.4972	0.4973	0.4974
2.8	0.4974	0.4975	0.4976	0.4977	0.4977	0.4978	0.4979	0.4979	0.4980	0.4981
2.9	0.4981	0.4982	0.4982	0.4983	0.4984	0.4984	0.4985	0.4985	0.4986	0.4986
3.0	0.4987	0.4987	0.4987	0.4988	0.4988	0.4989	0.4989	0.4989	0.4990	0.4990
3.1	0.4990	0.4991	0.4991	0.4991	0.4992	0.4992	0.4992	0.4992	0.4993	0.4993
3.2	0.4993	0.4993	0.4994	0.4994	0.4994	0.4994	0.4994	0.4995	0.4995	0.4995
3.3	0.4995	0.4995	0.4995	0.4996	0.4996	0.4996	0.4996	0.4996	0.4996	0.4997
3.4	0.4997	0.4997	0.4997	0.4997	0.4997	0.4997	0.4997	0.4997	0.4997	0.4998
3.5	0.4998	0.4998	0.4998	0.4998	0.4998	0.4998	0.4998	0.4998	0.4998	0.4998
3.6	0.4998	0.4998	0.4999	0.4999	0.4999	0.4999	0.4999	0.4999	0.4999	0.4999
3.7	0.4999	0.4999	0.4999	0.4999	0.4999	0.4999	0.4999	0.4999	0.4999	0.4999
3.8	0.4999	0.4999	0.4999	0.4999	0.4999	0.4999	0.4999	0.4999	0.4999	0.4999
3.9	**0.5000**	**0.5000**	**0.5000**	**0.5000**	**0.5000**	**0.5000**	**0.5000**	**0.5000**	**0.5000**	**0.5000**

Notice that at 3.90, the area under the curve is equal to 50% (0.5000). I can tell if I am on the left or the right side of the mean by the using the Z formula. If X is greater than μ then the value of Z is positive. If μ is greater than X, the value of Z is negative. Negative values are to the left of the mean and positive values are to the right of the mean. The negative and positive values are directional indicators only and should not be added or subtracted. The edges of the normal table are Z. The middle of the table is probability or percentage or area under the curve.

Tear-Out Sheet Chapter 5

Student Name: _____

Day and Time of Class: _____

Normal Curve Problems for Practice

Problems 1 though 7 will use the following narrative.

Assume that you own a telephone answering service. Over the past several years you have determined the following information about the length of telephone calls you receive. Your data set is normally distributed.

$$\mu = 150 \text{ seconds } \sigma^2 = 225.$$

Always draw a distribution when working problems of this nature, so you can visually see the area you are seeking.

1. What is the probability that a phone call will last between 150 and 180 seconds?
2. What is the probability that a phone call will last > 180 seconds?
3. What is the probability that a phone call will be between 125 and 150 seconds?
4. What is the probability that a phone call will be < 125 seconds?
5. What is the probability that a phone call will be between 145 and 155 seconds?
6. What is the probability that a phone call will be between 160 and 165 seconds?
7. What is the value below which 15% of the phone calls fall? (Bottom 15%) New Problem (Converting Area to Z):
8. You are a tire manufacturer. You have determined that the life of your tires is $\mu = 36,500$ miles and the $\sigma = 5,000$ miles. The distribution of tire life is normal.
   a. What percentage of tires will equal to or exceed 40,000 miles?
   b. You want to provide a minimum life warranty for the life of your tires, but it should not exceed more than 10% of your production. At what mileage value should the warranty be set?

Binomial Problem

The following narrative goes with the next three problems. There are five flights per day from Pittsburgh via Alleghany Airlines into Bradford, Pennsylvania Regional Airport. Suppose the probability that any flight arriving late is 0.20. Use the Excel BINOMDIST function or a table (Internet or textbook) to respond to the following questions.

9. What is the probability that none of the flights are late today?
10. What is the probability that exactly one flight is late today?
11. What is the probability that all five flights are late today?

Since $n = 5$ there are six possible outcomes: 0, 1, 2, 3, 4, or 5 flights late.

Inferential Statistics—The Basics

6

Attorney: How was your first marriage terminated?

Witness: By death.

Attorney: And by whose death was it terminated?

Witness: Take a guess.

Inferential Statistics

There are two types of statistics—descriptive and inferential; but I bet you have heard that before (of course some of you don't remember). In the first couple of chapters I introduced you to the idea of describing your data set by using measures of central tendency and dispersion. The two most useful measures are the mean and the standard deviation. Probability and probability distributions have moved you a step closer to understanding some of the basic ideas associated with inferential statistics.

So you might ask, what is inferential statistics?

Good question, I respond.

Inferential statistics involves the use of a statistic to form a conclusion, or inference, about the corresponding parameter.

To most, if not all, of you that definition means very little.

You're right, you silently think, and who really cares?

I astutely know you are beginning to question why in the world you are taking statistics, having to read a boring textbook and learn techniques you will most probably never use (apart from the valuable lessons on horse racing, craps, and Texas hold 'em).

Although I have given you some insight into this answer, I patiently move on believing your critical reasoning will, at some point, lead you to understand real business applications.

I continue: To understand the definition of inferential statistics, you must recall a statistic is a descriptive measure associated with the sample and a parameter is a descriptive measure associated with the population. Both are descriptive measures. You must recall that the mean and the standard deviation are both descriptive measures and usually those most often used.

In statistical terms I can state the relationship as follows:

Inferential statistics:

$$\overline{X} \text{ represents } \mu$$

Wait a minute, you say, that does not make any sense. I've studied probability and know that there is a small chance for the sample mean to exactly equal the population mean, so how can I say they are equal?

I agree with your logic; however, equal is not the assertion. If the population average age of the students reading this textbook is 20.2 and I select a random sample and determine that the average age of the sample is 19.5, am I asserting that 19.5 = 20.2? Hardly so!

What I am asserting is: I want the mean of the sample to be a fair representation of the mean of the population. As you will often hear (actually read) me say, you will never really know the true mean of the population. If you know the true mean of the population, there is no need for a sample is there?

I am asserting the two means are statistically equal on the basis of inferential statistics. I am inferring the sample comes from the population of interest to the researcher, thus the sample can represent the population. This does not imply the two are mathematical equivalents, but they are statistically equal (representative).

As a side note, *all inferential statistical testing is referred to as parametric testing*. I do not know the parameter (population mean), so I let a sample mean (statistic) represent the population mean.

As a preview of upcoming chapters, there are two very important techniques for using the concept of inferential statistics. One is confidence intervals and the other is hypothesis testing. There is a bridge between probability and these two techniques. It is referred to as the **sampling distribution of sample means.**

Good gosh, you say, what on earth does that mean?

Ignoring your slight impatience, I move on patiently. (Can I use both of those opposing words in the same sentence?)

Let's go back to the concept of permutations and combinations. Both of these concepts are arrangements of any data set into subsets. If I have a population size of "N," I can use permutations or combinations to determine how many arrangements (subsets) are possible. Given a population size of "N," how many subsets can I have of size "n"? Each subset would in fact have its own mean. The number of subsets can be referred to as "n," the number of possible samples from a population of "N."

For example, if I am interested in the average age of the students in a statistics class, I could survey 100% of the students and determine their age. My result would be a population mean. However, I might want to take a random sample of the students in the class to determine a sample mean, which I would then assert represents the population mean. If my sample size consists of three students, it should be quite clear I could develop many different samples of size three if I set my population size as 30 students. Using the combination approach (order is not important) there would be 4,060 possible arrangements of a population of 30 arranged three at a time. Each sample mean should represent the population mean. In essence, I would have 4,060 - samples, thus 4,060 sample means. N would yield many samples each with a sample mean – $\overline{X}_1$ or $\overline{X}_2$ or $\overline{X}_3$ or $\overline{X}_4$ or $\overline{X}_5$ ... $\overline{X}_{4,060}$. Inferential statistics asserts that each of the 4,060 sample means represents the true, unknown population mean. A statistic represents the parameter, and the distribution (listing) of the means of all samples would be the sampling distribution of sample means. (You are probably still confused, but let's move on.)

I hope this brief explanation starts clearing up what I mean by sampling distribution of sample means. In reality it is nothing more than a listing of the sample means possible for a population. Of course, I can never list all of the possible arrangements. In fact, there is really no need to do that. I need to find some method to assert with some degree of certainty that the sample mean is truly representative of the population mean.

Using confidence intervals and hypothesis testing will help determine how much I can rely on the assertion they are statistically equal, or the sample is representative of the population. Confidence Intervals and Hypothesis Testing will be explored in later chapters.

Sampling Distribution

Don't get too enamored with the stuff I am about to show you. While the conceptual idea is important, in practice, you will seldom have to make these calculations. However, when I show you the principle of substitution, you may find the idea helpful. In reality, there are too many software programs that will make your life much easier in making the needed calculations. Spend some time lightly reading through the next several paragraphs and tables to understand the conceptual ideas. I will tell you when to begin paying closer attention. For now, just read and absorb. Of course, your professor may want you to understand this material, so in that case, read it to learn it.

Let's assume I am the sales manager of a medium size corporation. My sales team is composed of five sales persons, whose last names are Adams, Baker, Collins, Davis, and Edwards. For the purposes of this example, I will refer to them by the first initials of their last names. What I want to do is determine the best combination of sales teams. I want to arrange the five salespeople into sales teams of two.

What do I do first, you ask?

The first thing I do is to determine how many possible arrangements of the five-person data set I can determine when putting them in teams of two. The question of order becomes important.

You should ask: Is order important?

The answer is "No." Sales team AB is the same as sales team BA, if you are measuring results in units sold. If A sold one unit and B sold two units, $1 + 2 = 3$ which is the same as $2 + 1 = 3$, so order does not make any difference.

I will use the combination calculation. I want to arrange the data set of five into arrangements two at a time ($5 - 2$ at a time). That calculation follows:

$$_nC_r = \frac{n!}{r!(n-r)!} = \frac{5!}{2!(5-2)!} = 10$$

I can arrange my five sales people into teams of two. I will have 10 possible arrangements of my data set into subsets.

Let's identify them.

Table 6.1   All possible arrangements of sales people into groups of two.

Combination #	Arrangement
1	AB
2	AC
3	AD
4	AE
5	BC
6	BD
7	BE
8	CD
9	CE
10	DE

Because these are all of the possible arrangements of my data set of five into subsets two at a time, I have developed the sample space. The probability of selecting any one sample (event) is 0.10 (there are ten). The sum of the probabilities of the entire sample space is 1.0 (adding up all 10 of the 0.10). The two rules of probability are met.

Let's further assume that the number of units sold by each sales person can be quantified as follows. These are very arbitrary and are useful only for making my point.

$$A = 1; B = 2; C = 3; D = 4; E = 5.$$

Let's complete another table similar to the one above, but this time I can determine the mean of each of the sales teams.

The formula for the grand mean is the sum of the column of means divided by the number of samples (here K, which is 10).

$$\overline{\overline{X}} = \frac{\sum \overline{X}}{K}$$

In Table 6.2, each value in the column headed "mean of the sample" (last column on the right) is determined. The first value in that column is 1.5. This is Team AB, where the total is 3.0. I will divide 3.0 by 2 to get the average of Team $AB = 1.5$. I repeat this process for the remainder of Table 6.2.

The grand mean is the same as the population mean, since I am working with all of the possible outcomes (sample space). Add up all the numbers in the last column on the right and divide by 10.

Remember, I will never know the true (population) mean, so what I am showing you is conceptual.

Table 6.2   The sales teams and their means.

Combination Number	Arrangement (Sample Space)	Sample Elements	Total	Mean of the Sample ($\overline{X}$)
1	AB	$(A = 1 + B = 2)\ 1 + 2 = 3$	3	1.5
2	AC	1 + 3	4	2.0
3	AD	1 + 4	5	2.5
4	AE	1 + 5	6	3.0
5	BC	2 + 3	5	2.5
6	BD	2 + 4	6	3.0
7	BE	2 + 5	7	3.5
8	CD	3 + 4	7	3.5
9	CE	3 + 5	8	4.0
10	DE	4 + 5	9	4.5
		Grand Mean	$\overline{\overline{X}}$	30.0/10 = 3.0

Now for a question: What is the probability of selecting any one combination from the sample space?

Since there are 10 possible outcomes, the probability is 0.10 or a 10% chance of selecting any one of the combinations #1 through #10. Combination #1 has a probability of selection of 0.10 as does combination #2 and so forth.

Of course, the question quite naturally arises (this may not really be that obvious to some of you, but pretend), how do I make certain each one has an equal chance of selection? Easy answer, I submit. Use the random selection process. (Where have you heard that before?). Each and every combination from 1 through 10 must have an equal and independent chance of being selected.

Let's look at the sample space a bit differently. Suppose I take the sample space in Table 6.2 and *consolidate the probabilities* of similar means.

What I am suggesting is shown below:

Table 6.3   (Combines last column of Table 6.2).

Means of the Samples	Number of Times Occurring	$F(x)$ or $P(x)$ Probability
1.5	1	0.10
2.0	1	0.10
2.5	2	0.20
3.0	2	0.20
3.5	2	0.20
4.0	1	0.10
4.5	1	0.10
Total	N/A	1.00

What I have done is to combine the probabilities of similar means. Since the mean of 1.5 appears only once, *the probability of drawing a sample whose sample mean is* 1.5 *is* 0.10. However, what is the probability of drawing a sample whose sample mean is 2.5?

Answer: 0.20. Check it out to make sure you find that number in Table 6.3. Notice this question is phrased differently.

My previous question was: What is the probability of drawing a particular combination from 1 through 10? Then answer was 0.10 (10%), since there are 10 combinations and any one may be selected at random at any time during the selection process.

However, the probability of drawing a sample whose sample mean is 2.5 is 0.20 or 20%, because I have two sample means that equal 2.5. (See Table 6.2 and count them).

This question is different.

Read it again.

Follow up question: What is the probability of drawing a sample whose sample mean is 3.5?

Answer: 0.20 since there are two samples with a sample mean of 3.5.

Sampling Error

How about another question?

What is the probability of drawing a sample which has no sampling error?

Whoa! (Those of us from Texas can use that term.) Wait a minute, you say.

That's impossible to answer.

Oh, really, I say.

Remember, the concept of sampling error?

Sampling error is the difference between the population parameter (mean in this case) and the sample statistic (also the mean).

Sampling error is

$\overline{X} - \mu$. (the difference between the mean of the sample and the mean of the population).

What is the population mean? 3.0.

One Word of Warning

In this example, I know the population mean. In real business situations, you never know the population mean.

If the population mean is 3.0, it is clear that all of samples that have a mean greater or lesser than 3.0 have some error. By looking back at Table 6.3, you can see the probability of drawing a sample that has sampling error is 0.80. If I wanted to know the probability of selecting a sample that had a sampling mean of 3.0 from Table 6.3, you would find it to be 0.20 (20%). There are only two choices—sampling error or no sampling error. This makes these two outcomes complementary events. The failure of one to occur means the other must occur.

The probability of a selected sample having sampling error (0.80) is greater than the probability of it having no sampling error (0.20). From this I can generalize there is a *higher probability of making an error* than *NOT making an error* when taking a sample.

How you handle sampling error is important. I will address that challenge in later chapters.

Sampling Distribution of Sample Means

The sampling distribution of sample means, like any other distribution, has a measure of central tendency (the grand mean $\overline{\overline{X}}$) and a variance or dispersion. Variance is the mean of the squared deviation from or around the mean, but you have heard that definition before.

Let's review symbols including symbols for the sampling distribution of sample means (SD of SM).

Table 6.4   Review of symbols.

	Mean	Variance	Standard Deviation	Size of the ...
Population	μ	σ^2	σ	N
Sample	$\overline{X}$	s^2	S	n
SD of SM	$\overline{\overline{X}}$	$\sigma^2_{\overline{X}}$	$\sigma_{\overline{X}}$	K

The following terms are all means: μ, $\overline{X}$, $\overline{\overline{X}}$. The mathematical calculation of each value is the same. You will add up a data set, then divide the sum by N, n, or K depending on which mean you are generating.

The variance column is composed of all variances. Variance by definition is the mean of the squared deviations around the mean. This is true for all three terms: σ^2, S^2, $\sigma^2_{\overline{X}}$. The first is the variance of the population. The second is the variance of the sample. The third is unique to the sampling distribution of sample means and is also a variance. It is called the variance of the standard error. All three are calculated the same way.

The standard deviation is the square root of the variance in all three cases and the symbols are shown in the second from the right column in Table 6.4. For the sampling distribution of sample means, the term is called the standard error.

N, n, and K are all sizes—population, sample, and possible arrangements of the sampling distribution of sample means.

Don't get confused by the terms sampling error, standard error, and standard deviation. All three mean different things and are used for different purposes.

The differences:

Sampling error is the difference between μ and $\overline{X}$.

A **standard deviation** is the square root of the variance.

The **standard error** is $\sigma_{\overline{X}}$.

Continuing what I told you earlier, don't get too involved with this approach, just read it for concept. I will tell you when to pay close attention. However, read it, because you may run into circumstances in the business world when you have to actually calculate the standard error using sample data sets.

Let's take some time to look at how to develop the standard error: $\sigma_{\overline{X}}$. Using Table 6.2 as a data set example, I can expand the columns so I use the following formula to determine the variance of the standard error.

$$\sigma^2_{\overline{X}} = \frac{\sum(\overline{X} - \mu)^2}{K} \quad \text{Variance of the Standard Error}$$

This formula should be familiar, since the variance from earlier chapters is as follows:

$$\sigma^2 = \frac{\sum(\overline{X} - \mu)^2}{N} \quad \text{Population}$$

Notice the formulas are quite similar; however, for the variance of the sampling error, let's look at Table 6.5 as expanded. From the first formula, I am looking for a column headed

$(\overline{X} - \mu)^2$. From Table 6.5 you can see the column of interest is to the far right of the table. How I get there is shown in the previous three columns. For example, I know the population mean is 3.0. I subtract the population mean (3.0) from the mean of the sample (1.5) and get -1.5 (1.5 minus 3.0 $= -1.5$). Then I square -1.5 to get 2.25; which is the first value in the last column to the far right of Table 6.5. Once I have completed those calculations, I will sum that column and then make the calculation of the variance of the standard error $\sigma_{\overline{X}}^2$.

Table 6.5   Variance of the standard error.

Comb. No.	Arrangement (Sample Space)	Sample Elements	Total	Mean of the Sample ($\overline{X}$)	μ	$\overline{X} - \mu$	$(\overline{X} - \mu)^2$
1	AB	1 + 2	3	1.5	3.0	−1.5	2.25
2	AC	1 + 3	4	2.0	3.0	−1.0	1.00
3	AD	1 + 4	5	2.5	3.0	−0.5	.25
4	AE	1 + 5	6	3.0	3.0	0	0
5	BC	2 + 3	5	2.5	3.0	−0.5	.25
6	BD	2 + 4	6	3.0	3.0	0	0
7	BE	2 + 5	7	3.5	3.0	0.5	.25
8	CD	3 + 4	7	3.5	3.0	0.5	.25
9	CE	3 + 5	8	4.0	3.0	1.0	1.00
10	DE	4 + 5	9	4.5	3.0	1.5	2.25
		Grand		Mean 30.0 ÷ 10 = 3.0	N/A	0	7.50

The actual formula for calculating the standard error as previously given is:

$$\sigma_{\overline{X}}^2 = \frac{\sum(\overline{X} - \mu)^2}{K}$$

The calculations:

$$\sigma_{\overline{X}}^2 = \frac{7.50}{10} = 0.75$$

The standard error is the square root of that value. Recall, all three (σ, S, $\sigma_{\overline{X}}$) are standard deviations, but each has a unique meaning.

$$\sigma_{\overline{X}} = \sqrt{0.75} = 0.866$$

In this example, I have a mean of the population of 3.0 and a standard error of 0.866.

When I calculate the standard error or refer to the standard error, I am making calculations for the sampling distribution of sample means ($n > 1$). When I deal with the standard deviation, I am working with a single sample ($n = 1$).

Standard Error (okay, start paying close attention from this point forward)

Okay, all of the stuff I just showed you is associated with the conceptual idea of the standard error. The standard error is different than sampling error. Do not get the two confused. The standard error is a calculated value, which is a cousin to the standard deviation. In both cases you would calculate the mean of the squared deviation around the mean to get a variance. The square root of the variance is, of course, the standard deviation. If working with the sampling distribution of sample means, the square root of the variance is the standard error. *Sampling error, on the other hand, is the difference between the population mean and the sample mean.*

If these terms don't totally confuse you, I will be amazed. Re-read them and try to make sure you understand the differences.

Now that I have showed you all of that stuff, you will find that 99% of the time in the real business world, you will not have to make the detailed calculations I just showed you. (That is why I told you to just read the material for clarity and not procedure). One major limiting factor is I must know the true population mean, which I will not ever know. Of course, I could make the calculation using sampling data, which often is necessary, since the population data are almost always unavailable.

There is, however, another very important relationship between the standard deviation of the population and the standard error of the sampling distribution of sample means. It is reflected in the following formula:

$$\sigma_{\overline{X}} = \frac{\sigma}{\sqrt{n}}$$

The standard error is equal to the standard deviation of the population divided by the square root of the size of the sample. Here too, what will most often happen is you will never know the standard deviation of the population (σ). You will usually have to use the sample standard deviation to make this calculation. In most cases you may substitute S for σ and $S_{\overline{X}}$ for $\sigma_{\overline{X}}$. While using sample values as an estimate of population values does create some error, it is usually not so large that your conclusions can be called into question. This estimate of the population standard error is quite often necessary in business settings.

Sample Size and Standard Error

There are two things which affect the standard error. One is the size of the standard deviation. If the standard deviation is large, the standard error will be large. The other is the size of the sample. If the sample size is large, the standard error will be reduced. Look, once again, at the formula:

$$\sigma_{\overline{X}} = \frac{\sigma}{\sqrt{n}}$$

Using the relationship stated just above, can $\sigma_{\overline{X}}$ ever equal σ?

Think about it.

If $n = 1$, what happens to the two values? They equal each other.

Let's do an important exercise. Using the standard error formula just above, calculate the following:

Table 6.6   Find the standard error.

If the Sample Size "n" Changes to the Following:	And you are Given $\sigma = 2$	Find the Standard Error $\sigma_{\overline{X}}$
$n_1 = 4$	$\sigma = 2$	?
$n_2 = 16$	$\sigma = 2$	?
$n_3 = 25$	$\sigma = 2$	?
$n_4 = 36$	$\sigma = 2$	?

Find the standard error when the standard deviation is 2 and the sample size increases in stages from 4 to 36.

Try making the calculation before looking at Table 6.7 below for the answers.

Look at the pattern in the last column. *As the sample size (n) increases the standard error decreases.*

This is an inverse relationship. One goes up and the other goes down.

This should make logical sense. Think about it.

If I did a 100% survey, how much sampling error would I experience?

I would have *no sampling error,* since I am not doing a 100% survey of the population; however, I would still have a standard deviation (variability).

Table 6.7   The standard error.

If the Sample Size "n" Changes to the Following:	And you are Given $\sigma = 2$	Find the Standard Error $\sigma_{\overline{X}}$
$n_1 = 4$	$\sigma = 2$	1.00
$n_2 = 16$	$\sigma = 2$	0.50
$n_3 = 25$	$\sigma = 2$	0.40
$n_4 = 36$	$\sigma = 2$	0.33

Let's look at one of the most, if not the most, important theorems in inferential statistics—the central limit theorem.

Central Limit Theorem and the Z-Process

As previously discussed in a prior chapter, the empirical rule is an important rule, but another crucial theorem is the central limit theorem (CLT). The essence of the theorem is as "n" (sample size) increases the *underlying distribution of sample means* will approach a normal distribution. In essence $\overline{X}$ provides an excellent estimate of μ as the standard error approaches $\sigma_{\overline{X}} = \dfrac{\sigma}{\sqrt{n}}$. When the sample size ($n$) is 30 or greater I can assert the distribution of sample means is normal or near normal. In fact, the larger my sample size the smaller the standard error will be.

This relationship can be empirically demonstrated, but I will not take time to illustrate it for you. Just accept it and move on.

What this means is: regardless of the distribution of the population, *the distribution of the sample means will be normal if "n" is equal to or exceeds 30.*

So what, you think to yourself.

Picking up on your mood, I comment, you are probably wondering why this matters.

This is important because, if the distribution is normal, you can use the Z-process in determining area under the curve (probability). Of course, you might expect the Z-process to change slightly. I will not disappoint you; it does.

When $n = 1$, the Z-process uses the following relationship.

$$Z = \frac{X - \mu}{\sigma}$$

When your sample size exceeds 1 ($n > 1$), the following modification is necessary. In this second formula, the sampling distribution of sample means is of interest to you. In the first formula, you are working with a single sample.

$$Z = \frac{\overline{X} - \mu}{\sigma_{\overline{X}}}, \text{ which is equivalent to } Z = \frac{\overline{X} - \mu}{\frac{\sigma}{\sqrt{n}}}$$

Because: $\frac{\sigma}{\sqrt{n}}$ can be substituted for the $\sigma_{\overline{X}}$.

There are two conditions when you can use the second Z-process. First, if the sample size is equal to or greater than 30 ($n \geq 30$) the sampling distribution of sample means is a normal distribution or is a near normal distribution. Second, if you are told the distribution is normal regardless of the size of the sample, you can use the Z-process. For example, the sample size could be 25, but if you are told the distribution is normal, then you can utilize the second. Z-process.

Let's pause for a second and look at a summary table of the symbols I am using.

Table 6.8 Review table.

	Mean	Variance	Standard Deviation	Size of the ...	Use of Z-Process
Population	μ	σ^2	σ	N	
Sample	$\overline{X}$	S^2	S	n	$Z = \dfrac{X - \mu}{\sigma}$ When $n = 1$
SD of SM	$\overline{\overline{X}}$	$\sigma_{\overline{X}}^2$	$\sigma_{\overline{X}}$	K	$Z = \dfrac{\overline{X} - \mu}{\sigma_{\overline{X}}}$ When $n > 1*$

*Note: When I get to Chapter 7, this concept will be adjusted slightly when using the t-distribution.

Finite Population Correction Factor

On occasion you must make a modification to the standard error, if "n" (sample size) is large relative to "N" (population size). Most statisticians use the 5% rule.

The adjustment is referred to as the **finite population correction** (FPC) factor and is applied to the calculation of the standard error under the following conditions.

1. Sampling is done from a finite population. *AND*
2. Sampling is done without replacement.

These two rules demonstrate the relationship between the sample draws is dependent (not independent).

However, if the samples are independently selected, then the CLT does not apply. To test for independence, one of two conditions must exist.

1. Sampling is done with replacement. *OR*

2. Sampling is done from an infinite population.

Independent selection means the samples are selected at random from the population and the selection of one sample does not depend on the selection of the second sample.

Under the condition of *dependent samples*, you must apply the FPC, if $n \geq 5\%$ of N. Do not use FPC if "n" is less than 5% of N.

Now the standard error becomes:

$$\sigma_{\overline{X}} = \frac{\sigma}{\sqrt{n}}\sqrt{\frac{N-n}{N-1}}$$

This will give you a better approximation of the standard error when $n \geq 5\%$ of N.

Use of the Z-Process

Primary Z-Process

Let's look at an example. Suppose you owned an answering service. During the last three years you have determined that the mean telephone call time is $\mu = 150$ seconds with a standard deviation of $\sigma = 15$ seconds. There is evidence the distribution is normal. You chose to use the Z-process.

You would like to know what the probability is for a single call lasting between 150 and 155 seconds.

What do you do?

I have told you the distribution is normal and the Z-process can be used, but which Z-process do you select?

$n = 1$ so, according to Table 6.8, you will use the following:

$$Z = \frac{X - \mu}{\sigma} = \frac{155 - 150}{15} = \frac{5}{15} = 0.33 \text{ standard deviations}$$

This is not my final answer, Regis. I still need to convert Z to probability. This is done by using the normal table to look up the Z-value, which is 0.33 or the same result can be determined by using the Excel function to calculate the probability. ($Z = 0.33$).

Looking up $Z = 0.33$ in the normal table, the probability of a call lasting between 150 and 155 seconds is 0.1293 (12.93%). See Figure 6.1 for a visual of the area of interest. As a good working rule, you should always draw a normal distribution and color in the area on the curve for which you have an interest. The $P(150 - 180) = 0.1293$, which comes from Table 6.12 (a normal table).

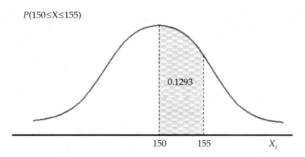

$P(150 \leq X \leq 155)$

0.1293

150   155 X_i

Figure 6.1   The probability of a call lasting between 150 and 155 seconds.

Secondary Z-Process

Let's pose a second question using the same numbers. What is the probability that a sample of 35 will yield a mean between 150 and 155 seconds?

Wait a minute, this sounds like the same problem, you say.

Is it really, I respond?

It is also a normal distribution which allows for the Z-process. How I know it is a normal distribution is because of the Central Limit Theorem since the sample size is greater than 30. The question is which Z-process will you select this time? Since $n > 1$ ($n = 35$), I will use the second Z-process.

$$Z = \frac{\overline{X} - \mu}{\sigma_{\overline{X}}} = \frac{155 - 150}{\dfrac{15}{\sqrt{35}}} = \frac{5}{\dfrac{15}{5.9161}} = \frac{5}{2.5355} = 1.97$$

$\dfrac{\sigma}{\sqrt{n}}$ is substituted for the standard error $(\sigma_{\overline{X}})$.

Next convert 1.97 to probability. You should get a probability of 0.4756. See Figure 6.2 for a visual of the area of interest.

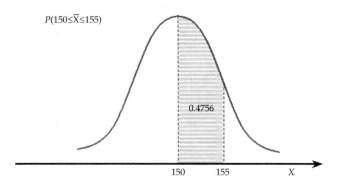

Figure 6.2   The probability that a sample of 35 will yield a call between 150 and 155 seconds.

What is the clue that tells you to use one Z-process versus the other Z-process?

Sample size, you respond. The first is a single sample ($n = 1$). The second is a sampling distribution of sample means ($n = 35$).

Very good observation, I encouragingly say.

Let's see how observant you are with the final discussion of alternate methods of selecting a sample at random.

Four Methods of Sampling Which Meet the Requirement of Randomness

Sampling Error (Luck of the Draw)

As I have often repeated and will once again repeat here: Sampling error is the difference between the mean of the sample (statistic) and the mean of the population (parameter). Sampling error may exist based on luck of the draw (random selection) or bias. If I am interested in making inferential assertions, my selection of a sample must be based on random selection. In random selection each and every element in the population must have an equal and independent chance of being selected.

Setting up the random selection process is important. Of course, there are many computer generated random number tables, but I want to have you look at a manual selection process so that you will understand the concept of random selection. There are four methods that meet the conditions of random selection.

#1 Random Sampling Using Excel Functions or Random Number Tables

I have written at length about the importance of random selecting of your sample. The easiest method for generating random numbers is Excel; but often a random number table may be available on the Internet or in a textbook. Let's look at how to use a random table to look up random numbers, then I will show you the Excel method. Typical random number tables are in column and

Table 6.9 A random number table.

Row/Column	1–5	6–10	11–15	16–20	21–25	26–30	31–35
1	64612	77930	16137	12927	89071	72799	41537
2	68866	19304	42847	17249	97332	86300	39716
3	50198	35604	77895	61969	51985	08141	33488
4	76698	11509	43552	41494	83724	01956	75786
5	73412	52071	43503	62873	53324	11284	43196
6	42295	74036	20944	62432	59331	89684	88553
7	14980	**35863**	**08297**	96342	19765	47025	29892
8	76350	78339	37830	**99947**	43444	98453	50998
9	**01581**	46405	52672	**46305**	08886	33547	38993
10	67238	13884	20162	80008	62569	**22205**	30546
11	66570	33762	21469	00199	27172	15397	82047
12	10557	21230	49179	29167	91844	51682	71808
13	09219	97504	31797	55465	99417	95123	17753
14	32543	64753	03363	75921	19893	88730	18290
15	05689	43380	65162	24128	11352	45001	03769
16	03507	88301	79068	65814	83846	19277	66548
17	28225	32562	80334	30146	61413	91111	43080
18	99646	08072	73891	72968	00687	38170	31209
19	26756	07050	27244	13452	53824	42973	53428
20	25235	65105	57132	92464	29317	60554	06727
21	25656	67440	05564	71519	49575	64287	00165
22	33390	91113	08488	81634	16286	46749	73217
23	43992	57138	00819	15070	20945	25400	57957

row format. This table is grouped into five numbers for ease of reading the table. Conceptually, each and every position, and there are 10, has an equal and independent chance of being a 0 through 9. All positions in the table are selected at random. The result is a random number table.

Okay that is a lot of numbers, how do I use a random number table and make any sense out of it?

Good question, I respond. Let's take it a step at a time.

1. Let's assume I have a population of 200 students and each student has been assigned a three-digit number from 001 to 200. Suppose I wish to select a random sample of six students. In practice, because of the central limit theorem, I would usually sample 30 or more, but will use six just to illustrate the process.

2. Since I have a population of 200 and 200 is a three-digit number, I will select the first three digits of the numbers listed on the chart. Of course it does not make any difference where I start since all of the numbers in the chart are generated randomly. However, once I choose a spot, I must continue in the same direction (horizontally reading across or vertically reading down or any other pattern).

3. I will arbitrarily select row 6 and column 31 and read horizontally across the table. The starting three numbers are 885, then 531, then 498, then 035. (Notice when I got to the end of row 6 I skipped down to row 7 and continued reading across). The first three students selected are beyond my limit of 200, so they are thrown out, but the fourth arrangement of three numbers is 035, which is within my population limit of 200. Student 35 would therefore be included in my sample. Continuing the process, you will find student 082, 099, 015, 050, and 053 are the next to be included. I would normally continue this process until it yielded my desired sample size of 30 or greater.

Just from this brief exposure to a random number table, you can see it is very cumbersome and if you lose your place in the table or in reading across, you have a nightmare.

You are right, Professor. I got confused and got off one entire row when trying to read the numbers. Isn't there a better way?

Ah yes, a simpler method does exist—Excel once again comes to your rescue.

Open an Excel spreadsheet.

I will wait.

Okay, now go to the $f(X)$ in the tool bar and double click on it. This will once again open the functions. You have a drop down window which allows you to select various organizations of functions. If you select "all" you will have hundreds of options. Scroll down the options until you find the "R" section. Under that section you have a function called RAND or RANDBETWEEN. These are the functions of interest.

You will use them as follows.

Go back to the Excel worksheet. Select a cell starting point anywhere on the worksheet.

Let's assume you have 400 students and you want to develop a sample size of 36 out of the 400. The first student would be number one (001) and the last student would be number 400.

Now type the following command into the function box.

= RANDBETWEEN (1,400).

Tab out of the function box. Do not hit enter, just hit tab.

Now in the cell you have selected as your starting point, you have one randomly generated number that is between 1 and 400.

But I need 36, you remind me.

You are correct, I respond.

You can move over one cell and repeat the process 36 times or you can catch the corner of the box and drag the formula across six columns. This will generate six random numbers between 1 and 400.

Next move to the first column and catch the corner of the cell and drag it down six rows. You would then take either each column or each row and catch and drag the cell to complete your 6 × 6 Excel box of random numbers. Don't worry about the fact that each time you drag a row or column all the numbers change.

This method is much simpler and faster. The result would look like Table 6.10. If you try this process, your random numbers will be different than my random numbers. That is okay, so do not concern yourself with the differences.

Table 6.10 Random numbers generated by Excel.

343	275	250	272	148	221
383	95	329	198	44	109
104	203	374	289	97	109
392	391	54	87	151	132
251	215	71	294	106	262
302	359	361	296	374	162

The number in each cell of the table represents the corresponding number of the student to be included in the sample.

Another command could have been possible.

$$= INT\ (400*RAND\ ()) + 1$$

This would have eliminated any decimal points, if your data set contained them.

There may be times when you are interested in proportions. I have not mentioned proportions yet, but they, too, are important. Some data sets will be in proportions or percentages such as the daily attendance at a baseball game measured against capacity. If you wanted to generate a random table of proportions, you would use the following command:

$$= RAND(),\ which\ returns\ values\ between\ 0\ and\ 1.$$

Table 6.11 shows the result of this command.

Table 6.11   The result of Excel command = RAND().

0.873580	0.779755	0.554737	0.065404	0.611094	0.630656
0.472831	0.455249	0.352476	0.725793	0.248568	0.298975
0.425663	0.456562	0.947050	0.332418	0.178236	0.549920
0.006089	0.157484	0.810563	0.733650	0.642303	0.422117
0.638979	0.521550	0.580328	0.762504	0.952939	0.791887
0.118257	0.605554	0.342322	0.479841	0.817381	0.093605
0.619287	0.344170	0.171888	0.817826	0.547588	0.706673

Random selection is one of the most important methods of generating randomly selected numbers. There are, however, three other important methods.

#2 Random Sampling Using Systematic Sampling

After you have taken the population and placed it in a random order, you would select a starting point (the first number) by selecting it randomly. You would then make further selections by taking every 5th or 10th or 15th or 20th or any item from the random order. This is called a **systematic sample**. Begin with a starting point that is selected at random, and thereafter select every "ith" item. This method permits some flexibility.

One could not arrange your population in alphabetical order, since you would be presupposing that the alphabet had a random distribution within each letter of the alphabet. This would be an unreasonable assumption.

For example, suppose you want to sample eight houses from a street of 120 houses. $120/8 = 15$, so every 15th house is chosen after a random starting point between 1 and 15. If the random starting point is 11, then the houses selected are 11, 26, 41, 56, 71, 86, 101, and 116.

In a random sample each and every element of the population has an equal and independent chance of being chosen, which is actually not the case with systematic sampling. However, in practice, a systematic sample is almost always acceptable as being random.

The advantage of a systematic sample is to spread the sample more evenly through the population and it is much easier to conduct than a simple random sample. The disadvantage is that the systematic sample may interact with some hidden pattern in the population such as the assumption that alphabetical listings contain the same pattern within each letter of the alphabet.

In other words, by using this method, I am assuming the distribution is randomly represented throughout the entire random order. I might end up with selection bias if a pattern exists in the groups (each letter of the alphabet).

To overcome this potential bias, stratified or cluster sampling may be used.

#3 Random Sampling Using Stratified Sampling

The population must be divided into strata or homogeneous subgroups according to some common characteristic. The strata must not have overlapping groups. Strata may include such things as geographical areas, age groups, or gender.

Stratification, properly done, offers some real advantages. Stratification will develop greater sample precision provided the groups or strata have been selected so members of the same stratum are as similar as possible with respect to the characteristic of interest (age, income, political preferences). The larger the differences between the strata, the greater will be the gain in precision. For example, if you were interested in Internet usage you might stratify by age; whereas, if you were interested in smoking you might stratify by gender or income level.

Because interviewers can be trained to handle specific strata such as age groups or ethnic groups or particular industry, it is often administratively convenient to stratify a sample. The results from each stratum may be of intrinsic interest and can be analyzed separately. It ensures better coverage of the population than simple random sampling.

Proportional Allocation of the Stratum

In general, proportional allocation will be used when determining the content of the sample. Let's assume that a company has the following administrative staff positions, as shown in Table 6.11.

Table 6.11 Administrative staff positions.

Gender/Job	Number of Employees	% of Total Employees
Male, full time	90	50%
Male, part time	18	10%
Female, full time	9	5%
Female, part time	63	35%
Total	180	100%

This simply means if you have a sample of 50: 25 should be male (50%), full time; 5 should be male (10%), part time; 3 should be female (5%), full time; and 17 should be female (35%), part time. This allows for a proportional representation of the strata within the company.

To illustrate this further, consider a sample that is to be taken showing the preference of voters for presidential candidates. If I know that the population of registered voters in a particular precinct is 58% men and 42% women, I might find it best to divide my sample into the same proportions. My sample would include 58% men and 42% women. Of course, if I want to be even more sophisticated, I would further subdivide the men into age groups such as 20 to 30, 31 to 40, 41 to 50, etc. If I know that 20% of the registered voters in the male category are between 20 and 30, 35% are between 31 and 40, and 22% are between 41 and 50, etc, I would then set up my sample to include those proportions in the substrata of the first 58% strata. The same would be done in the women strata of 42%.

While this process is a bit more detailed, the real advantage is to ensure members of the sample are represented in the same proportion as members of the population. The result will be more accurate than taking a sample without regard to the strata.

This is exactly what happened when Dewey ran against Truman in 1948. The sampling process was flawed and had a much larger proportion of Republicans in the sample than was actually on the registered voters list. Naturally, the Republicans felt Dewey would win. Because the newspaper did not consider the proper proportions of registered Democrats and Republicans, the opposite was true. The proper design of a sample would have prevented the embarrassment by the newspaper that printed a headline showing a win for Dewey even though Truman won the election.

#4 Random Sampling Using Cluster Sampling

Cluster sampling is sometimes useful if your population is too difficult to reach in normal ways. The population is divided into clusters, such as apartment complexes, election districts, city blocks, or other naturally related clusters. The clusters are then numbered and a random selection of clusters is made. Each of the clusters is then sampled 100%. Every item in the cluster is part of the sample. This is especially useful, if there is a geographic separation in the clusters such as farmers in four states. Just think about the problems of selecting the farmers to be sampled at random, and then setting out to visit each farmer selected. You might find yourself in a very costly venture just traveling to the location of each selected farm. You would first cluster your farmers into counties which are proportionate to the total number of counties in each state (stratified element). Next you would then select the counties of interest at random then conduct a 100% sample of the counties selected. This would minimize your travel time and your expense of collecting the sample. This approach is often combined with some element of stratified sampling to enhance the outcome.

Some disadvantages exist since units close to each other may be very similar and less likely to represent the whole population. When this occurs there is most likely a larger sampling error than in simple random sampling.

If the clusters are geographically separated, cost can be reduced because travel time can be reduced. Also cluster sampling is most useful when surveying employees in a particular industry, where individual companies can be the cluster.

The key to all sampling procedures is to try to make the sample, however selected, as representative of the population as possible. If this can be done, then the result will be a sample truly representing the population of interest. These four methods, if properly done, will not destroy the inferential process which is very important in a representative random sampling.

Quota or Mall Intercept Sampling

Would you think quota sampling or mall intercept sampling is random? The answer is "No," but from it the interviewer can gain some useful information about the subject of interest.

In quota sampling, the selection of the sample is made by the interviewer, who has been given quotas to fill from specified sub-groups of the population. For example, an interviewer may be told to sample 50 females between the age of 45 and 60.

There are similarities with stratified sampling, but in quota sampling the selection of the sample is non-random. Anyone who has had the experience of trying to interview people in the street knows how tempting it is to ask those who look most helpful. It is not the most representative of samples, although it may be extremely useful.

Quota sampling is quick to organize and relatively inexpensive to implement. It is not as representative of the population as a whole as are the other methods and because the sample is non-random it is impossible to assess the sampling error (cannot apply inferential techniques to the results).

Non-Sampling Error

Non-sampling error is a more serious error than sampling error. In a previous chapter, I have addressed this briefly. Sampling error can be reduced by increasing the sample size, but non-sampling error cannot be reduced by increasing the sample size. Non-sampling errors are due to mistakes either intentional or unintentional. Errors may be made in data acquisition when the wrong data are recorded or the respondent gives incorrect answers to questions because of misinterpretation of the question. For example, questions on sexual activity or possible tax evasion might lead to a respondent giving an incorrect answer. Bias can also increase the error when the respondent is not representative of the population of interest—a male responds to a questionnaire designed for a female response. If the interviewer cannot contact the designated person and opts for an alternate just to meet his or her goal, bias of the sample may result. This textbook will not address non-sampling errors other than to make you aware that errors associated with non-sampling exist. This can be a serious issue. If you take a course in marketing research, this issue will be developed in more detail.

Proportions

Proportions are associated with business decisions that have binary results. As such, you will be faced with developing percentages or ratios. These are referred to as proportions.

Just as there is a sample mean which estimates the population mean, there is a sample proportion which estimates the population proportion. The concept of proportions is exactly the same as the concept associated with means.

As you might imagine, the formulas are going to be different but not impossible to understand and solve. The confidence coefficients for proportions are the same as for Z and t-values, so those tables are appropriate to use. The confidence interval formula is as follows:

$$CI = p \pm Z_\alpha S_p \text{ where } S_p = \sqrt{\frac{p(1-p)}{n}}$$

This formula is the sample proportion—p is an estimate of π, the population proportion.

Let's look at an example. Suppose you have an auditor who wants to determine the frequency of errors in a company's invoicing. Assume that a sample of 100 invoices is selected at random. The auditor want to maintain a 95% confidence interval of the proportion of errors contained in the invoicing process. The sample yields invoices with 10 errors. What is the maximum and minimum invoice error this auditor might expect using a 5% alpha error?

Solution:

$$S_p = \sqrt{\frac{p(1-p)}{n}} = \sqrt{\frac{(0.10)(0.90)}{100}} = \sqrt{\frac{0.09}{100}} = \sqrt{0.0009} = 0.03$$

The confidence Interval is as follows:

$$0.10 \pm (1.96)(0.03) = 0.10 \pm 0.0588 = 0.0412 \le p \le 0.1588$$

Interpretation: My conclusion is I am 95% confident the true, unknown population proportion of invoices with errors will be between 4.12% and 15.88%. Management must now decide if this error range is acceptable. Proportions are important, so don't just gloss over them.

You know You are a Texan If:

- You only know five spices: salt, pepper, Ranch dressing, BBQ Sauce and ketchup.

- You have taken your kids out trick-or-treating when it was 90 degrees outside.

- You discover you get sunburned through your car window.

Tear-Out Sheet

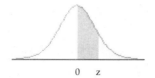

0   z

Normal Distribution Table
Area between 0 and Z

The following calculations may be made using the Excel formula NORMSDIST and subtracting 0.5000 from each result to get the area between 0 and Z, where Z is within two decimal points. In Excel find the $f(x)$ area. Double click on that symbol and the functions will appear. From that you can select the proper function. The NORMSDIST function is a cumulative distribution with a mean of 0 and a standard deviation of 1. *There is another helpful Excel function: NORMDIST (X, Mean, Standard Deviation, Cumulative). This calculation is for a specific Z value, but is cumulative also.*

Table 6.12   Normal table. Notice Z is down the left side of the table, but Z is also across the top of the table. I can now carry Z to two decimal points. Reading the table below: if Z, for example, is 1.96, the corresponding area between 0 and Z is 0.4750.

Z	0.00	0.01	0.02	0.03	0.04	0.05	0.06	0.07	0.08	0.09
0.0	0.0000	0.0040	0.0080	0.0120	0.0160	0.0199	0.0239	0.0279	0.0319	0.0359
0.1	0.0398	0.0438	0.0478	0.0517	0.0557	0.0596	0.0636	0.0675	0.0714	0.0753
0.2	0.0793	0.0832	0.0871	0.0910	0.0948	0.0987	0.1026	0.1064	0.1103	0.1141
0.3	0.1179	0.1217	0.1255	0.1293	0.1331	0.1368	0.1406	0.1443	0.1480	0.1517
0.4	0.1554	0.1591	0.1628	0.1664	0.1700	0.1736	0.1772	0.1808	0.1844	0.1879
0.5	0.1915	0.1950	0.1985	0.2019	0.2054	0.2088	0.2123	0.2157	0.2190	0.2224
0.6	0.2257	0.2291	0.2324	0.2357	0.2389	0.2422	0.2454	0.2486	0.2517	0.2549
0.7	0.2580	0.2611	0.2642	0.2673	0.2704	0.2734	0.2764	0.2794	0.2823	0.2852
0.8	0.2881	0.2910	0.2939	0.2967	0.2995	0.3023	0.3051	0.3078	0.3106	0.3133
0.9	0.3159	0.3186	0.3212	0.3238	0.3264	0.3289	0.3315	0.3340	0.3365	0.3389
1.0	0.3413	0.3438	0.3461	0.3485	0.3508	0.3531	0.3554	0.3577	0.3599	0.3621
1.1	0.3643	0.3665	0.3686	0.3708	0.3729	0.3749	0.3770	0.3790	0.3810	0.3830
1.2	0.3849	0.3869	0.3888	0.3907	0.3925	0.3944	0.3962	0.3980	0.3997	0.4015
1.3	0.4032	0.4049	0.4066	0.4082	0.4099	0.4115	0.4131	0.4147	0.4162	0.4177
1.4	0.4192	0.4207	0.4222	0.4236	0.4251	0.4265	0.4279	0.4292	0.4306	0.4319

(continued)

Table 6.12   Normal table (*Continued*).

z	0.00	0.01	0.02	0.03	0.04	0.05	0.06	0.07	0.08	0.09
1.5	0.4332	0.4345	0.4357	0.4370	0.4382	0.4394	0.4406	0.4418	0.4429	0.4441
1.6	0.4452	0.4463	0.4474	0.4484	0.4495	0.4505	0.4515	0.4525	0.4535	0.4545
1.7	0.4554	0.4564	0.4573	0.4582	0.4591	0.4599	0.4608	0.4616	0.4625	0.4633
1.8	0.4641	0.4649	0.4656	0.4664	0.4671	0.4678	0.4686	0.4693	0.4699	0.4706
1.9	0.4713	0.4719	0.4726	0.4732	0.4738	0.4744	**0.4750**	0.4756	0.4761	0.4767
2.0	0.4772	0.4778	0.4783	0.4788	0.4793	0.4798	0.4803	0.4808	0.4812	0.4817
2.1	0.4821	0.4826	0.4830	0.4834	0.4838	0.4842	0.4846	0.4850	0.4854	0.4857
2.2	0.4861	0.4864	0.4868	0.4871	0.4875	0.4878	0.4881	0.4884	0.4887	0.4890
2.3	0.4893	0.4896	0.4898	0.4901	0.4904	0.4906	0.4909	0.4911	0.4913	0.4916
2.4	0.4918	0.4920	0.4922	0.4925	0.4927	0.4929	0.4931	0.4932	0.4934	0.4936
2.5	0.4938	0.4940	0.4941	0.4943	0.4945	0.4946	0.4948	0.4949	0.4951	0.4952
2.6	0.4953	0.4955	0.4956	0.4957	0.4959	0.4960	0.4961	0.4962	0.4963	0.4964
2.7	0.4965	0.4966	0.4967	0.4968	0.4969	0.4970	0.4971	0.4972	0.4973	0.4974
2.8	0.4974	0.4975	0.4976	0.4977	0.4977	0.4978	0.4979	0.4979	0.4980	0.4981
2.9	0.4981	0.4982	0.4982	0.4983	0.4984	0.4984	0.4985	0.4985	0.4986	0.4986
3.0	0.4987	0.4987	0.4987	0.4988	0.4988	0.4989	0.4989	0.4989	0.4990	0.4990
3.1	0.4990	0.4991	0.4991	0.4991	0.4992	0.4992	0.4992	0.4992	0.4993	0.4993
3.2	0.4993	0.4993	0.4994	0.4994	0.4994	0.4994	0.4994	0.4995	0.4995	0.4995
3.3	0.4995	0.4995	0.4995	0.4996	0.4996	0.4996	0.4996	0.4996	0.4996	0.4997
3.4	0.4997	0.4997	0.4997	0.4997	0.4997	0.4997	0.4997	0.4997	0.4997	0.4998
3.5	0.4998	0.4998	0.4998	0.4998	0.4998	0.4998	0.4998	0.4998	0.4998	0.4998
3.6	0.4998	0.4998	0.4999	0.4999	0.4999	0.4999	0.4999	0.4999	0.4999	0.4999
3.7	0.4999	0.4999	0.4999	0.4999	0.4999	0.4999	0.4999	0.4999	0.4999	0.4999
3.8	0.4999	0.4999	0.4999	0.4999	0.4999	0.4999	0.4999	0.4999	0.4999	0.4999
3.9	0.5000	0.5000	0.5000	0.5000	0.5000	0.5000	0.5000	0.5000	0.5000	0.5000

Tear-Out Sheet Chapter 6

Student Name: _____

Day and Time of Class: _____

Use the Z-process for the sampling distribution of sample means to determine the following values.

$$Z = \frac{\overline{X} - \mu}{\dfrac{\sigma}{\sqrt{n}}}$$

1. According to a recent weekly report, the average years of experience for commercial airline pilots is 24.2 years with a standard deviation of 11 years. This year the pilot must make 36 business flights ($n = 36$). You want the average experience for the business pilots to be over 30 years. What is the probability this statement can be supported?

2. The average (mean) production level at a manufacturing plant is 46.5 units per day with a standard deviation of 10.5 units. If the plant manager takes a sample of 100 days and the mean production exceeds 49 units, all employees will receive a shift bonus. How likely are the employees to receive the bonus?

3. If a random sample of 64 is selected from a population whose mean is 50 with a standard deviation of 10, what is the probability of each of the following?

   a. $P(>52)$

   b. P(Between 48.5 and 52.4)

4. Find the probability of the following:

   a. $N = 250$; $n = 100$; $\mu_H = 35.6$; $\sigma = 4.89$; Find $P(\overline{X} \geq 36)$

   b. $N = 1{,}000$; $n = 60$; $\mu_H = 125$; $\sigma = 13.4$; Find $P(\overline{X} \leq 123)$

   c. Using the FPC term alone, explain why there is a difference in the FPC value in part a and part b just above.

5. Suppose the average checkout ticket at a department store is $64.28 with a standard deviation of $20.91. Twenty-two percent of the time (22%), when a random sample of 40 customer's tickets is examined, the sample average should exceed what value?

6. Suppose a sub-division in Southwest Fort Worth contains 1,200 homes. If a sample of 50 homes is selected at random and found to appraise at an average of $180,000 with a standard deviation of $8,750, what is the probability that the sample average will exceed $182,500?

7. A researcher wants to conduct a survey about a proposed shopping mall. According to the latest census, there are 500 households in the community in which the mall will be located. The researcher has numbered the households from 1 to 500. Use Excel to determine a random sample of 30 households.

7 Confidence Intervals—One Population Mean and Proportion Testing

Attorney:	Can you describe the individual?
Witness:	He was about medium height and had a beard.
Attorney:	Was this a male or female?
Witness:	Unless the circus was in town, I'm going with male.

Confidence Intervals

By way of review, let's look at a table to aid you in keeping the terminology straight. This is the same as Table 6.8 from the previous chapter.

The first row is associated with the population. The second row is a single sample ($n = 1$). The third row is the sampling distribution of sample means (*SD* of *SM* when $n > 1$). The second column consists of means. A mean is a mean is a mean. The third column is all variances. A variance is a variance is a variance. The fourth column is the standard deviation and the fifth is the size of the population, sample and *SD* of *SM*. All calculations are done the same way for a mean, for a variance, and for a standard deviation.

Table 7.1   Review Table for Symbols.

	Mean	Variance	Standard Deviation	Size of the...	Use of Z-Process
Population	μ	σ^2	σ	N	
Sample	$\overline{X}$	s^2	S	n	$Z = \dfrac{X - \mu}{\sigma}$ When $n = 1$
SD of SM	$\overline{\overline{X}}$	$\sigma_{\overline{X}}^2$	$\sigma_{\overline{X}}$	K	$Z = \dfrac{\overline{X} - \mu}{\sigma_{\overline{X}}}$ When $n > 1^*$

*Note: Use of Z will be modified when I discuss the *t*-distribution in this Chapter.

Because different concepts are stressed with each row of symbols, they are named differently to keep the conceptual confusion to a minimum.

Okay, I know you are thinking, "Getting confused is what I have been several times in this course." It will get better the more exposure you have to the language and concepts. The best method of leaning is to work the assigned homework problems.

I trudge on.

The last column in Table 7.1 shows two different Z-processes. One applies to a single sample and one applies any time $n > 1$.

$$Z = \frac{X - \mu}{\sigma}, \text{ when } n = 1.$$

Or $Z = \dfrac{\overline{X} - \mu}{\sigma_{\overline{X}}}$, where $\sigma_{\overline{X}} = \dfrac{\sigma}{\sqrt{n}}$ which allows me to re-write the formula

$$\text{as } Z = \frac{\overline{X} - \mu}{\dfrac{\sigma}{\sqrt{n}}}, \text{ when } n > 1.$$

I have two Z-processes. Use of either requires the distribution to be normal. Two things can make the distribution normal. First is the central limit theorem (CLT), which ensures the distribution of sample means is normal, if $n \geq 30$. Second, for sample sizes less than 30, you must be told the distribution is normal. If the distribution is not normal, a different statistical procedure is required, which I will cover a bit later.

How am I going to use all of this stuff, you ask? Remember, I have previously demonstrated that anytime I take a sample I have a very high probability of sampling error. Sampling error is defined as the difference between $\overline{X}$ and μ. My problem is what I do with the sampling error. Can I assert $\overline{X}$ represents μ or does $\overline{X}$ not represent μ?

Sampling error is NOT standard error, so don't let the two get jumbled up in your mind.

$$\text{Sampling error is } \overline{X} - \mu.$$

$$\text{Standard error is } \sigma_{\overline{X}} = \frac{\sigma}{\sqrt{n}}.$$

When I take a sample, I know I have sampling error. I want to assert that $\overline{X}$ is representative of μ. Two statistical methods are available to help me evaluate my assertion. One method is confidence intervals and the other method is hypothesis testing. In the next chapter, I will address hypothesis testing. In this chapter, I will address the use and interpretation of confidence intervals.

There are two types of estimators. One is a point estimate and the other is an interval estimate.

Okay, you have probably forgotten what a point estimate is, right?

The point estimate uses the *mean of the sample* as an *estimate of the mean of the population at a given point* ($\overline{X}$ is a point estimate of μ). Point estimates are estimates of the population parameter (mean in this case). One difficulty with a point estimate is the sample mean changes each time a new sample is selected. Remember, permutation or combination arrangements demonstrate the number of samples or subsets I can develop for any population data set.

To use the sample mean and expect it to exactly equal the true, unknown population mean is not a practical or realistic expectation. If I can place around the point estimate ($\overline{X}$) an interval that would be based on some statistically consistent procedure, I would have a better chance of the sample mean actually representing the true, unknown population mean. In essence, this is what confidence intervals accomplish.

The interval estimate begins with the point estimate and adds an interval based on an acceptable level of error. The relationship is as follows.

$$\overline{X} \pm Z_\alpha \sigma_{\overline{X}} \text{ which basically comes from solving } Z = \frac{\overline{X} - \mu}{\sigma_{\overline{X}}} \text{ for } \overline{X}$$

I begin with the point estimate of $\overline{X}$. Around the point estimate, an interval is calculated using $\pm Z_\alpha \sigma_{\overline{X}}$. The interval is Z at a chosen alpha error level times the standard error.

Also remember the standard error can be the following:

$$\sigma_{\overline{X}} = \frac{\sigma}{\sqrt{n}}, \text{ so the interval can be stated } \pm Z_\alpha \frac{\sigma}{\sqrt{n}}.$$

When everything is put together, the final formula looks like the following:

$$\overline{X} \pm Z_\alpha \sigma_{\overline{X}} \text{ or the mathematically equivalent formula, } \overline{X} \pm Z_\alpha \frac{\sigma}{\sqrt{n}}.$$

Okay, I have thrown a bunch of formulas at you, but the last two are the important ones to recall. Now let's talk about how using an interval estimate improves my ability to make a conclusion about the true, unknown population mean.

My process needs to be consistent. Confidence intervals provide me with that opportunity. Once I have determined the interval, I have two values, one below the mean (LCL) and one above the mean (UCL).

Graphed it looks like the following (Figure 7.1):

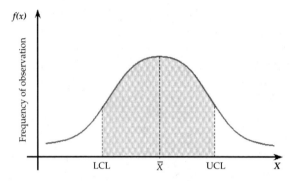

Figure 7.1   Area under the curve between the LCL and UCL.

Since I never know the true mean of the population, confidence intervals allow me to place around the point estimate (the sample mean) an interval. I can make certain statements about the true, unknown population mean (as long as the sample is selected randomly). Error can still occur, but the error is limited. There are three common error values (1%, 5%, and 10%). Each of these is referred to as an alpha error. Each alpha error has a corresponding confidence coefficient (CC, which are 99%, 95%, and 90%). These are also referred to as confidence limits (CL).

More on this shortly, so be patient. Just soak up the wonderful knowledge I am imparting to you.

Okay, knock off the snickering.

The **alpha error** by definition is the *rejection of a true, correct outcome.* In other words, the result of my study is true, but I erroneously say the results are false. An alpha error is the most serious error in many testing processes. Everything is okay, but I incorrectly conclude it is not okay. If

Table 7.2   Confidence coefficients and alpha.

Confidence Coefficients	Alpha Error	Total Area
0.99	0.01	1.00
0.95	0.05	1.00
0.90	0.10	1.00

I am in the manufacturing business, this might result in me shutting down my production line for an invalid reason. A shutdown when none is necessary could be a costly error.

When you use any particular confidence coefficient, there will be a corresponding alpha error level. Again, the alpha error is the *probability of rejecting a true statement.* If you have a CC of 95%, you will have a complementary alpha of 5%. Together they total 100% of the area under the curve. Table 7.2 summarizes the most common values.

Could I have other confidence coefficients?

Yes.

I could have anything from 1% to 100%, but the three most common are the 90%, 95%, and 99% confidence levels (confidence coefficients). Attorneys use a confidence interval of 51% to win a case, although they don't state it in that manner, nor do they probably consciously understand it that way.

Let's see if I can sort out what I am really trying to say.

A confidence interval is always a two-tailed rejection region test. The alpha value is in the tails of the curve. If alpha is 0.10, one-half will be in the right tail (5%) and one-half will be in the left tail (5%). My confidence statement will be associated with the chosen alpha value or the corresponding confidence level.

I know this is not clear yet, so keep reading.

The interval I develop will always begin with $\overline{X}$. I will choose an alpha value, which will be written Z_α. For instance, if alpha was 0.05, you would see $Z_{0.05}$. This means I have chosen the 95% confidence interval or confidence level.

To repeat the formula, I have the following:

$$\overline{X} \pm Z_\alpha \sigma_{\overline{X}}$$

The true mean of the population is unknown. By using confidence intervals, I am able to state how confident I am the true, unknown population mean is between the LCL and UCL. For example, if I use an alpha error of 0.05, I can make the following statement: I am 95% confident the true, unknown population mean is between the LCL and the UCL. This means I will be correct 95% of the time and wrong 5% of the time (the alpha error).

Another Example: In the formula, $\overline{X} \pm Z_\alpha \sigma_{\overline{X}}$, Z at any alpha level can be determined by looking up a value in a table or using software such as Excel. Knowing how to look up Z in the normal table is crucial. For example, if I were using an alpha level of 0.05, the area between the UCL and LCL would be 95%. Because a confidence interval is a two-tailed rejection region, this means 0.0250 of the area would lie in the upper tail (to the right of the UCL) and 0.0250 of the area would lie in the lower tail (to the left of the LCL).

Well, you have done it. You have me confused, you comment.

Okay, let's keep trudging on and see if I can clear this up for you. Maybe looking at it graphically will help you to visualize what I am trying so desperately to explain verbally.

Remember, a normal distribution is symmetrical, thus 50% lies to the right of the mean and 50% lies to the left of the mean. The entire distribution must total 100%. In my example, $0.9500 + 0.0250 + 0.0250 = 100\%$.

See the below graph.

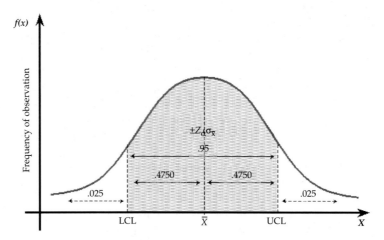

Figure 7.2   Area under the curve for alpha 0.05.

Okay, you say. I think I partially understand it, but go over the interpretation once more.

Good question, since many students struggle with two things—looking up the Z-value and interpreting the results.

Once I have established the UCL and the LCL, I can then interpret the outcome.

There are only two possible interpretations.

1. *I am 95% confident that the true, unknown population mean lies between the UCL and the LCL.*

   OR

2. *If I construct many confidence intervals, 95% of them will contain the true, unknown population mean; however, 5% will not.*

Don't get creative with your own interpretations. Mine are demanding enough. In either case, there is a 5% chance of error. Said differently, I will be correct in my assertion 95% of the time and wrong 5% of the time.

Confidence intervals have nothing to do with probability. The probability that the true, unknown population mean lies between the UCL and LCL is either 0 or 1. The true mean is either between the UCL and the LCL, or it is not there. You cannot interpret the result as that there is a 95% probability that the interval will contain the true mean. Probability and confidence levels are not the same.

Putting It Together (I hope)

Let's suppose that I am a manufacturer of a paper product that must measure 11.0 inches in length. This value is my specified value, so it is the target mean length for all of my sheets of paper (μ_H). Let us also suppose that I have determined that the standard deviation of my manufacturing process is 0.02 inches. I want to take samples on a periodic basis to determine if my production process is yielding paper that is 11.0 inches long within the limits of a tolerable error (one-half the interval width by definition). There may be times when the cutting blade may become dull, which may cause the paper to not be properly cut.

Suppose I determine I want to be 95% confident that the paper I am producing falls within tolerable error. Acceptable tolerable error is random error. I can calculate a 95% confidence limit. I take a sample of 100 sheets of paper ($n = 100$). For this sample, the sample mean is determined to be 10.998 inches. While the sample reflects my production process is less than the 11.0 inches desired, do I have enough information to assert the blade has become too dull? Am I producing paper outside an acceptable length (outside tolerable error)?

Said another way, can I be 95% confident my production process is in control and the difference between the 10.998 and 11.0 is due to random sampling error? Random sampling error is okay in explaining the difference.

To test this I calculate a 95% confidence interval. The calculation is as follows:

$$\overline{X} \pm Z_\alpha \sigma_{\overline{X}}$$

$$10.9980 \pm Z_{0.05} \left[\frac{0.02}{\sqrt{100}} \right]$$

$$10.9980 \pm (1.96) \left[\frac{0.02}{10} \right]$$

$$10.9980 \pm (1.96)[0.002]$$

$$10.9980 \pm 0.0039$$

$$10.9941 \text{ through } 11.0019$$

Interpretation: Since the interval contains the specified 11.0 inches, I can assert that I am 95% certain that the production process is in control and the blade is not too dull to cut the paper to the proper length.

Whoa, you say. I know where you got the 10.998, and I know how you got the standard error by using the standard deviation divided by the sample size, but where on earth did you get the 1.96?

Oh, how quickly you forget, I respond.

Go back and look at the Figure 7.2. A confidence interval is a *two-tailed rejection test*. One-half of alpha goes in each tail.

Okay, have you turned back to find that Figure 7.2 yet? It will give you a visual of the Z-calculation you must make. To find Z at alpha 0.05, you must look at the Z-table (normal table), which was given to you at the ends of Chapter 5 and Chapter 6. It is also in the back of the textbook. I will wait until you find that table, remove it from your textbook, and look at it as I tell you the following.

The alpha level is 0.05. This is a two-tailed rejection region test, so I will divide 0.05 by 2, which equals 0.0250 for each tail (since a normal distribution is symmetrical). Subtracting the 0.0250 from

0.5000 (50%), I have 0.4750 in the two equal center sections. $(0.4750 + 0.4750 = 0.9500)$. This is the 95% confidence interval.

Using the normal table, I will look up the 0.4750 in the *body of the table*. When I do, I get a Z-value of 1.96. Take a minute and see if you get the same Z-value. If you do not, you need to see the Professor or another student in your class who understands this process. You must have an absolute grasp of looking up Z-values. If you do not, you will not do well on examinations or understand the majority of the remainder of these next few chapters.

To repeat: Did you find the 0.4750? Good. Now trace that value back to the Z-value on the left side of the normal table and to the value above in the normal table. You should have now solved the mystery of the 1.96. **THIS IS A CRITICAL ISSUE AND YOU MUST UNDER-STAND HOW TO LOOK UP Z-VALUES.**

Let's look further at the application of the Z-process.

Z-Values

What I want you to do next is fill in the table below (Table 7.3). I want you to use the normal distribution table to determine the Z-values corresponding to the four listed confidence coefficients. I will give you some help on one of the values and let you determine the other two. (HINT: I just did the 95% area in the example problem just above.) The 90% CI would look like the following (Figure 7.3):

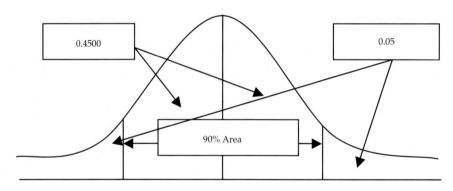

Figure 7.3   Area under the curve.

If I want to determine the Z-value associated with the 90% confidence limit, I would first divide 0.90 by 2. This gives me the value of 0.4500. This value of 0.4500 represents the area under the curve from the mean to the LCL or the UCL. I next look in the body of the table (not the edges of the table) to find the value closest to the 0.4500. I find the value 0.4505. I next move to the outer edges of the normal table to find the Z-value. The answer is 1.65. Actually you will find you are midway between 1.64 and 1.65. I usually take the conservative approach and round up when the value is between two values. Rounding is okay since interpolation will not yield significant differences. Of course, using Excel will yield more precise values.

Take a couple of minutes and fill out the Z-values for the following confidence coefficients (CC or CL). I have already done a couple of them for you.

Table 7.3 Exercise in looking up the Z-value.

Confidence Coefficient or Confidence Limits	Alpha Error	Z-Value
0.99	0.01	
0.98	0.02	
0.95	0.05	
0.90	0.10	

In general, to find the values, you will divide alpha by two and place it in each tail. Then you subtract the alpha value you just calculated from 0.5000. The resultant will be the value you look up in the body of the normal table. Usually use the closest value or round up. The same result can be obtained by dividing the CC or CL by two and looking up that value in the body of the normal table. Notice either approach yields the same result.

From the top of Table 7.3, the four answers are 2.58, 2.33, 1.96, and 1.65. The 2.58 is rounded up as is the 1.65. For the 2.33, the closest value in the body of the normal table is 0.4901 (you need 0.4900). I repeat, you must learn how to look up Z-values in the normal table. Before moving on, please make sure you know how to look up these values in the normal table.

I gave you an example just above about a paper manufacturer who wanted to develop a 95% confidence interval for his manufacturing process. Let's suppose that the manufacturer wanted to test his process control at the 99% level rather than the 95% level.

What would change? Think about it before reading the answer just below.

The Z-value would change from 1.96 to 2.58. Since the 2.58 is larger than the 1.96, it is logical to expect the interval to expand.

It does.

The new confidence interval is now the following.

10.9928 to 11.0032.

Make the substitution of 2.58 for the 1.96 and see if you come up with these same numbers. By comparing two intervals, I can see the 99% interval is wider.

95% Interval: 10.9941 to 11.0019 (width 0.0078)

99% Interval: 10.9928 to 11.0032 (width 0.0104)

Interpretation: My conclusion does not change, however. I have no reason to expect the process is not in control at the 95% level, and I have no reason to expect the process is out of control at the 99% level.

If I use the 90% level, the interval narrows from both the 99% and the 95% level, but my conclusion does not change. My statement of confidence changes (90%, 95% or 99% confident) in all three instances; however, the conclusion remains the same. There is no problem with the production process regardless of using the 99%, the 95%, or the 90% confidence levels. One word of warning: The alpha level is a value that should be determined *before* the study begins. Do not play with it to achieve a pre-conceived result.

For example, let's say I am the quality control inspector for a soft drink bottler. I want to ensure that I fill my 12 *oz* cans to the net weight level stated on the can. I do not want to put too much in the can or too little in the can. I can never know the true, unknown population mean of the 12 *oz* cans, because every time I fill a new can, the true mean changes.

You wonder, why isn't the true mean 12 *oz*?

I respond, some cans are under filled slightly and some are overfilled slightly. The only way I can determine the true mean is to dump out the liquid in every can and measure it. As you can see, this would be impractical, since I would have to destroy my product. This would lead to zero production, which would lead to a very unhappy sales force and stockholders. The point is you will never know the true, unknown population mean. If you know the true mean, there is no need for a sample. There is a true, unknown population mean (μ_T) and a hypothesized (unproven, but asserted) population mean (μ_H). The hypothesized mean is a representative of the true, unknown population mean.

Relationship Between Standard Error, Sample Size, and Interval Width

Remember, as the sample size increases, the standard error decreases. This relationship is demonstrated by looking at the formula for the standard error.

$$\sigma_{\overline{X}} = \frac{\sigma}{\sqrt{n}}$$

As "n" increases, $\sigma_{\overline{X}}$ decreases. This is an important inverse relationship.

The interval width is represented by the following formula:

$$\pm Z_\alpha \sigma_{\overline{X}}$$

Two things will affect the interval width. First, if you increase the sample size, the standard error will decrease. If the standard error decreases, the interval will become narrower assuming you hold Z constant. *Second,* if you select an alpha level of 0.01 ($Z = 2.58$) versus an alpha level of 0.10 ($Z = 1.65$), you will have a narrower interval at the 0.10 level than you will at the 0.01 level, assuming you hold the standard error constant. In summary, the interval width is controlled by the size of the sample (the larger the sample, the smaller the standard error) and by your selection of an alpha level. The lower the confidence interval, the narrower the interval will be. The higher the confidence interval, the broader the interval will be.

Okay, Professor, you have covered sample sizes which are equal to or greater than 30, but I can imagine a time when smaller sample sizes must be taken. What do you do in these instances when $n < 30$?

I have been working with the Z-test. This is known as a test statistic. There are other test statistics, however. There are several circumstances that must be considered as you determine the proper test statistic you will use in developing confidence intervals.

- First, you should always ask yourself "Is the population normally distributed?"
- Second, you should ask yourself "How large is the sample size?"
- Third, you should ask yourself "Is the standard deviation of the population known?"

Your answer to these three questions will tell you which test statistic to use. I have three choices of test statistics at this point: Z-test, *t*-test, and nonparametric tests. I won't challenge you with the nonparametric tests at this point, and you have been exposed to the Z-test. This only leaves one other: the *t*-test. Let's look at the *t*-test.

Wait, a minute, you ask. Tell me again, what is a test statistic?

Oh, I respond. Let me amplify it a bit more.

The term **test statistic** simply refers to the type of test you are going to conduct in solving any particular problem. The one to which you have been introduced is the Z-process. I am going to bring into focus the *t*-test, shortly. Others include nonparametric tests, the *F*-test, Chi square, ANOVA, and others, but don't worry about those just yet. There is plenty of time left in the text-book pages to muddle your thinking in those areas.

Let's briefly go back and look at the three questions I posed just above.

If the population is known to be normal and the sample size is 30 or greater and the standard deviation of the population is known, you *always use the Z-test.*

You would also use the Z-test if the population is known to be normal and the sample size is less than 30, but the *standard deviation of the population is known.*

I can give you an even broader picture of when you are to use the Z-test. *If the population is either normal or non-normal and **the standard deviation of the population is known**, use the Z-test statistic regardless of the size of the sample. The sample size may be equal to or greater than 30 or it may be less than 30.*

Good gosh, you say. This is getting confusing. Can't you simplify these statements in some way, so I can understand when to use what?

You are correct, I say. I am beginning to confuse myself, too.

Let's put the rules in a table and see if I can simplify the selection process. The three questions I ask form the headings of the columns.

This should simplify things for you.

Yeah, right, you comment. Maybe it makes is simpler for you, but I am still confused.

Okay, look down the right side of Table 7.4. Notice you *use the Z-test almost always, **unless** you are using the t-test or a nonparametric test.* Okay, so relax. As I have already said, you don't

Table 7.4   Conditions for using various test statistics (Z, t or nonparametric).

First Question	Second Question	Third Question	
Is the Population...?	Is the Sample Size ...?	Is the Standard Deviation of the Population...?	Use
Normal–If Yes	Greater than or Equal to 30	Known	Z-test
Normal–If Yes	Greater than or Equal to 30	Unknown	Z-test
Normal–If Yes	Less Than 30	Known	Z-test
Normal–If Yes	**Less Than 30**	**Unknown**	**t-test**
Normal–If No	Greater than or Equal to 30	Known	Z (CLT)
Normal–If No	Greater than or Equal to 30	Unknown	Z (CLT)
Normal–If No	Less Than 30	Known	**Nonparametric**
Normal–If No	Less Than 30	Unknown	**Nonparametric**

have to be concerned about the nonparametric tests at this point—that's later. The only one you have to learn is when to use the *t-test*, since *all other conditions* require you to use the Z-test. I could list each leg of Table 7.4 (normal distribution, $n \geq 30$, and σ is known = Z-test, for example), but listing all of the legs is not really necessary. In reality all you have to do is remember to use the Z-test in all circumstances, *unless* the distribution is normal, $n < 30$, σ is unknown. Under those three conditions and those three alone, you use the *t-test*. I will repeat them below.

There are three conditions which must *all, repeat all*, be met to use a *t-test*.

- First, the population must be normal.
- Second, the sample size must be less than 30.
- Third, the standard deviation of the population must be unknown.

When all three of these conditions are met, you use a *t-test* rather than a Z-test. Use Z *unless* all three conditions are met.

So now you wonder silently, what is a *t-test*?

Clairvoyance taking over again I say: Okay, let's look at the meaning and use of a *t-test*.

You continually are amazed at my ability to read your mind. There is a secret to this skill, but I will not disclose it until much, much later.

t-test

Quite naturally, the *t*-test has three conditions that must be assumed or stated in order for you to successfully use *t*-test values. It seems as though there are always assumptions, aren't there?

Those three conditions are repeated here a third time for emphasis: (Don't you just hate redundancy?)

- *The distribution is normal* through any statement in the problem that ascribes normality to the distribution.
- *The sample size is less than 30.* The *t*-test is used for small size samples.
- *The standard deviation of the population is unknown.* Notice this is the population standard deviation and not the sample standard deviation.

So what is the *t*-test, you ask again?

Essentially the *t*-test is the same thing as a Z-test, but for small samples ($n < 30$).

The *t*-distribution is driven by *degrees of freedom*. For now, the degrees of freedom are $n - 1$. In an earlier chapter, I introduced you to degrees of freedom.

Let's review the idea of degrees of freedom. Let's say that I have four numbers that equal 100.

$$X_1 + X_2 + X_3 + X_4 = 100.$$

I can set three of the values at any number that I wish. The first could be 20, the second could be 30, and the third could be 40. The total of these three is 90. However, once these three are selected, the fourth number is fixed and allows me no choice—it is 10.

By definition, the degrees of freedom are $n - 1$ or three degrees of freedom. I have three free choices out of four total choices. The fourth is not a free choice.

Solving Problems with the t-test

Okay, now that I know about the *t*-distribution or t-test, what do I do next?

The formula for the *t*-test is very similar to the formula for the Z-test.

$$\overline{X} \pm Z_\alpha \sigma_{\overline{X}}, \text{ where } \sigma_{\overline{X}} = \frac{\sigma}{\sqrt{n}} \text{ for the Z-test approach.}$$

The formula revised for the *t*-test approach is as follows:

$$\overline{X} \pm t_\alpha S_{\overline{X}}, \text{ where } S_{\overline{X}} = \frac{S}{\sqrt{n}}$$

Okay, you cheerily comment. These look much like the same formula. The only difference seems to be the *t*-value and the fact you use sample values and not population values for the standard deviation. I think I can do all of this formula, but do I look up the *t*-value in the normal table?

You are close to a breakthrough, dear student, very close. However, there is something called the *t*-distribution or *t*-table. It is different from the Z-table (normal table). I have reproduced one at the end of this chapter and the end of the textbook. You will need to go to it now or you will not understand anything about the next few paragraphs. It is a tear-out sheet, so remove it and place it side by side to the text material, so you can follow my comments.

Mark your place here and retrieve the chart. I'll wait.

Got it? Good!

Fortunately, the statisticians have provided a *t*-table for you rather than making you work with a complicated formula or use the very helpful Excel. (The command for the Excel function is TINV.) There is an explanation at the end of the table itself on how to look up values using the *t*-table. Read it. There are three keys to reading the table: know the alpha level desired; know the degrees of freedom; know if you have a one or two-tailed rejection region. For confidence intervals, the test is always two-tailed.

For example, let's suppose that I have set a 5% alpha value with a sample size of 20 and you want to find the appropriate *t*-value. You will look in the *t*-value table (Table 7.7) where the alpha of 0.05 intersects with the degrees of freedom of 19 $(n - 1)$.

Degrees of freedom $= (20 - 1 = 19)$.

The *t*-value is 2.093.

Find it. I will wait.

If you do not see this value, then get help. Make sure you understand how to get this value. **IT IS CRITICAL THAT YOU ARE ABLE TO LOOK UP *t* and Z-VALUES IN TABLES or USE THE EXCEL FUNCTION.** (I may have said this a time or two before.)

Substitutions

Most of the time, you will not have the population values. This will often require that you use sample values as estimates of the population values. I will present a brief review of the formulas of interest and the possible substitutions.

If you do not know $\sigma_{\bar{x}}$, then you may substitute $S_{\bar{x}}$. If you do not know σ, then you may substitute S. The following substitution is possible.

$$S_{\bar{X}} = \frac{S}{\sqrt{n}}$$

This, like Z, means that I could rewrite the *t-formulas* several ways.

$$\overline{X} \pm t_{\alpha}S_{\bar{X}} \text{ or the equivalent formula } \overline{X} \pm t_{\alpha}\frac{S}{\sqrt{n}}$$

Controlling or Affecting the Interval Width

You may do two things to control the interval width. Remember, the interval width is composed of two pieces—Z or t and the standard error.

The interval width is as follows:

$\pm Z_\alpha \sigma_{\overline{X}}$ if you know population values or $\pm t_\alpha S_{\overline{X}}$ if you know the sample values.

What two things might I do?

- Increase the sample size (as n increases, the standard error decreases, thus narrowing the interval width).
- Select a smaller or larger alpha value [as alpha decreases from 10% (1.65) to 1% (2.58), the interval increases, thus broadening the interval width].

Sample Size

As a quality control engineer or marketing research manager, proper sample size might be very important to you. You do not want to take too large a sample, especially if destructive sampling must be used and the cost of your product is quite expensive. Examples of destructive sampling are testing ammunition or wine tasting.

The formula is

$$n = \frac{(Z)^2 (\sigma)^2}{(e)^2}, \text{ where "e" is the sampling error } (\overline{X} - \mu).$$

Remember, the tolerable error allowable in most manufacturing operations is one-half of the interval range. In manufacturing operations, the interval might be three centimeters as you drill a hole into which you are going to fit a round part. The tolerance could not be three centimeters around the circumference, because this would make the interval six centimeters rather than the three centimeters as specified. The tolerable error is one-half of the interval or 1.5 centimeters, which leaves the interval at three centimeters. In this instance, however, $e = 3$ centimeters.

Often in real business settings, these three values (Z, standard deviation, and tolerable error) are not easily determined. The researcher may have to estimate them.

For example, the Z-value most often used is the one associated with the 95% level. This value would then be 1.96.

The standard deviation is often unknown, but can be estimated by using the range divided by six. The range is the difference between the high and the low, not the difference in the LCL and the UCL. The six is developed by using plus and minus three standard deviations on either side of the mean. This would, of course, assume a normal distribution and would encompass 99.7% of the area under the curve.

You might have to make an educated determination of the error you would find acceptable. Acceptable error is generally what a researcher can tolerate.

Once you have determined the value of "n", you would usually round the value up to the next integer, because it is always better to make the sample slightly too large rather than too small.

For example, let's assume I want a 95% confidence interval ($Z = 1.96$) and I know the standard deviation is 3 cm with sampling error of 0.5 cm. What sample size must I take to ensure these values are maintained?

$$n = \frac{(1.96)^2(3)^2}{(0.5)^2} = \frac{(3.8416)(9)}{0.25} = \frac{34.5744}{0.25} = 138.2976 = 139$$

My sample size would be 139 to hold a 5% alpha with sampling error of 0.5 cm and a standard deviation of 3 cm.

Four Properties of a Good Estimator

You will probably never be faced with these issues, but I toss them in to fill space. Don't get me wrong; these are important, but often not something you will ever see again unless your job requires this knowledge. Read about them if you want to. Some Professor somewhere may test you on these, but the only question I might ask is a multiple choice or true/false question on them, such as "The four properties of good estimators are unbiased, efficient, consistent, and sufficient". True or False?

Anytime you have an estimate, it will be composed of two parts—**the process** and **the result.** The *estimator is the process.* The *estimate is the results.* Estimators must be good in order to have acceptable and statistically accurate results. There are four properties of a good estimator (process).

In summary they are as follows:

The estimator must be **unbiased.** This tells me the mean of the sampling distribution of sample means must equal the population mean.

The estimator must be **efficient.** Given the first statement is true, then the estimator must have the smallest possible variance or standard error.

The estimator must be **consistent.** As "n" increases, the value of the statistic must approach the parameter. If you are using the mean as the parameter, then the mean of the sample must approach the mean of the population.

The estimator must be **sufficient.** No other estimator can provide more information about the parameter.

Okay, with that over, let's move on with one final subject—proportions. I have mentioned proportions one other time but have never developed the ideas associated with them. Now I have to take a paragraph or two to develop the idea of proportions.

Proportions (Same Material as in Chapter 6)

Proportions are associated with business decisions that have binary results. As such, you will be faced with developing percentages or ratios. These are referred to as proportions.

Just as there is a sample mean which estimates the population mean, there is a sample proportion which estimates the population proportion. The concept of proportions is exactly the same as the concept associated with means.

As you might imagine, the formulas are going to be different but not impossible to understand and solve. The confidence coefficients for proportions are the same as for Z and t-values, so those tables are appropriate to use. The confidence interval formula is as follows:

$$CI = p \pm Z_\alpha S_p \text{ where } S_p = \sqrt{\frac{p(1-p)}{n}}$$

This formula is the sample proportion—p is an estimate of π, the population proportion.

Let's look at an example. Suppose you have an auditor who wants to determine the frequency of errors in a company's invoicing. Assume that a sample of 100 invoices is selected at random. The auditor want to maintain a 95% confidence interval of the proportion of errors contained in the invoicing process. The sample yields invoices with 10 errors. What is the maximum and minimum invoice error this auditor might expect using a 5% alpha error?

Solution:

$$S_p = \sqrt{\frac{p(1-p)}{n}} = \sqrt{\frac{(0.10)(0.90)}{100}} = \sqrt{\frac{0.09}{100}} = \sqrt{0.0009} = 0.03$$

The confidence Interval is as follows:

$$0.10 \pm (1.96)(0.03) = 0.10 \pm 0.0588 = 0.0412 \le p \le 0.1588$$

Interpretation: My conclusion is I am 95% confident the true, unknown population proportion of invoices with errors will be between 4.12% and 15.88%. Management must now decide if this error range is acceptable. Proportions are important, so don't just gloss over them.

**You know
You are
a Texan
If:**

- You owe more money on your tractor than on your car.

- Hot water comes out of both taps.

Tear-Out Sheet

Table 7.7   *T*-Table.

Two-Tailed Test Alpha/C.L.	0.20/0.80	0.10/0.90	0.05/0.95	0.02/0.98	0.01/0.99
One-Tailed Test Alpha/C.L.	0.10/0.90	0.05/0.95	0.025/0.975	0.01/0.99	0.005/0.995
Degrees of Freedom					
1	3.077684	6.313752	12.70620	31.82052	63.65674
2	1.885618	2.919986	4.30265	6.96456	9.92484
3	1.637744	2.353363	3.18245	4.54070	5.84091
4	1.533206	2.131847	2.77645	3.74695	4.60409
5	1.475884	2.015048	2.57058	3.36493	4.03214
6	1.439756	1.943180	2.44691	3.14267	3.70743
7	1.414924	1.894579	2.36462	2.99795	3.49948
8	1.396815	1.859548	2.30600	2.89646	3.35539
9	1.383029	1.833113	2.26216	2.82144	3.24984
10	1.372184	1.812461	2.22814	2.76377	3.16927
11	1.363430	1.795885	2.20099	2.71808	3.10581
12	1.356217	1.782288	2.17881	2.68100	3.05454
13	1.350171	1.770933	2.16037	2.65031	3.01228
14	1.345030	1.761310	2.14479	2.62449	2.97684
15	1.340606	1.753050	2.13145	2.60248	2.94671
16	1.336757	1.745884	2.11991	2.58349	2.92078
17	1.333379	1.739607	2.10982	2.56693	2.89823
18	1.330391	1.734064	2.10092	2.55238	2.87844
19	1.327728	1.729133	2.09302	2.53948	2.86093
20	1.325341	1.724718	2.08596	2.52798	2.84534

Second Row is for One-Tailed HT

Top Row is for CI & Two-Tailed HT

(*Continued*)

Table 7.7   *T-Table (Continued).*

Two-Tailed Test Alpha/C.L.	0.20/0.80	0.10/0.90	0.05/0.95	0.02/0.98	0.01/0.99
One-Tailed Test Alpha/C.L.	0.10/0.90	0.05/0.95	0.025/0.975	0.01/0.99	0.005/0.995
Degrees of Freedom					
21	1.323188	1.720743	2.07961	2.51765	2.83136
22	1.321237	1.717144	2.07387	2.50832	2.81876
23	1.319460	1.713872	2.06866	2.49987	2.80734
24	1.317836	1.710882	**2.06390**	2.49216	2.79694
25	1.316345	1.708141	2.05954	2.48511	2.78744
26	1.314972	1.705618	2.05553	2.47863	2.77871
27	1.313703	1.703288	2.05183	2.47266	2.77068
28	1.312527	1.701131	2.04841	2.46714	2.76326
29	1.311434	1.699127	2.04523	2.46202	2.75639
30	1.310415	1.697261	2.04227	2.45726	2.75000
Infinity	1.281552	1.644854	1.95996	2.32635	2.57583

The t-table is driven by degrees of freedom ($n - 1$). Knowing the sample size, you will subtract one from n. This will give you degrees of freedom (free choices). You will then decide if you are using a two-tailed test or a one-tailed test. For now, I am using two-tailed rejection regions, since I am addressing only confidence intervals. Confidence intervals are always two-tailed tests. You will use the references in the top row and trace those to the intersecting cell for the proper degrees of freedom. For example, assuming $n = 25$, the degrees of freedom would be 24. At the alpha level of 0.05, I would trace the top row alpha level of 0.05 to the intersecting point of $d.f. = 24$. The value I find is 2.06390 as bolded in Table 7.7.

You can also use the Excel function to calculate each value for t. Open Excel. Double click on f(x) in the tool bar. Find the function TINV which returns the inverse of the t-distribution. You have two questions to answer—the probability desired and the degrees of freedom. In the above example, you would type in 0.05 as the probability and 24 as the degrees of freedom. The result will be 2.06390 from Excel which is the same as the table value.

Note one interesting fact (interesting to some of you, but to others a bore). See the last row? If reads "infinity." At infinity (wherever that is), the values in the Z-table (normal table) and the values in the t-table become the same. Notice for alpha 0.05, the value from the Z-table is 1.96 and from the t-table it is 1.95996 or rounded 1.96. Isn't that amazing?

Tear-Out Sheet Chapter 7

Student Name:_____

Day and Time of Class:_____

The following problems should be solved to aid you in understanding confidence intervals.

1. As the marketing director for TXU Electric, you are concerned about the change in average household consumption of electricity each month. You take a sample of 169 houses and find the mean usage to be 1,834 KWH per month. Previously you have determined that the *standard deviation of all consumption* (σ) has been 260 KWH. You decide to run some statistical tests using an alpha level of 0.10. You have reason to believe the household consumption is normally distributed.

    a. Calculate the standard error. Remember, the standard error is not the same as the sampling error.

    b. Calculate the 90% confidence interval.

    c. What can we say about the size of the sampling error with 90% confidence?

    d. Explain the meaning of the 90% confidence interval.

2. You are the proprietor of a New York city boutique. You want to know the average age of your customers. You take a *random sample of 25* customers, which yields an average age of 32 with a standard deviation of 8. You have good reason to believe the distribution is normally distributed.

    a. Determine a 95% confidence interval for the age of your customers.

    b. Explain the meaning of the interval.

3. In order to determine the life expectancy of the picture tubes of a particular brand of portable television, *a sample of six tubes* was selected randomly from a normal distribution. You want to determine a 90% confidence interval, but you do not have a population, sample variance, or standard deviation, which requires you to calculate a sample value. The results of the sample are shown in the following table.

    a. What is the first step in calculating a sample standard deviation?

Picture Tube	Life of the Picture Tube (X) (in thousands of hours)	$\overline{X}$	$X - \overline{X}$	$(X - \overline{X})^2$
1	8.2			
2	7.5			
3	9.5			
4	6.5			
5	8.5			
6	7.8			
Total	48.0			

    b. Calculate a 90% confidence interval for the life expectancy of all picture tubes for this brand of portable television.

    c. Explain the meaning of the interval.

4. A *random sample of 64 children* with working mothers showed the children were absent from school an average of 5.3 days per term with a standard deviation of 1.8 days.

    a. Provide a 96% confidence interval for the average number of days absent per term for all of the children.

    b. Explain the meaning of the confidence interval.

5. The monthly starting salaries of students who receive an MBA degree have a standard deviation of $70. *What size sample* should be selected so that there is 0.90 confidence of estimating the mean monthly income within a *sampling error* of $15 or less? Here again, remember, there is a difference between sampling error and standard error. Here I am interested in the sampling error and not the standard error.

6. The editor of a New York magazine wants to determine the proportion of magazines that have some sort of nonconforming attribute such as excessive rub off, improper page setup, missing pages, duplicate pages, typographical errors, etc. The editor commissions a 200-magazine study and finds 35 contain some type of nonconformance. Using a 90% confidence interval, estimate the true, unknown population proportion.

8

Applying Inferential Statistics —Hypothesis Testing One Population

Attorney:	Is your appearance here this morning pursuant to a deposition notice which I sent to your attorney?
Witness:	No, this is how I dress when I go to work.

Introduction: What Is Hypothesis Testing?

Hypothesis testing—sounds rather complicated, right? Yes and no is the correct answer. The concept is rather simple, but the difficulty lies in deciding how to set up your test process. You must learn about some things referred to as the null and alternate hypotheses. If you set those up incorrectly, you blow the entire problem. Sometimes logic does not seem to work.

If not logic, what then? I will explore a couple of ideas which may be helpful in setting up the alternate and null hypotheses.

First, what do I mean by **hypothesis test**?

Let's look at an example. I suspect some of you have a can of Coke or Pepsi or other soft drink in front of you now. The rest of you have purchased a can of Coke or Pepsi in the last few days.

Look at the label on the can. I will wait. Of course, without a soft drink, use your imagination.

How many net ounces of liquid does the can hold?

So you will not get too stressed out, the answer is probably 12 ounces.

My question to you: How did you know when you bought it that there were 12 ounces in the can?

You pause and think. I never thought about it before, you comment.

None of us do. You would not know unless you opened the can when you got it, poured the drink into a measuring device, and measured it. My bet is you did not measure it, but assumed the labeling was accurate.

What if the liquid measured 11.93 ounces or what if the liquid measured 12.15 ounces, what would you do?

Probably nothing, but Coke or Pepsi is asserting through their label, you are getting 12 ounces in the can.

What do you think the probability is of getting exactly 12 ounces in every can? It is pretty small, right? Why?

Well, first of all, no machine can fill the can to exactly 12 ounces each and every time. The machinery is not that accurate.

What do you think Coke or Pepsi is telling you?

They are telling you that they are filling each can to 12 ounces, plus a little bit or minus a little bit.

So, if this is not the true content of each and every can (12 ounces) that comes off the production line, what is the true weight?

The true weight is unknown and, in reality, is of no real interest to me.

Why so, you question? Can't I simply measure the liquid in each can of Coke and average it?

Yes, you could, I reply, but to get an accurate measurement you would have to destroy every can by opening it, pouring the contents into a measuring device, and recording and averaging it. This would make no practical sense because you would be destroying the entire production. The company's marketing department and the stockholders would not be very happy with you, but at least you would know the true mean of the entire production of Coke or Pepsi.

The true mean is unknown. The true mean changes each and every time another can of Coke or Pepsi is filled.

So what does the 12 ounces printed on the side of the Coke can suggest, you ask?

Good question, I remark.

The 12 ounces is the **hypothesized mean** of the population.

Webster's Ninth New Collegiate Dictionary defines a hypothesis as "an unproved theory that is accepted temporarily to explain certain facts." The theory is the liquid in the can measures 12 ounces. According to Webster, this is a tentative statement and subject to verification. Hypothesis testing is one method useful in inferential statistics when you are making assertions about the population mean using a sample mean or the population proportion using a sample proportion.

All companies who produce a product which claims to have a certain net weight or content level find hypothesis testing useful. This testing process aids them in deciding if they are going to add more to the package or reduce the contents in the package.

Confidence Intervals as Contrasted to Hypothesis Testing

Let's contrast confidence intervals and hypothesis testing. Both are derived from the Z-process formula which is solved for different terms. The following two graphs will help you make the proper distinction between the two processes (Figures 8.1 and 8.2).

Side Note

This chapter is reasonably complex and long, so I recommend you break your reading into a couple of sessions. Understanding this material will take you several hours of concentrated reading and doodling (trying to replicate some of the numbers).

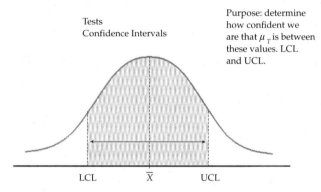

Figure 8.1   Confidence intervals.

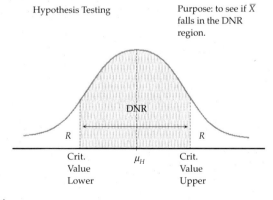

Figure 8.2   Hypothesis testing.

Figure 8.1 is a two-tailed confidence interval. The calculation of the UCL and LCL always begins with $\overline{X}$ and places around it an interval using $\pm Z_\alpha \sigma_{\overline{X}}$ (for a small sample Z-values would be replaced with t-values). The method of making these calculations is the subject of Chapter 7, so I will not dwell on the calculations here.

For confidence intervals, the interpretation is to assert with some statistical degree of confidence that the true, unknown population mean is between the LCL and UCL. In Chapter 7, I set three generally used confidence limits and their associated alpha error values. They are the 99%, 95%, and 90% CL with alpha values of 1%, 5%, and 10% respectively.

Figure 8.2 depicts the concept of hypothesis testing. I begin with μ_H in the middle and develop an interval around μ_H using $\pm Z_{\alpha/2} \sigma_{\overline{X}}$. In hypothesis testing, I want to know if my sample mean is between the two resultant values referred to as critical values (CV—one is a lower critical value and the other is an upper critical value). These two values are similar to the confidence interval values of the LCL and UCL.

There are three forms of hypothesis testing. Form I is a left-tailed rejection region. Form II is a right-tailed rejection region. Form III is a two-tailed rejection region. Confidence intervals are similar to hypothesis testing form III. I will share more on the other two forms shortly.

The main distinction between confidence intervals and hypothesis testing is the beginning point. With confidence intervals, I begin my calculations with $\overline{X}$ and with hypothesis testing I begin my calculations with μ_H. If you remember this one distinction, you will be well served as you make the actual calculations. Turn back to Figure 8.1 and Figure 8.2 so see the difference graphically.

But wait a minute, you say! You have told me the true mean will never be known, so what is this μ and how will I determine it, if it is truly unknown? This seems like a contradiction—almost like circular reasoning with no real answer.

Excellent observation, I remark. There is a true, unknown population mean (μ_T) and a hypothesized population mean (μ_H). I begin with the hypothesized mean and not the true mean, since I do not know or ever will know the true mean of the population.

To show the similarity, let's contrast the formulas for both confidence intervals and hypothesis testing.

Confidence Interval

$\overline{X} \pm Z_\alpha \sigma_{\overline{X}}$ yields an LCL and UCL for confidence intervals.

Hypothesis Testing (Form III)

$\mu_H \pm Z_{\alpha/2} \sigma_{\overline{X}}$ yields a lower critical value and an upper critical value.

Remember, μ_T will refer to the true, unknown population mean and μ_H will refer to the hypothesized mean of the population.

Example of Hypothesis Testing

It is often desirable to test certain assumptions regarding one's product or business. I might want to know if my assembly of radios is being done within specified limits. I can infer something about the population (parameter—all of my production) from a sample (statistic—

representative portion). Here I might be interested in how many defects I am producing given a desired defective rate of no more than 1%.

You might ask: Why don't I just obtain my information from the entire population rather than use a sampling? From earlier discussions, you may recall it is usually too costly or too time consuming to work with the entire population.

Business decisions are not made in a vacuum or under perfect conditions. There is always uncertainty. Learning how to reduce the uncertainty is an important business tool. I must minimize my risk of making a bad or uninformed decision, since I will not be able to work with the entire population. If I can properly draw a sample at random, I can then use a sample to accurately represent the entire population. This is inferential statistics at work.

The population is all of the observations of interest to me as the researcher; therefore, I may define the population in any way I wish. The sample must, however, be taken from the population of interest and not from a secondary population.

Suppose I have been collecting the IQs of students in a graduate school over a period of 10 years. My data suggest that the population's mean IQ is 115.

I can say that the hypothesized mean of the population is 115. $\mu_H = 115$.

Okay, one more time, why isn't this the true mean (μ_T), you ask?

Every time another student enrolls in the school, the average IQ changes, so (μ_T) is an elusive and moving target.

Okay, I understand (I think), you admit. I really don't know the real mean of the population (μ_T) because it constantly changes. I think I have the idea. The true, unknown population mean constantly changes.

So what am I supposed to do with this information, you silently wonder?

To take you to the next step and show you how to use hypothesis testing, I must verify that the hypothesized mean of the past few years (115) is still the mean of the population. To do this, I next take a sample of this year's class. The sample of 49 students is drawn *at random* with the following results:

$$\overline{X}_1 = 116 \text{ , which is the sample mean of this year's class.}$$

I have to decide if the hypothesized mean of 115 and the sample mean of 116 are statistically the same. Does the 116 sample mean represent the 115 population mean? Can the difference between the two (116 represents 115) be explained by sampling error alone or is the difference too great to be explained by sampling error alone? Sampling error is, by definition, the difference between μ_T and $\overline{X}$. Since I do not know μ_T I use μ_H as an estimate of μ_T. It is quite clear that the mathematical means are not equal, but I am interested in something other than mathematical means. Can I infer that 116 is representative of the hypothesized population mean of 115?

Okay, you think, this Professor has been sniffing too many tubes of glue, but you politely (since your mom would insist) wait for him to finish.

Do the two values come from the same population? Does the error between the 115 and 116 occur because of sampling error alone?

Said another way, is there a statistically significant difference between the 115 and the 116?

From observation, I would logically think they are close enough to statistically be the same.

Using inferential statistics, I can infer that 116 (the sample mean) is a good representative of the population mean (115), *but I cannot make this determination without first subjecting the two values to a consistent statistical procedure to evaluate my observation.*

Why, you ask? I know the difference between the population mean and the sample mean is, by definition, sampling error. This sampling error of one IQ point ($116 - 115 = 1$) seems really insignificant.

From observation, you might be correct, but let's take another example. What would your conclusion be if your sample mean had been 150? You would have a bit more difficulty in saying the two values appear to come from the same population. Does 150 statistically represent 115 such that the difference is explained by sampling error? Now it is not so obvious.

I need a procedure which is consistently applied to arrive at decisions. Fortunately, there is one available to me. This is where hypothesis testing becomes the procedure of choice.

An Overview of the Concept

First, I establish two hypotheses. One is called the null hypothesis (H_o) and the other is called the alternative hypothesis (H_a). Two things must be true for me to use this concept. I must assume that the distribution is normal or I must rely on the central limit theorem (sample size is 30 or greater) to insure that the distribution is normal. If either is true, then the *sampling distribution of sample means* is normally distributed. This allows me to use the Z-process (ignoring the t-process for now), and is one of the important tests for hypothesis testing. Without normality, hypothesis testing cannot be correctly used. As you can tell (well, maybe you can tell), these are important assumptions.

I am not going to make calculations at this point. I am going to make assumptions to illustrate the points I want to make. Later in this chapter, I will take you through the calculations using a specific example. The two hypotheses are set up as follows:

$$H_o: \quad \mu_H = 115.$$

This is the **null hypothesis.** I *always*, repeat, *always* test the null hypothesis (H_o). I *never*, repeat, *never* test the alternate hypothesis.

$$H_a: \quad \mu_H \neq 115.$$

This is the **alternate hypothesis.** It is always the opposite of the null. For simplicity often H_a (the alternate hypothesis) is set up first, but you never test H_a. Your test is always of H_o. What you do to the null will dictate what you do to the alternate hypothesis. If you DNR (do not reject) the null, you will reject the alternate. If you reject the null, you will accept the alternate. The conclusion must be applied in this sequence: H_o is DNR or rejected, then, and only then, will H_a be rejected or accepted.

I know this is confusing at this point, so just keep reading. I will pull this together (for most of you) in later paragraphs. Don't try to over read at this point. I will have to repeat this stuff over and over again, so be patient.

The Caveat

What I am trying to say is this, if the sample mean appears to come from the same population as the hypothesized mean, does this absolutely prove (big word) H_o is true?

No, it does not, as I answer my own question.

I can never totally accept the null hypothesis nor prove it to be absolutely true. The best I can do is to "do not reject" (DNR) the null hypothesis. Because DNR carries a double negative, it is often hard to comprehend, so thinking "accept the null" is okay. However, never write the conclusion as "accept" but always write the conclusion as DNR. The chance of making an alpha error keeps me from absolutely accepting the null. (The alpha error is rejecting a true hypothesis.)

Notice Figure 8.3 below, which is a picture of the concept. I have inserted a couple of assumed values. I will show you how to calculate lower critical values and upper critical values shortly. The values I show are arbitrarily chosen. They are 111.04 for the lower critical value and 118.96 for the upper critical value.

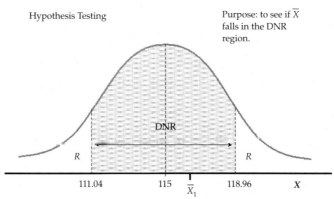

Figure 8.3 Example of IQ.

If the sample value of 116 is between the upper and lower critical values, I would DNR (do not reject) the null hypothesis.

Notice $\overline{X}_1$ (116) is between the two critical values of 111.04 and 118.96. Let's restate our null and alternate hypotheses at this point as a reminder.

$$H_o: \quad \mu_H = 115.$$

$$H_a: \quad \mu_H \neq 115.$$

Since $\overline{X}_1$ (116) falls between the upper and lower critical values, I will DNR the null hypothesis. The null hypothesis reads $\mu_H = 115$ and I DNR that statement (think accept that statement). I am asserting that the difference between 116 and 115 can be explained by sampling error alone.

Let's take a look at another possibility. Assume my sample mean is $\overline{X}_2$ (150). It is greater than the upper critical value of 118.96, so I *reject the null*. The difference between 150 and 115 CANNOT be explained by sampling error. In this instance the *true, unknown population mean* seems to have shifted. The true, unknown population mean appears to be higher than the hypothesized mean of 115. I do not know what it is, but the shift seems to be to the right (since 150 exceeds 115 and is statistically significant).

Critical values can logically be thought of as barriers or limits or thresholds. Any sample mean which occurs between the lower critical value (threshold) and the upper critical value (threshold) is okay. This means the difference between the sample mean and the hypothesized mean can be explained by sampling error. Anytime you take a sample, you have a high probability of error. This error is okay if the difference between the sample mean and the hypothesized mean is not significantly different. A sample mean falling outside (less than or more than) the critical value(s) is NOT explained by sampling error and is not okay.

So, you ask, how do I calculate the upper and lower levels of significance (upper and lower critical values)?

Wow, I am impressed. You just used a term (levels of significance) that you have never heard before and you used it correctly. You must be reading ahead.

In hypothesis testing, the term **levels of significance** carries the same idea as *confidence coefficients* (CC or CL) in confidence interval testing. In fact, confidence coefficients (CC) and levels of significance (LS) use the same three testing levels and have a common link—the alpha error. They are recapped as follows:

Table 8.1 Contrast *HT* and *CI* with common alpha error.

Hypothesis Testing Levels of Significance	Alpha Error	Confidence Intervals Confidence Coefficients
0.99	0.01	0.99
0.95	0.05	0.95
0.90	0.10	0.90

The one common feature between the two is the alpha error. In stating conclusions, this fact will be important, so remember it.

Type I and Type II Errors (Side Bar as a Judge Would Say)

Remember, anytime I test something, I can make an error. I have introduced you to one which is a **Type I error** or the alpha error (α). The alpha error is the probability of rejecting a null hypothesis when it is really true. I think there are problems and there are none.

There is a second error which is a **Type II** or beta error (β). This is the probability of accepting a null hypothesis when it is really false. I think things are okay and they are not.

As the probability of a Type I error increases, the probability of a Type II error decreases. The reverse is also true, as the probability of a Type I error decreases, the probability of a Type II error increases.

$$P(\text{Type I}) + P(\text{Type II}) = 1.0$$

Examples of Type I

Rejecting the null hypothesis when it does not need to be rejected, since it is true (rejecting a true hypothesis).

- Stopping a production line to recalibrate a piece of equipment when the operation is *within* tolerable limits.

Examples of Type II

Not rejecting the null hypothesis when it needs to be rejected, since it is false (accepting a false hypothesis).

- Not stopping a production line to recalibrate a piece of equipment when the operation is *outside of* tolerable limits.

While I will not ignore Type II error completely, the emphasis on Type I for manufacturing companies is more important, since the potential damage from making a Type I error is greater than a Type II error. Table 8.2 is a recap of both types of error and how they are defined.

Table 8.2 Alpha and beta errors.

		Actual Situation in the Population	
		H_o is True	H_o is False
Action Taken	Accept H_o (DNR)	**Correct Decision**	Type II Beta Error (β)
	Reject H_o	Type I Alpha Error (α)	**Correct Decision**

Notice in Table 8.2, I match the *action I am taking* (left-hand side of the table) with the *actual or real situation in the population* (top of the table). If I accept the null hypothesis and the null hypothesis is true, I have made a correct decision. In a similar manner, if I reject a false hypothesis, I have likewise made a correct decision. The intersection of those two decisions is shown in bold print.

If, however, I reject a hypothesis which is really true, I have committed a Type I, alpha error. What is happening in the real world is true (okay), but because of my sampling process I say it is not true. If I take something that is true and say it is not true, I have committed an alpha error. I do have some control over the alpha error, because I select it from among my choices (alpha error of 0.01, 0.05, and 0.10—the three most commonly chosen).

For example, let's assume I have a can of coffee labeled net weight of 3.0 pounds. Let's assume that I am filling the cans of coffee to three pounds plus or minus an acceptable sampling error. In other words, my filling process is okay and there is no need to do anything but to keep filling coffee cans. I take a sample and it leads me to believe I need to put more coffee in the cans. I reject a true hypothesis where everything is okay (true). When I reject an okay hypothesis (true hypothesis), I take action like any good manager would. However, I act on faulty information. I shut down my production line and add more coffee to the cans. I take action I do not need to take. This error is costly because of the work stoppage and the use of additional product when no more need be placed in the coffee can.

On the other hand, if I accept a hypothesis which is really false, I have committed a Type II, beta error. The chances of this happening are very high. The closer the true, unknown mean of the population (μ_T) and the hypothesized mean (μ_H), are to each other, the larger the beta error. For example, if the true, unknown mean of the population is 2.99 lbs, I stand a very large chance of making a beta error, since I have difficulty in making a distinction between 2.99 and 3.0. This error is not as serious as the alpha error for manufacturing, but can be the most serious error in medical research, when a dosage of medicine must be exact. The beta error is calculated. For each *true mean **possibility**,* (2.99, 2.98, 2.97, etc.) there will be a different beta error. As the true mean approaches the hypothesized mean, the beta error will approach 1.0. The closer μ_T is to μ_H, the higher the beta error.

All of the information I just shared with you is important, but you probably need to concentrate on the following *two statements*. The alpha error is the most important concept you should know. Any business decision is made under risk. There is always the risk of making a bad decision or drawing bad conclusions. You can have things going well in a manufacturing or service business, yet from a sample you determine there are problems. Based on the sample, you decide to take corrective action, but in reality you should not, because they are phantom issues. This may cause you to shut down your operation and make adjustments when none are needed. This is the alpha error—*the probability of rejecting a true hypothesis (Statement 1).* It is the probability of taking unneeded corrective action when you do not need to take the action.

In most business situations, you will not have to be too concerned about the beta error, just know it exists. It is the *probability of accepting a false hypothesis (Statement 2),* just the opposite of an alpha error. As the true, unknown population mean approaches the hypothesized mean, the beta error increases.

Okay, you say, I have all of this information and need to try to consolidate my thinking. Can you give me any hints on how to set up and work through a hypothesis testing problem?

As a straight "man" (generic term), you are amazing. You have led me into the next stage of my discussion. Hypothesis testing can be thought of as a five-step process.

Five Steps for Working Hypothesis Testing Problems

The process for solving null hypothesis problems is best approached using a five-step process. You will most likely abandon the formality of this five-step process at some point after you become comfortable with the concept. By always drawing a picture of the normal distribution and identifying the areas of interest to you, the five steps will be less useful. For now, however, you need to follow these steps.

Step One: Formulate the Null and Alternate Hypotheses. (H_o and H_a)

Step Two: Calculate the Critical Value(s) above or below which we will reject the null hypothesis.

Step Three: Determine the Decision Rule. This step will simply identify the rejection and the DNR regions. For example in a two-tailed test, if the sample value is to the left or to the right of the critical value(s), you will reject the null hypothesis. Rejecting the null hypothesis leads to accepting the alternate hypothesis.

Step Four: Compare the *Critical Value* to the *Sample Value* (CV to $\overline{X}$). This step and this step alone is the one you use in making a decision. The decision will be to DNR the null or reject the null. There are only two possible decisions. REPEAT: This step allows you to *make the decision by comparing the CV to $\overline{X}$*. The decision is NEVER made by comparing $\overline{X}$ to μ_H. Understanding what I have just said is crucial, so read it again until you have the concept mastered. Refer back to this step when working any hypothesis testing problem.

Step Five: State Your Conclusion. All decisions will contain five elements.

- The alpha error must be stated.
- A statement must be made that you *DNR or reject* the null hypothesis.
- A statement must be made that there *is or is not* a statistically significant difference between the hypothesized mean and the sample mean.
- A statement must be made that the difference between the sample mean and the population mean *can or cannot* be explained by random sampling error.
- A statement must be made about *adjusting* your production process *or not adjusting* your production process, if you are filling a coffee can, for example. This statement is problem specific depending on what is being asserted or claimed by the researcher. The conclusions must be stated in terms of a result supporting or not supporting a problem-specific assertion.

Whether or not you have realized it, so far I have been discussing Form III hypothesis testing, which is a two-tailed rejection region. In the Form III, the alpha error is divided in two with one-half of alpha placed in the right tail and one-half of alpha placed in the left tail. There are, however, two other forms. Let's summarize all three types of hypothesis testing.

Three Forms of Hypothesis Testing (Forms I, II and III)

To simplify things for you, there are only three useful forms for a hypothesis test. There is a left-tail rejection region test (Form I), where *all* of the rejection region is placed in the left tail. There is a right-tail rejection region test (Form II), where *all* of the rejection region is placed in the right tail. And there is a two-tailed rejection region test (Form III), where the rejection region is *divided into two tails*. Table 8.3 summarizes this concept.

Table 8.3 Summary of three forms of hypothesis testing (Using the Value Approach).

Steps	Form I Left-Tail Rejection Region	Form II Right-Tail Rejection Region	Form III Both Tails Rejection Regions
1. Set up H_o: Set up H_a:	$\mu_H \geq$ *a value* $\mu_H <$ *a value*	$\mu_H \leq$ *a value* $\mu_H >$ *a value*	$\mu_H =$ *a value* $\mu_H \neq$ *a value*
2. Calculate the critical value(s) (Value Approach)	$\mu_H - Z\alpha \sigma_{\overline{X}}$ one critical value	$\mu_H + Z\alpha \sigma_{\overline{X}}$ one critical value	$\mu_H \pm Z\alpha/2 \sigma_{\overline{X}}$ two critical
3. Decision Rule	DNR H_o if $\overline{X} \geq$ CV *Reject* H_o if $\overline{X} <$ CV	DNR H_o if $\overline{X} \leq$ CV *Reject* H_o if $\overline{X} >$ CV	DNR H_o if LCV $\leq \overline{X} \leq$ UCV *Reject*_ H_o if $\overline{X} <$ LCV or $\overline{X} >$ LCV
4. Compare the Critical Value to the Sample Value	One-Tail *Reject* Region in the Left Tail	One-Tail *Reject* Region in the Right Tail	Two-Tailed *Reject* Region in Both the Left and Right Tails

5. **State the Conclusion:** All three forms have the same general statements. Any conclusion reached must state the *alpha error* or *the level of significance*.

The decision is not the conclusion. The decision always compares the *sample mean* and the *critical value*. $\overline{X}$ compared to CV.

The conclusion always compares the *sample mean* and the *hypothesized mean*. $\overline{X}$ compared to μ_H

If you DNR *the null hypothesis*, you are concluding there is no statistically significant difference between the *sample value* and the *hypothesized value*. You are concluding that any error is due to sampling error alone.

If you *reject the null hypothesis*, then you are concluding there is too great a difference between the *null hypothesis* and the *sample mean* to be explained by sampling error alone.

Finally, the conclusion should be very specific about the action you should take—adjust the equipment, put more soda in the can, support a claim that sales average $2,000 per day, do not support the claim that extortion costs have increased, take soap product out of the container, etc. This is a **problem-specific conclusion.**

There are three solutions approaches – Value, Z-test and *p*-value. I will cover all three. So far I have concentrated on the Value Approach. No matter which you use, the conclusions must be the same. Don't get these three solution approaches confused with the three forms. They are different.

The Statement of Conclusion

Using a soft drink example, assume your lower critical value is 11.5 ounces. Your can of soda is labeled 12.0 ounces. You take a sample of 49 and find the mean of the sample is 11.4 ounces. This would lead you to reject the null hypothesis. I know this, because the 11.4 < 11.5. My critical value is 11.5 ounces, which acts as my lower threshold or barrier for my sample mean. If my sample mean is lower than the critical value mean, I have a problem. Further assume an alpha of 0.05 and the two hypotheses are set up as follows.

$$H_o: \quad \mu_H \geq 12.0 \text{ (rejecting)}$$

$$H_a: \quad \mu_H < 12.0 \text{ (accepting)}$$

In my example, I am rejecting the null, I am rejecting that μ_H is greater than or equal to 12.0 ounces, which means I must *automatically* accept the alternate that μ_H is less than 12.0 ounces. This is an inverse relationship. If I reject the null, I automatically accept the alternative, since I have only two possible outcomes.

The conclusion would read as follows:

At the alpha 0.05 level, there is a statistically significant difference between the sample mean (11.4) and the hypothesized mean (12.0) that cannot be explained by sampling error alone (the error is not random). Since I am under filling the cans of soda, I will adjust the fill levels and add more liquid to the cans.

Using the soda can example, which form did my hypothesis test set up take—Form I, Form II, or Form III?

Form I, you respond.

Right you are, Form I is the correct answer. Great job!

Graphically, a normal-distribution picture of my conclusion would look something like Figure 8.4 as follows:

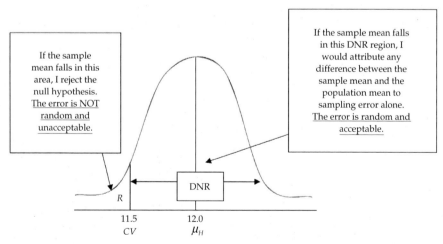

Figure 8.4   A normal-distribution graph of the soda can example.

Since the sample mean of 11.4 falls in the reject region, I make the conclusion stated above and repeated here.

Conclusion Repeated

At the alpha 0.05 level, there is a statistically significant difference between the sample mean (11.4) and the hypothesized mean (12.0) that cannot be explained by sampling error alone (the error is not random). Since I am under filling the cans of soda, I will adjust the fill levels and add more liquid to the cans.

How to Set Up the Null Hypothesis

Your most difficult task in hypothesis testing is setting up the proper hypotheses. If you reason through the set up, you may be correct, but often most students tend to set up the null just the opposite of what it should be.

Ask yourself the following question: "Am I conducting a left-tailed (Form I), right-tailed (Form II), or two-tailed (Form III) test?" The tail refers to the rejection region under the curve. The answer to this question is complicated. Answering this question will allow you to properly set up the null and alternate hypotheses.

I have found it easier to set up the alternate hypothesis before you set up the null hypothesis. This approach seems a bit awkward at first, but the nice thing is it WORKS. I am suggesting that you set up the *alternate hypothesis* (H_a) before you set up the null hypothesis.

I will share with you two different approaches for *setting up the alternate hypothesis*. First, I will show you the three-question approach and second, I will use the relationship between the sample mean and population mean (mean-mean approach) using the Z-test formula. More on the second approach later.

Before I address the three-question approach, I need to share with you a couple of observations about Table 8.3 (Step 2 is specific to the Value Approach). This information is general but is appropriate for use with either the three-question approach or the mean-mean relationship.

Let's first look at the three forms in a visual format (Figures 8.5, 8.6, and 8.7).

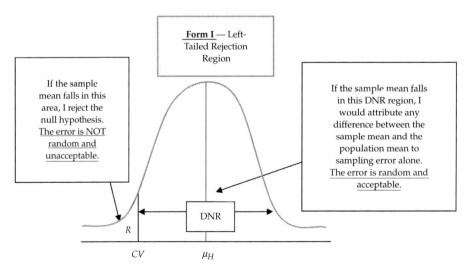

Figure 8.5   Form I Left Tailed Rejection Region

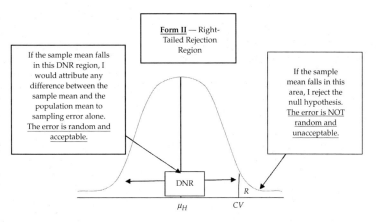

Figure 8.6 Form II Right Tailed Rejection Region

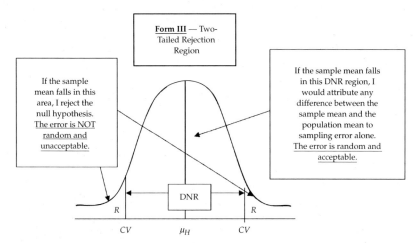

Figure 8.7 Form III Two Tailed Rejection Region

Using Table 8.3 and the three normal distributions shown just above, let's make some general observations. Remember, if I am to the left of the mean the sign is negative. If I am to the right of the mean the sign is positive. Signs are directional indicators only but important nonetheless.

Observation 1

The left-hand rejection region is on the left side of the curve and the *alternate hypothesis* has a *less than sign* pointing *left*. "See Table 8.3, Step 1".

Observation 2

The right-hand rejection region is on the right side of the curve and the *alternate hypothesis* has a *more than sign* pointing *right*. "See Table 8.3, Step 1".

Observation 3

The *equal sign* in both the left and right-tailed tests (Form I and Form II) is *always*, repeat, *always* in the H_o (the null hypothesis). In Form I and Form II, the equal sign is *never* in the H_a (the alternate hypothesis). "See Table 8.3, Step 1".

Observation 4

Form III is always written with H_o being equal to a specific value and H_a being not equal to a specific value. "See Table 8.3, Step 1."

Observation 5

The alpha value, which is the probability of rejecting a true hypothesis (making an error in judgment), is the rejection region in any of the three forms. Specifically, the full alpha value for the left or the right-tail rejection region is in the tail of the curve. For a two-tailed test this is not true. The alpha value is divided in two with one-half in the left tail and one-half in the right tail. For example, with an alpha value of 0.05, the following would be true.

Table 8.4 Value of alpha in one and two-tail rejection regions.

Form	Alpha in Rejection Region	DNR Region
Form I: Left-Tail Rejection Region	0.0500	0.9500
Form II: Right-Tail Rejection Region	0.0500	0.9500
Form III: Two-Tail Rejection Region	0.0250 in each tail	0.9500

The full alpha is in the tail for either a left or right tail rejection region test. One-half alpha is in each tail of the two-tail rejection region.

There is a relationship between the location of the rejection region (the tail) and the ALTERNATE hypothesis. From the above observations, the alternate hypothesis for Form I has a less than sign (<) pointing left. The alternate hypothesis for Form II has a more than sign (>) pointing right. Remember this.

I told you the hardest thing for you would be to learn how to set up the null and alternate hypotheses. I have given you three forms of hypothesis testing (Form I, Form II, and Form III). There are no other forms, so do not get creative and make up your own forms. Some statistics textbooks teach other arrangements, but they only confuse the issue. Stick with these three forms and your understanding will be greatly improved.

One of the approaches to setting up the hypothesis test is the three-question approach. I use the three-question approach to set up the *ALTERNATE hypothesis*, not the null. As a second aid (not discussed until later) approach, I can use the sign (plus or minus) of the Z-value to aid me in setting up the ALTERNATE hypothesis.

Logically, if there are only three forms and they are fixed, and if I can set up the ALTERNATATE hypothesis, I can automatically set up the NULL.

In spite of the fact you are completely numb at this point, let's see if I can demonstrate how the three-question method works. It aids us in setting up the ALTERNATE hypothesis, not the null.

Three Critical Questions That Will Aid in Setting Up the Alternate Hypothesis in Step I of the Process

These three questions will lead you to make a determination of the H_a (alternate hypothesis and rejection region), which in turn leads you to setting up the proper null hypothesis (H_o).

Notice, I have said repeatedly that these three questions aid in setting up H_a and NOT H_o. This is important.

The questions are quite simple.

$$\text{Is:} \quad \mu_H = \text{a specified value?}$$
$$\text{Is:} \quad \mu_H > \text{a specified value?}$$
$$\text{Is:} \quad \mu_H < \text{a specified value?}$$

Example #1

Let's quantify the specified value. Let's say you own a coffee company and have a can of coffee with a net, label weight of 3.0 pounds. The label weight is the hypothesized mean and not the true mean of the population. The three questions would read as follows:

$$\text{Is:} \quad \mu_H = 3.0?$$
$$\text{Is:} \quad \mu_H > 3.0?$$
$$\text{Is:} \quad \mu_H < 3.0?$$

Let's assume you believe it is important the coffee in the can not fall below 3.0 pounds, since you might get sued for false advertising. Your answers to the three questions would be as follows:

Is: $\mu_H = 3.0$? This is *not* the concern. It is okay if the can is filled to 3.0 lbs.

Is: $\mu_H > 3.0$? This is *not* the concern. It is okay if the can is filled greater than 3.0 lbs.

Is: $\mu_H < 3.0$? *This IS the concern.* It is not okay for the can to be filled less than 3.0 lbs.

The third issue is of interest to me. Notice, the less than sign ($<$) points to the left. This is significant. This means the rejection region will be on the left, so the *ALTERNATE* hypothesis would be as follows:

$$H_a: \quad \mu_H < 3.0$$

Knowing the alternate hypothesis (H_a), you can now set up both the null and the alternate hypotheses.

$$\text{If} \quad H_a: \quad \mu_H < 3.0 \text{ then } H_o: \mu \geq 3.0$$

It is always written in the following sequence (Form I):

$$H_o: \quad \mu_H \geq 3.0$$
$$H_a: \quad \mu_H < 3.0$$

There is a direct relationship between the sign in the correct question answer and the alternate hypothesis. If the question sign points left ($<$), the alternate hypothesis sign points left ($<$). This would lead to a negative sign in the formula solution, but more on that later.

If I know the alternate hypothesis points left, the null points to the right BUT the null also contains the equal sign. Setting up the null is a "no brainer," if you know the alternate hypothesis. Review the three forms as shown in Table 8.3, Step 1".

Example #2

If I bottled soft drinks and wanted 12 ounces in the can, I could use the three questions to set up my hypotheses. If the company is an ethical company, they would not want to under fill or overfill the can. Since you are interested in both under filling (left rejection region) and overfilling (right rejection region), the three questions would lead you to a two-tailed test (Form III).

$$H_o: \quad \mu_H = 12 \text{ ounces}$$

$$H_a: \quad \mu_H \neq 12 \text{ ounces}$$

Example #3

You might find that a manager or company may make a claim that sales are less than $5,000 per day. This claim is the basis for the alternate hypothesis—less than is a left-tailed test. The three questions are as follows:

Is: $\mu_H = $5,000? This is not the claim.

Is: $\mu_H > $5,000? This is not the claim.

Is: $\mu_H < $5,000? This is the claim.

In this example, your concern is sales are less than $5,000, not greater than or equal to $5,000, The answer to the question has a less than sign ($<$) which points to the left. The alternate hypothesis would be set up as follows:

$$H_a: \quad \mu_H < $5,000$$

I set up the alternate first; however, the set up of the null is automatic. The null and alternate should be in the following sequence (Form I).

$$H_o: \quad \mu_H \geq \$5{,}000$$
$$H_a: \quad \mu_H < \$5{,}000$$

You comment, I am beginning to see a glimmer of light, but do you always want to be able to explain the difference between the sample mean and the population mean by random, sampling error alone?

Absolutely great question, I respond. Let's look at three examples. The first is filling a coffee can to 3.0 pounds, the second is filling a soft drink can to 12 ounces, and the third is a claim sales are less than $5,000 per day. See Figure 8.8 for the coffee can fill level example:

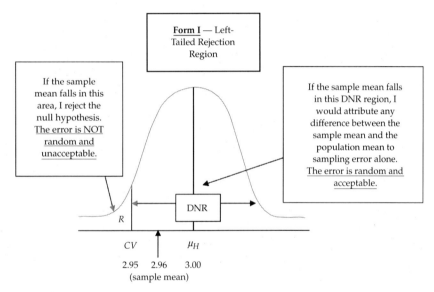

Figure 8.8   Example #1: Coffee can fill level.

Let's assume a sample mean of 2.96 ($\overline{X}$) and alpha of 0.05. The sample mean of 2.96 is in the DNR region. A restatement of the null and alternate hypotheses is as follows:

$$H_o: \quad \mu_H \geq 3.0 \text{ (DNR the null)}$$
$$H_a: \quad \mu_H < 3.0 \text{ (reject the alternate)}$$

Since, in this example, I have assumed the sample mean is 2.96, it falls in the DNR region (2.96 > 2.95). At alpha 0.05, I would conclude that the difference between the sample mean (2.96) and the population mean (3.0) can be explained by random, sampling error alone. There is no statistically significant difference between the sample mean and the population mean. Everything is cool, and I do not have to add more coffee to the cans.

Example #4 Soft Drink Fill Level

In this example, I am a soft drink manufacturer. I want to fill my cans of soda to 12.0 ounces (my hypothesized mean). I choose an alpha of 0.01 and take a sample. The sample yields a mean of 12.04. Assume I have previously calculated my LCV and my UCV as 11.97 and 12.03.

Because the sample mean is greater than the upper critical value (UCV), I will reject my null hypothesis and accept my alternate hypothesis. See Figure 8.9.

$$H_o: \quad \mu_H = 12 \text{ ounces (Reject)}$$
$$H_a: \quad \mu_H \neq 12 \text{ ounces (Accept)}$$

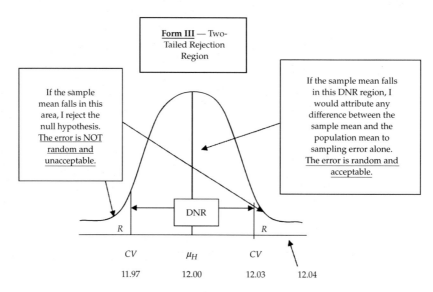

Figure 8.9 Example #2: Soft drink fill level.

My conclusion is as follows: At the alpha 0.01 level, I conclude there is a statistically significant difference between the sample mean ($12.04 = \overline{X}$) and population mean ($12.0 = \mu_H$) that cannot be explained by random, sampling error alone. I am currently overfilling the soda cans and must "turn the spigot" down to have less soda in the cans.

Example #5 Daily Sales

In this example, I am making the claim or assertion that my daily sales are less than $5,000. Assume an alpha level of 0.10. Further assume I take a sample and find the sample mean to be $4,925.46, and I have previously calculated my critical value to be $4,907.51. The null and alternate hypotheses are stated as follows:

$$H_o: \quad \mu_H \geq \$5,000$$
$$H_a: \quad \mu_H < \$5,000 \text{ This is the claim being made.}$$

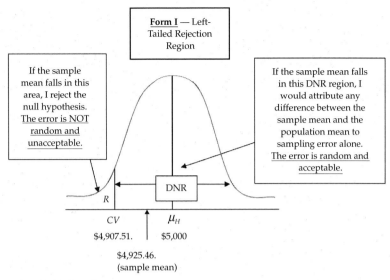

Figure 8.10 Example #3: Daily sales.

In this example, my claim is that the daily sales are less than $5,000. My sample mean falls in the DNR, so I DNR the null hypothesis that the sales are greater than or equal to $5,000 (go back and look at the null and alternate hypotheses). Since I DNR the null, I must reject the alternative.

My conclusion: At the alpha 0.10 level, I conclude there is no statistically significant difference between the sample mean ($4,925.46) and the population mean of $5,000. The difference can be explained by random, sampling error. This, in turn, means I cannot support the claim that daily sales are less than $5,000. For daily sales to be less than $5,000, my sample mean would need to fall in the reject region. For this to occur, the sample mean must be less than $4,907.51, (even by a penny).

Now I will answer your question.

Wait a minute, Professor, I have forgotten what I asked.

Using my perfect recall (and copy and paste), I will repeat your question.

You commented, *I am beginning* to see a glimmer of light, but do you always want to be able to explain the difference between the sample mean and the population mean by random, sampling error alone?

In the first two examples, I wanted the difference between the sample mean and population mean to be explained by random, sampling error alone so I was not overfilling the can of coffee or over or under filling the soda can. However, in the third example, I DID NOT want to explain the difference because of random, sampling error. If I wanted to support the claim that the sales were less than $5,000, I must have a difference between the sample mean ($4,925.46). and the hypothesized mean ($5,000). This is a problem-specific issue and can only be discerned by the information or claims or assertions in the problem itself.

Another Method of Setting Up the Alternate Hypotheses

The three-question approach is an important help when setting up the alternate hypothesis (H_a). There is another relationship to aid in setting up the alternate hypothesis. I call it the **mean-mean relationship.** It is from the relationship between the sample mean and the hypothesized population mean. The formula from which I can best show you the relationship is as follows:

$$Z_{\text{test}} = \frac{\overline{X} - \mu_H}{\dfrac{\sigma}{\sqrt{n}}}$$

If $\overline{X}$ is greater than μ_H, the sign of Z will be positive, which means the rejection region is on the right side of the curve. This equates to a right-tail rejection region with an *alternate hypothesis H_a* greater (>) than a specified value. This, in turn, sets up H_o as a $\leq$ test.

If μ_H is greater than $\overline{X}$, the sign of Z will be negative, which means the rejection region is on the left side of the curve. This equates to a left-tail rejection region with an *alternate hypothesis H_a* less than (<) than a specified value. This, in turn, sets up H_o as a $\geq$ test. The sign of the Z-test will determine the rejection tail or H_a. Setting up H_o is a no-brainer when I know H_a as long as I stick with the three forms of hypothesis testing (Form I, Form II, or Form III).

Using the negative or positive sign of the Z-test as a guide in setting up the alternative hypothesis works. If the sign of Z is negative, the alternative hypothesis is less than (<). If the sign of Z is positive, the alternative hypothesis is greater than (>). However, if there is over-riding language in the problem which requires a two-tailed test, you will set the null up as equal (=) and the alternate as unequal ($\neq$). Typical over-riding language would be the requirement for testing an average or testing to make sure a value is not less than or greater than certain values.

So far I have concentrated on setting up the hypotheses and interpreting the results, which are by far the most complicated issues. Let's go through a complete example with all of the calculations.

A Complete Example

Let's go back and pick up the idea of filling the coffee can. Let's say that I own and operate a company in the business of packaging coffee for distribution to supermarkets in the United States. The name of my company is Jones Coffee Company (clever name, right?). The Federal Trade Commission (FTC) is coming to my plant to test the fill weights for my three-pound can of coffee. They want to know if I am filling the can of coffee to an appropriate level. Because I have labeled the can of coffee as containing three pounds., the hypothesized net weight of the coffee in the can is three pounds. Both the FTC and I know that no manufacturing company has machinery that fills the coffee can to an exact level each and every time. They know there is a critical value or threshold value that will support the assertion there are three pounds in the coffee can.

There are three possible outcomes which might interest the FTC. Those three possible outcomes are listed in Table 8.5 in question format. Notice that if the fill level is greater than 3.0 pounds, no action is required. If the fill level is equal to 3.0 pounds, no action is required. However, if the fill level is less than 3.0 pounds, action is required. The FTC is only concerned if I am under filling the coffee cans.

Table 8.5   Three questions to set up H_a (alternate hypothesis).

Possible Outcomes	Conclusions that the Jones Coffee...	Actions by FTC will be to...
IF $\mu_H > 3$	...Co. is Exceeding Labeling Requirements	Take No Action.
IF $\mu_H < 3$	...Co. is *Not* Meeting Labeling Requirements	*Take Action.* **Shut Down the Production Line. Add More Coffee to each Can.**
If $\mu_H = 3$	...Co. is Meeting Labeling Requirements	Take No Action.

The alternate hypothesis is directly determined by looking at the less than ($<$) sign in Table 8.5.

Since the less than arrow ($<$) in the possible outcome column points to the left, I must conclude Form I (left-tail rejection region) is appropriate.

$$H_a: \quad \mu_H < 3.0 \text{ lbs} \quad \text{This is the alternate hypothesis.}$$

In the proper sequence, what are the null and alternate hypotheses?

$$H_o: \quad \mu_H \geq 3.0 \text{ lbs} \quad \text{Once the alternate is set up, the null is a "no-brainer"}$$
set up since there are only three forms.
$$H_a: \quad \mu_H < 3.0 \text{ lbs} \quad \text{Set this up first.}$$

Let me give you some additional information so you can work the problem.

Given: $\sigma = 0.18$; $n = 36$; $\overline{X}_1 = 2.91$ pounds; alpha is 0.01.

How would you now proceed with this test? That may be an unfair question, since you are probably somewhat confused at this point. Let me answer if for you.

Let's use the five-step process.

1. Set up the null hypothesis: Been there, done that—see above.

$$H_o: \quad \mu_H \geq 3.0 \text{ lbs.}$$

$$H_a: \quad \mu_H < 3.0 \text{ lbs.} \qquad \text{FTC is testing the cans for labeling accuracy and they do not want the cans to be under filled.}$$

2. Using the Value Approach in Table 8.3 Step 2, calculate the critical value: (There is only one critical value for a one-tailed test.)

$$CV = \mu_H - Z_\alpha \sigma_{\bar{x}} \text{ (Formula from Table 8.3)}$$

What is the critical value?

$$CV = 3.0 - (2.33)\left(\frac{0.18}{\sqrt{36}}\right) = 2.93$$

The critical value (CV) equals 2.93, if you do the math correctly. Remember to take the square root first then divide then multiply and lastly to subtract.

Wait a minute, you say, I pretty well follow you, but where did you get the Z-value of 2.33?

I reply, this is a table look up with alpha error of 0.01. I look up this value in the normal distribution table provided in Chapters 5 and 6 or the back of the textbook or make the calculation using Excel.

To get the Z-value, you subtract 0.01 from 0.5000 and get 0.4900. Go to the table and look up in the *body of the text* the value that is closest to 0.4900. The closest is 0.4901. By cross-referencing this value (0.4901) to the corresponding Z-value as shown in the margins of the table, you will find the value of 2.33. Don't bother interpolating, just select the closest value.

You really need to go to the normal table now and make sure you can find this value. If you cannot look up values of this sort, you will not understand how to make the calculations for hypothesis testing.

As a reminder, the standard error is calculated in the following manner.

$$\sigma_{\bar{X}} = \left(\frac{\sigma}{\sqrt{n}}\right)$$

$$\sigma_{\bar{X}} = \left(\frac{0.18}{\sqrt{36}}\right)$$

$$\sigma_{\bar{X}} = \left(\frac{0.18}{6}\right)$$

$\sigma_{\bar{X}} = 0.03$, which is the standard error.

3. Determine the decision rule:

If you look at Table 8.3, you will find the decision rules written in great detail. Basically the rules state the following: If the sample mean equals or is greater than the critical value (the threshold), DNR the null. For example, in this case if $\bar{X}$ exactly equals the critical value, you would DNR the null. This is not the situation in this example. You were given that $\bar{X} = 2.91$. The critical value is 2.93 and the sample mean is 2.91.

4. Next compare the critical value of 2.93 to the sample value of 2.91:

This comparison *alone* allows you to make the decision. When making the decision, always, repeat, always compare the sample mean to the critical value.

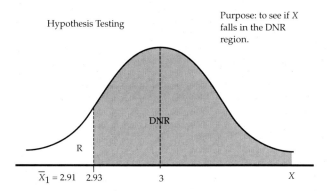

Figure 8.11 Value approach.

Since the sample value falls outside the DNR area, what conclusion is reached?

You think for a minute as the wheels of progress turn ever so slowly. I believe I will reject the null hypothesis and conclude the coffee company needs to add more coffee to the three-pound can.

Good thinking. Let's formally state your conclusion in the narrative in Step 5.

5. Conclusion:

At the alpha 0.01 level, there is a statistically significant difference between the sample mean of 2.91 pounds and the hypothesized mean of 3.0 pounds (the net weight label value). I cannot conclude the difference is due to random, sampling error alone. This means I am under filling the cans of coffee. The FTC would most likely take action by fining me. I would additionally have to put more coffee in subsequent cans of coffee produced. The null hypothesis is rejected and the alternate hypothesis is true (accepted).

Remember, I never directly reject the alternate hypothesis. I always accept (DNR) or reject the null hypothesis *and then and only then* accept or reject the alternate hypothesis.

Okay, let's change the focus a bit. What I have just shown you is from the viewpoint of the Federal Trade Commission. What form of testing would be done if Jones Coffee Company decided to run the same test from their viewpoint assuming Jones Coffee is an ethical company? If I am ethical, I do not want to overfill the cans of coffee nor do I want to under fill the cans of coffee. The test would be Form III (two-tailed rejection region). If I am interested in both tails (under filling and overfilling), I need to conduct a two-tailed rejection region test.

If you rework the problem using a two-tailed test, the results would be as follows:

$$H_o: \quad \mu_H = 3.0 \text{ pounds}$$
$$H_a: \quad \mu_H \neq 3.0 \text{ pounds}$$

$$CV = 3.0 \pm (2.58)\left(\frac{0.18}{\sqrt{36}}\right) = 2.92 \text{ to } 3.08$$

There are two critical values, a lower and an upper. If I assume the sample mean is still 2.91, my conclusion is still the same. I reject the null and accept the alternate. I am still under filling the coffee cans.

I bet you are having trouble with the 2.58, right? If alpha is 0.01, I divide 0.01 by 2 = 0.0050. You now take 0.5000 and subtract 0.0050 = 0.4950, which you look up in the body of the normal table. Got it?

Okay, let's change the problem slightly. What would happen if the sample mean turned out to be 3.09 (not the 2.91 as shown)? In this case, I would still reject the null hypothesis, but now I find I am overfilling the cans of coffee. (3.09 > 3.08)

What would happen if I drew a sample weighing exactly 2.92 pounds and approached the decision from the viewpoint of Jones Coffee Company (two-tailed test)? I would DNR the null because the sample value of 2.92 exactly equals the critical value. This is a rare occurrence; however, you should be aware it could happen. If I DNR the null, I conclude there is no problem and the difference between the sample mean and the population mean can be explained by random, sampling error.

Permitted Substitutions

At this point I need to make a general statement about substitution of values. Quite often you will not have values for the population (actually change the quite often to rarely). When you do not have the population value, you may make a substitution of the standard error of the sample $(S_{\bar{X}})$ for the standard error of the population $(\sigma_{\bar{X}})$. You may also substitute the standard deviation of the sample (S) for the standard deviation of the population (σ). There are exceptions to this permitted substitution, but for now I will not concern you with those exceptions.

To further blow your mind: There are two other approaches available to me—the **Z-test approach** and the **p-value approach.** I have been showing you the value approach exclusively. You will most often run into the p-value approach, especially when you use statistical software such as Excel.

The Z-Test Approach

There is actually a method that is shorter than the *value method* and it accomplishes the same result. In the example of the Jones Coffee Company, I have shown you the value method. The units are constant—pounds. The coffee is in pounds, the critical value is in pounds, and the sample is in pounds. The value approach is often more easily understood by your boss, who will probably be less knowledgeable about statistical processes. It is quite easy to understand that your threshold is 2.93 pounds, but your sample is 2.91 pounds. Even the most dense supervisor will be able to grasp the concept that 2.91 is less than the minimum threshold of 2.93 pounds, so there should be more coffee added to the can. For clearer communication, the value approach is often the best.

That makes sense you say; however, anything you can do to save me work will be appreciated. Can you share with me the Z-test approach?

Great question and great transition, I reply. I will not only show you the Z-test approach but will also show you the p-value approach.

The Z-test approach compares two Z-values—calculated value and critical value. This comparison is possible since the units of measure of Z are also constant—standard deviations. Based on that comparison, I can DNR or reject the null hypothesis. Depending on the information given in the problem, I will use one of the two forms of the Z-test as shown below.

$$Z_{test} = \frac{\overline{X} - \mu_H}{\sigma_{\overline{X}}} \text{ or}$$

$$Z_{test} = \frac{\overline{X} - \mu_H}{\dfrac{\sigma}{\sqrt{n}}}$$

These are mathematical equivalents.

Both of the formulas equal each other. Also remember the substitutions I told you were permitted. If you have sample values rather than population values, you may use the sample values in place of the population values.

Let's look back at the Jones Coffee Company example. Remember, I had a sample value of 2.91 and a hypothesized mean of 3.0, with a standard error of 0.03, a critical Z-value of 2.33, and an alpha level of 0.01. (If you need to go back and check these numbers, please do so.) The calculations for the Z-test would be as follows.

$$Z_{test} = \frac{2.91 - 3.0}{0.03} = \frac{-0.09}{0.03} = -3.00$$

The units of measurement for Z are standard deviations. This is 3.0 standard deviations to the left of the mean, since the sign is negative. The scale has shifted from a value scale to a Z-scale. The mean is zero using the Z-scale and the measurements around the mean are in standard deviations (negative to the left and positive to the right).

I can now compare the critical value of Z to a calculated Z-test value. This comparison will allow you to make a decision. The critical value of Z is a table look up value, which was previously shown to you. At the alpha level of 0.01, I look up 0.4900 (0.4901 is the closest) in the normal table. The critical value is−2.33 (left of the mean). The comparison is as follows:

$$-3.00 < -2.33 \text{ so I still reject the null hypothesis.}$$

The *calculated* value of Z (Z-test value) is −3.00. The *critical* table is −2.33 and is the value of Z previously determined from the normal table.

When I use this method of testing the null hypothesis, I shift to a Z-scale from the value scale. *The value scale is in common units—pounds in this problem. The Z-scale is in standard deviations (common units).* By using the Z-test approach, the mean on the Z-scale is converted to zero (0) and the measurements along the Z-scale are in terms of standard deviations.

Let's take a look at Figure 8.12 below, which reflects both the value scale and the corresponding Z-scale.

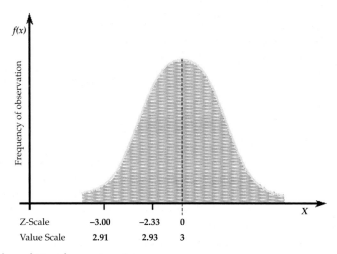

Figure 8.12   Value scale and Z-scale counterpoint.

Notice the value scale I used previously has a counterpoint associated with the Z-scale. Comparing the two Z-values (calculated and critical) allows me to shorten the process. With either the value process or the Z-process, the conclusion is the same. *No matter what process I use, the conclusion cannot vary*. In other words, if I reject the H_o with the value process, I must also reject the H_o with the Z-test process. The Z-test process is much simpler to calculate, but the value scale will be more easily understood by someone who is not statistically literate. Understanding the implications of critical Z-values (usually your boss) is a bit more challenging.

Have you ever wondered how your boss got to be a boss? There is a rule that is part of the Murphy's Law conundrums. It simply states *"A person rises to his or her level of incompetence."* I insert this sage comment into the course at no extra charge. My wife would tell you that my "sage" comments are worth what you pay for them, but what does she know? Her comments are questionable; after all, she married me. That fact by itself may disqualify her. (And she won't get a chance to read this unless someone squeals on me.)

The *p*-value Approach

I have shown you the value approach (units in pounds of coffee) and the Z-test (units in standard deviations). There is yet another method (Aren't you happy about that?) It is called the *p*-value approach. This method is the one most often used in statistical software such as Excel, SPSS, and MiniTab. A *p*-value is compared to the chosen alpha value to DNR or reject the null hypothesis. What is true about the value approach and the Z-test approach is also true of the *p*-value approach—the results will be the same. I cannot have different conclusions just because I chose a different approach from among the three options. Often the *p*-value will be referred to as the "observed level of significance." The *p*-value gives me additional insight into my decision about H_o (the null hypothesis). The *p*-value is helpful in understanding the *strength of my rejection of H_o*.

Rule One

If the *p*-value is *less than* the alpha level (conventionally 0.01, 0.05, or 0.10), then H_o is rejected. There is a saying that may help you remember this. If the *p*-value is low, the null must go. Kinda catchy, right?

Rule Two

If the *p*-value is *greater than or equal to* the alpha level, then H_o is not rejected (DNR).

Notice, once again I am comparing the *p*-value to the chosen alpha level to determine if I am going to DNR or reject the null hypothesis.

Let's take our Jones Coffee Company example again. As a reminder, the alpha was 0.01. I calculated a Z-test value of -3.00 as follows:

$$Z_{test} = \frac{2.91 - 3.0}{0.03} = \frac{-0.09}{0.03} = -3.00 \text{ (previously discussed)}$$

To find the *p*-value, I convert the -3.00 to a probability or *area under the curve*. This is done by table look up. I will use the normal table and convert -3.00 (standard deviations) to a probability, which is 0.4987. If you will look closely at the formula for the Z_{test}, this is the probability of obtaining a sample between 2.91 (the sample mean) and 3.0 (the hypothesized population mean).

Look the probability of 0.4987 up before reading on. Got it?

If you look at the formula, you will observe the measurement (see the numerator of the formula) is between these two values ($\overline{X}$ and μ_{H}); therefore, the area you have just looked up in the normal table is between those two values. The formula follows:

$$Z_{test} = \frac{\overline{X} - \mu_{H}}{\frac{\sigma}{\sqrt{n}}}$$

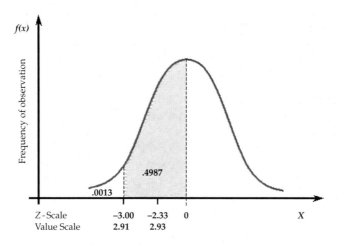

Figure 8.13 *p*-value.

The p-value is defined as the area in the tail *beyond the sample mean*. The area of interest is, then, the area *beyond 2.91*, which is on the left side of the curve. Since I know that a normal curve is symmetrical (50% on either side of the mean), I can determine the probability of obtaining a sample less than 2.91 by subtracting the 0.4987 from 0.5000 (50%). This yields a value of 0.0013. The 0.0013 is my p-value. This is the area in the tail *beyond* the sample mean.

See Figure 8.13 just above for a visual of the probability and the p-value.

Conclusion: I compare the p-value of 0.0013 to the alpha value of 0.01. Since 0.0013 < 0.01, I still reject the null hypothesis. The probability of obtaining a sample mean SMALLER than 2.91 is 0.0013 or 0.13%, which is very small. If this were a right-tail rejection region, this would be the probability of obtaining a sample mean LARGER than the current sample mean.

How strong is my decision to reject the null hypothesis, you ask?

Good question, I respond.

To review, Rule One states if the p-value is smaller than the alpha level (generally 0.01, 0.05, or 0.10), then H_o is rejected. Rule Two states if the p-value is greater than or equal to the alpha level, then H_o is not rejected (DNR). However, you need a measure of how strong your decision is to reject the null hypothesis. This can be shown in tabular format.

Table 8.6 Relative strength of rejecting any Null Hypothesis using the p-value.

If the *p*-value is less than...	The Evidence H_o is *NOT* True is...
0.10	Some Evidence
0.05	Strong Evidence
0.01	Very Strong Evidence
0.001	Extremely Strong Evidence

If the p-value is less than the following values, the evidence H_o is NOT true follows:

From this table, *the larger the p-value*, the more certain I can be that the H_o is true. *The smaller the p-value*, the more certain I can be that H_o is not true.

In the Jones Coffee example, the p-value is the probability of obtaining a sample that is smaller than the current sample mean of 2.91. The probability is very low (0.0013), so I have a low probability I will obtain a random sample smaller than 2.91. In this example, *the evidence is extremely strong that the H_o is not true.* The p-value approach, like the value approach and the Z-test approach, results in rejecting the null hypothesis (0.0013 < 0.01). The p-value is the area under the curve beyond the current sample mean (2.91). Remember, the null hypothesis stated the fill weight of the 3-lb coffee can was okay. Rejection of the null would tell me the fill weight of the 3-lb coffee can is not okay and some adjustment is needed.

Anytime you are working with a p-value, you will need to set up the null and alternate hypothesis. One warning is appropriate at this point. If the test is two-tailed, you would double the p-value. For example, when calculating the values associated with the Jones

Coffee Company using a two-tailed approach, the p-value would be 0.0026 (0.0013 $\times$ 2). I double the p-value because I only have one sample, but I am testing two tails. In this instance, 0.0026 is still less than the alpha value of 0.01, so I would still reject the null hypothesis.

Understanding the p-value is usually quite difficult for most students. Let me explain it a different way. If I refer to the p-value as the lowest alpha value I can set and still reject the null hypothesis, it may make more sense. If the alpha value is lower than the critical value, the null is not rejected (DNR). Said differently, if the critical value is less than the alpha, DNR the null hypothesis! By way of illustration, in the Jones Coffee Company example, I can set the alpha value as low as 0.0013 and still reject the null. However, if I move the alpha value to 0.0012, I can no longer reject the null (DNR). The p-value tells you exactly the point of indecision between rejecting and not rejecting H_o. The importance of the p-value in statistical software should be obvious (not to me, you quickly reply).

Using Excel for *p*-values

You can determine the p-value by using Excel rather than having to use a table look up approach. Go to Excel. Open a worksheet. Double click on *f(x)* in the toolbar. This opens a menu which allows you to find the function of interest. In this case, you need the cumulative standard normal function NORMSDIST. Open it. Now you have a screen that asks you to input a Z-value. From the above Jones Coffee Company example, the Z-test value was 3.00. Type this number in the Z. This will return a cumulative normal probability value of 0.99865. This is the cumulative value. To get the p-value, you can manually subtract 0.99865 from 1.00000 to get 0.00135. This value is one decimal point more accurate than the normal table look up value I manually determined (0.0013). Alternately, if you look at the formula bar, you will notice that it reads = NORMSDIST(3.00). You can insert a 1.0 just behind the equal (=) sign and in front of NORMS-DIST followed by a minus sign (−) In the function bar, it would look like the following: =1 − NORMDIST(3.00) This will return a value of 0.00135, which is the same as using the cumulative function just above.

I am sure you have not noticed it, but I have been working with a Z-test value.

I see that, you say.

So what happens if you are working with a t-value rather than a Z-value? Does this mean you cannot calculate a p-value, I ask?

I notice your hesitation, so I answer my own question. No, it does not. I can easily determine a p-value for a t-test by using the Excel function. Open Excel. Open a worksheet. Double click on the *f(x)* in the toolbar. In the menu, find the TDIST function. Here you will be asked to provide X, which is the t-value; Deg_freedom, which is $n - 1$ degrees of freedom; and tails, which would be 1 or 2 depending on whether you are using a one or two-tailed test. In the function bar you would have the following: =TDIST. If the t-value of interest to you is 2.15, type this value in for X. If $n = 21$, then degrees of freedom would be 20. Inserting "1" for tails returns a value of 0.021985. If you insert "2" for tails, Excel returns a value of 0.04397. Of course, one-half of 0.04397 would yield 0.021985, which is the same as using 1 for tails. This indicates the probability of a value exceeding +2.15 standard deviations is 0.021985. Using Excel can open the door for more accurate *p*-values.

Final Thought on the *p*-value

Okay, let's say the *p*-value is 0.0013. I can now compare it to any of the conventional alpha values (0.01, 0.05, or 0.10), and because the *p*-value is low, *Ho* must go. I reject the null at any of the three most conventional alpha values.

In my Jones Coffee example, all three methods, the value method, the Z-test, and the *p*-value lead to the rejection of the null hypothesis. I cannot vary my method of calculation and come to different conclusions. The conclusions will be consistent. If I reject the null using one approach, I must reject the null with the other two or I am making a mistake in my calculation. Re-check your work if you end up with opposite conclusions using any one of the three approaches.

"Professor, I Still Get Confused about What to Do with Critical and Calculated Values. Can You Help?"

Okay, I will give it another try. Let's first talk about the Value Approach. The values are in common units such as ounces, pounds, gallons, etc. This approach is the easiest to understand and explain to the lay person who has no clue about how to interpret statistical processes. The use of the value approach will be predicted on the company taking a sample. The sample mean ($\overline{X}$) will be compared to the critical value, which is determined by using one of the three formulas (left, right, or two-tailed rejection regions). The critical value is in a fixed position on the curve. It is the threshold or barrier to which you will make a comparison. The mean of the sample will be below, above, or equal to the critical value as calculated by the value approach formula. Where the sample mean falls on the curve will determine if you Reject or DNR the null hypothesis, which in turn, depends on which form of testing you do (Forms I, II, or III).

Now let's address the Z_{test} Approach. The Z_{test} itself is a formula calculation. It, however, is NOT the critical value. In the case of the Z_{test}, the critical value comes from a table lookup. If the problem meets the conditions for a Z-solution, the table will be the normal table. If the problem meets the conditions for a t-solution, the table will be the t-table. Again like the value approach, the critical value is in a fixed position on the curve. It is the threshold or barrier to which you will make a comparison.

No matter where you get the critical value (value approach as determined by a formula or table lookup as in the Z_{test} or t_{test} approach) it is a fixed value on the scale (normal curve). The sample mean and the Z_{test} CALCULATED value move and are compared to the critical value. For example, I will use a one-tailed right rejection region (Form II). If the Z_{test} calculated value or the sample mean is to the right of the critical value you will reject the null hypothesis. If the calculated value or the sample mean is to the left of (or equal to) the critical value, you will DNR the null hypothesis. Figure 8.14 below gives you the idea based on the right tailed rejection region (Form II).

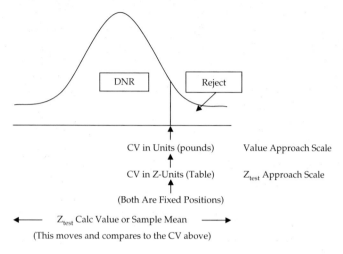

Figure 8.14   Comparison of Position of Two Values.

You are not through yet, however. Next you must determine if you can support the original claim or determine if there was a problem that must be solved (adjusting machine tolerance or not adjusting machine tolerance for example). This part of the decision has nothing to do with Rejecting or DNR the null. Rejecting or DNR is just a starting point. Your next step is to look at the null and alternate hypothesis to see what you have or have not rejected. For example, if the claim was sales exceeded a certain value (say $8,000) and you DNR the null, you could not support a claim sales is greater than $8,000. Think about it. The hypothesis would be set up as follows:

H_o: $\mu_H \leq \$8,000$ (arbitrary number to illustrate the point).

H_a: $\mu_H > \$8,000$ (to support the claim of exceeding a certain value, you must accept this alternate hypothesis, which means you will have first rejected the null).

By not rejecting the null (DNR), you are stating that sales are less than or equal to $8,000 (look at the null hypothesis for confirmation of this statement). The claim is that sales exceed $8,000. You have rejected that statement, if you DNR (think accepted) THE NULL (DNR the null of $\leq \$8,000$).

This is a two-step process. You must determine if you reject or DNR the null, then you must actually look at the two hypotheses to see if you can support a claim or make a modification. Remember, you always test the null and whatever you do to it (Reject or DNR), you will do the opposite to the alternate hypothesis.

I hope this helps. Oh yes, I forgot about the p-value approach. Guess I better give you a few thoughts about that approach. The p-value is compared to alpha (any alpha selected) and works this way. If the p-value is less than the alpha, you will reject the null. If the p-value is equal to or greater than the alpha, you will DNR the null. Once that is done you go back and look at the null and alternate and decide if you can support or not support a claim as detailed in one of the paragraphs just above.

How Do I Keep All of These Insane Rules Straight in My Mind?

By using Table 8.7 below as a reminder of the process, you should be able to keep the calculations and comparisons straight in your mind. Remember there are three forms of hypothesis testing and three different approaches to solving problems. This table is set up to address the five steps in Table 8.3 as they relate to the Value Approach, Z-test Approach and *p*-value Approach.

Table 8.7 Reminders for the value, Z-test and *p*-value approaches.

Action/Solution/ Steps	Value Approach	Z-test Approach Approach	p-value
1. Set up the Hypotheses. First identify and set up the ALTERNATE hypothesis, then the Null will be a no brainer if you are using the Three Forms I, II or III. You can identify the ALTERNATE by using one of the two approaches listed under each approach (three question or sign of Z). The *p*-value approach is not too helpful in setting up the ALTERNATE hypothesis.	Three Questions: $\mu_H < a\ value$ $\mu_H > a\ value$ $\mu_H = a\ value$ One of these will be the claim or assertion. This will make the alternate (not the null) equal to the answer to this question. If the claim is that a value is more than a certain value, this will be a right-tail rejection region, thus a Form II.	You can use the sign of Z to set up the ALTERNATE first, unless the problem language overrides the sign such as use of the word 'average'. $Z_{test} = \dfrac{\overline{X} - \mu_H}{\sigma_{\overline{X}}}$ • If $\overline{X} > \mu_H$ the sign of Z is positive, so this is a right tail rejection region (Form II). • If $\overline{X} < \mu_H$ the sign of Z is negative, so this is a left tail rejection region (Form I). • If you are interested in the average or in testing both ends, then a two-tailed rejection region is appropriate. (Form III).	No Help

Action/Solution/ Steps	Value Approach	Z-test Approach Approach	p-value
2. Determine the critical value.	This is determined by formula using one of the three formulas shown on Table 8.3, Step 2. Remember there are three Forms (I, II and III), so there will be three choices of formulas.	This is determined by looking up the critical value in the normal table.	The critical p-value is determined by manually converting the Z-test results to a probability (normal table lookup), then subtracting that from 0.5000 (50%). Excel can make this calculation for both the t-test and the Z-test.
3. Decision Rule	Table 8.3, Step 3 is the guide. The decision rule varies depending on the Form you are using (I, II or III).	Table 8.3, Step 3 is the guide. The decision rule varies depending on the Form you are using (I, II or III).	If the p-value is less than the alpha value, you will reject the null hypothesis. If the p-value is equal to or more than the alpha value, you will DNR (accept) the null.
4. Make Your Decision	Compare $\overline{X}$ to the Critical Value which has been determined by using one of the three formulas (Table 8.3, Step 4) (Left-tail, Right-tail or Two-tail rejection regions)	Compare the Z-test formula value to the critical value which comes from a normal table look up.	Compare the p-value to the selected alpha value (α). The p-value is the area under the curve BEYOND the current sample mean. If p is low, H_o must go (reject).
5. Conclusions	Same as Table 8.3, Step 5.	Same as Table 8.3, Step 5.	Same as Table 8.3, Step 5.

Remember: All conclusions are made comparing $\overline{X}$ to μ_H. Your interest lies in determining if the difference between the two means (sample mean and hypothesized population mean) is random and explained by sampling error alone. Conclusions are never stated by comparing $\overline{X}$ to the Critical Value. Comparing $\overline{X}$ to the Critical Value is how you make your decision, not state your conclusion.

Conclusions Include: A statement of the alpha level; there is or is not a statistically significant difference; the difference can or cannot be explained by sampling error; you can or cannot support the claim or assertion; and a statement about what you do such as fill the coke can with more liquid or adjust the lathe cutting length.

Proportions

Your life would not be complete unless I address one other subject—proportions.

Yeah, it would, Professor, but that is another story.

I briefly ignore you and move on. I have been working with the mean (μ_H) but I may encounter proportion problems. A proportion exists when you want to work with percentage relationships. Proportion solutions work exactly the same way as the mean solutions. The formulas are, of course, different.

For example, let's assume you believe 65% of your market will repurchase your product multiple times. You take a sample of 600 customers which reveals that 375 out of the 600 will repurchase multiple times (375/600 = 62.5%). You want to know if the difference between the sample mean (62.5%) and a hypothesized population mean (65%) is statistically significant or is just random. An alpha of 0.05 will be used to test the hypothesis.

$$H_o: \quad \pi = 0.65$$
$$H_a: \quad \pi \neq 0.65$$

The symbol π is proportions equivalent of μ_T. The Z-test is as follows:

$$Z_{test} = \frac{p - \pi_H}{\sigma_p}$$

where p is the sample proportion; π_H is the hypothesized population proportion; and σ_p is the standard error of the sampling proportion.

$$\sigma_p = \sqrt{\frac{\pi_H(1 - \pi_H)}{n}}$$

In the problem example, the calculations are as follows:

$$\sigma_p = \sqrt{\frac{0.65(1 - 0.65)}{600}} = \sqrt{\frac{0.2275}{600}} = \sqrt{0.0004} = 0.0195$$

$$Z_{test} = \frac{0.625 - 0.65}{0.0195} = \frac{0.0250}{0.0195} = -1.282$$

At the alpha level of 0.05, the critical value is ± 1.96, since I have set up the hypothesis as a two-tailed rejection region. (Look up the value closest to 0.4750, because one-half of the alpha goes into each of the tails.) The negative 1.282 falls between ± 1.96, so I DNR the null hypothesis and conclude there is no statistically significant difference between the 62.5% and 65%. The difference is due to sampling error and is random. The assertion 65%. of your customers will repurchase your product multiple times is supportable.

Two-Population Hypothesis Testing

Now that you have been introduced to hypothesis testing for a single population, I want to give you a preview of the next chapter—two-population hypothesis testing.

Oh, you say, I did not know I was dealing with a single population.

Well, you were, I respond.

There was one soft drink and one coffee can. By definition, this is a single population.

In your business, you may want to know how successful your product is compared to your competitors, or you may want to know if Plant A is producing at the same level as Plant B, or you may want to know if training process A yields better results than process B. All of these are examples of two populations and I will visit them in Chapter 9.

You know You are a Texan If:

- You think the start of Deer season is a national holiday.
- Your idea of a traffic jam is ten cars waiting to pass a tractor on the highway.
- It is noon in July, kids are on summer vacation and not one person is on the streets.

Tear-Out Sheet Chapter 8

Student Name: _____

Day and Time of Class: _____

Hypothesis Testing Problems—One Population

Special Note:

All hypothesis testing problems are assumed to be normal distributions. To aid you in your computations, draw a normal distribution for each problem before you do any calculations.

1. One of the major oil companies claims the average gasoline price of their brand is less than $1.25 per gallon. In order to test their claim, we randomly selected a sample of 49 of their gas stations and determined that the average price per gallon of the stations in the sample is $1.20. Furthermore, we assume that the standard deviation of the population is $0.14 from other studies. Using an alpha value of 0.05, test the company's claim.

   Determine your answers using the *value method*, the *Z-test method*, and the *p-value approach*. Are your conclusions the same with all three approaches? Explain the meaning of all three results, especially the *p*-value approach.

2. The manager of a local grocery store believes the store's average daily sales are *more than* $8,000 per day. To test his belief, a sample of 64 days of sales was selected, and it was found that the average sale was $8,250 with a sample standard deviation of $1,200. Test the manager's belief using an alpha value of 0.01.

   Determine your answers using the *value method*, the *Z-test method*, and the *p-value approach*. Are your conclusions the same with all three approaches? Explain the meaning of all three results, especially the *p*-value approach.

3. A lathe is set to cut bars of steel with a length of 6 centimeters. The lathe is considered to be in perfect adjustment if *the average length* of the bars is 6 centimeters. A sample of 25 bars is selected randomly, and their lengths are measured. The average length of the bars in the sample is 6.1 centimeters with a standard deviation of 0.2 centimeters. At an alpha value of 0.05, test to see if the lathe is in perfect adjustment. Clearly state your conclusion.

   Determine your answers using both the value method approach and the Z-test or *t*-test approach. Are your conclusions the same with both approaches?

4. Does your conclusion change on problem #2 if the alpha value is set at 0.05 rather than 0.01?

9

Hypothesis Testing and Confidence Intervals for Two Populations

Court Room Humor – Actual Exchanges Based on a Book by Charles M. Sevilla

Attorney:	Doctor, how many of your autopsies have you performed on dead people?
Witness:	All of them. The live ones put up too much of a fight.

Two Populations

What exactly do I mean by **two-population hypothesis testing?** In many business settings, the business manager will often find himself (not a gender statement) faced with asking questions about a product his company produces or a product his company wants to produce.

227

The question might be as simple as comparing the mean life of two products—his product and his competitor's product. The goal is to determine if his product is better or worse than the competitor's product.

Are North Slope Ski Boots more durable than Head Ski Boots?

Plant A is producing 200 metric tons and Plant B is producing 185 metric tons even though the two have similar equipment and processes. The question might be:

Do the workers in Plant A produce more than the workers in Plant B?

Your plant uses method A to produce products. A time and motion engineer claims if you switch to method B, the production output will increase significantly. Before spending the money on the switch over, you need to test the claim. The question might be:

Does production Method A yield higher output than Method B?

These are real questions asked often by the owner or manager of many businesses. To stay or become competitive, you must always be cognizant as to how your product or service compares to your competitor's product or service. The continual demand for your product and the proper pricing of your product will depend on how your product matches your competitor's product. If they are better and less expensive, you will lose market share. Often, consumer advocacy groups will test the claims made about the quality of products. This testing will serve to provide information to the general public so they can make informed decisions before they purchase a product.

In order to understand two-population testing, let's organize it into two general approaches—independent sampling and paired sampling. In both cases I am interested in the *differences in the two parameters* not the individual values generated from each of the samples. For example, assume there are two companies that produce tires. One tire has a mean life of 36,000 miles and the other comparable tire has a mean life of 33,000 miles. I have no interest in the 36,000 or the 33,000 but have a great deal of interest in the 3,000 difference.

The design of my experiment might compare two samples independently drawn at random from two separate and distinct populations (independent sampling). Alternately, the design of my experiment might match two separate pairs of data (dependent testing, or paired sampling).

Independent sampling collects separate samples from each population. The researcher would then evaluate the difference in the means of the samples. The sample sizes do not have to be equal. For example, if $n_1 = 25$ for one population and $n_2 = 50$ for a second population, the results will not be compromised because the sample sizes are unequal.

Paired Sampling, on the other hand, takes the same number of observations from each population. Each group is matched as closely as possible. These populations vary in only one relevant detail—the test characteristic being measured. Matched pairs are most often found in medical research, where for example two groups will be matched as closely as possible as to age, gender, weight, level of activity, cholesterol, and any other factor which might affect blood pressure. These two groups are often referred to as twins. One group would be given Medication A and the other Medication B. One of the two medications is a placebo and the other is the real medication. Neither the nurse nor the patient knows which group is receiving the actual medicine. Over a period of time, the blood pressure for each group is measured often and the result will determine if the group taking the real medication responds better than the group taking the placebo. Paired sampling can also work for on the job training programs with output before training being matched to output after training.

I can use hypothesis testing or confidence intervals with both independent sampling or paired sampling. Either hypothesis testing or confidence intervals testing will reveal if there is a statistically significant difference between the two populations. However, there is one main difference in the two approaches. If I am interested in knowing *how much the difference is*, I must (repeat *must*) use confidence intervals.

The hypothesis testing approach will answer the question—*yes*, there is a difference or *no*, there is no difference. Confidence intervals, on the other hand, will tell you if there *is a statistically significant difference and* **how much** *that difference is*.

The formulas used for confidence intervals and the formulas for hypothesis testing are essentially the same formulas.

Wait a minute, you say, while wiping the sweat from your brow. I do not understand how you can claim the formulas are the same.

Easily, I reply, since they are. All you do is solve the same equation for a different value.

You respond, I am not from Missouri, I still need you to "*splain* yourself" as Ricky Ricardo often said to Lucy (shows my age).

Let's look at the formulas associated with large sample sizes for confidence intervals as compared to the formulas for hypothesis testing.

Confidence Intervals—Large Samples

$$\overline{X}_1 - \overline{X}_2 \pm Z_\alpha \, S_{\overline{X}_1 - \overline{X}_2}$$ (Definition of terms later)

Hypothesis Testing—Large Samples

$$Z_{test} = \frac{\left(\overline{X}_1 - \overline{X}_2\right) - \left(\mu_1 - \mu_2\right)}{S_{\overline{X}_1 - \overline{X}_2}}$$ (Definition of terms later)

As you look at the above comparisons, notice that the hypothesis testing formula and the confidence interval formula are essentially the same. The hypothesis test formula solves the confidence interval formula for Z. All formulas in this chapter have the same mirrored image. There are two basic categories for two-population testing. Under independent testing there are two sub-categories, with two other ones under small samples.

Independent Testing:
    Large size samples
    Small samples
        Equal variances
        Unequal variances
Dependent Testing:
    Matched pairs

Given this similar relationship, the test statistic you select depends on the following question "*Am I interested in knowing if there is a difference or must I know the amount of the difference?*" The answer to this question will determine which solution—hypothesis testing or confidence intervals—you will use. Either the confidence interval or the hypothesis testing approach tells you if there is a difference. Confidence intervals is the only one, however, that tells you the amount of the difference. (I think I have said this before, right?)

A summary comparison of the respective formulas follows (Table 9.1), as well as some of the key factors associated with each of the methods. You may want to print this table for future reference.

Table 9.1   Comparison of CI and HT mirrored image formulas.

Confidence Interval	Hypothesis Testing
Independent Samples Large–CI:	**Independent Samples Large–HT:**
*Large samples.	*Large samples.
*Both n's must be ≥ 30.	*Both n's must be ≥ 30.
*Solution will use Z.	*Solution will use Z.
	*$\mu_1 - \mu_2 = 0$ (always)
$\overline{X}_1 - \overline{X}_2 \pm Z_\alpha S_{\overline{X}_1 - \overline{X}_2}$	$Z_{test} = \dfrac{\left(\overline{X}_1 - \overline{X}_2\right) - \left(\mu_1 - \mu_2\right)}{S_{\overline{X}_1 - \overline{X}_2}}$
$S_{\overline{X}_1 - \overline{X}_2} = \sqrt{\dfrac{S_1^2}{n_1} + \dfrac{S_2^2}{n_2}}$	$S_{\overline{X}_1 - \overline{X}_2} = \sqrt{\dfrac{S_1^2}{n_1} + \dfrac{S_2^2}{n_2}}$
Independent Samples Small–CI:	**Independent Samples Small–HT:**
*Small samples—equal variances.	*Small samples—equal variances.
*$\sigma_1^2 = \sigma_2^2$.	*$\sigma_1^2 = \sigma_2^2$.
*S_1^2 will not equal S_2^2.	*S_1^2 will not equal S_2^2.
*Either n is less than 30.	*Either n is less than 30.
*Variances may be pooled.	*Variances may be pooled.
*The pooled variance is a weighted average and will fall between the two sample variances.	*The pooled variance is a weighted average and will fall between the two sample variances.
*Solution will use t.	*Solution will use t.
*Degrees of freedom are $n_1 + n_2 - 2$.	*Degrees of freedom are $n_1 + n_2 - 2$.
$\overline{X}_1 - \overline{X}_2 \pm t_\alpha \sqrt{\dfrac{S_p^2}{n_1} + \dfrac{S_p^2}{n_2}}$	$t_{TEST} = \dfrac{\left(\overline{x}_1 - \overline{x}_2\right) - \left(\mu_1 - \mu_2\right)}{\sqrt{\dfrac{S_p^2}{n_1} + \dfrac{S_p^2}{n_2}}}$
Pooled Variance Calculation.	Pooled Variance Calculation.
$S_p^2 = \dfrac{S_1^2 \left(n_1 - 1\right) + S_2^2 \left(n_2 - 1\right)}{n_1 + n_2 - 2}$	$S_p^2 = \dfrac{S_1^2 \left(n_1 - 1\right) + S_2^2 \left(n_2 - 1\right)}{n_1 + n_2 - 2}$

Independent Samples Small–CI:	**Independent Samples Small–HT:**
*Small samples—unequal variances.	*Small samples—unequal variances.
*$\sigma_1^2 \neq \sigma_2^2$.	*$\sigma_1^2 \neq \sigma_2^2$.
*S_1^2 will not equal S_2^2.	*S_1^2 will not equal S_2^2.
*Either n is less than 30.	*Either n is less than 30.
*Variances cannot be pooled.	*Variances cannot be pooled.
*Solution will use t-prime.	*Solution will use t-prime.
*Degrees of freedom must be calculated.	*Degrees of freedom must be calculated.
*Always round degrees of freedom down.	*Always round degrees of freedom down.
$$\overline{X}_1 - \overline{X}_2 \pm t'_\alpha \sqrt{\frac{S_1^2}{n_1} + \frac{S_2^2}{n_2}}$$	$$t_{\text{TEST}} = \frac{\left(\bar{x}_1 - \bar{x}_2\right) - \left(\mu_1 - \mu_2\right)}{\sqrt{\frac{S_1^2}{n_1} + \frac{S_2^2}{n_2}}}$$
Degrees of freedom are calculated.	Degrees of freedom are calculated.
$$\text{d.f.} = \frac{\left(\frac{S_1^2}{n_1} + \frac{S_2^2}{n_2}\right)^2}{\frac{\left(\frac{S_1^2}{n_1}\right)^2}{n_1 - 1} + \frac{\left(\frac{S_2^2}{n_2}\right)^2}{n_2 - 1}}$$	$$\text{d.f.} = \frac{\left(\frac{S_1^2}{n_1} + \frac{S_2^2}{n_2}\right)^2}{\frac{\left(\frac{S_1^2}{n_1}\right)^2}{n_1 - 1} + \frac{\left(\frac{S_2^2}{n_2}\right)^2}{n_2 - 1}}$$
Dependent Matched Pairs–CI:	**Dependent Matched Pairs–HT:**

All matched pairs must have two distinct data sets which are matched as closely as possible for all characteristics, with the exception of the one characteristic which is the characteristic you wish to measure.

$$\bar{d} \pm t_\alpha \frac{S_d}{\sqrt{n}}$$	$$t_{\text{test}} = \frac{\bar{d} - \left(\mu_1 - \mu_2\right)}{\frac{S_d}{\sqrt{n}}}$$
$$\bar{d} = \frac{\Sigma d_i}{n}$$	$$\bar{d} = \frac{\Sigma d_i}{n}$$
$$S_d = \sqrt{\frac{\Sigma d_i^2 - n(\bar{d}^2)}{n - 1}}$$	$$S_d = \sqrt{\frac{\Sigma d_i^2 - n(\bar{d}^2)}{n - 1}}$$

Let's look at several examples. I will work through several examples of confidence interval problems. Let's begin with independent sampling with large size samples.

Independent Sampling—Large Size Samples–CI

Let's assume you have two answering devices you are considering for purchase. You are the purchasing agent of a Fortune 500 company, so your decision could have a major impact. These devices are useful in answering and queuing calls from your customers. You authorize an outside bureau to test the two devices. In the trial tests, you determine the following (Table 9.2).

Table 9.2 Answering device comparison.

Device A	Device B
n_1 = 75 calls	n_2 = 70 calls
S_1 = 4.8 seconds	S_2 = 3.8 seconds
$\overline{X}_1$ = 25.2 seconds	$\overline{X}_2$ = 21.3 seconds

First, I observe that the sample sizes both exceed 30. This is important. If the sample sizes equal or exceed 30, the central theorem may be assumed, which in turn assures the distributions are normally distributed. Both sample sizes must be equal to or exceed 30 for me to apply the large size sample approach. If one of the samples is less than 30, then I must apply a different technique (t-distribution and small size samples).

Second, I observe that I do not know the standard deviation or the standard error of the population. I do, however, know the standard deviation of the sample. This again is important because it determines the technique I will use.

The question is simply this: "Which device do I select?" Or, said differently, "Is there a statistically significant difference between the mean answering times of the two devices or can the difference be explained by sampling error?" I want to select the device that responds more promptly in servicing my customers. Price considerations are about the same, so this does not factor into my decision. From the initial observations, Device B looks as though it is faster (21.3 versus 25.2 seconds). I know enough about the comparison of products to know that I must test the results and *cannot rely on the sample means directly*. I want to look at the differences in the sample means rather than the value of each sample mean alone.

When I say I want to look at the differences, I am asserting that the difference in the two means is equal and that any error that occurs is due to sampling error alone.

This can be written as follows:

$$\mu_1 = \mu_2$$

or

$$\mu_1 - \mu_2 = 0 \text{ (This is an important concept. Remember this for later.)}$$

I want to perform my test using an alpha level of 0.10. Since this is a confidence interval, there is no need for a formal statement of the null and alternate hypotheses.

From Table 9.2 the confidence interval formula is as follows:

$$\overline{X}_1 - \overline{X}_2 \pm Z_\alpha \, S_{\overline{X}_1 - \overline{X}_2}$$

Go to Table 9.2 and make sure you can find this formula. It is a mirror image of the hypothesis formula.

$\overline{X}_1 - \overline{X}_2$ is the difference between the two means.

Z_α is the table look up Z-value at the chosen alpha level.

$S_{\overline{X}_1 - \overline{X}_2}$ is the standard error of the difference between the two means.

First, calculate the standard error of the difference.

$$S_{\overline{X}_1 - \overline{X}_2} = \sqrt{\frac{S_1^2}{n_1} + \frac{S_2^2}{n_2}}$$

Insert the values using the information given in Table 9.2.

$$S_{\overline{X}_1 - \overline{X}_2} = \sqrt{\frac{(4.8)^2}{75} + \frac{(3.8)^2}{70}}$$

$$S_{\overline{X}_1 - \overline{X}_2} = \sqrt{\frac{(23.04)}{75} + \frac{(14.44)}{70}}$$

$$S_{\overline{X}_1 - \overline{X}_2} = \sqrt{0.3072 + 0.2063}$$

$$S_{\overline{X}_1 - \overline{X}_2} = \sqrt{0.5135}$$

$$S_{\overline{X}_1 - \overline{X}_2} = 0.7166$$

Next, I return to the confidence interval formula for large size samples. Inserting the proper values I will have the following calculations.

$$\overline{X}_1 - \overline{X}_2 \pm Z_\alpha \, S_{\overline{X}_1 - \overline{X}_2}$$

$$(25.2 - 21.3) \pm (1.65)(0.7166)$$

$$3.9 \pm 1.18$$

2.72 to 5.08 seconds.

Incredible, you say, but I have a few questions.

Okay, shoot.

Well, first I understand where you got the 0.7166.

Good start.

I do not, however, know where you got the 1.65.

Okay, I say. This is a normal table look up of the Z-value at an alpha of 0.10.

I found it as follows: Since I am dealing with confidence intervals, I will divide the alpha by 2 (0.10 ÷ 2 = 0.05). One-half of alpha will be in the left tail and one-half will be in the right tail. I am assuming a normal distribution. Since both sample sizes are greater than 30, the central limit theorem applies. I know the normal distribution is symmetrical, so I can subtract 0.05 from 0.5000 (one-half of the area to the left of the mean and one-half to the right of the mean) to get a value of 0.4500. This is the area under the curve, so I will then go to the normal distribution table and find the area closest to 0.4500. I find this value in the body of the table and not on the edges. The edges are Z and the middle of the table is area under the curve. The closest value is 0.4505, which then cross references to a Z-value of 1.65.

Are there any other questions?

Yes, where did you get the 25.2 and the 21.3?

Oh, you are going to feel funny when I answer that.

Why, you ask?

Well, what was the mean of the sample of Device A?

You look and sheepishly say, oh, 25.2.

Okay, Okay, you say, enough already. I can see the mean of Device B is 21.3, too.

Great!

Now the rest of the solution is interpretation.

I will recap the calculations to this point.

The confidence interval is 2.72 seconds to 5.08 seconds. Both are positive values.

How do I interpret it, you ask?

Notice that the interval does not contain zero.

So what, you say.

For an interval to contain or not contain zero is significant.

If the interval *does* contain zero, I would conclude there is *no statistically significant difference* in the two devices. Both devices would be considered to be statistical equivalents. Any difference would be attributed to sampling error. Sampling error that is random is okay.

Remember I am really making the following statement: $\mu_1 - \mu_2 = 0$ (This was established just above in the chapter, and I suggested you remember it for later. Now is later).

However, since the interval *does not* contain zero, I will conclude that I am 90% confident there *is a statistically significant difference* between the two devices. At the alpha 0.10 level, the difference is too great to be explained by sampling error alone.

Having said that, I must now conclude which device is better. To answer that question I look at the means of the two samples. Device A had a mean response time of 25.2 seconds. Device B had a mean response time of 21.2 seconds. Device B is faster than Device A. *I can conclude at the 90% level of confidence that Device B will respond from 2.72 seconds to 5.08 seconds faster than Device A.* If the price consideration is not a real factor and speed is the determining factor, then Device B should be chosen over Device A.

One word about the signs of 2.72 and 5.08. Both signs are positive in this instance. If the signs were negative by subtracting Device B from Device A, I could actually conclude Device A responds 2.72 to 5.08 seconds *slower*, which is another way of saying the same thing. The point is this: when both signs are the same, the positive or negative sign really does not matter but is only an aid in interpreting the results. If you interpret the result from the viewpoint of Device B, you may say it is faster by 2.72 to 5.08 seconds. If you interpret the results from the viewpoint of Device A, you may say Device A is slower than Device B by 2.72 to 5.08 seconds. If you interpret the results as faster or slower, it makes no difference as long as your point of reference is understood.

Of course it goes without saying, but I am going to say it anyway: Any conclusion will depend on the question posed in the problem. Sometimes slower is better and sometimes faster is better. Sometimes higher is better and sometimes lower is better. The conclusion depends on the problem content and must be accessed individually at the time you make your final statement as to the meaning of the interval. Making a clear statement in your concluding remarks is extremely important in proper interpretation.

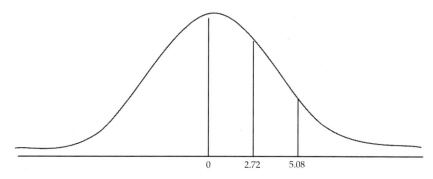

Figure 9.1 Answering Devices CI Solution.

Figure 9.1 shows zero is not in the interval, which indicates there is a significant difference between the two answering devices. Zero must be in the interval for there to be no significant difference. If there is no significant difference, any variation can be explained by random sampling error. This is not the case in this problem. Here, there is a statistically significant difference and random error has not occurred.

Independent Sampling—Small Size Samples–CI

Independent sampling can have both large and small size samples. I have just shown you the calculations for large size samples. Large samples use a Z-value. For small samples I will switch to t-values. There are, however, two approaches to small size sample calculations based on the *variances of the two populations*.

To use the small size sample and t-value approach, *at least one* of the samples must have a sample size less than 30. Both can be less than 30 but *one must be less* than 30. One sample size can be 40 and the second sample size can be 28. When this occurs, I will use the t-approach.

Small samples can have two approaches.

Approach One: The *populations* have *equal variances*.

$$\sigma_1^2 = \sigma_2^2$$

Approach Two: The *populations* have *unequal variances*.

$$\sigma_1^2 \neq \sigma_2^2$$

Note that the parameter in both approaches is the **population** *variance not the sample variance*. The sample variances $(S_2^2 \neq S_2^2)$ will *never equal* each other.

Approach One: Equal Variances (Small Sample)–CI

If the variances of the two populations can be assumed to be equal but unknown, you can pool the variances of the samples. Since I am using a t-solution, I need the degrees of freedom. Pooling the variances makes life much simpler, because I determine the degrees of freedom by $(n_1 + n_2) - 2$. Degrees of freedom are a necessary evil when I look up an appropriate t-value. Let's look at an example.

Let's assume a certain concession stand dispenses soft drinks at an event. A sample of 15 cups yields a mean fill level of 15.3 ounces with a *variance of 3.5 ounces*. This appears to be under the desired level of 16 ounces, so you make an adjustment to the dispensing equipment. After adjusting the fill level, a second sample of 10 cups is taken with a mean fill level of 17.1 ounces and a *variance* of 3.9 ounces. It is reasonable to assume the population variances are equal, since I am using one machine to fill the cups. I want to construct a 95% interval for *the difference* in fill levels.

Side Note

There is a statistical method you can use to determine if the variances are equal. It is the F-test. The F-test places the larger variance over the smaller variance. The formula and calculations are as follows:

$$F = \frac{S_1^2}{S_2^2} = \frac{3.9}{3.5} = 1.114 \text{ (This is my calculated value.)}$$

The null and alternate hypotheses I am testing are as follows:

$$H_o: \sigma_1^2 = \sigma_2^2$$

$$H_a: \sigma_1^2 \neq \sigma_2^2$$

I have the calculated value (1.114), but now need a critical value of F. Since I place the larger variance over the smaller variance, the F-value will be greater than 1. This forces a two-tailed test (see the null hypothesis) to become a one-tailed, right rejection region test. The procedure requires alpha to be divided by 2, so at the 0.05 alpha level, the alpha in the right tail would be 0.0250.

I now must find a critical F-value. The best approach is to use Excel. Go to Excel. Click on $f(x)$ in the toolbar. Scroll down and find "FINV." Open it. You have three questions to answer. First, the probability is 0.0250 (one-half of the alpha). Second, you are asked to provide two different degrees of freedom. One will be the numerator (degrees_freedom1) and the second will be the denominator (degrees_freedom2). Here the numerator has 9 degrees of freedom ($n-1$ or $10-1$). The denominator has 14 degrees of freedom ($n-1$ or $15-1$). After inserting these values, the resultant will be 3.2093.

Figure 9.2 shows the results of my example:

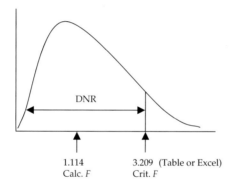

$$\begin{array}{cc} 1.114 & 3.209 \text{ (Table or Excel)} \\ \text{Calc. } F & \text{Crit. } F \end{array}$$

Figure 9.2 F-Distribution (Right Skewed Distribution).

Alternately, you can type into your browser "F distribution" to search the Internet for an F-table. I discovered one at *www.statsoft.com/textbook/sttable.html*.

Table 9.3 is an F-table and is partially reproduced by using the Excel function for alpha 0.0250. Other tables can be reproduced for other alpha levels—0.10, 0.050, or 0.010 for example.

To read Table 9.3, I use the degrees of freedom for the numerator of 9 ($10 - 1$) and the denominator of 14 ($15 - 1$). The critical F-value is 3.209. Since 1.114 (calculated F-value) is less than 3.209 (critical F-value), I would DNR (accept) the null hypothesis. The null hypothesis was stated above and the variances of the populations are equal, $H_o: \sigma_1^2 = \sigma_2^2$. I DNR the null and conclude the variances of the populations are equal. This allows me to pool my variances as intuitively suggested. To test the variance of the population I use the variance of the sample as representative of the population. Once again, this is parametric testing. I use a sample to test the population value.

I am now ready to determine my confidence interval using the following formula. I suggest you look at Table 9.1 and find the formula for small samples with equal variances.

Table 9.3   *F*-table for alpha 0.0250.

d.f. 2	d.f. 1	Numerator Degrees of Freedom for Alpha 0.0250									
		1	2	3	4	5	6	7	8	9	10
D	1	647.78	799.50	864.16	899.58	921.85	937.11	948.22	956.66	963.28	968.63
e	2	38.506	39.000	39.165	39.248	39.298	39.331	39.355	39.373	39.387	39.398
n	3	17.443	16.044	15.439	15.101	14.885	14.735	14.624	14.540	14.473	14.419
o	4	12.218	10.649	9.979	9.605	9.365	9.197	9.074	8.980	8.905	8.844
m											
i	5	10.007	8.434	7.764	7.388	7.146	6.978	6.853	6.757	6.681	6.619
n	6	8.813	7.260	6.600	6.227	5.988	5.820	5.700	5.600	5.523	5.461
a	7	8.073	6.542	5.890	5.523	5.285	5.119	4.995	4.899	4.823	4.761
t											
o	8	7.571	6.060	5.416	5.053	4.817	4.652	4.529	4.433	4.357	4.295
r	9	7.209	5.715	5.078	4.718	4.484	4.320	4.197	4.102	4.026	3.964
s	10	6.937	5.456	4.826	4.468	4.236	4.072	3.950	3.855	3.779	3.717
D	11	6.724	5.256	4.630	4.275	4.044	3.881	3.759	3.664	3.588	3.526
e	12	6.554	5.096	4.474	4.121	3.891	3.728	3.607	3.512	3.436	3.374
g											
r	13	6.414	4.965	4.347	3.996	3.767	3.604	3.483	3.388	3.312	3.250
e	**14**	6.298	4.857	4.242	3.892	3.663	3.501	3.380	3.285	**3.209**	3.147
e	15	6.200	4.765	4.153	3.804	3.576	3.415	3.293	3.199	3.123	3.060
s	16	6.115	4.687	4.077	3.729	3.502	3.341	3.219	3.125	3.049	2.986
o	17	6.042	4.619	4.011	3.665	3.438	3.277	3.156	3.061	2.985	2.922
f	18	5.978	4.560	3.954	3.608	3.382	3.221	3.100	3.005	2.929	2.866
F	19	5.922	4.508	3.903	3.559	3.333	3.172	3.051	2.956	2.880	2.817
r	20	5.872	4.461	3.859	3.515	3.289	3.128	3.007	2.913	2.837	2.774
e											
e	21	5.827	4.420	3.819	3.475	3.250	3.090	2.969	2.874	2.798	2.735
d	22	5.786	4.383	3.783	3.440	3.215	3.055	2.934	2.839	2.763	2.700
o	23	5.750	4.349	3.751	3.408	3.184	3.023	2.902	2.808	2.731	2.668
m	24	5.717	4.319	3.721	3.380	3.155	2.995	2.874	2.780	2.703	2.640

I will wait while you look for the formula.

I hope you found it. It is written below:

$$\overline{X}_1 - \overline{X}_2 \pm t_\alpha \sqrt{\frac{S_p^2}{n_1} + \frac{S_p^2}{n_2}}$$

You comment that this formula looks familiar.

You are correct. Great observation! The main differences are the use of a *t*-value and not a Z-value and the pooling of the variances.

Pooling the variances gives me a weighted average of the two individual variances. *The pooled variance will not be less than the smallest variance (3.5) nor higher than the highest variance (3.9).* The pooled variance is a weighted average of the individual sample variances. The sample variances do not equal (3.5 ≠ 3.9), nor will they ever equal. The variances I assume to be equal are the *true unknown, population variances.*

I have a question, Professor.

Okay, go ahead.

Why do I care about pooling the variances?

Good question. I have briefly addressed that issue but do not mind covering it again, since you are being bombarded by so many new ideas and terms. I am using a *t*-test. A *t*-test requires I know the degrees of freedom in order to look up the critical value. By pooling the variances, I can easily identify the degrees of freedom as $(n_1 + n_2) - 2$; $(10 + 15) - 2 = 23$ degrees of freedom.

Okay, you respond, but why did you subtract 2? Degrees of freedom in previous chapters has been $n - 1$.

Yes, but that was for one population. Now I have two populations, so I will subtract 2 rather than 1. I lose a degree of freedom for each population.

My first calculation is of the pooled variances. That formula and calculations are as follows:

$$S_p^2 = \frac{S_1^2\left(n_1 - 1\right) + S_2^2\left(n_2 - 1\right)}{n_1 + n_2 - 2}$$

$$S_p^2 = \frac{(3.5)(15 - 1) + (3.9)(10 - 1)}{15 + 10 - 2}$$

$$S_p^2 = \frac{49 + 35.1}{23}$$

$$S_p^2 = 3.66 \text{ (Falls between 3.5 and 3.9 and it must).}$$

Notice that I used 3.5 and 3.9 without squaring them. Why do you suppose I did not square the variances?

You respond, that's obvious, you gave us the variance. Variance is already squared. To square it again would not make it the variance, but variance squared.

My head is spinning, but excellent response and a bit scary! Could it be you are understanding this stuff? (Okay, I admit, maybe that is stretching things a bit.)

The next step is to determine the confidence interval using the pooled variance and the t-value. I need a critical value of t using an alpha value of 0.05 (95% CL). I have been able to pool the variances. With degrees of freedom of 23 ($n_1 + n_2 - 2$, which is $15 + 10 - 2 = 23$ degrees of freedom), I look up the t-value of 2.06866 (Round to 2.069).

Try it and make sure it does. The t-value table is Table 7.7 in Chapter 7 or is at the back of this textbook. Take a minute or two to check this out or use the Excel function to confirm the critical t-value.

The calculations are as follows:

$$\overline{X}_1 - \overline{X}_2 \pm t_\alpha \sqrt{\frac{S_p^2}{n_1} + \frac{S_p^2}{n_2}}$$

$$15.3 - 17.1 \pm (2.069)\sqrt{\frac{3.66}{15} + \frac{3.66}{10}}$$

$$-1.8 \pm (2.069)\sqrt{0.244 + 0.366}$$

$$-1.8 \pm (2.069)\sqrt{0.610}$$

$$-1.8 \pm (2.069)(0.781)$$

$$-1.8 \pm 1.616$$

$$-0.184 \text{ to } -3.416 \text{ (The values are both negative numbers;}$$
$$\text{same sign).}$$

Interpretation

From observation I do not find a zero in the interval. Both signs are negative, thus zero cannot be in the interval. Not finding a zero means that both fill weights are not statistical equivalents. I must, therefore, conclude there is a statistical difference in the fill weights before and after the adjustment. I wanted to make a slight adjustment in the fill level but apparently made a bigger one than I wanted. I wanted the difference before and after the adjustment to be explained by random sampling error. It is not.

What I must conclude is that there is a statistically significant difference between the 17.1 ounces and the 15.3 ounces. The difference cannot be explained by random sampling error alone.

Statement #1:   I am 95% confident the fill level of the cups, *after the adjustment,* is greater by between 0.184 to 3.416 ounces.

Statement #2:   I can also say I am 95% confident the fill level of the cups, *before the adjustment,* is less by between 0.184 to 3.416 ounces.

Either statement is correct. It depends on your point of reference—before or after the adjustment. The sign really does not affect the absolute value of the concluding statement.

Approach Two: Unequal Variances (Small Sample)–CI

Working with the assumption of unequal variances presents an entirely different problem. Statisticians have concluded that the distribution of unequal population variances does not fit a conventional t-distribution like equal variances do. *With unequal variances, I must calculate the degrees of freedom* rather than take the sum of the two variances less 2 $(n_1 + n_2) - 2$. Calculation of the degrees of freedom is done by using the following formula. Complicated as it looks, it is not. Tedious it is, but it is not complicated. You can make errors if you do not set the calculations up carefully and watch your order of operation.

$$\text{d.f.} = \frac{\left(\dfrac{S_1^2}{n_1} + \dfrac{S_2^2}{n_2}\right)^2}{\dfrac{\left(\dfrac{S_1^2}{n_1}\right)^2}{n_1 - 1} + \dfrac{\left(\dfrac{S_2^2}{n_2}\right)^2}{n_2 - 1}}$$

When I make this calculation the t-value is referred to as t'-value, which is called t-prime. I am still going to use the t-table (Table 7.7 in Chapter 7 or back of the textbook). Excel is also helpful as I have pointed out before.

The confidence interval formula for unequal variances is similar to the formula for equal variances. I have shown both below to you can visually compare them.

Notice the unequal variance formula uses the sample variance representing each population whereas the equal variance formula uses the pooled variance. The other difference is the manner in which degrees of freedom are determined. With the unequal variance approach, you calculate the degrees of freedom using the very tedious formula shown just above. With the equal variance approach, you determine degrees of freedom by $(n_1 + n_2) - 2$.

$$\overline{X}_1 - \overline{X}_2 \pm t'_\alpha \sqrt{\frac{S_1^2}{n_1} + \frac{S_2^2}{n_2}} \quad \text{unequal variances}$$

$$\overline{X}_1 - \overline{X}_2 \pm t_\alpha \sqrt{\frac{S_p^2}{n_1} + \frac{S_p^2}{n_2}} \quad \text{equal variances}$$

Also notice the unequal variances approach inserts a value called t-prime whereas the equal variances approach inserts a value called t. Fortunately, the use of t or t' is looked up the same way in the same t-table. I am personally not sure why the distinction needs to be made because they look up in the same t-table in the same manner. However, they are designated differently so just live with it and move on.

One word of caution is appropriate here. Let's say that you calculate the degrees of freedom as 24.65 (unequal variance approach). The rule is you round down to 24 degrees of freedom, never up to 25 degrees of freedom.

Let's look at an example. Babies To Go, Inc. is the manufacturer of car seats for children. They manufacture two distinct types of car seats. They want to test the car seats for durability. They take a sample of 15 car seats of Type 1 design and find the average life to be 11.4 months with a standard deviation of 1.2 months. A durability test of 10 car seats of Type 2 design yields an average life of 7.5 months with a standard deviation of 0.8 months. Here for illustration purposes, I will assume there is no evidence to suggest that the variances in the wear of Type 1 versus Type 2 are equal. For illustration purposes, this assumption overrides any results obtained using the F-test. The CEO wants to test the durability of each design using an alpha of 0.05.

Let's recap the data associated with the two samples:

Table 9.4   Babies To Go, Inc. data.

	Type 1	**Type 2**
Mean Life	11.4 months	7.5 months
Sample Size	15	10
Standard Deviation	1.2 months	0.8 months
Variance	1.44	0.64

Again the formula for determining degrees of freedom is as follows:

$$\text{d.f.} = \frac{\left(\dfrac{S_1^2}{n_1} + \dfrac{S_2^2}{n_2}\right)^2}{\dfrac{\left(\dfrac{S_1^2}{n_1}\right)^2}{n_1 - 1} + \dfrac{\left(\dfrac{S_2^2}{n_2}\right)^2}{n_2 - 1}}$$

Let's first calculate the degrees of freedom. You are going to substitute the values you know into the formula and *CAREFULLY* make the calculation as follows:

Numerator Calculation

$$\text{Numerator} = \left(\frac{1.44}{15} + \frac{0.64}{10}\right)^2$$

This is the numerator of the equation above. I will work the numerator then the denominator to keep the process from being too confusing.
Solving the equation:

$$\text{Numerator} = (0.096 + 0.064)^2$$

$$\text{Numerator} = (0.1600)^2$$

$$\text{Numerator} = 0.0256$$

Denominator Calculation

$$\text{Denominator} = \frac{(1.44 \div 15)^2}{15 - 1} + \frac{(0.64 \div 10)^2}{10 - 1}$$

This is the denominator calculation for the formula just above. Solving the equation:

$$\text{Denominator} = \frac{(0.0960)^2}{15 - 1} + \frac{(0.0640)^2}{10 - 1}$$

$$\text{Denominator} = \frac{(0.0092)}{15 - 1} + \frac{(0.0041)}{10 - 1}$$

$$\text{Denominator} = 0.0007 + 0.0005$$

$$\text{Denominator} = 0.0012$$

Putting Them Together

$$\text{Degrees of freedom} = \frac{0.0256}{0.0012} = 21.33$$

d.f. = 21 rounded down per the rule.

Okay, that tedious calculation is done, so what is next, you ask?

Well, since you have done such a great job with this one, let's push on.

Next, I need to look up the value of t' at alpha 0.05 and the degrees of freedom of 21. The corresponding t'-value is 2.080. Look it up yourself and make sure I am correct. This value is found in the t-table not the Z-table.

Let's look at the confidence interval formula once again.

$$\overline{X}_1 - \overline{X}_2 \pm t'_\alpha \sqrt{\frac{S_1^2}{n_1} + \frac{S_2^2}{n_2}} \quad \text{unequal variances}$$

Okay, now let's insert the numbers. I have been given in Table 9.4 or have developed by looking up the t-value (2.080).

$$11.4 - 7.5 \pm 2.080 \sqrt{\frac{1.44}{15} + \frac{0.64}{10}}$$

$$3.9 \pm 2.080 \sqrt{0.096 + 0.064}$$

$$3.9 \pm 2.080 \sqrt{0.160}$$

$$3.9 \pm 2.080(0.400)$$

$$3.9 \pm 0.8320$$

3.068 to 4.732 months (The 95% confidence interval)

Interpretation

Both values are positive, so the interval does NOT contain zero. I can conclude the two types are not statistical equivalents. *If I go back and look at the sampling data* (Table 9.4), *I can conclude that I am 95% confident that Type 1 lasts from 3.068 to 4.732 months longer than Type 2.* If the costs of manufacturing the two types are equal to each other, the CEO should prefer Type 1.

Let's change the problem slightly. Let's assume the CEO found that Type 1 was a lot more expensive to manufacture. The increased cost will lead to an increased sales price. Can the higher sales price be justified based on durability? Let us further assume that the CEO has determined if Type 1 lasts at least five months longer than Type 2, the cost of manufacture can be justified, and the Type 1 unit can be sold for enough to more than make up the additional costs. What decision do you make?

The numbers do not change. The calculations I have made remain the same. From those calculations, I have determined there is a statistically significant difference in the two types. Type 1 has a longer life than Type 2, but is it at least five months longer?

The answer is no. The calculated interval of 3.068 months to 4.732 months does not contain the five months. Therefore, I cannot conclude that the cost of manufacturing Type 1 can be justified at an increased sales price. Under these circumstances, I would opt for Type 2.

Wow, Professor. I can see this testing stuff as being very useful in making informed decisions rather than flying by the seat of your pants. I am beginning to understand some of this stuff.

I look at you in amazement, but say nothing, assuming your comment is rhetorical.

Let's move on with another helpful technique.

Dependent Paired Sampling–CI

As a recap, I have listed the main types of two-population tests.

Independent Testing:
    Large size samples
    Small samples
        Equal variances
        Unequal variances
Dependent Testing:
    Matched pairs

Large size samples, small samples with equal variances, and small samples of unequal variances have been examined. These three are associated with independent testing. Matched pairs (dependent testing) present a different challenge.

Suppose I want to evaluate *one relevant aspect* among two similar data sets. My method of testing choice would be paired sampling.

Paired Sampling offers several advantages.

- First, smaller samples may be used.
- Second, smaller variances are encountered.
- Third, fewer degrees of freedom are lost.
- Fourth, a smaller sampling error will occur.

Several examples will serve to help you understand the concept of paired sampling or matched pairs. The groups or pairs will have some common relationship. There will be an attempt to match the pairs as closely as possible.

Example 1

In medical research it is not uncommon to have control groups when a new medicine is tested. The groups will be matched as closely as possible. Let's say a new blood pressure medicine needs to be tested. Two groups of subjects are chosen. The groups are matched as closely as possible in such characteristics as gender, weight, age, activity level, cholesterol, and any other factor affecting blood pressure. The groups are essentially twins or mirrors of each other except for one relevant factor—the medicine given. Group 1 is given Medicine A and Group 2 is given a placebo (non-medication). The difference in the blood pressure after the study time period has lapsed will be due solely to the medicine or the lack of medication. I want to know if there is a difference in blood pressure between groups.

Example 2

Let's assume I have a product that I want to market. I have been presented with a choice of two different marketing programs by my advertising agency. I would select a sample from two matched test markets, which would be matched as to population size, socio-economic characteristics, demographic characteristics, etc. The purpose of the test is to determine which marketing program will yield the best sales results.

Example 3

End cap displays are generally sought by most vendors, since they tend to increase sales significantly. Often a vendor will pay a premium to the drug store or grocery store for a preferred display position. However, you want to know if you can justify the premium. Weekly sales for a soft drink product at a local supermarket are recorded before and after an end cap display is installed. Did the end cap display make enough of a difference in sales after the display is installed to justify paying a premium for the location?

The purpose of matched pairs is to control as many factors in the testing process as possible and then introduce an uncommon variable to determine the effect of the uncommon variable on the two groups.

Let's work through an example.

I want to test the effect of gender on starting salaries of graduates from a certain college in Texas. I select two groups—one male and one female. I gather the information on a large number of subjects by compiling a pool of males and a pool of females. I record the GPA and the major for each member of the pool. I will select all marketing majors or all economics majors. I would never mix majors such as marketing and education. I next select at random one male from the larger pool of males. I then select one female from the larger pool of females. I record this as matched pair number one (Table 9.5). I then continue this selection process nine additional times. The result is 10 matched pairs of males and females.

The confidence interval formulas I will used for matched pairs are as follows:

$$\bar{d} \pm t_\alpha \frac{S_d}{\sqrt{n}}$$

where $\bar{d}$ is the average difference in the matched pairs.

S_d is the standard deviation of the difference.

t_α is the critical t-value looked up in the t-table or found by Excel.

n is the sample size.

The two calculations are from the following formulas:

$$\bar{d} = \frac{\sum d_i}{n}$$

$$S_d = \sqrt{\frac{\sum d_i^2 - n(\bar{d})^2}{n - 1}}$$

The results of the study are recapped in Table 9.5 below.

Table 9.5 Matched pairs study of starting salaries.

Pair	Male Salary	Female Salary	d_i	d_i^2
1	$39,500	$39,000	500	250,000
2	$41,800	$41,900	−100	10,000
3	$40,200	$39,600	600	360,000
4	$38,500	$38,500	0	0
5	$43,400	$42,500	900	810,000
6	$37,800	$38,000	−200	40,000
7	$39,500	$39,200	300	90,000
8	$41,100	$40,000	1,100	1,210,000
9	$38,300	$38,100	200	40,000
10	$39,200	$38,500	700	490,000
Totals	$399,300	$395,300	$4,000	**$3,300,000**
Means	$39,930	$39,530	**$400**	$330,000

If you simply look at the data, the mean starting salary for males is $39,930 and for females is $39,530. This is a difference of $400.

I want to know if there is a statistically significant difference in the starting salaries of males and females with a certain GPA and a certain major or is the difference in $39,930 and $39,530 due to random sampling error alone? The test will be conducted at the alpha level of 0.05. This is a t-test, since the sample size is less than 30.

From observation, it appears as if there is no difference ($400 is not much). However, one of the things I hope you learn is to never trust your first impression without applying some sort of statistical procedure to test it.

I begin my calculations by determining the mean of the difference. That value is the sum of the column headed d_i divided by the number of matched pairs, which is 10 in this instance.

$$\bar{d} = \frac{\sum d_i}{n}$$

$\bar{d} = \dfrac{4{,}000}{10} = 400$ (This is also the difference in the $39,930 and the $39,530 starting salaries).

Next, I calculate the standard deviation of the difference.

$$S_d = \sqrt{\frac{\sum d_i^2 - n(\bar{d})^2}{n - 1}}$$

$$S_d = \sqrt{\frac{3{,}300{,}000 - (10)(400)^2}{10 - 1}}$$

$$S_d = \sqrt{\frac{3{,}300{,}000 - (10)(160{,}000)}{9}}$$

$$S_d = \sqrt{\frac{3{,}300{,}000 - (1{,}600{,}000)}{9}}$$

$$S_d = \sqrt{\frac{1{,}700{,}000}{9}}$$

$$S_d = \sqrt{188{,}889}$$

$$S_d = 434.61$$

The 95% confidence interval for the difference in the matched pairs is shown below. The t-value (2.262 with d.f. of 9) is determined from table look up (Chapter 7 table or back of the textbook). Check it out by looking it up yourself.

$$\bar{d} \pm t_\alpha \frac{S_d}{\sqrt{n}}$$

$$400 \pm (2.262)\left(\frac{434.61}{\sqrt{10}}\right)$$

$$400 \pm (2.262)\left(\frac{434.61}{3.1623}\right)$$

$$400 \pm (2.262)\left(137.435\right)$$

$$400 \pm 310.878$$

$$\$89.12 \text{ to } \$710.88$$

Interpretation

First I observe, there is no zero in the interval. This means there is a difference in the starting salaries that is significant. The difference in the starting salaries for men of $39,930 and women of $39,530 cannot be explained by sampling error alone. I am 95% confident the mean starting salaries for males are higher than the mean starting salaries for women ($39,930 is higher than $39,530). Were the interval to contain zero, I would have to conclude there is no statistically significant difference in the starting salaries—men are paid the same as women. Since this is not the case, do you have any idea *how much more* the men are paid than women?

Don't read the next sentence until you think about it.

On average, the starting salary for men is from $89.12 to $710.88 per year higher than the starting salary for women.

Test

Wow, you quickly say. I am not ready for a test.

Not so, I say.

Anyway, this is not really a test but a check of your understanding of when to apply an independent test or when to apply a matched pairs test. Let's look at a couple of examples.

Let's assume the following:

I am a manufacturer of tires. I would like to produce tires that last longer, so I conduct a test of the mean life of a certain tire. I have concluded that my tires should not be tested on the racetrack at Daytona by professional drivers. I want my test to include only the everyday, ordinary drivers driving on neighborhood streets. After all, the ordinary driver is my target market, so I better use him or her in my test.

The new tire is a steel-belted radial. I have two designs in mind, so I produce enough tires with both designs to accomplish the testing. The experiment is set up as follows. Twenty new cars were selected at random and two tires of the *same design* were installed on the rear wheels of those 20 cars. Twenty more new cars were selected at random and two tires of the *alternate design* were installed on the rear wheels of those 20 cars. The test as designed thus far includes 40 new cars split into two groups with 20 cars having one design on the rear wheels and the other 20 cars having the alternate design on the rear wheels. The drivers were told to drive their car as usual. Get the picture?

Okay, let's now say I conduct the test. How should I measure the results—independent sampling or paired sampling?

Think about it before reading on.

This experiment as set forth above would be the comparison of two independent populations. The experimental design as set forth above does not consider nor control the wear due to each driver. Each driver's driving style and driving habits provide an uncontrolled wild card in this experiment.

How could I have changed the experiment to better control this wild card?

Think about it before reading on.

I could have selected 20 new cars randomly and placed one design of each type on the same car. In this instance, the rear wheels would contain design A on one side and design B on the other side. Here the driving habits of the drivers are minimized. The *"mean life to wear-out"* is better established when the wild card is better controlled. This latter experimental design would use the matched pairs approach.

Do you see the difference? In the former, I leave the difference in driving skills and habits of each of the drivers as a wild card in the experiment. This allows me to designate each of the populations as independent. In the latter design, I tend to minimize the driving skills and habits of each of the drivers by matching the pairs of tires to the drivers.

Now that wasn't so bad was it? Design of the experiment is very critical as this example illustrates.

Okay, that wraps up confidence intervals, so let's move to hypothesis testing for two populations.

Hypothesis Testing versus Confidence Intervals

With hypothesis testing I have the same types of tests available to me.

Independent Testing:
    Large size samples
    Small samples
        Equal variances
        Unequal variances
Dependent Testing:
    Matched pairs

Go to Table 9.1. I will wait.

Okay, got it? I have been addressing confidence intervals. The formulas I have been using are shown in the left-hand column. There is a mirrored image formula for each left-hand test in the right-hand column. The right-hand column is the hypothesis test approach. The left-hand column is the confidence interval approach. The only difference between the formulas in the left column and the right column is one of solving for a different term. The formulas are essentially the same.

Both hypothesis testing and confidence intervals will reveal if there is a statistically significant difference between the means of the two populations. Confidence intervals will tell you the amount of the difference. Hypothesis testing can only reveal whether the difference is or is not statistically significant. If you have a problem that requires a conclusion about the amount of the difference, then you must use confidence intervals. If you are not interested in the amount of the difference and just want to know if the two population means are different, then use either.

Let's take a couple of examples of hypothesis testing.

Hypothesis Testing

As you can see from Table 9.1 created early in this chapter, the formulas for confidence interval and hypothesis testing are closely related. Remember, hypothesis testing can be done using a Form I test (left-tail rejection region) or Form II test (right-tail rejection region) or Form III test (two-tailed rejection region). If you need to review these three forms, you might return to Chapter 8.

In any hypothesis test, you compare a critical value of either Z or t to a calculated value of the corresponding Z or t. Let's work through an example of a hypothesis test using the following example.

A Texas study was commissioned to determine if there is a statistical difference between employees' contributions to two different types of retirement plans. Two sets of data are evaluated. One group of employees contributes to a tax-deferred annuity (TDA) while a second group of employees contributes to a 401(K) plan.

The TDA plan places deposits with an investment bank which invests the money in stock or bond portfolios. A second alternative is a standard 401(K) plan where the company matches all or a portion of the contribution by the employee. If the portfolios perform well, the retirement funds grow. Two groups are involved in making contributions.

The objective of the study is to determine if the two groups contribute the same or different amounts. It is felt that employees will contribute more to what is perceived as a favorable plan. The mean contribution for the TDA is $2,155 and the mean to the 401(K) is $2,040. Is there a statistical difference between the two means or does sampling error explain the difference? If there is a difference, it might be argued that employees see the TDA as a better plan than the 401(K).

A random sample of 12 people from the TDA plan is selected and a sample of 15 people from the 401(K) plan is selected. The results are shown in Table 9.6 below:

Table 9.6 Comparison of two plans.

Results	TDA Eligible	401(K) Eligible
Sample Size	12	15
Sample Mean	$2,155	$2,040
Sample Standard Deviation	$612	$695

This is an independent sample, since neither group influences the contribution of the other. Actually, the null hypothesis can take on any of the three forms of hypothesis testing.

Remember, Form I is a left-tail rejection region. Form II is a right-tail rejection region. Form III is a two-tail rejection region. Initially let's opt for a two-tail test—Form III.

$$H_0: \quad \mu_{TDA} = \mu_{401(k)}$$

$$H_a: \quad \mu_{TDA} \neq \mu_{401(k)}$$

This is a t-test since at least one of the samples is less than 30 (actually both are less than 30). Should you use the assumption of equal or unequal variances? In this instance, assume the variances are equal. The F-test supports this assumption (1.2896 if you care to calculate it) and there is no overriding statement to assume otherwise. The t-test formula can be found in Table 9.1 but is shown below.

$$t_{TEST} = \frac{(\bar{x}_1 - \bar{x}_2) - (\mu_1 - \mu_2)}{\sqrt{\dfrac{S_p^2}{n_1} + \dfrac{S_p^2}{n_2}}}$$

where $\bar{X}_1 - \bar{X}_2$ is the difference between the two means.

S_p^2 is the pooled variance.

$\mu_1 - \mu_2 = 0$ and is always zero.

n is the sample size.

Okay, Professor, why do you include $\mu_1 - \mu_2 = 0$, if it is always zero?

The only reason for including this in the formula is a conceptual one. The idea is associated with zero being important. If the means of the populations are equal, the difference in the means will equal zero (statistically speaking). Zero in the interval tells me everything is okay and the difference in the means is explained by sampling error.

The first step is to determine the pooled variance using the information given in Table 9.6. This formula and solution is as follows:

$$S_p^2 = \frac{S_1^2(n_1 - 1) + S_2^2(n_2 - 1)}{n_1 + n_2 - 2}$$

$$S_p^2 = \frac{(612)^2(12 - 1) + (695)^2(15 - 1)}{12 + 15 - 2}$$

$$S_p^2 = \frac{(374{,}544)(11) + (483{,}025)(14)}{25}$$

$$S_p^2 = \frac{(4{,}119{,}984) + (6{,}762{,}350)}{25}$$

$$S_p^2 = \frac{10{,}882{,}334}{25}$$

$$S_p^2 = 435{,}293.4$$

Using the information in Table 9.6 and the pool variance calculated just above, the calculated t-test gives us the following result:

$$t_{test} = \frac{(2{,}155 - 2{,}040) - 0}{\sqrt{\dfrac{435{,}293.4}{12} + \dfrac{435{,}293.4}{15}}}$$

$$t_{test} = \frac{115}{\sqrt{36{,}274.5 + 29{,}019.6}}$$

$$t_{test} = \frac{115}{\sqrt{65{,}294.1}}$$

$$t_{test} = \frac{115}{255.53}$$

$t_{test} = 0.4500$ This is the calculated t-value.

At the alpha level of 0.05, the *critical* t-value from Chapter 7 or the back of the textbook look up at 25 degrees of freedom ($n_1 + n_2 - 2$, which is $12 + 15 - 2 = 25$) is 2.05954 (rounded to 2.060). Excel will give you the same result. Look it up or use Excel to make sure I am correct before you move on with the rest of the problem. This is a two-tailed rejection region test.

Now you are ready to compare the calculated t-test value (0.4500) with the table look up critical value (2.060). The DNR (do not reject) range is from −2.060 to +2.060. The critical value is 0.4500. This value is less than +2.060 but greater than −2.060; therefore, it falls in the DNR region. I can now assert that there is no statistically significant difference at the 0.05 alpha level (95% level of significance) between the contributions of the employees to the TDA plan or the employees to the 401(K) plan. The contributions are statistically the same. The differences are due to sampling error and sampling error alone.

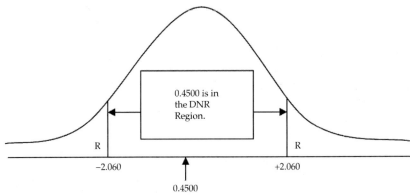

0.4500 is in the DNR Region.

R

R

−2.060

+2.060

0.4500

Figure 9.3   Two tail rejection region (TDA & 401k).

One-Tail Rejection Region

In hypothesis testing for two populations, I do have some latitude in using Form I, Form II, or Form III. I could have set this problem up as a right-tail rejection region test or as a left-tail rejection region test. How I state the null and alternate hypotheses would determine whether I use Form I, II, or III. For example, if I were to test that the TDA contributions are more than the 401(K) contributions, the hypothesis would be as follows.

$$H_o: \quad \mu_{TDA} \leq \mu_{401(k)}$$
$$H_a: \quad \mu_{TDA} > \mu_{401(k)}$$

In this case, the critical t-value becomes (one-tailed, right test rejection region) $+1.708141$ (Excel) (rounded to 1.708). The calculated t-value remains the same at 0.4500. You would reach the same conclusion. Because 0.4500 is less than 1.708, you would DNR the null hypothesis and conclude that the contributions to the TDA plan are less than or equal to the mean of the 401(K) plan.

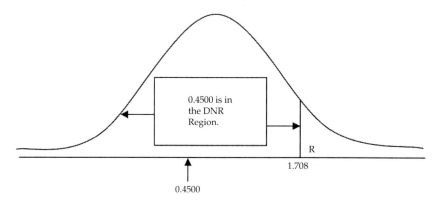

Figure 9.4   One tail rejection region (TDA & 401k).

What do you think would happen if I applied the confidence interval approach rather than the hypothesis testing approach? While Confidence Intervals are generally two-tailed rejection regions, here I am only interested in the right hand side rejection region.

I would hope I would reach the same conclusion, you say.

That would be a correct statement, I respond.

Let's go through that process and see what would happen. I am assuming the variances are equal, so the variances must be pooled. I will use the pooled variance, confidence interval formula for a small sized sample as follows:

$$\overline{X}_1 - \overline{X}_2 \pm t_\alpha \sqrt{\frac{S_p^2}{n_1} + \frac{S_p^2}{n_2}}$$

$$2{,}155 - 2{,}040 \pm (1.708) \sqrt{\frac{435{,}293.4}{12} + \frac{435{,}293.4}{15}}$$

$$115 \pm (1.708)(255.53)$$

$$115 \pm 436.4452$$

$$-321.4452 \text{ to } 551.4452$$

$$-321.45 \text{ to } 551.45 \text{ (Rounded)}$$

The interval contains zero. If zero is in the interval, you can assert that there is no statistically significant difference between the contributions of the two groups of employees. The difference can be explained by sampling error. I can conclude TDA contributions are from minus $321.45 less than the 401(K) contributions to plus $551.45 more than the 401(K) contributions, but the overall difference is not significant.

Strange how that works, isn't it? You get the same conclusion by using the hypothesis testing or the confidence interval process.

With confidence intervals I can determine how much the difference is, but with either confidence intervals or hypothesis testing, I can determine if the difference is significant.

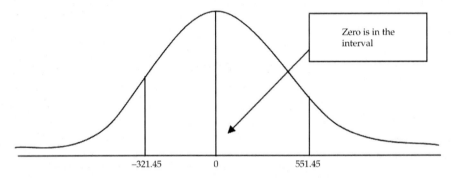

Figure 9.5 Confidence Interval (TDA & 401k).

Proportions

As you might suspect, you not only can determine if the means of two populations are statistically different, but you can test proportions in the same manner.

For example, let's suppose you wanted to determine the percentage (proportion) associated with two different manufacturing techniques. In this instance, I want to know if there is a difference in the defects produced by Process A versus the defects produced by Process B. I want to know which one yields the better result. This is a proportion problem. The only two outcomes are defective and non-defective.

The procedures associated with proportion and mean testing are essentially the same. The formulas are, however, different, as you might imagine.

The proportion formula for a confidence interval is as follows:

$$p_1 - p_2 \pm Z_\alpha S_{p_1 - p_2}$$

$$\text{Where } S_{p_1 - p_2} = \sqrt{\frac{p_1(1 - p_1)}{n_1} + \frac{p_2(1 - p_2)}{n_2}}$$

Compare the proportion formula to the mean formula.

$$\overline{X}_1 - \overline{X}_2 \pm Z_\alpha S_{\overline{X}_1 - \overline{X}_2}$$

Notice any similarity?

Yep, you say. They look like the same formula, but one is for proportions and one is for the means.

Actually, proportions work the same way as mean testing.

Let's work through an example. Assume I have a manufacturing plant and want to determine if shift 1 has more tardiness than shift 2. I take a sample of 100 workers from shift 1 and 125 from shift 2. The results show that 45 workers are tardy on shift 1 and 49 workers are tardy on shift 2. I want to determine a 95% confidence interval for the population proportion.

The proportions: $\qquad\qquad 45 \div 100 = 0.45$ for shift 1

$$49 \div 125 = 0.39 \text{ for shift 2}$$

First, calculate the standard deviation of the difference between the proportions using the information given above.

$$S_{p_1 - p_2} = \sqrt{\frac{p_1(1 - p_1)}{n_1} + \frac{p_2(1 - p_2)}{n_2}}$$

$$S_{p_1 - p_2} = \sqrt{\frac{0.45(0.55)}{100} + \frac{0.39(0.61)}{125}}$$

$$S_{p_1 - p_2} = \sqrt{\frac{0.2475}{100} + \frac{0.2379}{125}}$$

$$S_{p_1 - p_2} = \sqrt{0.0025 + 0.0019}$$

$$S_{p_1 - p_2} = \sqrt{0.0044}$$

$$S_{p_1 - p_2} = 0.0663$$

Next develop the confidence interval.

$$p_1 - p_2 \pm Z_\alpha S_{p_1 - p_2}$$

$$0.45 - 0.39 \pm (1.96)(0.0663)$$

$$0.06 \pm 0.1299$$

$$-0.0699 \text{ to } 0.1899$$

Interpretation

Zero is in the interval, so I must conclude that there is no statistically significance between the two population proportions. The difference can be explained by sampling error. I am 95% confident the true, unknown population proportion is between -0.0699 and 0.1899. There is no difference between the tardiness of shift 1 and shift 2 employees. This does not mean the level of tardiness is acceptable for either shift, just the difference is explained by sampling error.

Use of Excel

I have to share with you an answer one student gave on the exit examination for high school students. I am told the student was asked to *find "X" given certain information*. The answer was given by a blonde (not a slam at blondes since I know a number of really intelligent ones), female student as follows:

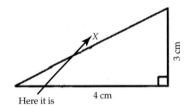

I personally love the answer. I understand she got credit for the problem on the examination. Do you suppose the testing bureau should be more specific?

Life with Excel is not quite that simple, but as you might expect, you can use Excel to make many of the computations for two-population testing.

For example, open an Excel worksheet > Tools > Data Analysis. Scroll down and find the following four possible Excel solution helps.

- *t*-test: Paired Two Sample for Means
- *t*-test: Two Sample Assuming Equal Variances
- *t*-test: Two Sample Assuming Unequal Variances
- Z-test: Two Sample for Mean

t-test: Paired Two Sample Means

The paired two sample *t*-test for means is the same as the dependent sample test shown to you above. As a reminder, I selected 10 males and 10 females who were matched as to GPA and major. I wanted to determine if the starting salary of males was equal to or greater than the starting salary of females.

To use Excel, I will enter all of my data from Table 9.5 into an Excel worksheet. Next I select the *t*-test, paired two sample for means. I am asked to enter the range for variable one (male salary) and the range for variable two (female salary). I place my cursor in the variable one box and then, using the mouse, highlight the entire data column for male salaries. Since I have a heading "Male Salary" for my column heading I include it in my variable one data range.

I now move the cursor to the second box and repeat the process for the column headed "Female Salary." I next input the difference in the hypothesized mean, which I want to be zero. In other words, I am asserting the difference in the means is zero. I check the box marked "Labels in the First Row." I choose the alpha level of 0.05. I will let the output be displayed in a new tab by selecting the second output choice. Then I click okay. The result is displayed in the following table (Table 9.7):

Table 9.7   *t*-test: Paired two sample test for means from Excel.

t-Test: Paired Two Sample Test for Means		
	Male Salary	*Female Salary*
Mean	**39,930**	**39,530**
Variance	3013444.444	2395666.667
Observations	10	10
Pearson Correlation	0.971436027	
Hypothesized Mean Difference	0	
Df	9	
t Stat	2.9104275	
P(T <= t) one-tail	0.008649604	
t Critical one-tail	1.833112923	
P(T <= t) two-tail	**0.017299209**	
t Critical two-tail	2.262157158	

If you go back and review the manual calculations associated with this problem, you will notice the *t*-value of 2.262 is the same. This approach determines a *p*-value, which for a two-tailed test is 0.0173 (rounded). Were this a Form III (two-tailed rejection region) test, the hypothesis that would be set up as follows:

$$H_o: \mu_1 = \mu_2 \text{ or } \mu_1 - \mu_2 = 0 \text{ (These have the same meaning.)}$$

$$H_a: \mu_1 \neq \mu_2 \text{ or } \mu_1 - \mu_2 \neq 0$$

Since 0.0173 < 0.05 (*p*-value < alpha value), the null hypothesis is rejected. The alternate hypothesis will be accepted, thus telling you the starting salaries of the males and females are unequal. The males have a higher starting salary. Using the Excel approach will tell you if there is a difference, but you cannot determine the amount of the difference like you can with confidence intervals. You would have to manually determine the confidence intervals as previously shown. Shown in the Table 9.7 is something referred to as a *t*-Stat (2.91). This is what I have referred to as the calculated *t*-value. Since this is a two-tailed confidence interval, the lower and upper *critical limits* are -2.262 and $+2.262$. Since $+2.91$ (*calculated value*) is greater than the upper *critical limit* of $+2.262$, you would reject the null hypothesis, just as I did using the *p*-value.

Just as a check, you can determine the *t*-test value by using the manual *t*-test formula.

$$t_{test} = \frac{\overline{X}_1 - \overline{X}_2}{\frac{S_d}{\sqrt{n}}} = \frac{35{,}930 - 35{,}530}{\frac{434.61}{\sqrt{10}}} = \frac{400}{137.535} = 2.9084 \text{ (Round to 2.91)}$$

You will have to refer back to the problem itself and the manual calculations to see where I got some of the numbers I am using. Using Excel is much faster than doing manual calculations, but as you can see the results are the same.

To use Excel, you need the entire, original data set. Without the original data set, you do not have anything to input. The other three processes using Excel ask about the same questions and work essentially the same way as demonstrated above. Additionally, if you have problems involving proportions, Excel works with their values as well as long as you have the entire data set from which the proportions are taken. Excel is helpful and much faster, so consider learning it and using it.

**You know
You are
a Texan
If:**

• You see people wear bib overalls at funerals.

• You refer to the capital of Texas as the "home of the Longhorns".

• You can actually burn your hand opening the car door.

Tear-Out Sheet Chapter 9

Student Name: _____

Day and Time of Class: _____

   Work the following problems in class if your professor allows or tear them out of the book and work them and turn them in to the professor.

Confidence Intervals

1. A sample of 35 textbooks was taken from the TCU bookstore. The average price of the books was $52.50 with a *standard deviation (S)* of $5.10. Forty textbooks were sampled from the SMU bookstore. The average price of those 40 books was $65.00 with a *variance* (S^2) of $18.06. Calculate a 90% confidence interval for the difference in the average prices for the two stores. Explain your findings.

2. Two car models are tested for a difference in average gas mileage. Ten cars of Model A averaged 32.1 miles per gallon with a standard deviation of 5.2 mpg. Twelve cars of Model B averaged 35.5 mpg with a standard deviation of 4.4 mpg. Calculate a 95% confidence interval for the difference between the two cars' mileage. There is no evidence to suggest the variances of the populations are equal. Explain your findings.

3. Bendix Fertilizer Company has two plants—one in LA and the other in Atlanta. Recent customer complaints suggest that the Atlanta shipments are underweight as compared to the LA shipments. Ten (10) boxes from LA average 96.3 pounds with a standard deviation (S) of 12.5 pounds and fifteen (15) boxes are selected form Atlanta with an average weight of 101.1 pounds with a standard deviation (S) of 10.3 pounds. Does a 99% confidence interval support those complaining? Assume equal population variances. Explain your findings.

4. The monthly starting salaries in thousands of dollars of 12 maintenance personnel at TCU are compared to those from SMU using the data in the table shown below. Develop and interpret a 95% confidence interval for the difference in mean starting salaries at TCU and SMU.

TCU	SMU
15.6	13.7
16.8	13.6
18.5	15.2
16.5	11.2

(Continued)

TCU	SMU
15.5	11.6
14.8	15.2
18.8	12.5
19.5	13.5
17.5	13.9
16.5	18.2
14.5	14.5
18.7	11.2

Hypothesis Testing

5. Each patient in Farmer's Hospital is asked to evaluate the service at the time of discharge. Recently there have been complaints that the resident physicians and nurses on the surgical wing responded too slowly to calls from the senior citizens. Other patients seem to be receiving faster service. Mr. Bob Anderson, Hospital Administrator, asked for a study by the quality assurance team. After studying the problem, the QA team, headed by Sharon Schwartz, decided to collect the following sample information and to test the claim at the alpha 0.01 level of significance. The question to be answered was: Are the other patients receiving faster service than the senior citizens? As a side calculation, Mrs. Schwartz decided to determine the p-value even though she knew she would have to explain its meaning to Mr. Anderson.

   Conduct the study by choosing the appropriate test statistic and explain your results.

   The data sets are as follows:

Patient Type	Sample Mean	Sample Standard Deviation	Sample Size
Senior Citizen	5.50 minutes	0.40 minutes	50
Other	5.30 minutes	0.30 minutes	100

6. Owens Lawn Care, Inc. manufactures and assembles lawnmowers, which are shipped to dealers throughout the United States and Canada. Two different procedures have been proposed for mounting the engine on the frame of the lawnmower. The question is: Is there a difference in the mean time to mount the engines on the frames of the lawnmowers? The first procedure was developed by Welles (#1) and the second was developed by Atkins (#2). To evaluate the two methods, it was decided to conduct a time

and motion study. A sample of five employees was timed using procedure #1 and six different employees were timed using procedure #2. The results in minutes are shown below. Is there a difference in the mean mounting times? There is reason to believe the population variances are equal. Use the 0.10 level of significance.

Procedure #1 in Minutes	Procedure #2 in Minutes
2	3
4	7
9	5
3	8
2	4
	3
Average = 4.0 minutes	Average = 5.0 minutes

10

Applying Inferential Statistics— Chi-Square as a Parametric Test, the F-distribution, One-Way ANOVA Tests

Attorney:	ALL your responses MUST be oral, Okay? What School did you go to?
Witness:	Oral.

Introduction

Sometimes the mean of the population and the mean of the sample may be statistically okay (representative). However, having a mean which is acceptable may not be the entire story. I might find the mean is okay, but the variability may not be acceptable. Both the mean and the variance are parameters, so I am still conducting parametric testing. The parameter of interest may change to the variance from the mean.

For example, let's suppose that I am a manufacturer of tennis rackets. During the past several years, I have determined the desired mean length for tennis rackets is 30 inches. I want to determine if my current production meets the 30-inch standard. I take a sample of 30 ($n = 30$) and find that the mean length of the sample is 30 inches. It looks like everything is okay, except after I ship the rackets, I begin getting complaints. Apparently 15 of the rackets are 15 inches long and 15 of the rackets are 45 inches long. The average is 30 inches; however, a length of either 15 inches or 45 inches is hardly acceptable. Obviously, I need to look further at my testing process. I cannot depend on a test of the mean alone. I need to look at the variability, namely the variance. Variance can be as important as the mean length.

There are three basic parametric methods which are useful. One is **chi-square,** which analyzes the variance of a *single population.* The second is the **F-Ratio,** which analyzes the variance of *two separate populations.* The third is **ANOVA,** which *analyzes the means by analyzing the variance of your data set.* **ANOVA** is useful for three or more populations. Some textbooks tell you two or more, but for two I find the *t*-test is possible thus negating the need for ANOVA. Let's look at each of these.

Chi-Square as a Parametric Test

Chi-square tests the hypothesis about the *variance of a single population.* Let's go back to our tennis racket example. Let's assume that the hypothesized mean is 30 inches long (my desired or specified length). Additionally, I do not want my tennis racket to have a variance greater than 0.71 inches squared. I take a random sample of 25 tennis rackets and find the length of the rackets to be 30.1" with a variance of 0.81 inches squared. The sample mean is very close to the hypothesized mean. Let's assume I performed the appropriate statistical test and determined there is no statistically significant difference between the hypothesized mean of 30 inches and the sample mean of 30.1 inches. The difference in the means can be explained by sampling error. However, I want to be doubly sure that the variances are equal.

This is a single population, so I can use a chi-square test. Is there a statistically significant difference between the population variance (0.71) and the sample variance (0.81)? In other words, does the sample variance serve as a good estimate of the population variance? Can the difference between 0.81 and 0.71 be explained by sampling error alone?

The chi-square distribution is a whole family of curves, which are driven by degrees of freedom much like the *t*-distribution. The formula is as follows:

$$\chi^2 = \frac{(n - 1)(S^2)}{\sigma^2}$$

What can you observe from the formula?

First, n = the size of the sample, which in this case is 25. Second, $n - 1$ is the degrees of freedom (24 in this case). Third, S^2 is the variance of the sample, whereas σ^2 is the variance of the population. So this means that chi-square is a weighted average of the sample variance divided by the population variance.

The five-step pattern developed in hypothesis testing applies here. The first step is to set up the null hypothesis. One of three situations could be true in this situation, so I can use the three-question approach. The answer to these questions will aid in *setting up the alternate hypothesis*, not the null hypothesis.

σ^2	<	0.71	This is okay. No action to be taken.
σ^2	>	**0.71**	**Out of control. Action must be taken.**
σ^2	=	0.71	This is okay. No action to be taken.

The answers to the three questions tell me that I am only concerned if the variance exceeds 0.71 inches squared.

But wait a minute, you interrupt. I can understand there not being a problem if the variance is equal to 0.71, but why would it not be a problem if the variance is less than 0.71 inches squared?

Good question, but bad reasoning, I respond. What am I testing, I ask?

The variance, you reply.

That is correct. So why is it a problem if the variance is less than a certain value, I ask?

I further comment: Would I be satisfied with zero variance? Less variance is okay and desirable, is it not?

Oh, you respond. I understand. I actually want less variance. The smaller the variance, the better my manufacturing tolerances are. Does this mean the chi-square test for variance will be a right-tailed rejection region test?

Yes and very astute observation, I comment.

If the variance is *less than or equal to* 0.71 inches squared, the manufacturer is operating within tolerance. However, if the variance can be shown to be *greater than* 0.71, the manufacturing process will have to be adjusted.

Reviewing the answer to my question, I notice that the greater than sign (>) points to the right, which indicates I need to develop a Form II, right-tailed rejection region test. The hypothesis would be as follows.

$$H_o: \quad \sigma^2 \leq 0.71$$
$$H_a: \quad \sigma^2 > 0.71 \quad \textbf{(right-tailed rejection region)}$$

This testing, like all other hypothesis testing, will compare a critical value (table look up) to a calculated value of chi-square (formula determined).

$$\chi^2 = \frac{(n-1)(S^2)}{\sigma^2}$$

$$\chi^2 = \frac{(25-1)(0.81)}{0.71} = 27.38 \text{ This is my calculated chi-square value.}$$

Assume alpha is 0.10. A chi-square table is shown below (Table 10.1). The degrees of freedom are $25 - 1 = 24$. At an alpha of 0.10 and 24 degrees of freedom, the *critical chi-square value is 33.196*. Make sure you find this value in Table 10.1 before continuing.

Table 10.1   Critical chi-square values for selected alpha levels.

d.f. / alpha	0.10	0.05	0.025	0.010	0.005
1	2.7055	3.8415	5.0239	6.6349	7.8794
2	4.6052	5.9915	7.3778	9.2103	10.5966
3	6.2514	7.8147	9.3484	11.3449	12.8382
4	7.7794	9.4877	11.1433	13.2767	14.8603
5	9.2364	11.0705	12.8325	15.0863	16.7496
6	10.6446	12.5916	14.4494	16.8119	18.5476
7	12.0170	14.0671	16.0128	18.4753	20.2777
8	13.3616	15.5073	17.5346	20.0902	21.9549
9	14.6837	16.9190	19.0228	21.6660	23.5894
10	15.9872	18.3070	20.4832	23.2093	25.1882
11	17.2750	19.6751	21.9201	24.7250	26.7569
12	18.5494	21.0261	23.3367	26.2170	28.2995
13	19.8119	22.3620	24.7366	27.6883	29.8195
14	21.0641	23.6848	26.1190	29.1412	31.3194
15	22.3071	24.9958	27.4884	30.5779	32.8013
16	23.5418	26.2962	28.8454	31.9999	34.2672
17	24.7690	27.5871	30.1910	33.4087	35.7185
18	25.9894	28.8693	31.5264	34.8053	37.1565
19	27.2036	30.1435	32.8523	36.1909	38.5823
20	28.4120	31.4104	34.1696	37.5662	39.9969
21	29.6151	32.6706	35.4789	38.9322	41.4011
22	30.8133	33.9244	36.7807	40.2894	42.7957
23	32.0069	35.1725	38.0756	41.6384	44.1813
24	**33.1960**	36.4150	39.3641	42.9798	45.5585
25	34.3816	37.6525	40.6465	44.3141	46.9279

Let's look at a curve to better see the results.

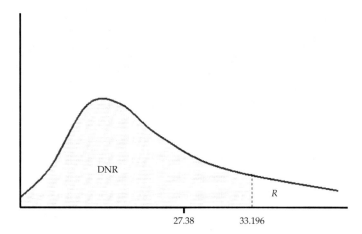

27.38   33.196

Figure 10.1   Tennis racket chi-square test.

Okay, you say, I got the numbers, but what about the conclusion? Do I have a problem or not?

Let's repeat the null and alternate hypotheses for reference.

$$H_o: \quad \sigma^2 \leq 0.71 \quad \text{(DNR)}$$
$$H_a: \quad \sigma^2 > 0.71 \quad \text{(reject)}$$

Interpretation

Since my calculated value is less than my critical value, I will not reject the null hypothesis (DNR). When I DNR the null hypothesis, the variance is less than or equal to 0.71. There is insufficient evidence for me to conclude there is a statistically significant difference between the variance of the sample and the variance of the population. The difference between 0.71 and 0.81 can be explained by sampling error alone at the alpha level of 0.10. I do not have a problem.

Confidence Intervals for Chi-Square

Just as I can use chi-square in testing hypotheses, I can use chi-square in developing confidence intervals. The confidence interval serves as an estimate of the unknown, true population *variance*. Confidence intervals are two-tailed tests. The confidence interval is determined using the formula below:

$$\frac{(n-1)(S^2)}{\chi^2_{\alpha/2}} \leq \sigma^2_H \leq \frac{(n-1)(S^2)}{\chi^2_{1-\alpha/2}}$$

Looks pretty complicated, doesn't it? Let's examine it and maybe it is not as tough as it looks. The sample size is "n," here 25; the degrees of freedom is $n - 1$, which is 24; the variance of the sample, S^2, is 0.81 inches squared. All of these values are given. The hypothesized variance, σ^2_H, is 0.71 and is also given.

The lower chi-square value is $\chi^2_{\alpha/2}$ and the upper chi-square value is $\chi^2_{1-\alpha/2}$. These values are determined by looking them up in a table. If alpha is 0.10, then you must divide it by 2 for the lower value. The $\chi^2_{0.05}$ is looked up at 24 degrees of freedom. The upper chi-square value ($\chi^2_{0.95}$) is also looked up at 24 degrees of freedom. Added together these two equal 1.0 ($0.05 + 0.95 = 1.00$). The upper is 13.848 and the lower is 36.415. Find them in the chi-square table before going on. Next I use them in the calculation as shown below:

$$\frac{(25-1)(0.81)}{36.415} \leq \sigma^2_H \leq \frac{(25-1)(0.81)}{13.848}$$

This will mathematically equal a confidence interval of 0.5338 to 1.4038. This is the 90% confidence interval. The interpretation: I am 90% confident the true, unknown population *variance* lies between 0.5338 and 1.4038.

Chi-square is a useful method of *testing the variance in a single population*. There are times, however, when I need to assess the equality of the variance for two populations.

F-distribution

Previously, (even though you may not remember it) one of the assumptions when analyzing the means of the distributions was that the variances were equal. Is this a reasonable assumption? It is probably not, because in most cases the variances will also vary. I need a test that determines if the variances of two populations are equal. The F-distribution or F-ratio fits the criteria for such a test.

The F-ratio is useful when I am working with *two different populations*. Since this is an inferential test, the assumption of normality is appropriate. The F-ratio divides one sample variance by another sample variance. These sample variances serve as an estimate of the corresponding population variances.

For example, let's say that I am interested in the variance of mean life of Goodyear tires as compared to the variance of Goodrich tires. These are two distinct and different populations even though they are both tires. The hypotheses tests for F-distribution problems are as follows:

$$H_o: \sigma^2_1 = \sigma^2_2$$
$$H_A: \sigma^2_1 \neq \sigma^2_2$$

Notice these are both population variances. This is still parametric testing, but instead of testing the means, I test the parameter (population variance) by using a statistic (sample variance). The F-ratio formula is as follows:

$$F = \frac{S^2_1}{S^2_2}$$

This determines the *calculated value*. Here, as in all hypothesis testing, I will compare the *calculated value* to a *critical value*. The critical value will come from a table look up. The calculated value is developed by using a formula.

The F-ratio is developed by using the variances of two different samples. These sample variances are estimates of the population variances. There is one quirk with this particular

F-ratio. The larger variance is placed over the smaller variance. This means that the *F*-value is always greater than 1. The only reason for this procedure is to prevent an inordinately large number of pages in the *F*-table. Placing the larger variance over the smaller variance forces a two-tailed test (as shown above in the statement of hypotheses) to be a one-tailed, right rejection region test. When this procedure is used, alpha is divided by two.

I am sure that is all about as clear as mud right now.

Yep, you admit. You lost me a couple of sentences ago.

Fair enough. Let's back up a bit. I will repeat the formula.

$$F = \frac{S_1^2}{S_2^2}$$

Where the larger variance is divided by the smaller variance or $\dfrac{Big}{Little}$

Making $F > 1$

Which requires alpha to be divided by 2

Side Note to Remember for Later

When I begin the ANOVA section below, you will see the calculated value will also be represented by an *F*-ratio; however, when developing the ANOVA *F*-ratio, you will *not* divide alpha by 2. Remember this. I will tell you again when I get to the ANOVA section.

The critical *F*-ratio is a value you looked up in the *F*-table. In the last chapter, I provided an *F*-table for alpha 0.025. Table 10.3 below is an *F*-table for alpha 0.05. The *F*-table requires you know the degrees of freedom for the numerator and the degrees of freedom for the denominator. Let's work through an example.

Suppose that you are an insurance company who believes that the repair cost for large automobiles is greater than the repair costs for smaller cars. As an insurance company, you want to take the results of a study to the Texas Department of Insurance in order to increase insurance rates for the larger automobiles. Your study has indicated the *mean repair costs are equal*, but you have some doubt about the variances. You have collected data for the variances of the two different populations—small and large cars. The repair cost data follows (Table 10.2):

Table 10.2 Repair cost for large and small vehicles.

Repair Cost Table	Type I Large Cars	Type II Small Cars
Sample Size	9	7
Degrees of Freedom	8	6
Sample Standard Deviation	$97	$83
Sample Variance	$9,409	$6,889

The first step is to set up the null and alternate hypotheses.

$$H_o: \sigma^2_1 = \sigma^2_2$$
$$H_A: \sigma^2_1 \neq \sigma^2_2$$

Second, you will determine the calculated F-ratio. Place the larger variance over the smaller variance.

$$F = \frac{S^2_1}{S^2_2} = \frac{9,409}{6,889} = 1.3658 \text{ This is the calculated F-ratio.}$$

Next, you need to look up the critical F-ratio using alpha of 0.10 in the F-table. Here the degrees of freedom of the numerator are 8 and the denominator of 6, which is 9 − 1 and 7 − 1 respectively. Since I have placed the larger variance over the smaller, I will divide alpha by 2 (0.10 ÷ 2 = 0.05). I look up the critical F-value under alpha 0.05 for 8 degrees of freedom for the numerator and 6 degrees of freedom for the denominator.

Go to Table 10.3 and look up the value. This gives us a value of 4.147. Make sure you can find this value.

Next, compare the calculated value (1.3658) to the critical value (4.147) and make a decision.

What is your decision?

You respond, I DNR the null hypothesis and conclude that the two variances are equal at the alpha 0.10 level. This means I will not obtain a price increase based on this study.

Congratulations, great answer. You may actually understand this stuff.

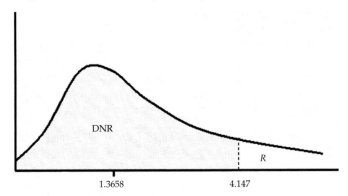

Figure 10.2 Comparison of critical F-value and calculated F-value.

From the above graph (Figure 10.2) you can see the relationship between the DNR region and the reject region. Remember, the use of the F-ratio is to *test the variance of two distinct populations*.

Okay, you say, you have shown me how to handle one population and two populations, but is there a method I can use to test three or more populations at the same time?

Great lead-in, I respond. Yes, there is. It is called ANOVA. Actually I could use this same technique for two populations but often the *t*-test is an acceptable approach.

Table 10.3 F-table for alpha 0.05.

d.f. 2	d.f. 1	Numerator Degrees of Freedom for Alpha 0.05									
		1	**2**	**3**	**4**	**5**	**6**	**7**	**8**	**9**	**10**
D	1	161.45	199.50	215.71	224.58	230.16	233.99	236.77	238.88	240.54	241.88
e	2	18.512	19.000	19.164	19.246	19.296	19.329	19.353	19.371	19.384	19.395
n	3	10.128	9.552	9.276	9.117	9.013	8.940	8.886	8.845	8.812	8.785
o	4	7.708	6.944	6.591	6.388	6.256	6.163	6.094	6.041	5.998	5.964
m	5	6.608	5.786	5.409	5.192	5.050	4.950	4.876	4.818	4.772	4.735
i	6	5.987	5.143	4.757	4.533	4.387	4.284	4.207	**4.147**	4.099	4.060
n	7	5.591	4.737	4.347	4.120	3.972	3.866	3.787	3.726	3.677	3.637
a	8	5.318	4.459	4.066	3.838	3.688	3.581	3.500	3.438	3.388	3.347
t	9	5.117	4.256	3.862	3.633	3.482	3.374	3.293	3.230	3.179	3.137
o	10	4.965	4.103	3.708	3.478	3.326	3.217	3.135	3.072	3.020	2.978
r	11	4.844	3.982	3.587	3.357	3.204	3.095	3.012	2.948	2.896	2.854
	12	4.747	3.885	3.490	3.259	3.106	2.996	2.913	2.849	2.796	2.753
	13	4.667	3.805	3.410	3.179	3.025	2.915	2.832	2.767	2.714	2.671
	14	4.600	3.739	3.344	3.112	2.958	2.848	2.764	2.699	2.646	2.602
D	15	4.543	3.682	3.287	3.056	2.901	2.791	2.707	2.641	2.588	2.544
e	16	4.494	3.634	3.239	3.007	2.852	2.741	2.657	2.591	2.538	2.494
g.	17	4.451	3.592	3.197	2.965	2.810	2.699	2.614	2.548	2.494	2.450
	18	4.414	3.555	3.160	2.928	2.773	2.661	2.577	2.510	2.457	2.412
	19	4.381	3.522	3.127	2.895	2.740	2.628	2.543	2.477	2.423	2.378
F	20	4.351	3.499	3.098	2.866	2.711	2.599	2.514	2.447	2.392	2.348
r	21	4.325	3.467	3.072	2.840	2.685	2.573	2.488	2.420	2.366	2.321
d	22	4.301	3.443	3.049	2.817	2.661	2.549	2.464	2.397	2.342	2.297
m.	23	4.279	3.422	3.028	2.795	2.640	2.528	2.442	2.375	2.320	2.275

One-Way ANOVA Tests

I have mixed emotions about how to teach ANOVA. In reality, if you are ever faced with having to simultaneously determine if three or more means are equal, you will not make manual calculations. You will use Excel or SPSS or Minitab or another software program. Therein lies my dilemma—should I merely teach you the Excel approach or should I teach you the Excel approach plus the manual approach?

Professor, you chime in, I have an opinion.

Okay, let's hear it.

Well it seems to me that you might consider teaching Excel, but give me the manual approach as if it were an appendix. Of course, do not forget to teach me how to interpret the results. For practical purposes, however, it sounds like I need to know how to calculate and read an Excel output.

I agree, your approach is probably a very balanced approach, so let's first discuss some of the basics.

First, understanding the meaning of ANOVA is a good starting point. Analysis of variance is a statistical method for analyzing *two or more population means* by analyzing the variance of those means. The word is an acronym. "ANOVA" comes from the following letters—**An**alysis **o**f **Va**riance.

There are *two types*.

One-Way ANOVA Test

Two-Way ANOVA Test

While Excel software addresses Two-Way ANOVA, I will not. One-way ANOVA focuses on one factor at a time. The procedure calls for developing a completely randomized design. This randomized design occurs when the experimental units are assigned randomly to the various treatments.

I know, I know, I have used several terms without defining them. Be patient and I will define them shortly. Just hearing them mentioned should help your comprehension. This section will prove to be one of those language nightmares until you grasp the concepts.

Two different models can be used.

Fixed-Effects Model: I will use the fixed-effect model. Specific levels of treatments are chosen *in advance* of the study. (more on this idea shortly)

Random-Effects Model: The levels of treatments will be chosen at random from a population of possible levels of treatments while the study is in process. This is a complicated approach and beyond the content of a basic statistics course and this textbook.

Definition of Some Terms

Don't you just love it when I throw more definitions at you? Remember, I warned you, statistics is a language course and not a mathematics course.

Experimental Units: These are the objects receiving the treatments.

Factor: This is the general type of category of treatments.

Levels of the Factor: These are the levels of the treatments.

You will learn more about these definitions as I work a sample problem.

Three assumptions are necessary for ANOVA to be applied.

- All populations are normally distributed.
- All populations have the same variance.
- The samples are independently chosen.

Let's take an example

Let's say that you are developing three training classes for students who wish to take the GMAT examination. You select 15 students as the test sample. The 15 students are the experimental units. There are three training classes available to your customers: 3-hour, 1-day, and 10-week classes. These are referred to as levels of the factor or treatments. The factor is training. Management has three levels of charges depending on which course the customer takes. Because of this, management would expect the differences in GMAT scores for each level of the factor (training class) to be significant. You charge more so the customer should expect better results.

Because the three levels of the factor are selected a priori, before the fact, the one-way ANOVA test can be used. Your next task is to assign the students to one of the three levels of the factor. This assignment must be done using random selection. *Random selection and assignment to a level of the factor are very important steps.* By random assignment, selection bias can be eliminated.

The first student out of the 15 students is selected at random and assigned to the 3-hour training class. The second student out of the 14 remaining is selected at random and assigned to the 1-day training class. The third student out of the 13 remaining is selected at random and assigned to the 10-week class. This process is then replicated four additional times. The end result is that five students are assigned *at random* to each of the three levels of the factor. This means the sample size in each level of the factor is five. This is known as a balanced design.

The students then proceed through the training programs. After the training program is complete, the students take the GMAT and their scores are recorded in the following table (Table 10.4). I will come back to this table to show you how to manually calculate ANOVA values after I first show you how to use Excel to make the calculations more efficiently.

Table 10.4 GMAT scores for 15 students.

GMAT Scores For 15 Students							
Training is the Factor							
Level of the Factor (i)	Observations (j)					Total	$\overline{X}$
3-Hour Class	491	579	451	521	503	2,545	509
1-Day Class	588	502	550	520	470	2,630	526
10-Week Class	533	628	501	537	561	2,760	552
Grand Mean						7,935	529

The study itself is training which is referred to as the factor. Levels of the factor are the three training options. There are three populations being tested, but I am using this experiment and the associated sample values as estimates of the unknown population values. Each level of the factor is considered to be a separate population.

I need to determine if the GMAT scores of the students are affected by the intensity of training. In other words, does it make a difference in the scores on the GMAT whether a student takes the 3-hour class, the 1-day class, or the 10-week class? I would hope the difference *cannot* be explained by sampling error, because I want to charge more for the more intensive training. This is a departure from the normal idea where you want the difference to be explained by sampling error.

Boy, is that confusing or what? Let's move on and try to amplify this issue.

I set up the hypotheses as follows:

$$H_o: \quad \mu_1 = \mu_2 = \mu_3 \quad \text{(Population means)}$$
$$H_a: \quad \text{Not all means are equal or at least two differ.}$$

Don't get creative, just state the null and alternate exactly this way. I am asking if there is a statistically significant difference between the paired means: 552 versus 509; 552 versus 526; 526 versus 509. Can the difference be explained by sampling error at the alpha 0.05?

Now is the point when I really get mixed emotions. In real, not academic, life, you will rarely be required to manually calculate the ANOVA values. Because you will probably never be faced with manual calculations, I will first show you the Excel approach. After you digest that approach, I will then show you the manual process. Let's hold the GMAT problem aside and look at two different Excel examples. I will come back to the GMAT problem shortly.

Excel Example 1

A pharmaceutical sales manager for Merck oversees sales representatives who make sales calls on doctors, hospitals, and emergency health care facilities. The manager has developed four different call frequency plans. He is not sure if the plans will help increase sales but wants to test the theory that all plans are the same. He selects thirty-six representatives who are chosen at random and assigned randomly to one of the four sales plans. The result is nine representatives are assigned to each plan. The frequency of usage of Merck products is tabulated for nine months. The results are shown in Table 10.5.

The null and alternate hypotheses are set up as follows:

$$H_o: \quad \mu_1 = \mu_2 = \mu_3 = \mu_4$$
$$H_a: \quad \text{Not all means are equal.}$$

This is the only way to set up the hypotheses in ANOVA. The only thing that can expand is the number of populations. It is not limited to three or four or five, etc.

Use Excel and test to see if there is a statistically significant difference between the frequency call plans at the alpha 0.05 level. To use Excel, open a worksheet. Select a random starting point and enter the data in Table 10.5 in columns or rows. Make sure you place a heading over the column or at the front of a row. Go to Tools > Data Analysis. Under Data Analysis, you will find three possible selections for ANOVA at the *top of the list*. The first is *ANOVA: Single Factor* followed by *ANOVA: Two Factor with Replication* and then *ANOVA: Two Factor without Replication*. The second and third options are associated with two-way ANOVA testing. Both of these are beyond the scope of this textbook, so ignore those choices.

Table 10.5   Frequency of usage for four sales calling plans.

Plan A	Plan B	Plan C	Plan D	Plan
36	39	44	31	
40	45	43	43	
32	54	38	46	Frequency
44	53	40	43	of use
35	46	41	36	During
41	42	35	49	9 months
44	35	37	46	of sales
42	39	37	48	Calls
40	51	42	44	
39.3	44.9	39.7	42.9	Averages

I am, however, interested in the first: *ANOVA: Single Factor.* Open it. Place your cursor in the Input Range Box. With your mouse, highlight **all four columns** of your data at the same time. Next check the box to reflect your use of columns or rows. Then check the box indicating you are using Labels in the first row or first column. Select the alpha. Select your preferred output location on the current worksheet by defining the starting cell location or on a separate tab (new worksheet ply) or in a location in a new workbook. Now click okay and get out of the way. The calculation will be almost immediate.

If you selected a new tab for output, you can right click on that tab and rename it to something creative like "output." Now you have to interpret the result. In this instance, do you have supporting evidence that there is a difference between the outcomes based on a particular plan? The ANOVA calculation is shown in the following table (Table 10.6), but you need to make sure you get the same result. Try using Excel and make sure you can duplicate this table.

Great numbers, you respond, and impressively quick. But what in the world do I do with them?

Interpret them, I respond.

Easy for you to say, but I need some help here, you indicate.

Okay, let's try it. Let's repeat the null and alternate hypothesis.

$$H_o: \quad \mu_1 = \mu_2 = \mu_3 = \mu_4$$
$$H_a: \quad \text{Not all means are equal.}$$

I am still doing parametric testing, so the test is of the population means. The population means are represented by the sample means which are shown in Table 10.6 as *average*. I am interested in knowing if a particular call frequency plan leads to increased use of Merck's products as measured by the four means shown in Table 10.6.

Table 10.6   ANOVA calculations for plan frequency calls for example #1.

SUMMARY: ANOVA: Single Factor						
Groups	**Count**	**Sum**	**Average**	**Variance**		
Plan A	9	354	**39.33333**	17.25		
Plan B	9	404	**44.88889**	45.36111		
Plan C	9	357	**39.66667**	9.5		
Plan D	9	386	**42.88889**	34.11111		
ANOVA						
Source of Variation	**SS**	**df**	**MS**	***F***	***P*-value**	**F-crit**
Between Groups	191.8611	3	63.9537	**2.408298**	**0.085304**	**2.90112**
Within Groups	849.7778	32	26.55556			
Total	**1041.639**	**35**				

In the table, you will find a *calculated F-value* of 2.408298 (2.41 rounded). You will also see a *critical value of 2.90112* (rounded to 2.90). I make my decision by comparing these two values—the calculated value of *F* and the critical value of *F*. Since the calculated value is less than the critical value (2.41 < 2.90), I will DNR the null hypothesis. The means are equal. At the alpha 0.05 level, there is no statistically significant difference between the population means. The difference in the population means can be explained by sampling error alone. None of the call frequency plans yields results that are different. They lead to the same frequency of usage or sales. Visually it looks like the following (Figure 10.3).

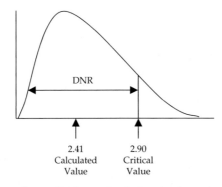

Figure 10.3   Comparison of critical value and calculated value.

I can also use the p-value to interpret the results. Notice, from Table 10.6, the p-value is 0.085304. If I compare the p-value to the alpha value, I can make a decision. In this case, the p-value is greater than the alpha value, so I DNR the null hypothesis. (0.085304 > 0.05) In fact, the p-value is the lowest level I can set the alpha and still DNR the null hypothesis. If I had selected the alpha 0.10 level, I would reject the null hypothesis.

Excel Example 2

Four different suppliers provide synthetic fibers to be woven into material used in making tents. As the manufacturer of tents, you want to test the tensile strength of the woven material to see if one particular supplier's synthetic fiber produces a woven product with higher quality than the other suppliers. The results of the tensile strength tests are shown in Table 10.7.

Table 10.7 Tensile strength test for tent material for example #2.

Supplier 1	Supplier 2	Supplier 3	Supplier 4	Supplier
18.5	26.3	20.6	25.4	
24.0	25.3	25.2	19.9	
17.2	24.0	20.8	22.6	Tensile Strength
19.9	21.2	24.7	17.5	
18.0	24.5	22.9	20.4	
19.52	24.26	22.84	21.16	Arithmetic Mean
2.69	1.92	2.13	2.98	Standard Deviation

The null and alternate hypotheses are set up as follows:

$$H_o: \quad \mu_1 = \mu_2 = \mu_3 = \mu_4$$
$$H_a: \quad \text{Not all means are equal.}$$

Notice the hypotheses are set up exactly the same as the example #1.

The ANOVA calculations are shown in Table 10.8 is in next page.

Repeating the null and alternate hypotheses, I have the following:

$$H_o: \quad \mu_1 = \mu_2 = \mu_3 = \mu_4$$
$$H_a: \quad \text{Not all means are equal.}$$

Use Excel and test to see if there is a statistically significant difference between the tensile strength of one supplier over another supplier using the alpha 0.05 level. Follow the same directions as shown in example #1. The question you are asking: Do I have supporting evidence there is a difference between the tensile strength based on a particular supplier?

Table 10.8   ANOVA calculations for tensile strength test.

SUMMARY: ANOVA: Single Factor						
Groups	**Count**	**Sum**	**Average**	**Variance**		
Supplier 1	5	97.6	**19.52**	7.237		
Supplier 2	5	121.3	**24.26**	3.683		
Supplier 3	5	114.2	**22.84**	4.553		
Supplier 4	5	105.8	**21.16**	8.903		
ANOVA						
Source of Variation	**SS**	**df**	**MS**	**F**	**P-value**	**F-crit**
Between Groups	63.2855	3	21.09517	**3.461629**	0.041366	**3.238872**
Within Groups	97.504	16	6.094			
Total	**160.7895**	**19**				

Interpretation

The calculated value of F is 3.46 (rounded) and the critical value of F is 3.24 (rounded). Since the calculated value is greater than the critical value, I will reject the null hypothesis. (3.46 > 3.24) At the alpha 0.05 level, there is a statistically significant difference between the means that cannot be explained by sampling error alone. At least two means differ but from this test alone *I cannot tell which two are different*. Visually, Figure 10.4 shows the results of this comparison.

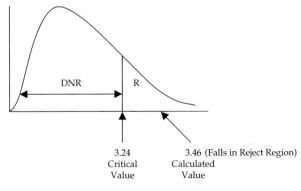

Figure 10.4   Comparison of critical and calculated value.

Also notice the p-value is 0.041366 (round to 0.041). The p-value is less than the alpha value, so I reject the null hypothesis (0.041 < 0.05). Rejecting the null hypothesis demonstrates the means are different but will not demonstrate which means are different. I must make the determination of which means are different by matching them two at a time (pair-wise comparison).

Special Note

The only time I must move to this next level of computation is when, and only when, *I reject the null hypothesis*. My purpose will be to determine the differences between the means using a paired comparison. In short, this will be done by determining the absolute differences and comparing those differences to a critical value calculated by one of three approaches. I know you have no clue what I just revealed to you, but hang in there.

The three approaches are the Tukey, the least significant difference (LSD) and the alternate LSD approaches. The first two (Tukey and LSD) are useful when the design is balanced (same sample size in each level of the factor such as all contain 5 or all contain 6). If the design is unbalanced (differences in the sample size for each level of the factor such as 5, 6, 5 or 5, 4, 7), then the alternate LSD is the formula of choice.

Once again, I move to this level of calculation only if I *REJECT the null* hypothesis. If I DNR, there is no need to take this step.

The following pair-wise comparisons are possible (Table 10.9). They come from Table 10.8. Go back to Table 10.8 and make sure you can find the source of these values. In Table 10.8, the means are labeled "averages". Find them.

Table 10.9   Pair-wise comparisons.

Pair-Wise Matches	Means	Absolute Difference	Critical Value	Significant
$\overline{X}_1 - \overline{X}_2$	19.52 − 24.26	4.74		
$\overline{X}_1 - \overline{X}_3$	19.52 − 22.84	3.32		
$\overline{X}_1 - \overline{X}_4$	19.52 − 21.16	1.64	To be completed shortly	
$\overline{X}_2 - \overline{X}_3$	24.26 − 22.84	1.42		
$\overline{X}_2 - \overline{X}_4$	24.26 − 21.16	3.10		
$\overline{X}_3 - \overline{X}_4$	22.84 − 21.16	1.68		

The means (averages) are shown in column 2 of Table 10.9. Column 3 shows the absolute value differences. When using absolute values, you will ignore the plus and minus sign. I am comparing mean one to mean two and mean one to mean three, etc. This is paired comparison or pair-wise comparison.

What I now need is a critical value for each of the pair-wise comparisons. Excel does not have the ability to make this calculation. Other software does have this capability, but because you probably do not have it available to you, I will show you how to make the calculations manually.

The problem exhibits a balanced design since $r = 5$ for each level of the factor (each supplier). The two formulas of interest are the Tukey and the LSD. They are as follows:

$$Tukey = q_{\alpha, c, n-c}\sqrt{\frac{MSE}{r}}$$ where $q_{0.05, 4, 16}$ is $\alpha = 0.05$, numerator is $c = 4$, denominator is $n - c = 20 - 4 = 16$.

$$LSD = \sqrt{\frac{2(MSE)F_{\alpha, 1, n-c}}{r}}$$ where $F_{0.05, 1, 16}$ is $\alpha = 0.05$, numerator $= 1$, denominator is $n - c = 20 - 4 = 16$.

If you look carefully at the two formulas, you will notice the Tukey and the LSD formulas include MSE and r. MSE comes directly from the ANOVA table (Table 10.8), here 6.094. By definition "r" is the sample size of each level of the factor, here 5. In the LSD formula, the 2 is a fixed integer.

This only leaves me needing a value for $q_{\alpha, c, n-c}$ to complete the Tukey formula or a value for $F_{\alpha, 1, n-c}$ to complete the LSD formula. The q-value comes from a table look up as does the F-value. For the q-value, $c = 4$; $n - c = 20 - 4 = 16$, which is 4.05. See Table 10.10 below for this look up.

Table 10.10   Selected critical values for Tukey factor at Alpha 0.05.

							$n - c$						
		5	6	7	8	9	10	11	12	13	14	15	16
	2	3.64	3.46	3.34	3.26	3.20	3.15	3.11	3.08	3.06	3.03	3.01	3.00
	3	4.60	4.34	4.16	4.04	3.95	3.88	3.82	3.77	3.73	3.70	3.67	3.65
	4	5.22	4.90	4.68	4.53	4.41	4.33	4.26	4.20	4.15	4.11	4.08	4.05
C	5	5.67	5.30	5.06	4.89	4.76	4.65	4.57	4.51	4.45	4.41	4.37	4.33
	6	6.03	5.63	5.36	5.17	5.02	4.91	4.82	4.75	4.69	4.64	4.59	4.56
	7	6.33	5.90	5.61	5.40	5.24	5.12	5.03	4.95	4.88	4.83	4.78	4.74
	8	6.58	6.12	5.82	5.60	5.43	5.30	5.20	5.12	5.05	4.99	4.94	4.90
	9	6.80	6.32	6.00	5.77	5.59	5.46	5.35	5.27	5.19	5.13	5.08	5.03
	10	6.99	6.49	6.16	5.92	5.74	5.60	5.49	5.39	5.32	5.25	5.20	5.15

To complete the Tukey formula, I would have the following calculations. Remember MSE comes from Table 10.8 and r is 5. I just looked up the 4.05 in Table 10.10.

$$Tukey = q_{\alpha, c, n-c}\sqrt{\frac{MSE}{r}}$$

$$Tukey = 4.05\sqrt{\frac{6.094}{5}} = 4.05\sqrt{1.2188} = 4.05(1.104) = 4.4712$$

The 4.47 (rounded) will be used as the critical value for determining which means are different. The revised Table 10.9 will look like the following (Table 10.11). The first three columns of Table 10.11 are the same as the first three columns of Table 10.9. The fourth column is the critical value I just calculated (4.47). The last column tells me if the difference is significant or not significant.

Let me review for you what I am doing.

Table 10.11   Pair-wise comparisons including critical Tukey value.

Pair-Wise Matches	Means	Absolute Difference	Critical Value	Significant
$\overline{X}_1 - \overline{X}_2$	19.52 − 24.26	4.74	4.47	Yes
$\overline{X}_1 - \overline{X}_3$	19.52 − 22.84	3.32	4.47	No
$\overline{X}_1 - \overline{X}_4$	19.52 − 21.16	1.64	4.47	No
$\overline{X}_2 - \overline{X}_3$	24.26 − 22.84	1.42	4.47	No
$\overline{X}_2 - \overline{X}_4$	24.26 − 21.16	3.10	4.47	No
$\overline{X}_3 - \overline{X}_4$	22.84 − 21.16	1.68	4.47	No

Great, you respond, because you lost me a bit back.

Oh, sorry, you should have spoken up. Okay, let's recap and see if I can fill in the missing pieces for example #2.

First, I have four suppliers who provide synthetic fibers which I use in weaving tent material. I want to know if there is a statistically significant difference between the suppliers measured in tensile strength of the tent material. I decide to use ANOVA since I have four populations (four suppliers) and one characteristic of interest—tensile strength. Since I have not shown you how to manually work problems, I enter my data into an Excel worksheet. I determine from the ANOVA calculation that I must reject the null hypothesis which states the means are equal.

$$H_0: \quad \mu_1 = \mu_2 = \mu_3 = \mu_4 \quad \text{(reject)}$$
$$H_a: \quad \text{Not all means are equal.} \quad \text{(accept)}$$

By rejecting the null hypothesis, I am stating there is a statistically significant difference between the means, but I cannot from this one test tell which means are different. From observation, I may have some clue which means appear to be different, but I must take my calculations one step further. I must use either the Tukey or least significant difference (LSD) method. I only need to take this step if I *reject* the null hypothesis.

To conclude which means are different, I compare the absolute difference between each pair of means (pair-wise comparison) to a critical value. I will first use the Tukey approach to determine a critical (threshold) value. Again, I will compare the absolute value of the difference in the paired means to this critical Tukey value. If the absolute value exceeds the critical Tukey value, I can assert at the chosen alpha level (here 0.05) that there is a statistically significant difference in the means that cannot be explained by sampling error.

Interpretation

In this instance, after developing the Tukey criterion, I find the tensile strength of supplier 2 exceeds that of supplier 1. The difference between the two suppliers cannot be explained by sampling error at $\alpha = 0.05$. Supplier 2 is the supplier of choice.

Whoa, you call out. How can you tell supplier 2 is better?

Easy, I respond. Look at the average tensile strength of supplier 2 (24.26) versus the tensile strength of supplier 1 (19.52). 24.52 > 19.52

I can actually go a bit further in my conclusion. I have stated that the tensile strength of supplier 2 exceeds that of supplier 1, but I can also state that there is no statistically significant difference between the other suppliers. The difference in the mean tensile strength of supplier 1 compared to suppliers 3 and 4 is due to sampling error. The difference in the mean tensile strength of supplier 2 compared to suppliers 3 and 4 is due to sampling error. And finally the difference in the mean tensile strength of supplier 3 compared to supplier 4 is due to sampling error. This can more easily be seen from Table 10.11 shown above. When the absolute difference exceeds the critical value, you can concluded there is a statistically significant difference. Looking at Table 10.11, this only occurs one time. Supplier 1 and Supplier 2 reflects a significant difference. Supplier 2 has a higher tensile strength, so it is better than Supplier 1.

Okay, you question, what happens if I use the LSD approach? I can use LSD as well as Tukey, right, since this is a balanced design?

Yes, you can use either. The result of solving the LSD formula is shown below:

$$\text{LSD} = \sqrt{\frac{2(\text{MSE})F_{\alpha, 1, n-c}}{r}} \quad \text{(The } F\text{-value is looked up in an } F\text{-table.)}$$

$$\text{LSD} = \sqrt{\frac{2(6.094)(4.49)}{5}} = \sqrt{\frac{54.7241}{5}} = \sqrt{10.9448} = 3.3083$$

Don't get confused by the numbers. You have been given most of them. The 2 is fixed, MSE comes from Table 10.8 as does r. The only value you look up in the F-value which comes from the F-table. Notice that the critical value is less than the critical value for Tukey. Here it is 3.31 rounded.

Table 10.12 Pair-wise comparisons including critical LSD value.

Pair-Wise Matches	Means	Absolute Difference	Critical Value	Significant
$\overline{X}_1 - \overline{X}_2$	19.52 − 24.26	4.74	3.31	Yes
$\overline{X}_1 - \overline{X}_3$	19.52 − 22.84	3.32	3.31	Yes
$\overline{X}_1 - \overline{X}_4$	19.52 − 21.16	1.64	3.31	No
$\overline{X}_2 - \overline{X}_3$	24.26 − 22.84	1.42	3.31	No
$\overline{X}_2 - \overline{X}_4$	24.26 − 21.16	3.10	3.31	No
$\overline{X}_3 - \overline{X}_4$	22.84 − 21.16	1.68	3.31	No

Interpretation

By using the LSD approach, I find two means reflect differences. Suppliers 2 and 3 when compared to supplier 1 reflect a statistically significant difference that cannot be explained by sampling error alone at the alpha 0.05 level. It is not unusual for the LSD to yield a higher number of significantly different comparisons than the Tukey method. The Tukey is a bit more conservative than the LSD method.

Unbalanced Design

Assuming your experiment turns out to be unbalanced 5 , 5, 4 or 5, 6, 7 or any other sample size for each level of the factor which is not the same, you would have to use a slightly different formula to determine which means are different. The formula is as follows:

$$\text{LSD}_{\text{ALT}} = \sqrt{\left[\frac{1}{r_j} + \frac{1}{r_k}\right](\text{MSE})\,(F_{\alpha,\,c-1,\,n-c})}$$

You should have no difficulty with this formula other than the calculation of "r." *MSE* is given in the ANOVA table and F is a table look up at a particular F-value. The value of r is associated with the sample size in each level of the factor. For example, if you had a 5, 6, 7 sample size, the first r sub j would be $1/5$ and the second r sub k would be $1/6$. This pattern is replicated for each possible sample size. For balanced designs I have one critical value, but for unbalanced designs I have *multiple critical values*. In fact, I have a different critical value for each pair-wise comparison.

With the two examples I just covered, I believe you should have a conceptual understanding of the use of Excel in ANOVA calculations. In reality, using Excel is the most efficient method. However, I am compelled to show you the manual method of calculating ANOVA.

Manual Calculations of ANOVA

Unless your Professor tells you to work through this section or you do not have access to Excel, the next few pages may be irrelevant since they address manual calculations for ANOVA. Reading through these pages may lead to a better understanding of the theory behind ANOVA, but manually calculating the values is slow and tedious. Were I you, I would read the material lightly. Reading it might clear up some conceptual confusion.

Let's go back to the original problem statement regarding the GMAT training. If you need to turn back to the problem, do so. In summary, there are three levels of the factor: 3-hour, 1-day, and 10-week training courses. I selected five students at random from among 15 and assigned them to each of the levels of the factor (training is the factor). The students completed the training and took the GMAT. Their scores are recorded in a table which is repeated below (Table 10.13).

Table 10.13 GMAT scores for 15 students (repeat of Table 10.4).

Level of the Factor (i)	Observations (j)					Total	Mean
GMAT Scores For 15 Students							
Training is the Factor							
3-Hour Class	491	579	451	521	503	2,545	509
1-Day Class	588	502	550	520	470	2,630	526
10-Week Class	533	628	501	537	561	2,760	552
Grand Mean						7,935	529

To get the means of each level of the factor, you simply add the scores for those taking the 3-hour class, which is 2,545. Next divide 2,545 by 5 to get the 509. Repeat this process for each of the other levels of the factor. These totals are shown on the far right of Table 10.13. The grand mean is an average of all 15 scores (7,935) divided by 15, which is 529.

Now for the question: *Is there a statistically significant difference between the training course and scores on the GMAT examination?*

In other words, is there a statistically significant difference between the 509 and the 526 and the 552 or can the difference be explained by sampling error? Since you charge your customer more for the more intensive course, you hope the differences shown are significant. From initial observation there appears to be a difference, since 552 is higher than either 526 or 509. But is this the case? Since there are three populations, ANOVA may be used.

Table 10.14 Comparison of GMAT scores developing absolute values.

Mean Comparisons	Absolute Difference
552 to 526	26
552 to 509	43
526 to 509	17

You saw how quickly Excel made the calculations with the results shown in an ANOVA table. The ANOVA table is the guts of understanding ANOVA. ANOVA partitions the total variation into two pieces—between and within. From these two pieces, I can calculate an F-ratio. I can then measure the calculated F-ratio to a table look up critical F-ratio to determine if I DNR (accept) the null or reject the null hypothesis.

$$H_o: \quad \mu_1 = \mu_2 = \mu_3$$

$$H_a: \quad \text{Not all means are equal.}$$

Table 10.15   ANOVA table for manual calculations.

Source of Variation	Sum of Squares	Degrees of Freedom	Mean Square	F-ratio
Between	SSTR	$c - 1$	MSTR	MSTR ÷
Within	SSE	$n - c$	MSE	MSE
Total	SST	$n - 1$		

Let's begin with the **total variation (SST),** which is referred to as **the sum of the squares total (SST).** The total variation (SST) is partitioned or divided into two pieces: SSE and SSTR. The equation is SST = SSE + SSTR. If I know SST and SSE, I know SSTR ($A = B + C$). Knowing any two values will allow me to automatically know the third. **SSE** stands for **sum of the square due to error** and **SSTR** stands for **sum of the squares due to treatments.**

The three manual formulas of interest are as follows:

$$SST = \sum\sum(X_{ij} - \overline{\overline{X}})^2 \quad \text{Where } \overline{\overline{X}} = \mu. \text{ (sum of the squares total} - \text{the largest piece)}$$

$$SSTR = \sum r(\overline{X} - \overline{\overline{X}})^2 \quad \text{(sum of the squares due to treatments)}$$

$$SSE = \sum\sum(X_{ij} - \overline{X})^2 \quad \text{(sum of the squares due to error)}$$

Most of the time these formulas contain sub-notations of "i" and "j." I will not show these notations in the formula since I believe they tend to confuse you. They refer to cell locations. I will show their location in Table 10.16 below. If you label the levels of the factor as "i" and the observations as "j," you will have the intersection of the ith items and jth items. Don't let these notations confuse you.

The calculations for these three formulas are best done *manually* using tables. I think you might have a better chance of understanding when you review the tables.

I will begin with the total variation of the entire study (SST). To reference some of the numbers I have already calculated, remember the grand mean as 529. The formula for calculating the grand mean is as follows:

$$\overline{\overline{X}} = \frac{\sum\sum X_{ij}}{n} = 7{,}935 \div 15 = 529.$$

To get SST, which is the sum of the squares total (SST), I would set up a table to solve the following formula:

$$SST = \sum\sum(X_{ij} - \overline{\overline{X}})^2 \quad \text{(I need the sum of a column headed this.)}$$

Table 10.16   Manual SST calculations.

Cell Location or Position of Student Score (i^{th}, j^{th})	Individual Student Score (X_{ij}) List of all 15 Scores	Grand Mean ($\overline{\overline{X}}$)	$X_{ij} - \overline{\overline{X}}$	$(X_{ij} - \overline{\overline{X}})^2$
1,1	491	529	−38	1,444
1,2	579	529	−50	2,500
1,3	451	529	−78	6,084
1,4	521	529	−8	64
1,5	503	529	−26	676
2,1	588	529	59	3,481
2,2	502	529	−27	729
2,3	550	529	21	441
2,4	520	529	−9	81
2,5	470	529	−59	3,481
3,1	533	529	4	16
3,2	628	529	99	9,801
3,3	501	529	−28	784
3,4	537	529	8	64
3,5	561	529	32	1,024
SST				30,670

This tells me to take each of the 15 scores and subtract them from 529, square the differences, and sum those squared differences. Table 10.16 does just that. The final total for SST is 30,670. I will insert this value into a summary ANOVA table shortly, so for now just remember the source.

Now let's set up a table for calculating SSTR. The formula is as follows:

$$SSTR = \sum r(\overline{X} - \overline{\overline{X}})^2$$

SSTR *refers to the sum of the squares due to treatments, which is 4,690 as shown in Table 10.17.* I will insert this value into a summary ANOVA table shortly, so once again just remember the source.

Table 10.17 Manual SSTR calculations.

Treatment Level Mean ($\overline{X}$)	Grand Mean ($\overline{\overline{X}}$)	($\overline{X} - \overline{\overline{X}}$)	($\overline{X} - \overline{\overline{X}}$)^2	r	($\overline{X} - \overline{\overline{X}}$)$^2r$
509	529	−20	400	5	2,000
526	529	−3	9	5	45
552	529	23	529	5	2,645
SSTR					4,690

Here I need to stop and give you a few definitions.

r This is the number of experimental units within each level of the factor. Or said differently, this is the *sample size* within each level of the factor. In this case $r = 5$. There are five students assigned to each of the levels of the factor.

c This is the number of levels of the factor. In this case, there are three levels of the factor. The three training class levels represent the three levels of the factor: 3-hour, 1-day, and 10-week training classes.

n This is the total number of observations (experimental units) in the experiment or factor (same word meaning). In this case, $n = r$ times c, which is $5 \times 3 = 15$. There are 15 students (experimental units) in the entire study. As long as the design is balanced, this formula works. If the formula is *unbalanced*, you will need to *observe the total value for n.*

The design of ANOVA is considered to be balanced when you have the *same number of experimental units* (students) in each level of the factor. In this example, I have five students in each level of the factor. This means the design is balanced with 5, 5, 5 in each level of the factor.

Let's, however, assume that during the course of the 10-week study, one of the students gets ill or has a family emergency and cannot continue with the course. Does this invalidate the study and cause us to start over again? No, it does not. I now have five students in the 3-hour class, five students in the 1-day class, but only four remaining students in the 10-week class. The design of the study now becomes unbalanced with 5, 5, 4 experimental units (students) in the levels of the factors. Any design that has a different number of experimental units in the level of the factor is considered unbalanced. Many studies actually begin with an unbalanced design. The ANOVA calculations are the same when developing SST, SSTR, and SSE for both the balanced and the unbalanced designs. The problem arises when the null hypothesis is rejected. The final solution for an unbalanced design requires a different solution than it does for a balanced design.

Man, what I am attempting to simplify seems to have gotten rather complicated. Don't worry too much about the details. Just pick up all the points you can, and I will reinforce the important concepts a bit later.

Let's go back to our calculations of SST, SSTR, and SSE. Remember, SST = SSTR + SSE. This means if I know SST and SSTR, I automatically know SSE. SST (30,670) − SSTR (4,690) = SSE (25,980). The only problem with using this approach is one of math. If I miscalculate either the SST or the SSTR, what happens to SSE?

You are correct if you said that SSE would be incorrect, which would render the entire problem wrong. So while, in theory, this idea works and works well, in practice there is some room for error. Heaven knows the calculations are tedious enough without having this built-in time bomb.

The calculation of SSE can be placed in tabular format also. **SSE** is the sum of the squares due to error. SSE is the variation within each level of the factor or within each treatment. The formula is SSE $= \sum\sum(X_{ij} - \overline{X})^2$. In order to develop SSE, I have three values which must be calculated—one for each level of the factor (each training class). After calculating these three values, I add them to get SSE. The three tables are set up below.

To get SSE, I total the three values calculated below in Tables 10.18, 10.19, and 10.20 (9,044 + 8,168 + 8,768 = 25,980), which is SSE.

Table 10.18   1st level of the factor: 3-hour class.

X	$\overline{X}$	$X - \overline{X}$	$(X - \overline{X})^2$
491	509	−18	324
579	509	70	4,900
451	509	−58	3,364
521	509	12	144
503	509	−6	36
Totals	N/A	Zero	8,768*

Table 10.19   2nd level of the factor: 1-day class.

X	$\overline{X}$	$X - \overline{X}$	$(X - \overline{X})^2$
588	526	62	3,844
502	526	−24	576
550	526	24	576
520	526	−6	36
470	526	−56	3,136
Totals	N/A	Zero	8,168*

Table 10.20   3rd level of the factor: 10-week class.

X	$\bar{X}$	$X - \bar{X}$	$(X - \bar{X})^2$
533	552	−19	361
628	552	76	5,776
501	552	−51	2,601
537	552	−51	225
561	552	9	81
Totals	N/A	Zero	9,044*

So now that you have the three values (SST, SSTR, SSE), what do you do with them, you ask?

Now I can determine the calculated F-ratio, which will in turn lead me to a decision. I need to insert the values of SST, SSTR, and SSE into the ANOVA table. The final end of the ANOVA table is a calculated F-ratio. You then compare the calculated value to a table look up critical value. You can complete the entire table just knowing the three values for the sum of the squares.

Table 10.21   Final ANOVA table.

Source of Variation	Sum of Squares	Degrees of Freedom	Mean Square	F-ratio
Between	SSTR	$c-1$	MSTR	MSTR ÷ MSE = 2,345 ÷ 2,165 = 1.08
	4,690	3−1=2	4,690 ÷ 2 = 2,345	
Within	SSE	$n-c$	MSE	Calculated F-ratio
	25,980	15−3=12	25,980 ÷ 12 = 2,165	
Total	SST	$n-1$		
	30,670	15−1=14		

I gave you the definitions for c and n earlier, but let's repeat them: "c" is the number of levels of the factor and "n" is the total observations (experimental units) or r times c. Notice that 12 + 2 is 14 (under the degrees of freedom column).

Next, I need to determine MSTR and MSE.

$$\text{MSTR is SSTR} \div c - 1.$$
$$\text{MSE is SSE} \div n - c.$$

Before I go forward with the conclusion, let's look at the null and alternate hypotheses once again.

$$H_o: \quad \mu_1 = \mu_2 = \mu_3$$
$$H_a: \quad \text{Not all means are equal or at least two means differ.}$$

The question is, can the differences in the three means be explained by sampling error alone, or are the differences in the means not explained by sampling error?

In simply looking at the mean values, I would have to say there appears to be a significant difference between at least the 552 and the 509. They simply look different, but are they statistically different?

My calculated F-ratio is 1.08. My critical F-value comes from a table look up.

If your mind is not too blown by this point, go to an F-Table. Let's set alpha at 0.05.

What is the critical F-value? Look this value up in the F-table.

If you came up with 3.89, you are correct. The only problem you may have experienced was the degrees of freedom associated with the numerator and with the denominator. Those are not too difficult to determine. Go back to the ANOVA table (Table 10.21). In this case, two (2) degrees of freedom are associated with 2,345 and twelve (12) degrees of freedom are associated with 2,165, so 2 is the degrees of freedom for the numerator and 12 is the degrees of freedom for the denominator. If you are trying to understand the manual calculations, do not move on until you understand this.

Assuming you understand, let's look at a graph of the solution (Figure 10.5).

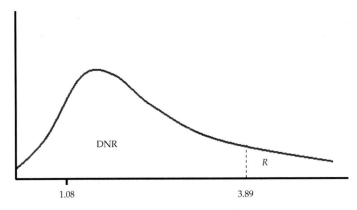

Figure 10.5 Comparison of critical F-value and calculated F-value for GMAT scores.

Interpretation

My conclusion is to DNR the null hypothesis which stated that $\mu_1 = \mu_2 = \mu_3$. I find this to be a true statement at the alpha 0.05 level. The difference can be explained by sampling error alone. The 552 compared to the 526 compared to the 509 are statistically the same.

In spite of the fact that the original observations appeared to reflect a difference in the GMAT scores as they were influenced by the training levels, when I apply a consistent statistical technique my conclusion does not reflect a difference. The difference can be explained by sampling error. It did not make a difference in the student's score if the student took the 3-hour class or the 1-day class or the 10-week class.

Wait a minute, you say. I would much rather have a 552 on my GMAT than a 509.

Duh, me too.

But that is not what I am measuring. *I am measuring the level of the training.* I am trying to see if my training programs will cause a person to score higher if he or she takes the more intensive the training classes. The answer to that question is no.

As the person who is responsible for developing the training in each of the classes, it appears that I have not done a good enough job in making the more expensive and more intensive classes good enough to cause the mean scores to be different. I need to go back to the drawing board and work on improving the more expensive (intensive) course levels.

But wait, you argue. There is over a 40-point increase in the average score from the 3-hour cram course to the 10-week intensive course (552 versus 509).

That is true, I acknowledge, but the difference can be explained by sampling error. The training company might make a claim that if you take the more expensive course, you will score about 8% higher on your test (40 points), but if a knowledgeable attorney looked at the advertising claim, the attorney might sue for false advertising and win. Just because one is higher or bigger than the other does not make them statistically different.

Excel Calculations of the GMAT Problem

Open an Excel worksheet and enter your data for the GMAT problem just completed manually. Start at any cell location. Follow the instructions given to you in Excel examples #1 and #2. The result will be the following ANOVA table.

Table 10.22   Excel calculation for GMAT problem.

ANOVA: Single Factor						
SUMMARY						
Groups	**Count**	**Sum**	**Average**	**Variance**		
3-Hour Class	5	2545	509	2192		
1-Day Class	5	2630	526	2042		
10-Week Class	5	2760	552	2261		
ANOVA						
Source of Variation	**SS**	**df**	**MS**	**F**	**P-value**	**F-crit**
Between Groups	4690	2	2345	1.083141	0.369447	3.885294
Within Groups	25980	12	2165			
Total	30670	14				

Looks familiar doesn't it? That is because the manual table and the Excel table are the same. Tables 10.21 and 10.22 reflect the same result, but I promise you the Excel process is much faster and easier.

Notice the p-value is 0.369 (rounded) and $0.369 > 0.05$, so I do not reject the null hypothesis. As a matter of fact, the p-value exceeds any of the three most commonly used alpha values (0.01, 0.05, and 0.10).

You know You are a Texan If:

- You learned how to shoot a gun before you learned how to multiply.

- Little Smokies are something you serve for special occasions.

Tear-Out Sheet Chapter 10

Student Name: _____

Day and Time of Class: _____

F-Ratio, Chi-Square Distribution, and ANOVA Problems

1. Your school board is trying to decide on awarding bus service contracts to the school district. Competition has narrowed to two competing firms: Madison and Abbott. All the financial considerations are approximately equal. The school board is especially sensitive to making the best non-political decision. You propose that the board evaluate the reliability of their service. Everyone agrees, so you commission two studies. The data gathered from the studies is as follows:

	Madison	Abbott
Sample Size	10	24
Means	Equal	Equal
Variance of the Sample	48	20

Since the means of the sample are equal, you notice that the variances are unequal. You must test to see if the variances are statistically the same and the difference is due to sampling error. Using an alpha level of 0.10, test the reliability of the two firms and make your recommendation as to who should be awarded the contract. Assume a normal distribution. Remember a variance is in units squared, so do not re-square a variance.

Do you use the F-ratio or the chi-square parametric testing approach?

2. The Dallas Transit Authority wants the public to think of them as a reliable transportation system. They consider it acceptable if their buses arrive with a variance level of four minutes squared. Again remember, variances are already squared so the units are stated in units squared. Do you use the F-ratio or the chi-square parametric testing approach?

   a. Using an alpha level of 0.10 and a sample size of 10 arrivals with a variance of the sample of 4.8 minutes squared, test the reliability claim of the Dallas Transit Authority. The mean arrival time is assumed to be the same. The distribution is assumed to be normal.

   b. Calculate the 90% confidence interval and explain its meaning.

   c. If you increase the sample size to 25, what happens to the confidence interval? What is the new interval?

3. Complete the table, set up the hypothesis, and draw your conclusions.

   Twenty-five (n) college freshmen are chosen from all the entering freshmen and randomly assigned to four (c) freshman English classes, those of Professors Q, R, S, and T. At the end of the semester, the same objective examination is given to all students who have taken freshman English. The grades of these twenty-five students are separated and SST and SSTR are calculated and put into the ANOVA table below.

Source of Variation	Sum of the Squares	Degrees of Freedom	Mean Squares	F-Ratio
SSTR	1,574			
SSE				
SST	4,817			

a. Complete the table and test the hypothesis that the mean grades between each professor are equal.
b. Set up the hypothesis and test it at an *alpha level of 0.05*.

$$H_o:$$

$$H_a:$$

c. Is there evidence that the differences in the means can be explained by sampling error alone?
d. Given the following information, apply the *alternate* LSD approach and determine which means are different given you reject the null hypothesis in the above problem.

Professor	Sample Size	Mean
Q	7	70.29
R	6	86.17
S	7	65.29
T	5	77.40
Grand Mean		74.12

Definitional Reminders

n = total number of observations for unbalanced design. For balanced design $n = r$ times c, where r is the sample size in each level of the factor and c = number of levels of the factor. For an unbalanced design, you cannot calculate n, but must observe it.

11

Forecasting— Simple and Multiple Regression

Attorney:	Do you recall the time that you examined the body?
Witness:	The autopsy started around 8:30 pm.
Attorney:	And Mr. Denton was dead at that time?
Witness:	If not, he was by the time I finished.

Regression

As in the last chapter on ANOVA, I am once again faced with a dilemma. Should I teach this strictly using Excel or should I throw in manual calculations as well? Actually I really do not have much of a choice. I have to do both, but in real life Excel is the best approach to use. The main reason you need to read the manual stuff is to better understand the ideas behind regression. With that understanding, you can interpret and understand the Excel results.

Let's get started.

Oh, great, you lament. I can hardly wait.

Ignoring your feigned excitement, I move forward.

Regression sounds rather Freudian. Maybe it is. If, however, I teach you something about Freudian regression I would have to bill you and you probably pay enough for this textbook and course as is, so I will limit my coverage to statistical regression.

Most textbooks will take one chapter to address simple regression (referred to as bi-variate regression) and another chapter to address multiple regression (referred to as multi-variate regression). I will use one chapter to cover both subjects, since they are closely related.

Linear and Nonlinear Regression

There are two types of regression—linear and nonlinear (curve type stuff). I will only address nonlinear in passing but will devote most of my time to simple linear regression. The curve stuff includes such things as logarithmic and S-curve calculations and is a bit more complex. Linear regression is not really that complicated. The theory behind regression is to use historical data to forecast future outcomes. The assumption you make is that what has happened in the past will repeat itself in the future. History does tend to repeat itself so the theory applies; however, you must be very careful not to think your forecast based on regression (history) is 100% reliable. It will not be but is a very useful tool in forecasting future events.

Oh, you comment, so regression is nothing more than a forecasting technique.

Great observation, I respond.

Estimating and forecasting are quite valuable tools for developing credibility in company planning. You would be shocked at the number of companies who "fly by the seat of their pants" in forecasting sales, for example. By understanding and applying regression and time series (next chapter), you will have tools far beyond those of most business professionals.

Simple and multiple regression have some similarities. In general, regression deals with a relationship between two or more variables.

Professor, will you give me some examples of what you mean by variables?

Yep, I can and will.

Let's say you want to *forecast your shipping cost* based on *number of orders* you expect to receive. It is logical that if I could track the number of orders I receive, I could track (forecast) the shipping cost. However, rather than list them in narrative form, maybe I can put several in a table for your review.

Notice in the third column, I have listed "causal variable." Regression is only effective if I can link two variables based on *cause and effect. The movement in one variable **causes** the other variable to move.* In Table 11.1, which variable is causal? Before you look at the answer in Table 11.2, try to fill in the last column of Table 11.1.

I have cleverly listed them so variable 1 is the cause and variable 2 is the effect (result). For example, shipping cost depends on number of orders received; changes in sales depend on

Table 11.1 Variables useful in forecasting.

Variable 1	Variable 2	Causal Variable
Number of Orders	Shipping Cost	
Hours Worked	Payroll Costs	
Advertising Expenditures	Sales	
Square Footage	Lease Revenues	
Number of Sales People	Travel Expenses	
Employee Training	Product Defects	
Number of Employees	Prescription Drug Costs	

Table 11.2 Identification of the causal variable.

Variable 1	Variable 2	Causal Variable
Number of Orders	Shipping Cost	**Number of Orders**
Hours Worked	Payroll Costs	**Hours Worked**
Advertising Expenditures	Sales	**Advertising Expenditures**
Square Footage	Lease Revenues	**Square Footage**
Number of Sales People	Travel Expenses	**Number of Sales People**
Employee Training	Product Defects	**Employee Training**
Number of Employees	Prescription Drug Costs	**Number of Employees**

changes in advertising expenditures; lease revenues depend on square footage; travel expenses depend on the number of sales people and so on. I am looking for movement in a variable that predicts the movement in another variable.

To forecast result I need there to be a relationship between two variables. Again, one variable responds to movement in the other variable. My cost of shipping responds to the number of orders I receive. Shipping cost is referred to as the **dependent variable** (response variable) and the number of orders received is referred to as the **independent variable** (predicting variable).

Cause and effect is the most important aspect of finding and utilizing two variables in forecasting. You can probably find two variables which seem to move together but upon examination do not posses cause and effect. Without cause and effect you cannot use the movement to accurately predict outcome (forecast). Shipping cost has a logical relationship to number of orders received. The movement in one variable (independent) will be used to predict the –movement in the other variable (dependent).

For example, suppose that you wanted to forecast the average annual sales of your retail store based on the square footage. The two variables of interest are average annual sales and square footage of the retail store. Let's further assume that the relationship between the two could be shown to be a positive linear relationship (upward slope to the right). Let's further assume that I have developed, using the *method of least squares* or *ordinary least squares method* (both procedures are the same), a forecasting equation. I will show you this process shortly, but for now assume the equation I developed is stated as follows:

$$\hat{Y} = 901.247 + 1.686X \text{ simple linear regression equation}$$

Here $\hat{Y}$ (pronounced Y-hat) is equal to average annual sales in (000). $\hat{Y}$ is also the *dependent variable*. The *independent variable* is X which, in this instance, is the square footage of the retail store. My cause and effect relationship logically exists. The bigger my store, the higher my average annual sales will be. Store size causes more sales.

Wait a minute, Professor, just because you have a larger store does not necessarily mean you will have greater sales.

True, I respond. There may be other factors, such as number of sales staff, level of inventory, and advertising. Logically, I know store size alone does not totally represent all of the variables that go into my ability to accurately forecast my sales. I will return to this thought shortly, but let me first wrap up my illustration of the two variables—store size and sales.

In order to use the forecasting equation, I must know or assume a value for X which would be the square footage of a chosen retail store. With this information, I can forecast average annual sales (dependent variable).

Let's assume that I want to open a store in the downtown area that is 4,000 square feet. This is X or the independent variable. If I substitute 4,000 for X_1 what is the forecast of my average annual sales? I find the sales by substituting 4 (000) for X in the predicting equation. The result will be a forecast of annual sales of 907.991 or $907,991. [The math: $\hat{Y} = 901.247 + 1.686(4)$].

It looks rather easy, doesn't it?

You are correct, Professor. The math is quite simple. However, is the predicting equation always given?

That would make life too easy, I respond, so the short answer is no. I must use historical data to develop a forecasting equation.

Let's return to the thought about size of store being the only variable which allows me to predict my sales. I listed some other possibilities: number of sales staff (X_2), level of inventory (X_3), and advertising (X_4). Let's assume I want to work these variables into my forecasting model. It might look like the following:

$$\hat{Y} = 901.247 + 1.686X_1 + 0.79X_2 + 2.46X_3 + 3.25X_4$$

Notice that X_1 is still square footage and is still an independent variable. Now I need values for sales staff, level of inventory, and advertising. Given those values, I can more accurately forecast my average annual sales ($\hat{Y}$). Also notice I did not add any more dependent variables. I still have only one dependent variable ($\hat{Y}$). I did, however, add more independent variables (more X's). I added to my square footage independent variable three other independent variables: sales staff levels, level of inventory, and advertising dollars spent.

What I have just shown you is the difference between simple linear regression and multiple linear regression. In **simple regression**, you have one dependent variable and one independent variable. In **multiple regression**, you have one dependent variable and two or more independent variables. The specific forms of a forecasting equation for both simple regression and multiple regression are as follows:

$$\hat{Y} = b_0 + b_1 X_1 \text{ (simple regression equation)}$$

$$\hat{Y} = b_0 + b_1 X_1 + b_2 X_2 + b_3 X_3 + b_4 X_4 + \cdots + b_n X_n \text{ (multiple regression equation)}$$

$\hat{Y}$ is the dependent (response) variable.
b_0 is the y-intercept. If all independent variables are zero, b_0 is the value of $\hat{Y}$.
b_1, b_2, b_3, b_4, b_n are all coefficients of their respective X-variable.

In short, what I must do is determine a value for each of the coefficients. If I can develop a value for b_0 and b_1, b_2, b_3, b_4, b_n , then given any value for each corresponding X-variable, I can develop a value for $\hat{Y}$. In order to accomplish this, I will use the process referred to as the *method of least squares* (MLS) or *ordinary least squares* (OLS) *method*. The calculation process is the same for either. They just have different names. Multiple regression is a bit more complex and contain a number of caveats, but I will address those issues later in the chapter. Before I move directly to the calculation process, let's visit a couple of issues.

There are two basic models used in simple linear regression—deterministic model and stochastic (random or probabilistic) model.

Deterministic Model

The first model is called a **deterministic model**. Let's say that I am leasing retail space in a strip shopping mall. I will pay base rent of $500 per month but my lease calls for me to pay 10% of my monthly sales as a rental premium. The best way to look at this model is to view it graphically. To do this I will use the Excel Chart Wizard in the Excel toolbar.

My equation for my study is $\hat{Y} = \$500 + 0.10(X_1)$. Using it I can determine my expected rent given different sales values for X, such as $1,000, $2,000, $3,000, $4,000, $5,000 and so on. Entering these solutions into an Excel worksheet ($600, $700, $800, $900, $1,000), I can highlight them, open the Chart Wizard and create the following graphic picture (Figure 11.1).

The math pattern for developing $600, for example, is to substitute $1,000 for X in the forecasting equation.

$$\hat{Y} = \$500 + 0.10(1,000) = \$500 + \$100 = \$600.$$

The other values are determined in the same fashion. Try a couple so you will understand the calcuations.

Now let's look at Figure 11.1.

From this graphic picture, you can see that all of the data points appear to fall on a straight line, which makes the model a deterministic model. Each and every point can be exactly and accurately determined. The $\hat{Y}$ value is rent and the X-variable is store sales. Rent is my dependent variable and sales is my independent variable. Movement in rent can be predicted very accurately by movement in sales. As sales increase, rent increases. As sales decrease, rent

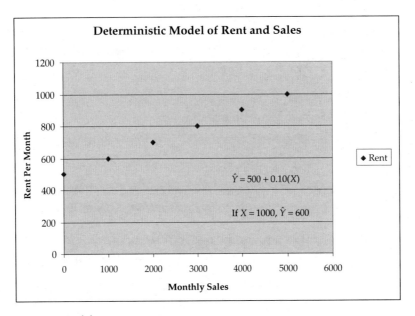

Figure 11.1 Deterministic model.

decreases. The movement is a positively sloped relationship in the same direction—one goes up and the other goes up, one goes down and the other goes down.

The actual form of the equation would be as follows:

$$\hat{Y} = b_0 + b_1X_1$$
$$\hat{Y} = \$500 + 0.10(X_1)$$

where b_0 is the y-intercept and b_1 is the slope of the line.
Here the slope b_1 is equal to 10% or 0.10, and it is positive. Positive slope is upward and to the right.

Professor, can you ever have a negative slope?

Absolutely. For example, the number of months you own exercise equipment and the number of hours of exercise per week may, in fact, be a negative relationship (think about it). In fact, negatively sloped predicting equations can be just as valid as a positively sloped relationship. When a person first purchases exercise equipment, the motivation is present to exercise for a longer period of time but the longer you own the equipment, the motive to exercise seems to lessen. Somehow our best intentions deteriorate over a period of time. I have a friend who claims to use his exercise equipment daily. In a recent conversation with his wife, she confirmed his claim. In fact, she confided, he always drapes his clothes over the equipment upon coming home in the evening. I am not sure that this is the use I expected when he made his claim, but at least he was telling the truth, misleading as it was. For most, this relationship reflects a negative relationship which might be described as a straight line.

In my deterministic example from just above, my monthly rent is *dependent* on my sales (independent). There is a clear and logical *cause and effect* relationship between the variables. Given any sales value, I can exactly forecast my rent. This relationship is a positive linear relationship.

Slope of the Line

Another example of negative sloped relationship is price elasticity. Price would be the vertical scale (*Y*-axis) and quantity would be the horizontal scale (*X*-axis). The slope of the line is from the left to the right in a downward direction. When price declines ($\downarrow$), the quantity purchased goes up ($\uparrow$). The opposite is also true: price$\uparrow$, quantity$\downarrow$. The amount by which the quantity increases is totally dependent on the slope of the line. A line that tends toward vertical (up and down) is an **inelastic demand.** A line that tends toward the horizontal (across) is considered to be **elastic demand.**

Inelastic demand tells you that a big change in price will result in a small change in quantity. The measurements of inelastic relationships are measured between 0 and -1.

An elastic demand simply reveals that a change in price will result in a much bigger change in quantity of purchases. The measurements of elastic relationships are measured above -1. Notice that I have used a negative sign to describe the values; however, in practice economists tend to ignore the negative signs and refer to the measurement as 1 or 3 or 0.5. This is done simply to prevent a discussion of which is larger, a negative 4 or a negative 5. As it applies to elasticity, the higher the value, the more elastic (sensitive) is the product to price changes.

In real practice, elasticity is hard to develop, since there is really no such thing as a single-company product elasticity (unless the company produces only one product with no different models). Elasticity is product, even model, specific and will depend largely on the stage in the life cycle of the product being studied. Elasticity can be long-range or short-range which further complicates life, but then who said life was simple? The product life cycles are introduction, growth, maturity, and decline. But I digress. However, my intent is to demonstrate negative relationships can be good and just as useful in predicting outcomes as positive relationships.

In real business situations, you do not often run into many deterministic models. What is most often seen is a random model, which is described below.

Probabilistic or Stochastic or Random Model (All the Same)

All three terms apply to the same type of model. Here all of the points do not fall on a straight line. The data set is random and, when plotted, the result will be a scatter diagram much like the one shown in the following graph (Figure 11.2). This graph reflects a study of ten pizza restaurants where the student enrollment in nearby colleges or universities seems to influence the sales at the nearby pizza restaurants. Let's say I own ten pizza restaurants and want to open an eleventh restaurant. I would like to be able to predict my sales for the eleventh restaurant with a reasonable degree of accuracy.

As I look at the data points (developed from Table 11.3 data below), a positively sloped, straight-line relationship between the two variables seems plausible. I need a procedure that enables me to develop a predicting equation. I need to fit a straight line to the scatter points. The straight line will enable me to forecast expected sales in any new restaurant I want to open. With this study, I am asserting a cause and effect relationship between pizza store sales (dependent) and student population on college campuses (independent). What I am trying to determine is if the sale of pizza near the college campuses is directly related to the student population at the school (cause and effect). Can movement in student college enrollment (cause) predict movement in pizza sales (effect)? The raw data for the 10 different pizza restaurants is tabulated below.

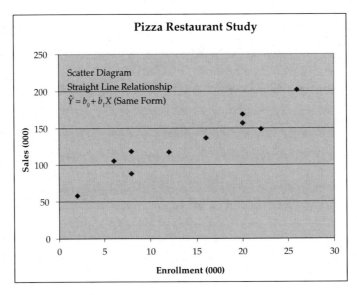

Figure 11.2　Pizza restaurant scatter diagram.

Table 11.3　Raw data for pizza restaurant sales.

Store Number	Student Enrollment (000) X	Restaurant Sales (000) Y
1	2	58
2	6	105
3	8	88
4	8	118
5	12	117
6	16	137
7	20	157
8	20	169
9	22	149
10	26	202
	$\Sigma X = 140$	$\Sigma Y = 1{,}300$
	$\overline{X} = 140 \div 10 = 14$	$\overline{Y} = 1{,}300 \div 10 = 130$

This table reflects that Store #1 was located in a town where the student enrollment at a nearby college was 2,000. Store #1 experienced $58,000 annual sales. The rest of the table should be reasonably simple to read in the same manner. For calculation ease, the 000 are removed from the data set.

If I can demonstrate a relationship between these two variables (student enrollment and pizza restaurant sales), I can develop a forecasting equation that would enable me to forecast the expected sales for a new restaurant I am considering. An accurate forecast will help me in planning the size of location, the number of employees, the capital required to do the leasehold improvement, the number of tables and chairs, the equipment required, etc. Many, if not all, of my managerial decision hinge on the expected sales.

As you look back at the scatter diagram shown in the Figure 11.2, there appears to be a positive relationship. It appears a straight line might fit the data set and best describe the relationship between the two variables. The next problem is to actually fit the straight line to the data set.

Remember, the general equation for a straight line is as follows:

$$\hat{Y} = b_0 + b_1 X_1$$

To fit a straight line, I must calculate the Y-intercept (b_0) and the coefficient associated with the slope of the line (b_1). How I do that is by using a technique called the *method of least squares*.

Here is where the mixed emotions arise. I can teach you the manual method, which most of you will not ever use or I can teach you Excel, which most of you will use if you are ever trapped into doing this stuff in real life. Actually it is pretty good stuff, so you really should pay attention to at least the Excel approach. The manual approach will give you insight into how the process works. Let's start with the good stuff—Excel.

Regression Using Excel

Open an Excel worksheet. Enter the raw data from Table 11.3 for the ten pizza restaurants. It makes no difference where you start. Pick a cell. Do not enter the totals; however, if you do, then do not highlight them when asked for your input range. Excel calculates the value you need from the data without totals. You also do not have to include the Store Number column since you will not need it. Just make sure the X and Y columns are shown in the Excel worksheet correctly.

Go to the toolbar and locate Tools > Data Analysis > Regression. Under regression you will be asked to input the range of the Y-variable. Highlight it (assuming you know which one it is). Remember, you are looking for movement in one variable (student enrollment—X) to predict the movement in sales (Y), so sales is my Y-variable I need to highlight. Next move your cursor to the X-variable box. Highlight these data also. Check the box that says labels, if you have included labels at the top of your column (which you should). Without including the column headings you will have generic names for the coefficients. Try it with and without labels being checked and see what happens.

You can check Confidence Interval box, but leave the Constant is Zero alone. Move to the Output Section where you have three choices where you want the data calculations (results) to be recorded. Usually, I will leave them as a separate tab in my existing worksheet (New Worksheet Ply). This allows me to keep the information close and allows me to rename the tabs by right clicking on the tab itself once the calculations are made. If you will notice, the worksheet will begin with three tabs (one, two, and three). It makes no difference which tab you enter your original data set under, but once you make the calculations you will have a tab number four. This tab will contain the results of the Excel calculations.

You can select the line fit plot since it tells you how your forecast lines up with your original data set. I probably would not mess with the Residuals, Residual Plots, Standardized Residual, or Normal Probability Plots for now. Click okay. The data calculation is rapid, if not instantaneous.

The Excel output is as follows (Table 11.4):

Table 11.4   Excel output for pizza restaurant study.

SUMMARY OUTPUT—Regression Output					
Multiple R	0.950122955	Coefficient of Correlation (Comment Added)			
R Square	0.90273363	Coefficient of Determination (Comment Added)			
Adjusted R Square	0.890575334				
Standard Error	13.82931669				
Observations	10				
ANOVA	**df**	**SS**	**MS**	**F**	**Signif. F**
Regression	1	14200	14200	74.24837	2.54887E-05
Residual	8	1530	191.25		
Total	9	15730			
Calculations	**Coefficients**	**Standard Error**	**t-Stat**	**P-value**	**Lower 95%**	**Upper 95%**
Intercept	60	9.22603481	6.503336	0.000187	38.72472559	81.2752744
Student Enrollment	5	0.580265238	8.616749	2.55E-05	3.661905963	6.33809404

Wow, that was quick, you comment.

Yes, it was, I respond.

How you interpret this output is important. I will address the main feature now and visit this output a bit later in the chapter for a broader interpretation. For now, remember, I set out to see if there was a relationship between sales and student enrollment. From my graphic plot shown as Figure 11.2, there appeared to be a linear relationship. I then took the next step to develop a forecasting equation of the form:

$$\hat{Y} = b_0 + b_1 X_1$$

I indicated if I could determine b_0 and b_1, I could then forecast $\hat{Y}$ (my sales). Take a look at the bottom section of the Excel output. Notice the values listed under Coefficients. They are 60 and 5. Notice to the left of those numbers the word "Intercept" associated with the 60 and "Student Enrollment" associated with the 5. The intercept is b_0, which in this case is 60 or $60,000 (since I have omitted the 000). The coefficient for student enrollment is b_1, which in this case is 5 or $5,000. Now I have my forecasting equation. It is as follows:

$$\hat{Y} = 60 + 5X_1 \text{ (omitting the 000)}$$

Remember, the intent of the entire exercise was for me to determine the sales of an eleventh restaurant I wanted to open. It so happens, I want to open a restaurant near a school with enrollment of 16,000 students. Ignoring the 000, I will use the 16 as my X-value in my forecasting equation.

$$\hat{Y} = 60 + 5(16) = 60 + 80 = 140 \text{ which is \$140,000 (inserting the 000)}$$

My forecast of sales for my new pizza restaurant is $140,000 per year.

This value is a *point estimate* of my expected sales. This is extremely helpful in my planning process. This gives me some idea about the level of sales I might expect given the relationship between sales and student population. This is an example of a **random** or **stochastic model.** This type of model is characterized by the fact that all observations do not fall on a straight line, but exhibit some sort of clustering pattern.

For another example, let's say that you wanted to use this equation to predict the sales in a college town with a student population of 50,000. What would the expected sales be for this town?

Your math should lead to expected sales of $310,000 but your answer would be wrong. $\hat{Y} = 60 + 5(50) = 60 + 250 = 310$ (right math, but wrong answer) To understand why, you need to go back to Table 11.3 and look at the range of your student enrollment data. The range is from 2,000 to 26,000. You have no data to support that the straight line relationship extends beyond 26,000 (the upper limit). Beyond the 26,000, I might find a curvilinear relationship. The point is this: I do not know what the relationship is between 26,000 and 50,000 student enrollment, so going very far beyond the 26,000 might lead to a flawed forecast.

Now back to the idea of the $140,000 being a point estimate of the annual sales given a student population of 16,000. The $140,000 is a **point estimate**—an estimate of the sales at a given point. I wonder if I can do anything more to improve my sales estimate, since I know that the probability of exactly hitting the estimate of $140,000 is close to zero?

The answer is yes. I will show you a quick and dirty use of the standard error. There is a more accurate approach, which I will cover shortly—global predicting values and individual predicting values. Just be aware that there are more sophisticated techniques to be used. Since I am working with sales dollars, the data set is continuous. Since it is continuous, I can use the empirical rule interpretation and develop a range for my sales. The empirical rule tells me if I move one standard deviation (standard error in this case) in either direction from the mean, I will encompass 68.3% of my observations. Two standard deviations (standard error) in either direction from the mean will encompass 95.5% of my observations, etc. Let's assume that I want to be 68.3% sure my sales will fall between two values. My formula begins with the $140,000 then adds and subtracts ($\pm 1, 2,$ or 3) standard errors. The formula is:

$\overline{X} \pm (1)S_e$ Using one standard error, I would have the following calculation.

140,000 $\pm$ (1)(13,829) = $121,171 to $153,829   (This approach gives you good planning information.)

Okay, you comment, I remember the empirical rule, but where in the world did you get 13,829 for the standard error?

Good question. I did blow by that, didn't I? Sorry about that. Go back to Table 11.4. Notice about halfway down the table on the left side there is something labeled Standard Error. To the right of it is 13.829, which has the (000) omitted. When (000) are added, you have the 13,829 I used for the standard error.

So I can be 68.3% certain my sales will fall between $126,171 and $153,829. This helps me better plan my staffing, equipment purchases, tables and chairs, rental space, and cash requirements. This tool is excellent in aiding you in forecasting no matter what the two variables may be.

I can probably make an argument that since I cannot demonstrate normality I might have to use Chebyshev's theorem to interpret the results. Were I to do this, I would have to use a K-value greater than one. Were I to use two as the number of standard deviations (K), my interval would widen. I would then only be *at least* 75% certain my sales would be between $112,342 and $167,658.

The calculation for what I just discussed is as follows: 140,000 $\pm$ (2)(13,829) = $112,342 to $167,658. *At least* 75% comes from using Chebyshev's formula of $1 - \dfrac{1}{(K)^2}$. By substituting 2 into the formula, the result is *at least* 75%. Remember using $K = 1$ will not work because the formula solution will equal zero.

My claim, using Chebyshev's interpretation, is that at least 75% of the time, my annual sales will fall between $112,342 and $167,658.

However, now that I have made all of these assertions about sales, I really need to know how well the forecasting line fits the actual data shown in the scatter diagram Figure 11.2. I can make this determination by looking at two different calculations as shown next.

Coefficient of Determination and Correlation

Two measures of interest to me are the **coefficient of determination** (goodness of fit) and the **coefficient of correlation** (strength). These are automatically calculated by Excel and are shown in the Excel output Table 11.4.

The *coefficient of determination* is referred to as *R-Square* in Table 11.4 and is shown as 0.9027 (rounded). The coefficient of determination is measured between 0 and +1. The closer the value is to 1, then the better the relationship between the variables. The closer the value is to 0, then the worse the relationship between the variables.

Wow, you say, I have no idea what you mean by a better or worse relationship between the variables. Can you take a minute or two and give me a hint?

Yes, I can, and good question. I love it when you stop me and ask questions. It makes me think you are really paying attention.

I will repeat Figure 11.2 which is the plot of the pizza restaurant study.

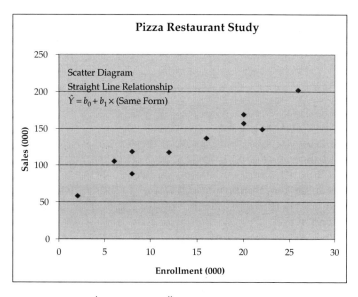

Figure 11.2 Ten pizza restaurants—sales versus enrollment.

Compare the pattern of this Figure (Figure 11.2) to the following figure (Figure 11.3).

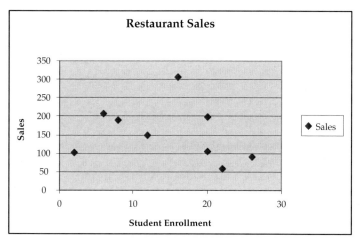

Figure 11.3 Adjusted restaurant sales to reflect wider dispersion.

Which graph depicts a better relationship between variables? Here the variables are the same. Sales is the dependent variable and student enrollment is the independent variable. Both use the same scale.

Looks to me like Figure 11.3 shows a much broader pattern and Figure 11.2 shows a much tighter pattern, you respond. It seems to me, this would make the relationship in Figure 11.3 worse than the data reflected in Figure 11.2.

That is an excellent observation and correct.

Which would you think would have a higher coefficient of determination (value closer to 1)?

My gut feel, you respond, is Figure 11.2 yields a much higher value.

You are correct. The coefficient of determination for Figure 11.2 is 0.9027 while the coefficient of determination for Figure 11.3 is 0.078 (I ran the numbers so trust me on this).

The *coefficient of determination* is measured between 0 and 1. At 0.9027, you can conclude *90.27% of the variation in pizza sales is explained by variation in student enrollment.* In the second example, only 7.8% of the variation in sales is explained by variation in student enrollment.

By the way, the interpretation I just shared with you is the *only interpretation* of the coefficient of determination. In the Excel output (Table 11.4) the coefficient of determination is referred to as *R*-Square (r^2). This is a measure of goodness of fit. It tells me how well the line fits (or explains) the movement.

The *coefficient of correlation* is the square root of *R*-Square. The coefficient of correlation is measured between −1 and +1. The closer the value is to 1 (either plus or minus), the better the *strength* of the relationship. In the Excel output, this value is shown as 0.9501 [$\sqrt{0.9027} = 0.9501$]. I determine if the coefficient of correlation is positive or negative by looking at the *sign of the slope* in the forecasting equation. If the sign of the slope is positive (+5 below), so too is the sign of the correlation coefficient. In the Excel output Table 11.4, the coefficient of correlation is shown as Multiple *R* (which I wish it were not, since I think the Excel term is confusing, but hey, that's just me).

$$\text{Repeating: } \hat{Y} = 60 + 5X_1 \quad \text{(positive slope)}$$

I need to discuss several other calculations shown in Table 11.4 but for now I will hold off. I will get to those comments shortly.

Three Y-Values

Actually there are three *Y*-values of interest to me. The use of the three will lead me to the theory associated with the manual calculations.

Oh boy, you say, I can't wait.

I glance over at you and wonder if you are serious. Oh well, I will give you the benefit of the doubt.

There is variation between the predicting equation line, the actual values, and the average values of *Y*.

Y = This is the Actual Sales and is represented by the free standing dots on the scatter diagram.

$\hat{Y}$ = This is the Predicted Sales and is represented by a straight line on the scatter diagram (dots on the straight line).

$\overline{Y}$ = This is the Average Sales of the entire data set (central line).

Figure 11.4 below shows the relationship between these three values.

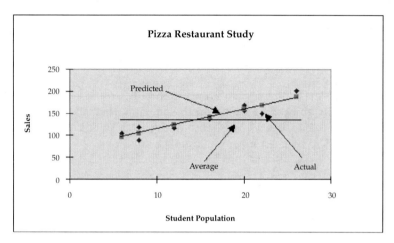

Figure 11.4   Three Y-values.

From the relationship between Y and $\overline{Y}$ and $\hat{Y}$, I will be able to develop three important variations: SST, SSR, and SSE. These are read sum of the squares total (SST), sum of the squares due to regression (SSR) and sum of the squares due to error (SSE). This is an $A = B + C$ relationship (SST = SSR + SSE). If I know any two, I know the third.

Table 11.4A   Comparison of manual formulas and Excel output (Same Results).

Output	Manual Formula	Excel Output
Coefficient of Determination	$r^2 = \dfrac{SSR}{SST} = 0.9027$	0.9027
Coefficient of Correlation	$r = \sqrt{\dfrac{SSR}{SST}}$ or $\sqrt{r^2} = +0.9501$	+ 0.9501
Standard Error	$S_e = \sqrt{\dfrac{SSE}{n-2}} = 13.829$	13.829

When these formulas are manually applied, the result will be the same as those values shown in the Excel output Table 11.4 and recapped in the last column of Table 11.4A.

Manual Approach to the Method of Least Squares or Ordinary Least Squares

This is the stuff you can probably read over for ideas unless your professor wants you to know how to manually calculate the coefficients, the forecasting equation, the coefficient of determination, the coefficient of correlation, and the standard error of regression. In my course, I usually require some knowledge of the manual calculations.

This procedure develops *a single line*, which is a best-fit line. *This single best-fit line minimizes the variation between the actual and the predicted values leading to a zero average deviation.* If you think about it, this is a very logical conclusion. The deviations around the mean are zero. The line acts as my mean line, so the deviations around it must be zero.

How do I start, you ask?

"Lotsa" columns, if I make these calculations manually.

Notice how I skillfully worked in my fluent Italian, since this is a pizza restaurant study. Of course, you real Italians are probably just shaking your head about now. Moving on, let's look at a completed Table 11.5 to be used for my manual calculations.

Table 11.5 Completed pizza restaurant table with manual calculations.

Restaurant Number	Student Enrollment—X (000)	Annual Sales—Y (000)	XY	X^2	Y^2
1	2	58	116	4	3,364
2	6	105	630	36	11,025
3	8	88	704	64	7,744
4	8	118	944	64	13,924
5	12	117	1,404	144	13,689
6	16	137	2,192	256	18,769
7	20	157	3,140	400	24,649
8	20	169	3,380	400	28,561
9	22	149	3,278	484	22,201
10	26	202	5,252	676	40,804
Totals	140	1300	21,040	2,528	184,730
	ΣX	ΣY	ΣXY	ΣX^2	ΣY^2
Averages of X and Y	$\overline{X} = 14$ *	$\overline{Y} = 130$ **			Use this column in the short-cut calculations.
Calculation of the Averages	*$\overline{X} = 140 \div 10 = 14$	**$\overline{Y} = 1300 \div 10 = 130$			

Pizza Restaurant Study

You should not have any trouble completing Table 11.5. XY is the product of X times Y, for example $2 \times 58 = 116$ for the first cell in the XY column. X^2 and Y^2 are the square of X and Y respectively. For example $2^2 = 4$ (first cell in the X^2 column) and $58^2 = 3,364$ for the first cell in the Y^2 columns. The totals at the bottom of the column are the sums of the columns. The averages of X and Y are shown below the table. Assuming you can duplicate this table, let's move on to the actual calculations.

Manual Calculation of the Predicting Equation

If I use the manual calculation method, I still have the same general form of the simple linear regression line.

$$\hat{Y} = b_0 + b_1 X_1$$

where the *coefficients* are determined by the following formulas:

$$b_1 = \frac{\sum XY - \frac{(\sum X)(\sum Y)}{n}}{\sum X^2 - \frac{(\sum X)^2}{n}} \quad \text{This is the formula for determining } b_1.$$

Looks pretty challenging, doesn't it?

Remember, the $\sum$ (capital Greek sigma) means "sum of a column headed ..."

$$b_0 = \overline{Y} - b_1 \overline{X} \quad \text{This is the formula for determining } b_0.$$

Next I will take the values created in Table 11.5 and substitute them into the formulas. By going back and forth from Table 11.5 to these formulas you should be able to follow my substitutions and calculations. Solving for b_1 and b_0 I have the following:

$$b_1 = \frac{21,040 - \frac{(140)(1,300)}{10}}{2,528 - \frac{(140)^2}{10}} = \frac{21,040 - 18,200}{2,528 - 1,960} = \frac{2,840}{568} = 5.0$$

[(which is actually 5,000 since I am working with (000)].

$$b_0 = 130 - 5(14) = 60 \text{ [This, too, is in (000), so this is actually 60,000.]}$$

Strangely enough, these two values are the same as shown in Table 11.4, which is the Excel output.

Now I simply substitute these two values into the general form of the equation to develop my forecasting equation which is the following:

$$\hat{Y} = b_0 + b_1 X_1 \quad \text{general form}$$

$$\hat{Y} = 60 + 5(X_1) \quad \text{specific equation for the pizza restaurant study}$$

Movement in sales (the dependent variable) can be explained by movement in student enrollment (the independent variable). As student enrollment increases (cause), sales will also increase (effect). Conversely, if student enrollment decreases (cause), sales will also decrease (effect). These two variables move in the same direction.

I can also manually calculate measures of goodness of fit and strength, which Excel has already done (Table 11.4). This is a pain in the 'you know what' to do manually, by the way.

Goodness of Fit (Coefficient of Determination and Standard Error of Regression)

$$SST = SSR + SSE$$

The sum of the squares total equals the sum of the squares due to regression + the sum of the squares due to error. The actual calculations are shown below and in the following tables.

$$SSE = \sum (Y - \hat{Y})^2 \quad \text{Table 11.6}$$

$$SSR = \sum (\hat{Y} - \overline{Y})^2 \quad \text{Table 11.7}$$

$$SST = \sum (Y - \overline{Y})^2 \quad \text{Table 11.8}$$

The best method of determining these values is to develop the following tables. However, this method is really unnecessary, so you can skip the calculations in the tables themselves. I put them into this textbook to fill pages. I am going to show you a short cut approach which you will exclusive use when making these calculations manually. Do, however, look at the totals for each of the three tables (11.6, 11.7, 11.8) since these are important.

The tables explain the theory, but there is a much, much less complex manual calculation of SSR and SST, and ultimately SSE. However, first let's walk through the manual calculation of SSE, SSR, and SST using the tables.

Wow, those are a pain in the "you know what" to do, you say.

Whoops, watch the language. I do not think you can say, "you know what" in a mixed company class room, I respond.

If you remember, I indicated the following relationship exists.

$$SST = SSR + SSE$$

From Table 11.6, 11.7, and 11.8, I have the following values.

$$15,730 = 14,200 + 1,530$$

Table 11.6   SSE = (actual less predicted)^2 $(Y - \hat{Y})^2$.

Student Enrollment (X)	Using $\hat{Y} = 60 + 55(X_1)$	Predicted Value Using	$(Y - \hat{Y})$	$(Y - \hat{Y})^2$
2	To get the predicted values, I substitute each X-value into the above formula, *for example:* $Y = 60 + 5(2) = 70$ $\hat{Y} = 60 + 5(6) = 90$	70	$58 - 70 = -12$	144
6		90	$105 - 90 = 15$	225
8		100	$88 - 100 = -12$	144
8		100	$118 - 100 = 18$	324
12		120	Etc −3	9
16		140	−3	9
20		160	−3	9
20		160	9	81
22		170	−21	441
26	Etc.	190	12	144
		Total	**0**	**1530**
			Average Deviation	SSE

Table 11.7   SSR = (predicted less average)^2 $(\hat{Y} - \bar{Y})^2$.

Average $\bar{Y}$	$(\hat{Y} - \bar{Y})$	$(\hat{Y} - \bar{Y})^2$
130	$70 - 130 = -60$	3,600
130	$90 - 130 = -40$	1,600
130	$100 - 130 = -30$	900
130	$100 - 130 = -30$	900
130	Etc $= -10$	100
130	10	100
130	30	900
130	30	900
130	40	1,600
130	60	3,600
Totals	**0**	**14,200**
	Average Deviation	**SSR**

Table 11.8   SST = (actual less average)^2 $(Y - \bar{Y})^2$.

Average $\bar{Y}$	$(Y - \bar{Y})$	$(Y - \bar{Y})^2$
130	58 − 130 = −72	5,184
130	105 − 130 = −25	625
130	88 − 130 = −42	1,764
130	118 − 130 = −12	144
130	Etc = −13	169
130	7	49
130	27	729
130	39	1,521
130	19	361
130	72	5,184
Totals	**0**	**15,730**
	Average Deviation	**SST**

If making manual calculations of these values (which you will most probably never do), you can accurately determine any two, and the third is known by adding (SSR + SSE) to get SST or by subtracting either SSR or SSE from SST.

My purpose, long since forgotten by you, is to know how well the forecasting line fits the actual data points. I have developed a forecasting model, so how well does it work? Just as in the Excel calculation, the three measures of interest to me are the coefficient of determination, the coefficient of correlation, and the standard error of regression. The coefficient of determination and the standard error are known as goodness of fit. The coefficient of correlation is known as the strength of the relationship.

The coefficient of determination (r^2) = SSR ÷ SST = 14,200 ÷ 15,730 = 0.90, which is the same as shown in the Excel output Table 11.4 (and 11.4A).

The standard error is $S_e = \sqrt{\dfrac{SSE}{n - 2}}$ where SSE is 15,730 − 14,200 = 1,530 so $S_e = \sqrt{\dfrac{1,530}{8}} = \sqrt{191.25} = 13.829$. This, too, is the same as shown in the Excel output Table 11.4 (and 11.4A).

The coefficient of correlation is the square root of the coefficient of determination. Here $r = \sqrt{r^2} = \sqrt{0.90} = +0.95$, which I repeat once again is the same as shown in the Excel output Table 11.4 (and 11.4A).

So what does this mean, you ask?

Glad you ask, I reply. This means the manual method of calculating b_0, b_1, r^2, r, and S_e are the same as the calculations shown in the Excel output Table 11.4. Using the manual calculation approach, I created three rather tedious tables: 11.6 (SSE), 11.7 (SSR) and 11.8 (SST). These three tables and the resulting values are necessary to calculate r^2, r, and S_e. Additionally, I created b_0 and b_1 using two formulas. These formulas allowed me to create the predicting equation $\hat{Y} = 60 + 5(X_1)$.

Well, the calculations are the same, I can see, you comment, but can I also conclude that the interpretation is the same?

Yes. Calculated manually or using Excel, the interpretation is the same. Excel is much faster, but the manual approach yields the same result.

As a recap: The coefficient of determination is a measure of goodness of fit. In our pizza restaurant study, it is interpreted as follows.

90% of the variation in sales (dependent variable) is explained by variation in student enrollment (independent variable).

How much variation can I ever explain?

100% is the short answer.

If I am explaining 90% of the movement in sales based on student enrollment, my relationship between the two variables is quite good. I can only explain another 10 percentage points (up to 100%).

Actually where you are doing manual calculations of SSR and SST, there is a much simpler approach than to use the tables (11.7 and 11.8).

Computational Ease for SSR and SST

In Table 11.5, I created a column headed Y^2. However, I have yet to use that column total. I know this has bugged you, right?

The answer is yes, in case this question almost stumped you. Okay, actually most of you did not even notice. Of course, some of you did not care. The simpler approach to computations includes using this column total ($Y^2 = 184,730$ from Table 11.5).

To use the short-cut calculation, what you do is the following:

You have already calculated a value for b_1. Let's use it. From the previous calculation:

$$b_1 = \frac{2,840}{568} \quad \text{Turn back to the complete calculation of } b_1.$$

You can directly calculate SSR by squaring the numerator of the b_1 calculation.

$$SSR = \frac{(2,840)^2}{568} = \frac{8,065,600}{568} = 14,200$$

Wow, you exclaim! Professor, you are brilliant and that was so simple!

I bow graciously and soak in your accolades. Wait, I humbly offer, there is more.

More, you question? My heart might now be able to stand up under this new information.

Give it a rest!!! Yep, I can also determine SST directly by using the Y^2 column previously discussed.

$$SST = \sum Y^2 - \frac{(\sum Y)^2}{n}$$

$$SST = 184{,}730 - \frac{(1{,}300)^2}{10}$$

$$SST = 184{,}730 - 169{,}000 = 15{,}730$$

These calculations are much easier and simpler than using the long form of the sum of the squares as shown in Tables 11.6, 11.7, and 11.8. You have a choice. You may work the problems the long way or work the problems the short way. I know which I would use. How about you?

Now that I know SSR and SST, I also know SSE. $(15{,}730 - 14{,}200 = 1{,}530)$

Standard Error of the Estimate

The standard error can be determined as follows.

$$S_e = \sqrt{\frac{SSE}{n - 2}}$$

$$S_e = \sqrt{\frac{1{,}530}{10 - 2}}$$

$$S_e = \sqrt{191.25}$$

$$S_e = 13.829$$

Coefficient of Correlation

The coefficient of correlation is the square root of the coefficient of determination. The purpose of the coefficient of correlation is to measure the strength of the relationship. As I have already shown you, the coefficient of correlation is measured between the values of -1 to $+1$.
In this instance, the coefficient of correlation is as follows.

$$r^2 = 0.90 \text{ from previous calculations}$$

$$r = \sqrt{0.90} = 0.95.$$

The strength of the relationship is excellent, close to the 1.0 which is the best. However, there is one thing. When I take the square root of any number, the outcome can be a plus or a minus.

The slope is positive in the forecasting equation $\hat{Y} = 60 + 5(X_1)$ so the sign of the coefficient of correlation is also positive.

Caveats

I have already shown you one warning. Do not go beyond the range of your data set in forecasting. One of my previous questions asked you to calculate sales using the predicting equation if I had a student population of 50,000. Your mathematical answer was $310,000. While mathematically correct, I pointed out that I did not know what happens to the relationship beyond the last data point of 26,000. Beyond that point, the relationship could be curvilinear or could have a different slope. I just do not know, so I must be careful to not go beyond the data in the data set. Does this mean that I could not forecast for a student population of 27,000 since this value is beyond the last data point of 26,000? No, it does not. What I would do is restrict my forecast to no more than 10% above my last data point. Using this rule of thumb, I could develop a forecast up to 28,600. Beyond that I would be very nervous about the outcome.

Secondly, regression and correlation cannot determine cause and effect. You must use common sense when you are determining the variables. For example, the number of salmon caught in Alaska may correlate very nicely to the number of brown bears in the zoo, but there is no relationship between these two variables. In short, two variables might yield high correlation values, but this does not mean that there is a cause and effect relationship. Use common sense.

Thirdly, the correlation in this example (salmon and bears) is known as spurious (false) correlation. Two unrelated variables can yield a high correlation coefficient.

Fourth, my predicting equation in the pizza restaurant study has been developed using 10 pizza restaurants located near 10 separate college campuses (or is that campi)? My results are very encouraging. My coefficient of determination is 0.90 (close to 1.0, which is the best). However, remember the idea of random selection where each and every element in the population has an equal and independent chance of being selected? How do you suppose that plays into my selection of the 10 pizza restaurants? To have a random selection, I would need to select the 10 pizza restaurants from the hundreds in the population. What does it do to my study if I don't do this? Well, it might invalidate my 0.90 coefficient of determination or my coefficient of correlation of +0.95. Suppose that my 10 restaurants are not selected at random from among the population. The real results from the population might not show such a strong relationship. Do you suppose there is a way I can test this issue?

Of course, you reply, or you would not have brought it up.

How astute of you, I reply.

Beta and Rho Testing

This stuff, while important, is probably not something you will use on an everyday basis, so read through it and learn the concept. It will be very important to validate your conclusions if you ever apply this to business decisions.

There are two tests I can conduct to see if my findings are supportable in the population. One is called the **beta test** and the other is called the **rho test.** Both beta and rho are Greek letters designating a test for the coefficient of determination (beta test) and a separate test for the coefficient of correlation (rho test). Usually you do not have to develop both tests, since the results should be identical in simple regression. However, the results in multiple regression may be different for the two values, so that is why the two exist.

Let's look at the calculations for beta and rho for the pizza restaurant study. Since I did not select the 10 pizza restaurants at random, I want to know if I can support my conclusion that pizza sales are a function of student enrollment. I want to know if a coefficient of determination of 0.90 and a coefficient of correlation of 0.95 are reasonable.

The beta test is appropriate for testing the coefficient of determination. Here, if I can assert that the slope of the *actual but unknown population regression line is zero,* I can then assert there is *no relationship between pizza sales and student enrollment.*

The hypothesis to be tested is as follows:

H_o: $\beta_1 = 0$ (beta)   If this is true, X cannot influence Y. (independence)

H_a: $\beta_1 \neq 0$ If this is true, X can influence Y. (dependence)

Here β_1 is representative of the population *coefficient* of the slope of my equation. Here I am testing for zero slope. (Boy, that probably confuses you, right?)

To test this hypothesis, I will use a t_{test}.

$$t_{test} = \frac{b_1 \sqrt{SS_x}}{S_e}$$

where SS_x is equal to the following.

$$SS_x = \sum X^2 - \frac{(\sum X)^2}{n}$$

$$SS_x = 2{,}528 - \frac{(140)^2}{10} = 568 \text{ This comes from Table 11.5.}$$

If you will notice, SS_x is the denominator of b_1 equation. You may have to turn back six to eight pages to verify what I am telling you, if you want to take the time, or just trust me on this.

The solution:

$$t_{test} = \frac{5\sqrt{568}}{13.829} = \frac{(5)(23.8328)}{13.829} = \frac{119.1638}{13.829} = 8.61$$

This is my *calculated t-*value. I match the calculated value to a critical value to make a decision.

At the alpha level of 0.05, I will look up the critical *t-*value in the *t-*table. The *critical t-*value is 2.306 using $n - 2$ degrees of freedom. Check this out before proceeding.

Since the *calculated* value of t is 8.61 and is greater than the *critical t-*value of 2.306, I reject the null hypothesis.

Great, you say, but what does this mean?

Glad you asked, I respond. Since I am rejecting the null, I can conclude that the population coefficient, β_1, is significantly different from zero. Since I reject the null, I can support that the population value would be different than zero. This allows me to assert that my pizza restaurant study can be supported in the general population. There is a dependent relationship between student enrollment and pizza sales because I am rejecting the null and accepting the alternate hypothesis. My coefficient of determination of 0.90 is supportable in the general population. Said differently, using my 10 pizza restaurants allows me to assert that my findings for those 10 are compatible with the population in general.

Let's test the coefficient of correlation. Here I use rho to represent the population correlation coefficient. Here the hypothesis being tested is as follows:

$$H_o: \quad \rho = 0 \text{ (rho)}$$

$$H_a: \quad \rho \neq 0$$

Here the formula is:

$$t_{\text{test}} = \frac{r\sqrt{n-2}}{\sqrt{1-r^2}}$$

The solution:

$$t_{\text{test}} = \frac{0.95\sqrt{10-2}}{\sqrt{1-(0.95)^2}} = \frac{(0.95)(2.8284)}{0.3122} = \frac{2.687}{0.3122} = 8.61$$

Notice that the calculated t-test value is the same for beta or rho test for simple regression (8.61). When you make these calculations for multiple regression, the values may differ, but for simple regression they should be the same.

Here again my conclusion is to reject the null hypothesis and conclude that the alternate is true. This means that my pizza restaurant study can support a positive coefficient of correlation.

Are you wondering why I have to go to this trouble to test the population values?

Not really, you comment, but I am sure you will tell me anyway, right?

Yep.

The need for these calculations is associated with my assumption about random sampling and inference. I am inferring that my coefficient of determination of 0.90 is representative of the population value of all pizza restaurants. I am demonstrating this to be the case. I do not want to choose a biased sample and draw incorrect inferential conclusions, so I should at least look at one of these two calculations (beta or rho). Does this absolutely mean that bias does not exist? Of course not! In statistics nothing is absolutely proven, but I can make assertions from the statistical tests.

More Accurate Uses of the Standard Error

This information on the use of the standard error, like beta and rho testing, is something you should do if you are going further into your studies. For now you should read through the information and know the process exists. Your professor may want you to know this stuff, so try to understand it. I generally require my students to have a working knowledge of the concepts.

Remember, I gave you a quick method of using the standard error in the pizza restaurant. I used the empirical rule since I was working with dollars (continuous data) to fit an interval around the point estimate of the sales of $140,000 given student enrollment of 16,000. Idetermined that I was 68.3% sure the sales should fall between $126,171 and $153,829. I do feel more comfortable about this range since my tests of beta and rho have been shown to support my assertions about the relationship between sales and student enrollment.

Now let's look at two approaches that are also useful. The standard error can be used in estimating two different values. One value is considered to be a **global value** (referred to as a **confidence interval**) and one is considered to be an **individual interval** (referred to as a **prediction interval**). Let me explain through an example and then through a real-life problem.

The Example

Let's say that I want to develop an estimate of the salary of all retail executives with 20 years experience. To do this, I would calculate a *confidence interval* (global implications). However, if I want an estimate of the salary of Curtis Bender, a particular retail executive with 20 years experience, I would calculate a *prediction interval* (individual implications). One is for all executives and one is for a particular executive.

The Real-Life Problem

Let's say that the Bradford Electric Company is studying the relationship between consumption of kilowatt-hours per month (in thousands) and the number of rooms in a private, single-family residence. A random sample of 10 homes yields the following information.

Table 11.9 Study of house consumption of KW hours.

House Included in Study	Number of Rooms	KW Hours (000)
1	12	9
2	9	7
3	14	10
4	6	5
5	10	8
6	8	6
7	10	8
8	10	10
9	5	4
10	7	7
Totals	91	74

I am going to give you the data you need rather than make you calculate it. Using the information from Table 11.9, you can calculate the values I am giving you, but why bother?

The Predicting Interval and Confidence Interval (Specific Names and Specific Solutions for Each)

Given the following information:

$$\hat{Y} = 1.333 + 0.667(X) \text{ (predicting or forecasting equation)}$$

$$\overline{X} = 9.1$$

$$\sum X^2 = 895$$

$$\sum X = 91$$

$$S_e = 0.898$$

$$N = 10$$

Bradford Electric is asking, "What is the predicted or forecasted usage of KWH for a six-room house?" Depending on what is desired, I can get two answers for this question—a *predicting interval* and a *confidence interval*. The predicting interval is for a specific six-room house (individual). The confidence interval is for any six-room house (global).

First, I am going to use the forecasting equation to determine the expected KWH usage for a six-room house. I will substitute 6 (for six rooms) into the forecasting equation. This yields the following calculation, which is a point estimate of the KWH usage for six room houses in general. I will begin my quest for the predicting interval (individual six room house) and the confidence interval (global − all six room houses) with this estimate point estimate.

$$\hat{Y} = 1.333 + 0.667(6) = 5.333 \text{ KWH}$$

At an alpha level of 0.05, I will calculate both the confidence interval (global) and the *predicting interval (individual)*. Again, the *confidence interval* is for *any six-room house* while the *prediction interval* is for a *specific six-room house.*

I will first address the confidence interval (global values).

The formula looks horrific. Go take some Rolaids and come back.

$$\hat{Y} \pm t_\alpha S_e = \sqrt{\frac{1}{n} + \frac{(x - \overline{x})^2}{\sum x^2 - \frac{(\sum x)^2}{n}}}$$

Oh, well, the Rolaids did not help because the formula still looks the same. Let's tackle it anyway.

The calculations are really not that difficult as long as you are careful about inserting values and not messing up the order of operation. All of the numbers I am showing below are from the values given in the problem statement on the previous page.

$$5.333 \pm (2.306)(0.898) \sqrt{\frac{1}{10} + \frac{(6 - 9.1)^2}{895 - \frac{(91)^2}{10}}}$$

$$5.333 \pm (2.306)(0.898) \sqrt{0.10 + \frac{(9.61)}{895 - \frac{(8,281)}{10}}}$$

$$5.333 \pm (2.306)(0.898) \sqrt{0.10 + \frac{(9.61)}{895 - 828.1}}$$

$$5.333 \pm (2.306)(0.898) \sqrt{0.10 + 0.1436}$$

$$5.333 \pm (2.306)(0.898) \sqrt{0.2436}$$

$$5.333 \pm (2.306)(0.898)(0.4936)$$

$$5.333 \pm 1.0221$$

4.3109 to 6.3551 KWH

This is the 95% global estimate of the KWH usage of all six-room houses.

Okay, you say. You told me all of the numbers came from the ones given, which I can pretty well follow, but you never gave me the 2.306, so where did you get that number?

Oh, I reply. This is a t-test with a sample size of 10. The alpha is set at 0.05 and the degrees of freedom are $n - 2$ or 8. You can verify the 2.306 in the t-table. Check it out. Confidence intervals are two-tailed tests, so look under the two-tailed alpha value of 0.05 and the degrees of freedom of 8.

Interpretation

I am 95% confident that the mean usage of all six-room houses (global) is between 4.3 and 6.4 KWH (rounded). This is known as a *confidence interval* because it applies to all six-room houses.

To determine an interval for a *specific* six-room house located at 1212 Avenue H, I would calculate a *predicting interval*.

The formula:

$$\hat{Y} \pm t_\alpha S_e = \sqrt{1 + \frac{1}{n} + \frac{(x - \bar{x})^2}{\sum x^2 - \frac{(\sum x)^2}{n}}}$$

Wait a minute, you say. This formula looks like the one for the *confidence interval* just above.

Good observation, I say. They are essentially the same with one difference. Can you find the difference?

Yeah, you reply. The formula for the *predicting interval* has an additional "one" (1) under the square root.

That's it, I confirm, how brilliant of you.

I can begin my calculations for the *predicting interval* by adding one to the 0.2435 (shown in the fifth step of the calculation for the *confidence interval* just above). My solution shown below picks up with that fifth step.

$$5.333 \pm (2.306)(0.898)\sqrt{1.2436}$$

$$5.333 \pm (2.306)(0.898)(1.1152)$$

$$5.333 \pm 2.3205$$

$$3.0125 \text{ to } 7.6535 \text{ KWH}$$

This is the predicting interval for a particular six-room house located at 1212 Avenue H.

Interpretation

I am 95% confident that the mean usage of a *particular* (located at 1212 Avenue H for instance) *six-room house* is between 3.01 and 7.65 KWH (rounded). This is known as a *predicting interval* and is broader than the mean usage for *all six-room houses*. The *predicting interval* should be wider (broader) than the *confidence interval* because it is much more difficult to accurately forecast the mean usage of a particular six-room house than it is for all six-room houses.

For those of you who are into baseball, it is much easier to predict the global batting average of a team than it is to predict the individual batting average of one player, so the interval for the team would be more narrow than the interval for one player. The same idea could be applied to an individual's batting average for the year or lifetime versus a single time he stepped up the plate. To be accurate, individual predictions must be much broader than global predictions.

Now, let's move back to stuff to which you really need to pay attention.

Multiple Regression

I want to spend a few pages addressing multiple regression (multi-variate). I have already shown you the primary difference. Simple regression has one independent (predicting) variable and one dependent variable (response). Multiple regression has more than one independent variable yet still only one dependent variable (response).

The linear regression forms for both simple and multiple regression are shown below:

$$\hat{Y} = b_0 + b_1 X_1 \quad \text{(simple regression equation)}$$

$$\hat{Y} = b_0 + b_1 X_1 + b_2 X_2 + b_3 X_3 + b_4 X_4 + \cdots + b_n X_n \quad \text{(multiple regression equation)}$$

$\hat{Y}$ is the dependent (response) variable.

b_0 is the y-intercept. If all dependent variables are zero, b_0 is the value of $\hat{Y}$.

b_1, b_2, b_3, b_4, b_n are all coefficients of their respective X-variable.

Solving Multiple Regression Problems

Quite simply, use Excel. The Excel process is the same for multiple regression as it was for simple regression. Let's assume I want to forecast the sales prices of homes. I take a sample of 15 homes and record the following information (Table 11.10) where price is the dependent variable and square footage, lot size, number of baths, and number of bedrooms are initially four independent variables.

Table 11.10 Characteristics of 15 homes.

Home	Price (000)	Sq. Ft.	Lot Size (000)	Baths	Bedrooms
1	499.5	2,196	18	2.5	3
2	729.1	3,475	25.7	3	4
3	650	2,846	18.9	3	4
4	692.5	2,995	21.5	3.5	4
5	710.1	3,025	22.6	3.5	4
6	595.5	2,596	21.8	3	3
7	644.3	2,985	17.2	4	4
8	790.3	3,602	22.9	4	5
9	668.8	2,825	26.4	3.5	4
10	540.6	2,612	19.9	3	4
11	828.9	3,690	29.5	5	5
12	635.6	2,785	24.2	4	3
13	615.9	3,051	20.9	3.5	3
14	619.5	2,665	21.9	3	3
15	495.3	2,090	15.5	2.5	3

Open an Excel worksheet. Enter your raw data from Table 11.10. It makes no difference where you start. Pick a cell. Do not enter totals; however, if you do, then do not highlight them when asked for your input range, since Excel will make the calculation you need. You also do not have to include the Home Number column since you will not need it. Just make sure the X columns and the Y columns are shown in the Excel worksheet correctly.

Which of the five variables do you believe is the causal variable?

You respond, it seems to me the price is a result of the other four, so Y (price) is the dependent variable and the other four are independent variables.

Very nicely done, I exclaim. Great job!

Now let's do the calculations. Go to the toolbar and locate Tools > Data Analysis > Regression. Under regression you will be asked to input the range of the Y-variable. Highlight it.

Then move your cursor to the X-variable box. Highlight **all four other variables at the same time,** including the labels at the top of each column. Check the box that says labels, if you have included labels at the top of your column (which you should).

You can check Confidence Interval box, but leave the Constant is Zero alone. Move to the output section where you have three choices of where you want the data calculations to be sent. Usually, I will leave them as a separate tab in my existing worksheet (New Worksheet Ply). This allows me to keep the information close and allows me to rename the tabs by right clicking on the tab itself once the calculations are made.

I probably would not mess with the Line Plots, Residuals, Residual Plots, Standardized Residual, or Normal Probability Plots for now. Click okay. The data calculation is rapid, if not instantaneous.

Selected Excel output follows in Table 11.11: (The ANOVA output section is excluded).

Table 11.11 Four independent variable multiple regression model—Excel (excluding ANOVA).

SUMMARY OUTPUT				
Regression Statistics				
Multiple R	0.96632891			
R-square	**0.93379156**			
Adjusted R-square	0.90730818			
Standard Error	29.053725			
Observations	15			
	Coefficients	**Standard Error**	**t-Stat**	**P-value**
Intercept	**37.2227913**	52.81280227	0.704806	0.497018
Sq. Ft.	**0.13012814**	0.036283835	3.586394	0.004959
Lot Size (000)	**4.84549928**	3.055740181	1.585704	0.14389
Baths	**12.2860177**	18.58011513	0.661246	0.523397
Bedrooms	**23.115558**	17.95882754	1.287142	0.227039

From this, several important conclusions can be drawn. The general forecasting equation is the following:

$$\hat{Y} = b_0 + b_1X_1 + b_2X_2 + b_3X_3 + b_4X_4$$

The specific forecasting equation is as follows:

$$\hat{Y} = 37.223 + 0.130X_1 + 4.845X_2 + 12.286X_3 + 23.116X_4$$

These values come from the Coefficients column in the Excel output (Table 11.11), which is highlighted for you.

Interpretation

The intercept is meaningless since you cannot have a house with no square feet, no lot, no baths, and no bedrooms. Each additional square foot added $130 to the price of a home (X_1 is square footage and 0.130 is the coefficient with price measured in thousands). Each additional 1,000 square feet of lot size will add $4,845 in sales price ($X_2$ is lot size). Each bath will add $12,286 to the sales price (X_3 is number of baths). And finally, each bedroom will add $23,116 to the sales price (X_4 is number of bedrooms).

Notice that the R-square (coefficient of determination) is good (output shows 0.9337), but the standard error is rather large (29.053725 which is $29,054) suggesting the interval is rather wide. I can state that 93.37% of the variation in sales price (dependent variable) is explained by variation in square footage, lot size, number of baths, and number of bedrooms (all four independent variables).

Parsimonious Model

Wow, what sort of word is that, you ask?

Parsimonious simply means stingy. The more independent variables I have in the multiple regression model, the more data sets I must maintain. I would rather keep up with as few data sets as possible, yet still explain as much of the variation as possible. This gives rise to the idea of the best model being parsimonious (stingy). The highest R-Square is not always the best, especially if a more complex model yields only very small gains in the models explanatory power.

Table 11.12   Bi-variate simple regression model using sales price and square footage—selected Excel output.

SUMMARY OUTPUT				
Regression Statistics				
Multiple R	0.9493009			
R-square	**0.9011723**			
Adjusted R-square	0.8935702			
Standard Error	31.132416			
Observations	15			
	Coefficients	**Standard Error**	**t-Stat**	**P-value**
Intercept	**71.917437**	53.49360655	1.344412	0.201806
Sq. Ft.	**0.1988383**	0.018262652	10.8877	6.65E-08

Let's play some "what if" games. What if #1: What if I begin with a simple linear regression model including only sales price and square footage? This would be a bi-variate model—one dependent variable and one independent variable. What I am going to do is to walk you through the use of one independent variable (bi-variate), then two independent variables, then three independent variables, and finally repeat the use of the four independent variables.

Going back to the simple regression approach of sales price and square footage, I have the following Excel output.

The model is as follows:

$$\hat{Y} = b_0 + b_1 X_1 \ (X_1 \text{ is square footage})$$

$$\hat{Y} = 71.917 + 0.199 X_1$$

Interpretation

Here, too, the intercept is not meaningful, since you cannot have a home with zero square feet. Each additional square foot, however, adds $199 to the sales price of a home. Here R-Square (coefficient of determination) is 0.9012, which means that 90.12% of the variation in sales price is explained by variation in square footage. Notice that the standard error is very large, so this gives rise to a very wide interval for your data set.

What if #2: What if I add X_2 or lot size to the simple model? The Excel output is below (Table 11.13):

Table 11.13 Multiple regression model using sales, square footage, and lot size—Excel output excluding ANOVA.

SUMMARY OUTPUT				
Regression Statistics				
Multiple R	0.9581326			
R-square	**0.9180181**			
Adjusted R-square	0.9043544			
Standard Error	29.51301			
Observations	15			
	Coefficients	**Standard Error**	**t-Stat**	**P-value**
Intercept	**46.776074**	53.178506	0.879605	0.396347
Sq. Ft.	0.1722961	0.0241957	7.120928	1.21E-05
Lot Size (000)	4.6805107	2.9806819	1.570282	0.14233

$$\hat{Y} = b_0 + b_1 X_1 + b_2 X_2 \ (X_1 \text{ is square feet and } X_2 \text{ is lot size}).$$

$$\hat{Y} = 46.776 + 0.172 X_1 + 4.681 X_2$$

Interpretation

The intercept is meaningless since you cannot have a home with no square footage and no lot size. Each additional square foot will add $172 to the sales price. Each additional 1,000 square feet in lot size will add $4,681 to the sales price. R-Square (coefficient of determination) is larger than the R-Square for Table 11.12 assumptions. At 0.9180 for R-Square, you can assert that 91.80% of the variation in sales price is explained by variation in square footage and lot size. The standard error is still large at 29.51301 ($29,513), so the predicting interval will still be wide.

Continuing our quest, for example #3, I add one more independent variable, number of baths, to the multiple regression model. The Excel output is as follows (Table 11.14):

Table 11.14 Multiple regression model using sales, square footage, lot size, and number of baths—Excel output excluding ANOVA.

SUMMARY OUTPUT				
Regression Statistics				
Multiple R	0.96063655			
R-square	0.92282258			
Adjusted R-square	0.90177419			
Standard Error	29.9084511			
Observations	15			
	Coefficients	**Standard Error**	**t-Stat**	**P-value**
Intercept	46.1419994	53.89648568	0.856123	0.410192
Sq. Ft.	0.15826446	0.029811895	5.308769	0.000249
Lot Size (000)	4.12965888	3.093099201	1.33512	0.20881
Baths	15.6684853	18.93444788	0.827512	0.425535

The model is as follows:

$$\hat{Y} = b_0 + b_1X_1 + b_2X_2 + b_3X_3 \text{ (X_1 is square feet, X_2 is lot size, and X_3 is number of baths).}$$

$$\hat{Y} = 46.142 + 0.158X_1 + 4.129X_2 + 15.668X_3$$

Interpretation

The intercept is meaningless since you cannot have a home with no square footage, no lot size, and no baths (I think I have said this a time or two, haven't I?). Each additional square foot will add $158 to the sales price. Each additional 1,000 square feet in lot size will add $4,129 to the sales price. Each additional bedroom will add $15,668 to the sales price of a home. R-Square (coefficient of determination) is larger than the R-Square for Table 11.13 assumptions. At 0.9228 for R-Square, you can assert that 92.28% of the variation in sales price is explained by variation in square footage and lot size. The standard error is still large at 29.9084511 ($29,908), so the predicting interval will still be wide.

This is getting boring, you volunteer. What are you trying to illustrate, Professor?

I am almost there and I really do have a point to make, so bear with me a bit longer.

I have already done the calculation for the full, four variable model. You can find that in Table 11.11, which I repeat here so you will not have to turn back to it.

Repeat of Table 11.11   Four independent variable multiple regression model—Excel (excluding ANOVA).

SUMMARY OUTPUT				
Regression Statistics				
Multiple R	0.96632891			
R-square	**0.93379156**			
Adjusted R-square	0.90730818			
Standard Error	29.053725			
Observations	15			
	Coefficients	**Standard Error**	**t-Stat**	**P-value**
Intercept	**37.2227913**	52.81280227	0.704806	0.497018
Sq. Ft.	**0.13012814**	0.036283835	3.586394	0.004959
Lot Size (000)	**4.84549928**	3.055740181	1.585704	0.14389
Baths	**12.2860177**	18.58011513	0.661246	0.523397
Bedrooms	**23.115558**	17.95882754	1.287142	0.227039

Now for my point: This continuum of calculations is under the heading "parsimonious model." A **parsimonious model** explains as much variation as possible with as few variables as possible. Before I go to the final conclusion, I must take a side trip to explain one more value in the Excel output. I have been referencing R-Square (the coefficient of determination) and Multiple R (coefficient of correlation). There is another value shown just below the R-Square and it is referred to as Adjusted R-Square. It, too, is a coefficient of determination, but a special one for multiple regression models.

That is great, you comment. Why do I need two coefficient of determination values and what is the difference between R-Square and Adjusted R-Square?

Good questions, I respond.

In simple regression there is no problem using R-Square. However, in multiple regression, there is a quirky thing that happens. As I continue to add independent variables, the value of R-Square is artificially driven up even if there is no additional explanatory power of the added variable. Let me illustrate with another ubiquitous table (which is taken from the Excel outputs).

Table 11.15 Comparison of R-Square and adjusted R-Square values.

Number of Independent Variables	R-Square	Adjusted R-Square	Comments—Dependent Variable Followed by the Independent Variable(s)
One	0.9012	0.8935	**Sales Price**: Square Footage (Comment #1)
Two	0.9180	0.9044	**Sales Price**: Square Footage, Lot Size
Three	0.9228	0.9018	**Sales Price**: Square Footage, Lot Size, # of Baths
Four	0.9338	0.9073	**Sales Price**: Square Footage, Lot Size, # of Baths, # of Bedrooms

Comment #1: This first value is a simple regression model using only sales price and square footage. The R-Square value of 0.9012 can be considered to be reliable, since the Adjusted R-Square phenomenon does not occur for simple regression.

Professor, what phenomenon?

How quickly you forget, I think, but do not utter my thought aloud. Smilingly I respond, I remind you that in multiple regression, the addition of another independent variable will artificially result in an increase in R-Square, even if the new independent variable does not explain additional variability.

You can actually see this pattern in the R-Square column in Table 11.15. R-Square (second column) gradually increases from 0.9012 to 0.9338. The Adjusted R-Square (third column) value shows a different pattern, which is pretty much flat. For multiple regression, the Adjusted R-Square value is more accurate.

With the Adjusted R-Square being so flat, this implies there is no additional significant explanatory value with any of the additional independent variables. In other words, since my goal is to have a parsimonious model, I would not need to add independent variable #2, #3, or #4. From my simple regression model which relates sales price to square footage, I can explain 90.12% of the variation in sales price by variation in square footage. By adding lot size, I am only increasing the explanation of the variability to 90.44% (increase of less than one-half of one percentage point). By adding number of baths, the explanatory values actually decrease to 90.18%. By adding the fourth independent variable, the explanation of the variability rises to 90.73%.

I do not know about you, but I don't think I want to develop and maintain data sets which do not change the explanatory nature of the model more than a little over one-half of one percent point (90.12% to 90.73%). You have as much information by using the simple regression model as you do by the addition of variables for the multiple regression model.

To support this concept, I can look at the p-value from the Excel output. I am once again repeating Table 11.11 to keep you from turning back to it.

If you page back to beta and rho testing, you can find the theory behind my conclusions stated below. You are going to determine if each coefficient (b_1, b_2, b_3, b_4) adds to the

Table 11.11   Four independent variable multiple regression model—Excel (excluding ANOVA).

SUMMARY OUTPUT				
Regression Statistics				
Multiple R	0.96632891			
R-square	0.93379156			
Adjusted R-square	0.90730818			
Standard Error	29.053725			
Observations	15			
	Coefficients	**Standard Error**	**t-Stat**	**P-value**
Intercept	37.2227913	52.81280227	0.704806	0.497018
Sq. Ft.	0.13012814	0.036283835	3.586394	0.004959
Lot Size (000)	4.84549928	3.055740181	1.585704	0.14389
Baths	12.2860177	18.58011513	0.661246	0.523397
Bedrooms	23.115558	17.95882754	1.287142	0.227039

explanatory power of your regression model. I compare the p-value to any alpha value I choose. Usually the alpha values will be the most common three: 0.01, 0.05, or 0.10. Since the p-value for the intercept (0.497), lot size (0.144), number of baths (0.523), and number of bedrooms (0.227) exceeds any of the three choices I would normally make, I can conclude I will not reject (DNR) the null hypothesis. Without going back and beating a dead horse (there is that phrase again), the null hypothesis would be as follows:

H_o: $\beta_2 = 0$ If this is true, X_2 (lot size) *cannot* influence Y. (independence)
H_a: $\beta_2 \neq 0$ If this is true, X_2 (lot size) can influence Y. (dependence)

Of course there would be a beta test for each of the coefficients (β_2, β_3, β_4) as well as one for β_1. For β_2, β_3, or β_4 I find that I DNR the null so lot size, number of baths, and number of bedrooms cannot significantly influence Y (sales price).

The opposite, however, is true for β_1. Here the p-value (0.004959) is less than any of the three most often used alpha values, so I will reject the null and conclude that X_1 (square footage) does influence Y (sales price). It is the only variable that does exert any significant influence.

What I saw from the coefficient of determination analysis is borne out by the p-value. I know most of you will not be challenged in real life with having to remember all of this beta stuff, but *you may find yourself in the position of having to use a p-value to make interpretations.* Let me give you a general statement to which you can actually relate.

If you have an Excel output like the one shown in Table 11.11, you can look at the p-value and know that the coefficient, and thus the variable, contributes or does not contribute by comparing it to the chosen alpha value. *If the p-value exceeds the chosen alpha value, the variable does not make a contribution to the explanatory power of the regression model.* Actually, all you really need to know, unless you get trapped into making a more detailed statement, is this simple idea.

So I can basically replace the last couple of pages of explanation by the preceding paragraph, you ask?

Hesitatingly, I respond, probably so. About all you need to know is if the *p*-value exceeds the alpha value, then the variable does not contribute to the model. Keeping this idea in mind will definitely place you at the front of the line in understanding how to interpret regression models. Because of Excel, you can collect the data and throw in all sorts of variables and quickly test them to see if they contribute to the model.

You have probably forgotten about it, but you really asked two questions a bit back, and all of this has answered only one of those questions.

You are right, Professor, by now I have forgotten the second question. Actually, I don't even know the day of the week much less the question.

Because I have perfect recall I will reproduce the questions you asked, I respond.

I said the following in reference to the Excel output: *"There is another value shown just below the R-Square and it is referred to as Adjusted R-Square. It, too, is a coefficient of determination."*

Your response: *"That is great. Why do I need two coefficient of determination values and what is the difference between R-Square and Adjusted R-Square?"*

Oh, my gosh, you gasp. Why did I even ask a question in the first place much less two questions? If the first question took you pages to answer me, how many more pages are you going to torture me with in answering the second question?

Torture? Torture?? Well, maybe, but relax, I think I can answer the second half of your question with not more than 50 additional pages (just kidding). Let's try for a lot fewer than that. My publisher has allotted me only so many pages for this book, so maybe I can be brief.

The difference between the *R*-Square and the Adjusted *R*-Square can be illustrated by the formula differences.

R-Square (Coefficient of Determination)

For simple or multiple regression, *R*-Square in the Excel output has the following concept:

$$R^2 = \frac{SSR}{SST} \quad \text{or} \quad R^2 = 1 - \frac{SSE}{SST}$$

In simple regression this would be written as small r^2 whereas in multiple it is capital R^2. Because of the phenomena in multiple regression of *R*-Square artificially increasing every time I add another independent variable, I must make an adjustment to the formula. Conceptually the adjustment is as follows:

$$\overline{R}^2 = 1 - \frac{\dfrac{SSE}{(n - k - 1)}}{\dfrac{SST}{(n - 1)}} \quad \text{(Which is read R-bar squared)}$$

I am glad you used the term "conceptually," Professor, because I have no concept about the second formula.

Let me simplify it for you. Notice the terms $(n - 1)$ and $(n - k - 1)$?

Yes, you respond.

Those are measures of degrees of freedom. You and I have discussed that idea before. It applies here. I simply adjust my formula to include degrees of freedom.

$$\text{The problematic formula is } R^2 = 1 - \frac{\text{SSE}}{\text{SST}}.$$

The adjusted formula inserts the degrees of freedom as follows:

$$\frac{\text{SSE}}{(n - k - 1)} \text{ and } \frac{\text{SST}}{(n - 1)}$$

Then the formula is re-written as follows:

$$\overline{R}^2 = 1 - \frac{\dfrac{\text{SSE}}{(n - k - 1)}}{\dfrac{\text{SST}}{(n - 1)}}$$

To shorten the page count for my publisher and get right to the explanation, I lose a degree of freedom every time I add another independent variable to my multiple regression model. The effect of this adjustment will cause the Adjusted R-Square (coefficient of determination) to either move sideways or actually decline if the new variable adds nothing to the explanatory power of the multiple regression model. You saw this demonstrated in the multiple regression model of sales price, square footage, lot size, number of baths, and number of bedrooms.

That's it. That is the answer to your second question. See that wasn't so bad, was it? That question is rhetorical by the way.

Well, enough of that stuff, I comment. Let's move on with some additional ideas about multiple regression. These concepts are necessary and important but for most basic statistics courses, all you need to know is that they exist. If your professor stresses them, then you should learn them.

Excel Output ANOVA Portion

So far I have ignored the ANOVA portion of the Excel output. Briefly, the **ANOVA table** is a measure of the entire regression model taken as a whole. Here I compare a critical F-value to a calculated F-value. If the calculated F-value is greater than the critical F-value, the model as a whole is good. If the calculated F-value is less than the critical F-value, the model as a whole is not useful as a predicting model. The higher the calculated F-value is above the critical F-value, the stronger the model as a whole.

Additional Concepts

Multi-collinearity for Multiple Regression Models

Multi-collinearity exists when one or more of the independent variables are themselves linearly related and the relationship between two independent variables is extremely high. Logic dictates that you would expect some sort of linear relationship between independent variables or you would probably not have included them in your forecasting model. Movement in the independent variables (2 or more) is used to predict movement in the independent variable (singular). Essentially if two independent variables are related, they both convey the same information (redundant information is present). This is a type of disturbance in the data. The major problem that occurs is if you want to know the contribution of each independent variable to the forecasting model. In other words, let's assume you have a multiple regression forecasting model with four independent (predictor) variables. I can determine an R_{bar}^2 or R value for the entire model, but if multi-collinearity is present, I cannot determine how much explanatory power each of the independent variables adds to the overall model. Additionally the standard errors are likely to be higher, if excessive multi-collinearity is present in the model. In short, if X_2 is linearly related to X_3 such that the relationship is significant, I cannot tell how much X_2 contributes to the overall model nor can I determine how much X_3 contributes to the overall model. A t-test of the match pair would be the normal test, but it would not yield accurate information about the contribution of each independent variable. This does not affect the overall goodness of fit and how well the model itself predicts movement in the dependent variable. For example, if you use X_1 to represent men and X_2 to represent women and X_3 to represent the entire population, it is easy to see there is a relationship between X_1 (men) and X_3 (total population) as well as a relationship between X_2 (women) and X_3 (total population). If multi-collinearity exists, one solution is to combine variables. For example, sales as one independent variable and square footage as a second independent variable could be combined to find sales per square foot. The other solution is to eliminate one of the offending independent variables.

Dummy Variables

I have two types of variables—quantitative and qualitative. The quantitative variable is not difficult to mathematically manipulate, but the qualitative variable has no value that can be manipulated. Variables that are not expressed in a quantitative fashion are difficult to use in the calculation procedures. Examples of these variables are gender, hair color, religious preference, etc. In order to offset this problem, a dummy variable is developed. The dummy variable accounts for the qualitative nature of a variable and incorporates its explanatory power into the model. If I had two data sets, one for females and one for males, I could use a zero to represent the female and a one to represent the male. I might want to use a zero to represent those who are single and a one for those who are married in another study of interest to me. By using a dummy variable, I can develop a predicting equation for both the males and the females separately or for single and married separately. This process helps overcome my inability to use qualitative variables in studies.

Curvilinear Relationships

Many of the relationships in dependent variables and independent variables cannot be explained by straight-line relationships. Often the relationship is that of a curvilinear relationship. For example, let's assume I am interested in the relationship between taxes and population. If I measure taxes in millions of dollars (dependent variable) and population in millions of people (independent variable), the data will probably support that as the population increases, the taxes will increase at a rate faster than linear. This is logical. When this case exists, the straight-line linear equations will not work. Most often a polynomial (usually second degree) will best describe the relationship. The polynomial simply says that as the independent variable increases, the dependent variable increases at an increasing rate.

The equation is as follows.

$$\hat{Y} = b_0 + b_1X + b_2X^2$$

I can have *S*-curves or logarithmic curves when working with curvilinear relationships.

Model Misspecification

I must be careful when developing a regression model to make sure to correctly specify relevant predictors (independent variables). Bi-variate models can experience this problem more often than multiple regression models, because I simply might not think of all possible explanatory variables. In bi-variate models, this can be a most serious omission or misspecification. It is less of a problem in multiple regression since I can add as many variables to the model as I choose. You can also cause a problem if you specify a linear model when a curvilinear model is required.

Heteroscedasticity (Non-constant Variance)

The regression line should fit equally well for all values of *X*. If the errors increase or decrease with *X*, this is known as **heteroscedasticity.** The error patterns will fan out or funnel in around the residual zero line. You hope for homoscedasticity where the error magnitude is constant for all values of *X*.

Autocorrelated Errors

Autocorrelation is a pattern of non-independent errors which are mainly found in time-series data sets. In the next chapter, I will cover time series. Positive autocorrelation is indicated by runs of residuals with the same signs (tend to be on one side of the residual zero line). Negative auto-correlation is indicated by runs of residuals with alternating signs, thus crossing the residual zero line more often.

You know You are a Texan If:

- You think stores don't have bags, they have sacks.
- You think people who complain about wind in their state are sissies.
- You realize that asphalt has a liquid state.

Tear-Out Sheet Chapter 11

Student Name: _____

Day and Time of Class: _____

Simple Regression Problems:

Given: The following exercise data and the months owned for equipment for ten people was obtained from a sample.

Person	Months Owned	Hours Exercised
1	5	5
2	10	2
3	4	8
4	8	3
5	2	8
6	7	5
7	9	5
8	6	7
9	1	10
10	12	3

Determine the X-variable (independent) and the Y-variable (dependent). Make sure you consider the cause and effect relationship.

1. Which variable do you suspect causes movement in the other?
2. Using the Excel Chart Wizard draw a scatter diagram.
3. Is there any apparent relationship between the variables?
4. Does the relationship appear to be negative or positive?
5. Using Excel determine the predicting equation.
6. Manually determine the predicting equation.
7. Determine how many hours of exercise you would expect, given that a machine was owned for 6 months.
8. From Excel find the coefficient of determination and explain its meaning.
9. Using the short-cut method, manually determine the coefficient of determination.
10. From Excel find the coefficient of correlation and explain its meaning.
11. Manually calculate the rho test and interpret its meaning. Use alpha 0.05.
12. From Excel use the standard error to calculate an interval around the value calculated in #7 above.

13. Let's suppose the data set matched cardiovascular fitness and the hours of work out time. What would be the independent and dependent variables—which causes the other to move? What would you think the slope would be—positive or negative?

Multiple Regression Problems

Using Excel and the following data, determine the regression for predicting all commodities using four of the major components of the index. The Bureau of Labor Statistics publishes information on food, shelter, apparel, and fuel and oil. The table below includes the percentage changes for a selected 20-year period.

Predicting All Commodities from Four Major Elements				
All Commodities	Food	Shelter	Apparel	Oil & Fuel
0.9	1	2	1.6	3.7
0.6	1.3	0.8	0.9	2.7
0.9	0.7	1.6	0.4	2.6
0.9	1.6	1.2	1.3	2.6
1.2	1.3	1.5	0.9	2.1
1.1	2.2	1.9	1.1	2.4
2.6	5	3	2.5	4.4
1.9	0.9	3.6	4.1	7.2
3.5	3.5	4.5	5.3	6
4.7	5.1	8.3	5.8	6.7
4.5	5.7	8.9	4.2	6.6
3.6	3.1	4.2	3.2	6.2
3	4.2	4.6	2	3.3
7.4	14.5	4.7	3.7	4
11.9	14.3	9.6	7.4	9.3
8.8	8.5	9.9	4.5	12
4.3	3	5.5	3.7	9.5
5.8	6.3	6.6	4.5	9.6
7.2	9.9	10.2	3.6	8.4
11.3	11	13.9	4.3	9.2

Percentage Changes over 20-Year Period (1985–2004).

1. Make the Excel calculations and interpret the results from the Excel output for all four independent variables.
2. Write the predicting equation.
3. Given a projected growth rate of 4.0% for food, 5.0% for shelter, 3.0% for apparel, and 7.0% for fuel and oil, what is the expected all commodities percentage change?
4. Are there any independent variables which are insignificant at any alpha level?
5. What is the adjusted R-square value using all four independent variables? Interpret it.
6. What happens if you eliminate any of the variables which do not contribute significantly to the four independent variable predicting equation? This will require you to recalculate using three variables using Excel.
7. Compare the results of the adjusted R-square value using three independent variables to the previous adjusted R-square value using all four independent variables. Interpret the difference.
8. Using 4.0% for food, 5.0% for shelter, and 7.0% for fuel and oil, what is the expected all commodities percentage change?
9. Compare the percentage change associated with the three independent variables model to the percentage change using the four independent variables model. Interpret this difference.
10. Which is the stronger model, the four independent variable model or the three independent variable model? Why?
11. Compare the standard error for each model. Which is higher?
12. Compare the ANOVA table for each model. Which appears to be the stronger model, the four independent variable model or the three independent variable model?

12

Smoothing Techniques and Time Series Qualitative and Quantitative Methods of Forecasting

Court Room Humor – Actual Exchanges Based on a Book by Charles M. Sevilla

Attorney: Are you qualified to give a urine sample?

Witness: Are you qualified to ask that question?

Business Forecasting and Planning

Business decisions are made under conditions of uncertainty, so naturally business professionals want to minimize the uncertainty. **Business forecasting** and **business planning** are two different processes. Forecasting will provide estimates of certain variables, which will then be used in the planning process. Planning is much broader than forecasting. For example, I might want to provide my company with a five-year plan of opportunities and challenges. However, I might like to include a forecast of my sales during that five-year period. The forecast might be developed by using the time series method or smoothing techniques or regression analysis. The processes associated with forecasting will provide the tools for quantitatively enhancing business decisions.

Forecasting involves the development and use of data sets and numbers. Planning on the other hand might include the use of any one of the following three non-numeric, qualitative approaches. **Qualitative approaches** incorporate the judgment of those participating, whereas **quantitative approaches** employ statistical techniques, which are usually applied to historical data to develop answers for future time periods. One implicit assumption is necessary when one applies statistical techniques to historical data sets. The assumption is that the history of yesterday is representative of the trend of tomorrow. Often this assumption is inaccurate. If there are bumps and warts in the historical data, there will be bumps and warts in the forecast. Too much reliance on historical data can lead to misleading forecasts of future results.

For example, in the late 1960's and early 1970's, the American automobile industry was on an upward sales trend of bigger, more profitable automobiles. In 1973 OPEC sharply curtailed the supply of oil. Prices rose and shortages of gasoline occurred. The result was disaster for Detroit. The American public turned away from the gas-guzzlers to the smaller cars of Japan. Detroit experienced a downturn in sales. The industry, which had largely relied on *historical forecasting* to build certain levels of inventory, found itself in a fight for its life as inventory failed to move as anticipated.

Time series forecasting (which had been used as a guide) depends on historical data, but it is not capable of easily seeing the turns in the road. Had Detroit used some of the qualitative approaches discussed below to supplement their strictly historical approach, the downturn might have been better anticipated. Interestingly, in the 1990's and early 2000's, the trend toward smaller automobiles reversed itself. The American public turned once again to the larger vehicles, and the SUV was born. During the 1960's and early 1970's, the United States imported some 30% of the oil needed to run the economy. Today as I write this textbook, the United States imports about 55% of the oil needed to run the U.S. economy. Could the future of the United States be once again held captive to oil? Qualitative issues must be factored into any quantitative forecast.

Let's look at three qualitative approaches (non-quantifiable), which add some qualitative validity to the quantitative forecasts.

Qualitative Approaches

Delphi Approach

This is a group consensus approach developed by the Rand Corporation. Opinions are gathered from a panel of experts, often managers of a company. The panel does not have to physically be in the same location. In today's instant communication world, the process can be conducted via email especially if the corporation is large and scattered throughout the United States. A moderator, selected by upper management, will develop a questionnaire based on upper management's identification of an important issue or issues for the future. The questionnaire might be as simple as:

1. What are the ten most important opportunities for *XYZ* Corporation in the next five years?

2. What are the ten biggest challenges for *XYZ* Corporation over the next five years?

As the moderator, you would send out the questionnaire to all of the pre-selected managers (experts). There would be a response time limit. Usually the response time is very short, perhaps a day or two at the most. The managers respond to your questions. Often all managers will not participate at the first level, but this does not void the study. As the moderator processes, summarizes, and condenses the answers, more and more managers will offer their opinions in later rounds. Late-comers do not void the study. The answers are returned to you as the moderator of the study. As the moderator, you tabulate the answers, noting the number of common responses for each answer. You then provide the answers received to all participants.

You then re-pose the questions giving the respondents an opportunity to adjust their answers after seeing the results from all other participants. Again, the time limit for response is short—usually a day. You will receive the modified answers, re-tabulate, condense, and re-submit the responses to the managers. Each time, you will find the answers will begin focusing on the best responses. This is essentially a process of prioritizing the most recent responses. You will probably have to administer this process up to six times before you have 10 to 15 good, consensus answers. These answers then form the nucleus for a moderated discussion forum in a face-to-face meeting with the managers. In such a meeting, rabbit chasing will be kept to a minimum and the focus of the meeting will be in the direction of the 10 to 15 responses which provide an agenda for the meeting. Out of that discussion group, you will be able to best identify the opportunities and challenges for the immediate future. Of course, the final discussion should include development of ideas on how the company should respond to each of the issues. The final outcome is a non-quantitative approach to planning.

The biggest drawback to the Delphi approach is the expertise of the experts. This is especially true if the process uses only internal managers to respond. The internal managers might not want to express opinions that run contrary to the perceived direction of upper management. To avoid this, outside participants should also be included in the survey process.

Scenario Writing Approach

This technique is much less structured than the Delphi approach. A set of well-defined assumptions is developed by a company's upper management. The assumptions act as a plausibility statement of what the future might hold. Often it is necessary to develop several sets of well-defined assumptions that correspond to a number of future scenarios. A panel of experts is asked to develop a conceptual scenario of the future based on each set of well-defined assumptions. Once the scenarios are written, management will select the scenario which seems most likely and then determine if the scenario is realistic. Often, pieces of each expert's scenario will be appropriated for a consensus result. This process is often restricted to just a few experts and involves more time to properly develop. I would be very surprised if Detroit does not include in their forecast a "what if" set of assumptions for both tightening and loosening of the oil supply.

Brainstorming Approach

This approach should be done as a very positive approach. No negative reasons or explanations should be given. No criticism of any person making a comment should be made. A group of managers will meet to discuss issues within the company. Part of the discussion will be to develop solutions to those issues. The managers will, without commenting negatively, list all of the possible outcomes (collectively exhaustive approach). At the end of the discussion, the alternatives will be prioritized and those suggestions that are less favorable will fall to the bottom of the list. This approach, if used in the positive manner, will encourage participation from all.

For example, during World War II, a panel of think-tankers was convened to develop options for the field commanders to use under certain battle conditions. Battlefield situations were presented to the group. One situation was to assume you are in a ship and the engines have gone dead. Your ship cannot move under its own power. Floating toward you is a water mine. If the mine hits you, the ship will blow up and perhaps be totally lost. What do you do?

There was much discussion of the issue. No acceptable response was reached. One individual, in sheer frustration, spoke out. There are over 300 sailors on the ship. Why not line them up on the side of the ship where the mine is approaching and have them all inhale at the same time, then exhale at the same time? The air will blow the mine away from the ship.

Suddenly the solution was clear. Take the water hose and create a stream of water to gently push the mine away from the ship. The point is this, had the frustrated individual not felt comfortable to make a silly comment, the solution could have gone without discovery. Positive brain-storming can be a good thing. Don't discourage even the simplest comment.

These three approaches are often very helpful in gaining a consensus opinion that is useful in planning the future of an organization. To supplement these qualitative approaches, there are the quantitative approaches.

Quantitative Approaches

Time Series Analysis

Time series analysis is an important quantitative tool for analyzing your data. This approach uses much the same approach that was used in simple regression. Remember, in simple regression I used one dependent variable (Y) and one independent variable (X). The example I used was that the sales in a pizza restaurant are linearly related to the number of students attending a college close to the restaurant. Sales was the *dependent variable* (Y) and number of students or student population was the *independent variable* (X). In regression, my purpose was to see if the movement in student population could forecast the movement in restaurant sales.

A similar approach is used in time series. The difference is that the *X-variable is time* (horizontal axis) rather than a specific variable. Examples would be the movement of stock prices, interest rates, sales, payroll, insurance claims, federal funds rate, or inflation over a period of time. Time may be daily, weekly, monthly, quarterly, bi-annually, or annually. Of course, if you are a day trader in the market, movement would be every few minutes.

There are four very important factors that influence all movements of time-related data sets. They are secular trend (T), seasonal variation (S), cyclical variation (C), and random (irregular) movements (R or I).

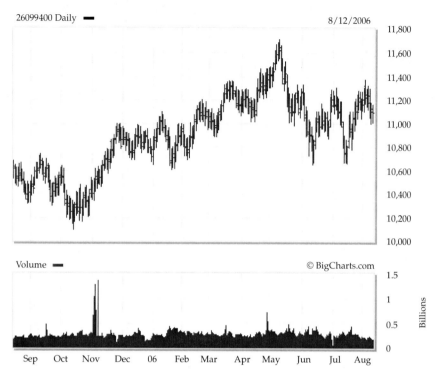

Figure 12.1   Dow Jones average one year 2005–2006.

These four components will be present in any actual time series data set (TSCR). Time series analysis involves the use of these four historical components to arrive at a future forecast for the data of interest. Most of you have seen charts for the Dow Jones Average or S & P or Nasdaq. These are time series charts. Figure 12.1 is an example of a time series (Dow Jones Average).

Definitions of T, S, C, and R

Linear Trend (T): Trend is *long-term* movement over an extended period of time. It is longer than one year. By observing the trend, you can detect the general direction of the movement—up, down, or even. The rate of change is relatively constant.

Seasonality (S): Seasons of the year bring on different sales. December brings on the Christmas sales frenzy. Spring brings on the sale of yard equipment and supplies. August brings on the sale of back to school purchases of clothing, books, and supplies. The seasonal pattern tends to occur at the same time each year. The movement is *short-term* and is complete in less than one year. I could not use annual data to determine seasonal movements.

Cyclical (C): This is a wavelike movement, which in general follows the business activity over a relatively long period of time. Usually three years or longer is involved in the cyclical portion of time series movements. There are four phases to the cycle—the upswing or expansion, the peak when the economy tops out, the downturn or contraction when employment declines and sales decline, and the trough, where the business activity is at the lowest point. These movements take longer than one year to develop and are considered *long-term* movement.

Irregular (R or I): Random or irregular movements are fluctuations caused by unusual occurrences and produce no discernible patterns. The movements are unlikely to reoccur in a similar fashion. Examples are earthquakes, wars, floods, oil embargoes, terrorist attacks, etc. These movements are also considered to be *long-term* movements, even though they will usually affect only one period of time.

Several Observations and Definitions

Forecasting Horizon

Often this is referred to as the forecast lead-time. This is the number of future periods covered by the forecast. Most of the time, three or four periods are identified. **Immediate-term** refers to less than one month. **Short-term** refers to one to three months. **Medium-term** refers to three months to two years. **Long-term** refers to two years or more. The accuracy of the forecast will often depend on the depth of the original data with which you are working. If you are working with two years of data, the accuracy of your forecast beyond a year is questionable. If you are working with 10 years of data, the accuracy of your forecast may extend beyond a year with less questioning.

Forecasting Period

The forecasting period might be for days, weeks, months, quarters, semi-annually, or annually. Historical data must be available in the appropriate units. For example, if you want monthly forecasts, the data must be available in months.

Forecasting Interval

If the forecasting period is for weeks, I would develop a weekly forecast. The frequency of the forecast must be for the same period as my data set.

Two Models

Even though there are two models, the additive and the multiplicative models, I will limit the discussion to the multiplicative model. The **multiplicative model** is known as the **ratio to moving average model**, which is helpful in *isolating* seasonal movement. The multiplicative model is as follows:

$$Y_t = T \times C \times S \times I$$

Where Y_t is the entire time series data set (the unadjusted actual value).

Since this is an equation, you can mathematically manipulate it. For example, if you divide one side of the equation by one of the components, you would also divide the other side of the equation by the same component. The purpose of this exercise is to demonstrate how you can isolate some of the movements. Three of the components have been identified as *long-term* movements (TCR) and one has been identified as *short-term* (S). What I would like to eventually do is to remove the *short-term* movements (seasonality), then prepare a forecast of the *long-term* movements, and then add back seasonality to the forecast. Before I take you to this tedious, painful and mind-numbing, yet helpful, solution, I want to introduce you to a couple of other methods of forecasting. There are three including the one I have just described (decomposition or de-seasonalization). Decomposition is the third of the three, so I will cover it last.

Three Methods of Forecasting

1. Smoothing Techniques
   a. Moving Averages
   b. Weighted Moving Averages
   c. Exponential Smoothing
2. Trend Projections
3. Decomposition—This is the process of isolating seasonal movement

Let's look at the three smoothing techniques.

1. Smoothing Techniques

There are three smoothing techniques—moving averages, weighted moving averages, and exponential smoothing. The purpose of a smoothing technique is to eliminate wild variations in the data set, which make it difficult to see any trend or cyclical movements in the time series. Moving averages is the least sophisticated and decomposition is the most sophisticated. Often business owners will not want to spend the time or resources on some of the more sophisticated techniques. If you cannot use the more complex techniques, use the less sophisticated techniques. A "guesstimated" forecast is not really a forecast. The point is this: use some technique, even if it is not the most sophisticated, to aid in your business forecasting and planning.

a. Moving Averages

A moving average is a series of arithmetic averages over a given number of time periods. This is an estimate of the long-run average of the variable.

Example of Moving Average

Let's say that I own a gasoline station and I want to use my current sales to forecast future sales. I do not want to be too sophisticated so I decide to use a three-week moving average to forecast the fourth week.

Table 12.1   3-week moving average gasoline sales.

Week#	Actual Sales (000)	3-Week Moving Average
1	17	
2	21	Plotting point if plotting the data set
3	26	
4	Need this week's forecast	This week's forecast

I will do the following.

The fourth period forecast = (17 + 21 + 26) ÷ 3 = 21.333

The forecast for my fourth week is 21,333 gallons of gasoline based on the three previous weeks.

Remember, I am using this method to forecast. Were I simply smoothing my data set, I would plot the value of 21.3 at the midpoint of my data set. Of course, this example is an oversimplified data set. Most data sets consist of many more data points. Okay, now let's repeat the chart from above.

Table 12.2   Recording of forecast and actual gasoline sales.

Week#	Actual Sales (000)	3-Week Moving Average
1	17	
2	21	
3	26	
4	If actual sales are 23, how would I adjust my forecast for the fifth week?	21.3—Forecast from above
5	What is this forecast?	I need this.

Let's say that the fourth week comes along and the actual sales are 23,000 gallons of gasoline. In other words, the forecast was 21,333 using the moving average approach, but the actual number of gallons sold was 23,000. Now I want to forecast the gallons using the same three-week moving average approach for the fifth week. What do I do?
You respond, a moving average implies to me that something moves.
That is a good start, I comment. If the average moves and the three weeks remains constant, I will drop the first week and add the fourth week, then re-average.

Moving Average = (21 + 26 + 23) ÷ 3 = 23.333 which is my forecast for the fifth week.

Table 12.3   Moving average forecast for fifth week.

Week#	Actual Sales (000)	3-Week Moving Average
1	17	
2	21	
3	26	
4	23	21.3
5	Unknown	23.3

Of course, there is nothing, except additional data, preventing me from making the moving average a four-week or five or six week moving average. The moving period of time is my choice and is subject to my own personal belief about my data set.

b. Weighted Moving Average

What if I believe that the most current week of actual data is of more value to me in forecasting than any other week? In other words, I believe the most current week of gasoline sales is more important than the actual sales from three weeks ago. I might want to use a weighted average of the actual gasoline sales. After studying the situation, the weights I decide to use are 1/6 for week one (earliest week), 2/6 for week two, and 3/6 for week three (most current week). Notice that the sum of my weights is equal to one. This will always be true. I now multiply the actual sales by the weights assigned to that week. Next I would sum the weighted values. Let's go back to the forecast for the fourth week.

Table 12.4   Weighted moving average.

Week#	Actual Sales (000)	Weight	Sales times Weights	3-Week Moving Average
1	17	1/6	2.8	
2	21	2/6	7.0	
3	26	3/6	13.0	
4			Sum	22.8
5				

The calculation:

$$(17 \times 1/6) + (21 \times 2/6) + (26 \times 3/6) = \textbf{22.8} \quad \text{fourth week forecast}$$

If the *actual* for the fourth week was *23,000*, the revised weighted moving average forecast would be calculated as follows:

$$(21 \times 1/6) + (26 \times 2/6) + (23 \times 3/6) = \textbf{23.7} \quad \text{fifth week forecast}$$

My un-weighted forecast was 21,333 gallons of gasoline for the fourth week, but my weighted forecast was 22,800 gallons of gasoline. Actually, if you stop and think about it, the un-weighted, three-week moving average forecast is also a weighted average. The weights in the "un-weighted" moving average are all *equal* (1/3 each), while the weights in the weighted moving average are *unequal*. I can choose any weights I believe to be relevant. I could use 10% for week one, 20% for week two, and 70% for week three. No matter what weights I choose, they must total 100%.

c. Exponential Smoothing

This is a weighted average of the current and past time period values. This is a better smoothing technique than either the moving average or the weighted moving average. This technique is, of course, more difficult to use, but the results are often more accurate. The basic model is as follows:

$$F_{t+1} = \alpha(Y_t) + (1 - \alpha)F_t$$

This can be read as the forecast for any time period plus one. (F_{t+1}) equals a weighted average of the actual $[\alpha(Y_t)]$ plus a weighted average of the forecasted period $[(1 - \alpha) F_t]$. The weights will be unbalanced with a smaller weight assigned to the actual and a larger weight assigned to the forecast, for example 0.2 for the actual (Y_t) and 0.8 for the forecast (F_t). The two weights [alpha and $(1 - \text{alpha})$] are complementary and add to 1.00 regardless of how they are set.

Formula Terms Defined Separately

Where α is the smoothing constant (not the same alpha value you have been using for CI and HT).

F_{t+1} = The forecast of the next time period (period $t + 1$)
Y_t = Actual value of the time series in period t
F_t = Forecast of the time series in period t

The difficulty with this method is the selection of α. Alpha (α) must be selected to minimize the mean square error (MSE). In reality, this can only be done by trial and error.

$$\text{MSE} = \alpha (F_t - Y_t)^2 \div (n - 1)$$

What I mean by trial and error is just that. You plug in a value for alpha (α), say 0.2, and solve the equation for the predicted values. You then calculate the MSE. You select another value for α, say 0.3. You next calculate the MSE. You then compare the two MSE values and select the one with the least value. You may have to repeat this process several times to develop the smallest value for MSE. If you actually try to calculate the MSE, I suggest you write an Excel program so you can adjust alpha up and down until your desired results are achieved.

Generally speaking, if the data are rather *volatile*, a *lower* α-value should be selected. This is because the smaller values for alpha assign less weight to the current period (more recent observations). Stable movements in the data may require a higher α-value.

Before moving to the next phase of forecasting, trend projections, I want to take a few paragraphs to discuss the use of Excel for some of these calculations.

Chart Presentations Using Chart Wizard and Smoothing Using Excel

Assume you have the following data shown in Table 12.5 collected for your retail sales business.

Using Excel, enter this data into an Excel worksheet. Note that the quarters have roman numerals, not numbers. Using numbers for the quarters confuses Excel. Start anywhere. Highlight all three columns including year and quarter information. Open the Chart Wizard and select line chart. Pick the one which reads "Line with Markers Displayed as Each

Table 12.5 Retail sales for five-year period.

Store Sales Five-year Period		
Year	Quarter	Sales (000)
2001	I	254.1
	II	290.4
	III	299.5
	IV	335.7
2002	I	286.7
	II	325.3
	III	333.6
	IV	354.4
2003	I	303.8
	II	349.2
	III	350.9
	IV	376.1
2004	I	321.4
	II	359.6
	III	371.2
	IV	401.4
2005	I	334.6
	II	387.4
	III	391.2
	IV	408.8

Data Value." On my version of Excel, this is the second one in the first column on the left. Click next. Verify the data range on this tab as well as indicating columns or rows. Most of the time, your data will be in columns. Click next. Input your desired title, X-axis and Y-axis. Click next. Select your output location—New Sheet or Object In Sheet 1 or 2 or 3. I usually select Object In Sheet 1, which places the graph beside my original data. Click Finish. A graph will appear which includes a legend on the right side. You may want to remove that legend by right clicking on it and selecting clear. You should see Figure 12.2. appear.

There are a number of other tabs and adjustments you may select, but for now leave them at default settings. Most of the time default will work for your presentation. After completing the graph, you may copy and paste it into your report or presentation.

Figure 12.2   Retail sales for five-year period by quarter.

One presentation adjustment you may want to make is to show the time series with a trend line. To accomplish that, click on one of the data points and select Fit Trend Line. You have several choices. Here you would want a linear solution. The result would be Figure 12.3.

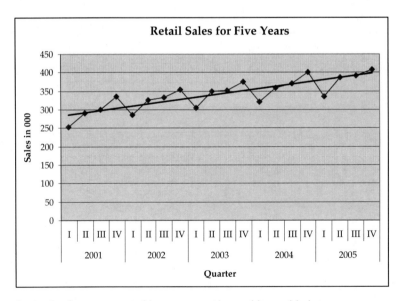

Figure 12.3   Retail sales for five-year period by quarter with trend line added.

I may want to show a moving average for my retail sales example. I can use the Data Analysis function under Tools to accomplish this. In an Excel worksheet you will enter the sales data from Table 12.5. Next select Tools > Data Analysis > Moving Average. Next is a departure from the normal. You will label the two columns next to the sales as MovAvg and StdError. This will be important when selecting your output. Highlight the sales column including the heading. Check the labels box. Set the interval at your desired level. Here I selected 4 since I wanted a four-quarter moving average. The output range selection is tricky. It needs to be the same column but one row just *BELOW your heading for MovAvg*. Here, my heading was in E3, so the output range would be E4 (just below my heading). Check the box Chart Output and Standard Errors. Click okay. The output should look like the following table (Table 12.6).

A simplistic approach to forecasting would use the last value in the MovAvg column as the forecast for the next time period, here 380.5. The error would be ±23.3338, so the interval of sales could run between 357.2 to 403.8 approximately 68.3% of the time.

Table 12.6   Moving average data table for retail sales.

Quarter	Sales (000)	MovAvg	StdError
1	254.1	#N/A	#N/A
2	290.4	#N/A	#N/A
3	299.5	#N/A	#N/A
4	335.7	294.925	#N/A
5	286.7	303.075	#N/A
6	325.3	311.8	#N/A
7	333.6	320.325	23.92288
8	354.4	325	19.30658
9	303.8	329.275	21.63222
10	349.2	335.25	21.70348
11	350.9	339.575	21.42542
12	376.1	345	22.01729
13	321.4	349.4	22.77097
14	359.6	352	22.00696
15	371.2	357.075	22.40807
16	401.4	363.4	24.92627
17	334.6	366.7	26.13276
18	387.4	373.65	26.75345
19	391.2	378.65	26.55643
20	408.8	380.5	23.3338

The chart graphic in the Excel output sheet needs to be expanded to better see the picture. Spread it to a desired width and height. Copy and paste it to your report or presentation. It would look like the following:

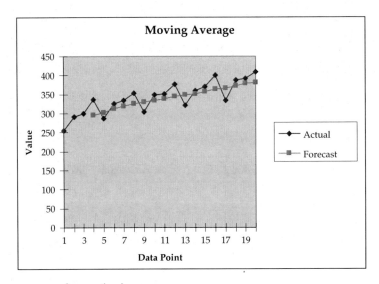

Figure 12.4   Moving average for retail sales.

In Data Analysis, you also have an option of using *Exponential Smoothing* rather than Moving Averages. Using the same data shown in Table 12.5, in an Excel worksheet select Tools > Data Analysis > Exponential Smoothing.

Here, as in the moving average approach, name the two columns immediately adjacent to your sales data entry column as Forecast and StdError. This is important in the output selection. Highlight the sales column as your input range.

The Damping Factor is from 0 to 1 and is 1-alpha. *Here I selected an alpha of 0.8. This is a damping factor of 0.2(1.0 − 0.8 = 0.2).* Check the Labels box. Select your Output Range as the same column but one row BELOW where you typed in the label Forecast. My entry cell was E26, so my output was E27. Check the Chart Output and Standard Error boxes. Click okay. The output is shown in Table 12.7 below.

Table 12.7   Exponential smoothing at alpha 0.8 (damping 0.2) for retail sales.

Quarter	Sales (000)	Forecast	StdError
1	254.1	#N/A	#N/A
2	290.4	254.1	#N/A
3	299.5	283.14	#N/A

(continued)

Table 12.7   (Continued)

Quarter	Sales (000)	Forecast	StdError
4	335.7	296.228	#N/A
5	286.7	327.8056	32.36963
6	325.3	294.9211	34.23136
7	333.6	319.2242	37.28532
8	354.4	330.7248	30.65512
9	303.8	349.665	23.73501
10	349.2	312.973	30.93418
11	350.9	341.9546	36.40744
12	376.1	349.1109	34.13704
13	321.4	370.7022	26.58838
14	359.6	331.2604	32.85897
15	371.2	353.9321	36.34211
16	401.4	367.7464	34.31237
17	334.6	394.6693	27.28782
18	387.4	346.6139	40.98399
19	391.2	379.2428	46.20387
20	408.8	388.8086	42.48452

Exponential smoothing uses the entire past history, whereas the moving average in my previous example uses four time periods as the average. If you will recall, a simplistic forecast using the *moving average* was 380.5. The exponential approach using a damping factor of 0.2 (alpha 0.8) would forecast the next time period as 388.8; however, the standard error has grown from 23.3 to 42.5.

The interval for exponential smoothing will be greater at 346.3 to 431.3 (68.3% of the time).

A graph of the chart would look like the following (Figure 12.5). Here, too, you will have to adjust the size so the data points can be more clearly seen. The exponential smoothing line fits the data set pretty well using an alpha of 0.8 (damping factor of 0.2).

I could have selected a damping factor higher than 0.2. Assuming I selected 0.8 for the damping factor (which would be an alpha of 0.2), the graph of that output would be Figure 12.6

The actual output would yield a simplistic forecast of 365.1 with a standard error of 30.5 for a 68.3% interval of 334.6 to 395.6. Clearly a larger damping factor does not fit the data set very well. A larger damping factor equates to a smaller alpha value.

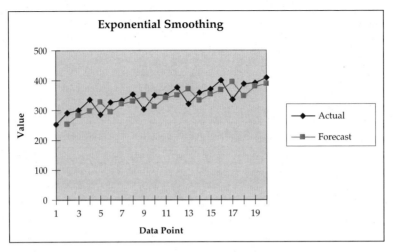

Figure 12.5   Exponential smoothing for retail sales at alpha 0.8 (damping factor of 0.2).

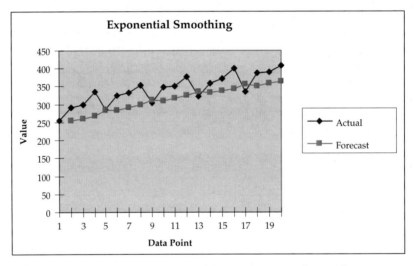

Figure 12.6   Exponential smoothing for retail sales at alpha 0.2 (damping factor of 0.8).

Professor, you finally comment, why is this true?

Actually, I have already given you an explanation of this. I will, of course, be glad to repeat it. Generally speaking, if the data are rather *volatile*, a *lower* α-value should be selected. This is because the smaller values for alpha assign less weight to the current period (more recent observations). Stable movements in the data may require a higher α-value. In my example, the movements in the retail sales example have minimal volatility, so the higher alpha is appropriate.

Another real life example is stock performance. While I will not attempt to explain all aspects of the following charts to you since this is not a finance textbook, I will point out two important tools often used by investors to make decisions about the purchase price of stocks. The following is a 50-day moving average of Sirius Satellite Radio for a year (Figure 12.7).

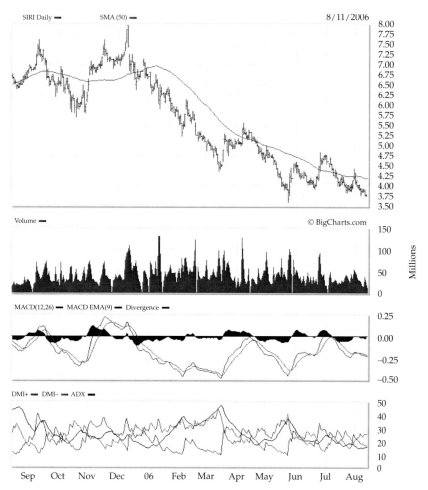

Figure 12.7   50-day moving average for Sirius stock prices.

From Figure 12.7, you can see the moving average indicates the average stock price over the past 50 days has been about $4.25. Since the stock is currently selling below the 50-day average, it might be considered to be under priced. Of course, you can't make a decision on stock prices from a chart alone, but you can get some indication of value.

Let's carry it one step further and look at a 200-day moving average to get some idea where the price could historically go.

From Figure 12.8, the 200-day moving average has a price of $5.25 or so. This is considerably above the 50-day moving average as well as the actual selling price. For an investor, this raised the possibility of a bargain in the current price of the stock. You would want to look at other factors before investing.

These charts were taken from the web site: *http://www.marketwatch.com.*

You can go there and sign up for an account and follow your favorite stock or perhaps find the next Microsoft. This is just an example of how moving averages work in real life decisions.

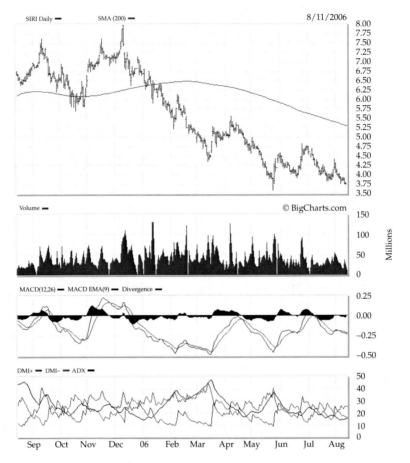

Figure 12.8   200-day moving average for Sirius Satellite Radio.

2. Trend Projections

A second method of forecasting is trend projections. This technique is identical to simple regression analysis. A trend line is fitted to the data set using the method of least squares or the ordinary least squares method (both the same). This line is a single best-fit line which minimizes the variation (average deviation concept = zero). Since I am using time as the X-variable, I must make some minor modifications to the formulas. They are notational only and have no bearing on solutions.

$$Y_t = b_0 + b_1 X \quad \text{for simple regression analysis}$$
$$T_t = b_0 + b_1 t \quad \text{for trend analysis}$$

where T_t is the forecast value of the time series in period t.

t is a period of time.

b_0 is the intercept of the trend line.

b_1 is the slope of the trend line.

Manual calculation of the time series is done the same way I approached regression. I set up the regression tables which would contain the t^2, tY_t, and Y_t^2 column headings. Additionally I need average Y_t and average t. I must make calculations for b_1 and b_0. Those formulas are also adjusted for time. Those adjustments are shown in the formulas below.

$$b_1 = \frac{\sum tY_t - \dfrac{(\sum t)(\sum Y_t)}{n}}{\sum t^2 - \dfrac{(\sum t)^2}{n}}$$

$$b_0 = \overline{Y_t} - b_1 \overline{t}$$

The solution to trend analysis formulas is the same as simple regression analysis. In simple regression, the variable along the horizontal axis was the independent variable. In trend analysis, the variable along the horizontal axis is time. Using time along this axis is the reason I adjusted the formulas above [shown with time (t) rather than X].

Excel is most helpful when determining the time series equation for forecasting. Even though Excel is relatively complex for time series use, I will explore the use of Excel when I get to the next section on decomposition. Trend analysis is an integral part of decomposition. For this reason, I will not work a problem here, but will postpone it to the next section.

3. Decomposition

Any time series data set contains four elements. Three are *long-term* and one is *short-term*. Remember, I told you earlier in this chapter it would be best if I could find some way to isolate the *short-term* movements in my data set, then fit a trend line to the *long-term* movements, and then re-insert the *short-term* movements. **Decomposition** is a process that does just that. Something that is decomposed is something that is taken apart.

I have two choices when working with a time series data set. I can use the original data set un-adjusted or I can use a data set that has seasonality (short-term movements) removed. To either data set, I can fit a trend line and determine a forecasting model similar to the regression model of the previous chapter.

Why would you care, you ask?

Good question, I reply.

If my data set has *no discernable seasonality* such as the use of insulin or salt, then I will use the original data set. If there *is discernable seasonality* such as the use of electricity or retail sales, I will use the decomposition approach.

Using the multiplicative model as previously presented, the relationship is as follows.

$$Y_t = T \times C \times S \times I$$

Mathematical manipulation might include the following:

$$\frac{Y_t}{S} = \frac{T \times C \times S \times I}{S}$$

$$\frac{Y_t}{S} = T \times C \times I$$

Let's look at an example. I will show you the manual process over the next few pages. This is a very tedious manual solution. The time series Excel process is not quite as tedious, but requires more knowledge of technique idiosyncrasies than does regression modeling. I will limit my presentation to the manual approach; however, I will use Excel to develop the trend forecasting equation. By showing you how easily Excel can determine the forecasting equation, you save you time. If you know that part of the technique, you can develop a quick forecasting equation for any time series data set. In short, part of the Excel process can be very useful, while part is too complex to be used at this point.

What I expect you to learn from the following pages is a very useful technique, which is available for your use. I am not naïve enough to believe you will come away from this section with full knowledge about how to apply this in a business setting. What I do hope is this will slide into your memory banks for later recall. At the time you need this technique, you can pick up a "How to Use Excel" book and fill in the details or simply work with the data set manually.

The example: Suppose you were the manufacturer of television sets. Over the past four years, you have accumulated the following quarterly sales data (Table 12.8).

Table 12.8   Original data set of TV set sales.

Year	Quarter	Sales – Y_t (000)
1994	1	4.8
	2	4.1
	3	6.0
	4	6.5
1995	1	5.8
	2	5.2
	3	6.8
	4	7.4
1996	1	6.0
	2	5.6
	3	7.5
	4	7.8
1997	1	6.3
	2	5.9
	3	8.0
	4	8.4

These sales, as stated currently, contain all of the four elements of time series data (TSCI). The first step is to review the data set. You need to ask yourself the question: Does this data set reflect any seasonality?

The answer is "absolutely." The third and fourth quarter sales are larger than the first and second quarter sales. If the data set had no seasonality, what would you expect? The answer: All four quarters of all four years reflect the same pattern, which would essentially be flat (5.0, 4.9, 5.1, 5.1 for example).

I am going to explain some of the steps in the process, but you will need to follow the tables inserted below to really understand what I am doing. There are a total of 12 steps to this process. The purpose and use of this technique will not become apparent until you read and re-read and study this section.

Step #1: I must isolate the seasonal movement by taking a four-quarter moving average, which is centered in the middle of the year. 4 Qtr. Moving Average $= (4.8 + 4.1 + 6.0 + 6.5) \div 4$ $= 5.350$. This value is reflected in Table 12.9 below.

Since it is a moving average, the next data point will be determined by dropping the 4.8 (first quarter of the first year) and adding 5.8 (first quarter of the second year). 4 Qtr. Moving

Table 12.9 Four-quarter moving average.

Year	Quarter	Sales – Y_t (000)	4 Qtr. M.A.	
1994	1	4.8		
	2	4.1	5.350	← $[(4.8 + 4.1 + 6.0 + 6.5) \div 4]$
	3	6.0	5.600	
	4	6.5	5.875	← $[(4.1 + 6.0 + 6.5 + 5.8) \div 4]$
1995	1	5.8	6.075	
	2	5.2	6.300	
	3	6.8	6.350	
	4	7.4	6.450	
1996	1	6.0	6.625	
	2	5.6	6.725	
	3	7.5	6.800	
	4	7.8	6.875	
1997	1	6.3	7.000	
	2	5.9	7.150	
	3	8.0		
	4	8.4		

Average = (4.1 + 6.0 + 6.5 + 5.8) ÷ 4 = 5.600. Continue this process until you understand how the moving average portion of Table 12.9 is developed.

Step #2: Unfortunately, the four-quarter moving average is centered in the middle of the year or the middle of the quarter. Centered here, the value is of no use to me. *I need values that are centered on the quarter itself.* In order to achieve this, I will *re-center* the four-quarter moving average. This is easily accomplished by averaging two quarters at a time.

$$\text{Centered Moving Average} = (5.350 + 5.600) ÷ 2 = 5.475.$$

$$\text{Centered Moving Average} = (5.600 + 5.875) ÷ 2 = 5.738.$$

Continue this process until you have completed Table 12.10. Notice four years of original data become three years of adjusted, useful data. I will not have data for the first and second quarters of the first year or the third and fourth quarters of the last year.

Table 12.10   Centered moving average.

Year	Quarter	Sales – Y_t (000)	4 Qtr. M.A.	Centered M. Aver.	
1994	1	4.8			
	2	4.1			
			5.350		
	3	6.0		5.475	← (5.350 + 5.600) ÷ 2
			5.600		
	4	6.5		5.738	← (5.600 + 5.875) ÷ 2
			5.875		
1995	1	5.8		5.975	
			6.075		
	2	5.2		6.188	
			6.300		
	3	6.8		6.325	
			6.350		
	4	7.4		6.400	
			6.450		
1996	1	6.0		6.538	
			6.625		
	2	5.6		6.675	
			6.725		
	3	7.5		6.763	
			6.800		
	4	7.8		6.838	
			6.875		
1997	1	6.3		6.938	
			7.000		
	2	5.9		7.075	
			7.150		
	3	8.0			
	4	8.4			

This second step smoothes the averages and effectively eliminates S and I from the equation. In other words, the centered four-quarter moving average *is defined as* $T \times C$. For now do not try to fully understand this column definition, just accept it. After you (if you ever want to) have a chance to think about the process, you will better understand the "minimization" process.

Step #3: Next, I must calculate the S and I. As I illustrated to you at the beginning of this section, I can mathematically manipulate the equation for time series.

$$\frac{Y_t}{T \times C} = S \times I$$

My original sales (4.8, 4.1, 6.0, 6.5, etc.) contains all four elements associated with time series (TSCI). Because I do not have a CMA (centered moving average) centered on the first and second quarter of the first year, I can divide the third quarter of the first year (6.0) by the centered moving average (CMA) of 5.475. The result will isolate seasonal movement (S) and irregular movement (I) (Table 12.11).

Table 12.11 Isolation of $S \times I$.

Year	Qtr	Y_t	4 QMA	CMA	S and I
1994	1	4.8			
	2	4.1			
			5.350		
	3	6.0		5.475	6.0/5.475 = 1.096
			5.600		
	4	6.5		5.738	6.5/5.738 = 1.133
			5.875		
1995	1	5.8		5.975	5.8/5.975 = 0.971
			6.075		
	2	5.2		6.188	0.840
			6.300		
	3	6.8		6.325	1.075
			6.350		
	4	7.4		6.400	1.156
			6.450		
1996	1	6.0		6.538	0.918
			6.625		
	2	5.6		6.675	0.839
			6.725		
	3	7.5		6.763	1.109
			6.800		
	4	7.8		6.838	1.141
			6.875		
1997	1	6.3		6.938	0.908
			7.000		
	2	5.9		7.075	0.834
			7.150		
	3	8.0			
	4	8.4			

Step #4: I next need to take the S and I and average them so I can remove (minimize) the irregular or random movements (I). I will average the quarterly values just computed above as follows (Table 12.12):

Table 12.12   Isolation of S I and development of seasonal index.

Qtr	1994 SI	1995 SI	1996 SI	1997 SI	Total Four Columns	Divide By	Seasonal Index	Adjusted Seasonal Index
1	None	0.971	0.918	0.908	2.797	3	0.9323	0.9308
2	None	0.840	0.839	0.834	2.513	3	0.8377	0.8363
3	1.096	1.075	1.109	None	3.280	3	1.0933	1.0915
4	1.133	1.156	1.141	None	3.430	3	1.1433	1.1414
							4.0066	4.0000

In step four, most students will wonder where I got the numbers in Table 12.12. Turn back to the Table 12.11. In the last column, find the 0.971. Now cross reference the 0.971 to the year and the quarter. You will notice the 0.971 is the first quarter of the second year (1995). Now look back to Table 12.12. Notice I have inserted 0.971 as a value in the first quarter for 1995.

Why did you skip the first quarter of the first year, you might ask?

Simple, I respond. There is no value for the first quarter of the first year (1994).

Remember, I told you that I would take four years of data and reduce it to three years of adjusted, usable data.

Keep looking back and forth at Table 12-11 and find the corresponding values in Table 12-12. Once you understand this process, let's move on.

There is a column headed *Total Four Columns* about the middle of Table 12.12. Find it. The value of 2.797 is the summation of three values (0.971 + 0.918 + 0.908). I repeat this process for quarters 2, 3, and 4.

The column headed *Seasonal Index* is the result of dividing 2.797 by 3 to get 0.9323. I repeat this process for quarters 2, 3, and 4. When I sum this Seasonal Index column, I get 4.0066. Find that value in Table 12.12. This value must equal 4.0000, since I have four quarters and each quarter is represented by the value 1.0000.

Since this total does not equal 4.0000, I must prorate the values in the Seasonal Index column down (reduce them) to make them add to 4.0000. This is called the **normalization ratio**. It consists of placing 4.0000 over the total of that column which results in the normalization ratio used in prorating the values down (or up if the total of the column is less than 4.000).

The ratio: 4.00 ÷ 4.0066 = 0.9984. (prorate down)

I next multiply each of the quarterly *Seasonal Index* numbers by 0.9984 to develop the very last column. Once I have made this multiplication, the new column will now add to 4.00. In this case, I prorate my values down (since the total is greater than 4.0000).

The results in the last column of Table 12.12 are the final seasonal index numbers.

What if my data set was expressed in monthly values? Would the total of the last column still be 4.00?

No, you respond. If your data set were in months, the last column would total 12.

Excellent answer, I respond. However, remember the proration issue would still apply.

Another word of caution is in order. When you are making your calculations, the total of the seasonal index numbers will not be significantly different than 4.00. What I am saying is this, if you calculate a seasonal index number *BEFORE* you apply any prorata adjustment, the value will be very close to 4.00, say 4.01076 or 3.9835 (arbitrary numbers to illustrate the point). The value before proration *WILL NEVER* be 4.656 or 3.564 (arbitrary numbers to illustrate the point). These last two numbers tell me I have a mathematical error somewhere. I better go back and check my numbers to see if I can find my mistake. In essence, the proration adjustment will be very small in all instances.

This process isolates the seasonal index. The averaging of the *S* and *I* values minimizes the effects of the irregular or random component.

How do you interpret the seasonal index of 0.9308, 0.8363, 1.0915, and 1.1414?

Professor, I don't have a clue. I am still reeling from the process, which I do not fully understand.

I know, I sympathize. To really understand it you will have to go over it again and again, but if you ever really find yourself in a job requiring forecasting and your data are highly seasonalized, you will need to know how to do this.

Now, back to the question: How do you interpret the seasonal index of 0.9308, 0.8363, 1.0915, and 1.1414?

Let's think about it. All these calculations have been for one purpose—to isolate seasonal movement (not to frustrate you). The last column in Table 12.12 is labeled *S*. This process has isolated the seasonal movement. My interpretation of the values in the last column of Table 12.12 is as follows:

The first quarter is approximately 7% below trend (100.00 less 93.08). The second quarter is approximately 16% below trend. The third quarter is approximately 9% above trend and the fourth quarter is approximately 14% above trend. Trend becomes my benchmark against which the seasonal index is measured.

Let's continue with the calculations. I still need to develop a forecasting equation for long-term movements, and then add back seasonality to get my final forecast. The fun is just starting. Table 12.13 is a combination of previously determined values and some new values in the last five columns. Don't get confused by this step. I think you can follow what I am doing if you pay very close attention.

Let's give it a try. I will repeat the year, quarter, and the original data set values (first three columns), but the fourth through eighth columns are new. I will describe them after

Table 12.13. They should be fairly easy to follow (at least to me and I hope to you too with a little concentration).

Table 12.13   Removal of seasonality from original data set and determination of manual forecasting columns to determine b_0 and b_1.

Year	Qtr	Orig. Data	S	De-Seasonalized Data Set $Y_t \div S = TCI$	t – Re-Numbered Quarter	$t\,Y_t$	t^2
1994	1	4.8	0.9308	$4.8 \div 0.9308 =$ 5.15	1	5.15	1
	2	4.1	0.8363	$4.1 \div 0.8363 =$ 4.90	2	9.80	4
	3	6.0	1.0915	5.50	3	16.50	9
	4	6.5	1.1414	5.69	4	22.76	16
1995	1	5.8	0.9308	6.23	5	31.15	25
	2	5.2	0.8363	6.22	6	37.32	36
	3	6.8	1.0915	6.23	7	43.61	49
	4	7.4	1.1414	6.48	8	51.84	64
1996	1	6.0	0.9308	6.44	9	58.05	81
	2	5.6	0.8363	6.70	10	67.00	100
	3	7.5	1.0915	6.87	11	75.57	121
	4	7.8	1.1414	6.83	12	81.96	144
1997	1	6.3	0.9308	6.77	13	88.01	169
	2	5.9	0.8363	7.05	14	98.56	196
	3	8.0	1.0915	7.33	15	109.95	225
	4	8.4	1.1414	7.36	16	117.76	256
	Totals			101.75	136	914.99	1,496

Step #5: The seasonal index column (S - last column in Table 12.12) is common to all four years. The index numbers 0.9308, 0.8363, 1.0915, and 1.1414 are repeated four times.

Step #6: Next, I will de-seasonalize my original data set (remove seasonality). I will divide the 4.8 (original data) by the seasonal index 0.9308 to get 5.15 television set sales. The 5.15

value has seasonality removed from it. This entire fifth column has no seasonality in it. Mentally match this de-seasonalized column against the original data set. You will notice that I am raising the first and second quarter of each year (4.8 raises to 5.15 and 4.1 raises to 4.90). I am lowering the third and fourth quarter (6.0 lowers to 5.50 and 6.5 lowers to 5.69). The same concept is true for the other quarters for the other years. I am removing the seasonality from my original data set. The logic makes sense. If my seasonal index is 0.9305 for the first quarter, this tells me I am approximately 7% below trend (100.0000 less 0.9305). If I adjust the original data, logically it would increase by approximately 7%. I need to total this column because I will use that total later.

Step #7: The sixth column in Table 12.13 is a renumbering of the quarters. I have four years each with four quarters, so $4 \times 4 = 16$. I number the quarters 1 through 16. I call this column "t," representing the quarterly time periods. I need to total this column also for later use.

Step #8: The next column in Table 12.13 is simply a multiplication of the t-column and the Y_t (as adjusted). For example, $5.15 \times 1 = 5.15$ and $4.90 \times 2 = 9.80$ etc. I need to total this column for later use.

Step #9: The final column in Table 12.13 which is the eighth column is squaring the t-value. 1 squared is 1, 2 squared is 4, 3 squared is 9, etc. I need to total this column for later use.

I have been referring to later and later has finally come. Of course by now I have probably lost most of you. If you are still reading, keep it up for a few more paragraphs. I will be finished shortly. Again, chances are you will not understand this unless you read and re-read it making the calculations as you read.

Here is where I am right now. I began this process with an original data set of TV set sales. There appeared to be high seasonality in the data set. I then created through several steps a measure of the seasonality (S). In the last table (Table 12.13), I removed the seasonality from the original data set and restated it as a de-seasonalized data set. This means I removed any seasonality from the data set. This is where I am at this point.

In regression in the previous chapter, I developed a straight-line predicting equation which enabled me to predict the movement in the dependent variable (Y) by variation in the independent variable (X). Here too I am interested in developing a straight-line predicting equation, which will enable me to forecast the value of my television set sales *beyond* my 16th quarter (fourth year).

Wait a minute, you say, as you recall a warning about regression. You told us in regression that I should not go beyond the range of my data set; however, here you are telling us to forecast beyond our data set.

Good grief, Charlie Brown (my age showing). I cannot believe you remember that warning. You are correct about regression, but in trend analysis I have replaced the independent variable with time. It is okay for me to go beyond my data set, but the caveat is: don't go too far beyond the time sensitive data set. There is no magic number, but for 10 years of data you might project two years ahead. Most bosses will want a five-year look at sales. I am sure you will be forced to make a five-year projection, but I caution you the five-year forecast (using trend analysis) is just about as good as the five-day weather forecast. You draw your own conclusions about that statement.

Step #10: Now apply trend analysis to develop a predicting equation.

$Y_t = b_0 + b_1 X_1$ my predicting equation for simple regression

$T_t = b_0 + b_1 t$ my predicting equation written for time series where T_t is the forecast value of the time series in period t.

t is a period of time.

b_0 is the intercept of the trend line.

b_1 is the slope of the trend line.

Re-writing the regression formulas, I have the following relationships.

$$b_1 = \frac{\sum tY_t - \frac{(\sum t)(\sum Y_t)}{n}}{\sum t^2 - \frac{(\sum t)^2}{n}}$$

$$b_0 = \overline{Y_t} - b_1\overline{t}$$

Solving for b_1 and b_0, I have the following results. (See the values in Table 12.13.)

$$b_1 = \frac{914.99 - \frac{(136)(101.75)}{16}}{1,496 - \frac{(136)^2}{16}} = \frac{914.99 - 864.875}{1,496 - 1,156} = \frac{50.115}{340} = 0.1474$$

$$b_0 = \frac{101.75}{16} - (0.1474)\left(\frac{136}{16}\right) = 6.3594 - (0.1474)(8.5) = 5.1065$$

The predicting equation can now be stated.

$$T_t = 5.1065 + 0.1474(t)$$

Great, you say, but how do I use it?

Good question. Now if I am given a value for any time period (t), I can forecast or predict the value for the time period plus one. For example, let's assume I am interested in forecasting the 17th, 18th, 19th and 20th quarters (the 5th year).

Step #11: Next, I simply substitute 17 for t in the predicting equation. This gives me the following solution.

$$T_{17} = 5.1065 + 0.1474(17) = 5.1065 + 2.5058 = 7.6123$$

I would then do the same thing for the 18th, 19th, and 20th quarters. The results of the calculations for the four quarters of 1998 are shown in Table 12.14.

Table 12.14   Forecast for year 1998 (quarters 17, 18, 19, and 20).

Quarter	Which is 1998	De-seasonalized Sales Forecast
17	Quarter 1	7.6123
18	Quarter 2	7.7597
19	Quarter 3	7.9071
20	Quarter 4	8.0545

Step #12: Gee whiz, I hope my 12-step plan does not drive you to drink. I just realized it is similar to those 12-step programs to sobriety. I assure you this is just a coincidence. Let's return to the twelfth step. Can I now conclude that the above figures represent my forecast for 1998? Should I start ordering television sets based on this forecast?

The answer to that question is "no." This forecast is de-seasonalized or sans seasonal movement. What I next need to do is reapply seasonality to my forecast. If you notice, my forecast in Table 12.14 is rather flat (7.61, 7.75, 7.91, and 8.05). This forecast does not at all reflect the same pattern as the original data set.

The following table re-seasonalizes the forecast (Table 12.15).

Table 12.15   Re-seasonalized forecast (final numbers).

Quarter	1998	Sales Forecast	S	Re-seasonalized Forecast
17	1	7.6123 times	0.9308	7.085
18	2	7.7597 times	0.8363	6.489
19	3	7.9071 times	1.0915	8.631
20	4	8.0545 times	1.1414	9.193

The fifth and last column in Table 12.15 is my re-seasonalized sales forecast. I can now begin manufacturing based on this forecast. Also, notice that this forecast resembles the pattern of the original actual data. In other words, the first quarter re-seasonalized forecast is higher than the second but lower than the third and fourth quarter. The original data set reflected the same pattern as the final forecast.

Why Do All of This or the "Who Cares" Question

By now, if you have been trying to follow this stuff at all, you may be asking, why go to all of this trouble just to get a forecast? Would I not do just as well fitting a trend line to the original data (the one that starts with the 4.8 and 4.1, etc.)?

That's a very good question, and I'm glad you asked.

In order to answer that question, I will use the original data set to develop a forecasting equation. The forecasted values for the 17th, 18th, 19th, and 20th quarters for the original data are shown in Table 12.16. Seasonality is still in the original data set. The final forecast from Table 12.15 is shown next to the original data forecast. The last column shows the difference in the Table 12.15 forecast and the original data forecast. Gee whiz, I hope this is clear. Maybe you will understand what I am saying by simply looking at Table 12.16.

Table 12.16 Comparison of two forecasts.

Quarter	Final Forecast Table 12.15	Original Data Forecast	Difference Greater or (Less)
17	7.085	7.910	0.825
18	6.489	8.090	1.601
19	8.631	8.270	(0.361)
20	9.193	8.450	(0.743)
Totals	31.398	32.720	1.322

Remember, my forecast is in thousands of units. The column total of 32,720 units is based on using the *unadjusted original data set*. The column total of 31,398 is based on the *very complicated decomposition process*. I hope you understand the columns so I can move to the illustration.

I will assume that the company has orders for the exact amount shown in the final forecast column (decomposed values). Let's further assume management did not use the de-seasonalized approach to forecasting. Okay, let me try to say this another way, because I am sure some of you do not yet understand what I am talking about.

I am making the assumption that my forecast was for 32,720 units (quarter by quarter) but that my actual sales are running 31,398 units (quarter by quarter). Is that better? I am also assuming that I am building product to the 32,720 unit level.

In my explanation, I will key off of the last column in Table 12.16 (the differences). Let's walk through the year with the management of the company. I forecasted 7,910 units would be sold in the first quarter, but actually the company sold only 7,085 units. I sold less than I forecasted. This left me with 825 units undersold (too much inventory). The president of the company calls me in and wants to know why I am not selling what I forecasted I would sell. With a lot of sweat and promises, I convince the president the second quarter will be much better.

Remember, I am building from a bad forecast base (the unadjusted original data).

The second quarter rolls around. I forecasted I would sell 8,090 units, but only sold 6,489. Again my forecasted sales are much larger than my actual (1,601 units go into inventory). This is 2,426 units (825 + 1,601) that have been placed into inventory because I am not meeting my sales goals. The president calls me in once again and now I have a problem. I am told to move the extra units. To move the inventory, I call my customers and offer special deals. Special deals will move the inventory, and the company gross margin will suffer, but I move the units and breathe a sigh of relief.

My forecast for the final two quarters (3rd and 4th) seems to be reasonable. I have forecasted 8,270 units and 8,450 units for a total of 16,720 units (from a bad base). However, when the quarters end, I find I have orders in hand for 17,824 units. This means I have orders for 1,104 units I cannot fill since I do not have them. Not being able to fill the orders drives my customer to competitors and costs me gross margin.

My company did not use the proper forecasting method. This led to improperly building the product which costs the company considerable gross margin. It makes more sense if my company used the proper (yet tedious) forecasting method. Because I did not, my stockholders, the president and employees should be very upset with me.

The point is this. By removing seasonal movement from the data set and then preparing a forecast based on long-term movement and then adding back seasonality (short-term movements), the forecast is much more accurate. Use this approach. It works.

Excel for Developing Forecasting Equations

As I indicated to you, the full use of Excel for trend decomposition is not going to be addressed in this textbook. It is too complex. I can, however, show you how to create the forecasting equation.

Go to an Excel worksheet. Enter the adjusted data from Table 12.13 including the quarters (1 though 16). It makes no difference where you begin. Go to Tools > Data Analysis > Regression. In regression, place your cursor in the Y-variable box. Now highlight the sales values including the label. Place your cursor in the X-variable box. Now highlight the quarter values (1 through 16). Check the Labels box. Since I am only interested in my predicting equation, I will not check any of the other boxes. Click okay and see Table 12.17 for selected output values.

Table 12.17 Selected Excel output for adjusted forecast.

	Coefficients	Standard Error	t Stat	P-value
Intercept	5.1065	0.112235336	45.49815	1.3E-16
Quarter	0.147397059	0.011607102	12.69887	4.51E-09

The forecasting equation from this output is as follows: $T_t = 5.1065 + 0.1474(t)$

Call me crazy, this seems to be the same equation I developed manually several pages back. This time it took five to ten minutes. Manually it took ages.

I can also do the same Excel exercise on the original data set. Using the same approach, I find the results can be shown in Table 12.18.

Table 12.18   Selected Excel output for original data set.

	Coefficients	Standard Error	t Stat	P-value
Intercept	4.8525	0.459871962	10.55185	4.78E-08
Quarter	0.1798529	0.047558826	3.781694	0.002023

The forecasting equation from this output is as follows: $T_t = 4.8525 + 0.1799\ (t)$

Excel can be useful even if you do not use it to fully develop the de-seasonalized values.

You know
You are a
Texan If:

- You listen to the weather forecast before picking out an outfit.
- You ask the restaurant for a sodee pop.
- You break into a sweat the instant you step outside at 7:30 A.M. before work.

Tear-Out Sheet Chapter 12

Student Name: _____

Day and Time of Class: _____

Moving Average

1. Given the following two-year data set, prepare a four-period moving average and forecast January of year three. Use Excel to make your calculations. You may do this manually, but it is recommended you use Excel.

Year	Month	Shipments
One	January	1050
	February	1340
	March	1382
	April	1200
	May	1253
	June	1362
	July	1109
	August	1335
	September	1415
	October	1285
	November	1345
	December	1380
Two	January	1065
	February	1355
	March	1399
	April	1225
	May	1275
	June	1381
	July	1120
	August	1346
	September	1425
	October	1296
	November	1365
	December	1392
Three	January	Forecast

Is this a reasonable forecast for January of year three when you examine the actual for January of year one and year two?

2. Using the same data set given in problem #1, use exponential smoothing to develop a forecast for January of year three. Try this with a high damping factor (0.8) (low alpha of 0.2) and then try it with a low damping factor (0.2) (high alpha of 0.8).

3. Is either a moving average approach or an exponential smoothing approach an effective tool for forecasting January of the third year? Why or why not?

Trend Analysis

4. The following sales data set has been collected for Wheels Bicycle Shop in Utica, New York since they have been in business. The owner wants to know what he can expect to sell next year, his eleventh in business. Using trend analysis, develop a point estimate forecast for the eleventh year of sales.

Year (t)	Sales (000) Y_t
1	$21.6
2	$22.9
3	$25.5
4	$21.9
5	$23.9
6	$27.5
7	$31.5
8	$29.7
9	$28.6
10	$31.4
55	$264.5
11th Year Forecast	

a. Can you de-seasonalize this data set? Why or Why Not?
b. Can you use Excel to solve this problem?
c. Can you use the manual approach to solve this problem?
d. Solve it using both and compare the outcomes.

Index Numbers

Attorney:	Doctor, before you performed the autopsy, did you check for a pulse?
Witness:	No.
Attorney:	Did you check blood pressure?
Witness:	No.
Attorney:	Did you check for breathing?
Witness:	No.
Attorney:	So then is it possible that the patient was alive when you began the autopsy?
Witness:	No.
Attorney:	How can you be so sure, Doctor?
Witness:	Because his brain was sitting on my desk in a jar.
Attorney:	I see, but could the patient have still been alive, nevertheless?
Witness:	Yes, it is possible that he could have been alive and practicing law.

Index Numbers

Index numbers are generally *price index* numbers. If you are interested in the unit quantity, such as inventory, it is certainly possible to compute quantity index numbers, but far more often you are interested in the change in prices, not changes in quantity. In this chapter, I will address only *price index* numbers.

A direct comparison of raw prices from time period to time period can be misleading. For example, if you were to compare the cost of a loaf of bread in 1982 to the cost of a loaf of bread today, you might find the 1982 price was $0.89 and today the cost is $1.29. This is obviously an increase, but how do you measure the increase? Let's say I want to compare, during the same time period, the cost of a gallon of milk. I find the price of milk in 1982 was $1.15 while today the price tag is $2.79. Again, I can see the price has gone up, but I have no comparative measurement of the increases. You cannot tell much from the direct comparison, but if you convert the prices to an index number, you could see immediately you are paying $1.29 ÷ $0.89 times 100 = 144.94 which is 44.94% higher for bread. For milk, I can say I am paying 142.61% more ($2.79 ÷ $1.15 × 100 = 242.61% − 100.00%). The cost of milk has risen much faster than the cost of bread: +44.94% versus 142.61%. By doing a very simple index number calculation, I can now compare the milk and bread price increases on a relative scale (percentage scale). This relative comparison is more meaningful than simply looking at the raw prices.

An **index number** measures the relative changes in price from one time period to another time period. The reference (current) period is chosen by the researcher as is the base period. When index numbers are published by the Government or some private organization, the reference period and the base period are selected by the publisher of the index.

Examples of Common Price Index Numbers

1. Consumer Price Index *http://www.bls.gov/cpi/* for more detailed information on the CPI than you can imagine.
2. Producer Price Index *http://www.bls.gov/ppi/* for more detailed information on the PPI than you can imagine.
3. Industrial Production Index.
4. Dow-Jones Industrial Average.
5. Standard and Poor's Composite Stock Index.

Other Links of Interest

http://www.bls.gov/   This links you to the Bureau of Labor Statistics. From there you can conquer the world with data. The site does contain a good summary section in the center of the home page that tells you the latest value of the CPI, Unemployment Rate, Payroll Employment Changes, Averaged Hourly Earnings, the PPI, the ECI, Productivity Changes and a U.S. Import Price Index.

http://www.bea.gov/   This links you to the Survey of Current Business/Bureau of Economic Analysis. Here you will be able to determine trends in industry, business, construction, manufacturing, and wholesale trade. The data are broken down by nation, region, country, and industry with GDP, personal income, corporate profits, and other excellent data.

http://www.bls.gov/news.release/pdf/eci.pdf   This links you to information on the Employment Cost Index in PDF format. Here you will find information on the cost of employment measured by changes in compensation costs including wages, salaries, and employee benefits cost for non-farm private and state and local government employees. This information is sorted in various manners.

http://www.bls.gov/opub/mlr/curlabst.htm   This is the Monthly Labor Review which includes historic and current information on the Employment Cost Index, the CPI, the PPI, the EPI (Export Price Index), and IPI (Import Price Index). You may have to move around in the site to find much of this information.

Consumer Price Index (CPI)

This index number is published monthly by the Bureau of Labor Statistics (U.S. Department of Labor). (*www.bls.gov*) It was originally established in 1914 to determine if wages were keeping pace with inflation. It was meant to be a measure of inflation. The CPI-W (pre-1978) consisted of a market basket of 400 goods and services purchased by urban and clerical workers. The pre-1978 index covered about 40% of the nation's total population. The CPI-U (from 1978 forward) is a market basket of about 3,000 consumer products covering about 80% of the nation's population. The previous base period for both the CPI-W and the CPI-U was 1967. In 1988, they were both updated to 1982–1984 base period. A **base period** is equal to 100 on the index number scale and provides a benchmark to which all subsequent comparisons are made.

The CPI is a weighted index. Weights are assigned to various categories; for example, food is 0.18, housing is 0.43, medical care and entertainment is 0.05, etc. The weights total 100%. The weights are updated about every 10 years. The calculation is slightly different than the Laspeyres Index shown below, because the weights are updated independent of any re-basing. This makes the CPI a fixed-weight, aggregate price index. I know some of these terms are absolutely meaningless to you at this point, so just bear with me and I will clarify most of them in the next few paragraphs.

Common Uses of the CPI

1. **The CPI Is Used as an Economic Indicator.**

   The CPI is the most widely used measure of inflation and is sometimes viewed as an indicator of the effectiveness of government economic policy. It provides information about price changes in the nation's economy to government, business, labor, and private citizens and is used by them as a guide to making economic decisions. In addition, the President, Congress, and the Federal Reserve Board use trends in the CPI to aid in formulating fiscal and monetary policies.

2. **The CPI Is Used as a Deflator of Other Economic Series.**

   The CPI and its components are used to adjust other economic series for price changes and to translate these series into inflation-free dollars. Examples of series adjusted by the CPI include retail sales, hourly and weekly earnings, and components of the national income and product accounts. An interesting example of this is the use of the CPI as a deflator of the value of the consumer's dollar to find its purchasing power. The purchasing power of the consumer's dollar measures the change in the value to the consumer of goods and services that a dollar will buy on different dates. In other words, as prices increase, the purchasing power of the consumer's dollar declines. Today's dollar is worth more than tomorrow's dollar, but this gets into the idea of present value/future value and is beyond the scope of current material.

3. The CPI Is Used as a Means of Adjusting Dollar Values.

The CPI is often used to adjust consumers' income payments (Social Security), to adjust income eligibility levels for government assistance, and to automatically provide cost-of-living wage adjustments to millions of American workers. The CPI affects the income of about 80 million persons as a result of statutory action: 48.4 million Social Security beneficiaries, about 19.8 million food stamp recipients, and about 4.2 million military and federal civil service retirees and survivors. Changes in the CPI also affect the cost of lunches for 26.5 million children who eat lunch at school, while collective bargaining agreements that tie wages to the CPI cover over 2 million workers. Another example of how dollar values may be adjusted is the use of the CPI to adjust the federal income tax structure. These adjustments prevent inflation-induced increases in tax rates, an effect called "bracket creep." Additionally the CPI will be found imbedded in many union or labor contracts knows as COLA's or Cost of Living Adjustments.

SOURCE: *www.bls.gov* website.

Weaknesses of CPI

1. Doesn't Contain Measures of Tax Payments. (The government is not interested in keeping track of increases in tax payments. Are you surprised?)
2. Doesn't Account for Quality Changes in Goods.
3. Doesn't Account for Leisure Time Available to Workers.
4. Doesn't Account for Improvements in the Variety of Goods and Services Available.

CPI as an Inflation Calculator

The Board of Governors of the Federal Reserve System uses the CPI to publish a measure of year-to-year inflation. Fourteen years of data are shown in the table below for all items and an all U.S. city average (Table 13.1).

Table 13.1 Inflation rate calculation through 2005.

Yearly—All Items	CPI	Inflation Rate
1992	140.3	N/A
1993	144.5	$(144.5/140.3) - 1.00 = 3.0\%$
1994	148.2	$(148.2/144.5) - 1.00 = 2.6\%$
1995	152.4	$(152.4/148.2) - 1.00 = 2.8\%$
1996	156.9	$(156.9/152.4) - 1.00 = 3.0\%$
1997	160.5	$(160.5/156.9) - 1.00 = 2.3\%$
1998	163.0	$(163.0/160.5) - 1.00 = 1.6\%$

(continued)

Table 13.1 *(Continued)*

Yearly—All Items	CPI	Inflation Rate
1999	166.6	$(166.6/163.0) - 1.00 = 2.2\%$
2000	172.2	$(172.2/166.6) - 1.00 = 3.4\%$
2001	177.1	$(177.1/172.2) - 1.00 = 2.8\%$
2002	179.9	$(179.9/177.1) - 1.00 = 1.6\%$
2003	184.0	$(184.0/179.9) - 1.00 = 2.3\%$
2004	188.9	$(188.9/184.0) - 1.00 = 2.7\%$
2005	195.3	$(195.3/188.9) - 1.00 = 3.4\%$

The effects of inflation can be determined by using the CPI as shown in Table 13.1. The current base for the CPI is 1982–84 = 100. To interpret the inflation rate from 1982–84 through 2005, I can conclude that what I spent $100 for in 1982–84, I must now spend $195.30 for the same items, which is a 95.3% increase in costs.

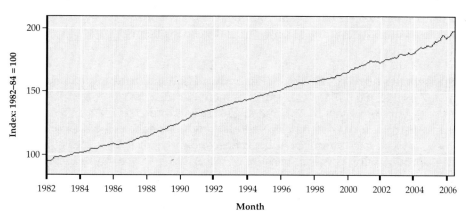

Figure 13.1   CPI growth since 1982 (urban wage earners).

SOURCE: *www.bls.gov.*

Figure 13.1 is a graphic representation of the inflation rate from 1982 to 2006. Notice inflation doubled from 100 to 200 in approximately 23 years.

The CPI as a Deflation Calculator

I can use the CPI to deflate a series. For example, let's suppose I want to know if my salary increases have grown at the same pace as inflation. My salary is in current dollars, but I am interested in deflating it to see if I have at least stayed up with the inflation growth rate.

For example, let's assume that my current salary for 2002 through 2005 is shown in the following table (Table 13.2). I can use the CPI to deflate my current salary. This removes the results of inflation on my current salary. I can then evaluate my current salary as compared to my salary in 1982–84. I want to know if my salary has grown at a pace that is rapid enough to offset the ills of inflation. Am I ahead of or behind the inflation curve? To illustrate the point, I will use four years.

Table 13.2   Deflation of a money series.

Year	Money Income	CPI with Base 1982-1984	Deflated Series Real Income
2002	$42,110	179.9	($42,110/179.9) times 100 = $23,407
2003	$46,000	184.0	($46,000/184.0) times 100 = $25,000
2004	$49,800	188.9	($49,800/188.9) times 100 = $26,363
2005	$53,500	195.3	($53,500/195.3) times 100 = $27,394

Your real money wages earned in 2002 were $42,110, but in terms of 1982–84 income it was only worth $23,407. Assuming you were making $25,000 in 1982–84, are you ahead of the earnings curve or behind it?

To interpret the result: Your current salary at $42,110 leaves you with *less disposable income* in 2002 than you had in 1982–84. Said differently, $42,110 in terms of deflated dollars is only worth $23,407 in 1982–84 dollars. Inflation has increased faster than your salary. If you look at the other years, you were even in 2003 but ahead in 2004 and 2005 (better than the $25,000).

Economists will deflate GNP (Gross National Product, which is the total monetary value of all final goods and services produced in the U.S. economy) to produce a measure of our nation's real output—productivity. This is a measure of the actual increase in production of goods and services. You may use the CPI to deflate (remove the effects of inflation) from any series. This helps you see if the growth is real or simply due to inflation.

Calculating the Relative Price Change Between Two Periods

There may be times when you want to determine the percentage change in the price of a reference period to a particular base period, but your data set is not in the correct form to view this percentage change easily. For example, the following table shows that the average product price increased by 23.2 percent between 1998 and 2003.

Let's assume I purchased a lathe for my factory in 2000. I paid $978 for the lathe at that time. Assume it is 2003 and the price quote for a new lathe is $1,200. When I complained about the higher price, the supplier told me inflation was driving the price up. I need a way to judge the accuracy of the supplier's statement, so I use my product index as reflected in Table 13.3.

Table 13.3   Relative price change.

Year	Product Index
1998	100.0
1999	105.3
2000	112.0
2001	116.5
2002	119.3
2003	123.2

The problem is my product index begins in 1998, so how do I convert it to 2000 year prices? I want to know how prices have changed from 2000 to 2003. To determine price inflation or defla-tion, you must be able to shift the base and reference periods as the need arises. Since my index numbers are all in common units (index numbers), I can re-arrange them by redefining a new ref-erence period and a new base period. I can determine how prices have changed between *any two time periods.* To calculate the percentage price change between any two time periods, I will select the price index number for the base period (112) and the price index for the reference period (123.2).

$$PI = (123.2 \div 112.0) \text{ times } 100 = 110.0$$

Based on the price index and this calculation, I can estimate that product prices in 2003 should be 1.10 times the prices in 2000 or 10.0 percent more than the prices in 2000. I can use this information as follows:

In 2000, I paid $978 for the lathe. Multiplying the $978 times my index of 110, I find inflation should have increased the price to $1,075.80. I am being quoted $1,200 which is a difference of $121.20. I can now ask the question of my supplier, what else is contributing to the higher price? Armed with this information, I am in a stronger negotiating position to seek a reduced price or some additional concessions such as free delivery, on site installation, on site training, etc. My negotiating position strengthens from knowledge.

Is the CPI the Best Measure of Inflation?

Inflation has been defined as a process of continuously rising prices or, equivalently, of the continuously falling value of money.

Various indexes have been devised to measure different aspects of inflation. The CPI measures inflation as experienced by consumers in day-to-day living expenses; the Producer Price Index (PPI) measures inflation at earlier stages of the production and marketing process; the Employment Cost Index (ECI) measures inflation in the labor market; the BLS International Price Program measures inflation for imports and exports; and the Gross Domestic Product Deflator (GDP Deflator) combines inflationary measurement of governments (federal, state, and local), businesses, and consumers. Finally, there are dozens of specialized measures, among which are interest rates and consumers' and business executives' expectations of inflation.

The "best" measure of inflation for a given application depends on the intended use of the data. The CPI is generally the best measure for adjusting payments to consumers when the intent is to allow consumers to purchase, at today's prices, a market basket of goods and services equivalent to one that they could purchase in an earlier period. The CPI also is the best measure to use to translate retail sales and hourly or weekly earnings into real or inflation-free dollars. The financial markets tend to look at GDP as a good measure of inflationary pressures.

SOURCE: *www.bls.gov.*

Estimating Prices or Cost Using CPI or Your Own Index Numbers

If inflation is the primary contributing factor to cost or price increases, you may use the CPI as a powerful tool in estimating your expected future costs or prices. This can be especially useful, for example, if you are going to be paid for a contract over several years (multiple time periods). Dollars today are worth more than dollars tomorrow because inflation reduces the time value of money. Using the CPI to adjust future payment on contacts will keep your payments in line with inflationary pressures.

There are times when your company may have a product which is made of expensive raw material. Because of the market driven forces, the prices of your raw material may exceed that of the CPI in general. Under these circumstances, you might want to create your own market basket of materials and develop your own index number for use in costing and pricing.

Producer Price Index

This index was formerly the Wholesale Price Index, which is published monthly by the BLS. It measures changes in the prices of goods in the primary market for raw materials used in manufacturing and covers about 3,100 producer goods. The base year is 1982.

Industrial Production Index

The Federal Reserve System publishes this index monthly and it tracks the changes in the volume of industrial output. The base period is 1977.

Dow-Jones Industrial Average

This is a Stock Market Index measuring 30 selected industrial stocks. The movement in these stocks represents the movement in the 1,800 stocks traded on the NYSE.

Standard and Poor's Composite Index

This Stock Market Index measures the price changes in 500 industrial stocks.

In General There Are Three Basic Types of Index Numbers

1. Simple Index Number
2. Composite Index Number
3. Weighted Index Number

Simple Index Number

This index measures the relative change in price of a *single good or service* from the base period to the reference period. Both the base and reference period are selected by a researcher or the company or government entity publishing the index.

$$PI_R = \frac{P_R}{P_B} \times 100$$

Table 13.4 is an example of how to calculate a simple index number. If I set the base period as 2001, then each of the subsequent periods are reference periods (2002 through 2005). Using the formula just above, I can create Table 13.4 for a base period of 2001. In the column to the far right, I shift the base period to 2003, which changes my index number reference points.

Table 13.4   Price index for gasoline.

Gasoline Price Index			
Year	Price Per Gallon	Index × 100 2001 as Base	Shift Base to 2003
2001	0.93	(0.93/0.93) times 100 = **100**	(0.93/1.35) times 100 = 69
2002	1.20	(1.20/0.93) times 100 = 129	(1.20/1.35) times 100 = 89
2003	1.35	(1.35/0.93) times 100 = 145	(1.35/1.35) times 100 = **100**
2004	1.30	(1.30/0.93) times 100 = **140**	(1.30/1.35) times 100 = 96
2005	1.15	(1.15/0.93) times 100 = 124	(1.15/1.35) times 100 = 85

What does this mean? Using a base period of 2001, I can assert if I spent $100 for gasoline in 2001, I would now be spending $140 in 2004. Additionally, if I wanted to shift the base (re-base) to a different year, I would divide all of the numbers by the new base. This is shown in the last column to the far right column of the table. *Any base period index number always equals 100.*

This is a **price index (PI)** for one good or service, but it may make more sense to calculate a price index for several goods and services at the same time. This can be accomplished by the use of a composite index number.

Composite Index Number

A **composite index** is a price index for a market basket of goods and services. The market basket may consist of two items or 3,000+ items like the CPI. The market basket may be of value to your company if you want to follow the cost of key components in your product. You can include in the market basket anything you can imagine. The market basket, however, should have some common relationship among those items included. This, like the simple price index, is an un-weighted index number. It may be calculated using the following formula. From the formula, I find I am looking for *the sum of a column headed* P_R, (ΣP_R) divided by *the sum of a column headed* P_B (ΣP_B). My market basket contains two or more items. The simple index calculated above consists of only one item.

$$PI_R = \frac{\Sigma P_R}{\Sigma P_B} \times 100$$

Example

Let's suppose I want to create an index number for the cost of driving my automobile. I will ignore depreciation and payments but will include four major costs—gasoline, oil, tires, and insurance. My market basket can contain any number of items. As the one who develops the index, I can also choose my reference period and my base period. Table 13.5 reflects the information I have collected on my four items and the prices for those items for the year 2000 (my chosen

Table 13.5 Composite index for the cost of driving an automobile.

Item	Unit	2000 (Base Period) Unit Price	2005 (Reference Period) Unit Price
Gasoline	Gallon	0.93	1.15
Oil	Quart	0.95	1.75
Tires	Single Radial	50.00	100.00
Insurance	Annual Policy	230.00	350.00
Totals		281.88	452.90

base period) and the prices for those items for the year 2005 (my chosen reference period). When determining the composite index number, I am interested in the total of two columns (the base period and the reference period).

The calculation of the index number itself uses the total of the column of the reference period (452.90) divided by the total of the column of the base period (281.88). Always multiple the result times 100 for proper index number formatting.

$$PI_R = \frac{452.90}{281.88} \times 100 = 160.67$$

For this market basket of goods and services, you would spend $160.67 in 2005 (reference period) for the same goods you spent $100 for in 2000 (base period). Since this is an un-weighted price index number, the index number is influenced by the change in the cost of insurance more than the increase in the cost of gasoline. However, if I consider quantity in my index number, the picture may change. In developing more accurate index numbers, quantity is an important addition.

It is very important, actually imperative, that the units of measure are the same for the base period and the reference period. In other words, if you are pricing gasoline by the gallon in the base period, then gasoline must be in gallons in the reference period also. You cannot measure in gallons one year and liters in another year. Also, remember, I could have many different reference periods such as 2004, 2003, etc.

Weighted Index Numbers (Including Quantity)

A simple or composite index omits one very important feature of index numbers—a weight. Often it is important to consider the *quantity consumed of each good or service*. Some products are consumed in larger quantities than other products. The simple and composite index numbers assume equal weights for each commodity (good or service) in the index number. It may be more accurate to assign a quantity-purchased weight to each product. Without this weight, the simple or composite index number may generate misleading conclusions.

This shortcoming is overcome by the use of a weighted index number. There are two types of weighted indices—the Laspeyres and the Paasche. One is weighted by use of *base period quantities* (**Laspeyres**) and the other is weighted by *reference period quantities* (**Paasche**). I am still going to take the price of a base period and divide it by the price of a base period, but I am going one step further to include quantities.

Look at the formulas and I think the difference will be more clearly understood. Q_B is the quantity of the base period while Q_R is the quantity of the reference period. Base and reference periods are selected at the prerogative of the developer of the index number.

$$L = \frac{\Sigma(P_R Q_B)}{\Sigma(P_B Q_B)} \times 100$$

$$P = \frac{\Sigma(P_R Q_R)}{\Sigma(P_B Q_R)} \times 100$$

Let's take the automobile cost used just above. The base period is 2000 and the reference period is 2005. However, I must now identify quantities consumed for both the base and the reference periods. The quantities are shown in the following table (Table 13.6).

Table 13.6 Quantities for automobile index example.

Item	Unit	2000 Quantity Base Period	2005 Quantity Reference Period
Gasoline	Gallon	1,000	1,500
Oil	Quart	15	20
Tires	Single Radial	2	2.5
Insurance	Annual Policy	1	1

Laspeyres Index Calculation

To calculate the Laspeyres, I need to multiply the price of the reference period times the quantity of the base period ($P_R Q_B$) divided by the price of the base period times the quantity of the base period ($P_B Q_B$). The information in Table 13.7 is taken from information in Table 13.6 (quantities) and Table 13.5 (price).

Table 13.7 Price-quantity Laspeyres index number.

Item	P_R (2005)	P_B (2000)	Q_B (2000)	$P_R Q_B$	$P_B Q_B$
Gasoline	1.15	0.93	1,000	1,150.00	930.00
Oil	1.75	0.95	15	26.25	14.25
Tires	100.00	50.00	2	200.00	100.00
Insurance	350.00	230.00	1	350.00	230.00
Totals				1,726.25	1,274.25

Notice that I have set up two columns which require me to cross-multiply each of the quantities of the base period times each of the prices of the reference period ($P_R Q_B$ which is the next to last column). For example, the 1,150 in the first column of the $P_R Q_B$ column is the product of 1.15 times 1,000. Take out your calculator and make sure you can determine the values shown in the $P_R Q_B$ column.

I also must cross-multiply each of the quantities of the base period times the prices of the base period (P_BQ_B which is the last column). For example, the 930 in the first column of P_BQ_B is the product of 0.93 times 1,000. Take out your calculator and make the above calculations, so you will know how they are developed. I total the two columns and use those totals in the Laspeyres index number formula as shown below.

$$L = \frac{1,726.25}{1,274.25} \times 100 = 135.47$$

Notice the change in the index number when I weight the prices by quantities purchased. The composite was 160.67, but the Laspeyres is 135.47. Inserting quantities shifts the price index from the higher priced item (insurance) back toward the most used item (gasoline).

Paasche Index Calculation

The Paasche index number is calculated in essentially the same way as the Laspeyres. The Paasche uses the reference period quantities whereas the Laspeyres uses the base period quantities.

Wait a minute, Professor. Why would I need to switch from base period quantities to reference period quantities? On the surface that switch makes no sense.

That is a very good thought. Let's explore it briefly. In this example, the quantity of gasoline consumed for the base period is 1,000 gallons. For the reference period, the gasoline consumed for the reference period is 1,500 gallons. In this instance, there has been a shift upward in the quantities used. The reference period quantities are 50% greater (1,000 to 1,500) than the base period.

Generally, if the base period quantities no longer represent what is being consumed then you should shift to a more representative period (reference period quantities).

Table 13.8 Price-quantity Paasche index number.

Item	P_R (2005)	P_B (2000)	Q_R (2005)	P_RQ_R	P_BQ_R
Gasoline	1.15	0.93	1,500	1,725.00	1,395.00
Oil	1.75	0.95	20	35.00	19.00
Tires	100.00	50.00	2.5	250.00	125.00
Insurance	350.00	230.00	1.0	350.00	230.00
Totals				2,360.00	1,769.00

With the Paasche index number, I cross-multiply each of the quantities of the reference period times each of the prices of the reference period (P_RQ_R) and the quantities of the reference period times the prices of the base period (P_BQ_R). This is same process I used in determining the Laspeyres index. Take your calculator out and make sure you can make these calculations. I next sum those columns and calculate the Paasche index number.

$$P = \frac{2,360}{1,769} \times 100 = 133.41$$

Since the quantity of gasoline increased from 1,000 gallons to 1,500 gallons from the base to the reference period, my index number dropped (as it logically should). By comparing these index numbers to the un-weighted composite number (160.67), you see the impact of the weights (L = 135.47 and P = 133.41). This example demonstrates the difference between the composite (un-weighted price index number) and two quantity weighted index numbers.

Let's see if I can demonstrate the use of these index numbers. Assume this market basket of goods and services is appropriate for negotiating a labor contract. Let's say you are negotiating a union contact with management. You have a choice of using the composite (160.67), the Laspeyres (135.47), or the Paasche (133.41). Which index number would you, as the union leader, use to argue for increased wages? This is not rhetorical.

Professor, as the union leader, I would want increased wages. Since the composite index number is greater than the other two (160.67), I would use it to argue my case.

Excellent answer, I comment.

The opposite would be true for management, however. Were I the management representative, I would argue for the lowest index number (Paasche = 133.41). Index numbers are guides and are useful in measuring relative changes in prices (and perhaps quantities). Without the use of index numbers, you must evaluate the raw numbers, which is difficult at best.

Advantages and Disadvantages of Both Weighted Indexes

Advantages of the Laspeyres Index Number

- Quantity data is for only one time period (base).
- This makes the quantity data constant so no other periods need to be tracked.
- Changes in the results of index number are all associated with price changes alone since quantities remain constant. (Only one variable moves at a time.)

Disadvantages of the Laspeyres Index Number

- Goods whose prices increase dominate the index.
- Buying pattern changes are not measured.

Advantage of the Paasche Index Number

- Reflects changes in buying habits.

Disadvantages of the Paasche Index Number

- Requires new quantity data each year (each reference period).
- Since there are two variables (price and quantity) which move at the same time, you cannot attribute changes in the index to prices alone. Part of the movement in the index number is due to price changes and part is due to changes in quantity. You cannot tell how much of each is involved.

Identifying Issues and Concerns

As you perform price/cost analyses using index numbers, you should consider time sensitive issues.

Inflation/deflation can mask underlying price changes. For example, if you are in the retail sales business and sales increase from 2004 to 2005 from $100,000 to $105,000 and you have increased prices by 5% can you say your sales have actually increased? Considering inflation and using price indexes will explain the effect of these general price changes.

The price index series selected for making the price/cost adjustment should be as closely related to the item being considered as possible. For example, you would not use the Consumer Price Index to adjust for changes in the price of complex industrial electronic equipment.

Why, you ask?

The CPI is a market basket of goods and services associated with the general public and should not be used with highly technical equipment. You would be much better off by creating a market basket of raw materials, parts, and sub-assembly parts more representative of the electronic equipment under price analysis.

Anyone can make a mistake in calculations. Do not assume that all adjustments are made correctly. Check your work. This is particularly important when the adjustment is part of a contract offer or part of an analysis performed by other government personnel.

It is common for a company to adjust supplier quotes to consider inflation/deflation between the time when the quote was obtained and the date that the product will be delivered. Make sure the supplier hasn't already considered the inflation/deflation in making the quote.

You can forecast any period into the future as long as you have a reasonable index estimate. The farther into the future that you forecast, the greater the risk that the economic factors affecting the index will change. Try not to get too aggressive in the process of projecting into the future.

Can Index Numbers Be Manipulated?

Businesses run in cycles. A researcher might be tempted to select a period in the business cycle when prices or quantities are low, thus making current values appear to be inflated. The opposite is also true. A researcher might select a base period with high prices or quantities thus causing the reference periods to appear deflated.

When selecting an aggregate index number, the choice of items can be crucial. An index bias will result if the researcher has a particular point of view to support. In this instance, there will be a tendency to select unimportant or unrelated items for inclusion. If, for example, you are developing an index number for the cost of transportation, you would not want it over weighted by the cost of clothing or electronic equipment.

Technological advances often create an issue for direct comparison of periods. For example, the VCR of today is much more complex and less expensive than the VCR of past years. The same is true about calculators or computers. You have more technologically advanced products at a lower price, but this cannot be reflected in an index number.

Make sure you consistently use either the wholesale or the retail prices of goods and services in the index number calculation. Do not use outlet prices as compared to department store prices. Always compare apples to apples. And lastly make sure you consider the regional difference in prices. Compare west to west, east to east, and so forth.

You know You are a Texan If:

- You no longer associate bridges or rivers with water.
- You can say 110 degrees without fainting.

Tear-Out Sheet Chapter 13

Student Name: _____

Day and Time of Class: _____

Given the following information:

Prices

Commodity	Unit	1982	1985	1992
Milk	Quart	0.26	0.31	0.56
Steak	Pound	1.05	1.17	2.15
Butter	Pound	0.75	0.85	1.40
Pepper	Pound	2.50	2.20	2.60

Quantities

Commodity	Unit	1982	1985	1992
Milk	Quart	728	735	737
Steak	Pound	312	320	350
Butter	Pound	55	56	56
Pepper	Pound	0.30	0.30	0.30

1. Develop a simple price index for 1992 as the reference period and 1982 as the base period for each commodity.
2. Develop a composite price index for 1992 as the reference period and 1982 as the base period for all commodities.
3. Develop both a Laspeyres and a Paasche index for 1985 as the base period and 1992 as the reference period.
4. Which of the two index numbers developed in #3 best describes the price index, if either?

14

Assumption Free Distributions Chi-Square as a Nonparametric Test

At Voir Dire the following took place

Attorney:	Okay, now is your feeling then that you have a fixed opinion that cannot be changed by the evidence or the charge of the Court based on the facts in this case?
Potential Juror:	May I say something?
Attorney:	Yes ma'am.
Potential Juror:	The questions you are asking are not fitting my answers.

Chi-Square as a Nonparametric Test

In Chapter 10, I showed you how to work with the variance of one population using chi-square as a parametric test. Parametric testing is stronger testing than the nonparametric testing I will cover in this chapter. Recall that, in parametric testing, I randomly select a sample (statistic) and use it to test the parameter (population value). Usually I work with the mean or the variance. Of course, when working with a parametric test, I must make the assumption the distribution is normal. This assumption is not always possible.

The appropriate tests under conditions where you cannot make the assumption of normality are called **nonparametric tests.** Nonparametric tests are used to test hypotheses when no assumptions about the parameters are possible.

One test is particularly useful. Chi-square was discussed in Chapter 10 as a parametric test. Chi-square can also be used as a nonparametric test. The chi-square distribution is much like the t-distribution in that it is influenced by the degrees of freedom. There are two common applications of the nonparametric chi-square test.

Test for Independence   If you need to determine if two variables seem to be related, the application of chi-square is used.

Test for Goodness of Fit   If you need to determine if a hypothesized distribution matches an observed distribution, this application of chi-square is used.

Goodness of fit tests might include the following hypothesized distributions:

- Uniform Distribution
- Specific Pattern
- Normal Distribution

Other Nonparametric Tests

Before I move directly into a discussion of tests of independence or goodness of fit, there are other nonparametric tests worth mentioning. Nonparametric testing does not require the same assumptions as parametric testing. Nonparametric tests are often referred to as distribution free tests. The parametric tests I have already discussed in previous chapters have counterpart nonparametric tests. Some of the most important are as follows:

Table 14.1 Nonparametric tests.

Major Nonparametric Tests	When to Use, Basic Description, and Counterpart Parametric Test
Signs Test	The signs test is useful in testing two populations. If you have data set A and wish to see if it *matches* data set B, the signs test is used when the assumption of normality is not possible. **The signs test is the nonparametric counterpart to the parametric t-test for matched pairs.** The t-test requires the assumption of normality and the signs test does not. My interest is in the sign of the difference ($\pm$), not the magnitude of the difference. The null hypothesis is stated that there is no difference in the data sets. The hypothesis can also take the form of a left or right tail rejection region as well as a two tailed rejection region.
Runs Test	By now you have grown tired of me stressing the need for randomness in testing. Sometimes I can look at the data set but cannot tell if the distribution is normal. I need a test for randomness. **The runs test accomplishes the test for randomness.** The runs (unbroken series) within a data set are tested to determine if randomness does or does not exist. If too many or too few runs occur, randomness may be absent. A run consists of an unbroken sequence of one or

Table 14.1 Nonparametric tests (*Continued*).

Major Nonparametric Tests	When to Use, Basic Description, and Counterpart Parametric Test
Runs Test	more similar symbols such as AA, BB, AAA, BBBB, AA, BBBBBB, AAAAA. Here there are seven runs. If there are two few or too many runs, randomness may not be present.
Mann-Whitney U-Test	This is often referred to as the *U*-test. **This test is the nonparametric counter part to the *t*-test for two independent samples** but does not require the assumption that the difference between the two samples is normally distributed. The median is substituted for the mean in this test process.
Spearman Rank Correlation	**This test is the counterpart to correlation that can be measured numerically.** This test measures the degree of correlation between two variables when the assumption of normality cannot be made and the data may not be measured numerically. In these instances, the ordinal rank of the data may be used (lowest to highest or highest to lowest).
Kruskal-Wallis Test	The Mann-Whitney *U*-test is for two populations. Often I will need to compare three or more populations to determine whether a difference exists in the distribution of the populations. **The Kruskal-Wallis test is the nonparametric counterpart to the parametric *F*-test used in ANOVA.**

While these nonparametric tests are important, I will not develop them any further. You should be aware that they exist. Your Professor may choose to stress them.

Back to Chi-Square as a Nonparametric Test

I will focus the majority of this chapter on chi-square as a nonparametric test. The formula calculations are the same for either the independence test or the goodness of fit test. The only difference in the two tests lies in how the degrees of freedom are determined. For goodness of fit testing, the degrees of freedom are $K - M - 1$, where K = the number of categories, M is the number of parameters estimated by a statistic, and 1 is 1. For independence testing, the degrees of freedom are determined by $(R - 1)(C - 1)$, where R is number of rows and C is number of columns.

Table 14.2 Two types of chi-square testing.

Chi-Square Testing	Description and When to Use
	Goodness of Fit Testing
Test for a Uniform Distribution	When you want to know if your data set fits a *uniform distribution*, use this approach. The hypothesis to be tested is *Ho*: The distribution is uniform. The alternate is H_a: The distribution is not uniform.

(Continued)

Table 14.2   Two types of chi-square testing (*Continued*).

Chi-Square Testing	Description and When to Use
Test for a Specific Pattern	When you want to know if your data set fits a *specific pattern*, use this approach. The hypothesis to be tested is H_o: The distribution fits a specific pattern. The alternate is H_a: The distribution does not fit a specific pattern.
Test for a Normal Distribution	When you want to know if your data set fits a *normal distribution*, use this approach. The hypothesis to be tested is Ho: The distribution is normal. The alternate is H_a: The distribution is not normal.
	Independent Testing
Contingency Tables	This process focuses on two variables, unlike the goodness of fit tests. This test allows you to determine if the relationship between the two variables is independent (H_o) or dependent (H_a).

For now, the goodness of fit testing will be set aside and I will concentrate on the independent testing process. Using a contingency table will be the best method to show you the process. Often in many business decisions, when you cannot assume normality, a contingency table is easily developed.

Even though I will concentrate on the independent testing process, there is some commonality between independent testing and goodness of fit testing. The formula is that common relationship. For either the test of independence or goodness of fit the formula is the same and is as follows:

$$\chi^2 = \sum \left[\frac{(O - E)^2}{E} \right]$$

For the independence test, the degrees of freedom are $(R - 1)(C - 1)$, where R is the number of rows and C is the number of columns. Depending on how you set up the contingency table, expected and observed frequencies are counted as one row or one column for each opportunity. This last statement will become clearer when I show you an example, so don't try to totally understand it right now.

The observed frequencies (O) are matched against the expected frequencies (E). If there is a large difference between what is actually observed in the sample and what you would expect, the relationship is dependent, which means you can draw conclusions about the relationship that might be helpful. The test I am applying determines if the observed versus the expected is significant. This test, while helpful, is, like all nonparametric tests, not as strong as parametric testing.

Let's look at an example. Suppose that I am a marketing research firm who has been hired to help a breakfast cereal manufacturer develop the best commercials to reach a particular target audience. With the aid of the manufacturer, three different TV commercials are developed. Before airing them and spending big bucks, you suggest that a focus group of children be formed to view each of the commercials. The results of the focus group should give you an indication which commercial(s) might reach the desired target audience most effectively. From past experience, you know that the distribution of data cannot be assumed to be normal. This rules out parametric testing but leaves room for using chi-square as a nonparametric test.

The focus group is established by selecting 125 children in the target audience age group. The focus group is asked to view the three commercials. The group is composed of 75 boys and 50 girls. They are shown the commercials and then asked to select the one they liked the best. Only one vote per child is permitted. Table 14.3 records the preferences (O) of the children after they viewed the commercials.

Table 14.3   Commercial preferences of focus group of children.

Gender	Commercial			
	A	B	C	Total
Boys	30	29	16	75
Girls	12	33	5	50
Total	**42**	**62**	**21**	**125**

Is the choice of commercial related to being a boy or a girl?

This is the same as asking in statistical language the following question: Are the two variables dependent? To be useful, I want there to be a relationship; however, I will set up the null hypothesis as an independent statement. The test I will conduct will be to test to see if there is an independent relationship. I hope to reject the null which will allow me to accept the alternate. The alternate will be the dependent statement, which means I have a useful tool. The two hypotheses are stated as follows:

H_o: **There is no difference in gender and commercial preferred.** If true, this would reveal an *independent relationship*, thus making the relationship between gender and commercial preferred not useful. Gender would not be a factor in commercial preference.

H_a: **There is a difference in gender and commercial preferred.** If I reject the null and accept the alternate, there would be a *dependent relationship* between the two variables. If the dependent relationship exists, there is some indication gender plays a role in the preference for the commercial. This relationship would allow me to use the commercial preferred as a guide in reaching a specific target audience.

When testing for independence, it is important to note that the null hypothesis will always contain the independent statement and the alternate hypothesis will always contain the dependent statement.

Table 14.3 above reflects my observed frequencies (O), which are the result of the children viewing the commercial and expressing their preference. The problem with the observed frequencies is they are gender biased. I need to come up with a process that effectively neutralizes the natural gender bias that exists in the observed frequencies. This is done by making use of the marginal probabilities (I bet you wish I would not go there again). Using marginal probabilities, I can determine expected frequencies. Table 14.4 reflects my calculation of the expected frequencies (E).

Table 14.4 Expected frequency calculations.

Gender and Commercial	Calculations	Expected Frequencies
Boys: Commercial A	(75 times 42) divided by 125	25.2
Boys: Commercial B	(75 times 62) divided by 125	37.2
Boys: Commercial C	(75 times 21) divided by 125	12.6
Girls: Commercial A	(50 times 42) divided by 125	16.8
Girls: Commercial B	(50 times 62) divided by 125	24.8
Girls: Commercial C	(50 times 21) divided by 125	8.4
	Total	**125.0**

Before you panic, let's look at how I made these calculations. Remember, I want to neutralize the gender bias when I calculate the expected frequencies. Notice that the marginal values are used. If you go back to Table 14.3 where the observed frequencies are recorded, you will find the 75 in the right margin for the total number of boys and you will find the 42 in the bottom margin for the total who preferred commercial A. If I multiply 75 $\times$ 42 (marginal values) and then divide that product by 125 (the total children in the study), I will have neutralized the gender bias for the boys for commercial A.

Try to follow the logic and calculation before going on.

This process is repeated for each gender and commercial. The expected results can be shown side by side with the observed frequencies in Table 14.5 below. The observed frequencies (O) from Table 14.3 are shown next to the expected frequencies (E) from Table 14.4.

Table 14.5 Observed and expected frequencies for commercial focus group.

Gender	Commercial						Total
	A		B		C		
	O	E	O	E	O	E	
Boys	30	25.2	29	37.2	16	12.6	75
Girls	12	16.8	33	24.8	5	8.4	50
Total	42		62		21		125

Notice that the marginal totals remain the same and, logically, this should be the case. If I add the observed frequencies (O) for the boys for all three commercials, I will find they total 75. If I add the expected frequencies (E) for the boys for all three commercials, I will also find they total 75.

Next I want to arrange the data in Table 14.5 into a format that will enable me to determine the *calculated* chi-square value. I repeat the formula to keep you from having to turn pages back.

$$\chi^2 = \sum \left[\frac{(O - E)^2}{E} \right]$$

This calculation requires me to eventually set up a column headed $(O - E)^2 \div E$. To best visualize this, Table 14.6 reflects that calculation.

Table 14.6 Determination of calculated chi-square value.

Gender and Commercial Preferred	Observed O	Expected E	O − E	(O − E)²	$\frac{(O - E)^2}{E}$
Boys: Commercial A	30	25.2	4.8	23.04	0.9143
Boys: Commercial B	29	37.2	−8.2	67.24	1.8075
Boys: Commercial C	16	12.6	3.4	11.56	0.9175
Girls: Commercial A	12	16.8	−4.8	23.04	1.3714
Girls: Commercial B	33	24.8	8.2	67.24	2.7113
Girls: Commercial C	5	8.4	−3.4	11.56	1.3762
Calculated Chi-Square Value					9.0982

What do you think the next step should be?

As your mind begins to turn, you respond. Well, I have a null hypothesis. The normal procedure is to DNR or reject the null hypothesis. To do this, I must have a calculated chi-square value, which I do (9.0982). I also need a critical value, right?

Excellent reasoning, and by now I thought you would be partially brain dead, I comment.

Recall, critical values for chi-square come from a table look up just like all critical values.

The table of interest is the chi-square table. Look for it in the back of the textbook.

If you found it, you will notice something.

Yeah, you reply sarcastically. There is a bunch of numbers just like all the other critical value tables.

I patiently reply, yes, that is correct, while shaking my head.

You will need to know the degrees of freedom to determine the critical value. Remember,

I spoke of the degrees of freedom briefly in the early part of this chapter. What I told you then, I will repeat now.

For independent testing, the degrees of freedom are $(R - 1)(C - 1)$, where R is the number of rows and C is the number of columns. Depending on how you set up the contingency table, expected and observed frequencies are counted as one row or one column for each opportunity. In this case there are two rows and three columns. Count the columns as one per each commercial. Do not count the observed and expected as separate columns. In other words, commercial A is one column, although it is made up of two sub-columns—observed and expected frequencies. The marginal totals are not counted as rows or columns.

The degrees of freedom are calculated as follows:

$$(2 - 1)(3 - 1) = 1 \times 2 = 2 \text{ degrees of freedom.}$$

Now, can you use the chi-square table and look up the critical value?

Professor, I could look up the critical value, if you would be so kind as to give me the alpha value.

There goes that small omission again. You are correct, so let's try alpha at 0.05.

Now what is the critical value?

If you got 5.991, you are correct.

Now what do you do, I ask?

You need to make a decision. Should you DNR (accept) the null or reject the null hypothesis?

Think about it and, if helpful, draw a picture of a distribution inserting the calculated value and the critical value before reading on. Figure 14.1 is a picture of the decision process. This is a right tailed test with a non-normal distribution.

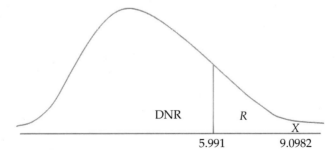

Figure 14.1 Comparison of critical value and calculated value for chi-square test.

The *calculated* value is 9.0982. The *critical* value is 5.991. The calculated chi-square value is greater than the critical value (9.0982 > 5.991) therefore, the calculated value falls in the rejection region. This means I reject the null hypothesis and accept the alternate hypothesis.

Let's restate the hypothesis again.

H_o: **There is no difference in gender and commercial preferred.**

H_a: **There is a difference in gender and commercial preferred.**

Since I am going to reject the null hypothesis, I must accept the alternate hypothesis. My conclusion is there is a difference in gender and commercial preferred. This means the relationship is dependent. A dependent relationship is useful to me in designing commercials to reach my target market.

However, I need to take the decision to a more practical level. It is not enough to simply say there is a relationship. What I want to know is which commercial(s) seems to be preferred by the boys and which commercial(s) seems to be preferred by the girls. The answer to this question will be very helpful as I begin the expensive process of developing the best commercial to reach my target market. To analyze this aspect, I am going to repeat Table 14.5.

Gender	Commercial						Total
	A		B		C		Total
	O	E	O	E	O	E	
Boys	30	**25.2**	29	**37.2**	16	**12.6**	75
Girls	12	**16.8**	33	**24.8**	5	**8.4**	50
Total	42		62		21		125

Let's look at the boys. I expected **25.2** boys to like commercial A. Thirty **(30)** actually liked commercial A; therefore, more boys liked commercial A than was expected.

I expected **37.2** boys to like commercial B, but I find that only **29** liked commercial B. Fewer than expected liked commercial B.

I expect **12.6** boys to like commercial C, but I find that **16** actually liked commercial C. More than expected liked commercial C.

From this I can generalize that boys liked commercial A and C better than commercial B. In fact, commercial A was the more preferred commercial for boys. I would, therefore, use the commercial A format to develop future commercials to reach the target market of boys in this age bracket. Since there was some preference for commercial C for the boys, I would probably ask the boys to tell me what they liked about commercial C. If there was a pattern or some consistent element, I might move that concept to commercial A, thus strengthening it as a marketing tool.

What about the girls?

Before reading on, try to form an answer by looking at Table 14.5 and make the same comparisons of expected and observed frequencies for the girls.

The Answer: The girls liked commercial *B* better than either *A* or *C*. This again aids me in making a decision on how to develop the best commercial to reach my target market.

Unfortunately, the girls liked one commercial and the boys another. It would have really been great if both the boys and girls preferred the same commercial. As it now stands, to best reach the target market of boys, I would use commercial *A* (modified with some elements from *C*), but to reach the target market of girls, I would use commercial *B*.

See how it works?

In reality, for chi-square to be helpful, you want to reject the null and accept the alternate. If you accept the null (DNR), you are asserting there is no relationship between gender and commercial preferred. When you DNR the null, you do not have a clue as to how to best design the commercials to reach the target markets.

What would happen if you tested the above hypothesis at the alpha 0.01 level?

Actually, none of the calculations change, so the only difference is the critical value of chi-square.

Looking this value up, you find it is 9.21. (Go look this up to verify it before moving on.)

Does your decision change?

The answer is yes. Now you DNR the null. At the alpha 0.05 level, I rejected the null. At the alpha 0.01 level, I accept (DNR) the null. This points out that the decision you made at the alpha 0.05 level is somewhat weak. However, at the alpha 0.05 level you can still generalize the conclusion I presented above.

Chi-square as a nonparametric test might be helpful for the following business decisions.
- A retailer may want to discover if there is a relationship between consumer income levels and consumer preference for a particular product.
- A production manager may want to determine if any relationship exists between the productivity of an employee and the type of degree or the job training the employee receives.
- Is there a relationship between GPA in college and salaries 10 years after graduation?
- A quality control manager operates three shifts (24-hour operation). The QC manager wants to know if there is a difference in quality on the three shifts. A sample of 500 parts from each shift is taken and the parts are marked acceptable or unacceptable.
- Does a male released from federal prison make a different adjustment to life if he returns to his hometown or goes elsewhere to live?

These are just a few examples of areas in which the contingency table and chi-square approach will be helpful.

The second use of chi-square is to test goodness of fit.

Goodness of Fit

Goodness of fit tests measure how closely the observed sample data set fits a particular hypothesized distribution. If the fit is close enough, the conclusion may be reached that the hypothesized distribution exists. There are three basic types of distributions of interest in goodness of fit testing.

- The normal distribution
- The uniform distribution
- A specific (desired) pattern distribution

Setting Up the Null and Alternate Hypotheses

The normal distribution null and alternate hypotheses are stated as follows:

H_0: The population distribution is normal.

H_a: The population distribution is not normal.

The uniform distribution null and alternate hypotheses are stated as follows:

H_0: The population distribution is uniform.

H_a: The population distribution is not uniform.

The specific (desired) pattern distribution null and alternate hypotheses are stated as follows:

H_0: The desired pattern is maintained. (proportions are maintained)

H_a: The desired pattern is not maintained. (proportions are not maintained)

Normal Distribution

The actual statement of the null and alternate hypotheses will depend on the specific problem being considered. For example, assume an interest lies in determining if the demand for a particular product fits a normal distribution. The two hypotheses would be stated as follows:

H_0: Demand for a product *is normally* distributed.

H_a: Demand for a product *is not normally* distributed.

If the interest lies in the fill level of a product, which permits a normal distribution, the hypotheses are stated as follows:

H_0: Fill levels for a product *are normally* distributed.

H_a: Fill levels for a product *are not normally* distributed.

If the interest lies in test scores matching a normal distribution, the hypotheses are stated as follows:

H_0:   Test scores *are normally* distributed.

H_a: Test scores *are not normally* distributed.

Uniform Distribution and Specific Pattern

Developing the specific null and alternate hypotheses for a uniform distribution or for a specific pattern will depend on the specific problem of interest.

Let's look at the hypotheses for a uniform distribution using the same concepts—demand, fill levels, and test scores. If you are interested in determining if the distribution fits a uniform distribution, the null and alternate hypothesis are stated as follows:

H_0:   The demand *fits a uniform* distribution.

H_a: The demand *does not fit a uniform* distribution.

H_0:   The fill levels *fit a uniform* distribution.

H_a: The fill levels *do not fit a uniform* distribution.

H_0:   The test scores *fit a uniform* distribution.

H_a: The test scores *do not fit a uniform* distribution.

Let's now look at the hypotheses for a specific pattern. Here, again, I will use the same concepts—demand, fill levels, and test scores.

The null and alternate hypotheses for a specific pattern would be stated as follows:

H_0:   The demand *fits a predetermined pattern* (proportion).

H_a: The demand *does not fit a predetermined pattern* (proportion).

H_0:   The fill levels *fit a predetermined pattern* (proportion).

H_a: The fill levels *do not fit a predetermined pattern* (proportion).

H_0:   The test scores *fit a predetermined pattern* (proportion).

H_a: The test scores *do not fit a predetermined pattern* (proportion).

Solutions to Chi-Square Problems

Goodness of fit solutions use the same formula as does a test for independence. There is no difference in the formula. After setting up the null and alternate hypotheses, you would calculate a value of chi-square using the same formula as was used in independence testing. It is repeated below.

$$\chi^2 = \sum \left[\frac{(O - E)^2}{E} \right]$$

Given an alpha level, you would next use the chi-square table and determine a critical value of chi-square. You next compare the calculated value from the formula and the critical value from the table look up to make a decision to DNR the null or reject the null. Of course, as always in hypothesis testing, if you DNR the null you are automatically rejecting the alternate. The opposite is also true, if you reject the null, you are automatically accepting H_a.

Difference in the Solutions

There is only one difference in the solutions for independent testing and goodness of fit testing. That difference is how you determine the degrees of freedom. For independent testing, you will use $(R - 1)(C - 1)$, where R = rows and C = columns. For goodness of fit, you will use $K - M - 1$, where K is the number of categories or classes and M = the number of parameters estimated by the use of a statistic. The interpretation depends on how you set up the hypotheses.

Excel

Quite naturally you might expect you could use Excel to make these calculations. You would be correct, but the process is rather cumbersome. If you have repetitive data sets so you can set up templates, you would be well served to use Excel. If you have a one-time data set contingency table, you will probably be just as effective if you manually determine the values.

In essence, setting up the templates would require you to enter the observed frequencies into an Excel worksheet without totals. This table would be labeled observed frequencies. You would then write the formula for determining the row and column totals. If you began your data entry in Column D Row 4 and ended the first row in Column F Row 4, the formula would be = Sum($D4:F5$) for the first row.

The next step would be to copy this table three or four lines below the observed frequencies table. Re-label this table expected frequencies. Now you must write the formula for each expected cell. The formula would be (Column Total * Row Total) ÷ Overall Total. Repeat this for each cell into which an expected frequency is needed. The totals of the rows and the columns of this expected frequency table will be the same as the totals for the observed frequency table.

Next you will determine a p-value for the entire chi-square problem. Find an empty cell and type in the label "p-value." Now select the cell to the immediate right of that label. Clicking on the $f(X)$ in the toolbar, find the CHITEST command. Open it. Now you will be asked to enter the observed frequencies (without totals) in the first box which reads Actual Range. With your cursor in this box, you will highlight all of the cells of the observed frequencies cells without the totals. Next place your cursor in the second box which reads Expected Range. Here you will highlight all of the cells of the expected frequencies cells without the totals. Press okay and you will have the p-value. The H_o set up process was shown to you earlier and that does not change when you use Excel.

I know this is relatively confusing, but the point is you can make these calculations using Excel. As I have already indicated, the use of Excel is most helpful if you have repetitive data sets and can use the template multiple times.

The results of the Excel calculations are shown below; although, of course, you cannot see the formulas, at least you can see the output.

Table 14.7 Results of Excel calculations of chi-square for commercial focus group of 125 children.

Actual Frequencies

	Commercial			
Gender	*A*	*B*	*C*	Total
Boys	30	29	16	75
Girls	12	33	5	50
Total	**42**	**62**	**21**	**125**

Expected Frequencies

	Commercial			
Gender	*A*	*B*	*C*	Total
Boys	25.2	37.2	12.6	75
Girls	16.8	24.8	8.4	50
Total	**42**	**62**	**21**	**125**

p-value	0.010577

At the 0.05 level the *Ho* is rejected.
At the 0.01 level the *Ho* is DNR.

The conclusions are the same as those shown in the manual calculation approach, although I used the *p*-value approach rather than the critical value approach. If you need to turn back you can double check those results.

You know You are a Texan If:

You know you are a Texan if you have ever had this conversion.

- "You wanna Coke?"
- "Yep"
- "What kind?"
- "Dr. Pepper"

Tear-Out Sheet Chapter 14

Student Name: _____

Day and Time of Class: _____

1. One thousand people are asked the following question:

   Which is your favorite type of television program: Comedy (C), Drama (D), Sports (S), or News (N)? The 1,000 people were also asked their age range. Since there are two variables of interest, age and viewing preference, the results may be shown in a tabular format as shown below.

Viewing Preference									
Preference	C		D		S		N		Total
Age Range	O	E	O	E	O	E	O	E	
Under 25	114		61		173		52		400
25-50	63		88		122		77		350
Over 50	58		75		49		68		250
Totals	235		224		344		197		1,000

   a. Is there a relationship between the age of the viewer and his or her preference at the $\alpha = 0.01$ level?

   b. Interpret the results in detail.

   c. You might try this using the Excel approach and see if you can do it. I know my instructions were sketchy, but give it a shot and see if you can follow them.

Quality Control Including Six Sigma™— Introduction

District Attorney: Judge, I object to the opposing Counsel's characterization of this disagreement. He is giving a one-sided view.

The Court: Of course he is. That is what you expect from an opposing trial attorney.

Quality Control

Quality control is a subject matter of hundreds of books. It does not seem unreasonable to ask, what is quality and why do I need to control it?

Quality has been defined as that which is necessary to attract and keep customers loyal to your product. Attached to this idea is a product that conforms to a set of specifications or to contractual requirements. Most companies want their product to attract and hold their customers. Appropriate quality is dependent on the sophistication of the consuming public. For instance, products produced for consumption in the United States will demand more and better quality than products produced for consumption in developing countries, where the consumer is less sophisticated and less demanding.

The control aspect involves those tools and techniques necessary to assure products meet the expectation of the consuming public even if they are sophisticated or less sophisticated. Control includes the techniques and actions taken by any organization to produce a quality product.

Quality control can be broken into two primary phases. First is the engineering phase where the product is *designed and developed*. A certain level of quality must be built into the product during this design phase. Because of the continued advancement of technology, a company will never build the ultimate quality into a product. Many products become obsolete within a short period of time. For example, cell phone or computer technology increases so rapidly that a company can never build in the ultimate quality. Management decisions will be made which determine an acceptable level of quality for any product. Two important considerations are marketability and pricing of the product.

Second is the management stage where the product moves into the production stage and the *process or the results* are inspected. There are two sub-parts to this management stage. First is process inspection during the manufacturing or assembly phase, and the second is lot acceptance of raw materials or sub-assembled components shipped to the company from suppliers. These are not necessarily sequential. The company is the consumer of those goods and the supplier is the producer of those goods. This distinction becomes important later. My first concentration during this chapter will be on the process inspection phase and secondly I will address lot acceptance.

Overall quality control of your products is extremely important in this international, competitive environment. Markets demand quality, so your company must influence the consumer and make the consumer believe your product is one of quality. The Industrial Revolution removed from the hands of the skilled artisan the ability to produce an individual product. Before the Industrial Revolution, skilled artisans took great pride in their workmanship and often signed their name to individual products (e.g., pianos and organs). After the Industrial Revolution, the skilled artisans became more and more rare. In the mid-1920's, Walter Shewhart made one of the first breakthroughs in product improvement when he recognized that variation in products was inevitable. However, he found by using a single graphic tool, he could monitor variation, thus determining when the control of the product is unacceptable (out of control). Today the manufacturer is forced to mass-produce, so more and more goods can be brought to the marketplace with competitive pricing and acceptable quality. In this process, many different hands will touch a single product. If quality errors occur, the manufacturer must have the ability to find the "hands" who commit the errors.

W. Edwards Deming was the leading pioneer in modern quality control techniques. He initiated the idea of TQM (total quality management). TQM involves quality control from the top of the organizational chart to the worker in the plant. From the Chief Executive Officer to the line worker, everyone must be committed to the concept of quality improvement. Usually an organization will form teams of well-trained individuals who are assigned the task of implementing quality management.

Deming is considered to be the father of the modern quality control process. He was instrumental in the late 1940's and 1950's in the miraculous recovery of the Japanese economy after WWII. Initially, only the Japanese seriously listened to Deming's ideas. The Japanese used his techniques in establishing superiority in the automobile market in the late 1970's.

In the 1980's, Motorola developed a quality measurement and improvement program that focuses on the control of a process to the point of ± six sigma (standard deviations) from a centerline. They trademarked the term Six Sigma to describe this approach to quality control. Prior to Motorola, the typical benchmark was ± three sigma from the centerline. With the advent of Six Sigma, quality control took giant leap forward.

Today a company who does not take quality control seriously will not long flourish and survive. There are many techniques which are used in quality control. Four important ones are just-in-time production, benchmarking, team building, and reengineering.

- **Just-In-Time Production:** Essentially, no extra materials and inventory are stored for use in the production process. Excess inventory is cut to the bare minimum. Supply chain management is helpful in effectively accomplishing this process.
- **Benchmarking:** A company will benchmark the best practices of the industry and adopt the best of the best. The goal is to achieve superior performance for your company as a market leader in your industry.
- **Team Building:** A group of employees is appointed to address and solve quality issues within the company. Many times the group will consist of cross functional members. The goal is to involve as many employees as possible in the quality process.
- **Reengineering:** Here the process is evaluated for revision. Essentially the evaluation begins with a blank sheet of paper and redesigns the core business process from scratch. The vision of the future dictates the direction of the reengineering process.

Control Charts

Quality management teams utilize many tools in their quest for quality. Among those tools are **process control charts**. In this chapter, I will concentrate on four charts—the **mean chart,** the **range chart,** the **p-chart,** and the **c-chart.** Additionally, I will look at the concept of **lot acceptance,** which involves a company deciding if they will accept or reject a shipment of goods from its supplier.

Let's first spend time on the idea of process control.

Process Quality Control

First, the company must realize that there are differences in products. There are no two products that are alike. Variation exists in all products. There are two types of variation—one is *acceptable* and one is *unacceptable.*

The acceptable variation is considered to be **common cause variation** or **chance variation.** There are subtle differences in all products. For example, a company may manufacture radios. Each radio is going to be slightly different, but the differences must not be so significant that they cause the product to be unacceptable to the company and the consumer. Companies are not interested in the small, insignificant, and expected differences in products as long as the differences do not render the product unusable to the consumer. As long as the product meets or exceeds the design specifications, the product may be sold without fear the customer will be displeased and refuse to purchase the product. *Common cause or chance variation* is variation the company and consumer will accept.

However, if variation exists that makes a product unacceptable, how does the company identify it and correct it? This type of variation is referred to as **assignable cause variation** or **special cause variation.** *Assignable cause variation* is of major interest to a company. Kaoru Ishikawa from Japan developed a diagram called the fishbone diagram, which is also referred to as the cause and effect diagram. This diagram identifies four major components which are associated with the root cause of assignable cause variation. Those components include machines, materials, methods, and manpower (people). For example, let's assume I have a saw blade that wobbles in a manufacturing process. I want to determine the reason. Assignable causes are those causes which can be located and corrected. Potential problems for the wobbly saw blade might include the following (Table 15.1):

Table 15.1 Assignable cause variation checklist.

Assignable Cause	Possible Issues
Materials	Damp or Wet Material
	Tensile Strength of Materials
	Inferior Lot
Machines	Lubrication
	Worn Bearings
	Crooked Blade
	Broken Teeth on the Blade
	Worn Teeth on the Blade
	Shaft is Worn
	Shaft is Off Center
Methods	Dust Collector Malfunction
	Humidity Control Malfunction
	Improper Training
	Improper Measurement
	Improper Inspection
Manpower	Inexperienced Worker
	Lack of Supervision
	Work Ethic (Attitude)
	Health of Worker
	Vision of Worker

Management should always prepare this list in advance, exploring all possible problems that could arise, as well as all possible solutions to those problems. This should all be done in advance, prior to any problem arising. The basic fishbone diagram (cause and effect) is shown in Figure 15.1.

The actual fishbone diagram looks like, well, a fishbone, if you have an amazing imagination. Under each of the potential assignable causes you would list all of the possible assignable causes similar to those listed In Table 15.1.

Once the problem has been identified, a quality management team should use the four major components as a guide to determine the detailed assignable causes. *All assignable causes*

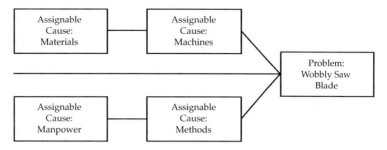

Figure 15.1   Fishbone diagram showing root causes of assignable cause variation.

must be correctable in a short period of time. Depending on the product, other assignable causes may be found such as raw material inferiority, power surges or brown-outs, software glitches, or many other causes. The job of the quality management team is to identify all possible causes, which allows the problem to be addressed and fixed in a short period of time when a quality problem arises. The process of brainstorming may be helpful. Having a collectively exhaustive list before a problem actually exists will decrease the solution-time cycle.

Charts as an Aid

To track the quality process, I can use the four typical charts (mean and range charts and p and c charts). Let's first look at the mean and range charts. These charts allow the company to monitor *quantitative data during the process.* The mean and range charts use an ordinal scale or a measurement scale. I measure the mean and the range and, from those measurements, I determine if I am meeting my specifications in the manufacturing or assembly process.

General Procedure

It is common to take a series of samples over time in order to determine if the quality of the product is within specification. The number of samples, K, taken should be in excess of 20. It is also important that the sample be broken into time elements with several sub-samples taken within those identified time elements (usually 5 to 15 sub-samples during the time element). The sub-samples are designated "n," while the sample size itself is designated "K."

Let's look at an example. Let's say that your manufacturing process is a continuous operation for 24 hours or three shifts. Let's say that you want to take a sample each hour. The sample each hour is designated "K," so each day you would have a sample size of 24. During each hour, you want to take 6 subgroup samples, which are designated "n." During an entire 24-hour period, you will identify 144 sample points (24 × 6 which is K times n).

Let's say the operation just described yields the following results. Measurements are in inches. See Table 15.2 for a recap of the results of production for one day (24-hour period).

Assuming that the samples are time sensitive, you would select a sub-sample each 10 minutes and measure the mean of that sub-sample. Based on the above table, you also need to calculate the mean of each of the samples (K). There are six sub-samples which would be averaged to give you a sample mean for hour 1 (K_1), hour 2 (K_2), and so forth. The average of those six measurements is called a sample mean. The value of the sample mean is shown in the next to last column of Table 15.2.

Table 15.2 Summary of manufacturing process for 24-hour period.

Sample (K)	Sample Measurements (n)						Mean $\overline{X}$	Range
1	15.2	14.5 low	15.4	16.5 high	15.9	16.2	15.6167	2.0
2	16.2	15.4	15.9	15.2	15.2	14.5	15.4000	1.7
3	15.6	16.5	15.9	16.2	15.9	16.2	16.0500	0.9
4	18.5	14.8	15.7	15.2	16.8	14.2	15.8667	4.3
5	17.5	15.7	14.5	14.2	14.5	15.2	15.2667	3.3
6	14.3	15.9	16.5	14.8	15.4	14.8	15.2833	2.2
7	15.4	15.2	15.4	15.8	14.2	15.7	15.2833	1.6
8	18.0	14.5	14.4	16.2	14.8	16.8	15.7833	3.6
9	14.2	15.6	14.5	16.1	15.7	15.9	15.3333	1.9
10	15.7	16.5	14.5	14.8	16.8	16.1	15.7333	2.3
11	14.8	14.5	16.5	14.9	15.8	16.3	15.4667	2.0
12	16.8	15.8	15.2	15.8	15.7	16.2	15.9167	1.6
13	15.2	15.9	14.5	15.1	15.9	14.7	15.2167	1.4
14	15.4	15.7	16.8	15.3	14.8	14.9	15.4833	2.0
15	18.4	15.7	15.9	14.8	15.5	14.8	15.8500	3.6
16	16.5	16.8	15.0	15.7	16.9	14.7	15.9333	2.2
17	15.2	16.9	16.8	17.0	17.1	15.4	16.4000	1.9
18	16.8	17.2	18.9	18.5	18.5	18.9	18.1333	2.1
19	13.5	17.6	18.7	21.1	17.2	16.0	17.3500	7.6
20	19.8	14.5	20.8	19.2	19.2	18.7	18.7000	6.3
21	18.7	17.9	18.7	20.8	18.4	17.5	18.6667	3.3
22	17.5	18.0	18.2	20.2	14.2	17.8	17.6500	6.0
23	14.9	18.9	20.0	16.8	16.2	18.5	17.5500	5.1
24	18.7	17.9	17.4	18.7	17.2	16.5	17.7333	2.2
Totals							391.6667	71.1

Next you would add the column headed $\overline{X}$ (the mean). That total is 391.6667 as shown in Table 15.2. If you divide 391.6667 by 24 (K), the result is called the grand mean ($\overline{\overline{X}}$), which in this case is 16.3194 (391.6667 ÷ 24). This grand mean is the centerline in developing the quality control chart for the mean. As a side note, if you are under contract to sell your product to another company, you might find this value (the grand mean) is specified by terms of the contract. In the example, I am using 16.3194 as calculated.

The last column in Table 15.2 is the range. The range is the difference between the high and the low. During sample 1, the first hour, the low measurement is **14.5** and the high is **16.5**. This yields a range of 2.0, so you will find the 2.0 in the far right-hand column. You now need the average range ($\overline{R}$). This is determined by adding the far right column to get 71.1 (shown in the last column of Table 15.2). Next you divide the 71.1 by 24 to get an average range of 2.9625. See the formulas and the calculations just below for both the grand mean and the average range.

$$\overline{\overline{X}} = \frac{\Sigma \overline{X}}{K} = \frac{391.6667}{24} = 16.3194$$

$$\overline{R} = \frac{\Sigma R}{K} = \frac{71.1}{24} = 2.9625$$

Rational Subgroups

It is important to divide the sampling process between **rational subgroups**. Do not develop your samples (K) so that they span either a shift change or a raw material change or a machine maintenance process. For instance, by spanning a shift change, you could not tell if the process is out of control because of operator 1 or operator 2. If the measurement bridged two raw material lots, you could not tell if the quality issue was because of raw material from lot A or lot B. Rational subgrouping will force the variation to be *between samples (K)* and *not within a sample (within n)*. Said slightly differently, any change in shift (personnel) should occur between the "$K's$" (in this example, between the hours) and not between the "$n's$" (the subgroup samples).

The Mean Chart

The mean chart is designed to determine if the mean of the process is in or out of control. If a pattern develops that shows it to be out of control, the process should be stopped and a search should be made for the assignable causes of variation. My calculation begins with the mean of my entire sample (the grand mean of a 24-hour period) as the centerline. Around the grand mean, I then determine an upper (UCL) and lower control limit (LCL). Quality control uses a three-sigma range (three standard errors) around the grand mean (99.7% area based on the empirical rule).

The formulas are as follows:

$$\text{UCL} = \overline{\overline{X}} + A_2\overline{R}$$

$$\text{LCL} = \overline{\overline{X}} - A_2\overline{R}$$

Quality control procedures currently use the adjusted range of each sample K as an estimate for the standard error. This is primarily because smaller sample sizes are most often used. For larger sample sizes, the distribution will approximate a normal distribution. The area between the UCL and LCL is based on $\pm\ 3\sigma_{\bar{x}}$, which according to the empirical rule is 99.7% of the area under the curve.

Using the grand mean and the average range, I can determine the upper and lower control limits of my mean measurement chart. Those calculations are shown as follows:

$$\begin{aligned} \text{UCL} &= \overline{\overline{X}} + A_2\overline{R} \\ &= 16.3194 + (0.483)(2.9625) \\ &= 16.6194 + 1.4309 \\ &= 17.7503 \\ \text{LCL} &= \overline{\overline{X}} - A_2\overline{R} \\ &= 16.3194 - 1.4309 \\ &= \mathbf{14.8885} \end{aligned}$$

Hold it, Professor. You omitted one small factor.

Oh, what is that, I ask?

Where do I get the value for A_2?

Okay, so there is a slight problem in my explanation. Thanks for pointing it out to me. Of course, you realize a professor never makes a mistake, but offers up intentional omissions to test your observance, right? Right!

A_2 is a table looked up value. Table 15.3 shows you the critical values for control charts. To use the chart, I need only know the value of n, not the value of K. If you will look under the heading A_2 and $n\ =\ 6$, you will find the value 0.483. This is the value for A_2 for the current problem.

The mean chart itself is plotted below. The Y-axis shows the average of the six subgroup measurements taken each hour. The X-axis is the number of samples during the day (24 in this case). The centerline is the grand mean which was calculated at 16.3194. The UCL is 17.7503 and the LCL is 14.8885 as calculated just above.

Notice that each *sample mean* (K) is plotted for each hour. By going back to Table 15.2, I look down the $\overline{X}$ column to see if I can find values which exceed the UCL (17.7503) or that fall below

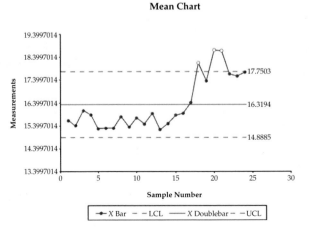

Figure 15.2 The mean chart.

Table 15.3 Critical factors for quality control charts.

n	Chart for Averages	Chart for Ranges	
	Factor for Control Limit	Factor for Control Limits	
n	A_2	D_3	D_4
2	1.880	0	3.267
3	1.023	0	2.575
4	0.729	0	2.282
5	0.577	0	2.115
6	**0.483**	**0**	**2.004**
7	0.419	0.076	1.924
8	0.373	0.136	1.864
9	0.337	0.184	1.816
10	0.308	0.223	1.777
11	0.285	0.256	1.744
12	0.266	0.284	1.716
13	0.249	0.308	1.692
14	0.235	0.329	1.671
15	0.223	0.348	1.652
16	0.212	0.364	1.636
17	0.203	0.379	1.621
18	0.194	0.392	1.608
19	0.187	0.404	1.596
20	0.180	0.414	1.586
21	0.173	0.425	1.575
22	0.167	0.434	1.566
23	0.162	0.443	1.557
24	0.157	0.452	1.548
25	0.153	0.459	1.541

the LCL (14.8885). Take a minute or two and go back to Table 15.2 and see if you can find the sample numbers which are out of control. I will wait.

You should have noticed the 18th, 20th, and 21st samples indicate that the process is out of control based on the mean chart. The 22nd, 23rd, and 24th samples are dangerously close to the UCL. Actually, when the first sample (#18) exceeded the UCL, the process was considered to be out of control. Production should have been stopped to look for the assignable cause(s) of variation. Of course, there must be a cost-benefit analysis to determine if the cost of stopping production exceeds the cost of correcting the problem.

As I look for the assignable causes, questions I should begin asking are: Was there a change in shifts and a new machine operator begin operating the machinery? Was a new shipment of raw materials opened only to find they are inferior? Did I experience some sort of machinery failure? Find out what happened before continuing to produce goods that are not meeting manufacturing standards. This mean chart as shown reflects that management allowed the production of inferior parts to continue for a period of five to six hours. This is not a proactive approach to finding the assignable causes of variation. Whatever production occurred from the 18th through the 21st hours was of inferior quality. When the cost of 30 minutes or so of shut down time is contrasted to a several hours of inferior production, the cost of shutting down may be relatively inexpensive.

Let's next look at a companion chart to the mean chart—the range chart. Both should be calculated.

The Range Chart

It is common to use both the mean chart and the range chart jointly to evaluate the control process. A process may exhibit a stable mean, but the variation (as measured by the range) may be so volatile that the process is producing defective parts. I discussed an extreme example several chapters back. I assumed I was producing tennis rackets. A sample of 30 was taken and found to be 30 inches long which was an acceptable length. Upon further inspection, however, 15 of the 30 had a mean length of 15 inches and 15 of the 30 had a mean length of 45 inches. This makes all of the tennis rackets produced useless, but the mean length of the overall sample is within tolerance at 30 inches. It is not enough to just look at the mean. You must also look at the variability. Quality control uses the range as the measure of variability.

The range chart begins with the average range in the middle and determines an upper and lower control limit. The formulas for the range chart using Table 15.3 data is as follows:

$$\text{UCL} = D_4 \overline{R}$$
$$\text{LCL} = D_3 \overline{R}$$

I have previously calculated the average range $(\overline{R})$ to be 2.9625. The values for D_4 and D_3 come from Table 15.2 or the tables in the back of the textbook. Go look them up. The value for D_4 is 2.004 and for D_3 is zero (0), given $n = 6$. Remember, you look these values up under n and not K. This makes the calculations of UCL and LCL as follows:

$$\text{UCL} = (2.004)(2.9625) = 5.937$$
$$\text{LCL} = (0)(2.9625) = 0$$

The range chart is shown in Figure 15.3 below.

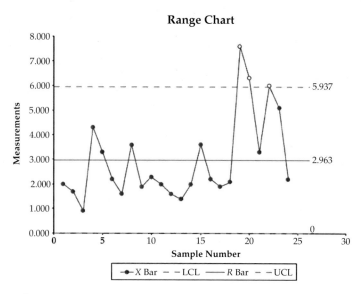

Figure 15.3   The range chart.

I return to Table 15.2 and look down the range column. I am looking for values which are below zero (which can't happen) and which are above 5.937. Once again there are problems with the control around the 19th, 20th, and the 22nd samples (hours). Actually had supervision stopped the production process based on the 18th hour (mean chart) and looked for assignable causes of variation, perhaps the range would not have been out of control at all. Once these assignable causes were identified and fixed, production should resume. Quality control should be proactive in looking for assignable causes of variation when the first hint of trouble arises. These two control charts reflect that management has not taken a proactive roll in finding the assignable causes of variation on a timely basis.

Often the R-chart will be constructed and interpreted first because the mean chart uses the range in calculating the UCL and LCL (look at the formulas). The theory is if the range chart is out of control, then the mean is most probably out of control. Both charts should be constructed. Both charts should be evaluated hourly and corrective action should be taken as soon as the charts show that the process is out of control or one that is tending toward being out of control. I will broaden this point shortly.

One thought needs to be reinforced at this point. Often your company will have the mean, the range, and the upper and lower control limits set by contractual obligation. In those instances, the mean of the process might be contractually set at 16 inches rather than the calculated value of 16.3194. The range might be contractually set at 2.5 inches rather than the 2.963 (rounded).

While the mean and range charts produce quantitative data for a process, I might find that I need to determine if the output is acceptable or unacceptable since I know there will still be random variation. In these instances, the ordinal scale is not appropriate. I must use the nominal or counting scale. I can calculate two different charts for evaluating attributes—the c-chart and the p-chart.

Control Charts for Attributes

The mean and range charts are measurement charts which measure height, weight, length, depth, etc. Measurements occur during the manufacturing process. After the product is completed, there needs to be some method of measuring acceptability. There are two useful charts for measuring attribute compliance—the p-chart and the c-chart. Often you will determine if a process is acceptable based on *the proportion of defects or the number of defects*. This testing occurs after the part is manufactured and ready to be shipped to the customer or ready to be used in an assembly process within your own plant.

These two charts determine if a product is acceptable or unacceptable based on proportions (the p-chart) or number of defects per unit (c-charts). These techniques measure the *quality of a process or the output of that process after the process is completed*.

P-Charts

All four charts (mean, range, p-charts, and c-charts) have a center line and an UCL and LCL. For p-charts, I take a sample and count the number of defects. I will develop a proportion of defects per sample. This process would be repeated several times by selecting several samples.

For example, suppose I was interested in how many hotel rooms were ready for check-in. I could measure the proportion of nonconforming (not ready) hotel rooms at check-in during a period of time. I could be interested in the proportion of nonconforming (inferior) sponges produced for a period of time or the proportion of flights late at the DFW Airport each day for a particular airline or the proportion of defects discovered in the production of guitars.

The calculations are similar to the mean and range charts; however, since I am working with a yes or no, acceptable or unacceptable, conforms or does not conform, defective or non-defective concept, I cannot determine a range. There are no measurements, only a proportion of defects or a number of defects.

The specific formulas are as follows:

$$UCL = \overline{P} + 3\sqrt{\frac{\overline{P}(1 - \overline{P})}{n}}$$

$$LCL = \overline{P} - 3\sqrt{\frac{\overline{P}(1 - \overline{P})}{n}}$$

where $\overline{P}$ is the $\dfrac{\text{Total Number of Defects in All Samples}}{\text{Total Number of All Items Inspected}}$

where 3 is a fixed number and n is the number of sub-samples and is not K (the sample size).

Here, $\overline{P}$ is an estimate of the population proportion (π).

Let's walk through an example. Assume you have taken 15 samples (K) with $n = 40$ for each sample. From this you have developed the following table.

Table 15.4 Proportion of defects in manufacturing process.

Sample (K)	Number of Defects	Proportion of Defects
1	10	0.250 (10/40)
2	12	0.300 (12/40)
3	9	0.225 (9/40)
4	15	0.375 (Etc.)
5	27	0.675
6	8	0.200
7	11	0.275
8	11	0.275
9	13	0.325
10	15	0.375
11	17	0.425
12	3	0.075
13	25	0.625
14	18	0.450
15	17	0.425
Total Defects = 211		

$$\overline{P} = \frac{211}{600} = 0.3517$$

The 211 is the total number of defects for the 15 samples. The 600 is the product of n times 15, which is 40 times 15 = 600.

The UCL and LCL are determined as follows:

$$\text{UCL} = \overline{P} + 3\frac{\overline{P}(1 - \overline{P})}{n} = 0.3517 + 3\sqrt{\frac{(0.3517)(0.6483)}{40}} = 0.3517 + 3\sqrt{\frac{0.2280}{40}}$$

$$= 0.3517 + 3\sqrt{0.0057} = 0.3517 + 3(0.0755) = 0.3517 + 0.2265 = 0.5782$$

The LCL formula subtracts 0.2265 from 0.3517 for an LCL of 0.1252.

The UCL is 0.5782 and the LCL is 0.1252. Next I will compare the UCL and the LCL to the far right column in Table 15.4. It reveals that samples #5 and #13 have proportions which are above the UCL (0.675 and 0.625). It also reveals that sample #12 is below the LCL (0.075). See Figure 15.4.

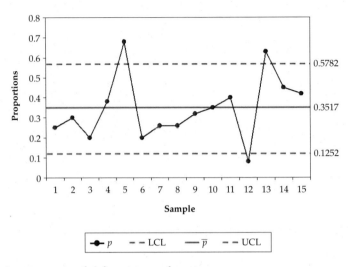

Figure 15.4   P-chart for proportion of defects in manufacturing process.

You would initiate a study to determine why samples #5 and #13 are out of control. Perhaps there is a problem with training or perhaps there is a problem because the computer software was inoperable and production had to be done manually rather than with computer-assisted software. The point is you would study the problem until you found the assignable cause.

Professor, why is being below the LCL not considered to be a problem? Aren't you interested in less variability and less variability is reflected in a lower proportion?

Good observation and always true. You always want less variability. One advantage of finding points out of control near or below the LCL is that of benchmarking. For example, if I find a point below the lower limit, I might have stumbled onto a new production technique which might improve my product or increase my competitive position. Perhaps this LCL violation (sample #12) occurred when superior material is being used. If so, then it might be appropriate to initiate a cost-benefit study of the superior materials. If the cost of materials is too excessive to allow for competitive pricing, you would not elect to adopt the new materials. However, if the cost is not too prohibitive, you might elect to adopt the superior materials.

The p-chart measures the proportion of defects in a series. However, often I will want to know if a single part is acceptable or unacceptable or I might want to know the number of defects in a product. In these instances I will use the c-chart. The p-chart and the c-chart are closely related to each other. The main difference is that p-charts use the proportion of defects while the c-chart would use the number of defects.

C-Charts

Another technique for measuring number of defects in a single part is the c-chart. C-charts are developed in a manner similar to the p-chart. A mean number of defects for all parts is determined. This value is used as the centerline around which you placed an UCL and LCL. The formulas are as follows:

$$UCL = \bar{C} + 3\sqrt{\bar{C}}$$
$$LCL = \bar{C} - 3\sqrt{\bar{C}}$$

where $\bar{C}$ is the mean number of defects in a unit and an estimate of C which is the population value and three (3) is a fixed number.

Assume a rug manufacturer wants to determine the number of defects in a batch of 20 new rugs. Table 15.5 is the result of counting the number of defects in each rug.

Table 15.5 Number of defects in 20 rugs.

Rugs	Number of Defects
1	5
2	4
3	3
4	5
5	16
6	1
7	8
8	9
9	9
10	4
11	3
12	15
13	10
14	8
15	4
16	2
17	10
18	12
19	7
20	17
Total	**152**

$$\bar{C} = \frac{152}{20} = 7.6$$

$$\text{UCL} = \bar{C} + 3\sqrt{\bar{C}} = 7.6 + 3\sqrt{7.6} = 7.6 + (3)(2.757) = 7.6 + 8.2710 = 15.871$$

$$\text{LCL} = \bar{C} - 3\sqrt{\bar{C}} = 7.6 - 8.271 = -0.671$$

The UCL is 15.871 and the lower limit is a negative 0.671, which is zero for all practical purposes. Next, I look at the values in the far right-hand column of Table 15.5. I want to identify any values which are above the 15.871. Samples #5 and #20 exceed that value. Rugs #5 and #20 have more defects than I expect, so I will transfer those to the secondary market and offer them for sale in discount retail outlets. The other rugs do not have enough defects to make them unacceptable to the primary market. I should be able to obtain full value for all rugs except #5 and #20. See Figure 15.5 for a picture of the number of defects.

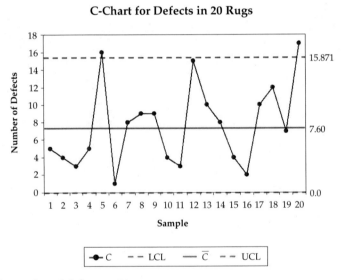

C-Chart for Defects in 20 Rugs

Figure 15.5 C-chart for number of defects in 20 rugs.

Other Examples

C-charts are useful when determining if a screw-on lid fits or does not fit or when a banker evaluates if loans are going to be paid or not paid or the number of accidents in a plant or the number of defects in a standardized section of continuous sheet metal or the number of defects in a production lot of goods. A c-chart is used in analyzing the number of defects per some unit.

Interpreting Control Charts

The interpretation of control charts is important. It is not difficult to interpret an out of control situation when a point or two goes beyond the upper or lower control limit, but more subtle patterns may indicate potential problems may exist even though your process is not beyond the upper or lower control limits.

Let's suppose that a single point during the 24-hour sample falls out of control. Do you have a problem?

Yes. Even one point outside the control limits indicates a problem. When a point is outside the control limits, management is responsible for immediately examining the process to identify the assignable cause of the variation. Let's say you cannot find any assignable cause, so what does this mean? It could simply mean that the process is okay and this single point is an anomaly. Further action may not be necessary. Of course, if you find an assignable cause, then you should take appropriate actions.

Two basic rules of thumb have been developed over a number of years. **The first rule: If you have 8 consecutive points that show a direction or trend, you have a process that is violating the rule of random variation.** The points do not have to be above or below the centerline, but may cut across the centerline. The points must show a direction or trend (up or down). When this occurs, there is evidence the process is out of control even though none of the points is above or below the upper or lower control limits. Trends must be investigated. Figure 15.6 shows a trend pattern which is exhibiting out of control tendencies.

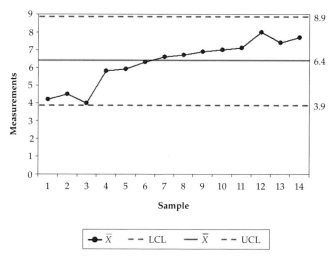

Figure 15.6   Trend showing out of control tendencies.

The second rule: If you have 8 consecutive points that are above the centerline or 8 consecutive points that are below the centerline, you may have a production situation that exhibits out of control tendencies. This pattern violates the rules of random variation and the process must be evaluated.

See Figure 15.7 for a visual of this condition.

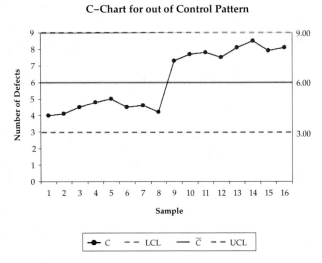

Figure 15.7   C-chart for Out of control pattern.

As I have just pointed out, it could be that all of the points in the sample are within the UCL and LCL for the mean, but you could still have a problem. Usually, you hope the sample data points randomly move back and forth from one side of the mean to the other side of the mean (centerline). If you develop a pattern on one side of the mean or the other side of the mean, there may a potential problem brewing. This would be especially true if the points are at or near the UCL or LCL. A pattern of points very close to the upper control limit or lower control limit could show that the process needs to be closely evaluated. Keep in mind that the three-sigma limit is used most often in control charts. What you might do is calculate a two-sigma limit and see if any points are out of control based on the 95% level of significance.

What you hope to see is no pattern at all in your control charts. Think about a thermometer. What if it were incorrectly calibrated to register three degrees warmer than normal? This might cause an incorrect diagnosis for a doctor, something you do not want. What you hope occurs is a random pattern with the sample points moving back and forth around the center line. An example of random, preferred variation is shown in Figure 15.8.

The process must exhibit random variation. As long as the pattern is random, your control charts are okay. If the pattern exhibits any tendency toward runs on either side of the center line or trends which cut across the center line (non-random variation), then examine the process to see if assignable causes of variation can be found.

Control charts are an ideal tool for the shop floor where quick and easy methods of evaluation are often necessary. Complicated statistical tools are not required, so these methods are the preferred methods of controlling quality.

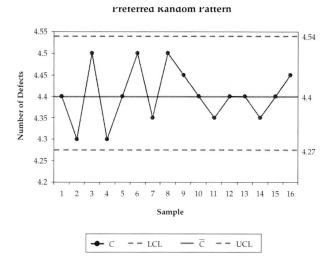

Figure 15.8   Preferred random pattern of number of defects.

Acceptance Sampling

I have shown you the four techniques used in evaluating a manufacturing process. Two of them (mean and range charts) are useful during the manufacturing process itself. The other two (p and c-charts) are useful after manufacturing is completed but before the part is used in an assembly process or shipped to the customer.

That brings up an interesting (to me) point. What do I do when I receive products from my supplier? Do I accept them assuming the supplier has met specification or do I test them? Quite simply, I test them using the random selection process. This procedure is called acceptance sampling or lot acceptance.

The question: When a shipment arrives at your loading dock, should you accept it or reject it?

Rarely does a firm inspect 100% of any shipment. Lot acceptance or rejection is determined by sampling part of the shipment to determine if there are too many defective parts in the shipment to warrant accepting the entire shipment. There are at least two important considerations in forming a lot. The lots should be homogeneous. Large lots are preferable to small lots.

Acceptance sampling is preferable to 100% sampling because of the following reasons. Sampling will be used because it is less expensive, less product damage will occur since there is less handling of the products, and fewer people are involved in the inspection process. Rejecting an entire lot can motivate the supplier to improve its own quality control. Sampling is the only approach that can be used if destructive testing must be used (wine tasting or test to failure of a critical aircraft part).

I set up the two hypotheses as follows:

H_o: Good quality lot
H_a: Poor quality lot

Like any other hypothesis test, I can make an error. The errors are the same as shown to you in prior material. The α **error** is the probability of rejecting a good lot and the β **error** is the probability of accepting a bad lot. The alpha error is called the **producer risk** and the beta error is called the **consumer risk.**

As the quality control manager, I want to accept H_o. The first step in acceptance sampling is to negotiate something called the AQL, acceptance quality level, between you and your supplier. In practice, the AQL may be negotiated in the following manner.

You say to your supplier, *I do not want your shipment of products to contain more than 1% bad parts (defective parts).* The supplier says to you, *okay, but in order to do that I need to increase the price from $1.38 to $1.65 per unit since the material I must use to ensure no more than 1% defective parts will have to be superior material.* You say to the supplier, *wait a minute. I cannot afford $1.65 per unit. That drives my price up too much, and I cannot sell my product.* The supplier says to you, *I can hold the $1.38 price, but you will have to accept a 5% AQL level.* You reply, *okay. I can live with that.*

This entire process has been a cost-value trade off analysis and is an important first step in the process of determining if you will accept or reject the lot of goods. For purposes of this example, let's assume the AQL is set at 5%.

What Does This Mean?

This simply means that you will reject the entire lot if there are more than 5% defective parts in all of the shipments. In other words, I will accept a lot if the shipment has no more than 5% defective parts. The AQL is referred to as π (pi) which is equal to 0.05 or 5%.

As a good quality control manager, I do not want to subject my manufacturing operation or the company supplier to unwarranted rejections of good lots. I will establish something referred to as the producer risk.

Producer's Risk

The **producer risk** is the probability that sampling error will cause me to mistakenly reject a shipment that is good. In English this means the following. I have a shipment of goods sitting on my loading dock. I must decide if I am going to accept or reject the entire lot. I do not want to send back to the producer a good shipment; however, as a human I am prone to errors. I do agree to limit this error. The percentage of error limit can be set based on my production needs, but is often set very high. I might set it at 1%. I do not want to send back good shipments more than 1% of the time. I want to limit my error to 1%. This error is referred to as the alpha error or a Type I error.

In this instance, I have set the producer risk at 1% or 0.01. Thus alpha is 0.01. Again, this means that only 1% of the good shipments will be returned.

Let's assume I order 1,000 parts from my supplier. They are shipped to me. I am going to sample the lot of goods to see if it is acceptable or unacceptable. I select a sample size, but need to know how many defects I can have in my sample before I reject the entire shipment of 1,000 parts.

The solution often uses a hypergeometric distribution, but the binomial distribution is often substituted in the search for the number of defective parts. The number of acceptable defects per sampling lot is defined as "C." C is the maximum number of defective parts you can have in your sample before the entire lot is returned to the supplier.

Let's carry my example a step further. The 1,000 parts are on my shipping dock, and I am trying to decide if I should reject or accept the entire shipment. Previously, you and I have agreed to a 5% AQL. The alpha I have agreed to is 1%. The lot size is 1,000 (N). I determine the correct sample size is $n = 50$. I need to know the *maximum number of defective parts (C)* I can have out of the sample of 50 before I return the entire 1,000 shipment.

Said a different way, I want to know the number of defective parts I can accept from the sample such that at least 99% of the good shipments contain 95% non-defective parts. (95% is $1 - $ AQL or $1.0 - 0.05 = 0.95$ or 95%)

Geez Louise, if you understand that you are doing real well, I exclaim.

I will actually use the AQL at 5% and the producer risk at 1% to make my calculations. Recall, the alpha error is a Type I error and is 1% in this example.

I will use a cumulative binomial table to look up the values I need. Find the cumulative binominal table in your textbook. (Actually one is reproduced a page or so below). I will wait. Oh, you're back.

In most tables, there must be some change made to the names/symbols as originally shown on the table. The "n" is still "n," so $n = 50$ in this instance, the sample size. I look up the desired value of "C" under $n = 50$. In this example, I have negotiated the AQL to be 5% or 0.05. I rename the π (pi) as shown in the table to AQL. So $\pi = $ AQL. I will look for my value of C using the π column of 5% (0.05). The term "X" must be renamed to "C." So $X = C$.

Okay, so how do I find the number of acceptable defective parts given AQL $= 0.05, n = 50, \alpha = 0.01$?

C (or X) is the unknown. I must now take the producer risk (α) and subtract it from 1. The calculation is 1.000 less 0.01, which will yield 0.9900.

I now go to the cumulative binominal table. I now look for the first value in the 0.05 column which *exceeds* the 0.9900 limit. Move down the column headed 0.05 (for the π value). The first value that exceeds 0.9900 is 0.9968. Now move to the left and look at the intersection of C (written as X in the table) and 0.9968. C is equal to 7. There is a more complete cumulative binominal table in the back of the textbook.

Table 15.6 Partial cumulative binominal table.

n	X or C	Pi or AQL of 0.05
50	0	0.0769
	1	0.2794
	2	0.5405
	3	0.7604
	4	0.8964
	5	0.9622
	6	0.9882
	7	**0.9968**
	8	0.9992
	9	0.9998

Maybe you had better stop and go back over what I just said again. Once you trace the values in the cumulative binominal table, you can move on.

Moving on, you have found that you *can have* 7 defective parts out of the 50 you are sampling *before* you will return the entire production lot of goods to the supplier. So only 7 defective parts may be found in $n = 50$, with an AQL of 0.05 (π) and an α of 0.01.

So if I draw a sample of 50 and find 7 parts defective, I will accept the entire shipment. If I draw a sample of 50 and find *8 parts defective, I will reject the entire shipment*. As soon as I reach the threshold of 8 defective parts, I can stop sampling and return the entire shipment. I do not have to tell the supplier there are 22 out of 50 which are defective. My threshold is 8.

Different Sampling Plans

The sampling plan just discussed above is a single sample plan. However, what if your shipments were very large and you wanted to set up other sampling plans? I could set up sequential (multiple) sampling plans or double-sampling plans.

In a double-sampling plan, I take the first sample. On the basis of the outcome of the first sample, I will do one of three things—accept the lot, reject the lot, or take a second sample. Let's say that I have a double-sampling plan set up such that the first sample is 100 parts. I decide to take a second sample of 100 if certain criteria are not met on the first sampling plan.

With the two sampling plans, I set two C-values. C is the number of defects I can have before rejecting the lot. In this instance, $n_1 = 100$ with C_1 set at 3, and $n_2 = 100$ with C_2 set at 8. In the first sample of 100, if I get 3 or fewer defective parts, I accept the entire lot and do not have to take the second sample. However, let's say that I found 5 defective parts in the first sample. At this point, I do not reject the lot. Finding more than 3 defective parts in the first sample will cause the second sample to be taken. The second sample must not yield defective parts in excess of 6 parts or else I must reject the lot.

Okay, wait a minute where did you get the 6, you ask?

Good question, I say. Let me put this in tabular format.

Table 15.7   Double-sampling plan.

Sample Size	Acceptable C	If when sampling you get the following number of defects ...	
#1 = 100	#1 = 3	Assume # of defects in #1 sample.	5
#2 = 100	#2 = 8	How many defects can you get in the #2 sample?	6
	Total 11	Because both must ...	Total 11

The total of both samples cannot exceed 11 defective parts. This approach is especially helpful if you must use destructive sampling in determining defective parts. If I find 7 defective parts in the first sample, I can then find no more than 4 defective parts in the second sample before I reject the entire shipment. Any combination of defective parts in sample #1 or #2 that exceeds the 11 total will cause me to reject the entire lot of goods and return it to the producer.

The process of quality control is extremely important. It is often said that quality control costs money. This is not totally true. Poor quality will kill a company. Good quality is expected. Good quality will involve some set up and training, but getting your company to think quality is well worth the investment.

One final idea—Six Sigma™. Let's review this concept briefly.

Six Sigma™ Commuting

I believe that the easiest way to explain the rudimentary concepts of Six Sigma™ is to show you a couple of examples.

For simplicity's sake, let us assume you want to get to work each day by 9:00 AM plus or minus two minutes. Your time of arrival must be between 8:58 AM and 9:02 AM each day. You leave the house each day at exactly 8:42 AM. You believe it takes you eighteen minutes to drive the distance from home to work.

Your acceptable range of drive time is from sixteen minutes to twenty minutes, which is eighteen minutes plus and minus two minutes. Sixteen minutes is your lower specification limit and twenty is your upper specification limit. Arriving in that interval is acceptable to you. Arriving too early or too late means you must make coffee or there will be no coffee left.

The question now before you is *"How much time does it actually take me to get to work?"*

To answer this question you collect data for a number of weeks. From that data you determine that the mean drive time is 18 minutes and the standard deviation is 2.7 minutes. Plotting this on a graph you see the following (Figure 15.9):

The calculation of the upper drive time is $18 + (1)(2.7) = 20.7$.

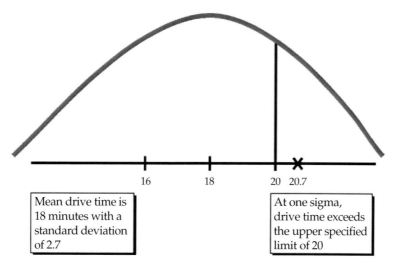

Figure 15.9 Unadjusted limits on drive time to work.

You notice that there is a lot of variation in your arrival time. It seems as though the standard deviation is quite high. You wonder if you can change the variability of the drive time so you can fall within the specified limits. At one standard deviation, you are outside the desired upper limit.

Professor, Why Don't You Just Leave Earlier?

I could, but quite often I would arrive at work too early, so that does not give me the desired result. [18 − (1)(2.7) = 15.3] If I leave earlier, I would end up arriving earlier than the 15.3 minutes which gives me even more time away from home.

I think: Because the variability is so high, perhaps I can find ways to limit the variation or improve the variability in my drive time.

Put in quality control language: The drive is considered to be your process and the drive time has too great a variability to allow you to have consistent arrival times within the desired levels of 16 to 20 minutes. I must improve (reduce) the variability of the drive time. You brainstorm what you might be able to do.

You might find a route that is consistently less congested.

Since you will be doing freeway driving, perhaps you can use cruise control to set the speed more precisely.

Once you get parked, you can promptly exit the car and stop listening to the radio for one more opinion or one more song.

You can park in approximately the same location every morning to ensure you have about the same distance to walk into the building each day.

You can find the most direct path from your car to the building.

You can set your walking pace at a reasonably consistent rate.

You take these actions and then collect data for several weeks. From the new data you have collected you determine the mean drive time is still eighteen minutes, but now the standard deviation is 0.33 minutes. This represents quite an improvement from the 2.7 minutes.

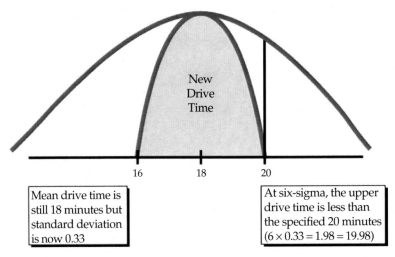

16   18   20

Mean drive time is still 18 minutes but standard deviation is now 0.33

At six-sigma, the upper drive time is less than the specified 20 minutes (6 × 0.33 = 1.98 = 19.98)

Figure 15.10 Six Sigma™ tolerance levels.

Now you draw the figure again and find out that you are within the Six Sigma tolerance limits.

Six times 0.33 = 1.98 standard deviations. (18 ± 1.98 = 16.02 to 19.98 minutes).

You are now well within the desired drive time limits because you took action to reduce the variability in the process. This means you can still leave at the same time (precisely 8:42 AM) and that you will have almost zero days when you are too early or too late.

This is an illustration of Six Sigma™ performance. You do not change the mean performance. It is still 18 minutes, but because of taking action with the process (drive time), you are now consistently within the desired limits. You improve the standard deviation.

Thinking of It a Different Way

My goal is to reduce the standard deviation of the process (narrowing the variability). The key to how much reduction is necessary is to know what the customer wants. Often these requirements are called CTQ's or "critical to quality" characteristics.

You can think of them as specification limits given to you by the customer.

A defect is defined as any event or error in which the product or process fails to meet a customer requirement.

Sigma levels of performance are also often expressed in "defects per million (of) opportunities" (DPMO). The chart tells me at six sigma you will have only 3.4 defects per million of opportunities (production levels). In case you are wondering that is very small.

Table 15.8 Defects per million.

Simplified Sigma Conversion Table		
If your yield is ...	**Your DPMO is ...**	**Your Sigma is ...**
30.9%	690,000	1.0
69.2	308,000	2.0
99.3	66,800	3.0
99.4	6,210	4.0
99.98	320	5.0
99.9997	3.4	6.0

A Second Example

Your first step in any business situation is to analyze the process you are currently using for meeting the needs of your current customers.

Let's say we are in the water transportation business. You row people across a small channel in a small boat every day. A typical customer currently is someone who wants to get across the channel in a leisurely manner to have a weekday picnic or a weekend outing. The customers never seem to be in any really big hurry. Your rowing time is good and provides the customer what he or she wants.

However, you notice that you are getting another type of customer during the weekdays who wants to get across the channel more quickly. The number of customers is also increasing, but you find you can only take three at a time because of the size limitation of the boat.

As you gather data you find it takes 7.5 minutes to make the trip across the channel in each direction. Your slow time (15 minutes round trip) is starting to cause a buildup of customers waiting at your dock. The boat is moving too slowly to meet the needs of your customers. The boat is analogous to your process in a business.

You get together with your neighbors (management team) and brainstorm solutions to develop a list of ways to improve the boat (process). You come up with a shopping list of potential improvements.

- Hire a person to help with the rowing.
- Increase the size of your oars.
- Buy more oars and get the passengers to help row.
- Get some help by putting up a sail on the boat.
- Repair any damage to the hull and repaint so the boat will glide through the water more easily.
- Limit the carry-on luggage to one bag per passenger.
- Buy a motor for the boat.

Notice, the decision is not to buy a bigger boat, because that is the same as scrapping the existing process and creating another process. *The decision is to make the current process (the boat) more efficient.*

You may not elect all of the possible changes you have listed so, after proper evaluation, you decide to increase the size of the oars and hire employees to help in rowing.

As a result, you cut your round-trip time by three minutes. This seems to work and your backup at the dock is eliminated and your customers seem to be happy with your performance.

However after a period of time, you find your business has increased. The customer line is back. You next decide to buy an outboard motor. This works quite well. The process (boat) is moving along nicely. Your round trip now takes six minutes.

You have now implemented two rounds of improving your process. Your customers are happy and your revenues and profits are up considerably.

Let's assume that, over a period of time, your customer base grows considerably. The lines at the dock begin to build once again. You also find that your customers are asking you to transport them further down the channel. This is something new for you. The trip now becomes one that is more dangerous and unreasonably time consuming for the small boat (process). It is becoming clear that your process (the boat) is too small and slow for the job your customers now want you to do. You have now reached the limits of the capability of your process as it is currently designed. You have hit the barrier—your process is not keeping up with changing needs or opportunities. You must now redesign the process (get a bigger boat). You cannot fix your existing process.

You are now faced with an investment and a redesign of your business model and process. You must address several issues. Do you have the skilled employees to be able to implement the new process? Can you implement training programs to bring your existing employees to the skill levels required for the new process? Is your new route and higher visibility going to attract competitors and, if so, how do you plan your response to those competitors? Will you need to set up ancillary facilities such as a telephone reservation system or ticket booths on the loading dock? Are you going to have to expand your marketing forces to make sure you attract as many new customers as possible?

Assuming you make the investment to buy the bigger boat and redesign the process, you still have challenges ahead of you. You must now learn how to manage your process. You find managing new employees to be quite challenging. In the past you have handled all of the business functions, but now you must hire an accountant, human resource personnel, maintenance personnel, a financial advisor, marketing specialists, operation personnel since you may want to expand your operation to two or three shifts, quality control specialists, and other key personnel.

Six Sigma™ involves evaluating the variability associated with any process. Six Sigma™ involves meeting your customer needs and adjusting the process to make sure you give them better and better service or products. When you have maximized the effectiveness of your existing process, you will want to look at a new process (meeting customer demand). Your process must be managed at all levels. You will find that, as your customer base grows, the complexity of your job will grow. Along the way, you are always striving to keep the variability of your service under control. You will continually ask the question: Can I do something different to improve my process? My target will be to operate within Six Sigma™ limits.

General Textbook Ending Comment

That does it. You have been exposed to statistical processes over the last 15 chapters that should influence your thinking. Now that you better understand the language of statistics, you can speak intelligently with your fellow workers or your boss about issues which involve statistical processes. The knowledge you have gained from this textbook and any course you are taking should make you listen more closely to television and radio personalities when they begin tossing around statistical conclusions. Hopefully, you will now begin to listen more intently and with some degree of skepticism. You should be able to deal with those who consider themselves statisticians and "hold your own" in meetings and discussions. You now have a competitive advantage over your fellow co-workers by understanding statistical concepts.

One Last Attempt at Humor

You know You are a Texan If:

- If you know everything goes better with Ranch and Tabasco.

- A bad traffic jam involves two cars staring each other down at a four-way stop, each determined to be the most polite and let the other one go first.

Tear-Out Sheet Chapter 15

Student Name: _____

Day and Time of Class: _____

1. Network Solutions offers a toll-free number where customers can call with problems involving the use of their products from 7:00 AM until 11:00 PM daily. It is impossible to have every call answered immediately by a technical representative, but it is important customers do not wait too long for help. Customers become upset when they hear the message "Your call is important to us. The next available representative will be with you shortly" too often. To understand their process, Network Solutions decides to develop a control chart describing the time from when a call is received until a representative answers the call. Yesterday, for the 16 hours of operation $k = 16$), five calls were sampled ($n = 5$) each hour. This information is recorded in minutes in the table below from the time a call was received until a call was answered by a representative.

Time	1	2	3	4	5	$\overline{X}$	R
7 AM	8	9	15	4	11		
8	7	10	7	6	8		
9	11	12	10	9	10		
10	12	8	6	9	12		
11	11	10	6	14	11		
12 PM	7	7	10	4	11		
1	10	7	4	10	10		
2	8	11	11	7	7		
3	8	11	8	14	12		
4	12	9	12	17	11		
5	7	7	9	17	13		
6	9	9	4	4	11		
7	10	12	12	12	12		
8	8	11	9	6	8		
9	10	13	9	4	9		
10	9	11	8	5	11		
Total							

    a. Develop a control chart for the mean and range for the mean duration of the calls.

    b. Do there appear to be peaks and valleys in the calling times?

    c. Are there any answer times which appear to be out of control?

    d. Is there a pattern which would lead you to believe your study conforms to random variation as measured by the mean and range charts?

2. A local bank is studying the loan activity for eight of its bankers. A subgroup sample of six loans is selected at random. The results are tabulated below.

Loan Amount in Thousands								
Banker	1	2	3	4	5	6	Mean	Range
1	14.1	9.1	7.0	6.7	6.1	5.9		
2	45.3	65.6	45.1	55.1	55.2	60.2		
3	22.9	31.4	36.2	30.5	32.5	29.6		
4	32.5	31.3	30.2	28.1	28.3	29.1		
5	56.8	65.4	45.2	55.6	57.9	60.5		
6	88.9	90.5	83.8	85.6	90.1	88.7		
7	110.0	101.9	114.6	99.6	150.4	119.8		
8	78.4	82.6	90.4	104.6	81.7	85.8		
						Totals		

    a. Develop a mean and range chart.

    b. Interpret the charts. Are there any patterns in the level of activity for any banker?

    c. Using the Wizard in Excel and the line chart, draw a picture of the loan activity of the bankers. Using Excel, you cannot draw in the UCL, LCL, or center point, but you can insert those manually after you print the graph.

    d. Given the following information, develop a p-chart to assess each banker's performance as it relates to defaults. Assume 20 loans were sampled.

Banker	Number of Defaults	Proportion of Defaults
1	8	0.4
2	6	0.3
3	6	0.3
4	4	0.2
5	2	0.1
6	6	0.3
7	18	0.9
8	12	0.6

e. Interpret the result of this p-chart. Does any banker appear to have more default loans as compared to the others?

f. Given the following information on mistakes made on loan applications by these same bankers, construct a c-chart on number of defects. Assume 12 loan applications were evaluated.

g. Interpret the result of the c-chart. Does it appear that any of the bankers should be asked to explain any particular loan application?

h. Using the Excel Chart Wizard, draw a graph of the c-chart. You cannot insert the UCL, LCL, or midline using the Chart Wizard, but can do so manually after drawing and printing the chart.

Loan Application	Violations of Bank Policy
1	3
2	4
3	2
4	3
5	10
6	1
7	2
8	0
9	3
10	4
11	2
12	3
Total	37

3. A local cereal manufacturer advertises there will be at least three scoops of fruit-flavored nuggets in each box of cereal. A customer will accept a maximum of 1% defective boxes (AQL). The producer's risk is limited to 5% (alpha). A sample of 100 boxes is selected from a shipment of 1,000 boxes. How many defective boxes (C) in the sample of 100 will the customer accept before returning the entire shipment?

Appendix I: My Personal Opinion on the Application of Probabilities to Evolutionary Theory – A Non-Testable Section

From the Goo to the Zoo to You

This material is only inserted to have you begin thinking about one application of probabilities to a controversial subject—evolution. There is no intent to try to persuade you to believe or not believe in evolution. Perhaps this section will cause you to want to know more about this subject, perhaps not. This Appendix is strictly my personal opinion and if you wish to discuss it and are taking a class from me, please wait until the class is completed to initiate any discussion on this issue. I will not discuss it as long as you are a current student of mine.

As the evolutionist's theme song, this is far too simplistic especially when you examine the probability of all the combinations which must happen for evolution to be plausible. If you have an interest in this subject, go to your browser and type in "evolution probability." You will be amazed at what comes up. Much of the material is highly technical and far beyond the few examples I will cite here. This material is presented as a study in probabilities.

Evolutionist usually side-step the subject of how life began and simply address the changes in life which they often refer to as evolution. While most will agree that evolution within species does exist, others would point out that evolution between species cannot be empirically demonstrated and does not exist. Evolutionist cannot demonstrate evolution between species. One species is said to evolve into a more complex organism through natural selection, survival of the fittest or mutations. If a rabbit evolved into a beaver, we have evolution between species. If a red rose is bred to yield an orange rose, we do not have evolution, but changes in the same species.

Life must begin somewhere. If you only address evolutions after the beginning of life, you are begging the question of how it all started. For evolution to be true, life had to arise from non-living matter. Many biologists tell us this cannot occur. While I will not develop the probabilities, I will cite other credible mathematicians and scientists who have made the calculations knowing the sequence of the building blocks of life including amino acids, RNA, DNA, and others.

In 1991 British astronomer Sir Fred Hoyle made the statement that the number of trial assemblies of amino acids required to give rise to enzymes, which are required for life to exist, is less than 1 in $10^{40,000}$. Dr. Emile Borel, a leading mathematician, has stated that the occurrence of any event with chances beyond 1 in 1^{50} is an event that will never happen no matter how much time passes. Remember, the probability of any event occurring is measured between zero and one. Zero means the event is highly unlikely and one means the event is highly likely. Nothing is asserted that an event will absolutely happen or will not absolutely happen.

The evolutionists argue that their theory can be supported empirically, but no one can support creation or evolution empirically, since the scientists of today were not present and cannot recreate the conditions in a laboratory environment. The only reasonable alternative to empirical observation is probability.

Other estimates of the probability of life evolving randomly (by chance) have been made by Dr. Harold Morowitz, former professor of biophysics, who estimated the chance probability of the smallest, simplest organism forming to be 1 in $10^{340,000,000}$. Carl Sagan, an outspoken evolutionist, estimated that the chance of life on any given single planet is one in $10^{2,000,000,000}$. The latter is a huge number and would take 6,000 books of 300 pages just to write the number with all of the zeros.

Sir Francis Crick, co-discoverer of the DNA molecule, stated that the great majority of sequences required for life can never be synthesized at all.

While you may believe in evolution, you must overcome the argument against evolution based on the very small probabilities that the complexity of humankind could have occurred by chance. These probabilities, as stated, apply to one complex organism. How do you answer the question that evolution must have occurred by species and by gender and the timing must have been exactly right?

Evolutionist claim that life arose from a primordial soup randomly developing into the complex creature called human.

For example, both man and woman must evolve from the same *random process* at the *same time*. If the evolutionary (beginning of all life) development of gender was out of phase by 100 years, there could be no reproduction which means there could be no human race. The same is true for dog genders and cat genders, etc. All would have to come out of the soup at the same time by gender and by species, with reproductive organs in place.

And the evolutionist always has the second law of thermodynamics to overcome. This law states that matter is in a state of entropy, which means that an ordered system moves toward disorder the more time passes. The universe is winding down and not regenerating itself. My body, as is yours, is decaying, not improving. I can do nothing permanently about the process. My body (the system) is living out the second law of thermodynamics. From a thermodynamic perspective, all natural processes are irreversible (closed system). Dollo's law states that evolution is not reversible (thus irreversible). Stephen Gould viewed the idea less strictly, suggesting that "irreversibility forecloses certain evolutionary pathways once broad forms have emerged: [For example], once you adopt the ordinary body plan of a reptile hundreds of options are forever closed, and future possibilities must unfold within the limits of inherited design." [Gould, Stephen J. (2007) "Eight Little Piggies," Vintage Books.]

Think about the logic—not necessarily the probability—of this scenario occurring. Let's take a couple of example of complex organisms. For example the human eye is enormously complex. Richard Dawkins, a leading contemporary evolutionist, and Charles Darwin, the father of evolution, would have us believe that infinitesimal small changes over millions of years caused the eye to develop in step-by-step plausible changes. For example, Dawkins paraphrases Darwin's argument with the following statement. "Some single-celled animals have a light-sensitive spot with a little pigment behind it. The screen shields it from light coming from one direction, which gives it some "idea" of where the light is coming from. Among many-celled animals. . . . the pigment-backed light-sensitive cells are set in a little cup. This give slightly better direction-finding capability . . . Now if you make a cup very deep and turn the sides over, you eventually make a lensless pinhole camera. . . . When you have a cup for an eye, almost any vaguely convex, vaguely transparent or even translucent material over its opening will constitute an improvement, because of it slight lens-like properties. Once such a crude photo-lens is there, there is a continuously graded series of improvements, thickening it and making it more transparent and less distorting, the trend culminating in what we would all recognize as a true lens." (Michael J. Behe, Darwin's Black Box, 2006)

Notice the starting point for the argument is a light-sensitive spot with pigment behind it and a cup for an eye. Neither Dawkins nor Darwin explains how the pigment or the cup was developed. The evolutionist begins an argument with major presuppositions about a starting point. Mr. Behe goes into much more detail in explaining the complex workings of just the eye. Dawkins does make a statement that some complex systems are just too complex to develop over time and that they just pop into existence as complete systems. This would explain (without real explanation) the reason species survived their natural predators without becoming extinct. An eye must have pupil, lens and cornea working properly to function at all as an eye. Without all three functioning properly, no animal would survive nor have a clue about being attack before it was too late.

Let's examine what Charles Darwin said about the eye.

"To suppose that the eye with all its inimitable contrivances for adjusting the focus to different distances, for admitting different amounts of light, and for the correction of spherical and chromatic selection, seems, I freely confess, absurd in the highest degree."—*Charles Darwin, The Origin of Species (1909 Harvard Classics edition), p. 190.*

Just how complex is the human eye?

"Consider the eye 'with all its inimitable contrivances,' as *Darwin called them, which can admit different amounts of light, focus at a different distance, and correct spherical and chromatic aberration. Consider the retina, consisting of 150 million correctly made and positioned specialized cells. These are the rods [to view black and white] and the cones [to view color]. Consider the nature of the light-sensitive *retinal*. Combined with a protein (*opsin*), the retinal becomes a chemical switch. Triggered by light, this switch can generate a nerve impulse. Each switch-containing rod and cone is correctly wired to the brain so that the electrical storm (an estimated 1000 million impulses per second) is continuously monitored and translated, by a step which is a total mystery, into a mental picture."—*Michael Pitman, Adam and Evolution (1984), p. 215.*

Is evolution at work in the development of the human eye? It seems to me an eye must come into existed all at once. Half of an eye is no good to anyone. Did the development of the eye occur by chance, natural selection or mutation? You be the judge.

Another example is the Bombardier Beetle who discourages his predators from attacking by mixing two chemicals—hydroquinone and hydrogen peroxide in a chamber and expels them at the predator at temperatures around 220 degrees (boiling). There are two holding and one mixing chambers involved and an enzyme that causes the mixture to become explosive in the mixing chamber. There is a tube to the outside which can direct the explosion outward. However there are also two openings facing the holding chambers (inside). These two holding chambers must be sealed off at the exact moment of explosion so the direction of the liquid is forced outward not inward. If forced inward as well as outward, the defense mechanism destroys the beetle and there is no survival of the species. If there is a force in one direction there is an equal action in the opposite direction. Were it not for the emission of the liquid to be in disconnected small spurts, the beetle would be forced backward away from the predator into who knows what. These short-spurts allow the beetle to remain in one place. There is much more about the Bombardier Beetle found in the Behe book, if you have an interest in pursing some of the ideas about the plausibility of evolution.

A third example is simply the coagulation of blood. The process is very complex. After an injury to any blood vessel platelets immediately form a plug at the site of the injury (hemostasis). A protein in the blood plasma acts simultaneously as a coagulation factor to form fibrin stands which strengthen the platelet plug. If this does not occur at the right time in the right order, there is the risk of continued bleeding and or the risk of clotting in the blood stream neither of which is good.

For me, it is very difficult to believe small changes over a long period of time could occur at random. For an evolutionist, the only way for these changes to occur is a long-period of time. Clearly evolution within a species occurs, but the theory must be challenged when the evolutionist asserts that the changes occur between species. Random chance and time is all the evolutionist has to demonstrate their theories as correct. The probabilities of random chance are too great for me to reconcile the complexities especially in light of findings in DNA to which Darwin did not have access. The DNA code is a barrier which evolution cannot cross. Creatures are born from their parents, but the variations are permitted by the DNA code for a particular species.

Appendix II

Tables

Internet Reference to Tables

(All links were live when this textbook was written)

http://www.statsoft.com/textbook/sttable.html

> Multiple Tables for such things as normal distribution, *F*, chi square, *t*-distribution and others and probably the cleanest site and most easily read.

Tukey: q-values

http://www.isds.duke.edu/courses/Spring98/sta110c/qtable.html

> Not a Very Good Table, but use it in case the best goes down.

http://cse.niaes.affrc.go.jp/miwa/probcalc/s-range/srng_tbl.html

> alpha levels 0.10, 0.05, 0.01.
> $k = c$ = Number of levels of the factor (treatment).
>
> n = total number of observations
>
> $n - k$ = d.f. or $n - c$ = d.f.

F, Normal, t, Binomial, Poisson, Chi Square & Others

http://davidmlane.com/hyperstat/chi_square_table.html

> Alpha level is 0.10, 0.05, 0.25, 0.01, 0.001. d.f. = 1–100. Additionally there are to other links of interest.

> Java Script Calculations by John Pessuillo where you will find a calculator for Normal Distribution, Student's *t*, Chi Square, and the *F* (Fisher) Distribution.

> CGI Calculator by Jan de Leeuw. There is a complex matrix for many distributions. Included are the Normal distribution, Student's *t*, Exponential, Chi Square, *F*-distribution, Uniform, Binomial, Poisson, and Random Number Generators for Each.

http://www.itl.nist.gov/div898/handbook/

> Click on Tools and Aids

> Click on #7 Tables for Probability Distributions

> The following will be available:

> > #2 Which is the upper Critical Values for Student's t at alpha 0.10, 0.05, 0.025, 0.01, 0.005, 0.001.
> > #3 Which is Upper Critical Values for *F*-Distribution at alpha 0.10, 0.05, 0.01 with numerator d.f. 1–20 and denominator d.f. 1–100
> > #4 Which is Both the Upper and Lower Critical Values for Chi Square, d.f. = 1–100; alpha 0.10, 0.05, 0.025, 0.01, 0.001. Scroll down to find the lower values or click the links.

http://cse.niaes.affrc.go.jp/miwa/probcalc/s-range/srng_tbl.html

> *F*-table. alpha 0.10, 0.05, 0.01. *k* or *c* from 1–20, where *k* or c is the sample size in each level of the factor. d.f. $= n - k$ from 1 to 100, where *n* is the total observations.

http://www.statsoftinc.com/textbook/sttable.html

> *F* table for 0.10, 0.05, 0.25, 0.01; Chi Square, *t* distribution, Standard Normal *Z* distribution.

http://www.itl.nist.gov/div898/handbook/eda/section3/ede3674.html

> More Chi Square links.

Cumulative Binomial Distribution

http://www.stt.msu.edu/~melfi/stt231/probdist/discrete/binom/cdfT.html

> Copy this site into your browser. This will be very useful when you are working with Quality Control and the concept of Lot Acceptance.

> This site is interactive. Here "*K*" is what my chapter identifies as "*C*", which is the maximum number of defects possible before you reject the shipment. Here "*m*" is the sample size, which in my chapter is "*n*". Here "*p*" is "AQL" or "π" in my chapter. Values should be entered in decimal form, i.e. 0.05 for 5%.

> From my example in the chapter, plug into this form the sample size of $m = 50$ and $p = 0.05$. Hit submit and you will be given a cumulative binomial distribution which allows you to come down that column until you find the value that first exceeds .9900. Cross referring that value to *k* (*c*) you will find 7 as the value of defects possible before you reject the entire shipment.

Quality Control A_2, D_3, D_4 and Other Links

http://www.robertluttman.com/Stat_table1.html

Other Sites

Type into your browser the name "normal distribution, *t*-distribution, *F*-distribution, chi square distribution" or any other table or concept of interest to you and multiple options will popup. Many sites are interactive and contain java demonstrations. The internet sites listed about are just samples of the type of material available on the internet.

Table A: Normal Distribution Table (Z-Table One-Half Area Approach)

Table A   The Normal Distribution.

Z	0.00	0.01	0.02	0.03	0.04	0.05	0.06	0.07	0.08	0.09
0.0	0.0000	0.0040	0.0080	0.0120	0.0160	0.0199	0.0239	0.0279	0.0319	0.0359
0.1	0.0398	0.0438	0.0478	0.0517	0.0557	0.0596	0.0636	0.0675	0.0714	0.0753
0.2	0.0793	0.0832	0.0871	0.0910	0.0948	0.0987	0.1026	0.1064	0.1103	0.1141
0.3	0.1179	0.1217	0.1255	0.1293	0.1331	0.1368	0.1406	0.1443	0.1480	0.1517
0.4	0.1554	0.1591	0.1628	0.1664	0.1700	0.1736	0.1772	0.1808	0.1844	0.1879
0.5	0.1915	0.1950	0.1985	0.2019	0.2054	0.2088	0.2123	0.2157	0.2190	0.2224
0.6	0.2257	0.2291	0.2324	0.2357	0.2389	0.2422	0.2454	0.2486	0.2517	0.2549
0.7	0.2580	0.2611	0.2642	0.2673	0.2704	0.2734	0.2764	0.2794	0.2823	0.2852
0.8	0.2881	0.2910	0.2939	0.2967	0.2995	0.3023	0.3051	0.3078	0.3106	0.3133
0.9	0.3159	0.3186	0.3212	0.3238	0.3264	0.3289	0.3315	0.3340	0.3365	0.3389
1.0	0.3413	0.3438	0.3461	0.3485	0.3508	0.3531	0.3554	0.3577	0.3599	0.3621
1.1	0.3643	0.3665	0.3686	0.3708	0.3729	0.3749	0.3770	0.3790	0.3810	0.3830
1.2	0.3849	0.3869	0.3888	0.3907	0.3925	0.3944	0.3962	0.3980	0.3997	0.4015
1.3	0.4032	0.4049	0.4066	0.4082	0.4099	0.4115	0.4131	0.4147	0.4162	0.4177
1.4	0.4192	0.4207	0.4222	0.4236	0.4251	0.4265	0.4279	0.4292	0.4306	0.4319
1.5	0.4332	0.4345	0.4357	0.4370	0.4382	0.4394	0.4406	0.4418	0.4429	0.4441
1.6	0.4452	0.4463	0.4474	0.4484	0.4495	0.4505	0.4515	0.4525	0.4535	0.4545
1.7	0.4554	0.4564	0.4573	0.4582	0.4591	0.4599	0.4608	0.4616	0.4625	0.4633
1.8	0.4641	0.4649	0.4656	0.4664	0.4671	0.4678	0.4686	0.4693	0.4699	0.4706
1.9	0.4713	0.4719	0.4726	0.4732	0.4738	0.4744	0.4750	0.4756	0.4761	0.4767
2.0	0.4772	0.4778	0.4783	0.4788	0.4793	0.4798	0.4803	0.4808	0.4812	0.4817
2.1	0.4821	0.4826	0.4830	0.4834	0.4838	0.4842	0.4846	0.4850	0.4854	0.4857
2.2	0.4861	0.4864	0.4868	0.4871	0.4875	0.4878	0.4881	0.4884	0.4887	0.4890
2.3	0.4893	0.4896	0.4898	0.4901	0.4904	0.4906	0.4909	0.4911	0.4913	0.4916
2.4	0.4918	0.4920	0.4922	0.4925	0.4927	0.4929	0.4931	0.4932	0.4934	0.4936
2.5	0.4938	0.4940	0.4941	0.4943	0.4945	0.4946	0.4948	0.4949	0.4951	0.4952
2.6	0.4953	0.4955	0.4956	0.4957	0.4959	0.4960	0.4961	0.4962	0.4963	0.4964
2.7	0.4965	0.4966	0.4967	0.4968	0.4969	0.4970	0.4971	0.4972	0.4973	0.4974
2.8	0.4974	0.4975	0.4976	0.4977	0.4977	0.4978	0.4979	0.4979	0.4980	0.4981
2.9	0.4981	0.4982	0.4982	0.4983	0.4984	0.4984	0.4985	0.4985	0.4986	0.4986
3.0	0.4987	0.4987	0.4987	0.4988	0.4988	0.4989	0.4989	0.4989	0.4990	0.4990
3.1	0.4990	0.4991	0.4991	0.4991	0.4992	0.4992	0.4992	0.4992	0.4993	0.4993
3.2	0.4993	0.4993	0.4994	0.4994	0.4994	0.4994	0.4994	0.4995	0.4995	0.4995
3.3	0.4995	0.4995	0.4995	0.4996	0.4996	0.4996	0.4996	0.4996	0.4996	0.4997
3.4	0.4997	0.4997	0.4997	0.4997	0.4997	0.4997	0.4997	0.4997	0.4997	0.4998
3.5	0.4998	0.4998	0.4998	0.4998	0.4998	0.4998	0.4998	0.4998	0.4998	0.4998
3.6	0.4998	0.4998	0.4999	0.4999	0.4999	0.4999	0.4999	0.4999	0.4999	0.4999
3.7	0.4999	0.4999	0.4999	0.4999	0.4999	0.4999	0.4999	0.4999	0.4999	0.4999
3.8	0.4999	0.4999	0.4999	0.4999	0.4999	0.4999	0.4999	0.4999	0.4999	0.4999
3.9	0.5000	0.5000	0.5000	0.5000	0.5000	0.5000	0.5000	0.5000	0.5000	0.5000

Notice down the left hand side of the table is Z. Also across the top of the table is more Z. The Empirical Rule allowed us to move ± 1 or ± 2 or ± 3 standard deviations from the mean. Now you have the ability to expand the Empirical Rule to two decimal points. Now you can move ± 1.06 or ± 1.96 or ± 2.33 or ± 2.58 or ± 3.06 standard deviations from the mean. This left side is the first digit plus one decimal place. At the top of the table is the second decimal place. For example, you would find that Z = 1.06 would convert to a probability of 0.3554. This can be written as 35.54% or 0.3554. Find Z = 1.0 on the left side of the table. Now move to the right until you line up with the 0.06 at the top of the table (1.0 + 0.06 = 1.06). The intersection of these two points is the area under the curve (0.3554).

The body of the table is area under the curve which is probability. The edges are Z. The Z-formula converts the mean of any normal distribution to 0 with the measurement around it in standard deviations.

For a single sample ($n = 1$), the formula is $Z = \dfrac{X - \mu}{\sigma}$

For $n > 1$ when the sampling distribution of sample means is being used, there are two formulas which are mathematical equivalents. They are as follows:

$$Z = \frac{\overline{X} - \mu}{\sigma_{\overline{X}}} = Z = \frac{\overline{X} - \mu}{\dfrac{\sigma}{\sqrt{n}}} \text{ because } \sigma_{\overline{X}} = \frac{\sigma}{\sqrt{n}}$$

Look at the value in the body of the table that is at the very bottom right of the table. It is 0.5000. The table is only one-half of the area under the curve or 50%. You can use this one-half approach because the normal distribution is symmetrical with 50% falling to the left of the mean and 50% falling to the right of the mean.

You know if you are on the left or right of the mean because of the sign of Z. If either X or $\overline{X}$ is larger than μ, the sign of Z will be positive thus you are on the right of the mean. If either X or $\overline{X}$ is smaller than μ, the sign of Z will be negative thus you are on the left of the mean. Remember, you never add or subtract Z-value. You must first convert Z to a probability (P), then and only then, add or subtract probabilities to determine area under the curve.

The chapters on confidence intervals and hypothesis testing will show you the following formulas.

$$CI: \overline{X} \pm Z_\alpha \sigma_{\overline{X}} \text{ or } HT: \mu_H \pm Z_\alpha \sigma_{\overline{X}} \text{ for a two-tailed rejection region.}$$

For a left and right, tail rejection region, you would have a negative or positive sign which replaces the ± sign; however, you do not need this last piece of information for me to illustrate my point.

For either confidence intervals (CI) or hypothesis testing (HT), you need a Z value at a chosen alpha level. Here use of the table is essentially the same, but you will run into either interpolating or rounding issues. For example, if you wanted to determine a confidence interval at an alpha level of 0.10, you would divide alpha by 2 for 0.05, which would be the value in the each tail. Since I know the normal distribution is symmetrical, I know I can subtract 0.05 from 0.5000 (50%) and get 0.4500, which is the area under the curve between the middle of the distribution ($\overline{X}$) and the critical value which is determined by using the CI formula just above.

The quirky thing is you look up the 0.4500 in the body of the table, not on the edges. You are looking for Z but have area. You are moving from the center of the table to the edges of the table rather from the edges to the center. What makes this difficult is there is no 0.4500 shown in the body of the table.

What to do? What to do? What to do, you lament?

Don't panic. Solution: Find the value closest to the 0.4500. Go look. What you will find is 0.4500 falls directly between 0.4495 and 0.4505. This is between a Z-value of 1.64 and 1.65. You can call it 1.645 and be technically correct; however, most of the time rounding up will work just as well. The final Z value would, therefore, be 1.65. Rounding will not materially alter your conclusions.

One final word: The CI formula and the HT formulas just above should look somewhat familiar.

You are correct, you say. They seem to be the same formula as the Z-formula shown just above, but just solved for a different term.

You are correct, they are. Good observation.

These few comments should show you how to properly read the Z-table more effectively.

Table B: *t*-Distribution

Table B   The *t*-Distribution.

	Two-Tailed Test					
	0.200	0.100	0.050	0.020	0.010	α value
	0.800	0.900	0.950	0.980	0.990	CL
	One-Tailed Test					
	0.100	0.050	0.025	0.010	0.005	α value
	0.900	0.950	0.975	0.990	0.995	CL
d.f.	Values of *t*					
1	3.078	6.314	12.706	31.821	63.657	
2	1.886	2.920	4.303	6.965	9.925	
3	1.638	2.353	3.182	4.541	5.841	
4	1.533	2.132	2.776	3.747	4.604	
5	1.476	2.015	2.571	3.365	4.032	
6	1.440	1.943	2.447	3.143	3.707	
7	1.415	1.895	2.365	2.998	3.499	
8	1.397	1.860	2.306	2.896	3.355	
9	1.383	1.833	2.262	2.821	3.250	
10	1.372	1.812	2.228	2.764	3.169	
11	1.363	1.796	2.201	2.718	3.106	
12	1.356	1.782	2.179	2.681	3.055	
13	1.350	1.771	2.160	2.650	3.012	
14	1.345	1.761	2.145	2.624	2.977	
15	1.341	1.753	2.131	2.602	2.947	
16	1.337	1.746	2.120	2.583	2.921	
17	1.333	1.740	2.110	2.567	2.898	
18	1.330	1.734	2.101	2.552	2.878	
19	1.328	**1.729**	**2.093**	2.539	2.861	
20	1.325	1.725	2.086	2.528	2.845	
21	1.323	1.721	2.080	2.518	2.831	
22	1.321	1.717	2.074	2.508	2.819	
23	1.319	1.714	2.069	2.500	2.807	
24	1.318	1.711	2.064	2.492	2.797	
25	1.316	1.708	2.060	2.485	2.787	
26	1.315	1.706	2.056	2.479	2.779	
27	1.314	1.703	2.052	2.473	2.771	
28	1.313	1.701	2.048	2.467	2.763	

The t-value from this table is determined by knowing the degrees of freedom (d.f. which is $n - 1$). All confidence intervals are two-tailed tests. Hypothesis testing can take the form of a two-tailed or a one-tailed test depending on the form used. Looking up values are reasonably straight forward. First determine it you are using a two-tailed or a one-tailed test. Next determine the alpha value. Then read straight down the alpha value column and cross reference the degrees of freedom. The intersection of the d.f. and alpha cell is the t-value you use in confidence intervals and hypothesis testing.

The t-test is very similar to the Z-test. The formula is as follows:

$$t_{test} = \frac{\overline{X} - \mu}{\dfrac{S}{\sqrt{n}}}$$

The confidence interval formula is as follows:

$$\overline{X} \pm t_\alpha \frac{S}{\sqrt{n}}$$

The hypothesis testing formula is as follows:

$$\mu_H \pm t_\alpha \frac{S}{\sqrt{n}}$$

Notice the similarities between the Z-formulas and the t-formulas. In fact, the basic difference is using t-values versus Z-values.

The t-values will always be larger than the Z-values for the same alpha level. The theory is that since the sample size is smaller using a t-test, you compensate for the higher error by widening the interval.

Table C: Binomial Distribution

Table C   Binomial Distribution.

n	X	π 0.05	0.10	0.15	0.20	0.25	0.30	0.35	0.40	0.45	0.50
1	0	0.9500	0.9000	0.8500	0.8000	0.7500	0.7000	0.6500	0.6000	0.5500	0.5000
	1	0.0500	0.1000	0.1500	0.2000	0.2500	0.3000	0.3500	0.4000	0.4500	0.5000
2	0	0.9025	0.8100	0.7225	0.6400	0.5625	0.4900	0.4225	0.3600	0.3025	0.2500
	1	0.0950	0.1800	0.2550	0.3200	0.3750	0.4200	0.4550	0.4800	0.4950	0.5000
	2	0.0025	0.0100	0.0225	0.0400	0.0625	0.0900	0.1225	0.1600	0.2025	0.2500
3	0	0.8574	0.7290	0.6141	0.5120	0.4219	0.3430	0.2746	0.2160	0.1664	0.1250
	1	0.1354	0.2430	0.3251	0.3840	0.4219	0.4410	0.4436	0.4320	0.4084	0.3750
	2	0.0071	0.0270	0.0574	0.0960	0.1406	0.1890	0.2389	0.2880	0.3341	0.3750
	3	0.0001	0.0010	0.0034	0.0080	0.0156	0.0270	0.0429	0.0640	0.0911	0.1250
4	0	0.8145	0.6561	0.5220	0.4096	0.3164	0.2401	0.1785	0.1296	0.0915	0.0625
	1	0.1715	0.2916	0.3685	0.4096	0.4219	0.4116	0.3845	0.3456	0.2995	0.2500
	2	0.0135	0.0486	0.0975	0.1536	0.2109	0.2646	0.3105	0.3456	0.3675	0.3750
	3	0.0005	0.0036	0.0115	0.0256	0.0469	0.0756	0.1115	0.1536	0.2005	0.2500
	4	0.0000	0.0001	0.0005	0.0016	0.0039	0.0081	0.0150	0.0256	0.0410	0.0625
5	0	0.7738	0.5905	0.4437	0.3277	0.2373	0.1681	0.1160	0.0778	0.0503	0.0313
	1	0.2036	0.3281	0.3915	0.4096	0.3955	0.3602	0.3124	0.2592	0.2059	0.1563
	2	0.0214	0.0729	0.1382	0.2048	0.2637	0.3087	0.3364	0.3456	0.3369	0.3125
	3	0.0011	0.0081	0.0244	0.0512	0.0879	0.1323	0.1811	0.2304	0.2757	0.3125
	4	0.0000	0.0005	0.0022	0.0064	0.0146	0.0284	0.0488	0.0768	0.1128	0.1563
	5	0.0000	0.0000	0.0001	0.0003	0.0010	0.0024	0.0053	0.0102	0.0185	0.0313
6	0	0.7351	0.5314	0.3771	0.2621	0.1780	0.1176	0.0754	0.0467	0.0277	0.0156
	1	0.2321	0.3543	0.3993	0.3932	0.3560	0.3025	0.2437	0.1866	0.1359	0.0938
	2	0.0305	0.0984	0.1762	0.2458	0.2966	0.3241	0.3280	0.3110	0.2780	0.2344
	3	0.0021	0.0146	0.0415	0.0819	0.1318	0.1852	0.2355	0.2765	0.3032	0.3125
	4	0.0001	0.0012	0.0055	0.0154	0.0330	0.0595	0.0951	0.1382	0.1861	0.2344
	5	0.0000	0.0001	0.0004	0.0015	0.0044	0.0102	0.0205	0.0369	0.0609	0.0938
	6	0.0000	0.0000	0.0000	0.0001	0.0002	0.0007	0.0018	0.0041	0.0083	0.0156
7	0	0.6983	0.4783	0.3206	0.2097	0.1335	0.0824	0.0490	0.0280	0.0152	0.0078
	1	0.2573	0.3720	0.3960	0.3670	0.3115	0.2471	0.1848	0.1306	0.0872	0.0547
	2	0.0406	0.1240	0.2097	0.2753	0.3115	0.3177	0.2985	0.2613	0.2140	0.1641
	3	0.0036	0.0230	0.0617	0.1147	0.1730	0.2269	0.2679	0.2903	0.2918	0.2734
	4	0.0002	0.0026	0.0109	0.0287	0.0577	0.0972	0.1442	0.1935	0.2388	0.2734
	5	0.0000	0.0002	0.0012	0.0043	0.0115	0.0250	0.0466	0.0774	0.1172	0.1641
	6	0.0000	0.0000	0.0001	0.0004	0.0013	0.0036	0.0084	0.0172	0.0320	0.0547
	7	0.0000	0.0000	0.0000	0.0000	0.0001	0.0002	0.0006	0.0016	0.0037	0.0078

(Continued)

Table C   Binomial Distribution *(Continued).*

n	X	0.05	0.10	0.15	0.20	0.25	0.30	0.35	0.40	0.45	0.50
8	0	0.6634	0.4305	0.2725	0.1678	0.1001	0.0576	0.0319	0.0168	0.0084	0.0039
	1	0.2793	0.3826	0.3847	0.3355	0.2670	0.1977	0.1373	0.0896	0.0548	0.0313
	2	0.0515	0.1488	0.2376	0.2936	0.3115	0.2965	0.2587	0.2090	0.1569	0.1094
	3	0.0054	0.0331	0.0839	0.1468	0.2076	0.2541	0.2786	0.2787	0.2568	0.2188
	4	0.0004	0.0046	0.0185	0.0459	0.0865	0.1361	0.1875	0.2322	0.2627	0.2734
	5	0.0000	0.0004	0.0026	0.0092	0.0231	0.0467	0.0808	0.1239	0.1719	0.2188
	6	0.0000	0.0000	0.0002	0.0011	0.0038	0.0100	0.0217	0.0413	0.0703	0.1094
	7	0.0000	0.0000	0.0000	0.0001	0.0004	0.0012	0.0033	0.0079	0.0164	0.0313
	8	0.0000	0.0000	0.0000	0.0000	0.0000	0.0001	0.0002	0.0007	0.0017	0.0039
9	0	0.6302	0.3874	0.2316	0.1342	0.0751	0.0404	0.0207	0.0101	0.0046	0.0020
	1	0.2985	0.3874	0.3679	0.3020	0.2253	0.1556	0.1004	0.0605	0.0339	0.0176
	2	0.0629	0.1722	0.2597	0.3020	0.3003	0.2668	0.2162	0.1612	0.1110	0.0703
	3	0.0077	0.0446	0.1069	0.1762	0.2336	0.2668	0.2716	0.2508	0.2119	0.1641
	4	0.0006	0.0074	0.0283	0.0661	0.1168	0.1715	0.2194	0.2508	0.2600	0.2461
	5	0.0000	0.0008	0.0050	0.0165	0.0389	0.0735	0.1181	0.1672	0.2128	0.2461
	6	0.0000	0.0001	0.0006	0.0028	0.0087	0.0210	0.0424	0.0743	0.1160	0.1641
	7	0.0000	0.0000	0.0000	0.0003	0.0012	0.0039	0.0098	0.0212	0.0407	0.0703
	8	0.0000	0.0000	0.0000	0.0000	0.0001	0.0004	0.0013	0.0035	0.0083	0.0176
	9	0.0000	0.0000	0.0000	0.0000	0.0000	0.0000	0.0001	0.0003	0.0008	0.0020
10	0	0.5987	0.3487	0.1969	0.1074	0.0563	0.0282	0.0135	0.0060	0.0025	0.0010
	1	0.3151	0.3874	0.3474	0.2684	0.1877	0.1211	0.0725	0.0403	0.0207	0.0098
	2	0.0746	0.1937	0.2759	0.3020	0.2816	0.2335	0.1757	0.1209	0.0763	0.0439
	3	0.0105	0.0574	0.1298	0.2013	0.2503	0.2668	0.2522	0.2150	0.1665	0.1172
	4	0.0010	0.0112	0.0401	0.0881	0.1460	0.2001	0.2377	0.2508	0.2384	0.2051
	5	0.0001	0.0015	0.0085	0.0264	0.0584	0.1029	0.1536	0.2007	0.2340	0.2461
	6	0.0000	0.0001	0.0012	0.0055	0.0162	0.0368	0.0689	0.1115	0.1596	0.2051
	7	0.0000	0.0000	0.0001	0.0008	0.0031	0.0090	0.0212	0.0425	0.0746	0.1172
	8	0.0000	0.0000	0.0000	0.0001	0.0004	0.0014	0.0043	0.0106	0.0229	0.0439
	9	0.0000	0.0000	0.0000	0.0000	0.0000	0.0001	0.0005	0.0016	0.0042	0.0098
	10	0.0000	0.0000	0.0000	0.0000	0.0000	0.0000	0.0000	0.0001	0.0003	0.0010

(Continued)

Table C   Binomial Distribution *(Continued)*.

n	X	0.05	0.10	0.15	0.20	0.25	0.30	0.35	0.40	0.45	0.50
11	0	0.5688	0.3138	0.1673	0.0859	0.0422	0.0198	0.0088	0.0036	0.0014	0.0005
	1	0.3293	0.3835	0.3248	0.2362	0.1549	0.0932	0.0518	0.0266	0.0125	0.0054
	2	0.0867	0.2131	0.2866	0.2953	0.2581	0.1998	0.1395	0.0887	0.0513	0.0269
	3	0.0137	0.0710	0.1517	0.2215	0.2581	0.2568	0.2254	0.1774	0.1259	0.0806
	4	0.0014	0.0158	0.0536	0.1107	0.1721	0.2201	0.2428	0.2365	0.2060	0.1611
	5	0.0001	0.0025	0.0132	0.0388	0.0803	0.1321	0.1830	0.2207	0.2360	0.2256
	6	0.0000	0.0003	0.0023	0.0097	0.0268	0.0566	0.0985	0.1471	0.1931	0.2256
	7	0.0000	0.0000	0.0003	0.0017	0.0064	0.0173	0.0379	0.0701	0.1128	0.1611
	8	0.0000	0.0000	0.0000	0.0002	0.0011	0.0037	0.0102	0.0234	0.0462	0.0806
	9	0.0000	0.0000	0.0000	0.0000	0.0001	0.0005	0.0018	0.0052	0.0126	0.0269
	10	0.0000	0.0000	0.0000	0.0000	0.0000	0.0000	0.0002	0.0007	0.0021	0.0054
	11	0.0000	0.0000	0.0000	0.0000	0.0000	0.0000	0.0000	0.0000	0.0002	0.0005
12	0	0.5404	0.2824	0.1422	0.0687	0.0317	0.0138	0.0057	0.0022	0.0008	0.0002
	1	0.3413	0.3766	0.3012	0.2062	0.1267	0.0712	0.0368	0.0174	0.0075	0.0029
	2	0.0988	0.2301	0.2924	0.2835	0.2323	0.1678	0.1088	0.0639	0.0339	0.0161
	3	0.0173	0.0852	0.1720	0.2362	0.2581	0.2397	0.1954	0.1419	0.0923	0.0537
	4	0.0021	0.0213	0.0683	0.1329	0.1936	0.2311	0.2367	0.2128	0.1700	0.1208
	5	0.0002	0.0038	0.0193	0.0532	0.1032	0.1585	0.2039	0.2270	0.2225	0.1934
	6	0.0000	0.0005	0.0040	0.0155	0.0401	0.0792	0.1281	0.1766	0.2124	0.2256
	7	0.0000	0.0000	0.0006	0.0033	0.0115	0.0291	0.0591	0.1009	0.1489	0.1934
	8	0.0000	0.0000	0.0001	0.0005	0.0024	0.0078	0.0199	0.0420	0.0762	0.1208
	9	0.0000	0.0000	0.0000	0.0001	0.0004	0.0015	0.0048	0.0125	0.0277	0.0537
	10	0.0000	0.0000	0.0000	0.0000	0.0000	0.0002	0.0008	0.0025	0.0068	0.0161
	11	0.0000	0.0000	0.0000	0.0000	0.0000	0.0000	0.0001	0.0003	0.0010	0.0029
	12	0.0000	0.0000	0.0000	0.0000	0.0000	0.0000	0.0000	0.0000	0.0001	0.0002
13	0	0.5133	0.2542	0.1209	0.0550	0.0238	0.0097	0.0037	0.0013	0.0004	0.0001
	1	0.3512	0.3672	0.2774	0.1787	0.1029	0.0540	0.0259	0.0113	0.0045	0.0016
	2	0.1109	0.2448	0.2937	0.2680	0.2059	0.1388	0.0836	0.0453	0.0220	0.0095
	3	0.0214	0.0997	0.1900	0.2457	0.2517	0.2181	0.1651	0.1107	0.0660	0.0349
	4	0.0028	0.0277	0.0838	0.1535	0.2097	0.2337	0.2222	0.1845	0.1350	0.0873
	5	0.0003	0.0055	0.0266	0.0691	0.1258	0.1803	0.2154	0.2214	0.1989	0.1571
	6	0.0000	0.0008	0.0063	0.0230	0.0559	0.1030	0.1546	0.1968	0.2169	0.2095
	7	0.0000	0.0001	0.0011	0.0058	0.0186	0.0442	0.0833	0.1312	0.1775	0.2095
	8	0.0000	0.0000	0.0001	0.0011	0.0047	0.0142	0.0336	0.0656	0.1089	0.1571
	9	0.0000	0.0000	0.0000	0.0001	0.0009	0.0034	0.0101	0.0243	0.0495	0.0873
	10	0.0000	0.0000	0.0000	0.0000	0.0001	0.0006	0.0022	0.0065	0.0162	0.0349
	11	0.0000	0.0000	0.0000	0.0000	0.0000	0.0001	0.0003	0.0012	0.0036	0.0095
	12	0.0000	0.0000	0.0000	0.0000	0.0000	0.0000	0.0000	0.0001	0.0005	0.0016
	13	0.0000	0.0000	0.0000	0.0000	0.0000	0.0000	0.0000	0.0000	0.0000	0.0001

(Continued)

Table C Binomial Distribution *(Continued)*.

n	X	0.05	0.10	0.15	0.20	0.25	0.30	0.35	0.40	0.45	0.50
14	0	0.4877	0.2288	0.1028	0.0440	0.0178	0.0068	0.0024	0.0008	0.0002	0.0001
	1	0.3593	0.3559	0.2539	0.1539	0.0832	0.0407	0.0181	0.0073	0.0027	0.0009
	2	0.1229	0.2570	0.2912	0.2501	0.1802	0.1134	0.0634	0.0317	0.0141	0.0056
	3	0.0259	0.1142	0.2056	0.2501	0.2402	0.1943	0.1366	0.0845	0.0462	0.0222
	4	0.0037	0.0349	0.0998	0.1720	0.2202	0.2290	0.2022	0.1549	0.1040	0.0611
	5	0.0004	0.0078	0.0352	0.0860	0.1468	0.1963	0.2178	0.2066	0.1701	0.1222
	6	0.0000	0.0013	0.0093	0.0322	0.0734	0.1262	0.1759	0.2066	0.2088	0.1833
	7	0.0000	0.0002	0.0019	0.0092	0.0280	0.0618	0.1082	0.1574	0.1952	0.2095
	8	0.0000	0.0000	0.0003	0.0020	0.0082	0.0232	0.0510	0.0918	0.1398	0.1833
	9	0.0000	0.0000	0.0000	0.0003	0.0018	0.0066	0.0183	0.0408	0.0762	0.1222
	10	0.0000	0.0000	0.0000	0.0000	0.0003	0.0014	0.0049	0.0136	0.0312	0.0611
	11	0.0000	0.0000	0.0000	0.0000	0.0000	0.0002	0.0010	0.0033	0.0093	0.0222
	12	0.0000	0.0000	0.0000	0.0000	0.0000	0.0000	0.0001	0.0005	0.0019	0.0056
	13	0.0000	0.0000	0.0000	0.0000	0.0000	0.0000	0.0000	0.0001	0.0002	0.0009
	14	0.0000	0.0000	0.0000	0.0000	0.0000	0.0000	0.0000	0.0000	0.0000	0.0001
15	0	0.4633	0.2059	0.0874	0.0352	0.0134	0.0047	0.0016	0.0005	0.0001	0.0000
	1	0.3658	0.3432	0.2312	0.1319	0.0668	0.0305	0.0126	0.0047	0.0016	0.0005
	2	0.1348	0.2669	0.2856	0.2309	0.1559	0.0916	0.0476	0.0219	0.0090	0.0032
	3	0.0307	0.1285	0.2184	0.2501	0.2252	0.1700	0.1110	0.0634	0.0318	0.0139
	4	0.0049	0.0428	0.1156	0.1876	0.2252	0.2186	0.1792	0.1268	0.0780	0.0417
	5	0.0006	0.0105	0.0449	0.1032	0.1651	0.2061	0.2123	0.1859	0.1404	0.0916
	6	0.0000	0.0019	0.0132	0.0430	0.0917	0.1472	0.1906	0.2066	0.1914	0.1527
	7	0.0000	0.0003	0.0030	0.0138	0.0393	0.0811	0.1319	0.1771	0.2013	0.1964
	8	0.0000	0.0000	0.0005	0.0035	0.0131	0.0348	0.0710	0.1181	0.1647	0.1964
	9	0.0000	0.0000	0.0001	0.0007	0.0034	0.0116	0.0298	0.0612	0.1048	0.1527
	10	0.0000	0.0000	0.0000	0.0001	0.0007	0.0030	0.0096	0.0245	0.0515	0.0916
	11	0.0000	0.0000	0.0000	0.0000	0.0001	0.0006	0.0024	0.0074	0.0191	0.0417
	12	0.0000	0.0000	0.0000	0.0000	0.0000	0.0001	0.0004	0.0016	0.0052	0.0139
	13	0.0000	0.0000	0.0000	0.0000	0.0000	0.0000	0.0001	0.0003	0.0010	0.0032
	14	0.0000	0.0000	0.0000	0.0000	0.0000	0.0000	0.0000	0.0000	0.0001	0.0005
	15	0.0000	0.0000	0.0000	0.0000	0.0000	0.0000	0.0000	0.0000	0.0000	0.0000

The column headers span under *π*.

(Continued)

Table C   Binomial Distribution *(Continued)*.

						π					
n	X	0.05	0.10	0.15	0.20	0.25	0.30	0.35	0.40	0.45	0.50
16	0	0.4401	0.1853	0.0743	0.0281	0.0100	0.0033	0.0010	0.0003	0.0001	0.0000
	1	0.3706	0.3294	0.2097	0.1126	0.0535	0.0228	0.0087	0.0030	0.0009	0.0002
	2	0.1463	0.2745	0.2775	0.2111	0.1336	0.0732	0.0353	0.0150	0.0056	0.0018
	3	0.0359	0.1423	0.2285	0.2463	0.2079	0.1465	0.0888	0.0468	0.0215	0.0085
	4	0.0061	0.0514	0.1311	0.2001	0.2252	0.2040	0.1553	0.1014	0.0572	0.0278
	5	0.0008	0.0137	0.0555	0.1201	0.1802	0.2099	0.2008	0.1623	0.1123	0.0667
	6	0.0001	0.0028	0.0180	0.0550	0.1101	0.1649	0.1982	0.1983	0.1684	0.1222
	7	0.0000	0.0004	0.0045	0.0197	0.0524	0.1010	0.1524	0.1889	0.1969	0.1746
	8	0.0000	0.0001	0.0009	0.0055	0.0197	0.0487	0.0923	0.1417	0.1812	0.1964
	9	0.0000	0.0000	0.0001	0.0012	0.0058	0.0185	0.0442	0.0840	0.1318	0.1746
	10	0.0000	0.0000	0.0000	0.0002	0.0014	0.0056	0.0167	0.0392	0.0755	0.1222
	11	0.0000	0.0000	0.0000	0.0000	0.0002	0.0013	0.0049	0.0142	0.0337	0.0667
	12	0.0000	0.0000	0.0000	0.0000	0.0000	0.0002	0.0011	0.0040	0.0115	0.0278
	13	0.0000	0.0000	0.0000	0.0000	0.0000	0.0000	0.0002	0.0008	0.0029	0.0085
	14	0.0000	0.0000	0.0000	0.0000	0.0000	0.0000	0.0000	0.0001	0.0005	0.0018
	15	0.0000	0.0000	0.0000	0.0000	0.0000	0.0000	0.0000	0.0000	0.0001	0.0002
	16	0.0000	0.0000	0.0000	0.0000	0.0000	0.0000	0.0000	0.0000	0.0000	0.0000
17	0	0.4181	0.1668	0.0631	0.0225	0.0075	0.0023	0.0007	0.0002	0.0000	0.0000
	1	0.3741	0.3150	0.1893	0.0957	0.0426	0.0169	0.0060	0.0019	0.0005	0.0001
	2	0.1575	0.2800	0.2673	0.1914	0.1136	0.0581	0.0260	0.0102	0.0035	0.0010
	3	0.0415	0.1556	0.2359	0.2393	0.1893	0.1245	0.0701	0.0341	0.0144	0.0052
	4	0.0076	0.0605	0.1457	0.2093	0.2209	0.1868	0.1320	0.0796	0.0411	0.0182
	5	0.0010	0.0175	0.0668	0.1361	0.1914	0.2081	0.1849	0.1379	0.0875	0.0472
	6	0.0001	0.0039	0.0236	0.0680	0.1276	0.1784	0.1991	0.1839	0.1432	0.0944
	7	0.0000	0.0007	0.0065	0.0267	0.0668	0.1201	0.1685	0.1927	0.1841	0.1484
	8	0.0000	0.0001	0.0014	0.0084	0.0279	0.0644	0.1134	0.1606	0.1883	0.1855
	9	0.0000	0.0000	0.0003	0.0021	0.0093	0.0276	0.0611	0.1070	0.1540	0.1855
	10	0.0000	0.0000	0.0000	0.0004	0.0025	0.0095	0.0263	0.0571	0.1008	0.1484
	11	0.0000	0.0000	0.0000	0.0001	0.0005	0.0026	0.0090	0.0242	0.0525	0.0944
	12	0.0000	0.0000	0.0000	0.0000	0.0001	0.0006	0.0024	0.0081	0.0215	0.0472
	13	0.0000	0.0000	0.0000	0.0000	0.0000	0.0001	0.0005	0.0021	0.0068	0.0182
	14	0.0000	0.0000	0.0000	0.0000	0.0000	0.0000	0.0001	0.0004	0.0016	0.0052
	15	0.0000	0.0000	0.0000	0.0000	0.0000	0.0000	0.0000	0.0001	0.0003	0.0010
	16	0.0000	0.0000	0.0000	0.0000	0.0000	0.0000	0.0000	0.0000	0.0000	0.0001
	17	0.0000	0.0000	0.0000	0.0000	0.0000	0.0000	0.0000	0.0000	0.0000	0.0000

(Continued)

Table C   Binomial Distribution *(Continued)*.

n	X	0.05	0.10	0.15	0.20	0.25	0.30	0.35	0.40	0.45	0.50
18	0	0.3972	0.1501	0.0536	0.0180	0.0056	0.0016	0.0004	0.0001	0.0000	0.0000
	1	0.3763	0.3002	0.1704	0.0811	0.0338	0.0126	0.0042	0.0012	0.0003	0.0001
	2	0.1683	0.2835	0.2556	0.1723	0.0958	0.0458	0.0190	0.0069	0.0022	0.0006
	3	0.0473	0.1680	0.2406	0.2297	0.1704	0.1046	0.0547	0.0246	0.0095	0.0031
	4	0.0093	0.0700	0.1592	0.2153	0.2130	0.1681	0.1104	0.0614	0.0291	0.0117
	5	0.0014	0.0218	0.0787	0.1507	0.1988	0.2017	0.1664	0.1146	0.0666	0.0327
	6	0.0002	0.0052	0.0301	0.0816	0.1436	0.1873	0.1941	0.1655	0.1181	0.0708
	7	0.0000	0.0010	0.0091	0.0350	0.0820	0.1376	0.1792	0.1892	0.1657	0.1214
	8	0.0000	0.0002	0.0022	0.0120	0.0376	0.0811	0.1327	0.1734	0.1864	0.1669
	9	0.0000	0.0000	0.0004	0.0033	0.0139	0.0386	0.0794	0.1284	0.1694	0.1855
	10	0.0000	0.0000	0.0001	0.0008	0.0042	0.0149	0.0385	0.0771	0.1248	0.1669
	11	0.0000	0.0000	0.0000	0.0001	0.0010	0.0046	0.0151	0.0374	0.0742	0.1214
	12	0.0000	0.0000	0.0000	0.0000	0.0002	0.0012	0.0047	0.0145	0.0354	0.0708
	13	0.0000	0.0000	0.0000	0.0000	0.0000	0.0002	0.0012	0.0045	0.0134	0.0327
	14	0.0000	0.0000	0.0000	0.0000	0.0000	0.0000	0.0002	0.0011	0.0039	0.0117
	15	0.0000	0.0000	0.0000	0.0000	0.0000	0.0000	0.0000	0.0002	0.0009	0.0031
	16	0.0000	0.0000	0.0000	0.0000	0.0000	0.0000	0.0000	0.0000	0.0001	0.0006
	17	0.0000	0.0000	0.0000	0.0000	0.0000	0.0000	0.0000	0.0000	0.0000	0.0001
	18	0.0000	0.0000	0.0000	0.0000	0.0000	0.0000	0.0000	0.0000	0.0000	0.0000
19	0	0.3774	0.1351	0.0456	0.0144	0.0042	0.0011	0.0003	0.0001	0.0000	0.0000
	1	0.3774	0.2852	0.1529	0.0685	0.0268	0.0093	0.0029	0.0008	0.0002	0.0000
	2	0.1787	0.2852	0.2428	0.1540	0.0803	0.0358	0.0138	0.0046	0.0013	0.0003
	3	0.0533	0.1796	0.2428	0.2182	0.1517	0.0869	0.0422	0.0175	0.0062	0.0018
	4	0.0112	0.0798	0.1714	0.2182	0.2023	0.1491	0.0909	0.0467	0.0203	0.0074
	5	0.0018	0.0266	0.0907	0.1636	0.2023	0.1916	0.1468	0.0933	0.0497	0.0222
	6	0.0002	0.0069	0.0374	0.0955	0.1574	0.1916	0.1844	0.1451	0.0949	0.0518
	7	0.0000	0.0014	0.0122	0.0443	0.0974	0.1525	0.1844	0.1797	0.1443	0.0961
	8	0.0000	0.0002	0.0032	0.0166	0.0487	0.0981	0.1489	0.1797	0.1771	0.1442
	9	0.0000	0.0000	0.0007	0.0051	0.0198	0.0514	0.0980	0.1464	0.1771	0.1762
	10	0.0000	0.0000	0.0001	0.0013	0.0066	0.0220	0.0528	0.0976	0.1449	0.1762
	11	0.0000	0.0000	0.0000	0.0003	0.0018	0.0077	0.0233	0.0532	0.0970	0.1442
	12	0.0000	0.0000	0.0000	0.0000	0.0004	0.0022	0.0083	0.0237	0.0529	0.0961
	13	0.0000	0.0000	0.0000	0.0000	0.0001	0.0005	0.0024	0.0085	0.0233	0.0518
	14	0.0000	0.0000	0.0000	0.0000	0.0000	0.0001	0.0006	0.0024	0.0082	0.0222
	15	0.0000	0.0000	0.0000	0.0000	0.0000	0.0000	0.0001	0.0005	0.0022	0.0074
	16	0.0000	0.0000	0.0000	0.0000	0.0000	0.0000	0.0000	0.0001	0.0005	0.0018
	17	0.0000	0.0000	0.0000	0.0000	0.0000	0.0000	0.0000	0.0000	0.0001	0.0003
	18	0.0000	0.0000	0.0000	0.0000	0.0000	0.0000	0.0000	0.0000	0.0000	0.0000
	19	0.0000	0.0000	0.0000	0.0000	0.0000	0.0000	0.0000	0.0000	0.0000	0.0000
20	0	0.3585	0.1216	0.0388	0.0115	0.0032	0.0008	0.0002	0.0000	0.0000	0.0000
	1	0.3774	0.2702	0.1368	0.0576	0.0211	0.0068	0.0020	0.0005	0.0001	0.0000
	2	0.1887	0.2852	0.2293	0.1369	0.0669	0.0278	0.0100	0.0031	0.0008	0.0002
	3	0.0596	0.1901	0.2428	0.2054	0.1339	0.0716	0.0323	0.0123	0.0040	0.0011
	4	0.0133	0.0898	0.1821	0.2182	0.1897	0.1304	0.0738	0.0350	0.0139	0.0046

(Continued)

Table C Binomial Distribution *(Continued)*.

						π					
n	X	0.05	0.10	0.15	0.20	0.25	0.30	0.35	0.40	0.45	0.50
20	5	0.0022	0.0319	0.1028	0.1746	0.2023	0.1789	0.1272	0.0746	0.0365	0.0148
	6	0.0003	0.0089	0.0454	0.1091	0.1686	0.1916	0.1712	0.1244	0.0746	0.0370
	7	0.0000	0.0020	0.0160	0.0545	0.1124	0.1643	0.1844	0.1659	0.1221	0.0739
	8	0.0000	0.0004	0.0046	0.0222	0.0609	0.1144	0.1614	0.1797	0.1623	0.1201
	9	0.0000	0.0001	0.0011	0.0074	0.0271	0.0654	0.1158	0.1597	0.1771	0.1602
	10	0.0000	0.0000	0.0002	0.0020	0.0099	0.0308	0.0686	0.1171	0.1593	0.1762
	11	0.0000	0.0000	0.0000	0.0005	0.0030	0.0120	0.0336	0.0710	0.1185	0.1602
	12	0.0000	0.0000	0.0000	0.0001	0.0008	0.0039	0.0136	0.0355	0.0727	0.1201
	13	0.0000	0.0000	0.0000	0.0000	0.0002	0.0010	0.0045	0.0146	0.0366	0.0739
	14	0.0000	0.0000	0.0000	0.0000	0.0000	0.0002	0.0012	0.0049	0.0150	0.0370
	15	0.0000	0.0000	0.0000	0.0000	0.0000	0.0000	0.0003	0.0013	0.0049	0.0148
	16	0.0000	0.0000	0.0000	0.0000	0.0000	0.0000	0.0000	0.0003	0.0013	0.0046
	17	0.0000	0.0000	0.0000	0.0000	0.0000	0.0000	0.0000	0.0000	0.0002	0.0011
	18	0.0000	0.0000	0.0000	0.0000	0.0000	0.0000	0.0000	0.0000	0.0000	0.0002
	19	0.0000	0.0000	0.0000	0.0000	0.0000	0.0000	0.0000	0.0000	0.0000	0.0000
	20	0.0000	0.0000	0.0000	0.0000	0.0000	0.0000	0.0000	0.0000	0.0000	0.0000

To work with the binomial distribution, you need to know a value of n, X and π. Binomial distributions are exact probabilities. Assuming sales calls of 20 and a probability of success (π) of 0.10, what is the probability of exactly 5 sales? Said differently: What is the probability of exactly 5 sales in 20 attempts given a probability of success on any one attempt of 10%? There is a formula which can make this calculation as well as using the Excel function, but when the values of interest are in the table, it is much easier to find them in the binomial table.

Using the binomial table, look up the exact probability. First, find $n = 20$. Next find the alpha level of 0.10. Now following the π value (10%) down the column and cross reference it to X (which is 5 here). The intersection shows a probability of 0.0319 or 3.19% chance of exactly five sales in 20 attempts with a probability of success on any one attempt of 10%.

Also notice something very important about the binomial distribution. Look at $n = 20$. Now look to the X column. What value is shown? $X = 1$, but as you follow the column notice it also reflects a value for $X = 2, 3, 4, 5, 6$, etc. up to 20. Beside each of those values is a probability. The total of the each of the π columns will be 1.0000, so this is obviously the sample space. Knowing the sample space enables me to answer most all questions about this distribution. For example, if I said, what is the probability of 3 or fewer sales given the same information from above. The correct answer would include the sum of the probabilities for 0, 1, 2, and 3, which would be $0.1216 + 0.2702 + 0.2852 + 0.1901 = 86.71\%$ or 0.8617 probability. The point is that I cannot ask you a question that you cannot answer since you have captured the sample space. Knowing the sample space will help determine any combination of probabilities.

Table D: Cumulative Binomial Table

Table D   Cumulative Binomial distribution.

n	X						π					
		0.01	0.05	0.10	0.15	0.20	0.25	0.30	0.35	0.40	0.45	0.50
20	0	0.8179	0.3585	0.1216	0.0388	0.0115	0.0032	0.0008	0.0002	0.0000	0.0000	0.0000
	1	0.9831	0.7358	0.3917	0.1756	0.0692	0.0243	0.0076	0.0021	0.0005	0.0001	0.0000
	2	0.9990	0.9245	0.6769	0.4049	0.2061	0.0913	0.0355	0.0121	0.0036	0.0009	0.0002
	3	1.0000	0.9841	0.8670	0.6477	0.4114	0.2252	0.1071	0.0444	0.0160	0.0049	0.0013
	4	1.0000	0.9974	0.9568	0.8298	0.6296	0.4148	0.2375	0.1182	0.0510	0.0189	0.0059
	5	1.0000	0.9997	0.9887	0.9327	0.8042	0.6172	0.4164	0.2454	0.1256	0.0553	0.0207
	6	1.0000	1.0000	0.9976	0.9781	0.9133	0.7858	0.6080	0.4166	0.2500	0.1299	0.0577
	7	1.0000	1.0000	0.9996	0.9941	0.9679	0.8982	0.7723	0.6010	0.4159	0.2520	0.1316
	8	1.0000	1.0000	0.9999	0.9987	0.9900	0.9591	0.8867	0.7624	0.5956	0.4143	0.2517
	9	1.0000	1.0000	1.0000	0.9998	0.9974	0.9861	0.9520	0.8782	0.7553	0.5914	0.4119
	10	1.0000	1.0000	1.0000	1.0000	0.9994	0.9961	0.9829	0.9468	0.8725	0.7507	0.5881
	11	1.0000	1.0000	1.0000	1.0000	0.9999	0.9991	0.9949	0.9804	0.9435	0.8692	0.7483
	12	1.0000	1.0000	1.0000	1.0000	1.0000	0.9998	0.9987	0.9940	0.9790	0.9420	0.8684
	13	1.0000	1.0000	1.0000	1.0000	1.0000	1.0000	0.9997	0.9985	0.9935	0.9786	0.9423
	14	1.0000	1.0000	1.0000	1.0000	1.0000	1.0000	1.0000	0.9997	0.9984	0.9936	0.9793
	15	1.0000	1.0000	1.0000	1.0000	1.0000	1.0000	1.0000	1.0000	0.9997	0.9985	0.9941
	16	1.0000	1.0000	1.0000	1.0000	1.0000	1.0000	1.0000	1.0000	1.0000	0.9997	0.9987
	17	1.0000	1.0000	1.0000	1.0000	1.0000	1.0000	1.0000	1.0000	1.0000	1.0000	0.9998
	18	1.0000	1.0000	1.0000	1.0000	1.0000	1.0000	1.0000	1.0000	1.0000	1.0000	1.0000
21	0	0.8097	0.3406	0.1094	0.0329	0.0092	0.0024	0.0006	0.0001	0.0000	0.0000	0.0000
	1	0.9815	0.7170	0.3647	0.1550	0.0576	0.0190	0.0056	0.0014	0.0003	0.0001	0.0000
	2	0.9988	0.9151	0.6484	0.3705	0.1787	0.0745	0.0271	0.0086	0.0024	0.0006	0.0001
	3	0.9999	0.9811	0.8480	0.6113	0.3704	0.1917	0.0856	0.0331	0.0110	0.0031	0.0007
	4	1.0000	0.9968	0.9478	0.8025	0.5860	0.3674	0.1984	0.0924	0.0370	0.0126	0.0036
	5	1.0000	0.9996	0.9856	0.9173	0.7693	0.5666	0.3627	0.2009	0.0957	0.0389	0.0133
	6	1.0000	1.0000	0.9967	0.9713	0.8915	0.7436	0.5505	0.3567	0.2002	0.0964	0.0392
	7	1.0000	1.0000	0.9994	0.9917	0.9569	0.8701	0.7230	0.5365	0.3495	0.1971	0.0946
	8	1.0000	1.0000	0.9999	0.9980	0.9856	0.9439	0.8523	0.7059	0.5237	0.3413	0.1917
	9	1.0000	1.0000	1.0000	0.9996	0.9959	0.9794	0.9324	0.8377	0.6914	0.5117	0.3318
	10	1.0000	1.0000	1.0000	0.9999	0.9990	0.9936	0.9736	0.9228	0.8256	0.6790	0.5000
	11	1.0000	1.0000	1.0000	1.0000	0.9998	0.9983	0.9913	0.9687	0.9151	0.8159	0.6682
	12	1.0000	1.0000	1.0000	1.0000	1.0000	0.9996	0.9976	0.9892	0.9648	0.9092	0.8083
	13	1.0000	1.0000	1.0000	1.0000	1.0000	0.9999	0.9994	0.9969	0.9877	0.9621	0.9054
	14	1.0000	1.0000	1.0000	1.0000	1.0000	1.0000	0.9999	0.9993	0.9964	0.9868	0.9608
	15	1.0000	1.0000	1.0000	1.0000	1.0000	1.0000	1.0000	0.9999	0.9992	0.9963	0.9867
	16	1.0000	1.0000	1.0000	1.0000	1.0000	1.0000	1.0000	1.0000	0.9998	0.9992	0.9964
	17	1.0000	1.0000	1.0000	1.0000	1.0000	1.0000	1.0000	1.0000	1.0000	0.9999	0.9993
	18	1.0000	1.0000	1.0000	1.0000	1.0000	1.0000	1.0000	1.0000	1.0000	1.0000	0.9999
	19	1.0000	1.0000	1.0000	1.0000	1.0000	1.0000	1.0000	1.0000	1.0000	1.0000	1.0000

(Continued)

Table D   Cumulative Binomial distribution *(Continued)*.

							π					
n	X	0.01	0.05	0.10	0.15	0.20	0.25	0.30	0.35	0.40	0.45	0.50
22	0	0.8016	0.3235	0.0985	0.0280	0.0074	0.0018	0.0004	0.0001	0.0000	0.0000	0.0000
	1	0.9798	0.6982	0.3392	0.1367	0.0480	0.0149	0.0041	0.0010	0.0002	0.0000	0.0000
	2	0.9987	0.9052	0.6200	0.3382	0.1545	0.0606	0.0207	0.0061	0.0016	0.0003	0.0001
	3	0.9999	0.9778	0.8281	0.5752	0.3320	0.1624	0.0681	0.0245	0.0076	0.0020	0.0004
	4	1.0000	0.9960	0.9379	0.7738	0.5429	0.3235	0.1645	0.0716	0.0266	0.0083	0.0022
	5	1.0000	0.9994	0.9818	0.9001	0.7326	0.5168	0.3134	0.1629	0.0722	0.0271	0.0085
	6	1.0000	0.9999	0.9956	0.9632	0.8670	0.6994	0.4942	0.3022	0.1584	0.0705	0.0262
	7	1.0000	1.0000	0.9991	0.9886	0.9439	0.8385	0.6713	0.4736	0.2898	0.1518	0.0669
	8	1.0000	1.0000	0.9999	0.9970	0.9799	0.9254	0.8135	0.6466	0.4540	0.2764	0.1431
	9	1.0000	1.0000	1.0000	0.9993	0.9939	0.9705	0.9084	0.7916	0.6244	0.4350	0.2617
	10	1.0000	1.0000	1.0000	0.9999	0.9984	0.9900	0.9613	0.8930	0.7720	0.6037	0.4159
	11	1.0000	1.0000	1.0000	1.0000	0.9997	0.9971	0.9860	0.9526	0.8793	0.7543	0.5841
	12	1.0000	1.0000	1.0000	1.0000	0.9999	0.9993	0.9957	0.9820	0.9449	0.8672	0.7383
	13	1.0000	1.0000	1.0000	1.0000	1.0000	0.9999	0.9989	0.9942	0.9785	0.9383	0.8569
	14	1.0000	1.0000	1.0000	1.0000	1.0000	1.0000	0.9998	0.9984	0.9930	0.9757	0.9331
	15	1.0000	1.0000	1.0000	1.0000	1.0000	1.0000	1.0000	0.9997	0.9981	0.9920	0.9738
	16	1.0000	1.0000	1.0000	1.0000	1.0000	1.0000	1.0000	0.9999	0.9996	0.9979	0.9915
	17	1.0000	1.0000	1.0000	1.0000	1.0000	1.0000	1.0000	1.0000	0.9999	0.9995	0.9978
	18	1.0000	1.0000	1.0000	1.0000	1.0000	1.0000	1.0000	1.0000	1.0000	0.9999	0.9996
	19	1.0000	1.0000	1.0000	1.0000	1.0000	1.0000	1.0000	1.0000	1.0000	1.0000	0.9999
	20	1.0000	1.0000	1.0000	1.0000	1.0000	1.0000	1.0000	1.0000	1.0000	1.0000	1.0000
23	0	0.7936	0.3074	0.0886	0.0238	0.0059	0.0013	0.0003	0.0000	0.0000	0.0000	0.0000
	1	0.9780	0.6794	0.3151	0.1204	0.0398	0.0116	0.0030	0.0007	0.0001	0.0000	0.0000
	2	0.9985	0.8948	0.5920	0.3080	0.1332	0.0492	0.0157	0.0043	0.0010	0.0002	0.0000
	3	0.9999	0.9742	0.8073	0.5396	0.2965	0.1370	0.0538	0.0181	0.0052	0.0012	0.0002
	4	1.0000	0.9951	0.9269	0.7440	0.5007	0.2832	0.1356	0.0551	0.0190	0.0055	0.0013
	5	1.0000	0.9992	0.9774	0.8811	0.6947	0.4685	0.2688	0.1309	0.0540	0.0186	0.0053
	6	1.0000	0.9999	0.9942	0.9537	0.8402	0.6537	0.4399	0.2534	0.1240	0.0510	0.0173
	7	1.0000	1.0000	0.9988	0.9848	0.9285	0.8037	0.6181	0.4136	0.2373	0.1152	0.0466
	8	1.0000	1.0000	0.9998	0.9958	0.9727	0.9037	0.7709	0.5860	0.3884	0.2203	0.1050
	9	1.0000	1.0000	1.0000	0.9990	0.9911	0.9592	0.8799	0.7408	0.5562	0.3636	0.2024
	10	1.0000	1.0000	1.0000	0.9998	0.9975	0.9851	0.9454	0.8575	0.7129	0.5278	0.3388
	11	1.0000	1.0000	1.0000	1.0000	0.9994	0.9954	0.9786	0.9318	0.8364	0.6865	0.5000
	12	1.0000	1.0000	1.0000	1.0000	0.9999	0.9988	0.9928	0.9717	0.9187	0.8164	0.6612
	13	1.0000	1.0000	1.0000	1.0000	1.0000	0.9997	0.9979	0.9900	0.9651	0.9063	0.7976
	14	1.0000	1.0000	1.0000	1.0000	1.0000	0.9999	0.9995	0.9970	0.9872	0.9589	0.8950
	15	1.0000	1.0000	1.0000	1.0000	1.0000	1.0000	0.9999	0.9992	0.9960	0.9847	0.9534
	16	1.0000	1.0000	1.0000	1.0000	1.0000	1.0000	1.0000	0.9998	0.9990	0.9952	0.9827
	17	1.0000	1.0000	1.0000	1.0000	1.0000	1.0000	1.0000	1.0000	0.9998	0.9988	0.9947
	18	1.0000	1.0000	1.0000	1.0000	1.0000	1.0000	1.0000	1.0000	1.0000	0.9998	0.9987
	19	1.0000	1.0000	1.0000	1.0000	1.0000	1.0000	1.0000	1.0000	1.0000	1.0000	0.9998
	20	1.0000	1.0000	1.0000	1.0000	1.0000	1.0000	1.0000	1.0000	1.0000	1.0000	1.0000

(Continued)

Table D Cumulative Binomial distribution *(Continued).*

							π					
n	*X*	0.01	0.05	0.10	0.15	0.20	0.25	0.30	0.35	0.40	0.45	0.50
24	0	0.7857	0.2920	0.0798	0.0202	0.0047	0.0010	0.0002	0.0000	0.0000	0.0000	0.0000
	1	0.9761	0.6608	0.2925	0.1059	0.0331	0.0090	0.0022	0.0005	0.0001	0.0000	0.0000
	2	0.9983	0.8841	0.5643	0.2798	0.1145	0.0398	0.0119	0.0030	0.0007	0.0001	0.0000
	3	0.9999	0.9702	0.7857	0.5049	0.2639	0.1150	0.0424	0.0133	0.0035	0.0008	0.0001
	4	1.0000	0.9940	0.9149	0.7134	0.4599	0.2466	0.1111	0.0422	0.0134	0.0036	0.0008
	5	1.0000	0.9990	0.9723	0.8606	0.6559	0.4222	0.2288	0.1044	0.0400	0.0127	0.0033
	6	1.0000	0.9999	0.9925	0.9428	0.8111	0.6074	0.3886	0.2106	0.0960	0.0364	0.0113
	7	1.0000	1.0000	0.9983	0.9801	0.9108	0.7662	0.5647	0.3575	0.1919	0.0863	0.0320
	8	1.0000	1.0000	0.9997	0.9941	0.9638	0.8787	0.7250	0.5257	0.3279	0.1730	0.0758
	9	1.0000	1.0000	0.9999	0.9985	0.9874	0.9453	0.8472	0.6866	0.4891	0.2991	0.1537
	10	1.0000	1.0000	1.0000	0.9997	0.9962	0.9787	0.9258	0.8167	0.6502	0.4539	0.2706
	11	1.0000	1.0000	1.0000	0.9999	0.9990	0.9928	0.9686	0.9058	0.7870	0.6151	0.4194
	12	1.0000	1.0000	1.0000	1.0000	0.9998	0.9979	0.9885	0.9577	0.8857	0.7580	0.5806
	13	1.0000	1.0000	1.0000	1.0000	1.0000	0.9995	0.9964	0.9836	0.9465	0.8659	0.7294
	14	1.0000	1.0000	1.0000	1.0000	1.0000	0.9999	0.9990	0.9945	0.9783	0.9352	0.8463
	15	1.0000	1.0000	1.0000	1.0000	1.0000	1.0000	0.9998	0.9984	0.9925	0.9731	0.9242
	16	1.0000	1.0000	1.0000	1.0000	1.0000	1.0000	1.0000	0.9996	0.9978	0.9905	0.9680
	17	1.0000	1.0000	1.0000	1.0000	1.0000	1.0000	1.0000	0.9999	0.9995	0.9972	0.9887
	18	1.0000	1.0000	1.0000	1.0000	1.0000	1.0000	1.0000	1.0000	0.9999	0.9993	0.9967
	19	1.0000	1.0000	1.0000	1.0000	1.0000	1.0000	1.0000	1.0000	1.0000	0.9999	0.9992
	20	1.0000	1.0000	1.0000	1.0000	1.0000	1.0000	1.0000	1.0000	1.0000	1.0000	0.9999
	21	1.0000	1.0000	1.0000	1.0000	1.0000	1.0000	1.0000	1.0000	1.0000	1.0000	1.0000
25	0	0.7778	0.2774	0.0718	0.0172	0.0038	0.0008	0.0001	0.0000	0.0000	0.0000	0.0000
	1	0.9742	0.6424	0.2712	0.0931	0.0274	0.0070	0.0016	0.0003	0.0001	0.0000	0.0000
	2	0.9980	0.8729	0.5371	0.2537	0.0982	0.0321	0.0090	0.0021	0.0004	0.0001	0.0000
	3	0.9999	0.9659	0.7636	0.4711	0.2340	0.0962	0.0332	0.0097	0.0024	0.0005	0.0001
	4	1.0000	0.9928	0.9020	0.6821	0.4207	0.2137	0.0905	0.0320	0.0095	0.0023	0.0005
	5	1.0000	0.9988	0.9666	0.8385	0.6167	0.3783	0.1935	0.0826	0.0294	0.0086	0.0020
	6	1.0000	0.9998	0.9905	0.9305	0.7800	0.5611	0.3407	0.1734	0.0736	0.0258	0.0073
	7	1.0000	1.0000	0.9977	0.9745	0.8909	0.7265	0.5118	0.3061	0.1536	0.0639	0.0216
	8	1.0000	1.0000	0.9995	0.9920	0.9532	0.8506	0.6769	0.4668	0.2735	0.1340	0.0539
	9	1.0000	1.0000	0.9999	0.9979	0.9827	0.9287	0.8106	0.6303	0.4246	0.2424	0.1148
	10	1.0000	1.0000	1.0000	0.9995	0.9944	0.9703	0.9022	0.7712	0.5858	0.3843	0.2122
	11	1.0000	1.0000	1.0000	0.9999	0.9985	0.9893	0.9558	0.8746	0.7323	0.5426	0.3450

(Continued)

Table D   Cumulative Binomial distribution *(Continued)*.

							π					
n	X	0.01	0.05	0.10	0.15	0.20	0.25	0.30	0.35	0.40	0.45	0.50
25	12	1.0000	1.0000	1.0000	1.0000	0.9996	0.9966	0.9825	0.9396	0.8462	0.6937	0.5000
	13	1.0000	1.0000	1.0000	1.0000	0.9999	0.9991	0.9940	0.9745	0.9222	0.8173	0.6550
	14	1.0000	1.0000	1.0000	1.0000	1.0000	0.9998	0.9982	0.9907	0.9656	0.9040	0.7878
	15	1.0000	1.0000	1.0000	1.0000	1.0000	1.0000	0.9995	0.9971	0.9868	0.9560	0.8852
	16	1.0000	1.0000	1.0000	1.0000	1.0000	1.0000	0.9999	0.9992	0.9957	0.9826	0.9461
	17	1.0000	1.0000	1.0000	1.0000	1.0000	1.0000	1.0000	0.9998	0.9988	0.9942	0.9784
	18	1.0000	1.0000	1.0000	1.0000	1.0000	1.0000	1.0000	1.0000	0.9997	0.9984	0.9927
	19	1.0000	1.0000	1.0000	1.0000	1.0000	1.0000	1.0000	1.0000	0.9999	0.9996	0.9980
	20	1.0000	1.0000	1.0000	1.0000	1.0000	1.0000	1.0000	1.0000	1.0000	0.9999	0.9995
	21	1.0000	1.0000	1.0000	1.0000	1.0000	1.0000	1.0000	1.0000	1.0000	1.0000	0.9999
	22	1.0000	1.0000	1.0000	1.0000	1.0000	1.0000	1.0000	1.0000	1.0000	1.0000	1.0000
50	0	0.6050	0.0769	0.0052	0.0003	0.0000	0.0000	0.0000	0.0000	0.0000	0.0000	0.0000
	1	0.9106	0.2794	0.0338	0.0029	0.0002	0.0000	0.0000	0.0000	0.0000	0.0000	0.0000
	2	0.9862	0.5405	0.1117	0.0142	0.0013	0.0001	0.0000	0.0000	0.0000	0.0000	0.0000
	3	0.9984	0.7604	0.2503	0.0460	0.0057	0.0005	0.0000	0.0000	0.0000	0.0000	0.0000
	4	0.9999	0.8964	0.4312	0.1121	0.0185	0.0021	0.0002	0.0000	0.0000	0.0000	0.0000
	5	1.0000	0.9622	0.6161	0.2194	0.0480	0.0070	0.0007	0.0001	0.0000	0.0000	0.0000
	6	1.0000	0.9882	0.7702	0.3613	0.1034	0.0194	0.0025	0.0002	0.0000	0.0000	0.0000
	7	1.0000	0.9968	0.8779	0.5188	0.1904	0.0453	0.0073	0.0008	0.0001	0.0000	0.0000
	8	1.0000	0.9992	0.9421	0.6681	0.3073	0.0916	0.0183	0.0025	0.0002	0.0000	0.0000
	9	1.0000	0.9998	0.9755	0.7911	0.4437	0.1637	0.0402	0.0067	0.0008	0.0001	0.0000
	10	1.0000	1.0000	0.9906	0.8801	0.5836	0.2622	0.0789	0.0160	0.0022	0.0002	0.0000
	11	1.0000	1.0000	0.9968	0.9372	0.7107	0.3816	0.1390	0.0342	0.0057	0.0006	0.0000
	12	1.0000	1.0000	0.9990	0.9699	0.8139	0.5110	0.2229	0.0661	0.0133	0.0018	0.0002
	13	1.0000	1.0000	0.9997	0.9868	0.8894	0.6370	0.3279	0.1163	0.0280	0.0045	0.0005
	14	1.0000	1.0000	0.9999	0.9947	0.9393	0.7481	0.4468	0.1878	0.0540	0.0104	0.0013
	15	1.0000	1.0000	1.0000	0.9981	0.9692	0.8369	0.5692	0.2801	0.0955	0.0220	0.0033
	16	1.0000	1.0000	1.0000	0.9993	0.9856	0.9017	0.6839	0.3889	0.1561	0.0427	0.0077
	17	1.0000	1.0000	1.0000	0.9998	0.9937	0.9449	0.7822	0.5060	0.2369	0.0765	0.0164
	18	1.0000	1.0000	1.0000	0.9999	0.9975	0.9713	0.8594	0.6216	0.3356	0.1273	0.0325
	19	1.0000	1.0000	1.0000	1.0000	0.9991	0.9861	0.9152	0.7264	0.4465	0.1974	0.0595
	20	1.0000	1.0000	1.0000	1.0000	0.9997	0.9937	0.9522	0.8139	0.5610	0.2862	0.1013
	21	1.0000	1.0000	1.0000	1.0000	0.9999	0.9974	0.9749	0.8813	0.6701	0.3900	0.1611

(Continued)

Table D   Cumulative Binomial distribution *(Continued).*

							π					
n	X	0.01	0.05	0.10	0.15	0.20	0.25	0.30	0.35	0.40	0.45	0.50
50	22	1.0000	1.0000	1.0000	1.0000	1.0000	0.9990	0.9877	0.9290	0.7660	0.5019	0.2399
	23	1.0000	1.0000	1.0000	1.0000	1.0000	0.9996	0.9944	0.9604	0.8348	0.6134	0.3359
	24	1.0000	1.0000	1.0000	1.0000	1.0000	0.9999	0.9976	0.9793	0.9022	0.7160	0.4439
	25	1.0000	1.0000	1.0000	1.0000	1.0000	1.0000	0.9991	0.9900	0.9427	0.8034	0.5561
	26	1.0000	1.0000	1.0000	1.0000	1.0000	1.0000	0.9997	0.9955	0.9686	0.8721	0.6641
	27	1.0000	1.0000	1.0000	1.0000	1.0000	1.0000	0.9999	0.9981	0.9840	0.9220	0.7601
	28	1.0000	1.0000	1.0000	1.0000	1.0000	1.0000	1.0000	0.9993	0.9924	0.9556	0.8389
	29	1.0000	1.0000	1.0000	1.0000	1.0000	1.0000	1.0000	0.9997	0.9966	0.9765	0.8987
	30	1.0000	1.0000	1.0000	1.0000	1.0000	1.0000	1.0000	0.9999	0.9986	0.9884	0.9405
	31	1.0000	1.0000	1.0000	1.0000	1.0000	1.0000	1.0000	1.0000	0.9995	0.9947	0.9675
	32	1.0000	1.0000	1.0000	1.0000	1.0000	1.0000	1.0000	1.0000	0.9998	0.9978	0.9836
	33	1.0000	1.0000	1.0000	1.0000	1.0000	1.0000	1.0000	1.0000	0.9999	0.9991	0.9923
	34	1.0000	1.0000	1.0000	1.0000	1.0000	1.0000	1.0000	1.0000	1.0000	0.9997	0.9967
	35	1.0000	1.0000	1.0000	1.0000	1.0000	1.0000	1.0000	1.0000	1.0000	0.9999	0.9987
	36	1.0000	1.0000	1.0000	1.0000	1.0000	1.0000	1.0000	1.0000	1.0000	1.0000	0.9995
	37	1.0000	1.0000	1.0000	1.0000	1.0000	1.0000	1.0000	1.0000	1.0000	1.0000	0.9998
	38	1.0000	1.0000	1.0000	1.0000	1.0000	1.0000	1.0000	1.0000	1.0000	1.0000	1.0000
100	0	0.3660	0.0059	0.0000	0.0000	0.0000	0.0000	0.0000	0.0000	0.0000	0.0000	0.0000
	1	0.7358	0.0371	0.0003	0.0000	0.0000	0.0000	0.0000	0.0000	0.0000	0.0000	0.0000
	2	0.9206	0.1183	0.0019	0.0000	0.0000	0.0000	0.0000	0.0000	0.0000	0.0000	0.0000
	3	0.9816	0.2578	0.0078	0.0001	0.0000	0.0000	0.0000	0.0000	0.0000	0.0000	0.0000
	4	0.9966	0.4360	0.0237	0.0004	0.0000	0.0000	0.0000	0.0000	0.0000	0.0000	0.0000
	5	0.9995	0.6160	0.0576	0.0016	0.0000	0.0000	0.0000	0.0000	0.0000	0.0000	0.0000
	6	0.9999	0.7660	0.1172	0.0047	0.0001	0.0000	0.0000	0.0000	0.0000	0.0000	0.0000
	7	1.0000	0.8720	0.2061	0.0122	0.0003	0.0000	0.0000	0.0000	0.0000	0.0000	0.0000
	8	1.0000	0.9369	0.3209	0.0275	0.0009	0.0000	0.0000	0.0000	0.0000	0.0000	0.0000
	9	1.0000	0.9718	0.4513	0.0551	0.0023	0.0000	0.0000	0.0000	0.0000	0.0000	0.0000
	10	1.0000	0.9885	0.5832	0.0994	0.0057	0.0001	0.0000	0.0000	0.0000	0.0000	0.0000
	11	1.0000	0.9957	0.7030	0.1635	0.0126	0.0004	0.0000	0.0000	0.0000	0.0000	0.0000
	12	1.0000	0.9985	0.8018	0.2473	0.0253	0.0010	0.0000	0.0000	0.0000	0.0000	0.0000
	13	1.0000	0.9995	0.8761	0.3474	0.0469	0.0025	0.0001	0.0000	0.0000	0.0000	0.0000
	14	1.0000	0.9999	0.9274	0.4572	0.0804	0.0054	0.0002	0.0000	0.0000	0.0000	0.0000
	15	1.0000	1.0000	0.9601	0.5683	0.1285	0.0111	0.0004	0.0000	0.0000	0.0000	0.0000
	16	1.0000	1.0000	0.9794	0.6725	0.1923	0.0211	0.0010	0.0000	0.0000	0.0000	0.0000

(Continued)

Table D   Cumulative Binomial distribution *(Continued)*.

n	X	0.01	0.05	0.10	0.15	0.20	0.25	0.30	0.35	0.40	0.45	0.50
							π					
100	17	1.0000	1.0000	0.9900	0.7633	0.2712	0.0376	0.0022	0.0000	0.0000	0.0000	0.0000
	18	1.0000	1.0000	0.9954	0.8372	0.3621	0.0630	0.0045	0.0001	0.0000	0.0000	0.0000
	19	1.0000	1.0000	0.9980	0.8935	0.4602	0.0995	0.0089	0.0003	0.0000	0.0000	0.0000
	20	1.0000	1.0000	0.9992	0.9337	0.5595	0.1488	0.0165	0.0008	0.0000	0.0000	0.0000
	21	1.0000	1.0000	0.9997	0.9607	0.6540	0.2114	0.0288	0.0017	0.0000	0.0000	0.0000
	22	1.0000	1.0000	0.9999	0.9779	0.7389	0.2864	0.0479	0.0034	0.0001	0.0000	0.0000
	23	1.0000	1.0000	1.0000	0.9881	0.8109	0.3711	0.0755	0.0066	0.0003	0.0000	0.0000
	24	1.0000	1.0000	1.0000	0.9939	0.8686	0.4617	0.1136	0.0121	0.0006	0.0000	0.0000
	25	1.0000	1.0000	1.0000	0.9970	0.9125	0.5535	0.1631	0.0211	0.0012	0.0000	0.0000
	26	1.0000	1.0000	1.0000	0.9986	0.9442	0.6417	0.2244	0.0351	0.0024	0.0001	0.0000
	27	1.0000	1.0000	1.0000	0.9994	0.9658	0.7224	0.2964	0.0558	0.0046	0.0002	0.0000
	28	1.0000	1.0000	1.0000	0.9997	0.9800	0.7925	0.3768	0.0848	0.0084	0.0004	0.0000
	29	1.0000	1.0000	1.0000	0.9999	0.9888	0.8505	0.4623	0.1236	0.0148	0.0008	0.0000
	30	1.0000	1.0000	1.0000	1.0000	0.9939	0.8962	0.5491	0.1730	0.0248	0.0015	0.0000
	31	1.0000	1.0000	1.0000	1.0000	0.9969	0.9307	0.6331	0.2331	0.0398	0.0030	0.0001
	32	1.0000	1.0000	1.0000	1.0000	0.9984	0.9554	0.7107	0.3029	0.0615	0.0055	0.0002
	33	1.0000	1.0000	1.0000	1.0000	0.9993	0.9724	0.7793	0.3803	0.0913	0.0098	0.0004
	34	1.0000	1.0000	1.0000	1.0000	0.9997	0.9836	0.8371	0.4624	0.1303	0.0166	0.0009
	35	1.0000	1.0000	1.0000	1.0000	0.9999	0.9906	0.8839	0.5485	0.1795	0.0272	0.0018
	36	1.0000	1.0000	1.0000	1.0000	0.9999	0.9948	0.9201	0.6269	0.2386	0.0429	0.0033
	37	1.0000	1.0000	1.0000	1.0000	1.0000	0.9973	0.9470	0.7024	0.3068	0.0651	0.0060
	38	1.0000	1.0000	1.0000	1.0000	1.0000	0.9986	0.9660	0.7699	0.3822	0.0951	0.0105
	39	1.0000	1.0000	1.0000	1.0000	1.0000	0.9993	0.9790	0.8276	0.4621	0.1343	0.0176
	40	1.0000	1.0000	1.0000	1.0000	1.0000	0.9997	0.9875	0.8750	0.5433	0.1831	0.0284
	41	1.0000	1.0000	1.0000	1.0000	1.0000	0.9999	0.9928	0.9123	0.6225	0.2415	0.0443
	41	1.0000	1.0000	1.0000	1.0000	1.0000	0.9999	0.9960	0.9406	0.6967	0.3087	0.0666
	43	1.0000	1.0000	1.0000	1.0000	1.0000	1.0000	0.9979	0.9611	0.7635	0.3828	0.0967
	44	1.0000	1.0000	1.0000	1.0000	1.0000	1.0000	0.9989	0.9754	0.8211	0.4613	0.1356
	45	1.0000	1.0000	1.0000	1.0000	1.0000	1.0000	0.9995	0.9850	0.8689	0.5413	0.1841
	46	1.0000	1.0000	1.0000	1.0000	1.0000	1.0000	0.9997	0.9912	0.9070	0.6196	0.2421
	47	1.0000	1.0000	1.0000	1.0000	1.0000	1.0000	0.9999	0.9950	0.9362	0.6931	0.3086
	48	1.0000	1.0000	1.0000	1.0000	1.0000	1.0000	0.9999	0.9973	0.9577	0.7596	0.3825
	49	1.0000	1.0000	1.0000	1.0000	1.0000	1.0000	1.0000	0.9985	0.9729	0.8173	0.4602
	50	1.0000	1.0000	1.0000	1.0000	1.0000	1.0000	1.0000	0.9993	0.9832	0.8654	0.5398
	51	1.0000	1.0000	1.0000	1.0000	1.0000	1.0000	1.0000	0.9996	0.9900	0.9040	0.6178

(Continued)

Table D Cumulative Binomial distribution *(Continued)*.

n	X	0.01	0.05	0.10	0.15	0.20	0.25	0.30	0.35	0.40	0.45	0.50
						π						
100	52	1.0000	1.0000	1.0000	1.0000	1.0000	1.0000	1.0000	0.9998	0.9942	0.9338	0.6914
	53	1.0000	1.0000	1.0000	1.0000	1.0000	1.0000	1.0000	0.9999	0.9968	0.9559	0.7579
	54	1.0000	1.0000	1.0000	1.0000	1.0000	1.0000	1.0000	1.0000	0.9983	0.9716	0.8159
	55	1.0000	1.0000	1.0000	1.0000	1.0000	1.0000	1.0000	1.0000	0.9991	0.9824	0.8644
	56	1.0000	1.0000	1.0000	1.0000	1.0000	1.0000	1.0000	1.0000	0.9996	0.9894	0.9033
	57	1.0000	1.0000	1.0000	1.0000	1.0000	1.0000	1.0000	1.0000	0.9998	0.9939	0.9334
	58	1.0000	1.0000	1.0000	1.0000	1.0000	1.0000	1.0000	1.0000	0.9999	0.9966	0.9557
	59	1.0000	1.0000	1.0000	1.0000	1.0000	1.0000	1.0000	1.0000	1.0000	0.9982	0.9716
	60	1.0000	1.0000	1.0000	1.0000	1.0000	1.0000	1.0000	1.0000	1.0000	0.9991	0.9824
	61	1.0000	1.0000	1.0000	1.0000	1.0000	1.0000	1.0000	1.0000	1.0000	0.9995	0.9895
	62	1.0000	1.0000	1.0000	1.0000	1.0000	1.0000	1.0000	1.0000	1.0000	0.9998	0.9940
	63	1.0000	1.0000	1.0000	1.0000	1.0000	1.0000	1.0000	1.0000	1.0000	0.9999	0.9967
	64	1.0000	1.0000	1.0000	1.0000	1.0000	1.0000	1.0000	1.0000	1.0000	1.0000	0.9982
	65	1.0000	1.0000	1.0000	1.0000	1.0000	1.0000	1.0000	1.0000	1.0000	1.0000	0.9991
	66	1.0000	1.0000	1.0000	1.0000	1.0000	1.0000	1.0000	1.0000	1.0000	1.0000	0.9996
	67	1.0000	1.0000	1.0000	1.0000	1.0000	1.0000	1.0000	1.0000	1.0000	1.0000	0.9998
	68	1.0000	1.0000	1.0000	1.0000	1.0000	1.0000	1.0000	1.0000	1.0000	1.0000	0.9999
	69	1.0000	1.0000	1.0000	1.0000	1.0000	1.0000	1.0000	1.0000	1.0000	1.0000	1.0000

Table D is for selected values of n from 20 up to 100 and π values of 0.01 through 0.50. For this textbook, it is suggested the use of Table D be restricted to acceptance sampling which in discussed in the chapter on quality control.

For those of you tempted to use it as binomial table, please remember there is one extra step in the process. The binomial Table C is the probability of an exact number of successes in a number of attempts given the probability of success on any one attempt. In Table C, this is a direct look up. In Table D, to get a value of exactly 5 successes (sales) in 20 attempts (sales calls) given a probability of success on any one attempt or 0.10, you would have to find $n = 20$ in Table D, then find $X = 5$ under the 0.10 column for π. That cell reads 0.9987. To find exactly 5 in 20, you would then move back one cell to find the value of 0.9568. Finally, you would subtract the values in the two cells (0.9987 less 0.9568 = 0.0319). The same value can be determined from Table C by direct look up as shown in the example in Table C. Using the cumulative binomial table is helpful under certain circumstances, but you need to remember to subtract the values. Table D can be somewhat confusing, so it is recommended you use Table C for looking up binomial values.

Using Table D in quality control acceptance sampling is quite useful. For acceptance sampling you must know the producer risk which is alpha, the AQL (acceptable quality level) and the sample size (n). In acceptance sampling you are looking for C, which is the maximum number of defects in the sample before you reject the entire shipment. To use Table D, you will rename some of the terms. (π becomes AQL; n remains as n; X becomes C). There is a full explanation of how to determine C in the chapter on quality control, so it will not be repeated here.

Table E: *F*-Distribution

Table E   The *F*-Distribution.

d.f. 2	d.f. 1	Numerator Degrees of Freedom for Alpha 0.0100 (1.0%)									
		1	2	3	4	5	6	7	8	9	10
D e n o m i n a t o r D e g r e e s o f F r e e d o m	1	4052.1	4999.5	5403.3	5624.5	5763.6	5858.9	5928.3	5981.0	6022.4	6055.8
	2	98.503	99.000	99.166	99.249	99.299	99.333	99.356	99.374	99.388	99.399
	3	34.116	30.817	29.457	28.710	28.237	27.911	27.672	27.489	27.345	27.229
	4	21.198	18.000	16.694	15.977	15.522	15.207	14.976	14.799	14.659	14.546
	5	16.258	13.274	12.060	11.392	10.967	10.672	10.456	10.289	10.158	10.051
	6	13.745	10.925	9.780	9.148	8.746	8.466	8.260	8.102	7.976	7.874
	7	12.246	9.547	8.451	7.847	7.460	7.191	6.993	6.840	6.719	6.620
	8	11.259	8.649	7.591	7.006	6.632	6.371	6.178	6.029	5.911	5.814
	9	10.561	8.022	6.992	6.422	6.057	5.802	5.613	5.467	5.351	5.257
	10	10.044	7.559	6.552	5.994	5.636	5.386	5.200	5.057	4.942	4.849
	11	9.646	7.206	6.217	5.668	5.316	5.069	4.886	4.744	4.632	4.539
	12	9.330	6.927	5.953	5.412	5.064	4.821	4.640	4.499	4.388	4.296
	13	9.074	6.701	5.739	5.205	4.862	4.620	4.441	4.302	4.191	4.100
	14	8.862	6.515	5.564	5.035	4.695	4.456	4.278	4.140	4.030	3.939
	15	8.683	6.359	5.417	4.893	4.556	4.318	4.142	4.004	3.895	3.805
	16	8.531	6.226	5.292	4.773	4.437	4.202	4.026	3.890	3.780	3.691
	17	8.400	6.112	5.185	4.669	4.336	4.102	3.927	3.791	3.682	3.593
	18	8.285	6.013	5.092	4.579	4.248	4.015	3.841	3.705	3.597	3.508
	19	8.185	5.926	5.010	4.500	4.171	3.939	3.765	3.631	3.523	3.434
	20	8.096	5.849	4.938	4.431	4.103	3.871	3.699	3.564	3.457	3.368
	21	8.017	5.780	4.874	4.369	4.042	3.812	3.640	3.506	3.398	3.310
	22	7.945	5.719	4.817	4.313	3.988	3.758	3.587	3.453	3.346	3.258
	23	7.881	5.664	4.765	4.264	3.939	3.710	3.539	3.406	3.299	3.211
	24	7.823	5.614	4.718	4.218	3.895	3.667	3.496	3.363	3.256	3.168

(Continued)

Table E The *F*-Distribution *(Continued)*.

	d.f. 1	Numerator Degrees of Freedom for Alpha 0.0250 (2.5%)									
d.f. 2		1	2	3	4	5	6	7	8	9	10
Denominator Degrees of Freedom	1	647.78	799.50	864.16	899.58	921.85	937.11	948.22	956.66	963.28	968.63
	2	38.506	39.000	39.165	39.248	39.298	39.331	39.355	39.373	39.387	39.398
	3	17.443	16.044	15.439	15.101	14.885	14.735	14.624	14.540	14.473	14.419
	4	12.218	10.649	9.979	9.605	9.365	9.197	9.074	8.980	8.905	8.844
	5	10.007	8.434	7.764	7.388	7.146	6.978	6.853	6.757	6.681	6.619
	6	8.813	7.260	6.600	6.227	5.988	5.820	5.700	5.600	5.523	5.461
	7	8.073	6.542	5.890	5.523	5.285	5.119	4.995	4.899	4.823	4.761
	8	7.571	6.060	5.416	5.053	4.817	4.652	4.529	4.433	4.357	4.295
	9	7.209	5.715	5.078	4.718	4.484	4.320	4.197	4.102	4.026	3.964
	10	6.937	5.456	4.826	4.468	4.236	4.072	3.950	3.855	3.779	3.717
	11	6.724	5.256	4.630	4.275	4.044	3.881	3.759	3.664	3.588	3.526
	12	6.554	5.096	4.474	4.121	3.891	3.728	3.607	3.512	3.436	3.374
	13	6.414	4.965	4.347	3.996	3.767	3.604	3.483	3.388	3.312	3.250
	14	6.298	4.857	4.242	3.892	3.663	3.501	3.380	3.285	3.209	3.147
	15	6.200	4.765	4.153	3.804	3.576	3.415	3.293	3.199	3.123	3.060
	16	6.115	4.687	4.077	3.729	3.502	3.341	3.219	3.125	3.049	2.986
	17	6.042	4.619	4.011	3.665	3.438	3.277	3.156	3.061	2.985	2.922
	18	5.978	4.560	3.954	3.608	3.382	3.221	3.100	3.005	2.929	2.866
	19	5.922	4.508	3.903	3.559	3.333	3.172	3.051	2.956	2.880	2.817
	20	5.872	4.461	3.859	3.515	3.289	3.128	3.007	2.913	2.837	2.774
	21	5.826	4.420	3.819	3.425	3.250	3.090	2.969	2.874	2.798	2.735
	22	5.786	4.383	3.783	3.440	3.215	3.055	2.934	2.839	2.763	2.700
	23	5.750	4.349	3.751	3.408	3.184	3.023	2.902	2.808	2.731	2.668
	24	5.717	4.319	3.721	3.380	3.155	2.995	2.874	2.780	2.703	2.640

(Continued)

Table E   The *F*-Distribution *(Continued).*

	d.f. 1	Numerator Degrees of Freedom for Alpha 0.0500 (5.0%)									
d.f. 2		1	2	3	4	5	6	7	8	9	10
D	1	161.45	199.50	215.71	224.58	230.16	233.99	236.77	238.88	240.54	241.88
e	2	18.512	19.000	19.164	19.246	19.296	19.329	19.353	19.371	19.384	19.395
n	3	10.128	9.552	9.276	9.117	9.013	8.940	8.886	8.845	8.812	8.785
o	4	7.708	6.944	6.591	6.388	6.256	6.163	6.094	6.041	5.998	5.964
m	5	6.608	5.786	5.409	5.192	5.050	4.950	4.876	4.818	4.772	4.735
i	6	5.987	5.143	4.757	4.533	4.387	4.284	4.207	4.147	4.099	4.060
n	7	5.591	4.737	4.347	4.120	3.972	3.866	3.787	3.726	3.677	3.637
a	8	5.318	4.459	4.066	3.838	3.688	3.581	3.500	3.438	3.388	3.347
t	9	5.117	4.256	3.862	3.633	3.482	3.374	3.293	3.230	3.179	3.137
o	10	4.965	4.103	3.708	3.478	3.326	3.217	3.135	3.072	3.020	2.978
r	11	4.844	3.982	3.587	3.357	3.204	3.095	3.012	2.948	2.896	2.854
D	12	4.747	3.885	3.490	3.259	3.106	2.996	2.913	2.849	2.796	2.753
e	13	4.667	3.805	3.410	3.179	3.025	2.915	2.832	2.767	2.714	2.671
g	14	4.600	3.739	3.344	3.112	2.958	2.848	2.764	2.699	2.646	2.602
r	15	4.543	3.682	3.287	3.056	2.901	2.791	2.707	2.641	2.588	2.544
e	16	4.494	3.634	3.239	3.007	2.852	2.741	2.657	2.591	2.538	2.494
e	17	4.451	3.592	3.197	2.965	2.810	2.699	2.614	2.548	2.494	2.450
s	18	4.414	3.555	3.160	2.928	2.773	2.661	2.577	2.510	2.457	2.412
o	19	4.381	3.522	3.127	2.895	2.740	2.628	2.543	2.477	2.423	2.378
f	20	4.351	3.499	3.098	2.866	2.711	2.599	2.514	2.447	2.392	2.348
F	21	4.325	3.467	3.072	2.840	2.685	2.573	2.488	2.420	2.366	2.321
r	22	4.301	3.443	3.049	2.817	2.661	2.549	2.464	2.397	2.342	2.297
e	23	4.279	3.422	3.028	2.795	2.640	2.528	2.442	2.375	2.320	2.275
e	24	4.259	3.402	3.008	2.776	2.620	2.508	2.422	2.355	2.300	2.254

(Continued)

Table E   The F-Distribution (Continued).

d.f. 2	d.f. 1	Numerator Degrees of Freedom for Alpha 0.1000 (10.0%)

d.f. 2		1	2	3	4	5	6	7	8	9	10
D	1	39.863	49.500	53.593	55.832	57.240	58.204	58.905	59.438	59.857	60.194
e	2	8.526	9.000	9.161	9.243	9.292	9.325	9.349	9.366	9.380	9.391
n	3	5.538	5.462	5.390	5.342	5.309	5.284	5.266	5.251	5.240	5.230
o	4	4.544	4.324	4.190	4.107	4.050	4.009	3.978	3.954	3.935	3.919
m	5	4.060	3.779	3.619	3.520	3.452	3.404	3.367	3.339	3.316	3.297
i	6	3.775	3.463	3.288	3.180	3.107	3.054	3.014	2.983	2.957	2.936
n a	7	3.589	3.257	3.074	2.960	2.883	2.827	2.784	2.751	2.724	2.702
t	8	3.457	3.113	2.923	2.806	2.726	2.668	2.624	2.589	2.561	2.538
o	9	3.360	3.006	2.812	2.692	2.610	2.550	2.505	2.469	2.440	2.416
r	10	3.285	2.924	2.727	2.605	2.521	2.460	2.413	2.377	2.347	2.322
D e	11	3.225	2.859	2.660	2.536	2.451	2.389	2.341	2.304	2.273	2.248
g	12	3.176	2.806	2.605	2.480	2.394	2.331	2.282	2.244	2.213	2.187
r	13	3.136	2.763	2.560	2.433	2.346	2.282	2.234	2.195	2.163	2.137
e	14	3.102	2.726	2.522	2.394	2.306	2.242	2.193	2.153	2.121	2.095
e	15	3.073	2.695	2.489	2.361	2.273	2.208	2.158	2.118	2.086	2.059
s	16	3.048	2.668	2.461	2.332	2.243	2.178	2.128	2.087	2.055	2.028
o	17	3.026	2.644	2.437	2.307	2.218	2.152	2.101	2.061	2.028	2.000
f	18	3.006	2.623	2.416	2.285	2.195	2.129	2.078	2.037	2.004	1.976
F	19	2.989	2.605	2.397	2.266	2.175	2.109	2.058	2.017	1.983	1.955
r	20	2.974	2.589	2.380	2.248	2.158	2.091	2.039	1.998	1.964	1.936
e	21	2.960	2.574	2.364	2.233	2.142	2.075	2.023	1.981	1.947	1.919
e	22	2.948	2.561	2.351	2.219	2.127	2.060	2.008	1.966	1.932	1.904
d	23	2.937	2.549	2.338	2.206	2.114	2.047	1.994	1.953	1.918	1.890
o											
m	24	2.927	2.538	2.327	2.194	2.103	2.035	1.982	1.940	1.906	1.877

Table F: Chi-Square Distribution

Below is the Table F for selected alpha values from 0.0100, 0.0250, 0.0500 and 0.1000. The F-table is a ratio of two chi square tables, which in nothing you need to know, but might be impressive to you (NOT). Notice there are two different degrees of freedom. One is the numerator and is stated first. The second is the denominator and is stated second. They are not interchangeable, so don't get them backward. Degrees of freedom of $F(6, 8)$ is not the same as $F(8, 6)$. Try looking up these under alpha 0.0100 and see what you get.

The F-distribution is useful when determining if the variance of two populations are equal or unequal, thus helping us choose the proper two population test for a small sample size. The formula is as follows:

$$F = \frac{S_1^2}{S_2^2}$$

Additionally the F-distribution is the final calculated value in an ANOVA table, which would be matched against the critical F-value from the tables below to determine if you DNR or Reject the ANOVA null hypothesis. The following example is at the alpha 0.05 level with d.f. of 3 and

Source of Variation	SS	df	MS	F-Calc	P-value	F-Crit
Between Groups	63.2855	3	21.09517	**3.461629**	0.041366	**3.238872**
Within Groups	97.504	16	6.094			
Total	160.7895	19				

16. F-Calc is the value calculated by the ANOVA technique. The F-Crit is the table look up which is shown as 3.239 below. Find it in the table.

In ANOVA when rejecting the null you would want to determine which means are statistically different. One of two methods for a balanced design is the Least Significant Difference (LSD) method and it requires an F-value be used in the calculation. The formula for LSD is as follows:

$$LSD = \sqrt{\frac{2(\text{MSE})F_{\alpha, 1, n-c}}{r}}$$

The table is fairly straight forward to read. Here you only have four choices of alpha, so select one of the four as given in the problem. Next find the degrees of freedom for the numerator (top set of degrees of freedom). Now find the degrees of freedom for the denominator (left side of the table). Where those two degrees of freedom intersect is the critical F-value. The distribution is right skewed.

Table F   Chi-Square Distribution.

d.f.	$\chi^2_{0.995}$	$\chi^2_{0.990}$	$\chi^2_{0.975}$	$\chi^2_{0.950}$	$\chi^2_{0.900}$	$\chi^2_{0.100}$	$\chi^2_{0.050}$	$\chi^2_{0.025}$	$\chi^2_{0.020}$	$\chi^2_{0.010}$	$\chi^2_{0.005}$
1	0.000	0.000	0.001	0.004	0.016	2.706	3.841	5.024	5.412	6.635	7.879
2	0.010	0.020	0.051	0.103	0.211	4.605	5.991	7.378	7.824	9.210	10.597
3	0.072	0.115	0.216	0.352	0.584	6.251	7.815	9.348	9.837	11.345	12.838
4	0.207	0.297	0.484	0.711	1.064	7.779	9.488	11.143	11.668	13.277	14.860
5	0.412	0.554	0.831	1.145	1.610	9.236	11.070	12.833	13.388	15.086	16.750
6	0.676	0.872	1.237	1.635	2.204	10.645	12.592	14.449	15.033	16.812	18.548
7	0.989	1.239	1.690	2.167	2.833	12.017	14.067	16.013	16.622	18.475	20.278
8	1.344	1.646	2.180	2.733	3.490	13.362	15.507	17.535	18.168	20.090	21.955
9	1.735	2.088	2.700	3.325	4.168	14.684	16.919	19.023	19.679	21.666	23.589
10	2.156	2.558	3.247	3.940	4.865	15.987	18.307	20.483	21.161	23.209	25.188
11	2.603	3.053	3.816	4.575	5.578	17.275	19.675	21.920	22.618	24.725	26.757
12	3.074	3.571	4.404	5.226	6.304	18.549	21.026	23.337	24.054	26.217	28.299
13	3.565	4.107	5.009	5.892	7.042	19.812	22.362	24.736	25.472	27.688	29.819
14	4.075	4.660	5.629	6.571	7.790	21.064	23.685	26.119	26.873	29.141	31.319
15	4.601	5.229	6.262	7.261	8.547	22.307	24.996	27.488	28.259	30.578	32.801
16	5.142	5.812	6.908	7.962	9.312	23.542	26.296	28.845	29.633	32.000	34.267
17	5.697	6.408	7.564	8.672	10.085	24.769	27.587	30.191	30.995	33.409	35.718
18	6.265	7.015	8.231	9.390	10.865	25.989	28.869	31.526	32.346	34.805	37.156
19	6.844	7.633	8.907	10.117	11.651	27.204	30.144	32.852	33.687	36.191	38.582
20	7.434	8.260	9.591	10.851	12.443	28.412	31.410	34.170	35.020	37.566	39.997
21	8.034	8.897	10.283	11.591	13.240	29.615	32.671	35.479	36.343	38.932	41.401
22	8.643	9.542	10.982	12.338	14.041	30.813	33.924	36.781	37.659	40.289	42.796
23	9.260	10.196	11.689	13.091	14.848	32.007	35.172	38.076	38.968	41.638	44.181
24	9.886	10.856	12.401	13.848	15.659	33.196	36.415	39.364	40.270	42.980	45.559
25	10.520	11.524	13.120	14.611	16.473	34.382	37.652	40.646	41.566	44.314	46.928
26	11.160	12.198	13.844	15.379	17.292	35.563	38.885	41.923	42.856	45.642	48.290
27	11.808	12.879	14.573	16.151	18.114	36.741	40.113	43.194	44.140	46.963	49.645
28	12.461	13.565	15.308	16.928	18.939	37.916	41.337	44.461	45.419	48.278	50.993
29	13.121	14.256	16.047	17.708	19.768	39.087	42.557	45.722	46.693	49.588	52.336
30	13.787	14.953	16.791	18.493	20.599	40.256	43.773	46.979	47.962	50.892	53.672

The Chi Square table is useful when you are working with Chi Square as a parametric or non-parametric test. The Chi Square values in the table are critical value against which you will match the calculated value to accept or reject a null hypothesis. Calculated values come from a formula.

Parametric Testing

$$\chi^2 = \frac{(n-1)S^2}{\sigma^2} \quad \text{for hypothesis testing}$$

$$\frac{(n-1)S^2}{\chi^2_{\alpha/2}} \leq \sigma^2_H \leq \frac{(n-1)S^2}{\chi^2_{1-\alpha/2}} \quad \text{for confidence intervals}$$

Non-Parametric Testing

$$\chi^2 = \sum \left[\frac{(o-e)^2}{e} \right] \quad \text{for tests of independence or goodness of fit}$$

The critical value is determined from the Table F by looking it up under the degrees of freedom $(n-1)$ for parametric testing. The degrees of freedom are determined differently for non-parametric testing. For independence testing, degrees of freedom would be $(r-1)(c-1)$. For goodness of fit, degrees of freedom would be $k - m - 1$. I give a full explanation of this process in the chapter on non-parametric testing. The degrees of freedom are on the right hand side of the table. Across the top are selected values of alpha. To find the critical value, first find the desired alpha column. Next you will move down that column to the cell location that corresponds to the degrees of freedom on the left of the table. The value at that intersection will be the critical value of Chi Square. Chi Square is a right tail rejection region test.

Table G: Tukey Factor

Table G   TUKEY FACTOR for $\alpha = 0.01$

$n-c$	C																		
	2	3	4	5	6	7	8	9	10	11	12	13	14	15	16	17	18	19	20
1	90.0	135	164	186	202	216	227	237	246	253	260	266	272	277	282	286	290	294	298
2	14.0	19.0	22.3	24.7	26.6	28.2	29.5	30.7	31.7	32.6	33.4	34.1	34.8	35.4	36.0	36.5	37.0	37.5	37.9
3	8.26	10.6	12.2	13.3	14.2	15.0	15.6	16.2	16.7	17.1	17.5	17.9	18.2	18.5	18.8	19.1	19.3	19.5	19.8
4	6.51	8.12	9.17	9.96	10.6	11.1	11.5	11.9	12.3	12.6	12.8	13.1	13.3	13.5	13.7	13.9	14.1	14.2	14.4
5	5.70	6.97	7.80	8.42	8.91	9.32	9.67	9.97	10.2	10.5	10.7	10.9	11.1	11.2	11.4	11.6	11.7	11.8	11.9
6	5.24	6.33	7.03	7.56	7.97	8.32	8.61	8.87	9.10	9.30	9.49	9.65	9.81	9.95	10.1	10.2	10.3	10.4	10.5
7	4.95	5.92	6.54	7.01	7.37	7.68	7.94	8.17	8.37	8.55	8.71	8.86	9.00	9.12	9.24	9.35	9.46	9.55	9.65
8	4.74	5.63	6.20	6.63	6.96	7.24	7.47	7.68	7.87	8.03	8.18	8.31	8.44	8.55	8.66	8.76	8.85	8.94	9.03
9	4.60	5.43	5.96	6.35	6.66	6.91	7.13	7.32	7.49	7.65	7.78	7.91	8.03	8.13	8.23	8.32	8.41	8.49	8.57
10	4.48	5.27	5.77	6.14	6.43	6.67	6.87	7.05	7.21	7.36	7.48	7.60	7.71	7.81	7.91	7.99	8.07	8.15	8.22
11	4.39	5.14	5.62	5.97	6.25	6.48	6.67	6.84	6.99	7.13	7.25	7.36	7.46	7.56	7.65	7.73	7.81	7.88	7.95
12	4.32	5.04	5.50	5.84	6.10	6.32	6.51	6.67	6.81	6.94	7.06	7.17	7.26	7.36	7.44	7.52	7.59	7.66	7.73
13	4.26	4.96	5.40	5.73	5.98	6.19	6.37	6.53	6.67	6.79	6.90	7.01	7.10	7.19	7.27	7.34	7.42	7.48	7.55
14	4.21	4.89	5.32	5.63	5.88	6.08	6.26	6.41	6.54	6.66	6.77	6.87	6.96	7.05	7.12	7.20	7.27	7.33	7.39
15	4.17	4.83	5.25	5.56	5.80	5.99	6.16	6.31	6.44	6.55	6.66	6.76	6.84	6.93	7.00	7.07	7.14	7.20	7.26
16	4.13	4.78	5.19	5.49	5.72	5.92	6.08	6.22	6.35	6.46	6.56	6.66	6.74	6.82	6.90	6.97	7.03	7.09	7.15
17	4.10	4.74	5.14	5.43	5.66	5.85	6.01	6.15	6.27	6.38	6.48	6.57	6.66	6.73	6.80	6.87	6.94	7.00	7.05
18	4.07	4.70	5.09	5.38	5.60	5.79	5.94	6.08	6.20	6.31	6.41	6.50	6.58	6.65	6.72	6.79	6.85	6.91	6.96
19	4.05	4.67	5.05	5.33	5.55	5.73	5.89	6.02	6.14	6.25	6.34	6.43	6.51	6.58	6.65	6.72	6.78	6.84	6.89
20	4.02	4.64	5.02	5.29	5.51	5.69	5.84	5.97	6.09	6.19	6.29	6.37	6.45	6.52	6.59	6.65	6.71	6.76	6.82
30	3.89	4.45	4.80	5.05	5.24	5.40	5.54	5.65	5.76	5.85	5.93	6.01	6.08	6.14	6.20	6.26	6.31	6.36	6.41

Table G TUKEY FACTOR for $\alpha = 0.05$

										C									
$n-c$	2	3	4	5	6	7	8	9	10	11	12	13	14	15	16	17	18	19	20
1	18.0	27.0	32.8	37.1	40.4	43.1	45.4	47.4	49.1	50.6	52.0	53.2	54.3	55.4	56.3	57.2	58.0	58.8	59.6
2	6.08	8.33	9.80	10.9	11.7	12.4	13.0	13.5	14.0	14.4	14.7	15.1	15.4	15.7	15.9	16.1	16.4	16.6	16.8
3	4.50	5.91	6.82	7.50	8.04	8.48	8.85	9.18	9.46	9.72	9.95	10.2	10.3	10.5	10.7	10.8	11.0	11.1	11.2
4	3.93	5.04	5.76	6.29	6.71	7.05	7.35	7.60	7.83	8.03	8.21	8.37	8.52	8.66	8.79	8.91	9.03	9.13	9.23
5	3.64	4.60	5.22	5.67	6.03	6.33	6.58	6.80	6.99	7.17	7.32	7.47	7.60	7.72	7.83	7.93	8.03	8.12	8.21
6	3.46	4.34	4.90	5.30	5.63	5.90	6.12	6.32	6.49	6.65	6.79	6.92	7.03	7.14	7.24	7.34	7.43	7.51	7.59
7	3.34	4.16	4.68	5.06	5.36	5.61	5.82	6.00	6.16	6.30	6.43	6.55	6.66	6.76	6.85	6.94	7.02	7.10	7.17
8	3.26	4.04	4.53	4.89	5.17	5.40	5.60	5.77	5.92	6.05	6.18	6.29	6.39	6.48	6.57	6.65	6.73	6.80	6.87
9	3.20	3.95	4.41	4.76	5.02	5.24	5.43	5.59	5.74	5.87	5.98	6.09	6.19	6.28	6.36	6.44	6.51	6.58	6.64
10	3.15	3.88	4.33	4.65	4.91	5.12	5.30	5.46	5.60	5.72	5.83	5.93	6.03	6.11	6.19	6.27	6.34	6.40	6.47
11	3.11	3.82	4.26	4.57	4.82	5.03	5.20	5.35	5.49	5.61	5.71	5.81	5.90	5.98	6.06	6.13	6.20	6.27	6.33
12	3.08	3.77	4.20	4.51	4.75	4.95	5.12	5.27	5.39	5.51	5.61	5.71	5.80	5.88	5.95	6.02	6.09	6.15	6.21
13	3.06	3.73	4.15	4.45	4.69	4.88	5.05	5.19	5.32	5.43	5.53	5.63	5.71	5.79	5.86	5.93	5.99	6.05	6.11
14	3.03	3.70	4.11	4.41	4.64	4.83	4.99	5.13	5.25	5.36	5.46	5.55	5.64	5.71	5.79	5.85	5.91	5.97	6.03
15	3.01	3.67	4.08	4.37	4.59	4.78	4.94	5.08	5.20	5.31	5.40	5.49	5.57	5.65	5.72	5.78	5.85	5.90	5.96
16	3.00	3.65	4.05	4.33	4.56	4.74	4.90	5.03	5.15	5.26	5.35	5.44	5.52	5.59	5.66	5.73	5.79	5.84	5.90
17	2.98	3.63	4.02	4.30	4.52	4.70	4.86	4.99	5.11	5.21	5.31	5.39	5.47	5.54	5.61	5.67	5.73	5.79	5.84
18	2.97	3.61	4.00	4.28	4.49	4.67	4.82	4.96	5.07	5.17	5.27	5.35	5.43	5.50	5.57	5.63	5.69	5.74	5.79
19	2.96	3.59	3.98	4.25	4.47	4.65	4.79	4.92	5.04	5.14	5.23	5.31	5.39	5.46	5.53	5.59	5.65	5.70	5.75
20	2.95	3.58	3.96	4.23	4.45	4.62	4.77	4.90	5.01	5.11	5.20	5.28	5.36	5.43	5.49	5.55	5.61	5.66	5.71
30	2.89	3.49	3.85	4.10	4.30	4.46	4.60	4.72	4.82	4.92	5.00	5.08	5.15	5.21	5.27	5.33	5.38	5.43	5.47

The Tukey solution is appropriate when the null hypothesis is rejected in an ANOVA problem. It is one of two solutions, the other being the Least Significant Difference Method (LSD). The LSD method uses the F-table for the factor, but Tukey uses Table G. There are two parts to Table G. One if for alpha 0.01 and the other is for alpha 0.05.

The Tukey formula is as follows:

$$T = q_{\alpha, c, n-c}\sqrt{\frac{MSE}{r}}$$

The factor you are determining is $q_{\alpha, c, n-c}$, where the alpha is given as 0.01 or 0.05 and c is the number of levels of the factor (number of populations being tested) and n is the total number of observations. Knowing c and n, you can look up the factor, q, in Table G. This value then becomes the value inserted outside the square root sign for $q_{\alpha, c, n-c}$. The MSE and r are available from the ANOVA table you will have calculated manually or done by using Excel.

Table H: Factors for Mean and Range Charts for Quality Control Charts

Table H   Factors for Mean and Range Charts for Quality Control Charts.

n	Chart for Mean Factor for Control Limit	Chart for Ranges Factor for Control Limit	
	A_2	D_3	D_4
2	1.880	0	3.267
3	1.023	0	2.575
4	0.729	0	2.282
5	0.577	0	2.115
6	0.483	0	2.004
7	0.419	0.076	1.924
8	0.373	0.136	1.864
9	0.337	0.184	1.816
10	0.308	0.223	1.777
11	0.285	0.256	1.744
12	0.266	0.284	1.716
13	0.249	0.308	1.692
14	0.235	0.329	1.671
15	0.223	0.348	1.652
16	0.212	0.364	1.636
17	0.203	0.379	1.621
18	0.194	0.392	1.608
19	0.187	0.404	1.596
20	0.180	0.414	1.586
21	0.173	0.425	1.575
22	0.167	0.434	1.566
23	0.162	0.443	1.557
24	0.157	0.452	1.548
25	0.153	0.459	1.541

Use of this chart is necessary when looking up the value for A_2 for calculating the upper and lower control limits for a mean chart and the values of D_3 and D_4 for calculating the lower and upper limits for a range chart. The sample size is designated K. The sub-grouping size is designated n.

All values for A_2, D_3 and D_4 are looked up under n not K. The formulas for the mean and range charts are as follows:

Mean Control Limits for Mean Chart	Lower Range Control Limits for Range Chart	Upper Range Control Limits for Range Chart
$\overline{\overline{X}} \pm A_2\overline{R}$	$LCL = D_3\overline{R}$	$UCL = D_4\overline{R}$

Simply look up the value of A_2, D_3 and D_4 in Table H and insert them into the formulas above. Given the other values, you can easily determine the upper and lower control limits for both the mean and the range charts.

Index